NEW TESTAMENT EPISTLES

HEBREWS

A CRITICAL AND EXEGETICAL COMMENTARY

_____ *by* _____

GARETH L. REESE

HEAD OF NEW TESTAMENT DEPARTMENT
CENTRAL CHRISTIAN COLLEGE OF THE BIBLE
MOBERLY, MISSOURI

Scripture Exposition Books, LLC
803 McKINSEY PLACE
MOBERLY, MISSOURI
65270

ACKNOWLEDGMENT

The Scripture quotations contained herein, unless otherwise noted, are from the New American Standard Bible, copyrighted 1960, 1962, 1963, 1971, 1972, 1975, 1977, 1995 by the Lockman Foundation. Used by permission.

SUGGESTED CATALOGING INFORMATION

Reese, Gareth L., 1932-
New Testament Epistles: Hebrews. A critical and exegetical commentary by Gareth L. Reese.

lxxxii, 368 p. : ill. ; 26 cm. (New Testament Epistles)
Bibliography: p. lxxiii, 276-279, 317-328
Indexes: p. 329-365

1. Bible. NT. Hebrews – Commentaries. 2. Covenants. 3. Bible. NT. Hebrews – Sermons. I. Title. II. Series: New Testament Epistles. III. Alt. Title: Hebrews.

BS2775.3.R33 1992   ISBN: 097-176-5219

I wish to thank my helpmeet

KATHLEEN

whose vision of a book like this being a tool in the hands of generations to come, not only leads her to encourage me to keep writing, but whose commitment to truth and quality has resulted in unselfish contributions to this book in the form of questions, discussions, editing and proofing.

CONTENTS

TO THE HEBREWS

Introductory Studies

The document entitled "To the Hebrews" is one of the greatest sources for instruction in Christian faith and for exhortations to faithfulness to Christ and His message. For all practical purposes, however, many have followed the lead of Luther, relegating Hebrews to the non-working section of their canons. We wish to show, first from our study of introductory matters and then by our comments on the text, that to ignore Hebrews (for any alleged reason) results in a great impoverishment of the soul!

In generations past, Restoration Movement preachers preached regularly from the book of Hebrews, their audiences committed great portions of this book to memory, and then lived daily in the light of what they had heard and learned. Yet in recent decades, fewer and fewer sermons and lessons from Hebrews are given to our congregations. Could one of the causes for the spiritual anemia and the decline of commitment to Christ found among the rank and file of contemporary congregations be traced to a deficiency of the nutrients and vitamins contained in Hebrews?

What is the source of this neglect of Hebrews? Perhaps it is traceable to the fact that the closely reasoned argument of the central portion of Hebrews does not lend itself to Saturday night, quickly-prepared messages by a preacher who has found his study time increasingly impinged on by all the pressing duties and expected meetings of a modern ministry. Perhaps the neglect of Hebrews is the (unconscious) result of the doubts and questions that remain about Hebrews' authorship, destination, or central message after reading the modern critics' and scholars' hypotheses as those scholars and critics have attempted (having first abandoned traditional views) to unravel the mysteries of these introductory matters. If modern neglect of Hebrews can be traced to what the scholars are doing, then we have too quickly abandoned the traditional views on matters of authorship, destination, purpose, since surely the price for abandoning the traditional views has been too high indeed!

In the past few hundred years, an amazing number of attempts have been proposed in an attempt to solve some of Hebrews' introductory questions. Each of these new attempts to arrive at a solution first gives what are thought to be convincing reasons for rejecting the traditional views, then each attempts to commend itself to Bible scholars as the more obvious solution, simply because it better explains certain verses the older theories did not. So far, none of these new "solutions" has managed to be convincing enough, or free enough from its own problems, to carry the day and win the general approval of scholars. What happens, instead, is this: Once a new theory has been introduced, it is not long before another scholar, interacting with the latest hypothesis, finds verses that do not match, or finds flaws in the major arguments given to substantiate the new theory, thus showing the new theory to be no more satisfactory than all the previous theories that didn't quite work either.

In this commentator's opinion, many of these attempts were doomed to failure from the start because their proponents have had one thing in common – they have held what appears to be a low view of revelation and inspiration. 1 Corinthians 2:6ff, especially verses 12,13, introduce us to how revelation and inspiration worked. Revelation is that help the Holy Spirit gave to Bible speakers and writers so they could learn truths from God that could not be learned by mere human investigation and research. While some truths could be learned only by revelation, this fact does not automatically rule out all human research, for Luke 1:1-4 certainly indicates Luke conducted personal interviews with eyewitnesses as part of his preparation for writing the two-volume history we know as Luke-Acts. Nevertheless, for those matters of God's wisdom which are beyond knowing by simple human research, revelation became the sole possible source of the information the Bible writers relayed on to their readers. Not only was there revelation, there also was inspiration. Inspiration is that help from the Holy Spirit which enabled the Bible speakers and writers to express in God-chosen words those truths they had learned by revelation.

In the early years of the church, when judgments were being made concerning what documents should be included in the New Testament Canon, "inspiration" was the final, indispensable criterion. If a book were deemed inspired, it was included in the collection, kept and guarded by the church. If the document was not inspired, it was not afforded a place in the Canon. The three tests by which the early church adjudged a work to be inspired or not were *authorship* (was it written by an apostle or a close associate of an apostle?), *contents* (does it teach the same doctrine as other already-accepted books?), and *universal acceptance* (did the churches all over the ancient world accept the work as Scripture?).[1] Concerning Hebrews, it is true that for at least one of these tests there were and are questions that cannot be answered with final certainty – and about which we shall have more to say in the course of these Introductory Studies. Yet as we study the scholars' efforts to explain Hebrews, it is certainly disappointing to see little, if any, mention of the idea that Hebrews is ultimately rooted in the revelation and inspiration from God, an idea that was one of the hallmarks of canonicity for Biblical books.

A low view of revelation and inspiration also will result in the assumption that the theology of the different New Testament writers is anything but a uniform body of doctrine. Instead of repeating some portion of the "faith which was once for all delivered to the saints" (Jude 3) by God, higher criticism believes each Bible writer had his own theology, and each writer, out of his own personal experience and understanding, contributed something unique to an ever-growing body of doctrine held and taught in Christian circles. Thus, contemporary critics think it a proper pursuit to try to ferret the sources of each writer's ideas out of his religious or cultural environment rather than looking ultimately to God as the source of the one body of pure, holy truth. Is it not more in harmony with New Testament verses[2] to affirm that

---

[1] A detailed examination of the whole matter of the canonicity of Hebrews occurs later in these Introductory Studies.

[2] Some verses promise the Holy Spirit would lead the apostles into all truth (John 14:26, 16:13), and Peter affirms it was done (2 Peter 1:3 – "His divine power has given us all things pertaining to life and godliness"). Jesus affirmed the Spirit would take what was His, which He had gotten from the Father, and reveal it to the apostles (John 16:14). Peter, James, and John did not add anything to the doctrines taught by Paul, Barnabas, and Titus at the Jerusalem conference. Rather, there was a harmony among them on the new covenant doc-

God, the Holy Spirit, has drawn on one divinely-known body of truth and then led all the Biblical writers into a parallel and complementary presentation of the different facets of that truth rather than posit a naturalistic, evolutionary growth for Christian doctrine? If God is the ultimate source of Christian doctrine (and remember, "God ... has spoken to us in His Son," Hebrews 1:1-3), then it is not quite true to say that John's theology differs from Peter's, and Paul's differs from that of any other inspired preacher or writer. From letter to letter, there may be different emphases, depending on the audience and situation being addressed, but certainly there are not different doctrines of faith, or repentance, or eschatology, or Christology.

Introductory matters usually ask such things as: What form did this manuscript originally take – was it a letter, a sermon, a theological treatise, or a combination of these? Can we say anything for certain about who the human penman was? Can we assign a date for its writing? To whom was it first addressed? Why was it written? The evidence marshaled to answer such questions as these is of two kinds – internal and external. For most New Testament books, we are given more internal information on these matters within the work itself than we are for Hebrews. Likewise, for most New Testament books, the external evidence bearing on introductory matters is of more uniform voice than it is for Hebrews. Because we have so little evidence to work with, and because of the possibility that some evidence may be explained in more than one way, scholars have struggled to give definitive and completely satisfactory answers to the different introductory questions.

Decisions made about one point of introduction affect conclusions in other areas. Great caution must therefore be taken before tentatively accepting any conclusion, knowing it will have far-reaching ramifications. For this reason, though very little attention has been given in the past century to the traditional views concerning the authorship, date, and destination of the document we know as "To the Hebrews," we think we should be slow to abandon the suggestions made by the early church on these questions. True, there are some verses that might be given a different interpretation from the one given by the traditional view, and thus might cause us to doubt or reject the traditional view. But so far, all the proposals (seen by this commentator) put forth in the place of the traditional interpretations have ultimately raised more questions than they have answered. When it comes to giving a coherent, consistent explanation to the phenomena, it certainly cannot be said that any of the modern hypotheses is an improvement on the traditional view. So, these introductory studies are written from this standpoint: Is there any compelling reason to abandon the traditional view, the view set forth by the early church?

I.   HISTORICAL ALLUSIONS (Internal Evidence Found in Hebrews)

"Historical allusions" are evidences given in the course of writing that help us identify who the author is, where he is when he writes, who the readers are, what time it is in history, and what has occasioned the writing of the document. In many first century letters, the majority

---

trines and practices they were teaching (Acts 15, Galatians 2). Thus, we believe modern attempts to isolate one writer's theology from another, as though each writer himself were the ultimate source of what he wrote, are ill-founded and inimical to the Christian faith.

of such allusions are found in the opening and closing verses, while a few may also be scattered here and there in the body of the document.

A. HISTORICAL ALLUSIONS IN CHAPTER 1

1. The Title

Most of the ancient papyrus and uncial manuscripts[3] have "to the Hebrews." This title is also found in Pantaenus (180 AD)[4] and in Tertullian (200 AD).[5] Titles, as far as we know, were not part of the autographed manuscript, but were added later by the churches when they were making collections of Scripture for reading in public worship services. The older the manuscript, the shorter the title, is the general rule for New Testament writings. Afterwards[6] the title was enlarged to "The Epistle to the Hebrews." Still later,[7] it was enlarged to "The Epistle of Paul the Apostle to the Hebrews," the title we find in the KJV.[8] This title reflects an ancient tradition of the churches regarding the authorship of the book.

What was the origin of this title, "To the Hebrews," and how reliable is it? Some suppose the title was included on the autograph copy of the manuscript. Some have supposed it was merely an educated guess based on some ancient reader's reflection on the contents of the work. Others suppose it genuinely represents the facts of the case, the title originally being added by those who made copies of it for use in churches other than the church which first received this manuscript from its writer. Early tradition offers no other title for the book, and thus the title, wherever it originated, represents the consensus of opinion in the early church that the document was addressed "to Hebrew people."

Is the word "Hebrews" to be taken literally or figuratively? Westcott and Delitzsch argued the title was to be taken literally. They posited, in the light of that term, that the recipients were Palestinian Jews and, in light of the notices later in the epistle, that the recipients had also become Christians.[9] A portion of the congregation at Jerusalem was once designated by the term "Hebrews" (Acts 6:1).[10] **The traditional view is that the recipients of this manu-**

---

[3] P[46], A, B, are a few of the important papyrus and uncial manuscripts.

[4] Eusebius, *Ecclesiastical History*, VI.14.4.

[5] *De Pudicitia* 20. Tertullian does not seem to have originated this title, but rather reflects an older tradition.

[6] Peshitto Syriac Version, c.425 AD.

[7] Philoxenian Syriac, P, L, and the Latin Vulgate.

[8] Concerning the title as carried by the KJV, Clarence Craig (one of the translators of the RSV) said, "Only three things are wrong with the title as given in the KJV -- it is not an epistle, it is not by Paul, and it was not to the Hebrews." What is one to think of Craig's affirmation? On what basis might one agree or disagree?

[9] B.F. Westcott, *The Epistle to the Hebrews* (Grand Rapids: Eerdmans, 1952), p.xxxv-xliii. Friederich Delitzsch, *Commentary on the Epistle to the Hebrews,* transl. T. Kingsbury (Edinburgh: T & T Clark, 1868), p.20.

[10] "'Hebrew' in the New Testament era normally designates the Jewish people of ancient times (e.g., Philo *Vit. Mos.* i.243; Josephus *Ant.* ii.201f.). The LXX speaks of Hebrews when distinguishing Jewish people from other peoples (Gen. 39:14; 43:32). Yet 'Hebrew' can (esp. in view of non-Palestinians) refer to Jews who are

script were Jewish Christians who lived somewhere in Palestine.[11]   Those who reject the traditional view have observed that a Jewish man didn't have to live in Palestine to be called a "Hebrew." There was a synagogue of the "Hebrews"[12] located in Corinth, presumably the place where "Jews" of that place worshiped; and also one in Rome.[13]   In the light of a wider use for "Hebrew" other than just for Jews living in Palestine, some have supposed "Hebrews" is addressed to Jews all over the ancient world.[14]   Still others have advanced the opinion that the title "Hebrews" was a symbolical designation for "pilgrims or sojourners," and thus even ethnic Gentiles might be figuratively called "Hebrews."[15]   Is there any valid reason for abandoning the traditional view of the meaning of the title?

2. Is Hebrews an "Epistle"?

The title, "To the Hebrews," tends to suggest this manuscript was sent by its writer to certain "Hebrew" readers. Is Hebrews, then, a 'letter' ('epistle'[16])? If it is a letter, where is the usual epistolary opening – signature, address, greeting – found on most other New Testament writings that were originally 'letters'? Was there one on the autograph manuscript? If so, did it accidentally get lost (e.g., the first page of the manuscript being lost due to wear and tear)? Was it deliberately suppressed, lest people pay an inordinate attention to the human penman and thus fail to rivet their attention on Jesus? Did this work first circulate with no epistolary opening because it never was intended to be a 'letter' – it was, instead, an essay or a treatise or

---

from Palestine, or are esp. connected with Palestine. An archaizing tendency is probably resonant in the word choice in NT times; in contrast to the (in the mouth of Gentiles) derogatory sounding *Ioudaios*, the name *Hebraios* is deliberately used as an honored name from the past." J. Wanke, "*Hebraios*, Hebrew" in *Exegetical Dictionary of the New Testament* (Grand Rapids: Eerdmans, 1990), Vol.1, p.369.

[11] "[T]he fact is universally presupposed in Christian antiquity as beyond doubt that the *Hebraioi*, whose name the epistle bears at its head, were the Palestinian Christians. The evidence for this statement is afforded by Pantaenus, Clemens Alexandrinus, Eusebius, Chrysostom, Theodoret, and many others." Gottlieb Lunneman, "The Epistle to the Hebrews," in *Meyer's Commentary on the New Testament*, Vol. 9 (Winona Lake, Ind.: Alpha Publications, 1980 reprint of the 6th edition of 1884), p. 370.

[12] Concerning the inscription on a broken lintel, see Jerome Murphy-O'Connor, "The Corinth Paul Saw," *Biblical Archaeologist* 47:3 (Sept. 1984), p.153. For a picture of the lintel, see Victor Paul Furnish, "Corinth In Paul's Time," *Biblical Archaeology Review* 15:3 (May-June, 1988), p. 26. Furnish dates the lintel from the fourth century AD.

[13] Wanke, *ibid.*

[14] The circumstances of the readers, their immediate past history, etc., found later in Hebrews, will make it difficult to picture Hebrews being a circular letter, intended from the first for a general audience, rather than one in a specific geographical location.

[15] Charles A. Trentham, "Hebrews," in *The Broadman Bible Commentary*, (Nashville: Broadman Press, 1972), Vol.12, p.7.

[16] G. Adolph Deissmann (*Bible Studies* [Winona Lake, Ind.: Alpha Publications, 1917 reprint of the 1901 English edition], p.3-12, 42-49) defined a "letter" as being a non-literary composition designed only for a particular group without any thought of publication, and an "epistle" as an artistic piece of literature carefully worked out in form as well as in content so as to present something literarily worthy of wide distribution. In this commentary on Hebrews we are following common usage, where "letter" and "epistle" are used as though they were synonymous terms.

a hortatory sermon?[17] Was there some other reason the author chose to write anonymously (if indeed, he did not sign his name at the beginning of the letter)? Chapter 13 will show the writer was known by the readers, so it cannot be said the authorship of the letter was deliberately withheld from the original readers.

If Hebrews doesn't have the usual epistolary opening, why did it come to be called a 'letter'? Partially because the closing verses of chapter 13 are typical of what is found in first century letters, and partially because early writers called the work an epistle. There are verses, as we shall see, which show that a certain community was addressed.

3. Hebrews 1:1-3

"God ... in these last days has spoken to us in His Son" tells us that Hebrews was written after the earthly ministry of Jesus was finished, for the passage also says that Jesus already, at some time in the past, "sat down at the right hand of the Majesty on high." His earthly ministry is over, and He has ascended on High, before Hebrews was written (see also Hebrews 12:2). Hebrews was therefore written sometime after AD 30.

No further information is given in the beginning of the letter that will be helpful to us on the matters of authorship, date, or destination, though the thesis presented (i.e., that Jesus is better than the prophets, Jesus is better than angels) may be of help determining the purpose for which this work was written.[18]

B. HISTORICAL ALLUSIONS IN CHAPTER 13

1. 13:3 – "Remember the prisoners." Does the writer have any particular prisoners in mind? Have some of the readers' brethren been imprisoned recently and thus were in need of the supplies (food, clothing) that prisoners depended on from their friends, lest they perish?

2. 13:7 – "Remember those who led you ... imitate their faith." Some former leaders, who had spoken the word of God to the readers, apparently are now dead. Did they die a natural death, or were they martyred? Whichever, they had been faithful to Jesus till the end. The readers are exhorted to follow their example of faithfulness. They have been gone long enough that a new group of leaders (13:17) has been selected to replace them, and these new leaders are now to be obeyed. These notes imply the "Hebrews" have been a congregation or community for some time. It is not a recently formed group that is addressed.

3. 13:9 – "Do not be carried away by varied and strange teachings ...." With "for" the writer goes on to explain what "strange teachings" he had in mind. They were teachings that emphasized "foods" rather than "grace." Shall we see in the word "foods" a reference to

---

[17] "Hebrews begins like a treatise, proceeds like a sermon, and ends like an epistle," R.C. Foster used to say. After noting the differences between Hebrews and first-century epistles, Professor Foster regularly went on to call Hebrews a "letter."

[18] An extended discussion of this document's "purpose" is included below in these Introductory Studies.

the (Pharisaic) Judaizers with their emphasis on clean and unclean foods? Or, shall we see here certain Gentile (Gnostic, Essene) ascetic practices?

4. 13:10,11 – "Altar, tabernacle, bodies ... burned outside the camp." This is language that shows the readers were of Jewish background. While Gentiles might have an "altar," it is not true that they had a "tabernacle" or rules (like Exodus 29:14, Leviticus 4:12,21, 9:11) about taking the bodies of animal sacrifices outside the camp after the blood had been offered as a sin offering in the Holy Place.

5. 13:12 – "Jesus also ... suffered outside the gate." As was already indicated by Hebrews 1:1-3, this verse likewise dates Hebrews after the death of Jesus outside the walls of the city of Jerusalem. How much time has elapsed between the death of Jesus in AD 30 and the writing of Hebrews? We shall keep looking for information that will help us date the letter.

6. 13:13 – "Let us go out to Him outside the camp." The writer summons the Hebrews to make an absolute break ("outside the camp") with their old religion.

7. 13:14 – "Here we do not have a lasting city." Is this a reference to any particular city (Jerusalem, for instance[19]) which is about to be destroyed? A failure to sit loose of the earthly city, a hankering for the 'good life' in the old city, cannot be harmonized with a "seeking *the city*[20] which is to come" (the New Jerusalem) which the readers are actually expected to be doing.

8. 13:15 – "Through Him then, let us continually offer up a sacrifice of praise to God." We shall see that Hebrews presents Jesus as our mediator with the Father, as our High Priest, and as our Man in Heaven. The exhortation to "continually offer" praises to God, is the very opposite of quitting the Christian religion in favor of turning back to the old "camp" (verse 13).

9. 13:17 – "Obey your leaders ...." The writer knows the readers' present attitude toward their present leaders. He knows the present leaders are keeping watch over the souls of the readers and will one day (likely, the final judgment) have to give an account for each of the readers. The implication in the words "joy" or "grief" is that the behavior of the readers will determine whether the account is one that can be given joyfully, or one that must be given with a broken heart.

---

[19] Some recent writers have suggested that Qumran, which was destroyed in June of 68 AD, was the city which was "not lasting." It is supposed the readers were ex-Essenes who were thinking of leaving the church and returning to the Qumran community. Shortly, we shall see that the readers have faced persecution in the past (10:32ff) and were facing it again in the future (12:3ff). The theory that suggests the "Hebrews" were really ex-Essenes takes note that the Essenes were persecuted in the past by the orthodox Jews before they became Christians, and now that they are Christians, they are facing persecution by the Roman military forces involved in putting down the revolt in Palestine that began in 66 AD. This attempt at identifying the "Hebrews" is open to the criticism that the first persecution was suffered because the readers were already Christians (10:32), not because they were Essenes.

[20] Compare Hebrews 2:5, 11:10,16, 12:22, and see Ephesians 2:19.

10. 13:18 – "Pray for us, for ... we have a good conscience ...." The readers knew who wrote this epistle; and if the "us" and "we" are more than an editorial plural, the readers knew the circumstances of those who were with the writer. If they didn't know before, they would have been told this information by whoever delivered the letter to its first audience. The readers will be able to offer up prayers for the writer since they know his circumstances. The affirmation concerning the writer's 'honorable conduct' may reflect the idea that someone has falsely accused the author of some crime, and the author is setting the record straight.

11. 13:19 – "(Pray for us) ... that I may be restored to you the sooner." The writer knows the readers, has been in their midst before, and looks forward to visiting them again. He even asks the readers to pray that this reunion may be accomplished "the sooner." Is the writer's absence due to imprisonment, illness, or something else? Did the hoped-for visit ever materialize?

12. 13:20,21 – "Now the God of peace ... equip you ... working in us ...." After asking for their prayers, in verses 20 and 21 the writer prays for the readers. The verses are a magnificent doxology which gathers up a number of the themes that have been unfolded throughout the course of the epistle. "Equip you" is a prayer that God would mend or restore in the readers whatever was necessary in order that they may continue to do His will. "In us" shows God's equipping work was somehow related to what God was doing in and through the writer, and is perhaps a reference to this very letter.

13. 13:22 – "Bear with this word of exhortation, for I have written to you briefly." With these words, the writer summarizes what he had in mind when he wrote as he did. Magnificent presentations of Christian doctrine, yes. Sobering warnings, yes. But behind it all was an "exhortation." Because of the use of the same expression the "word of exhortation" in Acts 13:15 to refer to a sermon delivered orally, some have supposed Hebrews was also originally a sermon, and that our epistle is either the manuscript prepared before the sermon was delivered or else is a later adaptation of the sermon into written form. If the verse ended with the word "exhortation," the case for this being originally a sermon might be stronger, but with the explanatory phrase "for I have written ..." immediately attached, it seems doubtful that we should style Hebrews as being "a sermon in search of an audience."

14. 13:23 – "Take notice that our brother Timothy has been released." The mention of Timothy's name (presuming this "Timothy" to be the one who travelled with Paul) shows the writing must be early, from the first century. "Take notice" suggests the writer is giving the readers some new information they did not before know.[21] But from what has Timothy been "released"? From his duties with some other church? From imprisonment? From some mission trip? If the writer here announces that Timothy is "released," the readers must have had knowledge of Timothy's duties, or imprisonment, or whatever – and this in turn implies that information about Timothy has come to the readers in some form or fashion, and may also imply that whatever Timothy was released from was neither insignificant nor of short duration. Since Timothy was known to the brethren in Jerusalem (he had helped bring the offering at the close of the Third Missionary Journey, Acts 20:4), this notice is not an argument

---

[21] This comment assumes the verb translated "Take notice" is to be understood as an imperative, rather than an indicative mood.

against the traditional view about the destination of this letter.

15. 13:23 – "With whom, if he comes soon, I shall see you." Timothy has been released, but he is not with the writer at the moment. The writer has hopes Timothy will soon join him, and then he plans that the two of them together will visit the readers. The readers and the writer are mutual friends or acquaintances of Timothy. Is the writer already free to travel at the moment he writes, i.e., he himself is not at the moment a prisoner? Is this simply the expression of a positive attitude that the writer, though presently in custody, soon will be free, as for example, we find in Paul's writings in the Prison Epistles? This planned visit to the readers tends to confirm the traditional conclusion reached about who the "Hebrews" were. After all, if the readers were Jewish Christians scattered in *all* lands, how could the writer promise his readers a speedy visit?

16. 13:24 – "Greet all of your leaders and all the saints." Is this an exhortation to the readers to carry the writer's greetings to leaders and church members who were absent when this letter was first read? Is this an exhortation to the readers to show their affection to and appreciation for their present leaders (cp. verse 17), and for the Christians generally? If the "leaders" are elders, we might expect them to be present at the meeting when this letter is read aloud. If the readers have been giving consideration to quitting Christianity, and forsaking the assembly of the brethren (10:25), this appeal has real force. Before they could heartily give such a greeting, they will have to give up all thoughts of forsaking Christ and His religion. Does "all the saints" reflect the view that the first recipients of this letter were just a small group – perhaps a house church, one among many such house churches in a large city or area?

17. 13:24 – "Those from Italy greet you." Is the writer in Italy? If so, then Italian Christians are sending greetings to the readers somewhere outside of Italy. Are there some Italians with the writer wherever he is? If so, they are sending greetings to the readers because they are mutual acquaintances. Is the writer sending greetings to Italy from some of its native sons? The phrase "from Italy" merely determines the people's place of origin; it does not determine their present place of residence.[22] Therefore, the "Italians" could be anywhere the writer is.

18. Subscription. Readers familiar with the KJV have noted (in small print) the words "Written to the Hebrews from Italy by Timothy"[23] following 13:25. Such subscriptions are post-apostolic, representing some early scribes' attempts to add brief introductory notes to the New Testament letters to help the readers understand from whence the letters had come and to

---

[22] See evidence of this in the notes offered on 13:24 in the commentary. In addition to what is written there, two things may be noted. First, the phrase *"from* (Grk. *apo)* Italy" occurs in Acts 18:2, where it indicates Aquila and Priscilla are "come from Italy." Etymologically, the preposition *apo* might be expected to have the same meaning here in Hebrews. Second, it must be noted that "those *in* (Grk. *en)* Italy" (cp. 2 that Timothy 1:15 and 1 Peter 5:13) is the Greek wording we might expect before we could unhesitatingly say that the "Italians" were still "in" Italy, from where they were sending greetings to the readers.

[23] Codex Alexandrinus (about 450 AD) reads "Written from (Greek, *apo)* Rome." The Peshitto Syriac (a revision made about 425 AD), and the uncials H (6th century), K and P (9th century manuscripts), and others, have "from (*apo)* Italy." One twelfth century minuscule, 1911, has "from (*apo)* Athens."

whom they were addressed. In these subscriptions the "by" notation does not indicate authorship; rather, the "by" indicates who (in the scribe's opinion) carried the letter to its original readers. That scribe's notion that Timothy was the bearer of this epistle seems to be contradicted by what is said about Timothy in Hebrews 13:23.[24]

C. OTHER HISTORICAL ALLUSIONS

2:1-3 – "Pay much closer attention to what we have heard ... so great a salvation" is a clear reference to the gospel of Christ. The readers were Christians who were becoming careless with the great gospel truths.

2:3 – "After it was at the first spoken through the Lord" tells us that Hebrews was written after the Lord Jesus had been on earth and had spoken about the "great salvation."

2:3 – "It was confirmed to us by those who heard" tells us that those who heard Jesus (i.e., think of the twelve apostles) "confirmed" the message to the writer and the readers. "Confirmed" means 'to verify, to corroborate,' not 'to hear for the first time.' The language does not say the readers are second generation Christians – it rather says the "great salvation" was authenticated as being from God as "those who (personally) heard (Jesus)" in turn told the gospel to the readers of Hebrews. God did the authenticating as He worked miracles and distributed the Holy Spirit in conjunction with the eyewitnesses' preaching.

This verse has often been appealed to as ruling out any possibility that the traditional view of authorship (i.e., Paul wrote it) is valid. It is claimed that what is said here contradicts what Paul himself says about where he got his gospel (Galatians 1:11ff) since Paul received his gospel by revelation from God. However, "*corroboration*" is different than "*source*." Paul was not one of the original twelve; yet for Paul, even as for the twelve, the *source* of the gospel is Jesus. Then, lest anyone doubt it is actually a message from God, God "confirmed" the message, to the readers as well as to the writers. So, if Paul wrote Hebrews, 2:3 would say nothing greatly different from what we read happened at the Jerusalem Conference (Acts 15, Galatians 2). Years after his conversion, and years after he has been faithfully preaching the message he received by revelation, Paul comes to Jerusalem, not knowing for sure what the twelve have been preaching in the interim but knowing that what he preached on the First Missionary Journey (i.e., gospel, not Law) was what God wanted preached. The miracles God wrought through Paul evidenced that fact (Acts 15:12). At Jerusalem, Paul and the original apostles compared notes, so to speak, and found they were preaching the same message (Galatians 2:6-9). Thus, in Paul's mind, the gospel was "confirmed" or "corroborated" even by the original twelve. Thus, Hebrews 2:3 is certainly no reason to abandon the traditional view of the authorship of Hebrews.

3:1 – "Holy brethren, partakers of a heavenly calling, consider Jesus, the Apostle

---

[24] If the verb in 13:23 were taken as an indicative, it would still be difficult to think of Timothy as the bearer of the letter, for, instead of Timothy coming alone, the writer indicates he and Timothy will together at some future time visit the readers.

and High Priest of our confession." This verse is another of many in Hebrews[25] which indicates the writer and readers were Christians. They have each shared in making a confession of faith in Jesus after hearing an invitation to do so. Again, we see that the date of writing must have been some time after Jesus' earthly ministry was concluded.

3:9 – "Forty Years ..." has been used by some to help date Hebrews. Just as the generation in the wilderness wanderings provoked God for 40 years, has it been about 40 years since Pentecost when Hebrews is written, so that the readers, like their ancestors in the wilderness, have been provoking God (by thoughts of unbelief) for a similar period of time?

3:12 – "Take care ... lest there should be in any one of you ... in falling away from the living God." Hebrews is full of language[26] that suggests the readers are in danger of forsaking the Christian religion. Is this danger the occasion for the writing of this letter?

5:6 – "Thou art a priest forever according to the order of Melchizedek." This prophecy made about the coming Messiah (Psalm 110:4) shows the Old Testament looked forward to the time when the Levitical priesthood would be superseded by a greater priesthood, the priesthood of the coming Messiah. Was this doctrine of a priestly order different from the Levitical a truth the readers had missed? The traditional view of Hebrews says the readers were going back to the Jewish religion because there they had a visible, functioning priesthood. This presentation of Messiah's priestly work was intended to show that should they go back, they would be going back to something that was only temporary, and completely unable (because of the lack of a perfect sacrifice for sins) to help the worshipers actually get to God.

5:12 – "By this time you ought to be teachers." The readers have been Christians for enough time that they should by now be teaching others about the excellencies of Christ. Does this language also indicate the letter is addressed to just a small group of church members rather than to the whole congregation in general since not all would be expected to be "teachers"?

6:1 – "Leaving the elementary teaching about the Christ, let us press on to maturity." The readers are to abandon the old "elementary principles of the oracles of God"

---

[25] The readers are Christians. They had been "enlightened" (i.e., converted), according to Hebrews 6:4 and 10:32. They are addressed as "brothers" (3:1, 10:19, 13:22), have shared a common Christian experience (3:1, 4:1,2,3, 8:1, 10:19-25), are described as having "become partakers of Christ" (3:14), and are described as "in the body" of Christ (13:3). The readers have fled to Jesus for refuge (6:18-20), and Jesus is functioning as the reader's great high priest (4:14).

[26] Their "confession" of Christ must be held firm until the end (3:14). There was danger the Hebrews would miss their promised rest, just as the disobedient and unbelieving Israelites missed the Promised Land (3:16-18). 4:1 again urges a healthy fear lest the Christian's promised rest be missed. 4:11 warns about falling through following the same example of disobedience we have seen in the Wilderness generation. 4:14-16 urges the readers to hold fast their confession. So does Hebrews 10:23, "Let us hold fast the confession of our hope (Jesus) without wavering." 6:11,12 repeats the need to show diligence, lest the readers become "sluggish" and fail to imitate those who "through faith and perseverance inherit the promises." There is the warning against drifting away (2:1), or throwing away their confidence (10:35), or growing weary and losing heart (12:3), and "falling away from the living God" (3:12). Hebrews 10:25 is an exhortation against forsaking the "assembling" of the saints. "You have need of endurance" the writer says (10:36 and 12:1), and expresses his optimism that neither he nor the readers will be among "those who shrink back to destruction" (10:39).

(i.e., the Old Testament institutions and shadows that pointed to the coming Messiah), and fully embrace what they have learned about Messiah from the New Testament preachers. The implication is the readers were being tempted to go back to the old Jewish way. In all the middle chapters of Hebrews, the writer presupposes his readers have an intricate knowledge of Jewish religious ritual. The whole point of his presentation of the superiority of Christianity (1:1-3, 2:1-3) is that it is superior to the Old Testament religion. It is difficult to explain the constant contrast between Old and New, between the Mosaic religion and Christianity, unless the audience was faced with just such a choice between the two as the traditional view of Hebrews has supposed.

6:4-6 – "Have fallen away ... crucify to themselves the Son of God, and put Him to an open shame." Anyone who treats what Jesus did at Calvary as though it were of little benefit personally, and really is not even needed personally, will find there is no other way of salvation ("it is impossible to renew them to repentance"). The Mosaic religion never offered a perfect sacrifice for sins; only Jesus has done that. To abandon Jesus is to abandon the only way of salvation there is.

6:9,10 – "... God is not unjust so as to forget your work and the love which you have shown ... in having ministered and still ministering to the saints." There was a time in the past when there was a noble service rendered by the readers to their brethren. In fact, such ministry continues to the very present. What is this referring to? Works of benevolence of some kind?

7:12 – "When the priesthood is changed, of necessity there takes place a change of law also." Something has happened in history that the Levitical priesthood is no longer a valid priesthood. That can only be a reference to Calvary and to Jesus' subsequent priestly activity (9:24, 25). Not only that, but the Law of Moses has been abrogated and set aside (7:18 and 10:9). Who, then, would even consider returning to that which was no longer valid?

8:6 – "He is also the mediator of a better covenant." Christians live under this new covenant, ratified by the sacrifice of Jesus (9:16ff). Why would they ever consider going back to something "faulty" (8:7) that was never intended to be anything but temporary (8:13, 9:10, 10:9).

8:13 – "Whatever is becoming obsolete and growing old is ready to disappear." What was going to happen shortly that would cause the Levitical priesthood and its sacrificial system to come to an end? The traditional view says it was the destruction of Jerusalem that effectively ended the Mosaic sacrificial system. This verse has been regularly used to help date the writing of Hebrews before AD 70.

10:11 – "Every priest stands daily ministering and offering time after time the same sacrifices, which can never take away sins." This language, the traditional view says, indicates the temple is still standing and the Levitical priests are still repeating the sacrifices commanded in the Law of Moses. If so, Hebrews is written before AD 70, the date of the destruction of Jerusalem by the Romans.

10:26-29 – "If we go on sinning willfully ... how much severer punishment do you think he will deserve?" In the Mosaic Age, the man who willfully set aside the Law of Moses was executed. The man who willfully abandons the Son of God and the new covenant religion will face something more severe than even physical death. The departure the readers proposed to make from the Christian religion back to the old religion was something that was a *willful* act on their parts.

10:32,33 – "Remember the former days, when ... you endured a great conflict of sufferings ...." The readers have passed through a time of persecution previous to the writing of this letter. They had been made a "public spectacle," a term which means, if taken literally, that they were put on display in some amphitheater,[27] and which means, if taken figuratively, the readers have been exposed to public disgrace because of their faith.

10:34 – "For you showed sympathy to the prisoners, and accepted joyfully the seizure of your property." The King James Version reads differently, "You had compassion of me in my bonds." This reading found in the Majority Text has often been used to corroborate the Pauline authorship of Hebrews, for we remember Paul was in prison in Jerusalem and Caesarea at the close of the Third Missionary Journey (Acts 21-26), and that imprisonment would have furnished opportunity for the Palestinian Christians to minister to him. It must be admitted, on the other hand, that Acts gives no record of any Palestinian believers having their goods and property confiscated because they helped Paul the prisoner.

12:3-14 – "Consider Him who has endured such hostility by sinners against Himself ... you have not resisted to the point of shedding blood ...." A persecution or time of testing (it is also called "discipline" in verse 5ff) seems imminent. "You have not resisted to the point of shedding blood" has been used to point to a date before the imperial persecutions, but this is not absolutely demonstrable. All it says is the current time of "hostility by sinners" has not cost any of the readers their lives; that is, the present persecution is no more severe than was the former one. They didn't quit then, why quit Christ now? Instead of thinking about quitting themselves, why not think about others by looking for some "hands that are weak" or "knees that are feeble" they could help to remain faithful.

D. SUMMARY OF INFORMATION FROM THE HISTORICAL ALLUSIONS

It is true that we have not yet studied in depth such matters as *style* or *theology* as we search for any internal evidence that would require us to reject the traditional views about the authorship, destination, and purpose of Hebrews; matters such as *style* or *theology* are not usually the purview of historical allusions. Yet it can thus far be rightly said that we have found no historical allusion in the book itself that is impossible to harmonize with the traditional view. The personal references (5:12, 6:10-12, 10:32ff, 12:4, 13:7,19, 23,24) suffice to show the writer had in mind a definite, locally-bounded circle of readers.

---

[27] Those who argue for a Roman destination for this letter explain the term literally and think it has reference to the Circus Maximus, in which Christians (for example, in Nero's time) were persecuted.

II. ATTESTATION AND AUTHORSHIP

"Attestation" has reference to evidence that may be found in Early Christian Literature for the use, canonicity, and authorship of any New Testament book, in this case the "The Epistle to the Hebrews." "Authorship" seeks to determine, from internal and external evidence, who the human penman was who wrote the document (recognizing that the ultimate source of the writing was God Himself).

A. INTERNAL MARKS AS TO AUTHORSHIP

1. The author of the epistle was a Jew. This, as far as this commentator can determine, has never been doubted. "The manner in which he addresses his readers, evidently themselves Jews, is such as to forbid the supposition that he was a Gentile."[1] Men who were Gentiles would then be eliminated as being the author.

2. The author habitually used the LXX for his Old Testament quotations. The use of the LXX is not exclusive, e.g., 10:30. In fact, the variety in wording of the quotations may imply there were several versions of the OT in circulation in the first century AD.[2] However, his heavy use of the LXX, at first, is surprising, especially when it is noted that some of the writer's arguments based on the Old Testament depend on the wording of the LXX (as compared to the Hebrew, from which it differs), e.g., 1:6,10, 2:7 and 10:5-7. Would a letter written to Palestinian Christians assume their familiarity with the LXX? Yes! It has recently been shown there was no great difference between what has been called Palestinian Judaism and Diaspora Judaism,[3] so that appeal to the LXX does not surprise us. It was the Bible used and held in high esteem in Palestine in the 1st century AD.[4] And the almost exclusive use of the LXX does not automatically rule out a Pauline authorship for Hebrews. If the apostle, in his signed letters, quotes from both the LXX and the Hebrew versions of the Old Testament, why could he not also, on occasion,[5] quote from just one translation?

---

[1] Henry Alford, "The Epistle to the Hebrews," in *Alford's Greek Testament*, Vol.4 (London: Rivingtons, 1871), p.51.

[2] See comments offered on Hebrews 13:5. G. Howard argued the writer of Hebrews seems to have used a variety of Greek Texts, some agreeing with our LXX and some differing from it ("Hebrews and the Old Testament Quotations," *Nov.Test.* 10 [2-3, 1968], p.208-216).

[3] One of the main working assumptions that governed New Testament studies of the life of Paul, at the turn of the 20th century was this – that it was possible to make a clear distinction between what was *Semitic* (or Palestinian) Judaism and what was *Hellenistic* (or Diaspora) Judaism in the 1st century. Well, "the old dichotomy between Palestinian and Diaspora Hellenistic Judaism is no longer tenable" (W.D. Davies, *Paul and Rabbinic Judaism* [Philadelphia: Fortress Press, 1980], p.viii-ix). L.H. Feldman, "Hengel's *Judaism and Hellenism* in Retrospect," JBL 96 (3, 1977), p.371-382, has shown that Hengel defends two basic theses: (1) We must cease to differentiate the Judaism of the land of Israel from Hellenistic Judaism since both show deep Greek influence; (2) This Greek influence was pervasive at a much earlier point than had been previously thought, in fact at least a century before the Maccabean revolt.

[4] "At that time [mid-1st century AD] the LXX ... enjoyed high esteem among the Judeans. It was even believed that the translators responsible for the Septuagint had been inspired by the Divine spirit." Solomon Zeitlin, *The Rise and Fall of the Judean State*, Vol 3, (Philadelphia: Jewish Publication Society, 1978), p. 198.

[5] What contemporary preacher has not at times quoted from the KJV, and at times from the NASB or NIV? There are even local congregations that prefer one over the other, and when preaching for those congregations,

3. There is much in the book of Hebrews that reminds us of Paul. The author was connected with Timothy, and therefore was Paul, or a close friend of Paul. Note, too, the close parallel to Paul's epistles in doctrine,[6] circumstances, appeal to Scripture to demonstrate the truth of Christian doctrine, and similarity of phraseology, diction, and style,[7] between the Epistle to the Hebrews and the thirteen signed letters of Paul.

4. The writer writes excellent Greek. The closely reasoned argument, the carefully interwoven use of key words ("hook words"), and the grammar itself (which closely approximates classical Greek), show this letter to be perhaps the finest example of the use of the Greek language we find in the New Testament Scriptures. None of this evidence, however, not even the appeal to the types and shadows of the Old Testament, can be used to demonstrate the author has been schooled in the philosophy and hermeneutical method of the Alexandrian School[8] (and Philo, in particular). The alleged "Alexandrian tone" many older commentators appealed to as one evidence of the authorship of Hebrews is probably no longer a valid point.

5. The author was not one of the original twelve apostles. From 2:3 ("confirmed to us") we learn the author was not one of the "eyewitnesses" of Jesus' earthly ministry. 2:3 does not exclude an *apostle* from writing the epistle to the Hebrews – only the original *twelve*.

6. The author was a male as the masculine participle "to tell" at 11:32 plainly shows. Had the writer been a female, the feminine participle would have been used.

B. THE TESTIMONY OF EARLY CHRISTIAN LITERATURE

There are allusions to Hebrews in the Apostolic Fathers which show the book was known and read before the close of the first century. For example, words from Hebrews are interwoven

---

the preacher is expected to use the version used by the majority in the congregation. In this use of differing versions, are we to suppose that our practices are so different from what may have been done in the 1st century?

[6] The similarity in theology between Hebrews and Paul is set forth in detail in "Theology of 'Hebrews'" by William Leonard, *Authorship of the Epistle to the Hebrews* (Rome: Vatican Polyglot Press, 1939), p. 45-106. Samuel Davidson, *An Introduction to the New Testament* (London: Samuel Bagster & Sons, 1848) Vol.3, p.211-214, lists fourteen points of doctrinal similarity between Hebrews and the Pauline epistles.

[7] See below, footnote #64, for documentation about style and diction.

[8] The Alexandrian School was a philosophical school combining Greek and Oriental thought, and emphasizing the allegorical (rabbinical) interpretation of Scripture, rather than emphasizing the literal and historical meaning. In the author's Commentary on Romans (p.xxx-xxxi), it has been shown how Platonic and Aristotelian philosophy had been imbibed by Philo. In addition, examples are given of how the Alexandrian School handled Scripture, and there is little similarity to the Hebrew writer's use of the Scriptures. Ceslaus Spicq (*l'Epitre aux Hebreux* [Paris: Gabalda, 1952], Vol.I, p.88-91) thought Hebrews so closely paralleled the thinking of Philo that the author of Hebrews most probably was a personal student of the famous Alexandrian philosopher. Ronald Williamson (*Philo and the Epistle to the Hebrews* [Leiden: E.J. Brill, 1970], p.575-576) examined each of Spicq's arguments on this issue and closed the door on anything more than superficial verbal similarity between Philo and Hebrews. For another excellent summary of the issues relating to the alleged similarity between Philo and the Epistle to the Hebrews, see J.C. McCullough, "Some Recent Developments in Research on the Epistle to the Hebrews," *Irish Biblical Studies* 2 (1980), p.141-165, and 3 (1981), p.28-45.

in the text of I Clement (96 AD) as the following quotation from chapter 36 shows:

> By Him the Lord has willed that we should taste the knowledge of immortality;
> "who, being the brightness [or, effulgence] of His majesty, is by so much
> greater than the angels, as He hath by inheritance obtained a more excellent
> name than they." For it is thus written: "Who maketh His angels winds [or,
> spirits], and His ministers a flame of fire." But concerning His Son the Lord
> spoke thus: "Thou art My Son, today have I begotten Thee. Ask of Me, and I
> will give Thee nations as Thine inheritance, and the uttermost parts of the earth
> for Thy possession." And again He saith unto Him: "Sit at My right hand, until
> I have made Thine enemies a footstool of thy feet."[9]

Hebrews was probably also used by Polycarp (*To the Philippians* 6; 12) and Hermas (*Visions* 2.3.2; 3.7.2; *Similitudes* 9.13.7). This shows the epistle was early regarded as authoritative and that the author was a first-century Christian.

1. The Eastern Church has generally received the letter as Paul's.

The Alexandrian Church

The earliest evidence comes from **Pantaenus**, bishop of Alexandria (180 AD). As quoted by Eusebius, the testimony reads:

> But now as the blessed presbyter [Pantaenus?] said, since the Lord, the apostle
> of the Almighty, was sent to the Hebrews, Paul, as having been sent to the
> Gentiles, on account of his modesty did not subscribe himself an apostle of the
> Hebrews, because of the honor belonging to the Lord, and also because he went
> beyond his bounds in addressing the Hebrews also, when he was herald and
> apostle of Gentiles.[10]

Next we have **Clement of Alexandria** (190 AD).

> To sum up briefly, he has given in the *Hypotyposes* [outlines] abridged
> accounts of all canonical Scripture, not omitting the disputed books – I refer to
> Jude and the other Catholic epistles, and [the Epistle of] Barnabas and the so-
> called Apocalypse of Peter. He says the Epistle to the Hebrews is the work of
> Paul, and that it was written to the Hebrews in the Hebrew language; but that
> Luke translated it carefully and published it for the Greeks, and hence the same
> style of expression is found in this epistle as in the Acts. But he says that the
> words, Paul the apostle, were probably not prefixed, because, in sending it to
> the Hebrews, who were prejudiced and suspicious of him, he wisely did not
> wish to repel them at the very beginning by giving his name.[11]

---

[9] Compare Hebrews 1:3ff and Clement's use of Hebrews becomes rather obvious. Also compare I Clement 17 with Hebrews 11:37 to see another allusion by Clement to Hebrews.

[10] Eusebius, H.E., VI.14.4.

[11] Eusebius, H.E., VI.14.1-3. Not many writers have accepted the idea that Hebrews, as it now reads in the Greek, is a translation from the Hebrew, as Clement suggests. Whether or not Hebrews is a translation is discussed in the notes below.

Origen (210 AD) thought Hebrews was a Pauline writing, but admitted various individuals and churches questioned whether it was written by Paul.

> In addition he makes the following statements in regard to the Epistle to the Hebrews in his Homilies upon it: "The style of the epistle, with the title `to the Hebrews,' has not that rudeness of speech which belongs to the apostle who confessed himself rude in speech, that is, in phraseology. But the epistle is purer Greek in the texture of its style, as everyone will allow who is able to discern differences in style." Again he says, "The ideas of the epistle are admirable, and not inferior to the acknowledged writings of the apostle [Paul]. Everyone will confess the truth of this who attentively reads the apostle's writings." Afterwards he adds, "I would say, that the sentiments are the apostle's, but the language and composition belong to someone who committed to writing what the apostle said, and as it were reduced to commentaries the things spoken by his master. If then any church receives this epistle as coming from Paul, let it be commended even for this; for it is not without reason that the ancients have handed it down as Paul's. But who wrote the epistle, God only knows certainly. But the account that has come down to us is various; some saying that Clement, who was bishop of Rome, wrote the epistle; others that it was Luke, who wrote the Gospel and Acts."[12]

Some comments on this long quotation are surely in order. (1) Origen himself believed Paul wrote Hebrews. In a letter to Africanus, Origen wrote, "But possibly someone pressed with this argument will have recourse to the opinion of those who reject this epistle as not written by Paul. In answer to such a one, we intend to write a separate discourse, to show that the epistle is Paul's."[13] (2) Origen admits different opinions were held in his day as to who the writer was. (3) Origen's own belief was the sentiments and ideas of the epistle belonged to Paul, but some other person wrote them down in the form and style they now possess.[14] (4) Agreeable with this last observation and his letter to Africanus, the expression "Who wrote the epistle, God only knows" can only mean *who the amanuensis was is uncertain*. (5) The "ancients" who handed the letter down as Paul's must refer to the ancient teachers at Alexandria.

Dionysius of Alexandria (250 AD) ascribes Hebrews without hesitation to Paul. In the epistle addressed to Fabius, bishop of Antioch, he writes, "They also took with joy the plunder of their goods, like those to whom Paul bore testimony (Hebrews 10:34)."[15]

In the same way Theognostos of Alexandria (280 AD), Peter (300 AD), Alexander (312), Hierax (310), Athanasius (350), Theophilus (400), Serapion, Didymus (400), and Cyril (440),

---

[12] Eusebius, H.E., VI.25.11-14.

[13] See *Ante-Nicene Fathers*, Vol.4, p.388. When appeal is made to Origen for testimony about the authorship of Hebrews, would that this statement of Origen's were as often quoted as are the words "who wrote the epistle, God only knows certainly."

[14] Some 200 times in his extant writings, Origen ascribes the authorship of Hebrews to Paul. See *Ante-Nicene Fathers*, Vol. 4, p.239, footnote.

[15] Eusebius, H.E., VI.41.6.

all of Alexandria, employ the epistle, ascribing it to Paul without question.[16]

The placement of Hebrews in the canon by the Eastern Church. The Chester Beatty Papyrus (P^{46}) is the earliest (early 3rd century AD) extant manuscript from Egypt. In it, the Epistle to the Hebrews appears in the collection of Paul's letters, in the order of Romans, Hebrews, 1 & 2 Corinthians, Galatians, etc. So, at that time and in that area, it was the firm belief that Paul the apostle was the author of Hebrews. In later manuscript history, Hebrews still appears exclusively in association with the letters of Paul. In several of the later codices (Aleph B A C H I K and P), not all of which came from Alexandria by any means, Hebrews is placed tenth in the order of Paul's letters, after the letters to churches (i.e., after 1 & 2 Thessalonians), and before the letters to individuals (i.e., 1 & 2 Timothy). This association of Hebrews with the epistolary order of the New Testament may be another thing that has encouraged readers to regard this document as a letter.

The Greek Church

The **Synod of Antioch** (264 AD) ascribed the letter to Paul in this language:

> "Now the Lord is that Spirit," according to the apostle Paul (2 Corinthians 3:17). And according to the same, "For they drank of the spiritual rock ..." (1 Corinthians 10:4) ... And of Moses the apostle writes, "Esteeming the reproach of Christ greater riches ..." (Hebrews 11:26).[17]

Methodius, bishop of Olympus in Lycia (290 AD), puts together two phrases, one from Romans 7:14 and the other from Hebrews 10:1, and attributes them both to Paul.

> "Since the Law, according to the apostle, is spiritual, containing images of good things to come ...."[18]

Gregory Thaumaturgus (d. 270 AD) ascribes Hebrews to Paul, and quotes or alludes to various passages, e.g., 2:3,4, 3:15-18.[19]

The Council of Nicea (325 AD) received the epistle as the authentic production of Paul. Eusebius, speaking in the name of the assembled bishops said, "Paul the chosen vessel, writing to the Hebrews, says ...."[20]

Eusebius of Caesarea (325 AD) frequently quotes the epistle, especially in his commen-

---

[16] Samuel Davidson, *Introduction to the New Testament*, Vol.3 (London: Samuel Bagster and Sons, 1848), p.191; and Alford, *Hebrews*, p.14,15, where the actual statements of these men can be examined. It is true that the Alexandrian Deacon Euthalius (460) again speaks of suspicions affecting its authenticity, but sets them aside, and declares it to be Paul's.

[17] Mansi Collect. Concil. Vol.I, p.1038.

[18] Galland, *Bibl. Patr., Vol. III, p. 703.*

[19] Davidson, *op. cit.*, p.192.

[20] Davidson, *ibid.*

tary on Psalms, attributing it to the apostle Paul without the least hint of doubt about its authorship. Several examples of such quotes:

> The fourteen letters of Paul are well-known and undisputed. It is indeed not right to overlook the fact that some have rejected the Epistle to the Hebrews, saying that it is disputed by the church of Rome, on the ground that it was not written by Paul. But what has been said concerning this epistle by those who lived before our time I shall quote in the proper place.[21]

> For as Paul had addressed the Hebrews in their own tongue, some think the evangelist Luke, others that Clement himself, translated the epistle. The latter seems more probable, because the epistle of Clement and the epistle to the Hebrews have a similar character in regard to style, and still further because the thoughts contained in the two works are not very different.[22]

In another passage, Eusebius refers to Hebrews as being classed (in the time of Clement of Alexandria) as among the *Antilegomena*, or disputed scriptures. However, in his principal passage on the canon, he numbers Hebrews with the *Homologoumena*.[23]

The Pauline authorship of Hebrews was commonly held in the Greek Church after the time of Eusebius. Thus Cyril of Jerusalem (386 AD), Gregory of Nazianzus (389), Epiphanius, bishop of Salamis in Cyprus (402), Basil the Great, bishop of Caesarea in Cappadocia (379), the council of Laodicea (360), Gregory bishop of Nyssa (c.370 AD), Titus of Bostra (371), Chrysostom (407), Theodore of Mopsuestia (428), and Theodoret bishop of Cyprus in Cilicia (457), held the Pauline authorship.[24]

The Syrian Church

The epistle is included in the **Peshitto Syriac** version. This does not really speak either for or against the Pauline authorship, but it does show the epistle was accepted as canonical in 150 AD. In position, the Peshitto shows nothing for or against its Pauline origin, because Hebrews follows the thirteen Pauline epistles.

A composition by the Synod of Antioch, addressed to Paul of Samosata, c. 264 AD, expressed the opinion that Paul wrote Hebrews. Jacob of Nisibis (325), belonging to the school there, and Ephraem the Syrian (378) quote Hebrews as being Paul's.[25]

---

[21] Eusebius, H.E., III.3.5. The "proper place" can be found at H.E. book VI, chaps. 14, 20, and 25.

[22] Eusebius, H.E., III.38.2-3.

[23] Eusebius, H.E., VI.25.2. The footnotes by Schaff explains that Hebrews is included in those "reckoned as the epistles of Paul." *Nicene and Post-Nicene Fathers,* Vol.1, p.155. "*Antilegomena*" is a technical term that means "some people in some places spoke against" this book being included in the canon. "*Homologoumena*" means "all people everywhere confess" this book should be included in the canon.

[24] Davidson, *op. cit.*, p.194. Gregory Nazianzus, in the *Jambi ad Seleucum*, inserts the remark "certain say that the Epistle to the Hebrews is illegitimate." Theodoret, in his *Prooemium* to the Epistle to the Hebrews, is still engaged in polemics against those of Arian sentiments, who rejected the Epistle to the Hebrews as "illegitimate (*nothos*)," denying its Pauline authorship.

[25] Davidson, *op. cit.*, p.195.

2. The Western Church only gradually came to hold the Pauline authorship.

The Testimony from Gaul

Irenaeus (180 AD) and **Hippolytus** (222 AD, a student of Irenaeus, who held the same opinion as his teacher) both denied the Pauline authorship. This fact we learn from Stephen Gobar, who in the 6th century wrote, "Hippolytus and Irenaeus say that the epistle of Paul to the Hebrews is not his."[26]

Victorinus of Pettau (303 AD, in Pannonia, north of the Adriatic Sea) speaks of seven churches to which Paul wrote, and speaks also of epistles to individuals, without the least mention of Hebrews.[27]

Hilary, bishop of Poitiers (368 AD), was the first known individual in the Western Church who was disposed to receive Hebrews as the production of the apostle Paul. He wrote, "Paul said to the Hebrews, 'being so much better than the angels'...."[28]

The Testimony from Africa (Carthage, Hippo)

Tertullian, bishop of Hippo (200 AD), ascribed the Epistle to the Hebrews to Barnabas. Tertullian quotes some verses from Hebrews 6, and assigns them to "the Epistle of Barnabas to the Hebrews." He goes on to say that this epistle of Barnabas deserves more respect than the *Shepherd of Hermas*.[29]

Cyprian (258 AD) speaks of seven churches (Romans, Corinthians, Galatians, Ephesians, Philippians, Colossians, Thessalonians) to which Paul wrote,[30] but does not mention the epistle to the Hebrews, nor quote it in any of his extant works. From this, some scholars have inferred that Cyprian did not look on Hebrews as Pauline. But in this place, as in several of these men's writings, this argument from silence is precarious.

Augustine, bishop of Hippo (430 AD), favored the opinion that Hebrews was written by Paul. He wrote,

---

[26] Davidson, *op. cit.*, p.174. That writer continues, "We learn from Eusebius that Irenaeus was acquainted with the epistle [to the Hebrews], and mentioned it in a work now lost: "There is also a book of Irenaeus of various treatises in which he mentions the epistle to the Hebrews, and the book called the Wisdom of Solomon, quoting some passages from them." It would appear from this passage that Irenaeus placed Hebrews on a level with the apocryphal 'Wisdom of Solomon.' He was not convinced that Paul was the writer, and therefore he did not quote it as a part of Scripture."

[27] Alford, *Hebrews*, p.20.

[28] *De Trinitate*, IV.11.

[29] *De Pudicitia*, chap.20. It is not easy to assign a proper value to this opinion advanced by Tertullian. (1) It may have been that which was current in all the African churches. (2) It may have been nothing but a guess on Tertullian's part. (3) It may have been derived from historical tradition. (4) It may have been a tradition of only limited extent.

[30] *De Exhortat. Martyrii*, XI.

> Paul has a like salutation at the beginning of all his epistles with the exception
> of that which he wrote to the Hebrews, where he is said to have omitted his
> ordinary form of salutation designedly, lest the Jews who were obstinately
> opposed to him, taking offence at his name, should either read with an
> unfriendly mind, or neglect altogether to read what he had written respecting
> their salvation. For which reason, some have been afraid to receive that epistle
> into the canon of Scripture.[31]

From the synods at which Augustine's influence was considerable, we find statements in agreement with Augustine's beliefs about the Pauline authorship of Hebrews. At the Synod of Hippo (AD 393), the third of Carthage (397), the fifth of Carthage (419),[32] it is specified as Paul's.

The Testimony of the Roman Church

There are evidences the letter was early received at Rome. **Clement of Rome** certainly used it as authoritative, and expected the church at Corinth to receive it in the same way.[33]

On the grounds of the **Jung Codex**, discovered at Nag Hammadi in 1945, it has been ascertained that around AD 150, Hebrews did not have lesser authority in Rome than, for instance, Paul's signed epistles.[34]

If it was received early at Rome, the time soon came when Hebrews was put aside by that same community. **Marcion** (140 AD) excluded Hebrews from his canon, but for what reason we cannot discover. The Epistle to the Hebrews has nothing in common with Marcionite errors. Marcion was very anti-Jewish. Hebrews, on the other hand, finds the Mosaic religion pointed forward to Christ and Christianity. It may well be that Marcion excluded Hebrews on doctrinal grounds, not on the grounds of authorship.

The information given in **The Muratorian Canon** (170 AD) has been interpreted to mean the author of that canon did not hold to the Pauline authorship of Hebrews. In this fragment it is stated Paul wrote epistles to seven churches, and his thirteen epistles are enumerated in a peculiar order. But the letter to the Hebrews is not named, unless it be either

---

[31] *Expos. ep. ad Roman. inchoat.*, sect.11. From this and other testimonies of Augustine, we learn: (1) It is certain that he knew of the fact that some Latin churches of his day, and some in Africa, denied the epistle to be Paul's, although the greater number received it to be his. (2) Augustine himself often quotes it as the apostle Paul's, speaks of fourteen epistles of Paul, calls it "Scripture," and was strongly inclined to believe it to be such. (3) At the same time, because Hebrews is unsigned, Augustine often introduced his quotations of the book in such a way as to avoid giving any opinion about the authorship.

[32] In the first and second councils of Carthage, Hebrews is mentioned separately from the other thirteen epistles of Paul. In the third council of Carthage, it is included in the fourteen epistles of Paul.

[33] See page xix above, and the discussion concerning canonicity below, in these Introductory Studies.

[34] The extant Nag Hammadi papyri are Gnostic documents. They try to prove Gnosticism is not heresy by appealing to Biblical writings, among them Hebrews and Paul's signed letters. The copies found at Nag Hammadi are supposed to be copies of documents that originally were made about the middle of the second century at Rome, and then taken to Egypt.

"the epistle to the Laodiceans" or "the epistle to the Alexandrians" which are named in the very next sentence in the Muratorian fragment.[35] The African Canon also omits Hebrews.

Attention is often called to the fact that **Novatian** (c.250 AD) never quotes or alludes to Hebrews, though two treatises of his are extant in which it was most suitable to his purpose. This silence does not prove much. Perhaps he had never seen Hebrews. Perhaps he had it and just chose not to quote it.

Caius (Gaius) of Rome (late 2nd or early 3rd century AD) rejected the Pauline authorship of Hebrews, as we learn from Eusebius.

> There has reached us also a dialogue of Caius, a very learned man, which was held at Rome under Zephyrinus, with Proclus, who contended for the Phrygian heresy. In this he curbs the rashness and boldness of his opponents in setting forth new Scriptures. He mentions only thirteen epistles of the holy apostle, not counting that to the Hebrews with the others. And unto our day there are some among the Romans who do not consider this a work of the apostle.[36]

Jerome (400 AD) evidently held to the Pauline authorship of Hebrews, though he recognized many Latin churchmen did not. In many places in his writings, Jerome quotes passages out of Hebrews and calls it "Paul's" or "the apostle's" (which amounts to the same thing). In other places he makes note of the peculiarities which caused some to distinguish it from the acknowledged letters of Paul. After enumerating Paul's signed letters, Jerome says:

> But the epistle called "To the Hebrews" is thought not to be Paul's because of the difference in style and language, but either Barnabas' (as Tertullian thought), or the evangelist Luke's (according to some), or Clement's, afterwards bishop of Rome, who they say arranged and adorned Paul's sentiments in his own language; or, at least, if it be Paul's, that he might decline putting his name in the inscription on account of the Hebrews being offended with him. But he had written as a Hebrew to Hebrews, in Hebrew, that is, in his own language most eloquently, on which account it was, that being translated it has more elegance in the Greek than his other epistles: this they say is the reason of its differing from the rest of Paul's Epistles.[37]

However, in his epistle to Dardanus (129), Jerome affirms his belief in the Pauline authorship and the canonicity of Hebrews.

---

[35] Both Westcott, *Hebrews*, p.xxviii, and Lunneman, *Hebrews*, p.371, reject the idea that Hebrews was ever called by either of these titles.

[36] Eusebius, H.E., VI.20.3. The last sentence in the quote is Eusebius' own statement that some among the Romans, from Caius' day down to his own, denied that Paul wrote Hebrews.

[37] *Catalog of Ecclesiastical Writers*, quoted in Davidson, *op. cit.*, p.180. The idea that Paul did not sign this letter because of possible antagonistic feeling toward him is a weak point. The epistle's recipients knew who wrote it; the one who carried the letter would have told them. Further, the writer says, "I'm going to visit shortly" (13:23). It would be ridiculous to say, "You don't know who I am, but I'm coming shortly." Again, it was not the Christians to whom this letter was written who were antagonistic to Paul – it was unbelieving Jews.

[After citing testimonies from Hebrews 11 and 12, Jerome proceeds] This must be said by ours, that this epistle which is inscribed "to the Hebrews," is received as the apostle Paul's not only by the churches of the East, but by all the ecclesiastical Greek writers of former times; though most ascribe it to Barnabas or Clement; and that it makes no difference whose it is, since it belongs to an ecclesiastical man, and is daily read in the churches. But if the Latins do not commonly receive it among the canonical Scriptures, the Greek churches do the same with the Apocalypse of John. We, however, receive both, not following the usage of the present time, but the authority of ancient writers, who for the most part quote both; not as they are wont to quote sometimes apocryphal books, but as canonical.[38]

That Jerome's own personal view was to favor the Pauline authorship of Hebrews can be seen from the title which he affixed to the letter in his Vulgate version, "The Epistle of Paul to the Hebrews" (*Epistola Pauli ad Hebraeos*). This title in turn influenced eleven centuries of belief in the Western Church.

This brief study of the early church fathers shows that after the middle of the fourth century the belief that Paul was the author of Hebrews gradually found acceptance in the West. The change of views may be traced to the preponderating influence of the Greek Church upon the Latin, and to the influence of Jerome's standardized Latin version, which became the official Bible in the West.

C. CONJECTURES CONCERNING AUTHORSHIP (If Paul's Authorship Is Denied)

1. Clement of Rome has been suggested as being the author. Arguments *for* this opinion: (1) That some ancients thought Clement was the author we learn from Origen. (2) If Clement of Rome is the same man who was an associate of Paul (Philippians 4:3), he could have known Timothy (Hebrews 13:23). (3) The earliest evidence of the existence of Hebrews is found in I Clement, where passages from Hebrews are found verbatim. Arguments *against* this opinion: (1) There is the possibility that what Clement refers to is not "authorship" but who put the author Paul's thoughts into its present Greek form. (2) It has never been shown the two Clements (Clement of Rome and the Clement named in Philippians) are the same man, though we admit it is possible. (3) The quotations from Hebrews could indicate no more than familiarity with the Epistle to the Hebrews because there was a copy of it in Rome, not that Clement of Rome is the author of both epistles.

---

[38] Concerning the writings of Jerome: (1) There is an ambiguity in his letter to Dardanus. Who are the "most (who) ascribe it to Barnabas or Clement?" Latins? Greeks? Are they from a former generation or contemporary with Jerome? (2) If the "most" are "ecclesiastical Greek writers," what did they mean when they "ascribed it to Barnabas or Clement"? Jerome likely means most Greeks ascribed the style and language of it to Barnabas or Clement, though the ideas and sentiments were Paul's. (3) What does the expression "an ecclesiastical man" mean? Apparently Jerome means the writer was a Christian, not a heretic. (4) From the testimony of Jerome, he evidently believed Paul wrote the epistle to the Hebrews. And though he seems to disapprove of the theory, he tells of Greeks who thought Hebrews was originally written by Paul in Hebrew and then put into Greek by someone other than Paul.

2. Barnabas has been, since the time of Tertullian, thought by some to be the author.[39] Arguments *for* this view: (1) Barnabas was a Cyprian by birth, and in times past when an "Alexandrian hue" was thought to be found in the epistle, it was noted that Cyprus was connected in many ways with Alexandria. (2) Barnabas was a Levite, and as such would have been accurately acquainted with the Jewish worship ceremonies. Note the many references to the priesthood and the sacrifices in Hebrews. (3) Barnabas was a companion of Paul (Acts 13,14), and this was thought to explain the similarity to Paul's thought found in Hebrews. (4) Barnabas was an "apostle" (Acts 14:14), and thus was a man of sufficient authority to have written the epistle, and to accord it a place in the canon. (5) It would be natural to find the "son of exhortation" (Acts 4:36) writing a "word of exhortation" (Hebrews 13:22). Arguments *against* this opinion: (1) No other writer than Tertullian adopted this opinion. (2) If Barnabas were the author, why did the knowledge of that fact so quickly disappear from the church's tradition? (3) The argument that one must be a companion of Paul to think similar thoughts reflects a low view of inspiration, if not a naturalistic source for theology. (4) Some think Hebrews 2:3 would exclude Barnabas since we find him in the church at a very early date (Acts 4). However, we just do not know whether Barnabas was an eyewitness of Jesus' ministry.

3. Luke was suggested as the author/translator by Clement of Alexandria, and is an opinion that has been preferred by others from time to time. Arguments *for* this hypothesis: (1) A considerable number of words and phrases unknown to every other New Testament writer are a feature common to both Hebrews and Luke's writings.[40] (2) Hebrews is good Greek – like that written by Luke. Luke's Greek is polished, whereas Paul's was rugged, though vigorous. (3) Luke was a constant companion of Paul's – thus the similarity to Paul's writings and thought, and the familiarity with Timothy, found in Hebrews. Arguments alleged to be *against* the Lukan authorship: (1) There are important differences of language and structure between Hebrews and Luke's writings.[41] (2) Luke was of Greek origin (cp. Colossians 4:11

---

[39] The usual arguments in support of Barnabas' authorship have been summarized in Theodor Zahn, *Introduction to the New Testament* (Grand Rapids: Kregel, 1953 reprint), Vol.2, p.354-355. Some writers have speculated about the relationship of Hebrews to the later Epistle of Barnabas. This conjecture is based on several factors: (1) Both works deal with somewhat similar motifs, though the Epistle of Barnabas is very marginal when compared with the magnificent book of Hebrews. (2) Codex Claromontanus has a *Versus scribturarum sanctarum* – an ancient stichometric catalog of the sacred writings of the Old and New Testaments – inserted between the Epistle to Philemon and the Epistle of Barnabas. (Claromontanus, in the first hand, does not contain any reference to a book called "to the Hebrews." So, some have supposed that "the Epistle of Barnabas" is another name for our Hebrews.) All Claromontanus has are the words *Barnabae epist. ver. DCCCL*; it names the Epistle of Barnabas and tells how many verses or lines *(stichoi)* it contains. Counts of the lines in the Epistle to the Hebrews vary from 703 to 830. The apocryphal Epistle of Barnabas is longer than Hebrews in all the manuscripts (e.g., Hebrews has 40 ½ columns in Codex Sinaiticus; Barnabas has 53 ½ columns.) The reader may examine this material from Claromontanus in detail in Lunneman, *Hebrews*, p.353-354. Lunneman attributes the failure of Claromontanus to list Hebrews as part of the canon to the debate in the West over its authorship, since this catalog comes to us from the West. (Hebrews was added to Codex Claromontanus by a later hand, but it was not part, originally, of the codex.)

[40] Lunneman (*Hebrews*, p.356ff) gives over six pages of the words and phrases allegedly found in Luke and Hebrews which allegedly point to the Lukan authorship of Hebrews. These are taken from Delitzsch's work on Hebrews. Delitzsch favored the Lukan authorship of Hebrews.

[41] "There is nothing in Luke of the rhetorical balance, nothing of the accumulated and stately period, nothing of the deep tinge ... [one finds in Hebrews]." Alford, *Hebrews*, p.53,54.

with 4:14), whereas Hebrews manifestly proceeded from a Jew by birth.

   4. Silas has been suggested as the writer.[42] The arguments *for* this view: (1) Silas (short for Silvanus) was a Jew, (2) a companion of Paul, and (3) is a writer of excellent Greek (if, as 1 Peter 5:12 seems to affirm, Silas is the penman of 1 Peter). (4) Silas was a member of the Jerusalem church (Acts 15:22), and was also a New Testament prophet (Acts 15:32). This latter fact would permit us to say his writings were inspired since prophets (by definition) spoke by inspiration. Arguments *against* this opinion: (1) Only a few, and those relatively modern, writers have advocated this hypothesis. If it were true, why didn't someone in the ancient church suggest it? (2) Earlier writers, who insisted the writer of Hebrews was a Hellenistic Jew, pointed to Silas' Palestinian provenance as being against his being the author of Hebrews. (Today, when there is no longer such a sharp distinction made between Hellenistic and Palestinian Judaism, this objection may have lost some of its force.)

   5. Apollos has also been proposed as being the author of Hebrews.[43] Arguments *for* Apollos: (a) Apollos was a Jew, born in Alexandria (Acts 18:24), and this would at once account for the "Alexandrian tone" of the letter and the uniform use of the LXX (which translation was made at Alexandria). (b) Alford thinks that in Apollos we have just that degree of dependence on Paul which is required, combined with that degree of independence which the writer must have had. (c) There was a rivalry at Corinth between the followers of Paul and those of Apollos (1 Corinthians 1:12). That Clement of Rome did not want to add fuel to this fire is the suggested reason why Clement does not give the name of the author of Hebrews, though he quotes Hebrews more extensively than any other New Testament book. (d) Apollos was "mighty in the Scriptures" (Acts 18:24), and Hebrews shows a real knowledge of the Old Testament. (e) Apollos also was an "eloquent man" (Acts 18:24), just the kind of rhetorician we'd expect to be the author of a rhetorical masterpiece like Hebrews. (f) Apollos "powerfully refuted the Jews ... demonstrating by the Scriptures that Jesus was the Christ" (Acts 18:28), and is this not what one finds also in Hebrews? Arguments *against* this view: (a) There is no early ecclesiastical tradition pointing to Apollos as the author. This conjecture was first introduced by Martin Luther, and has then been defended by some subsequent scholars.[44] (b) It would be very difficult to demonstrate the possibility of Apollos' being an Holy Spirit inspired speaker or writer, and this difficulty would hardly fit a book's being in the canon.

   6. Timothy is another who has been suggested as the author of Hebrews. Arguments

---

[42] See the case for Silas presented in Thomas Hewitt, *The Epistle to the Hebrews* (Grand Rapids: Eerdmans, 1960).

[43] Rotherham thought Apollos wrote Hebrews with Aquila and Priscilla looking on.

[44] Since Luther, this idea, which some have called a brilliant guess, has gained many followers, including such recent expositors as T.W. Manson and W.F. Howard, and E.H. Plumptre, "The Writings of Apollos," *Expositor*, New Series 1 (1885), p.328-348, 409-435. Ceslaus Spicq in his encyclopedic commentary has collected the chief arguments in behalf of Apollos' authorship. Twelve of these arguments have been followed and made available in English by Hugh Montefiore, *A Commentary on the Epistle to the Hebrews* (New York: Harper and Row, 1964). Taking note of the objection that the idea of Apollos' authorship is only as old as Luther, it is answered that because of the almost complete lack of ecclesiastical tradition through the first three centuries, we have as much right to make up our minds today as to the authorship of Hebrews as did the people living in the fourth century who chose Paul.

in *favor*: (1) Timothy had a Jewish mother (Acts 16:1-3). (2) From childhood he knew the Scriptures (2 Timothy 3:15). (3) He was a constant companion of Paul. Argument *against* this view: (1) Timothy seems to be excluded by the mention of him in Hebrews 13:23, as a different person from the author.[45]

7. Titus is another conjecture. An argument *for* this opinion is that he was a companion of Paul. *Against* it is the fact that Titus was a Greek (Galatians 2:3), not a Jew.

9. Philip, the deacon/evangelist was the one whom Ramsay suggested[46] as the author of Hebrews, but his view has found little support among the scholars.

10. Aquila is another New Testament personage whose name has been proposed as the author of Hebrews. Arguments given *for* the idea: (1) He was a companion of Paul. (2) He was a Jew, and (3) he was "at home" in Rome (a fact thought to help explain "those from Italy greet you" in Hebrews 13:24). *Against* the view: (1) From the usual method of mention of this man and his wife, with Priscilla the wife usually being named first, a method that is contrary to the custom of antiquity (it is claimed), most feel the wife was the more dominant of the two, and therefore Aquila would not have had the personality to write this letter.

11. The ideas that **Mary, the mother of Jesus,**[47] or **Priscilla,**[48] might be the author of Hebrews, both seem to be ruled out by the masculine pronoun at Hebrews 11:32.

12. Epaphras has recently been proposed as the author of Hebrews.[49] Assertions *for* this view include: (1) The epistle recommended in Colossians 4:16 is the writing we know as

---

[45] John D. Legg, "Our Brother Timothy," *Evangelical Quarterly* 40:4 (October-December, 1969), p.220-223, has urged that Timothy is the author of all of Hebrews except the last few verses (13:22-25). Legg sees the last few verses as being a gloss (post-script) added later by a different author, none other than by Paul himself. Legg's theory appears to be very inadequate, an attempt to claim Pauline authority for the book, by sacrificing the book's integrity. (We shall deal more fully with the matter of the integrity of the epistle at a later point in these Introductory Studies.)

[46] William Ramsay, *Luke the Physician, and Other Studies* (London: Hodder & Stoughton, 1908), p. 301-308.

[47] J.M. Ford, "The Mother of Jesus and the Authorship of the Epistle to the Hebrews," *Bib. Today* 82 (1976), p.684-694, proposes that Mary, perhaps in conjunction with John and Luke, was responsible for the content of Hebrews. Another hand wrote the Greek style, and the title was added even later. Mary was one who "treasured all these things in her heart;" her speech to Elizabeth (Luke 1:46ff) is full of references to Old Testament Scriptures, and Hebrews likewise is a treatise reflecting on the fulfillment of Old Testament texts. Ford defends her thesis on the basis of external probability and the content of Hebrews.

[48] Adolph von Harnack ("Probabilia uber die Adresse und den Verfasser des Hebraerbriefes," *ZNW 1* [1900], p.16ff), suggested the reason the author's name is suppressed is that Priscilla lived in a man's world, and there would therefore be every reason for keeping it quiet that a woman had written an epistle intended to be authoritative and to have wide circulation. Priscilla and her husband were cultured Hellenistic Jews, and the woman who could instruct Apollos in the faith (Acts 18:26) was no mean teacher. The interest in the tabernacle would be natural for a family whose living came from tent-making (Acts 18:3), and the emphasis in Hebrews on being a pilgrim would be natural to one who did as much travelling as this couple did. R. Hoppen, *Priscilla: Author of the Epistle to the Hebrews*, and Other Essays (New York: Exposition, 1969) is a contemporary defense of Priscilla's authorship of Hebrews.

[49] C.P. Anderson, "Hebrews Among the Letters of Paul," *StudRel/SciRel* 5:3 (1975-76), p.258-266.

the Epistle to the Hebrews. (2) The author of "my letter ... from Laodicea" was actually Epaphras, a major church leader in the Lycus river valley. (3) Epaphras lacked apostolic authority, but that authority was bestowed on Hebrews ("my letter ... from Laodicea") by Colossians 4:16. (4) A connection between Hebrews and Colossians in the minds of the earliest readers of Colossians could well have led to their joint circulation in some circles. (5) The Roman church probably knew Hebrews as an independent writing, while the Alexandrian church knew it in the context of a Pauline corpus. (6) When Hebrews was given its title ("to the Hebrews") and when the Pauline letters were arranged according to relative length, the connections with Colossians were broken. Objections that could be raised *against* this theory: (1) The "letter ... from Laodicea" is very likely the letter we now know as Ephesians, rather than being Hebrews.[50] (2) The idea that Hebrews is addressed to the Lycus river valley in the Roman province of Asia Minor is not easy to accept. (3) The conjecture about an original relationship between Colossians and Hebrews has not been accepted by scholars generally.

What has been noteworthy as we have examined these dozen hypotheses is how the same evidence can be given different interpretations, and how the championing of one theory of authorship seems to cancel all the arguments given by the champions of any other theory.

D. EXAMINE AGAIN THE POSSIBILITY OF PAULINE AUTHORSHIP

1. Arguments Against the Pauline Authorship

Arguments against the Pauline authorship from external evidence, often made in the past, include: (1) There is no evidence of the Pauline authorship in the apostolic fathers.[51] (2) The earliest testimony of the Western Church is opposed to the Pauline authorship of Hebrews. The Western Church fathers, with the exception of Tertullian, do not say who wrote the letter, only that Paul did not. (3) The earliest evidence for the Pauline authorship in the Eastern Church (Clement of Alexandria) appears to be inaccurate in at least one respect, namely, that Hebrews as we know it is hardly a translation from Hebrew to Greek, for the smoothness and artistic polish of the Greek argue that our Hebrews is an original composition. If Clement of Alexandria's reference is inaccurate in regard to the language, who is to say it is accurate in the claim to authorship? (4) It is not until the fourth century that the Western Church begins to speak of the Pauline authorship, and then perhaps it was because they had been so influenced by the Eastern Church.

---

[50] See J.B. Lightfoot, *St. Paul's Epistles to the Colossians and to Philemon* (Grand Rapids: Zondervan, a reprint of the 1879 edition published by MacMillan), p.244.

[51] The truth is there is no evidence one way or the other in the apostolic fathers. The Early Christian writers are often classified in three groups: the apostolic fathers (96-140 AD); the apologists (150-180 AD); and the early church fathers (190-400 AD). While the apostolic fathers make copious use of the New Testament, references to the authorship of any New Testament book are rare. The authors of only Matthew, Mark, 1 Corinthians, and Revelation are named by the apostolic fathers. If Marcion is included in this first group, then we would also have the authorship of Galatians and Romans stated in the apostolic fathers. For most other New Testament books, the first specific mention of authorship is found in Irenaeus (180 AD) or Clement of Alexandria (190 AD). In this light, the absence in the apostolic fathers of any statement of authorship for Hebrews is far from surprising, and the absence says precisely nothing for or against the Pauline (or anyone else's) authorship.

Arguments against the Pauline authorship from internal evidence, in the past, have included: (1) The alleged Alexandrian tone,[52] something (it was alleged) Paul could never have attained. (2) The writer of Hebrews quotes entirely from the Septuagint, whereas Paul quotes from both the Hebrew and LXX versions of the Old Testament.[53] (3) Would Paul, the apostle to the Gentiles, write to the Hebrews?[54] (4) Hebrews was not signed, as was Paul's custom.[55] (5) The writer of Hebrews depends on the apostles for information, whereas Paul received his gospel by revelation.[56] (6) Some have urged that the exquisitely balanced organization of Hebrews – with four doctrinal sections alternating with four exhortations or warnings – is quite unlike Paul, who typically divides his letters into two sections – a carefully argued doctrinal section, followed by practical applications.[57] (7) The theology of Hebrews differs from Paul's.[58] (8) The style of Greek in Hebrews is quite unlike Paul's writing.

The last argument against the Pauline authorship, the one based on style, is perhaps the strongest argument that can be marshaled. From the earliest times, Hebrews' diversity from the style of the acknowledged writings of Paul has been a matter of remark. The main difference for us, which will also set forth its characteristic peculiarity, is that whereas Paul is ever, as it were, struggling with the scantiness of human speech to pour forth his crowding thoughts, thereby falling into rhetorical and grammatical irregularities, the style of Hebrews flows regularly on, with no such suspended constructions.

---

[52] In addition to what was said earlier about the "Alexandrian tone" of Hebrews, an additional thought or two may be useful. (For a brief explanation of what the "Alexandrian tone" is, see T. Rees, "Hebrews, Epistle to," *International Standard Bible Encyclopedia*, edited by James Orr [Grand Rapids: Eerdmans, 1949], Vol.2, p.1361-62.) It has never been proven that a resemblance between Hebrews and the writings of Philo requires the author of Hebrews to have read or studied Philo. The "Alexandrian tone" is not as noticeable as is often represented. Philo indeed allegorizes the Pentateuch, but he allegorizes it much more than the author of Hebrews, and in a different way. Philo often undermines the historical reality of the Old Testament usages and acts, converting them into nothing but allegory; whereas the author of Hebrews points out the typical character of the Mosaic ritual without detriment to historical fact.

[53] The matter of how the author quotes the Old Testament has been discussed above on page xviii.

[54] We think so! Paul never lost his intense desire to win the Jewish people. In his evangelist work he went to Jews first. He sought the conversion of the Jewish leaders in Jerusalem. In Rome he sought to bring Jews to the salvation in Jesus Christ (Acts 28). Look at his intense longings in Romans 9-11. So we would expect him to write to the Hebrews, if the opportunity presented itself.

[55] Neither is anyone else's name appended to this manuscript. This argument could be used against any theory of authorship.

[56] Hebrews 2:3 does not say the author "received his gospel for the first time" from the twelve; it does say it was "confirmed" by the twelve. Hebrews 2:3 does not rule out Pauline authorship of Hebrews. See what was said on this verse under "Historical Allusions" earlier in these Introductory Studies, p. xiv.

[57] The analysis of the outline of Hebrews is considered at length in the notes below under "Outline."

[58] In recent years, it has been affirmed that Hebrews gives some "twists" to faith, the Law, to soteriology, and to the covenants that differ from Paul, and Hebrews omits almost any mention of themes that were dear to Paul, including the resurrection of Jesus from the dead. These reasons for rejecting Hebrews as Pauline (1) seem to reflect the idea that the human writers of Bible books each had his own theology, and that their own minds were the source of whatever they wrote; and (2) are often based on a denominational idea of "faith-only" as the God-approved condition of salvation, versus "faithfulness to the revelation one has" as being the condition. Now it is this commentator's position (see his Commentary on Romans, and the comments below on Hebrews 11) that the Bible has always taught "faithfulness" – both in Paul and in Hebrews, as well as everywhere else in the Sacred Writings.

> The careful syntax of the author of Hebrews differs radically from the bursting spontaneity of Paul. Paul was like a rushing mountain torrent, plunging over the rocks with no time for watertight syntax, rhythm, or polished innuendo. Paul's style was extreme freedom in the matter of style.[59]

Several things may be said in regard to this matter of style by the defenders of the Pauline authorship. (1) Some have appealed to the occasions and circumstances that called forth the letters.[60] When Paul's epistles were written, their occasion usually required a spur-of-the-moment letter, dictated to an amanuensis. Such a process of dictation might at times result in interruptions of the flow of thought, and thus account for the suspended constructions. In the case of Hebrews, if we envision the writer having time to compose this manuscript somewhat at leisure, working it over several revisions so that it would be perfect, in hopes that it will receive the best possible reception among the Hebrews, then the polished presentation is no longer surprising. (2) Others have appealed to the suggestion that the thoughts are Paul's, but the actual writing was done by someone else (e.g., Luke or Silas), which (it will be recalled) was Origen's view. If this indeed is what occurred, the argument from style is of little import.[61] (3) The arguments from style, though often made on both sides of the authorship question, actually must be weighed carefully. Assume for the sake of argument that the writer of Hebrews could be any one of the people suggested through the years. When none has left any other document wherein the questions addressed in Hebrews is addressed, we can properly ask: "Who can say what kind of vocabulary or method of reasoning Paul (or any other New Testament writer) would have used had he addressed himself to the subject of the epistle?"

2. Arguments for the Pauline Authorship of Hebrews

Arguments from external evidence include: (1) The Eastern Church has generally received the letter to be Paul's. If the traditional view as to destination (i.e., Palestine) is true, we would expect the churches in the East not only to have a copy of Hebrews for reading in the public worship services, but also to have a rather unbroken tradition about who the author was. These two things are exactly what we find when we examine the evidence. (2) The earliest extant collections of New Testament manuscripts included Hebrews exclusively among the Pauline epistles.[62] (3) There is a plausible answer as to why the Western Church, after first

---

[59] Trentham, *Hebrews*, p.4.

[60] Time, place, and circumstances have a very definite influence on style. For example, note the difference between the Gospel of John and the Book of Revelation (both by the apostle John), or between Leviticus and Deuteronomy (both by Moses).

[61] If a prophet (like Silas, for example) were the penman, the inspiration of the book is still assured. Further, if a penman is used, it can still be said to be the letter of the man whose thoughts and ideas are behind the manuscript. 1 Peter is signed by Peter, yet Silas was the penman. The interesting thing is that Greek style of 1 and 2 Peter are so different that the Petrine authorship is denied by certain critics of liberal theological persuasion. 1 Peter is good Greek; 2 Peter is rough Greek. The difference is usually explained in this fashion: Peter himself penned 2 Peter, whereas Silas put Peter's ideas into good Greek in 1 Peter. In a similar way, Hebrews can be attributed to Paul, even if someone else put the thoughts into writing.

[62] See above, page xxi, concerning "The Placement of Hebrews in the Canon of the Eastern Church." Peter does allude to a collection of Paul's letters as already having been made before 2 Peter is written (2 Peter 3:15,16). John Owen (*An Exposition of the Epistle to the Hebrews* [Wilmington, Del.: Sovereign Grace Publishers, a reprint of the 1668-1684 edition]) and J.A. Bengel (*Gnomon of the New Testament* [Edinburgh:

accepting the letter,[63] began to deny the Pauline authorship of Hebrews. Many suggest the reason Hebrews declined in the church's estimation was that the Montanists made use of Hebrews 6:4-6 to support their false teaching (i.e., that one sin committed after baptism caused the soul to be lost). The Latin church, unable otherwise to answer this proof text, denied that Paul wrote it, thereby lessening its authority.

Arguments for Pauline authorship, from internal evidence, include: (1) The historical circumstances alluded to in the letter (see the historical allusions in chapter 13) certainly fit Paul. (2) There are many terms and phrases similar to those found throughout Paul's writings.[64] Some of the main parallels noted in the past[65] in defense of the Pauline authorship of Hebrews include:

> Hebrews 1:5 and Acts 13:33 – The Old Testament verse "Thou art my Son, today I have begotten thee" is used with reference to Christ. This use of this Old Testament verse is found only in Paul and in Hebrews.

> Hebrews 2:4 and 1 Corinthians 12:11 – Both speak of the distribution of the gifts of the Holy Spirit.

> Hebrews 2:10 and Romans 11:36 or Colossians 1:16 or 1 Corinthians 8:6 – All speak of God as the One "for whom and through whom" all things exist.

> Hebrews 2:16 and Galatians 3:29 or 3:7 or Romans 4:16 – The only passages in the New Testament that designate the family of faith as being descendants

---

T & T Clark, 1860], Vol. 4, p.333) maintained Peter has reference to our Epistle to the Hebrews when he says to his readers that Paul wrote to them "some things hard to be understood" (cp. Hebrews 5:11ff). Such an identification, of course, would also affect our understanding about the destination of Hebrews.

[63] See above on page xxv, "The Testimony of the Roman Church."

[64] Perhaps these rather striking parallels have not been considered by scholars in recent years because the works in which they appeared are not readily available. For example, Samuel Davidson, "*Hebrews*" (p. 235ff) offers several pages of comparisons of parallels as they occur in the Greek phrases of Hebrews and Paul's epistles. Following that, he offers more pages which make these points: (i) Over 50 words are found in the LXX or Apocrypha that are found only in Paul and Hebrews in the New Testament. (ii) Over 20 words, found neither in the LXX or Apocrypha, are unique to Paul and Hebrews in the New Testament. (iii) Over 30 words, while appearing elsewhere in the New Testament, have a frequency of occurrence almost peculiar to Hebrews and Paul's letters. (iv) The same peculiarity of grammatical construction relative to the use of a passive verb (i.e., using a nominative as the subject of the verb) is found only in Hebrews and the epistles of Paul. (v) An adjective in the neuter gender is used to denote generic quality instead of a noun. (vi) The figure of speech termed paronomasia is a feature in the style of Hebrews, as it is one of the distinguishing marks of Paul's style. (vii) There is in Paul's style a species of digression which Paley calls "going off at a word." We have those same characteristic digressions of thought in Hebrews (2:1-4, 3:2 at the word "house," 12:18-29 at the words "voice, speaketh, shook," 12:5 at the word "chastening," and at Hebrews 2:7-9 at the word *hupotasso* [an example which exactly agrees with 1 Corinthians 15:27, because in both instances the digression is on the same word]). (viii) The epistle to the Hebrews exhibits certain modes of quotation characteristic of Paul.

[65] In the 1800's, Moses Stuart (*A Commentary on the Epistle to the Hebrews* [Andover, MA.: Warren F. Draper] p.120-253), defended the Pauline authorship of Hebrews. He devotes over 100 pages in his commentary to this topic, even offering a comparison in the Greek of verses in Paul and in Hebrews to show the similarities and parallels (p. 147-151). One of the last 20th century defenses of the Pauline authorship was by the Roman Catholic scholar William Leonard (*The Authorship of the Epistle to the Hebrews* [Vatican: Polyglott, 1939), p.3-43.)

or sons of Abraham are either all Paul or in Hebrews.

Hebrews 4:12 and Ephesians 6:17 – The comparison of the Word of God to a sword is found only in Paul and in Hebrews.

Hebrews 6:3 and 1 Corinthians 16:7 – These are the only places in the New Testament where the phrase "If God permits" occurs.

Hebrews 10:19 and Romans 5:2 or Ephesians 2:18 or 3:12 – Only in Paul or in Hebrews do we find the idea "access" or "introduction" into God's very presence so explained.

(3) The doctrinal content of Hebrews has been shown to be similar to Paul.[66] The person and work of Christ are similarly presented in Paul and in Hebrews. The Old Testament is considered to be temporary and a shadow of things to come, both in Paul (e.g., Colossians 2:17) and in Hebrews. The Pauline triad – faith, hope, and love – show up in Hebrews 10:22-24.

E. CONCLUSIONS REGARDING AUTHORSHIP

Recent years have seen the oldest of the breakfast cereals using the slogan in its advertising, "Try Kellogg's Corn Flakes Again for the First Time!" The background of that commercial is the fact that a host of different cereals are now on the market, all clamoring for the attention of the consumer. With all those other claimants, it is very possible to overlook the unique place and taste of the old one.

We propose something similar has happened regarding authorship studies for Hebrews. The book was early treated as canonical, both in West and East. In the East, the Pauline authorship was generally accepted. Then, because of debate over certain theological points, some people in some places began to question or doubt the Pauline authorship. Some even denied it. However, by the time of Jerome, AD 392, both East and West accepted the Pauline authorship. There is no solid tradition connecting the epistle with anyone else. The Pauline authorship of Hebrews was the accepted doctrine in the Roman Church until the time of the Reformation. Was the Reformers' doctrine of authorship also the result of a theological debate? Was it related to their total rejection of almost all the Roman church stood for? In any case, Reformers like Luther, Melanchthon, Calvin and Beza led the way in doubting or rejecting the Pauline authorship of Hebrews. In the most recent decades, with its scholarly rush to use the historical-critical method of interpretation, the Pauline authorship of the epistle has been more and more rejected, at least in the West (i.e., Europe, England, America). Today, it is difficult to find anyone who strongly defends the Pauline authorship. Instead, most commentators simply list all the reasons why the long-held Pauline authorship is to be rejected. Our appeal is to "Try the Pauline Authorship Again for the First Time!" The reasons for suggesting that Paul is the author of the book are at least as equally strong and convincing as any of those held up against the traditional view.

---

[66] Care must be exercised on this point, for all the New Testament writers held the same views!

The traditional view is that Paul was the author of Hebrews. If the writer of the epistle to the Hebrews had signed his name to the manuscript, then the whole topic of authorship would be a matter of faith. But in the absence of any such specific Biblical evidence, the final conclusion about the authorship of the book is really in the realm of opinion.

Our study of the evidence for and against the various suggested authors (Paul, and all the others), has shown several things: (1) Most of the internal and external statements are capable of being interpreted in at least two different ways, which renders the use of the evidence problematic at best. (2) The competing views about authorship almost cancel each other out, leaving no one as the author! What is not in question is: (3) Hebrews is included among the collections of Paul's letters in all the old manuscript traditions; (4) The traditional view was that Paul wrote it (though not all agree on the validity or the origin of the tradition); (4) There is no solid tradition connecting the epistle with any other writer; and, (5) Hebrews was recognized as having canonical authority from the first. For these reasons, this commentator will have to have more reason than has so far been found before rejecting the traditional view of Pauline authorship.

III. READERS AND DESTINATION

While authorship may not affect the interpretation of many verses in the epistle, the same cannot be said when it comes to the matter of destination. Who we suppose the original readers to be will have considerable influence on our interpretation of numerous verses.

One point to which attention should be drawn is the way in which the problems [of introduction] inter-lock. The questions of authorship, date, destination, and the identity of the addressees are all to some extent interrelated, and decisions about one may have a bearing on our conclusions about another. Equally, a false conclusion on one question may lead us into quite erroneous inferences regarding the others.[1]

So we must be methodical in our study, and very careful about any conclusions drawn. As was also true of authorship, many alternative views on destination rest on critical conclusions[2] that once were popular but now have been discredited. We must not use discredited arguments to support or reject any view of destination.

---

[1] R. McL. Wilson, "Hebrews" in the *New Century Bible Commentary* (Grand Rapids: Eerdmans, 1987), p. 11,12.

[2] Such critical conclusions include an alleged "Alexandrian tone or hue" thought to be found in Hebrews; the alleged difference between Palestinian and Diaspora Judaism; the idea that Christianity as Jesus left it was corrupted by an aberrant form of Judaism (read Hellenistic Judaism) into the religion we know today; the idea inherited from some Reformation teachers that "faith" in Paul is different from "faith" in Hebrews; and the present scholarly preoccupation with the Essenes and Qumran.

A. WHAT THE HISTORICAL ALLUSIONS TELL US ABOUT THE READERS

1. The readers were **Christians**.

"Jesus, the apostle and high priest of our confession" (3:1), Jesus our "hope" (6:18,19), "God ... has spoken to us in His Son" (1:3), "assembling together" (10:25), all point to the fact the readers were Christians. So does the fact that they were "new covenant" people, not old covenant people (Hebrews 8-10, and 12:24), and that they have come to Mount Zion, to the "church of the firstborn who are enrolled in heaven ...." (12:22ff).

The terms given in 6:4-6, and 10:32 – "enlightened ... tasted ... made partakers" – do not admit of any explanation other than that the circumstance envisioned is of complete conversion,[3] and that in the time past. The readers were already Christians.

The readers have been Christians for some time, and in that time some have gone backward (i.e., become sluggish) in their spiritual growth and understanding.[4] By now they ought, instead, to be "teachers" (5:11-14).

2. Ethnically, they were **Jewish** – *not* Gentile – as indicated by these evidences:

a. "To the Hebrews"[5] indicates the early opinion the readers were Jewish.

---

[3] A few writers have tried to explain Hebrews from the standpoint that the readers are **not yet converted**, and that Hebrews is written to encourage them to go on and become Christians, rather than failing to follow through into the faith toward which they have been leaning.

The discovery of the Dead Sea Scrolls near Qumran, an Essene community that existed in the first century AD (destroyed in the war which ended with the destruction of Jerusalem in AD 70), has led some to postulate a connection between "the Hebrews" and the Essenes. Hans Kosmala, in *Hebraer-Essener- Christen* (Leiden: E.J. Brill, 1959), has urged that the people addressed were not yet Christians, but Essenes who had stopped short of accepting Jesus and Christianity. Hebrews is written to encourage them to leave the Essene community, to take the final step with Jesus. (Essenes certainly did practice ceremonial washings -- see Hebrews 6:2, though the Essenes were not the only Jewish groups who practiced such ceremonial washings.)

F.C. Synge taught that *pros Hebraious* means "Against the Hebrews" (Jews), and that the primary thesis of the letter was to show the Law had been superseded by the Gospel of Christ. The letter "against Judaism" was addressed to Jews who were on the verge of accepting Christianity, but who had hesitated to take the final step. *Hebrews and the Scriptures* (London: SPCK, 1959), p.44.

[4] The historical allusions (about the origin and validation of the Gospel [2:3], and the replacement of the Mosaic covenant by the New Covenant, etc., because of the sacrifice of Jesus) in Hebrews "bear strongly against the theories of the Tubingen School. They furnish the historical proof that Christianity, as it stands vouched for in the canonical writings of the New Testament, was not gradually formed from a conflict of opposing tendencies, partly freer [Hellenistic influences, Paul and his school], and partly more restricted [Jewish influences, Peter and his followers]; but that defections from the primitive Apostolic faith took place at a very early period, and that partly by the relaxing, partly by the obscuring, of an already-existing but divinely-instituted life of spiritual faith, doctrinal and moral corruptions found their way into it. These of course stood in connection with other existing forms and tendencies of spiritual life. In this way might arise a division among the Jewish Christians, parallel to that among the Jews themselves; one tendency developing itself into heretical Ebionitism; the other into a Nazarite sect, whose incipient elements are assailed in this Epistle." C.B. Moll, "Hebrews" in *Lange's Commentary* (Grand Rapids: Eerdmans, nd.) p.12.

[5] We have already commented on the term "Hebrews" in our study of historical allusions, but more needs to be said here. This commentator freely admits that through the years the title has influenced his thinking about

The oldest title for which we have any evidence is contained in the words "to the Hebrews." Early tradition, east or west, knows no alternative title.[6] The consensus of opinion in the early period of the church was that this letter was addressed to "Hebrew people."

But what was it to be a "Hebrew"? (1) In some passages, the word is used to indicate physical descent. "Taken strictly, the term `Hebrew' indicates only *descent* (2 Corinthians 11: 22, Philippians 3:5), and implies nothing as to *residence* or language."[7] It was a term almost synonymous with "Jew."[8] The old title on this epistle surely indicates the belief then current that the letter was addressed to people who were of Jewish descent.

(2) In some places "Hebrews" are carefully distinguished from "Hellenists" – and both are ethnically "Jews." Acts 6:1 surely shows that both Hebrews and Hellenistic Jews lived in Jerusalem and were members of the same church. Yet there was a marked difference between the two, and the first-century people knew the difference.[9] (a) Was the strife between the two groups based purely on the difference of the language spoken – as though the Hebrews spoke Hebrew/Aramaic while the Hellenists spoke Greek? It is difficult to believe this conflict between the Hebrews and Hellenists was rooted simply in the language they preferred to speak. If the difference between the two is not based purely on language, then it would be possible to be a "Hebrew" and at the same time use the LXX version of the Bible, and to speak and read good Greek.[10] (b) Is, then, the difference between Hebrew and Hellenist something that goes

---

the destination of "Hebrews." Can we trust the title? What does it mean? Where would such people be living?

[6] Some contemporary scholars have written much in disparagement of this title. One approach is to say the present title is only someone's guess deduced from the contents. Another approach conjectures that when the Alexandrians first included Hebrews in the Pauline Corpus, they made up a title that matched the titles of the other letters in the corpus. It is this commentator's conviction that most of these aspersions against the traditional title arise from the logical necessity to minimize the force of these words in order to defend a destination other than the traditional view. We admit that sometimes the people in the early church got things wrong. When what they taught obviously does not match Scripture, we say the tradition is wrong. In this section concerning destination, we are deliberately approaching the topic from this standpoint -- Is there any Scriptural reason that can be found that demands a rejection of the traditional view? If "To the Hebrews" was such a wildly inaccurate guess (devoid of any relation to the truth) as some moderns have suggested, why did no one object to it in those sub-apostolic times when the title was first starting to be used?

[7] Moll, *op. cit.*, p.10

[8] According to Eusebius, *Preparation for the Gospel* VII.8, the name Hebrews (*Hebraioi*) belonged to the Israelites only previously to their receiving the law. In the same book, at VIII.12,14, the Jews (*Ioudaioi*) are called descendants of the Hebrews (*Hebraioi*), for which reason at IX.1, the two names are united as mutually supplementary. See also what was written above, pages viii-ix, especially footnote #10 on page viii.

[9] Surely, Acts 6:1, as well as modern scholarship which no longer makes a distinction between Hellenistic and Palestinian Judaism, would contradict the hypothesis, sometimes set forth and based on internal evidence, that the intended readers were not Hebrews, but Hellenistic Jews.

[10] If the difference between "Hebrew" and "Hellenist" is not just language, then the use of good Greek in Hebrews and the reliance on the LXX version for Old Testament quotations is no proof the readers were really Hellenistic Jews, and not "Hebrews" at all. Is it possible to be a "Hebrew" and at the same time use the LXX version of the Bible, and speak and read good Greek? We think so. James, the brother of the Lord, and for years the leader of the Jerusalem church, was considered to be a very pious man. Yet James was a man who knew and used his Greek. The Epistle of James is also excellent Greek, some say the best in the New Testament. Now James was written at Jerusalem and intended for Jewish Christians. Its excellent Greek is thought to be no hindrance to its intended readers, whether they lived in the Promised Land or in the Dispersion.

deeper than mere descent or language? When it came to being faithful to the revelation God had given, some of the descendants of Abraham had things right,[11] even if the Sadducees and Pharisees of Jesus' day didn't. In the light of this fact, might we call the Sadducees and Pharisees "liberals" (or "Hellenists," since they have adopted Hellenistic customs and culture), while the "Hebrews" were the old "conservatives" who eschewed the newer ways, when "new" included the embracing of the traditions of the elders which voided the Law of Moses (Matthew 15:3-6)? If the word "Hebrews" in the title of our book means the same thing that "Hebrews" means in Acts 6:1, there still is no doubt that the readers were ethnically *Jewish*.

(3) Is there another possibility? What about limiting the name "Hebrews" to one of the non-conformist Jewish sects that flourished during the first century AD? A non-conformist sect would be any of the sects other than the Sadducees and Pharisees who were the molders of Jewish religion and culture during the last century before Christ, as well as during the first century AD.[12] What are we to think of the proposal that the readers of Hebrews, before their conversion to Christianity, were members of such a non-conformist group? And what of the idea that Hebrews was written to squelch the temptation to return to the old non-conformist group?[13] Of course, in the eyes of some of these writers, it is supposed there wouldn't be anything wrong with going back to mainstream (Pharisaic, Palestinian, normative) Judaism, but to quit Christianity for some non-conformist sect would be a terrible sin! In the eyes of other writers, the "Hebrews" had been members of some non-conformist sect before their conversion. However, as they contemplated quitting Christianity, instead of going back to the old sect, or even to the religion of the rabbis, they had decided instead to go back to the old religion of Moses. Surely there is nothing wrong with that, they might have been thinking. Hebrews, by its appeal to the superiority of the new covenant to the old, is intended to put an end to any such option.

---

[11] We think of Simeon (Luke 2:25) who is described as "righteous and devout." We think of Zacharias and Elizabeth who, we are told, were "righteous in the sight of God, walking blamelessly in all the commandments and requirements of the Lord" (Luke 1:6).

[12] During the last century before Christ, as well as during the first century AD, Pharisaism was struggling with the Sadducees for the allegiance of the Jewish people. Gradually, Pharisaism became normative Judaism (also called Palestinian or Diaspora or Hellenistic Judaism). [NOTE: The distinction once made by scholars between Palestinian and Diaspora (Hellenistic) Judaism is now recognized to have been in error. Such a distinction is no longer a valid distinction. See page xviii, footnote #3 above for documentation of this fact.] If we take these two groups to represent "normative Judaism," then other sects besides the Pharisees and Sadducees might be classified as non-conformist. Is the term "Hebrews" then used of all those non-conformist groups because they have a similar background, or use similar thought forms, vocabulary, and hermeneutics?

[13] Since the discovery of the Dead Sea Scrolls, not a few writers have attempted to identify the "Hebrews" with the Essenes who lived at Qumran.

Yigael Yadin associated Hebrews and Qumran by asserting the epistle was addressed to current members of the Qumran sect, now scattered throughout the world, and who had not yet accepted Jesus as their Messiah. "The Dead Sea Scrolls and the Epistle to the Hebrews," *Scripta Hierosolymitana* 4 (Jerusalem: Magnes Press, 1958), p.36-55.

Otto Michael held a more moderate position. He found no direct historical connection between Hebrews and Qumran, but did find certain linguistic and conceptual similarities which he thought pointed to a common background for Hebrews and Qumran. *Der Brief an die Hebraer* (Gottingen: Vandenhoeck & Ruprecht, 10th edition), p.151-52, 376-78, etc.

See page xi, footnote #19 above for additional comments along this same line.

As intriguing as all this may be, we see no valid reason to limit "Hebrews" to some non-conformist group,[14] especially since the word "Hebrews" was used in early times to designate *Jewish Christians*.[15]

Continuing the evidences that the readers were ethnically Jewish, include these points:

b.   The readers were descended from Abraham (2:16). This has been taken to indicate the readers were ethnically Jewish.

c.   A familiarity with Old Testament sacrificial and priestly system characterized the readers.

The special emphases on Moses the lawgiver, on the Old Covenant, on Aaron the priest, on the Levitical priests, on their activities and sacrifices on the Day of Atonement, and on the tabernacle with its furniture and its ritual,[16] all show the readers and writer both were from the same Jewish roots.

Now, the "tabernacle" had not been used as a place for worship since the time Solomon built the first temple. Herod's temple was the building standing in Jerusalem in New Testament times. Yet, for some reason, Hebrews does not specifically speak of the temple.[17] Why, we

---

[14] F.F. Bruce published a significant article in *New Testament Studies* 9 (1962-63), p.217-232, entitled "`To the Hebrews' or `To the Essenes'?" in which he examines the alleged parallels between Hebrews and Qumran that had received so much attention from scholars in the 1950's. He concluded the differences between the materials considerably outweigh the similarities and that "it would be outstripping the evidence to call [the readers of the epistle] Essenes or spiritual brethren to the men of Qumran" (p.232). New articles which directly link Hebrews and Qumran have not been forthcoming since the work of Bruce.

[15] See this documented in M. Black, *The Scrolls and Christian Origins* (New York: Scribners, 1969), p.78. "Hebrews" means "Jewish Christians" in the title of the *Gospel According to the Hebrews* and in the Paris magical papyrus 574, 11, 3018f, which has phrases like "I adjure thee by Jesus the God of the Hebrews." In the Clementine Homilies, XI., 35, the Church of Jerusalem is called "The Church of the Hebrews," consisting, as it did, according to Eusebius H.E. IV.5, entirely of "Hebrew believers."

[16] Hebrews 9:4 and 10:11 have often been used to "prove" there is a contradiction between Hebrews and the Old Testament. But, there is no proof from Hebrews 9:4 where the "censer" or "altar of incense" seemingly is put in the wrong room of the tabernacle – or from the verse that says "daily" the priest stands offering sacrifices (10:11) – that the readers' or writer's knowledge of Old Testament institutions or of the ritual performed in the house of worship, was not derived from first-hand knowledge, or that this arrangement is in contradiction to what one reads in Moses. There is no need to understand these verses as implying the writer didn't know his Old Testament, or that the readers' were accustomed to a ceremony somewhat different from that derived from the instructions in the Law of Moses.

[17] Much has been made of the complete absence of any mention of a "temple." For example, see how this fact is used by the writer of the footnote (p.11,12) in *Lange's Commentary*. He writes:

It is difficult to see *what* in the Epistle requires us to suppose a temple in the neighborhood of its readers. The fact that *no single mention* of, or direct allusion to, the temple is made in the Epistle, from the beginning to the end, would seem to indicate the contrary; and it is, in fact, this utter silence of the Epistle regarding the temple worship, and *the complete carrying back* of the discussion to the arrangements and rites of the Mosaic tabernacle, which forms the chief *obstacle* to believing that it was addressed to those Jews, whose Judaistic associations all stood connected with the stately ritual of the temple. It seems difficult to explain how this complete ignoring of the temple could have taken place in connection with

wonder? Is this question to be answered by appeal to the fact that "Hebrews" – in distinction to Palestinian/Diaspora Judaism – would have had a higher regard for the tabernacle than they would for Herod's temple (built, as it was, with its court of women, and court of the Gentiles, on a Greek pagan-temple model, as much as on Old Testament instructions)?

Passages like 8:3ff, 9:6ff, 13:13ff, point clearly to the idea that the Old Testament priestly and sacrificial services were still in operation when Hebrews was written.[18] Such sacrifices had to be offered somewhere – at an altar, in a building, somewhere. This is not just a "spiritual" sanctuary, existing only in the readers' and writer's imagination. What is to keep us from explaining the absence of any reference to temple and reference instead to the ritual of the Pentateuch by this manner: Had the writer of Hebrews argued against the temple and the way the Sadducees ran things as a reason for not going back to Judaism, the readers could simply say "I never agreed with what they were doing, anyway. I'm going back to the way things were done in the Bible. What can be wrong with that?" The writer stops such an argument in its tracks by appealing to the ritual of the Pentateuch.

d.   Heroes of the Faith whose exploits are recounted in Hebrews 11 is very Jewish. They loved to have their history recounted.

e.   The contents and tone of our epistle do not allow us to regard it as addressed to Jewish Christians in general, nor to such Christians of Hebrew extraction as, united in one church with Christians of different origin, were living among the Gentiles.

Not a syllable points to relations with Gentile Christians as such. Everything indicates a purely Jewish community, and that, too, one in which many members still adhere to the Levitical temple service and sacrificial rites, as to a divine institution (13:9,10). Nowhere is there implied in the persons addressed, any mere *theoretical* preference of the Law. For this reason, the epistle can hardly be addressed to Jewish Christians in the Dispersion. A "Hebrew of Hebrews" might be born and live in the Dispersion (cf. Paul, Philippians 3:5), but this fact alone does not permit us to say that "Hebrews" was a general letter addressed to all "Hebrews" wherever they might be living in the ancient world.

Ethnically, the readers were Jewish, not Gentile.[19] "It must be said the particular type of

---

readers whose entire religious habits and associations clustered around it. Certainly, we must assume that either the *readers* or the *writer* had been more familiar with the Jewish ritual of the Pentateuch, than with that of Jerusalem and the temple. The *latter* supposition solves the problem, and leaves us at liberty to suppose the Epistle was addressed by a Jew of alien birth, and more familiar with Judaism in its historical records, than in its temple worship, to the Christian residents of Jerusalem and Palestine.

Later in these introductory studies, as the matter of "date of writing" is examined, more will need to be said about the absence of any mention of a "temple" in Hebrews.

[18] Below, in the discussion concerning the "Date" of the writing of Hebrews, documentation will be given concerning the debated matter of whether the sacrifices ceased when Jerusalem was destroyed, AD 70.

[19] In this century, a few scholars (e.g., James Moffatt *A Critical and Exegetical Commentary on the Epistle to the Hebrews*, ICC [Edinburgh: T & T Clark, 1924], p.xvi-ff) have argued the readers were GENTILES!   No

approach which we find in Hebrews is more naturally understandable if the author was a Jewish Christian writing to Jewish Christians and drawing upon their common background and heritage in the Old Testament Scriptures."[20]

3.   The readers formed a **definite community** of believers.

It does not seem to be a general epistle directed to Christians at large. Rather, the letter seems to be sent to a specific group to meet a specific need.[21] This idea of the readers forming a definite community is implied in several passages. 13:24 would be one, where the writer requests to readers to "greet all of your leaders and all the saints." This language about "leaders" (past and present) would certainly indicate that a congregation is addressed. "All the saints" nearby who are to be greeted (13:24), would indicate that a particular congregation, rather than the church at large, is addressed. The writer has visited the readers (13:19) and hopes to return to them soon (13:23). This too implies something other than a general destination. It implies a specific community.

Can anything be inferred from Hebrews concerning the relative size of this definite community? Can we say the readers formed one of the house churches in the city where they lived? Can we say the reference to the fact the readers should by now be "teachers" (5:12) is evidence that Hebrews is addressed to a relative small group? We are not ready to so affirm. That the readers by now ought to be teachers, in the context where the point is a distinction between old and new covenants, does not seem to prove they were something other than rank-and-file members of a church. Any Christian could be expected to be able to tell others the Old Testament, rather than being an end in itself, pointed to Christ. They should be able to tell the difference between Moses and Christianity!

---

one made any such claim for 19 centuries, but modern scholars will still propose this as a live hypothesis. They argue the title "to the Hebrews" was mistakenly tacked on to this work by someone in no real position to know, and that further "falling away from the Living God" (3:12) is not something a man would do if he left the church to go back to Judaism. Neither of these arguments is convincing. The title certainly reflects the contents of the letter. And it is precisely the point being made that to quit Christianity in favor of Judaism is "falling away from the living God," for unless we honor the Son, we cannot honor the Father! Further, why the author would try to dissuade a Gentile from leaving Christ by using an elaborate argument based on the Old Jewish ritual is unexplainable. But presume the readers to be Jewish – and the Epistle's argument at once makes sense.

A.B. Bruce has written on this matter, "If the readers were indeed Gentiles, they were Gentiles so completely disguised in Jewish dress ... that the true nationality has been successfully hidden for nineteen centuries, and even now, after the learned critics have done their best to show us the Gentile behind the Jews, we shake our heads in honest insurmountable doubt, and feel constrained to agree with Westcott when he pronounces the argument ... `an ingenious paradox'." ("Epistle to the Hebrews," HDB, II, p.337)

Further, Gentile Christians who were contemplating going back to their old religion, would not be greatly moved by an argument that began "Now if perfection was through the Levitical priesthood ..." (Hebrews 7:11). No Gentile ever thought it was. Only Jews thought that!

All this renders doubtful the suggestion of W.G. Kummel *(Introduction to the New Testament*, rev. ed. trans. H. Lee [Nashville: Abingdon Press, 1975], p. 399) and others that the recipients were *Gentile* Christians (or Christians in general) who are (in this new age) regarded by the writer as the true Israel or people of God. (It is true that Peter in 1 Peter and Paul in Romans and Ephesians, do teach that Christians, rather than the unconverted sons of Israel, are now the "Israel" of God. But it is doubtful that "Hebrews" is used as another name for this new people of God.)

[20] Wilson, *op. cit.,* p.11

[21] This is not to say that the principles and doctrines set forth are simply local in their application.

4. This community of Jewish Christians has **had some illustrious leaders** in the past (13:7).

Those leaders have died (were they martyred at the hands of hostile persecutors?), Hebrews 13:7, but their faithfulness till death is something the readers are called on to imitate.

5. They were people for whom **the LXX version was an authoritative Bible**, and who would not be offended by a letter addressed to them and written in excellent Greek.[22]

6. For the readers, **the gospel had been validated/corroborated** as God worked miracles through the apostles of Jesus (Hebrews 2:3,4).

Whoever the readers were, there have been apostles working among them, and by God's help doing the signs of an apostle while preaching.

Does the phrase "confirmed to us by those who heard [Jesus]" (2:3) imply that neither the writer[23] nor the readers learned anything from Jesus personally? It has been so interpreted,[24] but is the inference justified? And even if so, can the inference be used as evidence to help determine the destination of Hebrews? Our answer to these questions is, No. Remember, the whole point of the passage concerns the *guarantee* the readers have about the truth of the gospel. The guarantee is that the gospel which was first spoken by *Jesus* has been just as much validated as was the Law of Moses. In that context, it would *not* also be an important part of the emphasis whether or not the readers had personally heard Jesus during His earthly ministry.

7. They had **given practical evidence of their faith** by serving their fellow Christians, especially caring for those of their number who suffered most in a past time of persecution.

The Hebrews writer refers to the readers' long-standing practice of ministering "to the saints" (6:10). "Amidst the excitement of their new-found faith in Christ, they had demonstrated practical concern and love by ministering to fellow believers in need (6:10) and comforting others who had been harassed for their faith (10:34)."[25]

8. They have been **persecuted in the past**.

---

[22] See page xviii, footnote #4. The Jews in Palestine not only spoke Greek, they preferred the LXX version of the Bible.

[23] Hebrews 2:3 has no real force for or against the possible Pauline authorship of this work. See comments on the historical allusions given at the very beginning of these Introductory Studies.

[24] "The readers appear to be a group of Jewish Christians who had never seen or heard Jesus in person, but learned of Him from some who had themselves listened to Jesus." F.F. Bruce, *The Epistle to the Hebrews*, p.xxx.

[25] Bruce Demarest, "Hebrews" in *Baker Encyclopedia of Bible* (Grand Rapids: Baker Book House, 1988), Vol.1, p.943.

They had endured public abuse, imprisonment, and the looting of their property (10:32). The present readers had not yet been called on to die for their faith (12:4). This persecution resulted from the fact they had become Christians (10:32ff).

9.   They are **now facing a new opposition**.[26]

This current wave of opposition seems to have caused many to seriously consider quitting Christianity in favor of returning to the old religion. Some have already stopped attending the assembly (likely, the Sunday assembly[27] of believers), Hebrews 10:25. The opposition was so persuasive, it seemed the obvious thing to do was to change religions and no longer be the object of this persecution.

Who was the cause of this opposition – government or religion? (1) Some would say *government* – and the inducement to abandon Christianity was that of going back to a religion that enjoyed government protection.   (a) Not many Jews would agree being Jewish automatically provided insulation from persecution.   (b) What are we to think of the presentation made by some that these Jewish Christians have begun to waver and abandon hope, threatening to renounce Jesus Christ and to revert back to the security of the Jewish religion because it enjoyed the protection of Roman law? Indeed, there were religions licit and illicit. But it was not till after 64 AD and the burning of Rome that Christianity was looked on by the empire as a new religion rather than a sect of the Jewish religion. This commentator is not sure we should bring up the idea of the protection of Roman law as one of the motives the Hebrews might have had for abandoning Christianity. (2) Above, we've shown the possibility that the persecution of the readers resulted from *religious* intolerance – and if they re-embraced the Jewish religion, no more opposition from that quarter was to be faced.

10. They **knew Timothy and the writer**.

Not only have the readers been united with the writer in the past (13:19), they also have had some common experience with Timothy in the past, and there is the possibility of renewed acquaintances in the future (13:23).

How many places do we know where Timothy has been? If Paul, as the traditional view has it, is the writer, how many places can we name where Timothy and Paul together have visited? One of these places would be the destination of our letter.

11. They found **something very attractive in the old Jewish religion**, attractive
     enough to give serious thought to rejoining its devotees.

Is this devotion something similar to what we read about the Christians at Jerusalem in Acts 21:20, where James says to Paul, "You see, brother, how many thousands (tens of thou-

---

[26] It is a rather difficult decision to choose between "discipline" (12:7-11), "persecution," or "hostility by sinners" as the term to express what Hebrews 12:3ff warns about.

[27] This hardly is to be interpreted to mean that the members of one house church were no longer willing to associate with other house churches in the same town in the city-wide meetings held from time to time.

sands) there are among the Jews of those who have believed, and they are all zealous for the Law ...." If following Christ brought persecution, and the older way of the Jewish practice did not, why not return to the old religion, a religion that after all, was divinely given?

12. While at first sight it might be attractive, **such a return was fraught with problems**.

They would be going back to a city that was about to be destroyed (Hebrews 13:14). What cities besides Jerusalem (and, perhaps, Qumran) were threatened with destruction in the middle of the first century AD?

They would be going back to a sacrificial system that never could take away sins, and to a religious ritual that was about to be ended by force (8:13). What sacrificial system that we know about was "ended" in the middle of the first century AD? If we can identify it, we can identify our readers and where they lived because that was the religion they were tempted to return to.

Worse, such a defection from Christianity would be tantamount to "falling away from the living God" (3:12), or falling away from their Christian faith altogether. The writer identifies what they were in danger of doing (2:1, "drift away") as being apostasy, and he indicates the real cause was found in unbelief (3:12). Such continual refusal to believe has eternal consequences! The writer warns them they have everything to lose if they fall back (apostatize from the Christian faith), and encourages them with the assurance that they have everything to gain if they press on (2:1-4, 3:12-13, 6:4-8, 10:26-31, 12:15-17).

To forestall such a defection, the writer stressed the superiority of Jesus in a series of contrasts to the prophets (1:1-3), angels (1:4-14), Moses (3:1-6), Aaron (5:1-6), and the Levitical system (7:11,12). The object of such contrasts was to show the inferiority of Judaism and the superiority of the religion introduced by Jesus.

13. They needed to **consider Jesus**!

Fix their thoughts on Him! Meditate profoundly on Who He is, on what He does, on the religion He established (3:1, 12:3).

The writer calls attention to "the Old Testament, with its elaborate ceremonies, its types and shadows, and its great historic figures like Moses and Aaron. His finely-wrought argument runs thus: We will grant the dignity of Moses and Aaron, and the authority of the Old Covenant. But Christ is supreme over all; His dignity and authority cannot be compared with others. Therefore, honor and hold only to Him. So the main drift of the argument in the epistle, more than anything else, shows that its original readers had grown up with the religion of Israel as their background and way of life."[28] By carefully considering Jesus, they will be weaned from any further desire to return to the old way.

---

[28] Neil R. Lightfoot, *Jesus Christ Today: A Commentary on the Book of Hebrews* (Grand Rapids: Baker, 1976), p. 32.

A study of the historical references shows that the readers were Jewish Christians. They have been Christians for some time, but recent circumstances have tempted them to quit Christianity, in favor of reverting to their old Jewish ways.

B. WHERE DID THE READERS LIVE?

The world of the New Testament was the Mediterranean world, and in the absence of a specific city being named in the letter, proposals for the location where the readers lived have ranged from Spain in the West, to Jerusalem in the East.

> 1. Did the readers live somewhere in the Roman Province of **Syria** (as distinct from Jerusalem or Judea)?

Bowman has the letter addressed to Samaria.[29] Spicq has it addressed first to Alexandria, then to Caesarea, then to Antioch of Syria.[30] His choice of Antioch assumes Barnabas is the writer. Caesarea would be Spicq's choice if Luke were the writer. Still others have it addressed to Christians living all over Palestine.[31]

Arguments *against* this attempted identification of the destination include: (a) Do "Hebrews" live in Samaria? Are the readers contemplating going back to the old worship of the Samaritans? (b) When was Timothy ever in Antioch? (c) Shall we give up the traditional view of authorship just to defend one of these alternative views on destination? (d) The view that Hebrews was addressed to Jewish Christians in *Palestine* generally, while making it possible to apply many of the characteristic marks contained in the epistle, does not fit the ones that seem to imply the readers made up a definite community.

> 2. Did the readers live in **Asia Minor** or **Greece**?

T.W. Manson suggested *Colossae*, or some neighboring place in the Lycus River Valley, as the destination.[32] He was convinced he had found in Hebrews references to the same Colossian heresy Paul deals with in that letter.

---

[29] J.W. Bowman, *Hebrews, James, 1 & 2 Peter* (Richmond: John Knox, 1962), p. 13-16, thinks the book is addressed to readers who were influenced to some extent by the Essenes in Qumran, and that their understanding of the gospel had some serious defects that the Hebrew writer attempted to correct.

[30] C. Spicq, *L'Epitre aux Hebreux* (Paris: Gabalda, 1952), Vol. 1, p.227ff. and 250ff., for his earlier views, and "L'Epitre aux Hebreux, Apollos, Jean-Baptiste, les Hellenistes et Qumran," *Revue de Qumran* 1 (1959), p.365-390, for his later views.

[31] Coffman, Hebrews, p.15ff, and C.B. Moll, "Hebrews" in *Lange's Commentary*, p.12. See also, F.S. Delitzsch, *Commentary on the Epistle to the Hebrews*, translated by T. Kingsbury (Edinburgh: T & T Clark, 1868), p.20.

[32] *Studies in the Gospels and Epistles* (Philadelphia: Westminster, 1962), p.242. The chapter in the book, "The Problem of the Epistles to the Hebrews," is reprinted from BJRL 32 (1949), p.3ff.

W.F. Howard identified *Ephesus* as the destination.[33] He believed the readers were a group of wealthy and cultivated Jews, a large number of whom were converted during Paul's Ephesian ministry, but whose faith waned after Paul's Roman imprisonments and subsequent execution in Rome.

Antony Snell opted for *Cyprus*.[34] This is consistent with his ascription of the authorship to Barnabas, whose close association with Cyprus is well-attested.

The view that the readers lived in *Corinth* was advanced by Montefiore.[35] On the view that the letter was written from Ephesus by Apollos to Corinth, "those from Italy" might be a reference to Aquila and Priscilla, the only people in the New Testament described as "from Italy" (Acts 18:2). Further, the word "confirmed" in Hebrews 2:3 would be matched by what is written in 1 Corinthians 1:6.

Several problems are not answered if one of these views is adopted: (a) Can we show the original believers in Colossae had been evangelized by apostles who worked miracles while in their town? (b) Where is there evidence that only *Jewish* Christians faced opposition and persecution in Ephesus? (c) When did *Jewish* Christians at Corinth face the despoiling of their property, and what do we know about the deaths of any of their early leaders?

3.   Did the readers live in **Egypt**?

Alexandria has been the suggestion by many as the place where the readers lived. Supporters of this view call attention to these points: (1) The writer of Hebrews – often thought to be Apollos, by proponents of this theory – is alleged to show a familiarity with the literature of Alexandrian Judaism (like Wisdom, IV Maccabees, and the writings of Philo). This would help him to find a ready audience in Alexandria, it is supposed. (2) The Muratorian Canon, as indicated above, makes no mention of Hebrews. However, it does refer to an epistle "to the Alexandrians." Might it be possible that what we call Hebrews was called "to the Alexandrians" in the Muratorian canon?[36] (3) Appeal is made to the fact there was a Jewish temple at Leontopolis, not far from Alexandria. One writer has argued the deviations in the description of the worship found in Hebrews (e.g., the *daily* ministration of the high priest, 7:27) from that prescribed in the Old Testament and followed in Jerusalem, reflected the practice at Leontopolis. Therefore Hebrews must be addressed to Alexandria![37] (4) The earliest referen-

---

[33] "The Epistle to the Hebrews," *Interpretation* 5 (1951), p.80ff.

[34] *New and Living Way* (London: Faith Press, 1959), p.19. E. Riggenbach, *Der Brief an die Hebraer* (Leipzig: A. Deichert, 1913), p.xlvii, previously offered this same suggestion.

[35] H.W. Montefiore, *The Epistle to the Hebrews* (New York: Harper and Row, 1964), p. 18. Also F. Lo Bue, "The Historical Background of the Epistle to the Hebrews," *Journal of Biblical Literature* 75 (1956), p.52-57.

[36] In the Muratorian canon itself, this epistle "to the Alexandrians" is described as being forged in Paul's name to support Marcion's heresy. It takes a powerful stretch of the imagination to identify such a work with our epistle "to the Hebrews." There is little or nothing about Hebrews that would support Marcion's heresy. If there had been, he would have included it in his canon.

[37] It is hard to accept the idea that the temple at Leontopolis is the temple to which the readers of Hebrews were tempted to return. "The temple of Onias at Leontopolis in Egypt, built under Ptolemy Philometor, and es-

ces to our letter are found in Rome and Alexandria. The letter was known in Rome by the end of the first century, as its use by Clement of Rome attests. The letter was known and valued in Alexandria in the second century, as the references in Clement of Alexandria and Origen show. Was it perhaps written from Rome to Alexandria? If a copy was retained by the author, this might account for its presence in both cities.[38]

Arguments *against* the view that Hebrews was originally addressed to Egypt: (1) It is in Alexandria that belief in its Pauline authorship first was stated, but with hesitation as to the actual penman. Are we to suppose the city that originally received the letter so soon forgot who wrote it? (2) We have no real knowledge of Christianity in Egypt until well into the second century. Alexandria, with its large Jewish population, might seem an obvious and natural field for an early Christian mission, but our oldest sources have nothing to say. Tradition links the founding of the church in Alexandria with the name of Mark, but the fact that neither Clement nor Origen says anything about it makes this tradition one of very doubtful value.[39]

4.   Did the readers live in **Rome** or **Italy**?

The belief that Hebrews was addressed to Rome is becoming the most widely accepted view in the 20th century.[40] The reasons usually given in defense of this view include: (1) The first place where Hebrews was known and quoted, according to our extant literature, was Rome. See I Clement.[41] (2) The greetings in the book ("Those from Italy greet you") could be made to fit this destination. Christians away from their native land are sending greetings back home.[42]

---

tablished exclusively (Josephus, *Ant.*, XIII.3.1) for Jews dwelling in Egypt, with reference to Isaiah 19:18,19, and in part obscurely described by Josephus *(Wars* VII.10.3), was not merely held in light esteem in Palestine, but also in Egypt. Even Philo knows but one *patron hieron*, that of Jerusalem, to which also Alexandrian Jews directed their sacred gifts and their festal journeys." Moll, *op. cit.*, p. 12.

[38] We admit that copies of letters often were retained by the author. But there are other possible explanations for how copies of Hebrews were early found in both Alexandria and Rome, not the least of which is the collection of apostolic books for use in the public worship services. 1 Timothy 5:18 (which quotes Luke's Gospel, thus showing it is in circulation) and 2 Peter 3:16 show that such collections were being made prior to Paul's death in 68 AD.

[39] Wilson, *op. cit.*, p.9.

[40] For the best defense of Rome and a single congregation as the destination of the letter, see Wm. Manson, *The Epistle to the Hebrews, An Historical and Theological Reintepretaton*. Manson's ideas are refined and presented by F.F. Bruce, *The Epistle to the Hebrews* in the NICNT. See also, M.C. Tenney, "A New Approach to the Book of Hebrews," *Bibliotheca Sacra* 123 (491, July-December 1966), p.230-236, who concludes the letter was written to Jewish Christians living in Rome, between AD 65 and 70.

[41] Of course, acquaintance with Hebrews would not prove a Roman destination, for by this time Christian writings were circulating rather freely. By no means does his acquaintance with the other New Testament books prove a Roman destination for them. Furthermore, Clement presupposes the Corinthians also are acquainted with Hebrews. Does that prove Corinth was the original destination? Hardly.

[42] It has even been suggested that Aquila and Priscilla, who years earlier left Rome, have asked for their greetings to be conveyed to friends in Rome. After all, they had come from Rome in the first place (Acts 18:2). There is evidence from the epistles they were a well-travelled couple. (According to Romans 16:3, it is evident they were back in Rome when Paul wrote that letter. And from 1 Corinthians 16:19, written from Ephesus, we learn they were in Ephesus when that letter was written.) There would be nothing unusual if they were in the town where this letter was written, and so send their greetings to old friends in Rome. (See further information on "those from Italy" in the commentary at 13:24, in footnote #22 on page xiii, and above on page xlvi.)

(3) Romans 11:13,18 has been used to prove the church at Rome included a Jewish-Christian minority. Perhaps so, but before we could suppose Hebrews was written to that minority, we would have to know the theological position of these Jewish Christians in Rome. Were the "Hebrews" in the church at Rome converts from normative first-century Judaism (if we can speak of such a thing), or were they ex-members of some non-conformist Jewish group?[43] (4) The allusions to the ministry of the readers in supporting other Christians (Hebrews 6:10,11, 10:33-34) has been thought to agree with the history of Christianity in Rome.[44] (5) The Hebrew writer uses an unusual word (*hegoumenoi*) to designate the leaders of the community (Hebrews 13:7,17,24). The same term is found in early Christian literature connected with Rome,[45] and this has led some to think the use of the term points to a Roman destination. (6) The existence of house churches (or individual congregations) in Rome is confirmed by Romans 16:5,14,15. This would fit the "definite community" idea if the verses in Hebrews indeed speak of something like a house church.[46]

Problem verses that cannot be answered well given a Roman destination include: (1) Who is persecuting the readers so that they are thinking of quitting the church? Jewish Christians in Rome had been banished from Rome by the Edict of Claudius, but will that explain the reference to persecutions past? Do we know anything about the spoilation of goods at Rome, about which 10:32 speaks? What were the persecutions presently being faced? We cannot appeal to the Domitianic persecution because, on any dating of the letter, that was yet

---

[43] Some defenders of a Roman destination for Hebrews affirm that it is at Rome that we have the best attestation of the survival for several generations of non-conformist Jewish groups in the Christian community. For example, "The Jewish community in Rome preserved certain features of non-conformist or sectarian Judaism that would explain several notable similarities between the theology and praxis of the Qumran community and that expressed in Hebrews" (Demarest, *op. cit.*, p.944.) Even if this is true, does "Hebrews" mean the same thing as "non-conformist Jewish sect"? (See footnote #12 on page xxxix.) Other defenders of a Roman destination for Hebrews affirm the Jews in Rome were the old conservative, main-line Jews. Manson, in the Baird lecture, 1950, suggested the Roman Church had both Jewish and Gentile converts in it. From the positions taken by the strong and weak brothers in Romans 14,15, it might be argued a portion of the congregation held to the more conservative principles of mainline Judaism, and that (if the hypothesis of a Roman destination is true) it is to that small group this letter is addressed. 'Give up those old Jewish practices for the harmony and unity of the whole church in Rome!' then becomes the thrust of Hebrews.

[44] See Dionysius of Corinth as cited by Eusebius H.E. IV.23.10. Of course, we would expect Christians, in whatever town they lived, to minister to the saints, for that is what Jesus taught His followers to do. Just because the Romans were benevolent, does not prove Hebrews was addressed to Rome.

[45] I Clement 21:6; Hermas, *Visions* II.2.6, and III.9.7.

[46] The number of people the average "upper room" would accommodate was probably somewhere between 20 and 40 people. "House churches" likely would not have more members than this. "An impression of what such early house churches in Rome may have been like is conveyed by the remains of buildings of several stories that date to the second and third centuries, but which have been modified over the course of time. Incorporated into the walls or preserved below the floors of at least three of the existing titular churches in Rome are the remnants of large tenement houses (cf. Peterson, *Exp. Times* 84 [1973], p.277-279; id. VC 23 [1969], p.264-272). The ground floors appear to have been occupied by shops, and the upper levels by prosperous families. The connection of these buildings with the social world of craftsmen and artisans is suggestive in the light of the reference to the church in the house of Aquila and Priscilla (Romans 16:5), whose property must have served as a worship, residence, and meeting place. As yet there has been no excavation of common housing from the days of the early empire in Rome, but J.E. Packer's work on the *insulae*, or apartment buildings, points to the existence of amorphous blocks of tenements, one building abutting another ("Housing and Population in Imperial Ostia and Rome," JRS 57 [1967], p.80-95)." Lane, *Hebrews 1-8* (Waco, Tex.: Word Books, 1991), p.lix.

a future event. Christians in Rome were facing governmental persecutions in the mid-60's AD (i.e., the Neronian persecution), but that was not limited just to the "Hebrew" portion of the church. So that hardly fits the allusion in Hebrews to the current wave of persecutions. (2) Assuming the traditional view of authorship, where in Paul's missionary journeys would he and Timothy be thinking of a second trip to Rome that he would ask for their prayers to that end? (3) If Paul is not the author, still, when would the Romans be expecting another visit from Timothy, with whom they have previously become acquainted? Can we harmonize such an acquaintance with Timothy before he comes to Rome during Paul's first imprisonment? Did Roman Christians come to the city from elsewhere in the empire, and so know Timothy from elsewhere, as well as they knew Paul from elsewhere,[47] before they moved to Rome? Are we to think of some trip by Timothy to Rome subsequent to the writing of 2 Timothy? If so, the writer of Hebrews is not Paul, because either he was already in Rome, or he was already dead. It is not easy to explain the references to Timothy on the hypothesis that Rome is the destination. (4) Certainly Hebrews 2:3 is very difficult to explain on the hypothesis that the letter was sent to Rome. Not many authors attribute the origin of the church at Rome to eyewitnesses of Jesus' earthly ministry.[48]

That Hebrews was sent to Rome (or Italy) is an appealing suggestion, simply because the other possible destinations are thought not to explain all the allusions to the situation in which the readers find themselves. But upon careful scrutiny, the Roman theory has more problems which are more difficult to answer than does the traditional interpretation.

5.   Did the readers live in **Jerusalem**?

The traditional view, and the most natural view if "to the Hebrews" is an authentic title,[49] is that the addressees were Jewish Christians, tempted to relapse into Judaism. The traditional view also has the letter addressed to Jerusalem. Only later did writers begin to suggest the "Hebrews" might be living somewhere other than Jerusalem.

Care must be exercised when trying to reconstruct what life was like for Christians in Jerusalem. We must remember the first congregation (Acts 2-7) was scattered by the persecution that arose after the death of Stephen (Acts 8:1). We therefore suppose the church we read about in later chapters of Acts was a new congregation made up of converts won from among the citizens after the persecution of Acts 8 ended. It is this new congregation about which we read in Acts 9ff and with which the historical allusions in Hebrews (assuming a Jerusalem destination) should be harmonized.

---

[47] Gareth L. Reese, *New Testament Epistles: Romans* (Moberly, Mo.: Scripture Exposition Books, 1987), p.xii, xx, and the comments on the names in chapter 16.

[48] Defenders of a Roman destination urge that, before they moved to Rome, a small group, now a house church at Rome, could be spoken of as having been evangelized by eyewitnesses of Jesus' ministry. Therefore, 2:3 would not be so much of an argument against a Roman destination.

[49] B.F. Westcott, *The Epistle to the Hebrews* (Grand Rapids: Eerdmans, 1952), p. xxxv-xliii, and William Leonard, *Authorship of the Epistle to the Hebrews* (Vatican: Polyglot, 1939), are the best defenses of the Jerusalem destination for Hebrews.

Almost all the historical allusions are easily explained if Jerusalem was the original destination of this letter. (1) Some of the more difficult allusions to explain are the ones concerning opposition or persecution. More will be said on this matter as we discuss "Date" below in these Introductory Studies. The new congregation certainly faced opposition from the Pharisees, who in this and the following decades became more and more militant in their attempts to stop the *minim* ("heretics," read "Christians").[50] Only in Jerusalem, in the first century AD, would Judaizing influences have been felt in sufficient force to provoke the need for such a book as Hebrews and its warnings against defecting from the gospel in favor of re-entering Judaism. (2) The Jerusalem church had, in the past, some illustrious leaders (13:7). Think of Stephen (Acts 6,7) and James (Acts 12), who, though persecuted, were faithful to death. Tradition has it the apostles stayed at Jerusalem until about the time of the Jerusalem Conference. These might be the "past leaders" Hebrews 13:7 has in view. The Jerusalem church also, at an early date, had an eldership (Acts 11:30, 15:4). These leaders, then, might be the ones in view in Hebrews 13:7. (3) Did the Jerusalem church have a prison ministry? Did they minister to Paul when he was arrested at the close of the third missionary journey and during his subsequent incarceration at Caesarea? Was Paul's nephew, who overheard the plot of the Jews, on a mission of mercy to Paul on behalf of the church when he overheard the plot? (4) The readers have been Christians for some time (5:12). Believers at Jerusalem would have been Christians for some time, on any accepted date for this letter. (5) Jerusalem was about to be destroyed, AD 70. This would satisfy the reference that they have no continuing city here – and, for that matter, the prediction concerning no continuing ritual based on the instructions found in Moses.[51] (6) Those "from Italy" who send their greetings would then be a statement from Italian Christians living in Rome from where the letter is written, and addressed to their fellow believers in the city of Jerusalem. (7) Jewish Christians in Jerusalem would have had a warm feeling for Paul and Timothy, especially after those two were involved in bringing the offering from the Gentile churches at the close of the third missionary journey. Certainly there was no lingering animosity or suspicion toward Paul in the Jerusalem church.

Those who deny the traditional destination have usually raised these points as being weighty evidence proving Jerusalem was not the city where the original readers lived: (1) Some have thought that 2:3 rules out a Jerusalem destination. Would not some of the Jerusalem Christians have heard the Lord personally rather than having gotten their information from the apostles? Even at the latest reasonable date for this epistle, there would still have been a few members of the Jerusalem church who would have been personal witnesses of the ministry of Jesus.[52] (2) Some have thought a Jerusalem destination is ruled out by the fact that nothing is

---

[50] In the decades either shortly before, or shortly after, the Fall of Jerusalem in AD 70, the line to accurse the "heretics" was added to the benedictions usually recited in the Jewish Synagogue services. See Sol. Zeitlin, *The Rise and Fall of the Judean State* (Philadelphia: Jewish Publication Society, 1978), Vol.3, p.187.

[51] Some have tried to make a case for the view that the Levitical sacrifices continued to be offered at Jerusalem, even after the destruction of the city and Temple in AD 70. See this matter discussed below under the section dealing with the date when Hebrews was written.

[52] In previous notes we have already shown the real thrust of Hebrews 2:3. The thrust is not from whom someone *heard* the gospel. The emphasis is on the fact that the gospel was *corroborated*. Even people who heard Jesus or the apostles personally would need a "validation/corroboration/guarantee" for the gospel, before they would (being good Jews) be ready to think of the gospel in the same terms as they thought of the Law (which had been validated/corroborated, Hebrews 2:2).

specifically said about the temple; Hebrews instead refers to the tabernacle. While more will be said on this later, this is not as convincing an objection as it first appears.[53] (3) Some have thought a Jerusalem destination is ruled out by the contrast between the known poverty of the Jerusalem Church and what is said in Hebrews 6:10, 10:34, 13:16. If we suppose the letter is addressed to Jerusalem, how shall we harmonize this with the fact that at least twice (Acts 12 and Acts 21) during its existence, the church at Jerusalem was the recipient of aid from others, rather than a giver of such ministry? The simple reply to this objection is, Did not the Jerusalem church, when they were able, generously give aid to others, as they did in the early days (Acts 2 and Acts 4)? And then when they had need, there was a kind of equality as others who had been helped by them were able to help them in return. (4) Some have argued the excellent Greek of Hebrews would be a barrier to the idea that it was written to Jews living at Jerusalem, and who would be more likely to be Aramaic speaking. Not so! Jews in Jerusalem did speak Greek, and fluently.[54] (5) Of all the historical allusions, the hardest one to harmonize with a Jerusalem destination for the letter is the one about Timothy's release and coming visit. The traditional view of authorship also has Paul asking for their prayers that he, too, might soon visit them. About all that can be said is there are other plans made by Paul that apparently never were within the will of God. He said to the Ephesian elders that he doubted he would ever see them again (Acts 20:38), yet 1 Timothy 1:3 indicates he did see them at a later time. Before his first Roman imprisonment, Paul's plans included a trip to Spain. It would appear the imprisonment changed his plans; he never did get to Spain.[55] In a like manner, we might suppose his hopes of visiting Jerusalem were disappointed. We also must admit that what it was Timothy is released from is left unexplained. (This latter problem, however, is not limited to those who accept the traditional destination for this letter.)

What is our conclusion regarding the letter's destination? Jerusalem best fits the intimations in the book itself. We find no reason to abandon the traditional view that "to the Hebrews" means "Hebrew people living in Jerusalem."

IV. PLACE OF WRITING

"Those from Italy greet you" (13:24) is the key. As indicated in the historical allusions, this has been taken two ways.

Many attempt to show that 13:24 proves the letter was not written from Italy. This is the theory currently making the rounds amongst theologians who accept the assured conclu-

---

[53] When this point is advocated, attention is sometimes called to the fact that the New Testament offers another example of someone defending Christian doctrine and practices against Judaism. Stephen, it is affirmed, spoke of the "temple," not the "tabernacle" like Hebrews does. When he addressed the Sanhedrin on charges (among others) that he had blasphemed "this holy place," Stephen did indeed make reference to the "house" Solomon built for God (Acts 7:47). But Stephen also made reference to the tabernacle (Acts 7:44) as part of his same defense.

[54] See above, footnote #10, page xxxviii, concerning the excellent Greek in the Epistle of James.

[55] See Gareth L. Reese, "Epilogue: The Last Labors and Letters of Paul," in New Testament History: Acts (Moberly, Mo. Scripture Exposition Books, 1987), p. 951ff.

sions of higher criticism,[1] though it by no means is an opinion held exclusively by commentators of liberal persuasion.[2] "Those (away) from Italy" are the ones sending their greetings, the theory goes.[3] Moffatt thought the letter was written from *Alexandria*, and that it was Italians living in Egypt who were sending greetings to their fatherland.[4] Certainly, if the letter did originate in Alexandria, we would have expected the Eastern Church which did champion the Pauline authorship to claim the letter as having originated in their part of the world. Alford, who identified Apollos as the author, opted for the view the letter was written from *Ephesus*.[5] Another suggestion for the place of writing, which has some attractive features, is *Caesarea*.[6] The two years Paul spent in prison there (Acts 24:1ff) would have provided sufficient time to produce this polished work. The proximity to Jerusalem would have given Paul a more intimate knowledge of the temptations and difficulties the church there was facing. Since Caesarea was the Roman administrative capital of Judea, "those from Italy" could be understood as a reference to many of the Italian officials in residence there who also were converts to Christianity.[7] The most difficult reference to harmonize with Caesarea as the place of writing is the reference to Timothy. As far as Acts is concerned, we know little about Timothy from this particular period in Paul's life. Another difficulty to explain, if we opt for Paul writing from Caesarea, concerns the references to persecution. At the time Paul is imprisoned in Caesarea (c.58-60 AD), the persecution that resulted in James' the Lord's brother's death was still about two years in the future; James' death is usually dated about AD 62.[8] Before that, the last persecution of Christians by the unconverted Jews which we know

---

[1] One of the reasons liberals want a place of writing other than Rome is related to another assured conclusion to which their studies have led them. Liberal theologians regularly note that the book of Hebrews has the blood atonement in it. According to their thinking, the idea of a "slaughter-house religion" is a late development, much after Paul is dead. If they can show Hebrews was written from some place other than Italy, it greatly helps their case against the Pauline authorship. And if they are to date the doctrine of the blood atonement as a late doctrine, introduced into Christianity after Paul's death, they must deny Paul had anything to do with Hebrews.

[2] Alford, a conservative, held the view that Hebrews was not written from Rome.

[3] Barclay, for example, notes that the expression "those from Italy" has the preposition *apo* in it, which he interprets to mean "people away from (*apo*) Italy." Acts 10:23 and 21:27 are examples of *apo* meaning "away from" while John 11:1 and Acts 17:13 are examples of *apo* meaning "in" that place, so the phrase is ambiguous. Moffatt (International Critical Commentary, *ad loc.*) documents examples from the papyri of *apo* meaning "in that place." Church fathers (e.g., Theodoret) as well as the title and subscription affixed to Hebrews indicate the belief that Italy was the place of writing. When writing from Ephesus, Paul used the simple genitive (no preposition), "the churches of Asia greet you" (1 Corinthians 16:19).

[4] There were other groups of foreigners in Alexandria who were Christians also. How would they feel if only the Italians among them were included in sending greetings to cosmopolitan Rome? The idea the letter was written from Alexandria was more believable when scholars thought to find "Alexandrian hue" in Hebrews. Now that this view has been discredited, there is less evidence that Alexandria was the place of writing.

[5] Montefiore, too, who believes the letter was written (by Apollos) from Ephesus and addressed to Corinth, thinks the "Italians" are none other than Aquila and Priscilla, who are sending their greetings to Corinth through Apollos, just as they did through Paul when he wrote 1 Corinthians 16:19.

[6] P.L. Suarez, "Caesarea, Lugar de Composicio de la Epistole a los Hebreos?" *CB 13* (1956), p.26-31.

[7] On the other hand, if the writer is writing from someplace other than from Italy, why send greetings from the Italians rather than from the Christians living in the place where he wrote?

[8] The Lord's brother, leader of the Jerusalem church, was martyred by the Jewish religious leaders about the time Annas the younger was inaugurated as High Priest, in the time between the departure of the Procurator Porcius Festus and the coming of his successor, Albinus. See Josephus, *Antiquities* XX.9.1.

anything about is recorded in Acts 12, when James the son of Zebedee was martyred and Peter was imprisoned. The use of the Hebrew letter by Clement of Rome is no argument against a possible Caesarean place of writing. Even if the letter were written from Caesarea in the 60's AD, there would be time for copies of the letter to be in Rome before it was used by Clement of Rome in his letter to Corinth. The usual view is that it took about 25 years after a book was written for it to be known and used in the churches all over the Empire.

The traditional view is that 13:24 indicates the place of writing was Italy (Rome). The Christians in Italy where the writer himself was are thus seen to be sending their greetings to the readers. One of the objections often raised against the traditional view concerns the identity of the Italians. To speak of "Italians" would be a rather unusual way to refer to Christians in Rome. (Italians would certainly include more than just people living in Rome.) But what do we know of Christians outside of Rome at this early time? Acts 28:13-14 mentions Christians in Puteoli in the early 60's AD. Were there other Christians in Italy outside of Rome[9] at this early period? Another objection to the traditional view is the reference to Timothy (13:23). Admittedly, it is not easy to explain from what Timothy has been released on the hypothesis the letter was written from Rome.[10] But then neither is the reference to Timothy easy to explain on any other hypothesis. The argument sometimes raised against a Roman origin for the letter, drawn from the West's second-century refusal to acknowledge the letter as Pauline, is perhaps overwrought. We've shown that at an earlier date the letter was known and acknowledged in Rome. The *silence* of the Western Church concerning the place of authorship is the only thing that can be affirmed.

Several verses might be seen as support for the traditional view as to place of writing. (1) The traditional view of destination has some bearing on the question of place of writing. If the letter was written to Jewish Christians in and around Jerusalem, then "those from Italy" could well be a note that the writer is in Italy when he writes. (2) The subscriptions found in some old manuscripts "written from Rome"[11] or "written from Italy,"[12] likely are educated guesses based on 13:24. (3) The traditional view of authorship for the letter also has some bearing on the place of writing. If Paul wrote it, then "sympathy to the prisoners" (10:34) could be explained as being reference to help Paul received while he was in prison in Caesarea, before his voyage to and first imprisonment in Rome. Further, the anticipation of shortly being able to visit the readers (Hebrews 13:18,19) is language similar to that written by Paul from the first Roman imprisonment (Philemon 22, Philippians 1:19).

In regard to place of writing, we see no compelling reason to abandon the older majority view that the letter was written from Rome.

---

[9] A *Sator* square, found in the ruins of Pompeii, has been interpreted to mean that there were Christians in that town before it was destroyed by the eruption of Mount Vesuvius. Compare F.L. Cross, *The Early Christian Fathers* (London: Gerald Duckworth and Co., 1960), p.200f.

[10] Many of the older interpreters supposed Hebrews 13:23 was to be explained by reference with Philippians 2:19. That older interpretation suggested that the trip anticipated in Philippians is finished, so Timothy is now free to make a trip to Jerusalem shortly.

[11] This reading is found in Codex Alexandrinus.

[12] This reading is found in Codices H, K, P, and the Peshitto Syriac.

V. DATE OF WRITING

Lacking firm information as to the author or destination of the letter, no certainty exists concerning the date of writing. There are, however, some general indicators.

A. What do the HISTORICAL ALLUSIONS tell us?

Hebrews was written after the crucifixion and resurrection of Jesus (Hebrews 1:3; 2:17, 18; 5:8,9; 9:14-16; 13:20). Indeed, Jesus is already enthroned at the right hand of the Majesty on high when Hebrews is written (Hebrews 1:3). Since AD 30 is the year of Jesus' death, resurrection and coronation,[1] Hebrews must have been written after AD 30. The readers and the writer had the gospel corroborated to them by people who were eye-witnesses (Hebrews 2:3). This suggests the letter was written before people who were eyewitnesses of Jesus' ministry were dead. However, this does not, as some have described them, make the readers "second generation Christians" in the strict sense of the term. There is no need to suppose some 25 or so years have passed since Jesus was here before these people became Christians; it would not require a date much after Pentecost for their initial acquaintance with the gospel.

Jewish sacrifices, it would seem, are still being offered when Hebrews was written. The present tense verbs in Hebrews 5:1-4, 7:8,21-28,[2] 9:6-10, and 10:1-4,11-14 plainly suggest the temple is still standing and the Jewish sacrifices are still being offered, as they have been for centuries.[3] The destruction of Jerusalem by the Romans in AD 70 brought an end to the Jewish ritual and sacrifices in that city.[4] If this is true, we would expect Hebrews to have been written

---

[1] See the author's *New Testament History: Acts*, p.i-x.

[2] In 7:21 and 23, the Greek construction is a periphrastic perfect (*eisin gegonotes*). The periphrastic use of the present tense of the verb "to be" (*eisin*) with the perfect participle (*gegonotes*) defines a state that is still in existence when both verses 21 and 23 were written.

[3] We are well aware that many point out the fact that Hebrews makes no direct reference to the temple. Rather, Hebrews speaks of the tabernacle and does so in language taken from the Old Testament Scriptures rather than first-century historical Jewish worship practices. From this use of language, it has been urged that the "present tense verbs and the Old Testament vocabulary should not be pressed into service when one tries to find evidence for the date of Hebrews." We are not greatly impressed by this argument. In principle, the tabernacle and temple were one. The worship ritual of the former was the ritual of the latter; the floorplans and furniture of the one were the floor plans and furniture of the other. No author we have read attempts to take the Old Testament vocabulary in an absolutely literal sense, as though the tabernacle itself were still standing when Hebrews is written. In fact, there is no way one could argue (from the use of the word "tabernacle") that Hebrews was written in the times before Christ when there was an actual tabernacle still in use among the Jews. The terms must be used with reference to the cultus in use at the time Hebrews was written.

[4] Josephus, *Wars* VI.2.1, records the cessation of the daily sacrifice on August 5, 70 AD. He does so with a precision that some have interpreted to mean Josephus saw a fulfillment of Daniel 9:27 in this traumatic event. Wilson, in his commentary on Hebrews (p.6) has urged us to be cautious about saying the sacrificial system based on the Old Testament Scriptures ceased when the Romans destroyed the city in 70 AD. K.W. Clark, "Worship in the Jerusalem Temple after AD 70," NTS 6 (1959-60), p.269-80, has tried to make a case for the view that sacrifices continued to be offered in Jerusalem even after the destruction of the temple in AD 70. Attention is also called to the fact that Clement of Rome (I Clement 32:2 and 40:5) speaks of the Levitical ritual of the temple in the present tense, and yet most writers date I Clement well after the fall of Jerusalem. From these observations it is sometimes claimed that what appears to be a telling argument (the present tense verbs in Hebrews, and the cessation of the sacrifices in AD 70) proves on further examination to be not so compelling.

Solomon Zeitlin, however, documents the fact the old system really was for all intents and purposes ended when Jerusalem was destroyed. As early as AD 71, the Pharisees, sitting in Jabneh under the leadership of

somewhere between AD 30 and 70.

Other historical allusions tell us the readers of Hebrews were facing a current wave of persecutions, but those have not yet resulted in deaths of any Christians (as "you have not yet resisted to the point of shedding blood" is regularly interpreted to mean, 12:4). Timothy is still alive (13:23). The readers have been Christians for some time ("For though by this time ..." in 5:12 and "remember the former days ..." in 10:32-34), and their first generation of leaders is gone ("Remember those who led you ... considering the result of their conduct", 13:7). The absence in Hebrews of any mention of the destruction of Jerusalem or of the temple is significant for the dating of the letter. If those events had occurred, they would have made a great point in the argument.[5] The extended exegesis of Jeremiah's new covenant prophecy in Hebrews 8-10, and the emphasis that it has superseded the former Mosaic covenant, and that the former is "becoming obsolete and growing old," and "is ready to disappear" (8:13) is very aptly put if we consider a date a few years before AD 70 for the writing of this letter.

Some scholars point to Hebrews 3:7-19 (quoting Psalm 95:8-11), suggesting the argument of Israel's 40 years of wandering in the wilderness would be more forceful if the 40th year from the Lord's death was approaching at the time when the Epistle was being written.[6]

The historical allusions and the general tenor of the letter point to a date somewhere between AD 30 and 70, and more precisely, to a time in the early 60s AD. Is there any firm evidence that would cause us to reject this tentative conclusion?

Rabbi Johanan ben Zakkai, were obliged to made new rules (*takkanot* – amendments to earlier laws, Pentateuchal or halakhic) to meet religious problems created by the destruction of the Temple and the dispersion of the Jews. Not a few of these new rules had to do with modifications concerning sacrifices that used to be offered (as the Scriptures required) at the Temple. In *The Rise and Fall of the Judean State* (Philadelphia: Jewish Publication Society, 1978), Vol. 3, p. 155, 161ff, Zeitlin cites numerous references from the Mishna to establish that indeed new rules had to be made: (1) About the blowing of the trumpet (shofar) on Rosh Ha-Shanah when that day fell on the Sabbath. (2) About the carrying of a palm branch on the Sabbath during the festival of Tabernacles. (While the temple stood, it was permissible to carry the branch only in the temple.) (3) Concerning the rule about not eating any of the new barley harvest till the first sheaf had been offered *in the temple*. (It was ruled permissible to eat of the new harvest on the 16th of Nisan, with no offering being made at all, now that the offerings of first fruits had ceased.) (4) About how to figure the first day of each month. (Witnesses used to report to the presiding officer of the Sanhedrin before the time of the afternoon sacrifice that they had seen a "new-born" moon. After AD 70, ben Zakkai ruled the report could be accepted any time of day by any member of the Bet Din.) (5) After AD 70, proselytes to the Jewish religion were no longer required to sacrifice turtle doves, or set aside a money offering of equal value. (Before AD 70, such converts were required to offer a sacrifice of two turtle doves.) (6) Following the destruction of the temple, the daily sacrifices were replaced with a fixed ritual of prayers which were to be recited at set hours each day. All these new rules surely are evidence the old ritual centering around the temple had been ended. It certainly is true that when the Romans destroyed Jerusalem in AD 70, the sacrificial system there ceased.

[5] In terms of his argument that the Old Covenant had passed away and the Levitical priesthood had been superseded, the writer would scarcely have omitted mention of the temple's destruction had that event occurred before he wrote. "The whole argument of Hebrews is to the effect that the types and shadows of the Hebrew institution were due to be replaced by the more spiritual verities of which those types were but the copies; and, if all those types and shadows had already been swept away, it is hardly conceivable the author of Hebrews would have overlooked such an opportunity to mention the passing of the old order." Coffman, *op. cit.*, p.10.

[6] See page xiv, and in the commentary at Hebrews 3:9, for an explanation of the possible historical allusion in "forty years," especially in the light of the fact that there is a textual variant which puts the "40 years" in a slightly different place in Hebrews than we find it in the Old Testament text being quoted.

B. WE REJECT CERTAIN HIGHER CRITICAL ARGUMENTS concerning the possible date of writing for Hebrews.

One of these, that time must be allowed for the development of the Christological thinking that Hebrews reflects, is a specious argument. Doctrine about Jesus did not slowly develop along naturalistic lines (with the more miraculous themes being added by later generations). The Christology of the New Testament was revealed, and that first by Jesus Himself. Higher critical presuppositions, including form and redaction criticism, in this area just lead us in a wrong direction.

Another higher critical argument often advanced as having a bearing on the date of the epistle is the writer's use of the Pauline epistles. That there is such a use is nothing more than an allegation; there is no real proof. Nevertheless, some have argued from the writer's alleged use of the Pauline epistles, which would require a sufficient interval for these to have circulated, that the date of Hebrews must be pushed to a time considerably later than the death of Paul. In reply, we have rejected, (1) the *religionsgeshichte* view that the writers of our New Testament books were simply copyists of earlier sources, and (2) that there is anything of permanent value to be gained from a diligent search for such sources of Christian doctrine. Furthermore, few scholars would date Hebrews after I Clement, so we would be incorrect to say that Hebrews was written considerably later than the death of Paul.[7]

The evidences alluded to by the higher critics are not of sufficient weight to cause us to think we must reject or modify the tentative conclusion reached earlier, that Hebrews was written in the early 60s AD.

C. What can we learn from EXTRA-BIBLICAL SOURCES?

The latest possible date for the writing of Hebrews is generally admitted to be AD 96, because it seems clearly settled by the fact that Clement of Rome apparently possessed a copy of Hebrews and seems to have had the work in mind when he wrote I Clement, which is traditionally dated at AD 96. If he did, then Hebrews was written sometime before AD 96.[8]

---

[7] It is admitted that some scholars suggest that Hebrews was received in Rome only a short while before Clement wrote. Indeed, Goodspeed *(Introduction to the New Testament*, [1937], p.258ff) suggested Clement's letter was written in response to Hebrews 5:12. The *Interpreter's Bible* (Vol. XI, p.593,594) is one of the better presentations of the late date. Using I Clement as a point of reference, a date somewhere between the late70's and very early 90's is chosen.

[8] Instead of the traditional AD 96 date for I Clement, some have urged that Clement was actually written before AD 70. "If J.A.T. Robinson, persuaded by the arguments offered by George Edmundson in his Bampton Lectures for 1913 (G. Edmundson, *The Church in Rome in the First Century* [London: Longmans, Green, 1913]), is right in his conclusion that the Epistle of Clement to the Corinthians should be dated early in AD 70, just before the destruction of Jerusalem, rather than in the last decade of the century (J.A.T. Robinson, *Redating the New Testament* [Philadelphia: Westminster, 1976], p.327ff), this would serve only to confirm the plain indication of the internal evidence that the epistle to the Hebrews was written prior to the catastrophe of AD 70, because of the unmistakable manner in which Clement quotes from this epistle." [One of these writers' chief arguments for the early date of I Clement is the use of present tense verbs by Clement when speaking of the Levitical ritual and the continual daily offerings in Jerusalem.] See Hughes, *The Epistle to the Hebrews, p.31-32*.

Is there anything concerning the pending persecutions (Hebrews 10:32-36) to be found either in extra-biblical sources or in the New Testament itself that might help us decide on the date of writing? What persecutions between these roughly fixed limits for the writing of Hebrews (i.e., between AD 30 and 96) do we know about?

Interestingly, most scholars who have examined the evidence for the dating of Hebrews have come up with roughly the same decade (i.e., somewhere in the 60s AD) as the likely time of writing.

For example, those who opt for the view that the letter was addressed to Rome also tend to opt for the view the persecutions alluded to in Hebrews were governmental. It is not unusual, among these writers, to identify the earlier persecution of Hebrews 10:32ff with the disturbances over one "Chrestus" that led to the banishment of all Jews from Rome about AD 49 (see comments at Acts 18:2). The more deadly persecution that was still pending when Hebrews was written (Hebrews 12:4ff) is then identified with the Neronian persecution, AD 64. Christians were martyred during this persecution. Once these identifications are made, they point to a date before the mid-60s AD for the writing of the epistle.[9]

Those who opt for the view that the persecutions were religious in nature and that Hebrews was addressed to Jerusalem or Palestine have some difficulty explaining when and where these persecutions took place. However, most feel they can find enough information about conditions faced by Christians before AD 70 to satisfy the requirements of Hebrews concerning an earlier persecution that resulted in public ridicule and confiscation of personal property, and then a pending persecution, more serious in consequences (i.e., martyrdom is threatened). The truth is, once we have passed AD 44, with the persecution recorded in Acts 12, we have precious little information about what was going on in Jerusalem. Chapters 13ff of Acts take us away from Jerusalem and the Holy Land as we travel with Paul on the missionary journeys that eventually took him to Europe. The epistle of James may give us a glimpse of life in the church at Jerusalem, about AD 60. However, nothing is said about persecution in the epistle of James, unless the "manifold trials" (1:2ff) are persecutions, a possibility that should not be quickly dismissed. After he wrote his epistle, there was a persecution that resulted in at least the death of James and certain other brethren, about AD 62.[10] Some have supposed this persecution was the "serious" one threatened in Hebrews.

---

[9] Some students of first-century history note there was also a persecution when Domitian was emperor, from AD 81 to the late AD 90's. Some have tried to make the "earlier" persecution in Hebrews be a reference to the Neronian persecution and the pending one a reference to the Domitianic persecutions. In reply, it is difficult to think the Neronian persecution is in view for the earlier one since a huge number of Christians died in that persecution. Second, it is not easy to reconcile what Hebrews says with a government-sponsored persecution like Domitian's – in which Domitian was attempting to force everyone to worship the emperor (something Christians steadfastly refused to do). No attempt that we've yet seen to date the epistle to the Hebrews after AD 70 has carried the ring of conviction once the evidences used to "prove" it have been heard.

[10] C.M. Kerr, "James: ... (3) the Lord's brother," in the *International Standard Bible Encyclopedia*, edited by James M. Orr (Grand Rapids: Eerdmans, 1929), Vol.3, p.1561, and D. A. Hayes, "James, Epistle of," ISBE, p.1563, give documentation [Josephus, *Antiquities*, XX.9.1] of the death of James and some of his companions at the hands of the high priest Annas.

Perhaps we could look in another direction for the persecution yet pending against the readers of Hebrews. In the years following AD 48, at the close of Paul's first missionary journey, the Pharisees certainly put pressure on the Christians to conform to the old Jewish rules. They even pretended to become "believers" (Galatians 2:4) in order to infiltrate the church and bring about conformity to the traditions of the elders from within. We have a record – in Acts and Galatians, and perhaps 1 & 2 Corinthians) of their fanatical efforts outside of Palestine. What must have been their frenzy and fury inside the land? While we have no written record of such pressure on the church, it is not hard to imagine. Perhaps such pressure is one reason the Christians at Jerusalem (30 years after Pentecost) were still "zealous for the Law," including the making of sacrifices (Acts 21:20ff).

In any case, a consensus is emerging. Many of those who opt for a Roman destination for Hebrews, and those who opt for the traditional Jerusalem destination, both date the letter in the early 60s AD.

D. NON-TRADITIONAL CONCLUSIONS ABOUT OF AUTHORSHIP AND DESTINATION tend to affect the date assigned to Hebrews.

Montefiore, who has Hebrews written by Apollos and sent to Corinth, dates Hebrews about AD 52 or 54, before 1 Corinthians was written. Such a date is too early to satisfy all the evidence. The church at Corinth was first planted during Paul's second missionary journey, AD 51-54. Not enough time has passed to satisfy the allusions to being a Christian for some time and for the death of the first generation of leaders. Nor is it easy to get Apollos and Timothy to Corinth this early, then have them leave town, so that Hebrews could anticipate their return (as 13:23 calls for).

Spicq, who has Hebrews written by Apollos to ex-Essene priests, dates Hebrews about AD 68 corresponding with the time of the destruction of Qumran by the Romans.

Manson, who has the epistle addressed to a Jewish Christian minority group at Rome, dates the epistle AD 65-70. But at this time the church in Rome would still be suffering from the Neronian persecution. According to tradition, it was in AD 68 that both Peter and Paul lost their lives in Rome. Countless Christians were dying in the Circus Maximus and in Nero's gardens. It is not easy to reconcile these facts with the idea that Hebrews was written and received at Rome in the midst of this situation. The problem with this suggested date is it requires us to give other than the traditional interpretation to Hebrews 12:4 ("you have not yet resisted to the point of shedding blood"). If the letter were written to Roman Christians in the post-Neronian times, some of their brethren certainly had resisted so much it cost them their blood! If the people addressed were Roman Christians, a date not later than AD 64 is indicated in Hebrews 12:4, for Nero surely did shed the Christians' blood.

Kummel and others suggest the epistle's alleged links with Luke-Acts suggest a post-Pauline period – say a date between 80 and 90 AD. This requires either that we take "to the Hebrews" to mean "Gentiles," or we must think that groups of the brethren in Rome continued to ignore Romans 14-15 and maintained their independent ethnic identities. Again, it is hard to explain how such a late date, after the Neronian persecution, can be reconciled with Hebrews

12:4. Furthermore, it is nearly impossible to document the hypothesis that Hebrews shows evidences of literary linkage with Luke-Acts that would allow us to extract a separate strain of theology (as distinguished, say from Peter or John or Paul).

Perhaps influenced by the restudy of second-temple Judaism currently occupying the attention of the scholars, Walter Schmithals has recently introduced another element into the discussion by suggesting Hebrews is to be interpreted in the light of the situation that resulted from the post-70 AD re-organization of Jewish religious life at Jabneh.[11] As noted above (page *li*), it was about this time that a benediction against "heretics" was added to the prayers regularly offered during the synagogue services. Once this occurred, the threat of excommunication from the synagogue loomed more and more as a fact of life for the followers of Messiah Jesus. Schmithals dates Hebrews c. AD 80-100 and has it addressed to God-fearing *Gentile* Christians (i.e., proselytes) who were just then being driven out of the synagogue. This excommunication, he thinks, accounts for the persecution Hebrews warns was coming. In reply to Schmithals, are God-fearing Gentiles ever designated as "Hebrews"? The title affixed to the epistle is hard to explain if Schmithals view is correct. And what about the epistle's destination being a definite community, an idea we've discerned in Hebrews. Contrary to the demands of Schmithals' proposal, Hebrews does not appear to be a circular letter to a number of ex-synagogue attendees across the empire.

It begins to become evident that accepting a non-traditional view of authorship or destination creates more problems for determining the date of writing for the letter than does accepting the traditional view.

E. What effects do the TRADITIONAL CONCLUSIONS ABOUT AUTHORSHIP AND DESTINATION have on the possible date of writing?

Jerusalem was destroyed in AD 70 and the church there fled the city before the final campaign by the Romans began in earnest.[12] If the traditional view is correct, which has Hebrews addressed to Jewish Christians in Jerusalem, the letter must be dated before AD 70.

Paul's death is dated in the spring of AD 68.[13] If the traditional view of the Pauline authorship is correct, then Hebrews must be dated before AD 68.

The writer's request for the readers' prayers that he might soon visit them again (13:18,19) sounds much like the requests made in Paul's Prison Epistles (Philemon 21,22, Philippians 1:19), which come from Paul's first Roman imprisonment in AD 61-63. By contrast, Paul did not expect to be released from the second imprisonment (2 Timothy 4:6ff). On this basis, the traditional date for Hebrews is during Paul's first Roman imprisonment, somewhere between AD 61 and 63.

---

[11] *Neues Testament und Gnosis* (Darmstadt: Wissenschaftliche Buchgesellschaft, 1984), p.138ff.

[12] Eusebius, H.E. III.5.3. Jesus gave His followers warnings (Mark 13, Matthew 24, Luke 21) that enabled them to recognize when it was time to leave the city of Jerusalem.

[13] For documentation of this date, see Reese, *New Testament History: Acts*, p.953.

There are good reasons to date Hebrews in the early AD 60s. The whole tone of the epistle – its historical allusions and theological arguments – calls for a date in the years prior to the destruction of Jerusalem in AD 70, as do the traditional conclusions about authorship and destination.

VI. PURPOSE

Any conclusions made concerning the purpose the writer had in mind will necessarily have some bearing on the interpretation of many passages in the book. Care must be taken, therefore, in the conclusions reached about the purpose for writing.

The traditional view is that Hebrews was written to encourage the Jewish Christian readers to remain faithful to Jesus Christ rather than reverting to the old Jewish religion. The encouragement is based on the fact that the new covenant is superior to the old, a truth that can be demonstrated from a careful study of the old covenant Scriptures themselves. These old covenant Scriptures looked forward to their own abrogation and replacement by something "better" – a better priest, a better tabernacle, a better sacrifice, a better cleansing, and a better redemption.[1] What else could it mean, when we are told the Mosaic institutions were but shadows and types, but that something better – the realities to which the types and shadows pointed – was to come and replace them?

The traditional view is also based on several other factors found within the book itself. The "camp" the readers are encouraged to leave (13:13) is most naturally explained as being a reference to the camp of ancient Israel as it was pitched around the tabernacle as they traveled through the wilderness, i.e., it is a reference to the Mosaic religion. The five warning passages (2:1-4, 3:7-4:13, 5:11-6:20, 10:26-39, 12:18-29) interspersed throughout the epistle form an unusual feature of this letter, a feature not found in any other New Testament book. Some note must be taken of this unique feature as we discuss purpose.[2] They are hardly viewed as optional extras that merely interrupt the thread of doctrinal argument, extras we could just as well do without. It must also be asked how the doctrinal sections of the letter serve the writer's purpose. Usually, in the New Testament, the exhortations flow from the doctrinal portions – *if* the doctrine is true, *then* here is the expected response from the reader.

If we take 13:22 as the writer's own purpose statement, we will view Hebrews as a "word [message] of exhortation."[3] The exhortation running through the whole letter is the encourage-

---

[1] Not a few writers have noted one of the key words in Hebrews is the word "better," occurring a dozen times. We have taken note of this fact as we have drafted a statement about the purpose of the letter.

[2] In certain circles, it is fashionable to use the word "paraenesis" to identify the literary genre into which Hebrews falls. "Paraenesis" is another way of saying "exhortation," while "thesis" is another way of saying "doctrinal section." We see little to be gained by using the language of literary criticism as it is spoken in secular humanistic circles as we attempt to explain the epistle to the Hebrews.

[3] The other place in the New Testament where we encounter this expression "word of exhortation" (Acts 13:15) is followed by the record of a sermon preached by Paul in the synagogue at Antioch. Should we let this fact influence us into thinking Hebrews was originally a sermon delivered at some particular place or on some particular occasion which was then (either with or without editing) turned into an epistle? One could even sup-

ment to remain faithful to Jesus Christ. What makes apostasy from Jesus so bad (see the strong language in Hebrews 6:6 and 10:29) is that a man who has turned his back on Jesus Christ has repudiated the only real, working, efficacious, propitiatory sacrifice for sins that ever will be offered. What happens at the judgment to a man whose sins are not covered?

One could even rationalize and find plausible reasons why embracing the Mosaic religion again would not be so bad. After all, the old covenant had been given by God Himself, some of it even written by the finger of God on tables of stone. The tabernacle (and later the temple building itself, both the one built by Solomon and the one rebuilt by Herod, which were magnificent by any worldly standards) as well as the impressive services repeatedly held therein had been the divinely-revealed way to worship God for over 1,400 years. Jews with their greater knowledge of God were certainly a light for the Gentiles. With all these things being true, people might easily be tempted to think it would not be abandoning God, would it, if they were to quit Christianity and revert to Judaism? Against such erroneous thinking it is the burden of the whole epistle that what a man has in Christ is better. The new covenant is superior to the old in every way! In every chapter of the letter in our Bibles, we can see this proposition advocated, analyzed, illustrated, and proven from Scripture beyond a shadow of a doubt. The readers need to be aware of the danger inherent in becoming dull in hearing (5:11), of imitating Israel in the wilderness (3:7-12), of yielding thorns and thistles (6:7,8), and of neglecting so great a salvation (2:3). The need for faithfulness (6:12 and chapter 11) and endurance (10:36, 12:1), and "hold[ing] fast our confidence ... until the end"(3:6,14) are also key to understanding the message of Hebrews.

Such has been the traditional explanation of the purpose of Hebrews. Nothing in recent studies has shown any real need to abandon the traditional view. Nor have any of the recent hypotheses accounted for the emphases found in the book as well as the traditional view does.

Theories regarding the author's purpose, of course, are integrally related to the decision that has been made about the destination of the letter. If the letter is addressed to Jewish believers in Jerusalem, the purpose is likely to be conceived in different terms than if the letter were addressed to Jewish believers in Rome, or to Gentile believers. Let us illustrate.

Those who have supposed the letter is addressed (as already noted in the earlier treatment of "destination") to a certain group of Jewish believers, say ex-priests,[4] or former members of the Qumran sect,[5] or to a small group of Jewish Christians in Rome, offer a slightly different explanation of the letter's purpose. While it may be true that ex-priests forfeited the positions they once held, and might be tempted to revert to Judaism to resume their old status, it is also true of all converts to Christianity from Judaism that there was much they gave up in everyday

---

pose the five warning passages interspersed throughout the letter are the exhortations that close or drive home each major point of the sermon. (More on this later as we discuss the outline of the book.) In any case, only someone who has a personal and passionate concern for another will offer him a word of exhortation, of earnest appeal. The use of "exhortation" suggests just such a relationship between writer and readers.

[4] C. Sandegren, "The Addressees of the Epistle to the Hebrews," EQ 27 (1950), p.221ff.

[5] Y. Yadin, "The Dead Sea Scrolls and the Epistle to the Hebrews," *Scripta Hierosolymitana* 4 (1959), p.36-55.

life that would be just as tempting to resume. Whatever might be singled out in Hebrews as applying to priests – e.g., the discussion about the high priesthood of Jesus – would be just as true of the rank-and-file Jewish convert. Furthermore, where is there any evidence that there were churches made up wholly of converted ex-priests. Perhaps the Qumran sect did have trouble exegeting the Old Testament Scriptures as they tried to make them relevant to the contemporary situation they were in (Hebrews is supposed to show them the right way to do it, instead of using the method called *pesher*[6]). Yet it is just as true that an ex-Pharisee or ex-Sadducee who thought the old covenant was better also needed help with his Bible interpretation. And what are we to think of the idea there was a small group of Jewish Christians who were failing to embrace the idea that Christianity was worldwide in its scope,[7] so that the Hebrew writer's purpose was to get the readers to see that God was interested in Gentiles as well as in Jews? Is being narrow minded racially the same as "forsaking our own assembling" or "falling away from the living God" that Hebrews 10:25 and 3:12 warn against? Obviously, there was something other than racial prejudice behind the warnings in Hebrews. Each of these slight modifications of the traditional view of purpose may take into account one or two of the features exhibited in Hebrews, and thus have a bit of truth in them, but none account as satisfactorily for all the features of Hebrews as the traditional view does.

Those who have supposed the letter is addressed to Gentiles have found the discussion of purpose to be a topic fraught with many difficulties. As explained earlier, those writers who reject the title "to the Hebrews" and posit a Gentile address for the letter, have not convinced their fellow students of the truth of their hypotheses, either as to destination or as to purpose.

---

[6] "Pesher" is a term that has come into vogue among some Bible scholars since the discovery of the Dead Sea Scrolls. Some of the most fascinating texts found in the caves near Qumran are the ones called "Pesharim" (from the Hebrew *pesharim*, plural of *pesher*, meaning "solution or interpretation"). The Pesharim are usually grouped into two categories. (1) Thematic pesharim explain a central theme by taking selected texts from the Hebrew Bible and attempting to make a contemporary application. *11QMelchizedek* is one example of thematic pesharim, whose isolated Old Testament texts are interpreted as actually having reference to "the end of days" rather than to the historical past. (2) Continuous pesharim are verse-by-verse "explanations" of a Hebrew text. The original text was thought to be written in a kind of code, which could only be decoded by the Teacher of Righteousness after God provided him with the key. The *Commentary on Habakkuk* is an example. It is unconcerned with the literal sense of the text of Habakkuk, relying instead on metaphor, allegory, and paronomasia to make the intended interpretation clear. For example, the judgment spoken against Babylon (Habakkuk 2:7,8) is explained as referring to a wicked priest in Jerusalem who caused trouble for the Qumran community (1QpHab. 8:13f.).

The discovery of these scrolls has given new impetus to a study of Jewish hermeneutics in the intertestamental period. This in turn has led some scholars to try to prove such methods were used by early Christian writers as they interpreted certain Old Testament passages Messianically. The *pesher* method is an imaginative interpretation or expansion based on some Old Testament text, usually in an attempt to show the particular Old Testament text has contemporary relevance. The presupposition behind the whole theory is that the text itself contains a mystery communicated by God that is not understood until the solution is made known by some inspired contemporary interpreter. (This idea may come from the use of the word *pesher* in the book of Daniel, where it is often translated "interpretation".) As a result of this presupposition, the pesher method evidenced in the Dead Sea Scrolls often has little regard for the original historical context; Old Testament passages are explained in terms of the present or imminent experience of the interpreter. What is important is the present historical event or person; if we can find some reference to it in the Bible, do it, even if the original meaning of the Old Testament text must be ignored. (See F.F. Bruce, "Pesher" in the *Encyclopedia Judaica*, [Jerusalem: Encyclopedia Judaica, 1972] V. 13,, p.331-332, and M. Horgan, *Pesharim: Qumran Interpretations of Biblical Books* [Washington, DC.: Catholic Biblical Association, 1979]).

[7] See Wm. Manson, *The Epistle to the Hebrews*, for a presentation of this view.

(1) One hypothesis was that the purpose of Hebrews was to prove that Christianity was the only valid religion in the world. According to this suggestion, Hebrews was addressed to Gentile readers who were being influenced by some sectarian Jewish people, whose views were developed after they had deliberately chosen to abandon the normative Judaism of the day. There was a time when the history of early Judaism was explained much as George F. Moore explained it (*Judaism in the First Centuries of the Christian Era*). He thought he discerned both a normative and a heterodox Judaism. Today, such a dichotomy is held by few scholars. It seems rather to be more in harmony with the evidence to speak of the pluriformity of early Judaism.[8] But while Moore's dichotomy held, some did urge that the purpose of the writer of Hebrews was to combat one of the heterodox and speculative strands of Judaism. The Hebrew writer allegedly did so by showing that Christianity was the only valid religion, and he proved his point by appealing to the very Scriptures the speculative sect themselves used. Once he had shown from Scripture that the sect was wrong, then perhaps the Gentile readers who were being influenced by that sect would be less inclined to continue to hold those wrong views. Two problems are faced by this reconstruction of the purpose of Hebrews. One is that there is little in the epistle that could be attributed to something other than mainstream understanding of the Old Testament teaching about tabernacle, priesthood, or worship. The other is that Christianity *is* the only valid religion in the world, and if that point is made in Hebrews, it is not just to counteract some heretical group but because it is gospel truth! (2) Another hypothesis has been that Hebrews was written for the purpose of counteracting a new heresy. The new heresy is identified as the incipient Gnosticism (with Jewish overtones) which was invading a Gentile church somewhere.[9] The identification was made because of the emphases on angels (Hebrews 1 and 2), and washings (Hebrews 6), and restrictive dietary rules (Hebrews 13:9), all of which can be demonstrated as being emphasized in Gnostic thinking. While admitting that some of the parallels between Hebrews and Gnosticism are true (i.e., Gnosticism, in some places, was a mixture of Jewish and pagan beliefs), we also do not see that this attempt at identifying the purpose of Hebrews satisfactorily explains the features and emphases we find in the whole book. (3) A slight variation on this theme that the purpose of Hebrews is to counteract incipient Gnosticism, affirms that chapters 3 and 4 of Hebrews are the key to understanding the whole book. Allegedly, the writer of Hebrews has been influenced by the Gnostic redeemer myth which included the idea that the redeemer himself had to be redeemed before he could redeem others. Against this idea that the redeemer had to be redeemed is the meaning of "perfect" when we are told that Jesus had to be made "perfect" before He could be our Redeemer (see notes at Hebrews 5:9).

One writer has noted that in all likelihood, some of the recent nontraditional suggestions about destination and purpose have a hidden agenda behind them, that agenda being the doctrinal dispute about the possibility or impossibility of apostasy. If a Christian enjoys unconditional eternal security, then the letter cannot be a warning about the dangers of apostasy; or, if it is about apostasy, it cannot be addressed to people who are Christians (since

---

[8] James A. Sanders, "Understanding the Development of the Biblical Text," in *The Dead Sea Scrolls After Forty Years,* edited by Hershel Shanks (Washington, DC.: Biblical Archaeology Society, 1991), p.60.

[9] T.W. Manson supposed that Hebrews was written to the church at Colossae, and that the Colossian heresy is exactly what Hebrews reflects. See *BJRL*, 32 (1949-50), p.1-17.

they can never fall).[10]

> We have seen no compelling reason to abandon the traditional explanation of the writer's purpose for writing "to the Hebrews." If these converts to Christianity from the Jewish religion will just "consider Jesus," the new covenant His death ratified, and the truth to which their own Scriptures pointed, they will certainly be dissuaded from rejecting Christianity and reverting to the old Jewish religion.[11]

VII. CANONICITY

Faith is based on evidence. In each generation, Christians have had the responsibility before God to re-examine the evidence on which their faith rests. As the evidence is re-examined, one topic that needs to be explained is the process by which books were and continue to be included in the collections we call the Bible. How does a 21st century believer know in fact and with certainty that Hebrews should be included in his New Testament?

When it comes to a detailed presentation of why certain books were included in our New Testaments and why certain ones were excluded, the presentation usually includes such topics as factors that led to the collection of a body of authoritative books (including the influence of the Hebrew Scriptures on the formation of a body of Christian Scriptures and the vacuum left by the death of the apostles), the criteria used in the determination of the status of any book, and the formation of lists of accepted books in order to combat heresies and heretics.

The Greek word translated canon (*kanon*) literally means "rule or standard," or the limits of a sphere of action or influence. It was also used in the second century church with reference to the rule of faith. The word then came to mean something that has been measured and which in turn becomes the standard by which others are measured. Thus the books included in the canons of our Old and New Testament Scriptures are books which have been measured, and then become the standard by which others are measured. Such a collection of books becomes the yardstick by which the church's beliefs and practices are measured because the writings are recognized as authoritative and binding, having come from God Himself.

A. BRIEF OVERVIEW OF HOW THE CANON WAS DECIDED

Before any of the books of the New Testament were written, the earliest Christians had

---

[10] See footnote #3, page xxxvii, for writers who view the letter as addressed to people not yet converted. For a special study concerning the security of the believers, see "Once Saved, Am I Always Saved?" in Gareth L. Reese, *New Testament Epistles: Romans* (Moberly, Mo.: Scripture Exposition Books, 1987), p.280ff.

[11] A word of caution is necessary. When one reads the five warning passages, it is true that they say nothing about reverting to the Mosaic religion; all they do speak about is apostasy from the covenant and religion introduced by Jesus the Messiah. It is inference from the context of the warning passages that the danger being warned against was that of reverting to Judaism. In this commentator's opinion, no other suggestion offered as to what the danger was satisfies the general thrust of the whole epistle as well as the traditional statement of purpose does. Nor, for that matter, when we read about the persecutions the readers have faced and still do face, are we told specifically that it is fanatical adherents to the old Mosaic religion who are the persecutors – yet the whole tenor of the letter suggests this indeed is the source of the persecution.

such a canon. It was made up of (1) the Old Testament Scriptures interpreted Christologically, and (2) the preaching of the apostles. When the New Testament books came to be written, they simply recorded in writing what Jesus and the apostles had been saying orally. It was a rather straightforward thing for the listeners who knew the apostles to compare what they had just received in writing with the Scriptures and the doctrine preached by the apostles.

The time when the book was first accepted should be distinguished from the later time when re-evaluations were made of what had already been done by a former generation. A book was first accepted or rejected as apostolic and authoritative the moment it was received.[1] We would even suggest that in an age when spiritual gifts still pertained, this would be a suitable function for the person who had the gift of discerning of spirits. A Christian with this spiritual gift could look at the letter and immediately pass judgment on its authenticity as being from God. Paul and John insisted in the first century that it was necessary to "test the spirits [prophets]" (1 Corinthians 12:1-3, 1 John 4:1-3) and make sure their utterances were consistent with the gospel as they themselves had received and delivered it.

It might even be proper to say the canon was closed when the last inspired letter was written and received.[2] Hindsight would tell us the canon (i.e., the list of books accepted as inspired and included in a church's collection) was actually completed when John wrote the last book of the Bible about AD 96. But it took time for this fact to be recognized by all the churches.

After the initial acceptance of the various books, it became necessary, as time passed, for the church to re-evaluate what the original readers had done. Collections of apostolic works were being made for use in the public worship services.[3] When men could no longer hear the

---

[1] The 27 canonical books were written between AD 45 and 96. Thus, by the end of the first century, all New Testament books were accepted as divine by believers somewhere. No writing of an apostle was knowingly rejected by the church, nor has any apostolic book been proven lost. The apostolic fathers and the apologists (i.e., the church leaders living from about AD 96 to 180) viewed the apostles as a fixed group with a now finished work. The extra-biblical authors who were closest in time to the apostles claimed to be far beneath them, equating the apostles' words with the words of Christ Himself. Within a generation after John, all 27 books were cited as Scripture by some church leader. Within 200 years, all but 11 verses of the New Testament were quoted in more than 36,000 citations that have been preserved for us.

[2] This statement is deliberately made since it is rather common in present-day works on the canon to read that the New Testament canon was finally closed in the 4th century. Such language implies men are the sole determiners of what is to be included in the Bible. We must be careful when we say the "New Testament Canon was closed when the last apostolic book was written and received," or "it was finally closed in the 4th century," for it was not *men* who determined when it closed; *God* is the ultimate author and determiner of the books. Canonicity is determined by God's actions, not men's decisions. Humans do not determine canon, they merely discover the already existent canon which God has given by inspiration. If the book was recognized as inspired by God, it was included in the canon. Just as in early Judaism when the Hebrew canon was considered closed when it was recognized that the period of classical prophecy was over, so too in early Christianity the New Testament canon was considered closed when it was eventually recognized the divine authority resident in the apostolic writings could not be reproduced.

[3] Before the last third of the 1st century, some of the Gospels were circulating and being collected; see Paul's citation of Luke's Gospel as Scripture (1 Timothy 5:18). By the time Peter wrote, Paul's letters were circulating, collected and designated as "Scripture" (2 Peter 3:16). The parts of the collection of Paul's writings were labeled "To the Romans," etc. Not long after John wrote, the four Gospels were brought into one group called "The Gospel," each of its four parts entitled "According to Matthew," etc. Since these collections were made at differ-

apostles speak personally, there would be a felt need for having the writings of the apostles available.[4]   Heretical books were clamoring for inclusion among the books deemed authoritative by the church.[5]   Which ones should be translated into other languages for missionary purposes? Persecutions would demand the Christians know which books were worth dying for. So a deliberate restudy of the limits of the canon became a necessity.

As we look back at how this reassessment was done by the next generations of believers, as they accepted or rejected books as being canonical, we see their key test for continued inclusion in the canon was *inspiration*, and there were three criteria by which inspiration was recognized: 1) authorship, 2) contents, and 3) universal acceptance.[6] *Authorship* means, Was it written by an apostle or a close associate of an apostle? (Remember, spiritual gifts were passed on by the laying on of an apostle's hands.) *Contents* has to do with doctrine. Do the teachings match the doctrine of the already-accepted books? After all, truth cannot contradict truth. *Acceptance* asks, Was the book generally received and accepted by the orthodox church? Again, it must be emphasized, the decisions recorded in the church fathers, and those made by the early councils, are not the first time the canon was ever being decided.

B. HOW DOES HEBREWS FARE WHEN THESE CRITERIA ARE APPLIED?

1. Authorship

Our earlier study of the question of authorship shows that, no matter who is finally thought to be the author, it was an apostle or a close associate of an apostle who wrote Hebrews. Whether or not the traditional view of the Pauline authorship is accepted, Hebrews passes this test for canonicity.

Had Hebrews been signed by an apostle, or a close associate of an apostle, it likely would have met with no resistance as far as canonicity is concerned. But it was not signed. This should not cause us hesitation, for Hebrews is not the only unsigned book included in the canon. The Gospels are not signed. 1 John is not signed. Simply because a book was unsigned is not an automatic reason to reject its canonical status.

---

ent times and places, their contents were not always the same; each location didn't have copies of all the same books yet. This limited circulation of some books helps explain why they were later questioned by some.

[4] Among the Hebrews, and even among some early Christians (see Papias' statement [Eusebius, HE. III.39.3-4] about preferring the living voice rather than writing), perhaps oral communication was deemed more trustworthy than written. "But in a society like the Graeco-Roman world of the early Christian centuries, where writing was the regular means of preserving and transmitting material worthy of remembrance, the idea of relying on oral tradition for the recording of the deeds and words of Jesus and the apostles would not have generally commended itself." F.F. Bruce, "Some Thoughts on the Beginning of the New Testament Canon," BJRL 65:2 (Spring 1983), p.44,45.

[5] Paul and John insisted in the 1st century that it was necessary to "test the spirits [prophets]" and make sure their utterances were consistent with the gospel as they themselves had received and delivered it. Such testing was all the more necessary a century later. The Montanist challenge from one direction and the Marcionite and Gnostic challenges from another made it necessary for the limits of Holy Scripture to be carefully defined.

[6] These three tests for inspiration can be documented from early Christian literature as tests *consciously* employed at the time the early Christian writers were writing about their contemporaries' views on canon.

2. Contents

Orthodoxy had little problem with the contents of Hebrews until about the time of the Reformation. There was some question about whether Hebrews 9:4 has a mistake about the location of the altar of incense (or golden censer), and there was a question about Hebrews 7:27, which seems to have the high priest entering the Holy of Holies "daily," but the key doctrinal points in Hebrews agree with what Jesus and the apostles regularly taught.

The church in the western part of the Mediterranean world seemed to have some dispute over Hebrews, but it was not so much over Hebrews itself as over the use made of certain passages in Hebrews by heretics after the heretics had misinterpreted the passages. This was true of two passages in particular. 3:2 was used to support Arianism and 6:4 was used both by the Novatianists[7] and the Montanists[8] to support their particular heresies. Rather than counter those arguments by properly explaining the Hebrews' passages, some churches in the western part of the Mediterranean world chose to reject Hebrews as canon.

In the Reformation, Luther took issue with the contents of Hebrews[9] and as a result relegated Hebrews to a less-than-canonical place in his Bible. Cardinal Cajetan expressed doubts concerning the canonicity of Hebrews, James, 2 and 3 John, and Jude. Erasmus expressed doubts about Revelation, as well as the apostolicity of James, Hebrews, and 2 Peter. In direct response to the Reformers' doubts about the canonicity of Hebrews, the Council of Trent declared emphatically the epistle was written by Paul and was indeed canonical.

Since the sixteenth century, when Protestants and Roman Catholics debated the extent of the Biblical canon, there have been no changes in the shape of the Christian Bible. Protestants and Catholics still differ over the Old Testament Apocrypha; they remain in agreement on the canonical status of the twenty-seven books of the New Testament.

---

[7] Novatianism was a debate over the proper treatment which the church should afford to Christians who denied their faith in times of persecution. Novatian maintained the church must be kept pure of defilement. Because Hebrews says it is "impossible to renew them to repentance," the church should therefore deny forgiveness for such a serious offence.

[8] Montanism originated when Montanus (c. AD 170) began to utter prophecies while in a state of convulsive frenzy. His supporters claimed this ecstatic condition was the result of being totally under the power of the Holy Spirit, and that his prophecies were inaugurating a new dispensation of divine revelation. Of course, this movement provoked a debate on whether the church should expect further revelations now that the apostolic age had ended. Montanists failed to convince the church that their prophecies were a valid addition to Scripture. The Montanists made use of Hebrews 6 to prove one of their new doctrines was not unscriptural, namely, that one sin committed after baptism results in the soul being lost.

[9] Luther's doctrine (which he found at Romans 3:20,28) that God saves by faith, not works, was attacked by agents of the papacy. Their most telling weapon used against Luther was the epistle of James, with its doctrine of works, epitomized by the text, "Faith, if it has no works, is dead" (James 2:17). Luther sometimes defended himself by trying to explain the true relationship between faith and works; on another occasion he took a bolder step of denying that the epistle of James was written by an apostle. Later, he asserted that if the epistle was not written by an apostle, it did not belong in the canon. His objections were doctrinal, not historical. He rejected Hebrews because he thought the contents (especially Hebrews 6:4ff, 10:26ff, 12:17) were not in harmony with what the other books of the Bible teach. B.F. Westcott, *A General Survey of the History of the Canon of the New Testament* (London: McMillan, 1870), p.438ff, has a good summary of the discussion of Hebrews place in the canon at the time of the Reformation until the Council of Trent.

Except for some scattered instances of doubt in some people's minds, Hebrews has passed the "contents" criterion for inclusion in the canon.

3. Universal Acceptance

We have no written record of how Hebrews was first received by those to whom it was addressed. If our decision about the destination is correct, we know that many of the Jerusalem Christians remained faithful to Jesus, for Eusebius (H.E. III.5.3) tells us they fled the city just ahead of the Roman destruction that trapped the Jewish non-Christians.

Furthermore, the book has been recognized as canonical from nearly the first days that the original readers accepted it as genuine and authoritative. A brief review of the historical facts about its acceptance or non-acceptance will be helpful to our understanding of this point.

Hebrews in the Eastern Mediterranean world was accepted into the canon from the first. By the middle of the second century (i.e., c. AD 150) we have evidence from the East that Hebrews was already accorded canonical recognition.

One line of evidence for this is the treatment of Hebrews in early Christian writings. Pantaenus (c. AD 170), Clement of Alexandria (AD 150-215),[10] and Origen (AD 185-254)[11] all taught the canonicity of Hebrews. Origen's great influence in the Eastern Church was sufficient to insure the continued canonical acceptance of Hebrews. Eusebius of Caesarea (AD 260-340) included Hebrews (reckoned by him as a Pauline letter) among the books whose canonicity was obvious and plain.[12] Ephraem (c. AD 350) and the other Syrian fathers accepted Hebrews without question as canonical. Athanasius of Alexandria was a respected leader in the East. In AD 367 he wrote his *Festal (Easter) Letter* 39, in which he defends the present 27-book New Testament canon as the acceptable writings for use in the churches.[13] His judgment eventually came to be the majority's opinion concerning the canon.

---

[10] The recorded beliefs of Pantaenus and Clement of Alexandria have already been shown above in the discussion about *Authorship*. Clement evidently knew and used all 27 books of the present New Testament canon (as well as other Christian writings which he held to be inspired in some cases). See J.A. Broadus, *Commentary on the Gospel of Matthew* (Valley Forge, Pa.: Judson Press, nd), p.xxvi.

[11] Origen, in his *Homily on Joshua* 7:1 speaks of 14 letters (i.e., including Hebrews) by Paul as being among the works later included in Scripture. In Origen's earlier works, he classified sacred writings into three categories: acknowledged, disputed, and spurious. He included 21 New Testament books in the first group, 6 (Hebrews, James, 2 Peter, 2 & 3 John, and Jude) in the second, and various heretical gospels in the third. Origen himself included the disputed books in the canon, though he acknowledged some had reservations.

[12] Eusebius, H.E. III.3.5. (See above on page *xxiii*.) Eusebius was a good compiler of lists. One such list was of the various books read as Scripture in the different churches. He divided these into three categories: *homologoumena*, *antilegomena*, and *notha*, that is, acknowledged, disputed, and spurious. The books everyone acknowledged as New Testament canon were the four gospels and Acts, Paul's 14 letters, 1 Peter, 1 John, and (according to some) Revelation. The books most churches accepted but some disputed were James, 2 Peter, 2 & 3 John, and Jude. In the class of spurious books were the Shepherd of Hermas, the Apocalypse of Peter, the Didache, the Epistle of Barnabas, the Gospel according to the Hebrews, and (according to others) Revelation. Eusebius, like Origen, divides the books into three categories, and Eusebius' list of acknowledged books includes Hebrews. In the acknowledged and disputed classes, Eusebius has the 27 books of our present New Testament canon. He thus shows what the church was thinking about the canon around AD 325.

[13] For the text of Athanasius' letter, see *Nicene and Post-Nicene Fathers* [Grand Rapids: Eerdmans, 1953], V. 4, St.Athanasius, p.551-552.

Jerome (AD 347-420), who studied in Rome and Antioch before spending the last half of his life in a monastery near Bethlehem, tells us the "epistle to the Hebrews is received by all Greeks and not all Latins ...."[14] He also wrote,

> If the usage of the Latins does not receive [Hebrews] among the canonical Scriptures, neither indeed by the same liberty do the Churches of the Greeks receive the Revelation of John. And yet we accept both, in that we follow by no means the habit of today, but the authority of ancient writers, who for the most part quote each of them.[15]

Jerome's translation (now known as the Latin Vulgate) of the Greek Scriptures into Latin about AD 385 at the request of the Roman bishop Damasus, was likewise a notable landmark. In it are included the 27 books of our present New Testament canon.

Another line of evidence from the Eastern Church is found in the codex collections of New Testament books. Early in the first century the codex (or book form) became the acceptable way of binding manuscript sheets together. This had an advantage over the older scroll form in that many small letters or books could now be bound together in one volume. From the first, in the East, Hebrews is included in these collections of writings intended for reading in the churches. That Hebrews appears in most of the old manuscripts and versions speaks to the church's view on the canonicity of the epistle.[16] In the Chester Beatty Papyri(P[45], P[46], P[47]), dated about AD 200, Hebrews is included in the Pauline epistles, between Romans and 1 Corinthians. We include it here among the Eastern witnesses to the canon since the Chester Beatty Papyri seem to have been part of a Bible of a Greek-speaking church in Egypt. In Codex Sinaiticus (dated about AD 325-350), Hebrews is included before the Pastoral epistles. In Codex Vaticanus (dated c. AD 325-350), Hebrews is included after Galatians. In the Sahidic version, it stands after 2 Corinthians. Hebrews is also included in the Syriac Bibles. The Old Syriac Bible, at the beginning of the 3rd century, employed only the *Diatessaron* (in place of the four Gospels), Acts, and the Pauline epistles, with Hebrews among them.[17] During the early fifth century, the Peshitto Syriac version was produced and became the standard Syriac version. In it the *Diatessaron* was replaced by the four gospels, 3 Corinthians was removed, and three Catholic epistles of James, 1 Peter and 1 John were included. Revelation and the other Catholic epistles were excluded, resulting in a 22-book canon. The point is this:

---

[14] Ep. 125 *ad Evagrium.*

[15] Ep. 129 *ad Dardanus.* Some twenty years earlier, Jerome was somewhat less certain. "The apostle Paul writes to seven churches, for his eighth letter to the Hebrews is by many excluded from the number." The older Jerome gets, the more he quotes Hebrews as a letter of Paul.

[16] Hatch ("The position of Hebrews in the Canon of the New Testament," HTR 29 [1936], p.133-51) has shown that among the numerous New Testament manuscripts, Hebrews occupies three different positions: (1) Among the epistles addressed to churches, after Romans or after Corinthians, etc. (2) After 2 Thessalonians, that is, after the epistles addressed to churches but before those addressed to individuals; (3) After Philemon, that is, after the epistles written to individuals and at the end of the Pauline group. But it is uniformly included! The placement reflects different opinions about its authorship -- not its canonicity.

[17] The Catholic epistles and Revelation were omitted; Hebrews, viewed as Pauline, was accepted; Philemon was either unknown or rejected. The fourth century Syrian fathers also included 3 Corinthians as canonical. (Concerning 3 Corinthians, see A. Robertson, "Apocryphal Correspondence of St. Paul and the Corinthians" in his article on 2 Corinthians in *Hastings Dictionary of the Bible* (New York: Scribners, 1908), Vol.1, p.498.)

Hebrews was included in the Syriac Bibles since the very beginning of translations into Syriac. That indicates their view of its canonicity.

The evidence of Hebrews' acceptance in the East is uniform from the first and is in favor of its inclusion in the New Testament canon.

In the Western Mediterranean world, Hebrews was at first accepted, then rejected, and then later accepted as being authoritative and canonical.

Evidence of its early acceptance comes from Clement of Rome, the Jung Codex,[18] Justin Martyr, and Tertullian. I Clement gives evidence of Hebrews' authority being recognized at the close of the first century, both at Rome and at Corinth.[19] True, Clement's quotations or references are anonymous, but so are they for all the New Testament books he quotes. He quotes Hebrews the same way he did other books included in the canon. Justin Martyr, a native of Palestine, went to reside in Rome in the mid-second century. Martyr, quoting words found only in Hebrews right along with Old Testament references, affords a presumption that he regarded Hebrews on a par in authority with Old Testament Scriptures.[20] The evidence from Tertullian points in two different directions. In one place,[21] Tertullian bears witness to a fixed canon of 22 books (four gospels, Acts, 13 epistles of Paul, 1 Peter, John, Jude and Revelation). Hebrews was missing from this list because of the question of authorship; a writing had to be by an apostle or composed under apostolic authority to be acceptable. However, in another place,[22] Tertullian tells us that, unlike Marcion, Valentinus (who flourished in the middle of the second century) "seems to use the entire *instrumentum*" – meaning the whole New Testament. Is there any evidence which writings Valentinus used? One of the Nag Hammadi writings, the *Gospel of Truth*, which many think was the work of Valentinus himself, alludes to Matthew and Luke (possibly with Acts), to the gospel and epistles of John, to the Pauline letters (except the Pastorals), Hebrews and Revelation.[23] If the *Gospel of Truth* represents the "whole instrument" used by Valentinus which Tertullian alludes to, then we may say this: Tertullian may not have accepted Hebrews, but he knew of people who did.

It is not until late in the second century that we begin to hear some doubts in the west about Hebrews.   Hebrews was apparently omitted from some collections of New Testament

---

[18] See page xxv for details concerning the Jung Codex.

[19] "It seems certain that Clement, as he refers to Hebrews, is not introducing a novel document. It would appear that the church at Corinth knows something of the epistle, for why would Clement employ its language again and again if it were completely unfamiliar to them? It may be that Hebrews was better known and more frequently used in the first century than has often been allowed." Neil R. Lightfoot, *Jesus Christ Today: A Commentary on the Book of Hebrews* (Grand Rapids: Baker Book House, 1976), p.30.

[20] J. Barmby, "Hebrews," in *Pulpit Commentary* (Grand Rapids: Eerdmans, 1962 reprint), p.xv.

[21] *Against Marcion* IV.5. Another argument sometimes advanced is Hebrews, quoted only once by Tertullian in all his writings, did not possess the same authority as the epistles of Paul, which are quoted many times.

[22] *De praescriptione haereticorum* 38:7.

[23] W.C. van Unnik, "The `Gospel of Truth' and the New Testament," in *The Jung Codex*, ed. F.L. Cross [London: Mowbray, 1955], p. 50-100.

books made by the Western Church. Hebrews was omitted from Marcion's canon, but this can hardly be used as credible evidence of what all Rome thought. In fact, it was Marcion's action of publishing a new, abbreviated version of the canon that likely led to serious reassessment of what books should be included in the New Testament canon.[24] Hebrews was omitted from the Muratorian canon,[25] although this may be due to the corrupt state of the text of that canon. Hebrews was also likely omitted from the African Old Latin version, c. AD 170. Irenaeus of Lyon (c. AD 180), despite being a native of proconsular Asia, had reservations about Hebrews; he may have given it deutero-canonical status comparable to Wisdom.[26] Cyprian, who may be regarded as a fair representative of the Western Church in the mid-third century, did not accept the epistle. Finally, as noted above, in Eusebius' time the church at Rome did not accept Hebrews as Pauline, and therefore tended to exclude it from their canon.

The attitude toward the canonicity of Hebrews began to shift back in its favor in the mid-fourth century. Hilary of Poitiers regarded the epistle as canonical. He has been called "Doctor of the Church" and "Athanasius of the West," and his influence in this matter of the canonicity of Hebrews had to be considerable. Hebrews was then included in the canon promulgated by the synods of Hippo (393) and Carthage (397) in this form, "Of Paul the apostle, thirteen epistles; of the same to the Hebrews, one."[27] Augustine defined the New Testament canon as the same 27 books we have in our Bibles. It was Augustine who finally swayed the council at Carthage, and through it the Western Church, toward the renewed acceptance[28] of the letter

---

[24] Efforts to define again which books were to be received into the New Testament canon received help from an unexpected source -- Marcion the heretic. Marcion (AD 85-160) came to Rome c. AD 140. While in Rome, Marcion taught and won disciples to his peculiar views. "Marcion preached the doctrine of two Gods: the OT was the work of the Just God, the Creator, harsh judge of men: Jesus was the emissary of the Good (or Kind) God, higher than the Just, sent to free men from that God's bondage: crucified through the malice of the Just God, he passed on his gospel, first to the Twelve, who failed to keep it from corruption, and then to Paul, the sole preacher of it." (*Illustrated Bible Dictionary*, p.242). He taught that Jesus came straight down from heaven and had suddenly appeared full grown in the synagogue at Capernaum. Jesus taught the previously unknown existence of a good God who wanted to save men. This God was different from the harsh God whose actions fill the pages of the Hebrew Bible. Therefore anything connected with the Jewish religion or their Bible should be repudiated by Christians. The Old Testament could not be authoritative for the followers of Jesus; for them a new volume of sacred writings was provided. Marcion set about to produce this new volume. When he was finished, Marcion's canon included 10 letters of Paul, and the Gospel of Luke heavily edited. This truncated canon was supposed to represent what the apostle Paul taught. Of course Hebrews, which makes much use of the Old Testament to establish its thesis, would be rejected.

[25] This is a listing of New Testament books, thought to be dated c. AD 170 and to represent the beliefs of the church at Rome at the time of its composition. As it now reads, it contains no reference to Hebrews, though it does speak of 13 letters of Paul. Zahn and others have conjectured that our extant copy of the Muratorian canon is a translation from the Greek, and they also suggest textual emendations, so that some books now excluded are shown to have appeared in the Greek original.

[26] Eusebius, H.E. V.26. Irenaeus cites Hebrews and the book of Wisdom in a way that seems to equate the two. He alludes to Hebrews in another place (*Adv. Haer.* II.30.9), yet makes no use of it whatever in his refutation of the heretics.

[27] The wording of the council likely reflects an attempt at compromise between those who thought Paul was not the author and those who wanted to include Hebrews in their canon.

[28] The Roman Catholic church often affirms, "We gave you Protestants the Bible. We decided what books should be included in it." It should once more be emphasized that the councils in North Africa at Hippo and Carthage did not decide for the first time what books should be in our Bibles. They merely reaffirmed what was already the accepted practice in most of the ancient church.

into the canon.[29]

The evidence of Hebrews' acceptance in the West is not as uniform as was the evidence from the East; nevertheless the evidence for the inclusion of Hebrews in the canon is greater than is the evidence that the letter should be excluded.

C. SUBJECTIVE TESTIMONY -- THE WITNESS OF THE SPIRIT

Hebrews, as indeed is true for all canonical books, reads differently from apocryphal or pseudepigraphical books. It has a majesty about it that is noticeably absent from the books excluded from the canon.

> The marked distinction between the writings of the NT and the few that have come down to us from the sub-apostolic age has often been observed and commented on. The difference consists, not only in the tone of authority that pervades the former, but also in their entire complexion as compositions of a higher order. We feel ourselves, as we read them, as if walking in a purer and more heavenly atmosphere, peculiar to the apostolic age. Without attempting to define this difference further, which none can fail to recognize, we may say, without hesitation, that the Epistle to the Hebrews takes rank in this regard with writings of the NT canon.[30]

CONCLUSION

Hebrews is classed either among the accepted books or among the books disputed by some, but never as spurious in the ancient lists. When the criteria used by early Christians to reaffirm canonicity are examined, we can see why Hebrews is included in the canon.

The evidence for including Hebrews in the collection of authoritative books we call New Testament Scriptures is not as strong as the evidence for some of the other books. Yet it is strong enough that higher critics in the 20th and 21st centuries have not attacked its canonicity.

Those who doubted its canonicity, whether in the West in the early centuries or in Europe during the Reformation, have done so, for the most part, on doctrinal grounds. In every case, it would appear, the letter has been misinterpreted and the misinterpretation was what caused its rejection.

It is, by almost two thousand years, too late for the canon of the New Testament to be altered. **Hebrews has a secure place among our New Testament Scriptures.**

---

[29] Early in his career, Augustine unhesitatingly accepted Hebrews as Pauline. He included Hebrews among the canonical writings (*de doct. Christ.* II.8), and occasionally made use of it; but he apologizes for it because of the then-existing opposition by some in the Western Church to the already widely-spreading conviction of its Pauline origin. As the years pass, and the older Augustine becomes, the less he quotes Hebrews as by Paul. A. Souter, *Text and Canon of the New Testament*, 2nd Ed. (London: Duckworth, 1965), p. 174.

[30] Barmby, *op. cit.*, p. xvi.

SELECTED BIBLIOGRAPHY ON THE CANON OF THE NEW TESTAMENT

The Feb.5,1988 issue of *Christianity Today* included five brief articles covering different issues and perspectives on the subject of the canon.

Bruce, F.F., "Some Thoughts on the Beginning of the New Testament Canon," *Bulletin of the John Rylands University Library* 65:2 (Spring, 1983), p.37-60.

Dayton, Wilbur T., "Factors Promoting the Formation of the New Testament Canon," *Bulletin of the Evangelical Theological Society* 10:1 (1967), p.28-35.

Harris, R. Laird, *Inspiration and Canonicity of the Bible*, rev.ed. (Grand Rapids: Zondervan, 1969).

Hatch, Wm. H.P., "The Position of Hebrews in the Canon of the NT," HTR 29 (1936), p.133-55.

Bruce M. Metzger, *The Canon of the New Testament* (Oxford: Clarendon Press, 1987).

Wm. G. Oliver, "Origen and the NT Canon," *Restoration Quarterly* 31:1 (1989), p.13-26.

Sawyer, M. James, "Evangelicals and the Canon of the New Testament," *Grace Theological Journal* 11:1 (1991), p.29-52.

Hans von Campenhausen, *The Formation of the Christian Bible* (Philadelphia: Fortress, 1972).

Warfield, B.B., "The Formation of the Canon of the New Testament," *Revelation and Inspiration* (New York: Oxford University Press, 1927. Reprinted Grand Rapids: Baker Book House, 1981).

VIII. OUTLINE

A satisfactory outline for Hebrews is one that should help us easily remember both the main points of the author's thesis and also how the minor points contribute to the whole thread of the argument. It would also be helpful if breaks between the main points of the outline corresponded with the chapter divisions in our Bibles. Attempts at producing such a satisfactory outline of the arguments presented in Hebrews have proven to be a difficult undertaking.[1] The letter writer's own arrangement or outline is not easily ascertained, for at times he seems to repeat the same arguments, while at other times he pauses in the presentation to deliver a stern warning or hearty exhortation, only to return to the topic he previously was presenting. As a result, a multitude of outlines have been proposed.

---

[1] After struggling to reproduce the letter writer's outline, some have concluded that the structure of Hebrews remains an unsolved problem or that the arrangement the author had in mind as he developed his thesis is not easily perceived by today's students of Hebrews. Yet as one puts proposed outlines side by side for comparison, it can be seen most writers agree somewhat on the outline through chapter four. After that, however, there is no such agreement, either as to what title should be assigned to the paragraphs or as to the chapters and verses included in each topic. As a result, the outlines presented are almost harder to remember than the actual chapter themes in Hebrews.

Attempts to outline Hebrews must take into account more than the fact that the writer's own arrangement is not easy to ascertain. Answers to other questions, such as form and integrity, will have an effect on the final product.

Some have debated the *form* this writing "to the Hebrews" originally took. It has often been repeated that "Hebrews begins like a treatise, proceeds like a sermon, and ends like an epistle." Was Hebrews a treatise,[2] a sermon,[3] or a letter[4]? Perhaps, if it could be determined whether it was a sermon or a letter, that would give help in deciding which tools to use in an effort to outline the letter. A "word of exhortation" it may have been, but it was a *written* exhortation, from the first, according to 13:22.

Some have also questioned the *integrity*[5] of Hebrews as they have tried to discern the author's original outline. Perhaps if certain verses or chapters have been added later, and we were to ignore them now, it would be easier to outline the book. Some have therefore identified 13:22-25 as one section that likely was added later.[6] Another adds 13:19 as a second passage

---

[2] A treatise (the word comes from a Latin root which means to draw along or lead along) is "a book or article which treats a subject, especially in a systematic manner and for an expository or argumentative purpose; a methodical discussion of the facts and principles involved and conclusions reached" (Webster). Deissmann urged Hebrews is an example of a first century "written treatise" (*Bible Studies*, p. 49; *NT in the Light of Modern Research,* p.51). The problem with this view is how to explain the historical allusions that abound in Hebrews. Written treatises did not usually have such definite historic situations in view. Furthermore, the idea that Hebrews is a treatise which develops one central idea – the high priesthood of Christ – has little in its favor.

[3] To prove that the greater part of Hebrews was originally a sermon, appeal is made to several features found in Hebrews. The most compelling is the comparison of Hebrews 13:22 with Acts 13:15 (the only two passages in the New Testament where we find the expression "word of exhortation"). The theory is then advanced that Hebrews is a typical example of the kind of sermon preached in the synagogues by Christian preachers. They would take the Old Testament Scriptures (the Law and the Prophets) that were read for the service of the day and expound them Christologically. Other features that point to the idea that Hebrews was originally a sermon are the frequent pauses for exhortation, just as a preacher is often wont to do. "Time will fail me if I tell ..." (Hebrews 11:32) is also said to fit a sermon more than a written document.

[4] First century letters usually followed a standard format: Signature, address, greeting, thanksgiving, body, and closing salutations and greetings of a personal nature. Hebrews exhibits the closing salutations and greetings but not the usual epistolary opening. It is because of the missing signature, greeting, and thanksgiving that writers are hesitant to classify Hebrews as a "letter." The absence of the usual epistolary beginning has led some writers to ask some speculative questions and then try to answer them. Was there once a greeting and thanksgiving? Did those portions fill a whole page that was subsequently and accidentally lost from the manuscript? Would a whole page be lost without any trace at all? Not even that is true of Mark 16:9ff. [The closing verses of Mark would make up a whole page, and the accidental loss of the last page through wear and tear may account for its absence in some of our early manuscript copies of Mark.] There is not the slightest indication in any of the extant manuscripts of any textual variation in the beginning of Hebrews. Well, if it was not lost accidentally, was it dropped off deliberately? If it was deliberately removed, what was the motive? To make the letter suitable for circulation among many churches? Why didn't the editor remove the definite historical allusions in chapter 13, too, for would these not have been just as unsuitable in a circular letter as was the original statement of destination?

[5] "Integrity" (a technical term used in introductory studies) has to do with the wholesome preservation of the text substantially in the same form as it proceeded from the writer's pen. Specifically, Hebrews enjoys integrity if it originally contained the same number of sentences (we might say "chapters and verses," though the division into chapters and verses was a later addition to the text) that our present editions do.

[6] For example, J.D. Legg, who argued the book (except for 13:22-25) was written by Timothy, also suggested these last few verses were added by Paul. This is an attempt to rescue some Pauline authority for the book by sacrificing its integrity. We should be slow to sacrifice the book's integrity. If Pauline authority is desired, would not the readers have been more convinced by a Pauline signature and introduction at the letter's beginning?

that was not part of the original.[7] Still another suggests that all of chapter13 does not enjoy integrity.[8] There does not appear to be adequate evidence (other than that certain scholars' theories demand it) for suggesting any part of chapter 13 is not original.[9] So our study of the outline of the book will have to make explanation for the form we now have.

BRIEF OVERVIEW OF PAST ATTEMPTS TO OUTLINE HEBREWS

For the sake of these introductory studies, it seems useful to classify the attempts to outline Hebrews into four broad categories: (1) Those who have accepted the traditional view of a Pauline authorship often have tried to impose the traditional two-point division of Paul's letters (doctrinal and practical sections) onto Hebrews. The break between the two points is usually located at 10:18. (2) Those who identify Hebrews as being a treatise (or some other first-century literary effort) have tried various literary criticism and analysis tools in an effort to discern a satisfactory outline. (3) Those who identify Hebrews as a sermon have tried various speech and rhetoric analysis tools in their effort to extract some satisfactory outline. (4) A fourth approach takes the major themes (along with the Old Testament Scripture passages used to substantiate the themes) and the exhortations (warnings) that predominate from chapter to chapter and try to extrapolate an outline suggested by these themes and warnings.

The **traditional two-point outline** has found many proponents, so it must have some commendable things about it. (1) It does make for an easily-remembered outline. John Brown is an example of commentators who divide Hebrews into two major parts. Brown spoke of "the great doctrine" and "the great duty" taught in Hebrews, referring to the superiority of Christianity over Judaism and the believer's need for continued faithfulness.[10] (2) Quite a few outlines, whether traditional two-point or not, make some kind of break at 10:18.

---

[7] Albert Vanhoye found he must remove this verse, along with 13:22-25, if he was to be able to show the perfect symmetry and concentric outline he thought pertained to the original writing of Hebrews, where chapter 1 and chapter 13 each made a unit of thought with but one section in it. See this French scholar's writings explained in English in David A. Black, "The Problem of the Literary Structure of Hebrews: An Evaluation and a Proposal," in *Grace Theological Journal* 7:2 (1986), p.163-77.

[8] This proposal is part of the view that Hebrews was originally a sermon, and that for some reason, it was later reworked into a letter by adding chapter 13.

[9] Two sources for further study concerning the integrity and authenticity of chapter 13 are, R.V.G. Tasker, "The Integrity of the Epistle to the Hebrews," *Exp.Times* 47 (1935-6), p. 136-138, and Floyd V. Filson, "Yesterday": *A Study of Hebrews in the Light of Chapter 13*, Studies of Biblical Theology, 2nd Series, Vol. 4 (Naperville: Allenson, 1967). The main themes found in chapters 1-12 (the abrogation of the Mosaic covenant and sacrificial worship; the superiority of Jesus' priesthood and sacrifice; the need for faithfulness to the new revelation) are echoed in chapter 13, and this strongly supports the unity of the book. In addition, there is little evidence of change of style in chapter 13, certainly not enough to support the view that this chapter was added later, and perhaps by another hand.

[10] John Brown, *An Exposition of the Epistle of the Apostle Paul to the Hebrews* [NY: Carter and Brothers, 1862], Vol.1, page 8. The doctrinal section demonstrates the superiority of Christianity over Judaism by calling attention to Jesus, the Son of God. The Son's superiority to angels through whom the Law of Moses was given, His superiority to Moses, the lawgiver and mediator of the Old Covenant, and His superiority to the Jewish high priest Aaron and his ministry, are all boldly displayed. Jesus as Son, Apostle, and Great High Priest infinitely transcends them all; so does the new covenant of which He is the mediator.

There are, to be sure, some difficulties with the traditional outline that have kept it from being universally adopted. (1) The neat, two-point outline does not fit Hebrews as well as it does, say, Romans, Galatians, or Ephesians. As the critics have pointed out, if we outline Hebrews this way (doctrinal and practical), we end up with exhortations in the midst of the doctrinal section and doctrine in the midst of the practical section. Advocates of the two-point outline reply that it should be remembered 1 and 2 Corinthians, Philippians, and Colossians, regularly outlined as doctrinal and practical, also have hortatory sections intermingled with the doctrinal elements. If Paul could intermingle an occasional exhortation to duty in his doctrinal presentations in those letters, why could he[11] not have done so in Hebrews? (2) Some advocates of the two-point outline have been too strong in their comments on certain verses. It is not exactly in harmony with the repeated warning passages dispersed all through Hebrews to write at 10:19, as Boll does, that "the application of the preceding doctrinal section begins here." (3) Nor are the personal notes found in chapter 13 easily fitted into the traditional two-point outline. Quite a few attempts at outlining Hebrews actually have a three point outline – doctrinal, practical, and personal.

What of the idea that **literary analysis or discourse criticism** is the key to unlocking the outline of Hebrews? Acceptance of the historical-critical method of interpretation of the Bible is basically what, since 1940,[12] is behind the rush to attempt to use discourse analysis, literary criticism or linguistic analysis on Hebrews. Pages and pages have been written attempting to ascertain the genre of first century writing with which Hebrews is to be compared. Is it a dialogue, a diatribe, an epistle,[13] a running midrashic commentary,[14] or a treatise? Reams have been written defending first this then that attempt at analyzing the document according to the canons of that discipline's procedures. Almost every new discipline that comes along in the field of scientific inquiry into literature has been attempted on Hebrews. Linguistics is the latest discipline to be tried.[15] Albert Vanhoye, a noted Jesuit scholar, has produced an enormous

---

[11] We have often observed that the folk who most strongly reject the traditional two-point outline for Hebrews are the same ones who have denied any possibility that Paul was the author of Hebrews.

[12] L. Vaganay, "Plan de l'Epitre aux Hebreux," in *Memorial Lagrange* (Paris: Gabalda, 1940) has been called "the beginning of the modern discussion of the literary structure of Hebrews." Wm. Lane, "Hebrews" in *Word Biblical Commentary* (Dallas: Word, 1991), p.lxxxvi shows the five point outline that Vaganay offered for Hebrews, once Vaganay had completed his literary studies.

[13] See "Is Hebrews an 'Epistle'?" on page ix.

[14] See footnote #6, page *lxiii*, concerning "continuous pesharim." Now the imaginative midrash pesharim such as are found in the commentaries on Habakkuk, Micah, and Zephaniah, among the Dead Sea Scrolls, are not to be compared with the straightforward expositions of the Biblical texts as done by the writer of Hebrews. Nor are the *pesher* interpretations found in the Dead Sea Scrolls to be compared with the types and shadows the writer of Hebrews calls attention to as he exhorts his readers to remain true to the realities to which they pointed. It just will not do to try to identify Hebrews as being another example of first century *pesher*.

[15] Linguistics is a young discipline (Ferdinand de Saussure, 1915; Noam Chomsky, 1957). It is a study of human language, and especially the inner dynamics (speech sounds, word meanings, grammar) within a network of relationships (word grouping in phrases, sentences and paragraphs) which must come together harmoniously in order for communication to take place. Scholars attempting to utilize this discipline as a tool useful in the interpretation of the Biblical text are still endeavoring to develop the perspectives, tools, and applications that would be suitable to Bible study. "The fact is that at present there are no firm conclusions, no generally accepted formulae, no fixed methodology, not even an agreed upon terminology" (P. Cotterell and M. Turner, *Linguistics and Biblical Interpretation* [Downers Grove, Ill.: Inter-Varsity Press, 1989], p.233).

amount of literature defending, modifying, and improving his original work (published 1963), in which he tried to use structural linguistics as a tool to help us understand Hebrews.[16] Scholars still working within the historical-critical system now insist that Vanhoye's work must be the starting point for all future work on Hebrews.[17] The reality is that all the work with hook words, chiasmus, inclusio, etc. contributes little to a study of Hebrews that follows the grammatical-historical method of interpretation. The same topics and paragraph breaks, the same warning passages, can be discerned. New Testament scholarship is rightly hesitant to employ literary criticism methods. Literary criticism leaves us with not much on which to build our faith, nor does it give our faith any content.

What about the idea that **rhetorical criticism or rhetorical analysis** is the key to unlocking the outline of Hebrews? Shall we identify Hebrews as being a sermon, yea, indeed, a fine example of first-century rhetoric, and then try to outline it by using the tools employed in rhetorical criticism[18] or rhetorical analysis? Above, as we considered the form and integrity of Hebrews, we listed certain objections to its being classified as a sermon.[19] Not only are these points against this whole approach to Hebrews, so is the fact that it is difficult to know whether any of the New Testament writers were trained in ancient rhetoric. When the rhetorical devices are known (*narratio, probatio*, etc.), it is difficult to find these in Hebrews.

---

[16] A. Vanhoye, "Structure litteraire et themes theologique de l'Epitre aux Hebreux" in *Studiorum Paulinorum Congressus Internationalis Catholicus* 1961 (Rome: Pontifical Biblical Institute, 1963), 2:175-81. It has been released in a revised edition in 1976. Vanhoye's fundamental principle is that nothing in a text like Hebrews has resulted from chance. The writer consciously and deliberately did each thing we can note (rhythm, alliteration, choice of words, arrangement of different themes). Vanhoye's identification of certain linguistic features like hook words, chiasm, inclusion, announcements, etc., has resulted in a five point outline.

> 1:5 - 2:18   -- Jesus has a better name than the angels.
> 3:1 - 5:10   -- Jesus is a merciful and faithful high priest.
> 5:11-10:39   -- The sacerdotal work of Christ, a priest like Melchizedek.
> 11:1-12:13   -- The endurance of faith.
> 12:14-13:18 -- Specific ways the readers can make "straight paths for your feet."

In a previous footnote (#7, page lxxvii), attention was called to the fact that Vanhoye's approach can be studied in English in Black, GTJ 7 (1986), p.168-73.

[17] Two recent works on Hebrews have shown special indebtedness to Vanhoye. They are Neil Lightfoot, *Jesus Christ Today* (Grand Rapids: Baker, 1976), who makes Vanhoye's structural analysis easy to understand, and William Lane, "Hebrews" in *Word Biblical Commentary* (Dallas: Word, 1991).

[18] Rhetoric (the art of persuasion, or the means of argumentation) developed among the Greeks about 4 centuries before Christ, and Aristotle's master work, "The Art of Rhetoric," can still be studied. The Romans borrowed and modified what the Greeks had been doing, and textbooks on rhetoric from the New Testament era are still extant. It was debated (Cicero, Quintillian) whether there were four or six parts in a proper speech (including the *exordium* or introduction, the *narratio* which states the proposition being discussed and provides background information, the *partitio* or enumeration of the points to be made, the *probatio* or *confirmatio* which presents the logical arguments for the case, the *refutatio* which seeks to disprove opposing views, and the *peroratio* or *conclusio* which summarizes the major points and appeals to both reason and the emotions on behalf of the thesis). For more detail, see "Excursus on Rhetorical Criticism" by Grant R. Osborne, in *The Hermeneutical Spiral* (Downers Grove, Ill.: Inter-Varsity Press, 1991), p. 121-126.

[19] Chapter 13 does not harmonize with the idea that Hebrews originally was a sermon, nor has anyone successfully explained why it had to be reworked into its present letter form by the alleged addition of chapter 13. If Hebrews was not originally an oral address, it is difficult to agree with B. Lindars who wrote, "Once it is recognized that Hebrews belongs to the class of deliberative rhetoric, every detail of the letter falls into place" ("The Rhetorical Structure of Hebrews," *New Testament Studies* 35 [1989], p.382-406).

Because of dissatisfaction with the traditional two-point outline, and because of a studious refusal to use the historical-critical methodology, conservative scholars have begun to propose an outline that reflects the **major themes** presented in the epistle. This is the method of outline used in this commentary.

When commentaries already written are examined, several features of the proposed outlines quickly become obvious. There is general agreement that major breaks between topics occur in the closing verses of chapters 4 and 10, and perhaps also at the end of chapter 7. There is general agreement concerning the theme developed in each of the resulting sections. There is general agreement that the writer, having introduced his main theme, systematically documents the truth of his theme by appeal to the Old Testament Scriptures in order to win acceptance of his basic theme, and to lead the readers to appreciate what they have in Jesus, and then to act upon this truth. There is general agreement that the hortatory units should be assigned an important role in framing the structure of the major divisions of Hebrews. However, there is no general agreement when it comes to the exact verses to be included in some sections,[20] nor is there any agreement on how to title either the major sections or the paragraphs[21] that make up the sections.

One thing yet needs to be done before we can make an attempt at an outline. We must attempt to write a sentence that will serve as the **theme** for the whole book. R.C. Foster used to teach this sentence: "The New Testament is better than, and takes the place of the Old, because the Messenger (Jesus) who gave the New is greater than the messengers (prophets, angels, Moses) who gave the Old."[22] While this is good, it tends to put more emphasis on the change of covenants[23] than it does on who Jesus is. It seems to this commentator that the emphasis in Hebrews centers more on the superiority of Jesus and the effect that superiority has for many matters in religion – matters such as priesthood, sacrifice, covenant, sanctuary, rest, etc. Accordingly, we would offer this theme sentence:

---

[20] For example, does the introduction include 1:1-3, or 1:1-4? Or should we treat 1:1-4 as part of the first major point of the outline, rather than introduction? What shall be done with 4:14-16? Should they be included in the close of part one of the outline, or in the opening verses of part two? And what about chapter 10? Does the break come after 10:17, or after 10:31, or after 10:39?

[21] How shall we outline 8:1-13, as one point or two? What title shall we give to chapters 8, 9, and 10, when it seems the emphasis fluctuates back and forth between Christ's better service, the better sanctuary in which He serves, the better covenant He has inaugurated, then returns to the sacrifice again?

[22] See R.C. Foster, *Class Notes on Hebrews and James* (Cincinnati: Standard, 1925). Chapters 1 through the middle of chapter 7 explain the Son's superiority to the Old Testament messengers. Beginning in the middle of chapter 7 and continuing through chapter 10 is the discussion of the abrogation of the Mosaic covenant and its replacement by the new and better covenant.

[23] At the time Foster taught and wrote, the religious world in general was confused about the relationship of the Law and the Gospel. Therefore, the emphasis on the abrogation of the Old Covenant and the superiority of the New after it was inaugurated by the death of Jesus was a very needed corrective if men were to rightly divide the word of truth (2 Timothy 2:15 KJV). Good as it was, Foster's theme sentence did not make for an easily remembered outline after you had completed chapter 4. This can be seen in the fact the titles he assigned to the following paragraphs did not (in many cases) help the student to remember how the overall theme was being developed by this particular paragraph.

> *Let the superiority of the Son of God and of the revelation God gave through Jesus motivate you to continued faithfulness to Christianity!*

With this theme in mind it is possible to propose titles for the major sections of Hebrews.

1. Exhortations based on the Superiority of the Son of God to the Messengers whom God used in Former Ages. 1:1 - 4:13

2. Exhortations based on the Superiority of the Son of God's Priestly Office (which is after the order of Melchizedek). 4:14 - 7:28

3. Exhortation based on the Superiority of the Son of God's Priestly Work. 8:1 - 10:31

4. Exhortations based on the Imperative of Faithfulness to the Superior Revelation made through Jesus, the Son of God. 10:32 - 13:17

There are some definite advantages to this four point outline. (1) It takes into account the "Scripture exposition" which pervades each section. For example, Messianic Psalms are reflected in chapters 1 and 2, while Psalm 95:7ff is emphasized in 3:7 to 4:7. Again, the Scriptures about Melchizedek form the heart of the argument in 5:6 to 7:17. Jeremiah 31:31ff is the passage being unfolded in 8:1 to 10:18. (2) The titles given to the four major points take into account 13:22, which describes Hebrews as being a "word of exhortation." (3) The writer's own summary statement at 8:1, "now the main point in what has been said," is not ignored. (4) It is also possible to give the paragraphs that make up each section a title that shows its relationship to the main topic of the whole section, as the following partially expanded synopsis of the outline demonstrates.

SUGGESTED OUTLINE FOR HEBREWS

I.   Exhortations based on the Superiority of the Son of God to the Messengers whom God used in Former Ages. 1:1 - 4:13

    A. Jesus is Superior to the Prophets. 1:1-4
       1. God's progressive revelations made through the prophets. 1:1
       2. God's final revelation made through the Son. 1:2a
       3. The evidences of the Son's superiority. 1:2b-4

    B. Jesus is Superior to the Angels. 1:5 - 2:18
       1. The Son's superiority to angels was asserted by the Old Testament. 1:5-14

      WARNING #1 -- 2:1-4
         ▪ Exhortation to pay closer attention to what we have heard. 2:1
         ▪ The penalty for disobedience in the Old Testament. 2:2
         ▪ The present obligation to "pay attention" to the Gospel. 2:3,4

2. The Son's superiority to angels is not contradicted by His humanity. 2:5-9
3. The Son's superiority to angels is not contradicted by His suffering. 2:10-18

C. Jesus is Superior to Moses. 3:1 - 4:13
1. Both Jesus and Moses were faithful to God. 3:1,2
2. The Son's superiority to Moses is asserted by appeal to their positions in God's house. 3:3-6
   a. Jesus is builder of the house; Moses was but a part of the house. 3:3,4
   b. Jesus is the Son over the house; Moses was but a servant in the house. 3:5,6

WARNING #2 -- 3:7-4:13
   - Warnings & exhortations with respect to our pilgrimage. 3:7-19
   - Warnings & exhortations with respect to the promised "rest." 4:1-13

II. Exhortations based on the Superiority of the Son of God's Priestly Office (which is after the order of Melchizedek). 4:14 - 7:28

A. Encouragement to "Hold Fast Our Confession" and "Draw Near With Confidence to the Throne of Grace." 4:14-16

B. Jesus is Better Qualified than Aaron to be our High Priest. 5:1-10

WARNING #3 -- 5:11-6:20
   - Rebuke for having become dull of hearing. 5:11-14
   - Exhortation to go forward to spiritual maturity. 6:1-3
   - Warning against the consequences of continued spiritual defection. 6:4-8
   - Encouragement to persevere based on the certainty of God's promises. 6:9-20

C. Further Teaching About Messiah's Priestly Office (after the order of Melchizedek). 7:1-28
1. Jesus' priesthood is a higher order of priesthood than Aaron's. 7:1-11
2. Jesus' priesthood means the Law of Moses has been abrogated! 7:12-19
3. Jesus' priesthood is so important that was announced with an oath. 7:20-22
4. Jesus' priesthood is a permanent priesthood. 7:23-25
5. It is a priesthood for which Jesus, being sinless, is perfectly qualified. 7:26-28

III. Exhortation based on the Superiority of the Son of God's priestly ministry. 8:1 - 10:31

A. His Ministry is Superior Because it Involves a Better Covenant. 8:1-13

B. His Ministry is Superior Because it Occurs in a Better Sanctuary. 9:1-28

C. His Ministry is Superior Because it Offers a Better Sacrifice. 10:1-18

WARNING #4 -- 10:19-31
- Encouragement to use the new access to God that Christ's priesthood affords. 10:19-25
- A reminder of the fearful consequences of apostasy. 10:26-31.

IV. Exhortations based on the Imperative of Faithfulness to the Superior Revelation made through Jesus, the Son of God. 10:32 - 13:17

A. Encouragement to Endurance in the Faith. 10:32-39.

B. A Reminder that Faithfulness has Always been the Characteristic of God's People. 11:1 - 12:3
1. Preliminary view of the consequences of faithfulness. 11:1-3
2. Faithfulness in the age before the flood. 11:4-7
3. Faithfulness in the Patriarchal Age. 11:8-22
4. Faithfulness in the Mosaic Age. 11:23-40
5. Jesus, the perfect example of faithfulness. 12:1-3

C. Exhortation Concerning Perils that Threaten a Life of Faith. 12:4-17
1. Misunderstanding of the nature and value of suffering. 12:4-13
2. Failure to pursue peace and sanctification. 12:14-17

WARNING #5 -- 12:18-29
- The joy and happiness associated with Mount Zion (compared with the terrors associated with Mount Sinai). 12:18-24
- The consequent responsibilities of Christians. 12:25-29

D. Exhortation Concerning the Performance of Christian Duties. 13:1-17
1. Social duties. 13:1-6
   a. Brotherly love. 13:1-3
   b. Fidelity in the marriage relation. 13:4
   c. Contentment. 13:5,6
2. Religious duties. 13:7-17
   a. Imitate the faith of former leaders. 13:7,8
   b. Be steadfast in the teachings of Christianity. 13:9-15
   c. Benevolence encouraged. 13:16
   d. Obedience and submission to spiritual authority. 13:17

Conclusion: Instructions and Greetings. 13:18-25
A. A Request for Prayer. 13:18,19
B. A Prayer for the Readers. 13:20,21
C. An Exhortation to Heed the Things Just Written in this Epistle. 13:22
D. Information about Timothy. 13:20
E. Final Greetings and Benediction. 13:24,25

COMMENTARY

I. *EXHORTATIONS BASED ON THE SUPERIORITY OF THE SON OF GOD TO THE MESSENGERS WHOM GOD USED IN FORMER AGES.* Hebrews 1:1 - 4:13

A. Jesus Is Superior to the Prophets. 1:1-4

1. God's progressive revelations made through the prophets. 1:1

1:1 -- God ... has spoken – In one of the most beautifully constructed and expressive sentences found in the New Testament, we are immediately reminded "God ... has spoken". Instead of any form of address or greeting as was common in first century letters, the writer plunges directly into his theme, that "God ... has spoken to us in His Son."[1] The reader should let nothing detract from this tremendous theme. Few books in the New Testament Scriptures use the word "God" as often as it is used in Hebrews. Right from the beginning, we are confronted with the reality of God, and with the fact that "He is there and He is not silent!"[2] A person who permits himself to consider the possibility of quitting Christianity should recall this sobering truth – he is actually thinking about putting himself in opposition to God, the powerful One, the One who has arranged things as they are, the One who has revealed Himself[3] and His will through the ages. Is it wise to consider defying the living God by your actions?

After He spoke long ago to the fathers in the prophets -- The time frame covered by these words includes all the ages before the coming of Jesus into the world.[4] In the Patriarchal Age God not only spoke with men face to face, but there were also prophets like Enoch, the seventh from Adam, who prophesied (Jude 14). In the Mosaic age, God revealed himself to men through prophets like Moses, and Samuel and his successors (Acts 3:21-24). A "prophet" is one who speaks for God, and who speaks by inspiration.[5] "Long ago" might be intended to

---

[1] One helpful Bible study method is to "parse" the sentence -- that is, identify subject, verb, and object. In the original, the first sentence runs to what is the end of verse 4 in our Bibles, but stripped of all its modifiers, the subject is "God" and the predicate is "has spoken in His son."

[2] "God" is used 68 times in the epistle, an average of once about every 73 words. *He Is There and He Is Not Silent* is the title of a book on epistemology by Francis Schaeffer (Wheaton, IL: Tyndale House, 1972).

[3] A God who speaks His will to men is one of the distinguishing marks of true religion. Of the world's great religions, only the Hebrew and Christian religions were so given, and the epistle to the Hebrews will demonstrate that of these two, only Christianity is valid for this age and time. What is the guilt of one who repudiates such a religion?

[4] "Fathers" may include all from Adam to Christ, as Robert Milligan, *Commentary on Hebrews* (St. Louis, MO: Christian Board of Publication, nd), p.49 thought; or it may refer to the Hebrew fathers from Abraham to Malachi ("father" is used specially of the patriarchs in John 7:22 and Romans 9:5).

[5] The inspiration of the Old Testament prophets is affirmed in the expression here used, that God spoke "in" the prophets. However, the wording of this affirmation of inspiration must not be used to prove the prophets were mere automatons, or passive instruments. The prophets were more than simply a public address system. 2 Peter 1:21 explains God's messengers were themselves also active in the process of bringing God's message to the world.

This verse throws light on the office and function of prophet. The prophet is not merely one who predicts the future (though sometimes he did that); he was a preacher of righteousness, a messenger of God, one who rep-

suggest God's older revelation was no longer sufficient, that a newer one was needed (cp. Hebrews 8:13).

In many portions and in many ways -- "Many portions" would tell us God revealed Himself little by little, bit by bit, in those Old Testament ages. God gave progressive revelations of Himself and His will.[6] No one person nor no one prophet received a complete picture. Some basic revelations were made to Adam and Eve, Cain and Abel, Enoch, Noah, and others. Abraham was the recipient of further revelations; David received some more; Isaiah, Jeremiah, Ezekiel, and Daniel provide still more as God revealed more and more of His truth to them and they in turn passed on what had been revealed to them. "Many ways" would remind us that God employed dreams, visions, direct communications, object lessons, burning bushes, storms, thunder, gently flowing streams and a Euphratean flood, angels (Gideon), dumb animals (Balaam). He gave Law, history, poetry, and prophecy, yet, none of these revelations or methods came up to the fullness of what God had yet to say in His Son.

2. God's final revelation made through the Son. 1:2a

1:2 -- In these last days -- The marginal note tells of a manuscript variation. Some manuscripts read "at the end of these days." If we read as does the margin, verse 2 points to the close of the Old Testament era as the time when God spoke in His Son.[7] If we read as does the text, this is one verse that suggests the Christian Age is the last of the series of ages in God's management of history.[8]

(God) has spoken to us in *His* Son -- God's earlier speaking, presented in numerous forms and fashions, cannot compare with His final revelation in Jesus, the Son. The Old Testament was preliminary, destined to be superseded from the outset. It was preparatory, awaiting a final, definitive speaking. The claim for the finality of the revelation in Jesus ("God *has spoken*!" – past tense, completed action) should not be ignored or missed. By the time the letter to the Hebrews was written, God's revelation in His Son was a thing completed and in the past.[9] There is no "the" or "His" before "Son" in the Greek. Such a grammatical construction causes

---

resented God before men, one who spoke for God, whether the content of the message dealt with the past, present, or future. Genesis 20:7; Deuteronomy 34:10; 18:18; Acts 2:30; Psalm 105:15.

[6] Liberal theologians have used the expression "progressive revelation" to denote what they think was an alleged evolutionary development of doctrine from Moses (who they think first gave us monotheism), to the prophets (who finally showed us that sacrifices were no longer necessary), to Jesus (who improved on the prophets), to the apostles (who improved on Jesus), to us (we can even improve on what the apostles gave us!). Such evolutionary development of doctrine is not synonymous with "progressive revelation."

[7] The manuscripts that read "on the last of these days" remind one of the expression found in the Septuagint (e.g., Numbers 24:14) that refers in some way to the days when the Messiah would come. Such a meaning here in Hebrews would mean that in Jesus the new age, the Messianic Age predicted in the Old Testament, has appeared.

[8] The concept of the Christian Age being the "last days" is shared by other New Testament writers. See, for example, Acts 2:16,17; James 5:3; 1 Peter 1:20; 2 Peter 3:3; 1 John 2:18; Jude 18.

[9] The reader should be clear in his thinking here. It is *not* affirmed Hebrews was the last of the books of the New Testament to be written (thus making it possible to say "God *has spoken*" – the revelation is already complete and final). It *is* affirmed the revelation had already been completed before many of the books of the

emphasis to be given to the word "Son"[10] He was not a *prophet* (great as many of them were) who was entrusted with God's final revelation – He was One who was of the nature and quality of "*Son*"! It has often been pointed out that the kind of messenger entrusted to deliver a message may have direct relationship to the importance of the message.[11] If the messenger God chose for His final revelation was no less than "Son!" then the message must be of exceeding value and importance. Eight[12] phrases immediately follow, wherein the writer elaborates the incomparable superiority of the "Son"[13] to any prophet or angel or any other agent.

3. *The evidences of the Son's superiority. 1:2b-4*

Whom He appointed heir of all things -- The *first evidence* given to prove Jesus' exalted position is the fact God appointed Him heir of all things. "Heir[14] of all things" is most likely a title of dignity, and shows Jesus has the supreme place in all the mighty universe.[15]   Several

---

New Testament were written in the decades from the 60's to 90's AD. What we find in those books written in the last half of the first century is a record of that revelation already fully given in the Son and which, before it was written down, had been handed on by word of mouth by the New Testament apostles and prophets. Hebrews 1:1,2 is but one of several New Testament passages which affirm the finality of the revelation before the close of the first century -- a truth that reflects strongly and convincingly against certain 20th century claims to continuing revelation from God similar to what one finds in Jesus and the New Testament writings.

[10] The emphasis is all the more striking, as Westcott has called to our attention, because the word "the" is used with "prophets," the other member of the comparison. Translators must try to reproduce the sense of the Greek construction for which there is no English equivalent. The RSV may under-translate it; the KJV may over-translate it. Now, at times, the Old Testament prophets were called "sons" (e.g. Ezekiel 2:1), but the very contrast here with the prophets would be enough to prove Jesus is not considered by the Hebrew writer to be just "a son" (in the sense that he is just one of many). Jesus is in a unique sense God's *Son*; there are no others like Him. That Jesus is not just "a Son" can be seen from the terms and qualities immediately ascribed to Him in the following context here in Hebrews.

[11] One can see this truth illustrated in 2 Samuel 18:19-30, where the runner who carried the sad message about Absalom's death was not Ahimaaz (the good runner), but the Cushite. The type of messenger indicates the type of message he carries.

[12] There are *eight* phrases given if we include verse 4 as part of the first sentence of the letter, as indeed it is in the Greek. Those who start a new point of the outline to the book of Hebrews at 1:4 will tell us that in the first three verses there are *seven* phrases given to describe the "Son."

[13] It is probably true that we would not call "Jesus" the "Son" were it not for the incarnation (Luke 1:35). We are aware that John 3:16 tells us that God so loved that He sent His "Son." That language could, on first sight, be construed to mean that Jesus was the "Son" before He was sent. Furthermore, Matthew 3:17 and 17:5 indicate Jesus already is God's beloved "Son" before the crucifixion and resurrection. But was He the "Son" back in eternity before creation, or did He become the "Son" as a result of the virgin birth and incarnation? In our opinion, the latter is the correct view. (Of course, all views that use "Son" to prove Jesus was a created being – that, so to speak, back in eternity God had a baby and it was a "boy"! – are to be rejected since the New Testament everywhere presents Jesus as an eternal being. Loraine Boettner, *Studies in Theology* [Grand Rapids: Eerdmans, 1953], p.158ff, has an excellent chapter on the *eternal* pre-existence of Jesus, in which he appeals to John 8:58, Colossians 1:16,17, Isaiah 9:6, Micah 5:2, John 17:5 and Philippians 2:6 as evidence for the eternal pre-existence of Jesus.

[14] "Heir" in our language often implies the entering into possession of some valuable property after the death of a testator. However, in the New Testament, this word often is used simply to mean 'get possession of' without any reference to the specific way the property in question came into possession.

[15] Psalm 2:7 will be quoted in verse 5. Perhaps this verse also is intended to remind us of Psalm 2:8, "Ask of Me, and I will surely give the nations as Your inheritance, and the very ends of the earth Your possession."

opinions have been advanced in an attempt to explain when this appointment was made by God. (1) The appointment was made after Jesus completed His redemptive work on earth and had returned to the Father's right hand. (2) The better suggestion is that the appointment took place in the divine counsels in eternity before creation. The following phrases would then describe the successive steps by which Jesus accomplished God's eternal purpose – steps that included making the ages, making purification of sins, and sitting down on high.

Through whom also He made the world -- This is the *second evidence* showing the superiority of the "Son." Before He ever became incarnate, the Son was active helping the Father[16] create the "worlds" or "the ages" (NASB mg.). To present Jesus as creator is to ascribe to Him a divine function quite apart from the ability of any prophet. The plural Greek word *aionas*, telling what it was Jesus helped create, is rendered both "worlds" and "ages" in other places in the New Testament.[17] If we opt here for the meaning "worlds" (and so it is translated in Hebrews 11:3), then Jesus helped create the sun, moon, earth, stars, and entire universe. If we opt for the meaning "ages" (and the previous verses spoke of "long ago" and "these last days"), then this verse suggests Jesus has been the agent who determined when the ages (Patriarchal, Mosaic, and Christian[18]) began and ended. Jesus has been the manager of the ages of history – something no mere prophet could do.

1:3 -- And He is the radiance of His glory -- The *third evidence* proving Jesus' superiority to any prophet is the fact that Jesus Himself exudes the very glory of God. "Glory" is often used of the dazzling sphere of light one sees emanating from God as He sits on His throne (cp. Revelation 4:2,3). The Father is often called the "God of glory" (as in Acts7:2), calling attention to this well-known phenomenon.[19] The Hebrew writer now tells us Jesus is the "radiance" of this glory, that Jesus Himself also shines[20] with dazzling light just like the Father

---

God places His anointed one (the Messiah) upon the Messianic throne, and grants Him the earth and its people for His inheritance, thus fully assuring the Son that the Messianic office will be His. Compare Daniel 7:13,14, Matthew 11:27 and 28:18, where the same truth is taught. During His earthly ministry, Jesus claimed "all things that the Father has are Mine" (John 16:15).

[16] The preposition translated "through whom" is *dia*, a construction that indicates Jesus was an intermediate agent in the creative work. God created "through" Jesus. Cp. John 1:3, 1 Corinthians 8:6, and Colossians 1:16.

[17] *Aionas* is translated "worlds" at 1 Timothy 6:17, and "ages" at Ephesians 2:7. Those writers who suppose they can find Gnostic sources for some of the ideas found in Scripture are quick to point out the word *aion* (or "aeons") was a word used by the Gnostics to designate the demigods and other beings superior in rank to men (Mosheim, *Eccl. Hist.*, V.1, p.63). Trying to reconcile the Scriptures with the then contemporary Greek philosophy, which included the dualistic notion that spirit was good while matter was evil, the Gnostics suggested God (good spirit) created Jesus, who in turn created some lesser beings (aeons), who in turn created lesser beings, who several generations later created the devil (an evil demiurge), who then created this material world. It is hardly likely the writer of Hebrews, when he tells us it was through Jesus that God created the *aionas* (aeons), has here adopted a Gnostic idea. Hebrews was written before even incipient Gnosticism had made much headway in the church.

[18] Concerning history being divided into "dispensations," and being managed (like a steward managed his owner's estate), see Ephesians 1:10, 3:11; Galatians 3:24,25; Colossians 1:25,26; and 1 Corinthians 2:7.

[19] "Glory" is used to speak of God's shape, His form, His splendor. *"Doxa* ["glory"] is the glorious appearance of the absolute holy nature of God." See Franz Delitzsch, *A System of Biblical Psychology* (Grand Rapids: Baker, 1966), p.60,61.

[20] The Greek word *apaugasma* could be translated "reflection" as well as "radiance or effulgence." It would

does. Of no prophet can it be said that "He *is*[21] the radiance of God's glory," not even of Moses, whose face, when he came down from Mt. Sinai with the tables of Law, emitted or reflected a glow which lasted only for a while and then gradually faded (2 Corinthians 3:13). Jesus, like no other (save perhaps the Holy Spirit), radiates the glory of God.[22]

And the exact representation of His nature -- The *fourth claim* supporting the superiority of Jesus is this, that Jesus is an exact likeness to all that one finds in the Father. "Nature" is a better translation of the Greek *hupostasis* than was the KJV's "person."[23] "Nature" speaks of the constituent elements of which anything is made up (e.g., the "nature" of water is H_2O – that is, a molecule of water is made up of two parts hydrogen and one part oxygen). "Exact representation"[24] tells us that whatever "elements" one finds in the Father, that is precisely what one finds in the Son. They match exactly! If the Father is omnipotent, omniscient, omnipresent, infinitely holy, wise, just, and good, then so is the Son.

And upholds all things by the word of His power -- *Fifth*, Jesus the "Son" is superior to the prophets because He upholds and moves all things toward the goal God had in mind when He created. And He does it simply by speaking the word! "Upholds" is one possible meaning of *phero*, a word that can also mean "bear or carry along."[25] If we take the meaning "upholds," the idea is similar to Colossians 1:16,17, where we are told that in Jesus Christ "all things hold together (or endure)." This fifth claim says that one of Jesus' continuing tasks[26] is to sustain this universe in its existence and operation, and to carry it forward until it arrives at the consum-

---

hardly do to say Jesus is simply *reflecting* the glory of God, like the moon in our solar system reflects the light of the sun; hardly, that is, in the light of what else Hebrews says about the deity of Jesus. So, we agree with the ancient Patristic interpretation of this passage -- they favored the sense of effulgence or direct shining (see "Apaugasma," in *Theological Dictionary of the New Testament*, edited by Gerhard Kittel, trans. Geoffrey W. Bromiley [Grand Rapids: Eerdmans, 1964], Vol.I, p.508.).

[21] The significance of the present participle translated "is" should not be missed. Not that Jesus *was* or that He *is going to* be the brightness of God's glory, but that He always has been, *is*, and always will be that. It is in harmony with the Son's eternal relationship with the Father, that the writer says "is."

[22] The exalted dignity of the Son depends not just on world-making. It also involves the eternal order of deity. There was a time when God was without a world, but there never was a time when He was without glory. Likewise, Jesus continually radiates the same glory.

[23] The translation "person" was an unfortunate mistranslation, first introduced in the German Testament in deference to Beza. "Previous to the Arian controversy [in which it was debated whether or not Jesus was a created being, and not equal with nor eternal like the Father], in the beginning of the fourth century, this word (*hupostasis*) was seldom used in the sense of person (*prosopon*). But then [Arian's chief opponent] Athanasius ... so explained it because [he] thought it necessary to make a distinction between the *ousia* (essence, being) of the Deity, and his *hupostasis* ("person"). [He] alleged that in the Godhead there could be but one essence; that the essence of the Son is of necessity the same as the essence of the Father and of the Holy Spirit; though [he] supposed each might have his own proper personality. Hence [he] inferred that it is the personality, and not the essence or substance, of Christ which is here compared with that of the Father." Milligan, *op. cit.*, p.54.

[24] The Greek word *charakter* was used for the imprint or image made by a die or an engraving tool. The "imprint" perfectly represented the same shape or image as the tool that made it. A similar assertion is made in Colossians 1:15, where Christ timelessly exists in the "image" (*eikon*) of God. Compare also John 14:9.

[25] An interesting use of the verb *phero* is found in the Septuagint at Numbers 11:14, where Moses states, "I alone am not able to carry all this people alone." The word there may connote the idea of being responsible for governing and for guiding them to the promised land.

[26] The word translated "upholds" (or "carrying") is a present tense participle, implying continuing action.

mation God has planned. Jesus is so great He can do all this merely by speaking, for His word is that powerful! In the days of creation, God said "Let there be light!" and light existed just because He spoke. He said, 'Fishes, swim!' and fish came into being and began swimming, just because He spoke. Now Jesus says to all things, 'Hold together!' or 'Move along!' and it happens, just because He speaks.[27] No wonder then, while in the days of His flesh, He could just speak and a storm would be stilled, or a sick person healed, or a dead man raised.

When He had made purification of sins -- As we near the end of this long sentence, we have our attention directed toward what the Son has done to help the world with its sin problem.[28] He provided, or produced, or made purification for sins.[29] The reference is to Christ's redemptive work on the cross of Calvary, and this *sixth proposition* showing the Son's superiority is also something no prophet could ever do. Making purification of sins was a priest's work; so we have introduced one of the great themes of Hebrews, namely, the high priesthood of Jesus. Jesus came to earth to deal with the problem of man's sin. His once-for-all sacrifice is another of the great themes of Hebrews.[30] Of course, this purification is not automatically granted to all men, but is conditioned on men's faithfulness to God's revelation to them, a theme that also will be developed in due time in Hebrews. Another to-be-developed theme introduced by "purification of sins"[31] is that neither the Levitical priesthood and procedures nor the blood of bulls and goats which they offered could ever take away sins.

He sat down at the right hand of the Majesty on high -- The *seventh assertion* about the "Son" is that, following His redemptive work, He is sitting at the highest place of honor and

---

[27] The picture is not of "an Atlas holding up the weight of the world," but of Jesus just speaking and it is so! The impact of what is here said on the theory of evolution should not be overlooked. The evolutionary idea of a universe and mankind developing from a primary organism by inherent forces, contradicts completely the declarations of Hebrews that God created and that Jesus sustains the world and moves it towards its goal. The idea here in Hebrews is in harmony with what is called the "providence" of God (i.e., the care, preservation, and government God exercises over His creation so that it accomplishes the purposes for which He made it).

[28] The word "sin" occurs 25 times in this epistle. Only in Romans (48 times) is this total exceeded. "Sin" is man's great problem.

[29] The KJV reads "when he had *by himself* purged our sins." "By Himself" probably lacks textual support, but the idea might be included in the middle-voice participle *poiesamenos*. The middle voice usually presents the subject as acting for his own benefit. This idea would fit here -- when Jesus offered Himself on Calvary's tree as a sacrifice for sins, He was acting not only for men, but also to benefit Himself. Back in eternity, the Godhead wanted a family of men who would praise Him, not because they had to, but because they wanted to. By Jesus' giving Himself to redeem men, Jehovah God could still have that family and those praises!

[30] Because there is no equivalent in Latin for the Greek perfect tense verb, the Latin Vulgate read *"makes* purification of sins" -- a translation which may well have given rise to the Roman Catholic idea that Christ is continually sacrificed for sins each time the Mass is offered. What Hebrews clearly teaches throughout is the finality of Christ's finished work. There will never be another Calvary. His once-for-all sacrifice was all that was needed to take care of sin.

[31] "Made purification of sins" is a much more satisfactory rendering than Rotherham's "discovered purification for sins." Rotherham's rendering here at 1:3 is based on a rigid translation of Hebrews 9:12 which does literally read "discovered eternal redemption." What is objectionable about Rotherham's rendering is it suggests God first tried this, then that, and finally found the method of making purification through Jesus Christ after a long trial-and-error search. This completely destroys any foreknowledge or deliberate planning on God's part, such as Romans 8:28 and other verses affirm. In our opinion, it is better to translate *poieo* here at 1:3 literally as "make," and to give *euramenos* at 9:12 its secondary meaning of "achieved" or "obtained."

authority in the universe, namely, at God's right hand. "Majesty on high" is a periphrasis for "God." The Hebrews so reverenced God they would not pronounce His name. Instead they would use such expressions for God as "throne of the Majesty" (Hebrews 8:1), or "heaven" (Luke 15:18), or "power" (Mark 14:62). That Jesus would be exalted to such a place of honor and dignity was predicted in the Old Testament (Psalm 110:1, a verse that will be quoted at Hebrews 1:13) and by Jesus Himself during the final week of His public teaching (Matthew 22:42,44). The fact that Jesus "sat down" after making purification is an indication that His atoning work for sins was finished.[32] No prophet or Levitical priest could ever thus sit, for their duties were never finished. Nor were any of those mere men ever on an equal with God so that they dared to sit in the Father's presence!

1:4 -- Having become as much better than the angels -- Here is the *eighth evidence* of the Son's superiority to prophets, and at the same time it introduces the theme of the remainder of chapter 1, the superiority of Jesus to angels. "Better" is one of the Hebrew writer's favorite words. He uses it 13 out of the 19 times the word appears in the New Testament. That Jesus *became* better is a somewhat unexpected statement after those seven previous strong statements about the excellence of Jesus' person. We might have expected the writer to describe Jesus as eternally superior to the angels, rather than as *becoming* superior to them. But the writer words it this way because he was thinking of what the Son did in becoming man in order to make purification of sins. While He was incarnate, He was made a little lower than the angels (Hebrews 2:7).[33] But He is no longer lower. He was not lower in eternity before the creation and He is not now lower (as Hebrews 2:9 will explain). He is superior! No one doubts angels[34] were superior beings to even the Old Testament prophets. If Jesus is superior to angels, He certainly is superior to the prophets.[35]

As He has inherited a more excellent name than they -- The "name" Jesus inherited,[36] as the following context seems to show, was the name "Son."[37] The name "Son" was more excellent than the name "angel" (a word that means "messenger"). In antiquity, "name" meant much more than it does in our day; we use it as little more than a label to distinguish one person or thing from another. But in the world of the Bible, the person's name concisely summed up all

---

[32] With the exception of Acts 7:56, in every other place in the New Testament (and it is more than a dozen times the language occurs), we are told that Jesus is *sitting*. Chrysostom declared that the one exception, when Jesus was described as *standing* at the time of Stephen's death, was indication of His intense interest in the death of the first Christian martyr.

[33] Compare what is said of Jesus "emptying Himself" at Philippians 2:6-8. What He temporarily gave up, as He became temporarily subordinate to the Father, was the independent exercise of the prerogatives of deity.

[34] The student should make use of a good Bible dictionary at this place in order to make a study of "angels."

[35] Some of the major world religions in the 20th century have claimed Jesus was just a prophet, like Moses or Elijah or (as it is claimed) even Mohammed. Hebrews 1:1-4 is an excellent passage to use to show such a claim for Jesus is not at all in harmony with the Biblical presentation that He is God!

[36] What was written about "heir" at verse 2 is also true here of the word "inherited." It does not connote, as our English word does, that one enters into possession as the result of the death of someone. Neither the word "inherit" nor the context which spoke of Christ's death on Calvary ("made purification of sins") should be used to prove that the time when Jesus inherited the better name was at His ascension and exaltation following His death and resurrection.

[37] Rotherham, noting what is written in Hebrews 1:8, believes the name Jesus inherited was "God." Whether we pick "Son" or "God" as the name Jesus inherited, this verse proves to be a molding force on our Christology.

that the person is. His whole character is somehow implied in the name.[38] Now if Jesus was "Son" by virtue of His incarnation (see Hebrews 1:2), in what sense did He come to obtain this more excellent name at the close of His earthly ministry, as this verse seems to say? The exaltation of Jesus by the Father, when He raised Him from the dead and seated Him at His right hand (Ephesians 1:20,21; Romans 1:1-4; Philippians 2:9,10), was the Father's acknowledgment or public declaration that Jesus, in spite of His time of earthly humiliation, was truly the unique Son, with the prerogatives that belong to such a Son. Only Jesus has the right to the title "Son" in the sense in which it is here ascribed to Him.

B. Jesus is Superior to the Angels. 1:5 - 2:18

1. The Son's superiority to angels was asserted by the Old Testament. 1:5-14.

1:5 -- For -- From here to the close of chapter one, seven different Old Testament Scriptures are cited to prove the statement that the "Son" is superior to angels. An eighth quotation is found in Hebrews 2:6-8.[39]

To which of the angels did He ever say -- The implied answer to the question, of course, is "none!" God said things to Jesus He never said to angels. That the writer spends so much more time showing Jesus' superiority to angels than was spent showing His superiority to the prophets must reflect the readers' thinking. It will be remembered the readers were tempted to defect from Jesus and return to the Old Testament Jewish religion. What will cause them to resist the temptation to defect? Only if the readers recognize who Jesus really is – that He is not just greater than the prophets, He is above the realm of ordinary mortals, yea, even above the realm of angels – will they be caused to hesitate in their intent to quit confessing Him before

---

[38] Consider the change of names from Abram (meaning, the father is high) to Abraham (meaning, the father of a people) indicated all that Abraham was intended to become, i.e., a father of a multitude. Or again, to see that names imply character, consider that Joshua (Greek, *Jesus*) means Jehovah saves.

[39] The New Testament's use of the Old Testament is a highly important and interesting study. In the last quarter century, much scholarly research has gone into the question of whether the New Testament writers respected, modified, or violated the original passages and their contexts. C.H. Dodd, *According to the Scriptures* (London: James Nisbet & Co.,1952), and R.V.G. Tasker, *The Old Testament in the New Testament* (Grand Rapids: Eerdmans, 1963), while both giving up too much to theological liberalism, run counter to the now generally popular view that the New Testament writers tended to look high and low for "proof texts" without regard for the original meaning of the passages they quote. C.B. Caird, "The Exegetical Method of the Epistle to the Hebrews," *CJT 5* (1959), p.45, reacts strongly against any view that would represent the New Testament writers as using far-fetched exegesis. "I should like to suggest that, so far from being an example of fantastic exegesis which can be totally disregarded by modern Christians, Hebrews is one of the earliest and most successful attempts to define the relation between the Old and New Testaments, and that a large part of the value of the book is to be found in the method of exegesis which was formerly dismissed with contempt."

    The use of the Old Testament in the epistle to the Hebrews exhibits a number of distinctive features. (1) Prominence is given to the book of Psalms. (Is this one reason the New Testament Scriptures and Psalms are often bound together?) (2) Just as Jesus taught his listeners to "take all the verses on a subject" (see His treatment of divorce in Matthew 19 and who the son of David was in Matthew 22) in order to learn what the Bible teaches, so the writer of Hebrews does. He takes a verse from Genesis, for example, and a verse from Psalms, which may be tied together only in the use of one word, and puts them together in order to deduce what Biblical doctrine is. He does it over and over in Hebrews. (3) He also explains that certain events and topics in the Old Testament were types and shadows of the things to come in the New Covenant age.

men. What has been said before about Jesus being God (in the 8 descriptive phrases of verses 2-4) is now plainly set forth in unequivocal fashion. God the Father calls the Son "God"!

"YOU ARE MY SON, TODAY I HAVE BEGOTTEN YOU"? -- Two passages from the Old Testament are cited in verse 5, and it seems that the point of both is that in them Jesus indeed is God's "Son." The first comes from Psalm 2:7. Psalm 2 is a Messianic psalm, and in it God calls Messiah "Son." Now it is true that angels are sometimes called "sons of God" (Job 1:6; 38:7), and so is Israel (Exodus 4:22; Hosea 11:1), and even Solomon (2 Samuel 7:14; 1 Chronicles 28:6). But none of these is ever singled out and given the kind of status given to Jesus when He is called by God, "My Son." Commentators have not been able to agree as they try to explain what day God had in mind when He said, "Today I have begotten thee." Either the time of the incarnation[40] or the resurrection[41] would fit the needs of the context here in Hebrews.[42] The former is the more likely option, in this commentator's opinion.

And again -- These words introduce a second quotation from the Old Testament. It too will call Messiah "Son." It too is part of the question "to which of the angels did He ever say?" And the implied answer is again, "none!" Jesus is obviously superior to angels if He is "Son."

"I WILL BE A FATHER TO HIM, AND HE SHALL BE A SON TO ME"? -- This language comes from 2 Samuel 7:14, and occurs in the midst of God's promise that one of David's seed (namely, Solomon) would succeed David on the throne and that God would graciously provide for that successor ("I will be a father to him"). Milligan suggests it must have been a double reference prophecy, with a near fulfillment in Solomon[43] and a later fulfillment in Messiah.[44] Messiah would have a special relationship to the Father[45] – He would be a "Son," the very name that Jesus has inherited, a name no angel can claim because Jesus is superior to the angels.

---

[40] Luke 1:35 speaks of "the holy thing begotten" (NASB margin) by the Holy Spirit in Mary's womb. Acts 13:33 also quotes Psalm 2:7, and there it most likely refers to the incarnation. "He raised up Jesus" (Acts 13:33) is a reference to His entrance into the world; it is not till verse 34 of Acts 13 that the resurrection from the dead is alluded to, and for that another passage (about the sure blessings of David) is quoted from the Old Testament.

[41] Romans 1:4 has been appealed to as evidence that at the resurrection Jesus was declared to be God's "Son" in a special way.

[42] Primasius held the view that "today" ("this day") refers to that which is eternal and timeless. This is hardly satisfactory. Justin Martyr in his *Dialogue with Trypho* quotes "This day have I begotten thee" as referring to Jesus' baptism and explains it as offering an explanation for the voice from Heaven which said "You are My beloved son" (Mark 1:11). However, the idea Jesus became the "Son" at His baptism smacks of the adoptionist heresy of the early Christian period, the theory that the divine Christ came upon the human Jesus at His baptism, and that just before His death on Calvary, the divine essence left Him, so it was only the human Jesus who died on the cross. The need for such an elaborate theory was found in the attempt to make the Bible fit Greek philosophy (how can God [who is spirit] have a body [which is matter] and how can God die?).

[43] The verse talks about the "son" sinning and being "chastened," language hardly applicable to Messiah but true of Solomon.

[44] F.F. Bruce, *The Epistle to the Hebrews* (Grand Rapids: Eerdmans, 1964), p.14 documents the suitability of applying 2 Samuel 7:14 to Messiah, for some modern critics have questioned it. In many passages, one of David's descendants is identified as the coming Messiah (cp. Matthew 22:42). That unique "Son" of God, the Old Testament everywhere suggests, will be One Who is a special concern to the Father in heaven.

[45] This and Hebrews 12:9 are the only passages in Hebrews where the term "Father" is applied to God.

1:6 -- And when He again brings the firstborn into the world -- It is rather easy to see that "He" is a reference to God the Father. But the rest of the verse is not so easy to understand, for there are three problems connected with the explanation of this verse: (1) Where shall we insert the word "again"? (2) What is the meaning of the term "firstborn"? (3) What Old Testament passage (where angels are commanded to worship Him) is quoted?

Where we insert the word "again" has a strong influence on our understanding of the meaning of the verse. (a) If we follow the NASB text which inserts "again" before the verb "brings," the verse is made to refer to some coming into the world by Jesus (the firstborn) other than His first coming at His incarnation. Tentative explanations offered to identify what this return into the world might be include Jesus' entrance into His public ministry,[46] the resurrection,[47] Pentecost,[48] or the Second Coming.[49] Angels' activities are clearly included in the passages that speak about His resurrection and His Second Coming, and were we limited to this translation, one of these two options would be most likely. (b) If we follow the suggestion of the NASB margin, the verse reads "And again, when He brings the firstborn into the world ...." According to this translation, "again" simply serves to introduce another quotation, the very same function the word serves in the middle of verse 5, and at 2:13.[50] We would then be free to explain the words about bringing the firstborn into the world as a reference to Jesus' first coming (the incarnation). Angels did worship and sing praises over the plains of Bethlehem as they announced Jesus' birth to the shepherds (Luke 2:8-20).

---

[46] Where is there any mention of angels worshiping Jesus at the beginning of His public ministry?

[47] Angels are specifically mentioned in the accounts that tell about Jesus' resurrection (Matthew 28:1ff, Mark 16:5ff, Luke 24:4ff, and John 20:11ff). One might even conjecture that Mary turned around because the angels with whom she had been speaking suddenly bowed in the presence of the risen Lord. Other than this, it is not easy to find angels "worshipping" at the resurrection. More plausible would be the suggestion that just after He spoke to Mary Magdalene ("I have not yet ascended to the Father"), He returned to heaven, to the Father's presence, and all along the journey the angels were worshiping Him, and celebrating what He had done while on earth (see Psalm 24:7-10, which many suppose pictures Jesus' return to heaven at the ascension).

[48] Grotius, Wetstein, and Milligan (who gives several arguments to defend this choice) opt for this interpretation. The problem with it is trying to answer where, when, and how angels worshiped Jesus at Pentecost, let alone how what happened at Pentecost could be described as a bringing [again] of Jesus "into the world." Even if angels did sing and rejoice at the time He was enthroned, it probably will not do to say that Jesus was not enthroned in heaven until the day of Pentecost (10 days after His ascension and 50 after His resurrection). Nor is it entirely satisfactory (when trying to show angels did worship Jesus at Pentecost) to call attention to the fact that after Pentecost Messiah reigns in His mediatorial kingdom, and of course all knees are to bow to Him then (Philippians 2:11).

[49] Westcott, Dods, Lenski, Kent, Alford, Delitzsch, and Hewitt agree with the ASV/NASB translators that the reference is to the second coming. Some have objected that the writer of Hebrews has nowhere in the preceding verses spoken of the *first* coming, so how could verse 6 be a reference to His *second* coming? This objection ignores what is implied about the incarnation in verses 3, 4, and likely clearly referred to in 5 ("begotten"). As far as angels being involved at the time of the second coming, this is the teaching of Matthew 13:41, 16:27, 25:31 and 2 Thessalonians 1:7, so this detail would fit. Kent urges the Greek word order suggests that "again" be taken with the verb; that the subjunctive mood of the verb "brings in" argues the event is still future; and the use of the conjunction "whenever" all tend to confirm the "second coming" interpretation for this verse.

[50] This method of understanding the passage is reflected in the KJV, RSV, NEB, and in comments by Bruce and Lightfoot.

A study of the lexicons will show that "firstborn" can have different connotations. (1) It can have a temporal significance, but to give it such a meaning here, as though Jesus were the first being to be created, would be to make this verse contradict what Scripture elsewhere affirms about Jesus' eternality.[51] (2) It can have a positional significance. (a) In Hebrew culture, the "firstborn"[52] received a double portion of the inheritance and certain other prerogatives and responsibilities with regard to the rest of the family. That Jesus is here called "firstborn" might be an indication He has certain prerogatives and responsibilities in relation to the rest of mankind. (b) The term "firstborn" sometimes is used as though it meant "chief."[53] This is exactly the meaning of Psalm 89:27 where Messiah is called "firstborn." It is a way of referring to His primacy of position, His dignity, His pre-eminence.[54] In a passage where Jesus' superiority to angels is the topic, it is exactly as we would expect to have Jesus called "firstborn" – i.e., He is pre-eminent! It asserts His superiority in position in the eyes of God Himself.

He says -- The third problem to struggle with in verse 6 is identifying the source of the Old Testament passage about to be quoted? At Deuteronomy 32:43, there is a verse in the Septuagint that reads exactly as the verse here quoted, but there is no corresponding verse in the Hebrew (Masoretic) text.[55] Perhaps the source of the quotation is Psalm 97:7. In that passage, the wording is "Worship him, all you gods" (Heb., *elohim*), but the Septuagint translated "gods" as "angels."[56]

"AND LET ALL THE ANGELS OF GOD WORSHIP HIM" -- How does this Old Testament verse prove the superiority of Jesus to angels? Why, *all* the angels are commanded to worship Jesus. Only God is to be worshiped, never angels. Clearly if He is to be worshiped by all[57] the angels, Jesus is superior to them.

----

[51] See footnotes #13 and #21 above, and the comments on verse 3.

[52] It was not always the oldest son who was designated "firstborn." At times a younger son might be elevated to this rank (e.g., Genesis 48:17-20; Exodus 4:22).

[53] When so used, there is often no thought of age at all. See Job 18:13, "firstborn of death," or Isaiah 14:30 (ASV), "firstborn of the poor."

[54] The title "firstborn" given to Jesus in Colossians 1:15,18 is another example where the word emphasizes Jesus' rank and position and pre-eminence.

[55] Early Christians made extensive use of the LXX version as they did evangelistic work among the Jews. The readings of the LXX in those passages that were Messianic were so clear that early in the second century the Jews put out a new translation of the Bible in Greek (Aquila's Version) in order to blunt the Messianic proof-texting done by the Christians. Was it passages like this one from Deuteronomy the new official Jewish version corrected? Before we can answer this question for sure, more work needs to be done on the Hebrew text in order to determine just what was the text (or texts) behind the Septuagint, and why it differed (if it did) from the present Masoretic text.

[56] This is not the only place where the LXX translators "interpreted" the Hebrew *elohim* as if it had reference to angels rather than to the members of the Godhead. In the Old Testament, beings who were "superior" were sometimes called *elohim* even though they were not deity. See, for example, Jesus' use of one such instance during His earthly ministry, when He referred to human judges as *elohim* (John 10:34,35).

[57] That the Father commands *all* the angels to worship Jesus shows that this is no small affair. All the angels in heaven are to offer homage to the Son because He, being God, is superior to them.

1:7 -- And of the angels He says -- Verses 7 and 8 open with the same words, calling attention to what God says concerning angels versus what He says concerning the Son. Unless all three verses (verses 7, 8 and 9) are read together, the contrast between angels and the Son will be missed. Verse 7 contains the fourth passage quoted from the Old Testament to prove Jesus' superiority to angels. The passage quoted is Psalm 104:4, and relates to the place of angels in the administration of the universe. Earlier, the writer alluded to Jesus' "upholding all things by the word of His power." So (once what Psalm 104:4 says is recalled) it might appear, on first sight, that both angels and Jesus have equal responsibilities. Not so! Without downgrading the angels, the writer, in verses 8 and 9, shows that they are immeasurably lower than the Son.

"WHO MAKES HIS ANGELS WINDS, AND HIS MINISTERS A FLAME OF FIRE" -- Twice the angels are called "His," that is, they belong to God; they serve at His beck and call. They are His "messengers" (*aggelos*), His "ministers," because that is what the Father "makes" them. Sometimes He makes them "winds"[58] and sometimes He makes them to be "a flame of fire."[59] But, none of them are given a throne and a scepter (verse 8), nor are any of them "anointed ... with the oil of gladness" (verse 9) like the Son was.

1:8 -- But of the Son *He says* -- Here begins the second half of the contrast between angels and the Son that began in verse 7. The verses quoted are taken from Psalm 45:6,7, a Psalm the Jews recognized as Messianic.[60]

---

[58] It is not easy to decide exactly what this expression means. (1) The word translated "winds" is the same word elsewhere translated "spirits" (indeed, that is the translation in the KJV). Some have understood the first part of Psalm 104:4 to be an affirmation that God created ("makes" translates *poieo*, a word often translated "create") the angels as "spirit" beings. Others, while believing angels are created beings (created before the universe was), think this verse is not the verse to prove that doctrine since the verb *poieo* is present tense, thus speaking of continuing action rather than some past-completed action. (2) Milligan preferred the translation "spirit" since "God is spirit." He thought the writer of Hebrews was using this designation to more effectually exalt the angels in the estimation of his Hebrew readers. Yes, they are "spirits" – beings who excel in strength, and who are wholly removed from all the weaknesses, impurities, and imperfections of the flesh. Yet, great as they are, Jesus is still superior. (3) Taking the word "winds" literally, some think the verse says God is able to do with the angels whatever He desires. He can change them into winds, or into flames of fire. Angels, at their highest, are mere servants. They have no will or rule of their own. They do not give orders; they just follow them. (4) Since there are times angels seem to have some control over the elements (see Revelation 7:1, for example, where the physical elements are under some angels' control), there are some commentators who think a similar "administration" is here ascribed to angels. (5) Closely related to this view is the one which would render the phrase "He makes His angels *like* winds." So translated, the verse would mean God uses angels as His instruments to carry out His will just like He uses the winds and flaming fire to carry out His will.

[59] The two clauses of the verse quoted from Psalm 104 are a fine example of the phenomenon in Hebrew poetry called "Hebrew parallelism." Just as "angels" and "ministers" are both names for angels, so "winds" and "flame of fire" are parallel. The way we interpret one, we probably should interpret the other. If we take "winds" literally, then perhaps "flame of fire" is a reference to lightning. If "spirits" recalls their exalted position, then "flame of fire" would do the same. Milligan reminds us that in the presence of angels the enemies of God have always melted away as wax or stubble before a fire. Examples of angelic discomfiture of men would be the overthrow of Sodom and Gomorrah (Genesis 19), the destruction of the Egyptian firstborn (Exodus 12), the overthrow of the hosts of Benhadad the Syrian (1 Kings 20), and the army of Sennacherib (2 Chronicles 31).

[60] In the Targum (an Aramaic paraphrase) of this psalm, verse 7 is taken as a direct reference to the Messiah. Although the Psalm celebrates a royal wedding of a king in David's line (perhaps Solomon), certain portions of it cannot be limited to any earthly king, not to Solomon or any other. The Psalmist addresses first the groom and then the bride. The words quoted in Hebrews are part of the address to the groom. Milligan urges that it is hard to apply many of the expressions of the Psalm to any human king -- it is therefore wholly Messianic -- and speaks of the union between Christ and the church.

"YOUR THRONE, O GOD, IS FOREVER AND EVER" -- Jesus is superior to the angels because He is here addressed as "God"[61] and His "throne" lasts forever and ever.[62] The Father, speaking to Jesus, calls Him "God" and affirms that His reign ("throne") is eternal.[63] He is sovereign, and there is nothing temporary about His rule. Nothing like this was ever said to any angel. Therefore, Jesus is superior to angels.

"AND THE RIGHTEOUS SCEPTER IS THE SCEPTER OF HIS KINGDOM" – "Righteous" here in verse 8 translates *eutheutetos* which means "uprightness, rectitude." Jesus' administration is one of absolute justice and rectitude. When He extends His scepter, you can be sure only what is absolutely right is being done. Christ's reign is not just something in the future; it is something that was already occurring even as Hebrews was being written.[64]

1:9 -- "YOU HAVE LOVED RIGHTEOUSNESS AND HATED LAWLESSNESS" "Righteousness" here is used to translate *dikaiosune*, a word sometimes used of God's way of saving men, sometimes used of one of God's attributes, and sometimes used of the right kind of living (the kind of living in harmony with the absolute norm and standard of right which God Himself has decreed to be in keeping with His holy character). Likely it was during Jesus' ministry on earth that He is said to have loved righteousness and hated iniquity. Thus, it could refer to His own sinless life, or it could refer to what He did on Calvary to insure a way of salvation. Either way, the next phrase tells what God did to reward such a life.

"THEREFORE GOD" -- Here again, for the second time in the span of two verses, Jesus is called "God"[65] by the Father Himself! The Father says, 'Because You have loved righteousness and hated lawlessness, God, I'm going to exalt You!'

"YOUR GOD HAS ANOINTED YOU WITH THE OIL OF GLADNESS ABOVE YOUR COMPANIONS" -- That the Father should be called Jesus' "God" should not be thought incongruous. Jesus Himself used such an expression on the cross when He prayed, "My God,

---

[61] While it is admitted "God" can be either in the nominative case or the vocative case, we also are aware that vocative is the way the Jewish writers and the ancient versions almost unanimously understood it. Taking it as nominative ("God is your throne ...") makes little sense and is contrary to the analogy of Scripture language. The Hebrew at this place is *'elohim*; in the LXX, *theos* is regularly used to translate *'elohim*.

[62] The RSV rendered this verse "Your divine throne endures forever and ever." F.F. Bruce, in a footnote on page 19, shows this translation to be barely defensible. It certainly robs the Psalm of any Messianic content and is another instance of the anti-supernaturalistic bent often observed in the RSV, especially when it comes to the deity of Jesus.

[63] Compare Daniel 7:14 and Luke 1:33 which speak of an eternal reign. There is no contradiction between this concept and what is affirmed in 1 Corinthians 15:24, which speaks of an end to Jesus' *mediatorial* reign. That reign will come to an end at the second coming, but the whole Godhead will continue to reign throughout eternity.

[64] Eschatological theories that do not have Jesus' reigning until after His second coming (say, an earthly reign during a millennium) find numerous verses against them, for time after time the New Testament depicts Jesus as reigning even now during the church age before the second coming (e.g., Acts 2:30-33).

[65] We take the first "God" in this verse to be another vocative case, just as in the preceding verse. The punctuation in the NASB, which puts a comma after each occurrence of the word "God" ("Therefore God, Your God, has anointed You ...") treats the first "God" as though it were nominative, the subject of "has anointed." The phrase "Your God" then identifies the Father as being the God of Jesus.

My God, Why?" (Matthew 27:46). We suppose the anointing took place after Jesus' earthly ministry, at the time of His coronation and exaltation.[66] "Oil of gladness" would be a figurative expression derived from the oriental custom of anointing the head at important festivals (Psalm 23:5). In this context, the "companions" would have reference to the angels, and thus the emphasis of this whole section, namely, that Jesus is superior to angels, is flatly affirmed by an appeal to the Old Testament Scriptures.

1:10 -- And -- The word "and" is used to connect the three following verses to the presentation being made. The writer of Hebrews alludes to another Scripture from the Old Testament, Psalm 102:25-27, to demonstrate his thesis that Jesus is superior to angels. And just as verses 8 and 9 had the Father speaking to the Son, so these verses are introduced in such a way that the writer of Hebrews has them spoken by the Father to Jesus.

"YOU, LORD -- As these words stand in their original setting in the Psalm, the words appear to be addressed directly to the Father. Some feel there is a problem with the way the writer of Hebrews uses them, for he takes words addressed to the Father and applies them to the Son.[67] The truth is, we have a problem only if Jesus is *not* deity. If, as the early verses of Hebrews 1 have clearly shown, Jesus is God, where is there any problem? Language addressed to one member of the Godhead can just as well be addressed to the other.

"IN THE BEGINNING LAID THE FOUNDATION OF THE EARTH -- Jesus is presented as being the agent of the creation about which one reads in Genesis 1 and following.[68] Jesus' pre-existence – He was here before the earth was created – is called to mind. The writer is beginning to build his case for the unchanging character of Jesus by quoting verses about the changing character of all things created.

"AND THE HEAVENS ARE THE WORKS OF YOUR HANDS -- It likely speaks of the material universe, including the galaxies of stars and the reaches of space. We suppose the Psalmist had the Genesis verse in mind that says "In the beginning God created the heavens and the earth" (Genesis 1:1).

1:11 -- "THEY WILL PERISH, BUT YOU REMAIN -- "Perish" does not mean annihilate.[69]

---

[66] Noting that "anoint" is a word often used with reference to the Holy Spirit, Milligan supposes the time when Jesus was "anointed" above His companions was at His baptism, when the Spirit descended in the form of a dove. We rather suppose the words of verse 9 are explanatory of how the Son got to be on an eternal throne (as verse 8 introduced).

[67] Here is another place where the Hebrew and LXX texts differ. In the Hebrew, the words are addressed to God in prayer. In the LXX, God is the one speaking and the person addressed is the Lord (i.e., Jesus). The reader may wish to review what was explained above in footnote #55. Kent offers this suggestion to explain the insertion of *kurie* ("Lord") by the LXX translators: "Apparently the Septuagint inserted it for clarification, having drawn it from earlier occurrences in the psalm (e.g., Psalms 102:1,12)."

[68] Even though at Genesis 1:1 "beginning" translates the Hebrew *breshith*, while in Psalm 102:25 "beginning" translates *l'panim* (which simply means "of old"), the two expressions must be almost synonymous since the Septuagint used *arche* ("beginning") in both places.

[69] One of the best passages to show that *apollumi* does not mean annihilate is 2 Peter 3:6,7,11. "The world that then was (Noah's time) perished" (KJV). Now if "world" means "globe," the globe is still here, though not in the same outward shape it was before the flood. And if by "world" one means people, even the wicked were

The next phrase will explain that what is in the future for the heavens and earth is renovation, not annihilation. Yet in contrast to the change that will come over the creation, Jesus remains the same! Jesus is superior to the angels because He is the creator, the one who has power to change all created things, because He is unchanging in His existence.

"AND THEY ALL WILL BECOME OLD LIKE A GARMENT -- The second law of thermodynamics says the universe is running down. Things are decaying, becoming old. The process is slow but certain. Yet however the universe changes, Jesus does not!

1:12 -- "AND LIKE A MANTLE YOU WILL ROLL THEM UP -- Jesus is the One Who not only began the universe (verse 10), He is the One Who will finish it. The Son will deal with the parts of the universe as one deals with clothing, rolling them up and changing them.

"LIKE A GARMENT THEY WILL ALSO BE CHANGED -- The Bible teaches the renovation of the universe, not its annihilation.[70] Clearly the final transformation of all things is in mind (cp. Isaiah 66:22; Revelation 6:14; 21:1). The universe that seems so solid and permanent will be rolled up, changed, and replaced by a new heavens and a new earth (2 Peter 3:13).

"BUT YOU ARE THE SAME -- Through all the change and decay of the universe, the Son remains unchanged! This unchanging quality is one of the things that makes the Son superior to the angels.

"AND YOUR YEARS WILL NOT COME TO AN END" -- The eternality of Jesus is here affirmed. Our years will come to an end; His never will! It is Jesus, not any angel, who will bring the universe to its consummation. The point of verses 10-12 is this: like the other passages cited in Hebrews 1, Psalm 102:25-27, when carefully studied, points to Jesus' superiority to any angel.

---

not annihilated, but still exist in Hades awaiting the final judgment (1 Peter 3:19,20).

[70] See the author's commentary on Romans 8:21, a passage which can only be explained on the basis of renovation. Since many Christian Church readers are familiar with Milligan's commentary on Hebrews, several explanations and corrections must be offered concerning his writings on these phrases. On page 71, Milligan's notes reflect the old "gap theory" that was sometimes used to explain Genesis 1-3. In an attempt to harmonize what it was supposed Genesis taught and the modern theories of science about millions of years for the age of the earth, it was proposed that the words in Genesis 1:2 should be translated "the earth *became* null and void," i.e., became something it wasn't to begin with. One could then insert millions of years between verses 1 and 2 if he were of a mind to do so. Then, beginning with verse 3, God started over to bring order out of chaos. Bernard Ramm, *Christian View of Science and Scripture* (Grand Rapids: Eerdmans, 1955), p.195ff, has a good chapter refuting the "gap theory."

Milligan also writes (p.71) about what he calls "aerial heavens" and "sidereal heavens." Sidereal pertains to the stars; aerial speaks of the atmosphere. Milligan makes this distinction as he tries to explain 2 Peter 3 (which speaks of the heavens being "burned up") on the assumption that it predicts annihilation by fire. He has referred to the Peter passage as a parallel to the verses here in Hebrews 1:11,12. Something, he supposed, had to be annihilated -- it must be the atmosphere, not the starry heavens. When offering comments on 2 Peter 3, we would not use the same explanation Milligan tried. We would speak of a "renovation" by fire resulting in a "new heavens and a new earth" (2 Peter 3:13; Revelation 21:1).

1:13 -- But to which of the angels has He ever said -- Again the implied answer is, "To none!" Instead, what angels really are will be explained in verse 14. This seventh passage in the series that began back at verse 5 is taken from Psalm 110:1.[71] Psalm 110 was a Messianic Psalm. It was so recognized in Old Testament times, and Jesus' usage of it (Matthew 22:43-45) assumes the religious leaders of His day also were aware of its Messianic import. Jesus later, during His trials, applied this passage to Himself (Mark 14:62), and His enemies rejected His claim as blasphemy. But on Pentecost and after, the apostles again quote the Psalm and affirm that Jesus' claim to be the very One predicted was vindicated by His resurrection, ascension, glorification, and the subsequent events (e.g., Pentecost, Acts 2) that happened because He was on the throne. In fact, Psalm 110 is uniformly applied to Jesus throughout the New Testament.

"SIT AT MY RIGHT HAND, UNTIL I MAKE YOUR ENEMIES A FOOTSTOOL FOR YOUR FEET"? -- When Jesus used this passage on the Great Day of Questions (Matthew 22:43ff), He was trying to help the religious leaders see the Old Testament taught that He, the Messiah (David's descendant), would be Deity. That is exactly the point the writer of Hebrews uses it to make. Jesus is superior to any angel, not only by virtue of Who He is (God), but by virtue of where He is sitting! Angels may stand before God (Luke 1:19; Revelation 8:2; Daniel 7:10), but no angel was ever invited by the Father to sit down at His right hand. Yet that is precisely where Jesus is sitting.[72] And He will sit there, and reign from there, until the last enemy (which is death) is destroyed (1 Corinthians 15:25,26).[73] In other words, He will sit at the Father's right hand until it is time for the second coming and the final resurrection, the means by which the last enemy is defeated.

1:14 -- Are they not all ministering spirits -- This question expects a "yes!" answer. That is exactly what angels are – they are servants. They are spirits who minister.[74] At times, they may appear as if they are rulers (e.g., "prince of Persia" or "prince of Greece" in Daniel 10:13,20), but when we see the whole picture, it is clear that angels are not independent sovereigns. They are merely the King's agents, the King's messengers, the King's servants.

---

[71] Psalm 110 is alluded to several times in the course of this epistle to the Hebrews. (E.g., 5:6,10; 6:20; 8:1; 12:2. See also chapter 7, in relation to Melchizedek.) Jesus said that David was the author of Psalm 110, and He also affirms its inspiration (Matthew 22:43).

[72] Certain eschatological schemes have this reign of Jesus still future, say after His second coming. Such schemes contrary to 1 Corinthians 15:22 which has Jesus' reign before His *parousia*, and contrary to what Peter said on the day of Pentecost (Acts 2:34-37) when he used Psalm 110 to show how what had occurred that day happened because Jesus was already sitting at the right hand of the Father. We also affirm such an attempted futuristic application of the present verse would rob this passage of its force, which is to prove that Jesus is *right now* superior to angels, and that therefore it is a behavior fraught with great peril to think of quitting Christianity to go back to Judaism. Just think of Who it is that you would be repudiating!

[73] To use one's defeated enemy as a footstool is a figure of speech drawn from the ancient practice (cp. Joshua 10:22-25) of a conquering king sitting on his throne and forcing the vanquished to lie (often, face up) on the floor while the conqueror uses the prone form of his helpless victim for a footstool. Such behavior emphasized the complete triumph of the victor, and the complete defeat of the vanquished.

[74] "Minister" both at verse 7 and here in verse 14 translates the Greek *leitourgos* or *leitourgika*, a word that does *not* denote slavery or even what might be called common service, such as a domestic might do. It speaks of serving God in a special office or function. It was a word used of the work a priest did as he stood at the altar and functioned for God in a special way. The angels' ministry is a special work done for God, but it is still ministry. They are still just servants.

Sent out to render service for the sake of those who will inherit salvation? -- In verses 13 and 14, we have the argument of verses 7-9 repeated, but in reverse order. The "Son" is co-ruler with the Father. The angels – at best – are but servants whom the King sends out repeatedly as the occasion demands.[75] The people whom the angels are sent to help are "those who will inherit salvation."[76] It is awe inspiring to contemplate what this verse asserts. Angels, highest as well as lowest, are servants who minister as Jesus wills them to. And more remarkable still, their tasks[77] are performed to benefit us human beings[78] who are the heirs of salvation!

---

[75] The present tense verb form here indicates continuous action. The word translated "sent forth" is *apostello*, which means commissioned to do a special task. They are sent forth continually, repeatedly, as the occasion demands.

[76] "Salvation" has several meanings in the New Testament. Sometimes it refers not to forgiveness from sin, but simply to deliverance from physical peril and danger. When it is used of forgiveness of sins, salvation is something that can be past, present, or future. In the *past* time, salvation might refer to what Jesus did on Calvary, or it might look back at the time the sinner was converted and initially forgiven of his sins. Salvation is sometimes pictured as a *present* possession, since the faithful Christian is in the process of being saved right now. Salvation sometimes is a *future* prospect, even for the faithful Christian, for the believer will be invited to share in the blessings of heaven, and that too is called "salvation." Which use of salvation is it that is in the Hebrews writer's view? Is it a reference to angels being sent to help unbelievers become Christians (like in the case of Philip and the Ethiopian, Acts 8, or like in the case of Cornelius, Acts 10)? Is it a reference to angels being sent to help those who are already converted, but for whom heaven is yet future? Most commentaries take it in the latter sense, but we cannot be sure.

[77] The Scriptures allude to some of the tasks of angels. Milligan (*op. cit.*, p.73,73) tries to sum up several of these passages in this way: "Some of them may be sent to frustrate the wiles and devices of Satan and his fallen compeers (Jude 6); some, to punish wicked men (Genesis 19:1-26; 2 Kings 19:35; Acts 12:23); some, to preside over the councils and courts of princes (Daniel 10:20, 21; 11:1; 12:1); some, to aid providentially in bringing men to repentance (Acts 10:1-8); some, to take care of the living saints (2 Kings 6:15-23; Psalms 34:7; 91:11; Daniel 3:25-28; 6:22; Matthew 18:10; Acts 5:19; 13:7-10); some, to comfort dying saints and to bear their spirits home to glory (Luke 16:22) ...."

Hebrews 1:14 (with its present tense verb) has often been enlisted as proof that Christians have guardian angels assigned to them. Other passages that may imply there are guardian angels are Acts 12:15 (Rhoda, reporting Peter at the door, is told it can't be Peter, but "it is his angel"), and Matthew 18:10 (Jesus, warning His followers to be careful about despising "little ones" [little children, or new converts?] says "their angels in heaven continually behold the face of My Father who is in heaven").

[78] These angels who minister to the saved are clearly a different class from those "world rulers and elemental spirits" alluded to in Paul's epistles, whose influence is harmful to the lives of the unredeemed, and whose influence over the unredeemed is broken when the unredeemed "die with Christ" (Ephesians 6:12; Colossians 2:8,15,20; Romans 8:38; and perhaps 1 Corinthians 2:8).

FIRST WARNING PASSAGE. 2:1-4

- ### *Exhortation to pay closer attention to what we have heard. 2:1*

2:1 -- For this reason -- The exhortation that follows is closely related to what has been written in chapter 1. Because God has spoken in His Son, who Himself is God and superior to both prophets and angels, because God had no greater messenger than His Son, the message from God delivered by the Son is of paramount importance and must be heeded! The writer has more yet to say about Jesus' superiority to angels and will continue that topic shortly, once this warning has been voiced.

We must pay much closer attention to what we have heard -- "The things which we have heard" (KJV) are the facts, commands, warnings, and promises[1] of the gospel – what will be designated as "so great a salvation" in verse 3. "We" includes both writer and readers in this necessity to "pay much closer attention." The writer proceeds here in this warning on the assumption that wherever much has been given, much also is always justly expected and required by God.[2] The verb *prosechein* translated "pay attention to" means not only to focus the mind on a thing, but also to act upon what is perceived.[3] Failure to think and act on such important spiritual things as those which the Son has delivered is fatal!

So that we do not drift away *from it* – It is not the gospel which drifts away from men; it is men who drift away from the gospel. The verb *pararuomen* can have several meanings. It is sometimes used as a nautical term, meaning "to drift away," as a ship not tied securely slips from its mooring and drifts away from shore to destruction. It can mean "to let slip away," like a valuable ring slipping off the finger of a careless swimmer. It sometimes means "to take a wrong course," like a crumb going into the windpipe and choking the person. All these usages have one thing in common – a tangible loss is sustained because of a failure to "pay much closer attention," a failure to think. Making application to the readers of Hebrews, the warning seems to say those readers should not let the persecution and opposition to Christianity they were facing cause them to quit thinking aright about who Jesus is and how great the gospel is.[4]

---

[1] See the footnote on page 15 of the author's commentary on Romans for a summary of some of the salient points of the gospel.

[2] Luke 12:47,48; Matthew 11:20-24. The new covenant is a greater revelation than the Old. Our writer is telling his readers that there rests on every man who hears the gospel an obligation to receive it and obey it, an obligation commensurate with the infinitely exalted character of Jesus the Christ.

[3] The double idea of thinking and action can be seen at Acts 8:6 and 16:14 where this same verb appears. This same verb is used in Greek literature of "bringing a ship to land," an endeavor that requires careful attention and action or the ship will be lost.

[4] This warning passage has considerable bearing on the matter of the security of the believer. The Christian who would make his calling and election sure has an obligation to pay close attention lest he drift away from the things he has heard. Unless the mind is held closely to the words God has spoken, the man will take a wrong course. (The warning passages in Hebrews have always proven hard to explain for those commentators who have the notion that the security of the believer is unconditional. The Bible never did teach once saved, always saved. This first warning assumes the danger of drifting is real for the writer and readers both.)

▪ *The Penalty for Disobedience in the Old Testament. 2:2*

2:2 -- For if the word spoken through angels proved unalterable -- The "word" or message, as the context shows, is what we call the Law of Moses. That this earlier revelation was given "through angels"[5] is a mark of its inferiority to the gospel.[6] The same word here translated "unalterable" (or "steadfast," NASB margin) is translated "confirmed" in the next verse. What is affirmed is that the Law was binding, fully valid, validated, credentialed. In fact, when we put verses 2 and 3 together, we see that both revelations – both Law and gospel – were "confirmed" or guaranteed by God.

And every transgression and disobedience received a just recompense – Every commandment which God gave also had the appropriate penalty ("recompense") prescribed for its infringement. Alongside the commands and prohibitions He gave in the Law, God had included provisions for the proper punishment of transgressions[7] or disobedience.[8] After God had validated the message which angels had delivered, men could not just ignore it and get away with it.

▪ *The Present Obligation to "Pay Attention" to the Gospel. 2:3,4*

2:3 -- How shall we escape if we neglect so great a salvation? -- The obvious answer to the question is, "We[9] shall not escape, if we neglect what God has spoken to us in His Son." The

---

[5] That angels were messengers whom God used to deliver the Mosaic Law was a point the writer assumes his readers knew to be true, and so makes no effort to prove it. Stephen makes reference to the fact that the Law was "ordained by angels" at Mt. Sinai (Acts 7:53), and Paul does also at Galatians 3:19. Josephus (*Ant.* XV.5.3) has Herod remind the Jews that the noblest of the ordinances contained in the Law had been learned by them from God through angels. Before the days of Moses, angels were sent to Abraham; Jacob wrestled with an angel all night; Lot was warned by an angel to flee. But as for angels being active in the giving of the Law, about the closest we can come is Deuteronomy 33:2 ("The Lord came from Sinai ... He came from the midst of ten thousand holy ones" [the LXX adds "At His right hand were angels with Him"]) and Psalm 68:17 ("The chariots of God are twenty thousand, even thousands of angels: the Lord is among them, as in Sinai, in the holy place" [KJV]).

[6] This statement about the angels being God's Old Testament messengers may explain why so much time was spent (chapter 1:5ff) showing Jesus' superiority to the angels.

[7] "Transgression" translates *parabasis,* a deliberate stepping over the line. For example, the man who gathered sticks on the Sabbath, deliberately violating God's command not to do such work, was to be stoned to death, Numbers 15:32-36.

[8] "Disobedience" translates *parakoe,* a disobedience which results from a failure to hear. For example, the man who would presumptuously neglect to hear the instructions and warnings of the priest touching the requirements of the Law was to be put to death, Deuteronomy 17:12, 27:26.

[9] The first "we" (*hemeis*) is emphatic in the Greek. Now the emphatic pronoun is found only 5 times in Hebrews; therefore its use here is significant. When an emphatic pronoun is used, there is an implied contrast. Perhaps it means "*we*, who are so very privileged to have the gospel, in contrast to those who had only the Law." The "we" refers to the same people ("us") to whom God had spoken in His Son (Hebrews 1:2). That includes the writer, the readers of this letter, and in a general way all men who live this side of the incarnation.

context suggests that it is punishment of some kind[10] that we will not escape. From the Law of Moses, with its "recompense" for disobedience and transgression, we certainly can learn that God punishes neglect of His revelation. The Hebrews' writer did not write "reject"; he used the word "neglect." The same word appears in Matthew 22:5 where the guests "made light of (KJV)" or "paid no attention" to the invitation to the marriage feast. What an outrage that the invited guests should disdain the king's gracious invitation! "So great a salvation" is synonymous with "[the things which] we have heard" (Hebrews 2:1), which is synonymous with what "God ... in these last days has spoken ... in His Son" (Hebrews 1:1,2). What must a man do to lose[11] his salvation? Just neglect[12] it, and he will lose it! Why is salvation called "great"? Perhaps the three phrases that follow explain what is so "great" about it.

After it was at the first spoken through the Lord – The point of verses 3b and 4 is this: the Hebrews had been convinced of the validity of the Mosaic Law (verse 2). Now they were beginning to doubt the validity of the gospel message. So the writer gives three proofs of its validity: (1) it was first spoken by the Lord (i.e., Jesus[13]); (2) it was confirmed by those who heard Him; (3) it was certified as from God by the God-wrought miracles accompanying its apostolic announcement. "First spoken through the Lord" reminds us of the emphasis of chapter 1; namely, that the gospel was brought to earth by no prophet nor any angel, but by the Son of God Himself.[14]

It was confirmed to us by those who heard -- Jesus' earthly ministry was not done in secret. It was very public, and those who had been present when Jesus spoke, and who had seen His

---

[10] When the revelation that is neglected is greater, then the punishment is greater. If it was physical death that recompensed neglect of the Law of Moses, then it is something worse than physical death that is threatened upon those who neglect the "great salvation" offered in the gospel.

[11] What the Hebrews were tempted to do, namely, to quit Christianity and revert to the Jewish religion, is here identified by the word "neglect." In this commentator's opinion, this is not a verse to use when one wishes to attempt to show that people who have never heard the gospel are all lost. It does express the utter impossibility of being saved for anyone who once confessed Jesus and then "neglect(s)" the salvation which God has so graciously offered to us in the gospel. For nearly 2000 years, faithfulness to the gospel has been the condition of salvation, and will continue to be so until Jesus comes again.

[12] The aorist tense verb "neglect" speaks of a completed action, a finished act. It does not say one sin causes a saved man to be lost. In the light of the rest of Hebrews, it does say that one who quits Jesus finally and completely will be lost. If the state of mankind was such that only the Son of God could save them, then what hope can there be for any who neglect the salvation which He offers?

[13] "Lord" was a title of divinity used by Jesus Himself (e.g., Luke 19:31), and also used by His followers even during His earthly ministry (e.g., John 13:13), as well as immediately after His resurrection and ascension (e.g., Acts 1:7). The LXX had used "Lord" to translate the name par-excellence for God, "Jehovah" or "Yahweh."

[14] The affirmation that the "great salvation" was "first spoken" by Jesus does not contradict verses elsewhere that say it had been promised to the Old Testament worthies. What Hebrews claims is that what had before just been *promised* (cf. Genesis 3:15; 12:3; Isaiah 53) has given place to *fulfillment*, and Jesus was the first to announce this fulfillment. After John the Baptist's imprisonment, Jesus came into Galilee "preaching the gospel of God, and saying, 'The time is fulfilled, and the kingdom of God is at hand: repent ye, and believe the Gospel'" (Mark 1:14). Compare His preaching in the synagogue at Nazareth, early in His earthly ministry. After reading the prophecy from Isaiah 61, Jesus declared "Today has this Scripture been fulfilled in your ears" (Luke 4:18ff). So, while actual fulfillment was first announced by Jesus, there also is a sense in which the Gospel was preached beforehand (Galatians 3:8; 1 Peter 1:10-12).

miracles, were able to corroborate what had happened by their own testimony. For "us" who could not be there in person,[15] such testimony from eyewitnesses helps guarantee[16] the truth of the gospel. We regularly identify "those who heard" by the name "apostles."[17]

2:4 -- God also bearing witness with them -- If the Hebrews were ever going to be weaned from the idea of quitting Christianity in favor of going back to the old Jewish religion, they would first have to be convinced of the surpassing validity of the gospel. "God also bearing witness" is the third of the reasons why our salvation can be called "so great" (verse 3). "Bearing witness with them" says that even while the apostles were speaking, God also was acting to attest the truth of what they were preaching.[18] How God acted to convince men of the validity of the gospel is explained in the following phrases.

Both by signs and wonders and by various miracles -- Each of these three synonyms are but different ways of looking at the same miracles. Any one supernatural act[19] done to bear witness with the apostles could at the same time be both a sign, a wonder, and a miracle. "Sign" emphasizes the purpose of the miracle, to point men to something God wants them to hear. "Wonder" tells of the effect on the people who beheld the miracle. The word translated "miracle" calls attention to the power it took to accomplish the supernatural act. "Various" is a vivid word, telling us there was no flat uniformity about the mighty deeds accompanying the apostolic preaching.[20]

---

[15] In the Introductory Studies, the use of this verse in the discussion of the authorship of the epistle has been alluded to. While not a few writers have urged this verse as proof that Paul could not have been the author of Hebrews (as the title of the KJV has it), we are not convinced by their representations. All this verse affirms is that neither the writer of the letter nor its original readers were eyewitnesses of Jesus' earthly ministry. Although Paul was not an eyewitness (which is the likely meaning of 2 Corinthians 5:16 in its context) of Jesus' earthly ministry (AD 26-30), he did get his gospel by direct revelation from Jesus (Galatians 1:11-24) sometime after AD 34. The inspiring truth about all this is that Paul's message and the message of the original twelve exactly match. If Paul is the author of Hebrews, he, too, can say that the consistent voice of the twelve, which matched what he had received by revelation, "confirmed" the truth of the gospel even for him.

[16] The verb "confirm" (*bebaioō*) is the same word used of the Old Testament in Hebrews 2:2. It is a legal term, meaning to guarantee, to validate. The uniform testimony of the eyewitnesses is one of the proofs of the truthfulness and validity of the gospel message.

[17] Indeed, one of the qualifications to be an apostle of Jesus, i.e., to be numbered with the original apostles (Acts 1:26), was that the person had to be an eyewitness of the earthly ministry of Jesus, Acts 1:21,22.

[18] The modern-day reader should not miss the point here. This is one of the verses in the New Testament that tells the purpose of miracles at the beginning of the church age. They were wrought by God to attest or validate the truth of the gospel claims. It should also be clear that the language of Hebrews 2:3,4 indicates the miracles done to confirm the message were already a thing of the past at the time when Hebrews was written, for "confirmed" is an aorist tense verb — indicating completed action in the past time. The validating of the message was past and done.

[19] In the author's *Commentary on Acts* (p.91), attention is called to the distinction between *providence* (God's everyday activity in His world) and *miracle* (miracle is not something that happened every day). C.S. Lewis' definition of miracle also was given: "The divine art of miracle is not the art of suspending the pattern to which events conform, but of feeding new events into that pattern" (Lewis, *Miracles* [New York: Macmillan, 1948], p.72). (Lewis' book is a very readable presentation of "miracles" to a world that tends to be biased against the possibility of any supernatural intervention.)

[20] "Various" translates *poikilos*, "many colored, variegated, diverse." The writer of Hebrews can appeal to the readers' common knowledge of the accompanying miracles to remind them that the Gospel has been validated by God Himself! Such an appeal could not have been made if there were any possibility that the readers

And by gifts of the Holy Spirit according to His own will -- The margin shows the word translated "gifts" can properly be translated "distributions." Exactly what distribution is in view is hard to identify with certainty. Of all the measures of the Holy Spirit available, we would doubt that the one called the indwelling gift is the only one in mind.[21] The context calls for something which accompanied the gospel preaching by the eyewitnesses that would have evidential value. What this likely refers to is to the apostles' ability to pass on spiritual gifts[22] by the laying on of their hands (cp. Acts 8:17,18, 19:6; 1 Corinthians 12:11). As in 1 Corinthians 12:11, "according to His own will" tells us the distributions were given as the Spirit willed them to be given.[23] The first warning passage thus is concluded. When God speaks through His Son, and then validates the message as He did the gospel, that message must be given very close attention.

2. The Son's superiority to angels is not contradicted by His humanity. 2:5-9.

2:5 -- For -- Now that the warning has been given, the topic begun at 1:5 is continued.[24] It seems likely that this paragraph and the next are intended to answer standard Jewish objections to the Christian doctrine of who Jesus is – i.e., the He is God and superior to angels. The first objection likely contained these ideas: Men, in rank, are lower than the angels (cf. verse 7). If Jesus became a man, some might argue, is He not less than the angels? The writer will answer by showing that Jesus, during His earthly stay on earth, when He was perfectly human, was temporarily subordinate in rank to angels. But, since His resurrection and glorification, He is not subordinate any more.

He did not subject to angels the world to come -- The "world to come" is Bible language for the church age, the Messianic Age[25] foretold in the Old Testament prophets, the age since the cross, in which we now live. The following verses (especially verse 9), and even the final phrase of this verse, make it clear that the period referred to is that which followed the exalta-

---

could reply that they had never seen or heard of such things. The present-day critic, who would deny the facticity of miracles in the beginning of the church, must stubbornly reject evidence not only from the Gospels and the Epistles but the evidence found in the common experience of both believers and non-believers as well.

[21] The prepositional phrase "of the Holy Spirit" may mean either the Spirit Himself *is* the gift (an objective genitive), or that the Spirit *gives* the gift (a subjective genitive). Likely the point made here in Hebrews is similar to the one made in Galatians 3:2-5, where "Spirit" can cover both the indwelling of the Holy Spirit and the measure called "spiritual gifts."

[22] See 1 Corinthians 12:4-10 for one listing of such miraculous spiritual gifts.

[23] If the Spirit Himself is the "gift," then "according to His own will" might refer to the will of the Father. On the other hand, if the Spirit is the giver, then "according to His own will" speaks of the Spirit's will.

[24] There is a very clear connection between Hebrews 2:5 and 1:14. Angels are "ministering spirits ... *for* he did not subject to angels the world to come." There is also a connection with 2:3,4. The salvation that is now given has been proclaimed not by angels, but by Jesus the Son, and has even been validated by God Himself as He works with the apostolic preachers of the gospel whom Jesus sent. God does not so work with angels, "*for* it was not to angels that He has subjected the world ..." (NIV).

[25] It is admitted the Greek translated "world to come" (*ten oikoumenen ten mellousan*) is not the usual Greek for Messianic Age. In fact Arndt-Gingrich (p.564) note this is the only usage of this expression to mean the Messianic Age, and that the usual word for "age to come" is *aion* (e.g., Matthew 12:32).

tion of Jesus.[26] It was to Jesus, not to any angel, that the "world" was subjected.[27] This is another mark of Jesus' superiority to angels.

Concerning which we are speaking -- Where has the writer spoken of the "Christian age" before this, so that he can say "concerning which we are speaking"? He has called attention to "these last days" and "heir of all things" (1:2), "sat down at the right hand of the Majesty on high" (1:3), "kingdom" (1:8), and "sit at My right hand until I make Your enemies a footstool for Your feet" (1:13). All these expressions are true of the church age. So, too, is the message spoken first by the Lord, and then confirmed to us by eyewitnesses (2:2,3).

2:6 -- But one has testified somewhere, saying -- "But" marks a contrast between angels (to whom the world to come was not subjected) and Jesus (Who is crowned with glory and honor). The writer is going to appeal to an Old Testament passage to prove his point about the exalted position of Jesus. At first sight, the somewhat indefinite introduction of the verses from Psalm 8 is surprising.[28] So is the use of the word "testified."[29] But, further thought leads us to see the indefinite introduction focuses our attention on the words, and also warns us to take them with all seriousness. Be careful you don't miss what the Scriptures say about subjection and who it is to whom all things are subjected!

"WHAT IS MAN, THAT YOU REMEMBER HIM? – The quotation is of Psalm 8:4-6. The Psalmist, reflecting on the glories of the creation and on God's dealings with man, is recognizing that man is somebody special to God!

"OR THE SON OF MAN, THAT YOU ARE CONCERNED ABOUT HIM? -- Psalm 8 was not considered by the Jews to be a Messianic psalm. Nor is it likely that "son of man" is

---

[26] To make the "world to come" refer to the age following Jesus' *second* coming, would be to rob the present argument of any meaning. What the author is trying to do is show Jesus' superiority *now*, not at some future age, say either a millennial reign after the Second Coming, or a reign in Heaven. Only if Jesus is exalted *now* would the readers be deterred from quitting Jesus to go back to the Jewish religion.

[27] Angels do have, or did have(?), a certain "administrative" function in our world. Deuteronomy 32:8 tells us, "When He separated the children of men, He set the bounds of the peoples according to the number of the angels of God [LXX]." See also Daniel 10:13,20,21, and 12:1. Ephesians 6:12 speaks of "world-rulers of this darkness" (ASV) -- a reference to evil angels and their administrative activities. See also Revelation 16:1ff. But whatever their administrative functions, and whether or not they functioned only in the Old Testament age over *peoples*, this much is certain -- the whole universe, including the angels, is under the Lordship of Jesus! Angels may function from time to time in tasks entrusted to them, but they are never the all-powerful controlling agent who is entrusted with the administration of the whole universe, as was Jesus.

[28] The writer of Hebrews usually introduces a Scriptural quotation by some such formula as "God says" or "the Holy Spirit says," or "He (God) says." In none of the seven quotations given in chapter 1 is the human speaker identified; in the Hebrew writer's view, God was the speaker of all Scripture, no matter who the human spokesman was (see 1:5b, 3:7). Furthermore, the language of Psalm 8 was originally addressed to God. It would take the writer far afield to have to defend how the passage could be inspired and at the same time be addressed to God before he actually quotes from Psalm 8. "One has testified somewhere" does not indicate a lapse of memory as to the source, for the LXX of Psalm 8 is quoted verbatim.

[29] "Testified" is a word used when someone is put under oath before he speaks. It shows the solemnity of the testimony about to be given.

intended to make us think the Psalm had reference particularly to Jesus.[30] "Concerned about" has the idea of looking after, taking care of, and is rather synonymous with "remember" of the previous phrase, a word that includes the idea of helping. That God should help and care for man, as He does, is evidence that of all the created beings, man is somebody special to God.

2:7 -- "YOU HAVE MADE HIM FOR A LITTLE WHILE LOWER THAN THE ANGELS – Having asked a question to get us to pause and reflect about man, the Psalmist now answers his own question. God has given man an outstanding position, just a little lower[31] than that of angels,[32] and has also given him a special responsibility.

"YOU HAVE CROWNED HIM WITH GLORY AND HONOR -- The exact import of this phrase is rendered somewhat doubtful[33] by the phrase or phrases[34] from Psalm 8 yet to be quoted. Nevertheless, this very phrase is one of the more important taken from Psalm 8, for (in verse 9) it is one of but two phrases from that whole passage which the writer of Hebrews uses concerning what happened to Jesus.

---

[30] Hebrew parallelism would cause us to think that "man" in the first member of the poetic pair is synonymous with "son of man" in the second member of the pair. Even though we recognize that "Son of Man" was Jesus' favorite Messianic title, we think the parallelism of Hebrew poetry rather requires that the two expressions here be taken in the same sense. "Son of..." would then emphasize quality, as "son of strength" means "the strong man." "Son of man" would emphasize the quality of humanity, the quality of being man.

[31] "Little" in the Greek can refer to space, time, or degree (rank). The Hebrew word seems to favor "degree", i.e. "a little lower." This is the interpretation favored by Delitzsch, Alford, Moll, and Milligan, who think "son of man" refers to mankind in general. Those writers who think "son of man" is a specific reference to Jesus construe the word "little" to be expressive of "time," i.e., Jesus was for a "little while" lower than the angels, but He isn't any more. This is the view of Macknight and Clarke.

[32] There is a difference of readings here. The Hebrew has "a little lower than *'elohim* ("God," "gods"). The LXX has "a little lower than angels." For the LXX use of "angels" to translate *'elohim*, see chapter 1, footnote #56. If the LXX translators' interpretation of Psalm 8:5 was wrong, then the understanding we get from their translation (that man is a little lower than *angels*) is wrong. Perhaps it means, as the Hebrew might be translated, that man was made a little lower than *God* -- and so, even now, man holds an exalted position to the angels.

The decision to limit "son of man" to mankind in the previous verse now takes on added significance. If "son of man" is Jesus, then the words "you have made him (Jesus) a little lower than angels" would mean one thing -- during the time of His incarnation He was temporarily subordinate in rank even to the angels. But if the Hebrew means "you have made him (Jesus) a little lower than God" -- that might be supposed by some to mean that Jesus was a created being, whose rank was a little less than that of the Father. Such a supposition, however, is ruled out when one remembers all that has been said about Jesus in Hebrews 1 and 2. The only possible time when Jesus might be considered to be temporarily subordinate in rank to the Father is after He emptied Himself (Philippians 2:7) to become incarnate.

The Hebrew writer seems to settle this problem (verse 9) when he uses the word "angels" (not "God") in his argument about Jesus. His use of "angels" there seems to confirm that the LXX translation was the right way to understand the Hebrew of Psalm 8.

[33] *When* does the crowning of man take place? Was it in the past? If the last phrase of verse 7 enjoys integrity, then a case could be made that man was "crowned with honor" when he was given dominion over all the works, over the animals, etc. (Genesis 1:26ff). Is the crowning of man future? Many of the Old Testament prophecies are written in the past tense (cf. Isaiah 53). They are written in the past tense because when God predicts, it comes to pass! If it is future, then perhaps a parallel passage would be one that speaks of a "crown of righteousness" which awaits those who are faithful (2 Timothy 4:8).

[34] There is a manuscript variation at the end of verse 7. Not all manuscripts carry the last phrase that appears in our NASB version. Its inclusion or omission has some bearing on the meaning of "crowned him with glory and honor."

"AND HAVE APPOINTED HIM OVER THE WORKS OF YOUR HANDS -- The NASB margin indicates some manuscripts of Hebrews omit this phrase.[35] Since it did appear in the Old Testament Psalm, we suppose it had reference to what we can read in Genesis 1:26, "Let ... man ... rule over the fish of the sea and over the birds of the sky ... and over every creeping thing that creeps on the earth."

2:8 -- "YOU HAVE PUT ALL THINGS IN SUBJECTION UNDER HIS FEET" -- This phrase, we suppose, is the Psalmist's way of wording what we read in Genesis 1:28, "Be fruitful and multiply, and fill the earth, and *subdue* it; and *rule* over the fish of the sea and over the birds of the sky, and over every living thing that moves on the earth." This first phrase of verse 8 is still a part of the quotation from Psalm 8, and brings out even further the dignity of man. What a responsibility man was given!

For in subjecting all things to him – Here begins the Hebrews writer's comment on the implications of Psalm 8. At the creation, God did subject all things to man. The Bible says so.

He left nothing that is not subject to him -- God's original intention was that man exercise a dominion over the whole creation. That's an awesome responsibility! Man is somebody special!

But now we do not yet see all things subjected to him – Something happened after the dominion mandate was given to man. Man sinned and lost his dominion. Sin, with its curse, has prevented man from exercising the dominion that God intended, which subjection Psalm 8 holds forth as the ideal. That's why "now," when we look around us, we do not see man subduing and ruling creation as he once did. "Not yet" shows the writer's optimistic outlook. One day, the subjection will be fully realized again.

2:9 -- But we do see Him -- We must read the last part of verse 8 and the first part of verse 9 together to see the contrast. It is this. When we look around us, we don't see man doing what the Psalm pictures (God's original intent), but we do see Jesus ("Him")! Furthermore, we see Jesus crowned with glory and honor! What we see is that Jesus went to work to restore what man lost in the Fall. In doing that work, for a while He was made a little lower than the angels, but He is not anymore!

Who has been made for a little while lower than the angels, *namely,* **Jesus** -- While Jesus was in the flesh,[36] just like all men in rank are, He was a little lower[37] than the angels.

---

[35] The clause is omitted by the Nestle[26] and UBS[3] texts. The omission is given a "C" rating in the UBS textual apparatus, which means there is a considerable degree of doubt whether the phrase should actually be omitted. The phrase is in the Hebrew text of Psalm 8; it is found in the LXX of Psalm 8; and it is found in the codices Sinaiticus, A, C, and D of Hebrews.

[36] That Jesus is *God*, the creator of both man and angels, is clearly taught in Hebrews 1. That He was also (for a while) *man* is just as clearly taught in Hebrews 2. Note the use of His human name ("Jesus") here, and what is said in verses 11-14 below. In our comments, we have regularly been using the name "Jesus," but the careful student will observe that this is the first time the writer of Hebrews has used His personal name. "Jesus" means "Jehovah saves" or "salvation is of Jehovah." After speaking of "Jesus" (salvation is of Jehovah), the writer speaks about the death of Jesus.

[37] The comments on the language "little while lower" made at verse 7 apply here, too.

Because of the suffering of death -- This phrase likely should be taken with what follows rather than with what precedes.[38] So construed, it says Jesus is crowned with glory and honor precisely because He died.[39] This is the first mention of the death of Jesus in this letter.

Crowned with glory and honor -- What Psalm 8 holds out as God's intention for man, Jesus has already received. And He received it after His death, after He successfully accomplished the mission for which He became incarnate. Since He is crowned with glory and honor,[40] then it follows He is no longer "a little ... lower than the angels" – and the first objection the Jews were wont to use to counter the Christian doctrine of who Jesus is has been answered. His superiority to angels is not contradicted by His humanity.

That by the grace of God He might taste death for everyone -- The writer of Hebrews asserts that, by dying,[41] Jesus has achieved something for fallen man. In fact, since the word translated "everyone" may just as well be rendered "everything," we can say the death of Jesus had cosmic significance! In God's good grace,[42] the death Jesus experienced[43] (which resulted in His glori-

---

[38] The preposition is *dia* and usually means "on account of" in such constructions as this. Some have attempted to show that it was "on account of the suffering of death" that Jesus was made a little lower than the angels," but that idea ("in order to suffer") would better be written with the preposition *eis* or *hina*, not *dia*.

[39] What is here said then would be similar to what is written in Philippians 2:5-11.

[40] How do we know Jesus has been crowned with glory and honor? Hebrews 1:6 and 13, among other verses, have already said so! Furthermore, before He came into the world, God had promised that Messiah should be abundantly rewarded for His sufferings (Isaiah 52:13 and 53:12). Luke tells us Jesus was taken up into heaven after His passion (Acts 1:1-11). Peter tells us "angels and authorities and powers have been subjected to Him" (1 Peter 3:22). Jesus is crowned Lord of all! Moulton has said, "It is noteworthy that we do not read, 'We behold all things put in subjection to Jesus,' for that would conflict with Hebrews 10:13." Physical death is an enemy yet to be subdued, but it will be at the final resurrection!

[41] The order of the clauses, at first sight, might cause the reader to think that Jesus was "crowned" *before* or *so* that He could "taste death for everyone." Such an interpretation has chronological difficulties, for the Scriptures elsewhere have the cross before the crown (cp. Hebrews 12:2).

[42] Instead of *chariti theou* ("by the grace of God"), some manuscripts (M, 424mg, 1739mg), versions (one manuscript of the Vulgate, and a few Syriac mss.), and early church fathers exhibit the reading *choris theou* ("apart from God"). Morris (*op. cit.*, p.25) has written, "This *[choris theou]* reading has strong patristic support." Among Origen, Jerome, Theodore of Mopsuestia, Theodoret, and Ambrose, the reading "apart from God" received various interpretations. It was said Jesus died "apart from God" in the sense that (1) it reflects His sense of being forsaken on the cross (Mark 15:34); (2) He died apart from His divinity (the human Jesus died, but His divine nature survived [the Adoptionist heresy?]); (3) He died for everyone or everything with the exception of God. Two studies of this problem are R.V.G. Tasker, "The Text of the 'Corpus Paulinum',' NTS 1 (1954- 55), p.84, who concludes "grace of God" was the original reading, and J.K. Elliott, "When Jesus was Apart from God: An Examination of Hebrews 2:9," *Expository Times* 83 (1971-72), p.339-341, who favors "apart from God' as the original reading.

   If "by the grace of God" is the true reading for verse 9, then this verse affirms that it was because of God's grace that Jesus died for all, and that His saving work is made available to all. "Grace" here would be both an attitude and an action on God's part, by which He provided the atonement for a fallen world. (See the author's commentary on Romans for a special study on the Biblical doctrine of "Grace" [p.47-65].)

[43] "Taste" (Jesus did "taste death") was a common metaphor meaning 'to experience.' It does not suggest a mere sampling of something (the same word is translated "eat" at Acts 10:10), or a sip from a glass (rather than a full and satisfying drink). This is one of several passages in the New Testament where someone is said to "taste death" (see Matthew 16:28; Mark 9:1; Luke 9:27; John 8:52). Because men learn through the senses (including taste), the verb *geusetai*, "taste, eat," also has the meaning "come to know, to experience fully." Also, since some things are bitter to the taste, several writers have offered the opinion that this expression is used of

fication) not only permits Him to exercise dominion, but to make available the beneficial consequences of His death to fallen man,[44] and ultimately to reverse the effects of the Fall on the whole creation.

3. The Son's superiority to angels is not contradicted by His suffering. 2:10-18.

2:10 -- For -- The thought that begins in verse 10 is closely connected with the preceding expression, "by the grace of God He tasted death for every man." It also, we suppose, is a refutation of another (see verse 5 above) standard Jewish argument used to refute Christian doctrine that Jesus is superior to angels. This one perhaps said, "Jesus lived on earth, and suffered greatly. He was humiliated and executed like a common felon. No angel ever suffered like that. How can you say Jesus is superior to angels?" The writer of Hebrews will make three points as he explains the necessity of Jesus' suffering: (1) suffering was necessary to complete His identification with humanity (verses 10-13); (2) suffering was necessary to destroy the devil and deliver believing men (verses 14-16); and (3) suffering was necessary to qualify Him to be a merciful high priest (verses 17-18).

It was fitting for Him -- "Him" is a reference to God the Father. "Fitting" says there was an inner fitness, something perfectly proper, in what the Father has been doing in history – in trying to bring many sons to glory, and asking Jesus to suffer for fallen men. Usually, we do not think of things being "fitting" for God, but in this place the word is appropriate. The way of salvation is not something arbitrary; it is something befitting[45] the very character[46] of the God we know, the One "for whom are all things, and through whom are all things."

For whom are all things -- God the Father is the goal toward which all things are moving (cp. Romans 11:36, 1 Corinthians 8:6). All things are ultimately intended to benefit Him. So what was done at Calvary will permit even fallen man to yet praise and glorify Him.

And through whom are all things -- The Father is the author of all things. In Him everything

---

death because death is not often a pleasant thing to experience. On the other hand, Primasius and Theodoret supposed the verb "taste" is used because of the brief duration of Jesus' death.

[44] If we translate the last word in the verse "everyone," and note that Jesus "tasted death for *(huper,* in behalf of) everyone," we can certainly say there is no doctrine of limited atonement here. It is not that every man will be saved (it is not universalism), but the potential is there. After Jesus has provided the salvation through His death, if men will heed the message that was also first spoken through the Lord and then by the eyewitnesses (see Hebrews 2:3,4), the effects of Jesus' atoning death will be imputed to them.

[45] The verb is *prepo* ("fitting," seemly, becoming), not *dei* (it is necessary) or *opheilo* (ought, a moral obligation). The salvation God has provided was not an obligation that grew out of the circumstances, nor something that God was morally obliged to provide. Rather, it was provided because it matches beautifully with God's great eternal purpose to have a family who would love Him (Ephesians 1:4ff).

[46] God is love (1 John 4:16). Such a way of redemption shows His love. God cares for His creation. Such a redemption shows how much God is mindful of men. God is holy, and cannot overlook sin. At the same time, His mercy and grace lead Him to provide a way of salvation for sinners. The death of Jesus allows God to forgive sin, without impinging on His perfect justice. He could at the same time be both just and justifier of those who believe in Jesus. The way God has chosen to solve men's sin problem is an act worthy of God.

finds its reason. The suffering of Jesus that was intended to benefit all men finds its cause or its reason in Him and His purposes.

In bringing many sons to glory -- God's grand purpose, bringing[47] many sons to glory, fully warranted the drastic actions taken, including the suffering and death of Jesus. In such a noble cause, Jesus' suffering was not foolish; it was sinners' only hope! The "glory" to which God is bringing His "many sons"[48] includes the blessings of heaven as well as a new, resurrected, glorified body for each. The Father's plan of redemption that is but briefly outlined here in Hebrews can be read in greater detail in Ephesians 1:3-12. There we are told that before the creation of the world, God wanted a family who would love Him, not because they had to, but because they wanted to. He wanted the family members to be holy and blameless in His sight. If the man He was going to create should sin, He would send the Son to provide redemption. God also planned to adopt as "sons" each one who would choose (of his own will) to be "in Christ." Of course, as sons, each of the redeemed will share in the same inheritance[49] Jesus (the "Son") received when He returned to the Father's presence after His sojourn on earth.

To perfect the author of their salvation through sufferings -- It is a striking description to call Jesus the "author" of salvation. The Greek word means "to go first" and has been rendered as pioneer,[50] captain,[51] leader,[52] author or originator.[53] "Their salvation" introduces the idea that will be developed later, that Jesus did not need to save Himself from sin, because He had

---

[47] The fact that "bringing" translates an *aorist* participle leads us to pause and reflect on its possible meaning. Aorist tenses refer to one act, and in this context the one act is likely Calvary (including all that the death of Christ meant in the mind and plan of God). The *participle* does not need to be restricted to some past event, as though it referred to Old Testament saints already glorified, or to New Testament saints who have died before Hebrews is written.

[48] For the first time in Hebrews, "sons" is used of Christians. Before it has been used of Jesus, God's unique Son. Christians become "sons," as is made clear elsewhere in the New Testament, only by the process of adoption (Romans 8:15, Galatians 4:5). "Many" tells us not so much how many people will be in heaven as it emphasizes that it was God's purpose to have not one Son, but *many* sons to share His glory.

[49] Redeemed men do not become gods like Jesus is God, but they will have a glorified body like the one He now has (Philippians 3:20,21), and they will share in the "glory" of God like He now does.

[50] The pioneer blazed the trail along which others later came. Jesus blazed the trail along which God's "many sons" could be brought to glory. Hebrews 6:20 will remind us that Jesus has gone as a "forerunner" into heaven.

[51] This was the choice of the KJV translators. In their time, in the old world armies, the captain led the other soldiers into battle. He showed his men how and where to fight. At the same time he had an authority over them. So it is with Jesus. Jesus' superior position is what the translators thought was in mind when this same word was rendered "Prince" or "ruler" at Acts 5:31.

[52] Translators who have chosen "leader" as a translation of *archegos* have supposed that in the background is an idea similar to 1 Corinthians 15:22. As the first Adam led all to physical death, the Second Adam (Jesus) leads all to life. By using "leader" they hoped to help readers recall this great truth.

[53] In secular Greek writings, *archegos* was used of the hero who founded a city, gave it its name, and became its guardian. Similarly, it was used of one who was head of a family or the founder of a school of philosophy. Because this same word is used again at Hebrews 12:2, and there it seems to have the sense of originator or founder since it is contrasted with "perfecter" or completer, the NASB translators chose the word "author" as the meaning here. Jesus began our salvation (think of Calvary), and He will finish it (think of all He will do at the second coming).

no sin. It was men who needed the salvation. When we recall that Jesus is God, we are surprised by the term "perfect." Was Jesus not perfect, if He were God? Yes, He was perfect as far as committing any sin is concerned; He was sinless perfect. But as far as being qualified to be a *savior*, that was not something that was His simply because of who He was. It took the suffering and death at Calvary to "perfect" or "qualify"[54] Him for that task.

2:11 -- For -- The necessity for Jesus to become man in order to suffer and be qualified to be the "author" of salvation is now further explained.

Both He who sanctifies and those who are sanctified are all from one *Father* -- "He" who sanctifies is Jesus, the "author" of salvation who tasted death for everyone (verses 9 and 10). "Those" who are being sanctified are the "many sons" who are being brought to glory (verse 10). "Sanctify" means to set apart, to dedicate, to make clean, to purify, and the sanctifying is in both cases a present tense verb indicating continuing action. Over and over again throughout history, as men become believers, they are consecrated to God, set apart to be His holy people, qualified to enter into the presence of the Father. Sanctification is a condition essential for access into God's presence (Hebrews 12:14). "All" (both Jesus and believers) are said to be "of one" or "from one."[55] "One" is an adjective and we must supply the noun.[56] The NASB translators have chosen to supply "Father," thereby suggesting the reference is to God the Father. Perhaps "father" (small "f") is also a viable suggestion, since Adam or Abraham would also accord (along with God) with all the terms and conditions of the context. The thing being emphasized here is the unity between Jesus and "those" whom He sanctifies.

For which reason He is not ashamed to call them brethren -- Since they all are "from one" – since they have the same Father – Jesus is not ashamed to call the ones who are sanctified[57] His "brethren."[58] The particular passages from the Old Testament where men are called Jesus'

---

[54] The Greek word is *teleioō*, a word used 14 times in Hebrews. (The most the term occurs in any other New Testament Book is 5 times in John.) Whenever the word is used in Scripture, the context must explain in what sense the word is being used. It means "end, goal, to finish (for example a tower or work of art), mature, full-grown, to bring to completeness (as opposed to incomplete or partial)," and it never has the connotation of moral perfection or sinless perfect. Lightfoot supposes the use of the term in the LXX is in the background here. In the Pentateuch, *teleioō* was used to refer to the consecration of priests (Exodus 29:9,29,33, 35). As the Old Testament priests were perfected or consecrated into office by various rites, so Jesus was perfected or consecrated or qualified by His sufferings to be the "author" of men's salvation.

[55] The writer does not say they are one, but rather that they are "from one." Believers are not gods like Jesus is God. While it is true that Jesus is exalted above the others, yet He is a "Son." He even calls God His Father, John 17:1,5,11,21,24,25. Compare 1 Peter 1:3.

[56] Besides "Father" we might supply race or seed or blood.

[57] It is important to identify the "them" of whom it is said Jesus is not ashamed to call *them* brethren. It is not men in general whom He calls brothers, but only those who are sanctified.

[58] It is not unusual to find the term "brothers" (or "brethren") applied to all the followers of Jesus (a figurative use of the term, as at Acts 1:15,16; Matthew 12:49,50; Mark 3:33-35). Rarely in the New Testament, however, are Christians called *Jesus'* "brothers" (Romans 8:29 may be an example). Indeed, sometimes Jesus and His followers are clearly differentiated, for example, Matthew 23:8, when Jesus says to the twelve, "For One is your Teacher, and you are all brothers." The word "brothers" is also used in its more literal sense referring to the children born to Joseph and Mary (Matthew 12:46-48; Luke 8:19,20; John 2:12; Acts 1:14). So, while this language in Hebrews is somewhat unusual, there is a sense in which Jesus is a "brother" to all who have the same Father.

"brothers" will be quoted in the following verses. That there is no shame in giving such an appellation implies there is an infinite disparity between them and Him, as far as His deity is concerned.

2:12 -- Saying -- Three Old Testament proofs are submitted to point up the common tie between Jesus (the author of salvation) and the redeemed (those who are sanctified).

"I WILL PROCLAIM YOUR NAME TO MY BRETHREN -- This first quotation comes from Psalm 22:22, a Messianic Psalm.[59] In the words of the Psalm, Messiah (and Jesus is Messiah) calls men "my brethren," and vows to tell those men what the Father is like.[60] Again, we emphasize the Old Testament verses quoted in Hebrews 2:10-12 are building a case for the *humanity* of Jesus. These verses make sense only if the incarnate Jesus shares a common humanity with all other men.

"IN THE MIDST OF THE CONGREGATION I WILL SING YOUR PRAISE" -- Not only will Messiah reveal the Father to men whom He acknowledges as His brothers, He will make that revelation right in the midst of a congregation of those men. He will not be off in some distant place handing down decrees for others to deliver. He will do it Himself, identifying Himself with them as a part of their "congregation."[61]

2:13 -- And again -- The phrase about to be quoted is found in three places in the LXX, 2 Samuel 22:3, Isaiah 8:17, and 12:2. The point of this second quotation is to prove how much the Sanctifier and the sanctified are alike in their humanity.

"I WILL PUT MY TRUST IN HIM" -- Jesus and His "brethren" are so alike that both felt the need to put their trust in God.[62] They all had to depend on Him.

---

[59] Verses 1,8,15,16 and 18 of Psalm 22 are quoted in the New Testament and applied to Jesus. On the cross, Jesus spoke the words of verse 1, "My God, My God, Why have You forsaken Me?" (Mark 15:34). The words of Psalm 22:18 about dividing of garments by casting lots were fulfilled in Jesus (John 19:24). Some commentators have classified Psalm 22 along with Psalm 110 as being simply and directly prophetic, having no fulfillment before they were fulfilled by Jesus. Others have urged that some of the language in certain verses is so descriptive of an actual experience of the Psalmist that they treat the Psalm as a double reference prophecy, or as typico-prophetic.

[60] While there are New Testament passages which affirm the perfect humanity of Jesus, the original readers of Hebrews, who had the most implicit confidence in the divine origin and plenary inspiration of the Old Testament Scriptures, would more likely be convinced of the truth of the claims of Christianity for Jesus if those claims could be shown to be clearly enunciated in those Old Testament Scriptures. In fact, since few of what will become the New Testament Scriptures have been committed to writing at the time Hebrews was written, the Christian who wanted "Scripture" to convince a doubter was almost required to point to Old Testament texts.

[61] "Congregation" translates *ekklesia,* a word that means "assembly" or "called out." See the word explained in the author's commentary on Acts at 5:11 and 7:38. In its Jewish sense, "congregation" spoke of the nation of Israel assembled in Jerusalem, where David and his brethren often celebrated the praises of Jehovah. Jesus declared the Father to the Jews first. He, likewise, while on earth before and after His resurrection, declared the Father to the twelve (compare John 5:17-23, 17:26).

[62] If the quotation comes from 2 Samuel 22:3, the original speaker is David. David certainly knew how to depend on God to deliver him out of the hand of his enemies and out of the hand of Saul. David's actions and words are often typical of Christ. If the quotation is taken from Isaiah 8:17 or 12:2, then the writer of Hebrews regards Isaiah as typifying Jesus in these words. Isaiah often presented himself as part of the faithful remnant which was looking to God for salvation in the midst of a rebellious nation.

And again -- The familiar formula "and again"[63] introduces a third quotation, taken from Isaiah 8:18, to show the incarnate Jesus shares a common humanity with all other men.

"BEHOLD, I AND THE CHILDREN WHOM GOD HAS GIVEN ME" -- In its original setting, this remarkable passage occurs in connection with the memorable message (Isaiah 7:3-25) God sent to king Ahaz, on the occasion of the confederacy of Rezin of Damascus and Pekah of Israel against Judah. After an interval of perhaps a year has passed and Jerusalem and Judah have in fact since been plundered by Rezin and Pekah, it looks like the comforting prophecy against Rezin and Pekah, made earlier and recorded in Isaiah 7, will not come true. Should Isaiah and his listeners begin to doubt the truth of the prophecy uttered earlier? No! Isaiah will make new prophecies (Isaiah 8:1ff) in which he again affirms that Assyria will come and Rezin and Pekah will be no more. In the meantime, Isaiah says he will continue to trust in the Lord (Isaiah 8:17), and in the midst of the people's general dismay and disbelief of his earlier message, the prophet (accompanied by his children) travels around (Isaiah 8:18) calling attention to himself and to his children,[64] and says that together they are presenting God's message to the king and to Israel. This identity or togetherness is the idea the writer of Hebrews is emphasizing as he applies the passage to Jesus and His "brethren."[65]

2:14 -- Since then the children share in flesh and blood -- Turning from the idea that Jesus' suffering was necessary to complete His identification with humanity (verses 10-13), the writer now turns to the topic that suffering even unto death was necessary for Jesus to render power-less him who had the power of death, namely, the devil. And in order for Jesus to experience

---

[63] Compare the use of this formula at Hebrews 1:5, 1:6, and at the beginning of 2:13.

[64] "Isaiah" means Jehovah is salvation. One of Isaiah's sons was named Shear-Jashub, which means "a remnant shall return." The other son's name was Maher-shalal-hash-baz which means "speed to the spoil, haste to the prey." "Immanuel" (Isaiah 7:14, 8:8) means "God with us." Israel could hardly say God had not given sufficient revelation about the future. Assyria was hastening toward the spoil that plundering Rezin and Pekah would provide. Judah, too, would be passed through by the flood waters of Assyria. Many in Judah would be taken captive, but a remnant would return because salvation is in Jehovah. After the remnant returned, the days would come when the virgin would conceive and "Immanuel" would be with us. Just seeing Isaiah and his children would remind the people of the dominant themes of the prophet's message.

[65] A number of commentators have questioned whether the writer of Hebrews has made a legitimate use of the Isaiah 8:18 passage. Statements like the following are not uncommon: "The citation of the words, 'I and the children whom thou hast given me' in Hebrews 2:13, is noticeable here chiefly as showing how little the writer of that Epistle cared in this and other quotations for the original meaning of the words as determined by their original context." Now the writer of Hebrews does interpret Isaiah 8:18 (and perhaps 8:17) typologically of Jesus. But must it be said the writer of Hebrews has to ignore the context of Isaiah 8 in order to make such a typological application? Hardly. Even in Isaiah 8, these words are introduced rather abruptly, as a message from God. This commentator is not ready to affirm that when God inspired Isaiah to speak the words he did (recorded in Isaiah 8) that God did not also intend them to be true of the Messiah whom Isaiah has also been told is coming (see "Immanuel" in both Isaiah 7:14 and 8:8). F.F. Bruce (*The Epistle to the Hebrews*, p.46,47) has pointed out another linkage between the passages quoted in Hebrews 2:12,13. He shows Isaiah 8:17 (the second quotation's source in his opinion) speaks of Jehovah hiding His face from Jacob, and reminds us that this provides the link with the Messianic Psalm 22 (the first quotation), which speaks of Jehovah as temporarily hiding His face from the righteous sufferer of the seed of Jacob (note Psalm 22:1,2,12,24). Thus the Isaiah and Psalm passages are tied together in thought, and the writer of Hebrews is not to be criticized for his use of them typologically as referring to Jesus the Messiah.

death, He had to become a partaker of the same flesh and blood[66] that all humanity shares.[67]

He Himself likewise also partook of the same -- The verb tenses are significant. The children "share" (perfect tense, did share and still do) in flesh and blood; Jesus "partook" (aorist tense, he partook once, but does *not* now still partake) of their humanity. The two different verbs used are also significant. Hebrews does not say men *are* flesh and blood, but that they *share it*[68] in common with all other men. Jesus, on the other hand, of His free choice, *took part* in these, so becoming a brother to mankind.

That through death – Why did Jesus become a partaker of flesh and blood? In order that He might die. God cannot die, but men can. Only by becoming a man could Jesus experience death.

He might render powerless him who had the power of death, that is, the devil -- This phrase explains one of the reasons Jesus came to die. The devil's death grip on mankind had to be broken. Most likely the "death" here in view is the physical death that became the common lot of the race when Adam sinned (Romans 5:12; 1 Corinthians 15:22). It is the teaching of this verse that what happened at Calvary rendered inoperative[69] the devil's power to inflict death.[70]

---

[66] "The children" in verse 14 picks up the word "children" found in verse 13 and continues the idea contained in it. Who are these "children" with whom Jesus identifies Himself? Men and women, creatures of flesh and blood. (The word order in Greek is "blood and flesh," but we doubt that the word order has any significance as compared to the word order "flesh and blood." We are not convinced that the former has reference to the physical substance of man, whereas the latter, when it occurs, emphasizes the weakness and fallenness of humanity. If the distinction is valid, then the word order as it actually appears in the Greek would make even more vivid the point the writer of Hebrews is making, namely, that Jesus shared common physical humanity while He was incarnate.)

[67] If Jesus' solidarity with other humanity is real, then Jesus must be a true human being, a genuine partaker of flesh and blood. No docetic (He just appeared to be human, but wasn't really) or Apollinarian (Jesus was not completely human), "Christ" will satisfy men's need of a Savior, or God's determination to supply that need.

[68] The writer of Hebrews thus implies that there is more to a man than simply flesh and blood; there is also soul and spirit that are part of man's makeup. Flesh and blood simply make up the house in which man now lives.

[69] Jesus is not here said to have as yet *abolished* death, only to have rendered it inoperative or ineffective (even though the word is *katargeo*). There is one sense in which death is no more: in and through Jesus death is already destroyed (2 Timothy 1:10). In another sense, complete victory over death awaits the final consummation, for "the last enemy to be destroyed (*katargeo*) is death" (1 Corinthians 15:26; cf. Revelation 20:14).

[70] A number of difficult questions suggest themselves as one ponders all that verse 14 says. (1) Is it physical death, or spiritual death, or both, over which the devil has some control? (2) Did the devil have this power only until Calvary, or does he still have it? (3) This is the first time the devil has been introduced by name in the book of Hebrews. What else do we know about him and his work?

(1) It has been this commentator's understanding of the verses dealing with the Fall that what was passed on to the race as a result of Adam's sin was physical death. The doctrine of an inherited sinful nature does not seem to be supported by either Old or New Testament Scriptures. Nevertheless, when the devil tempts men and they sin, they do die "spiritually," and so in a sense it might be maintained that the devil has the power to cause men to die spiritually. If that is the doctrine here taught in Hebrews, then what Jesus did at Calvary had as one of its intentions to reverse (at least for believers) the effects of the devil's work. Once there has been a

2:15 -- And might deliver those -- Here is another reason Jesus came to die. The men for whom Jesus died were subject to a bondage, or slavery, to the devil.[71] Jesus' death and resurrection[72] delivered men (believers, at least) from this slavery. He set the prisoners free!

Who through fear of death were subject to slavery all their lives -- Why do men fear death? Because of the pain and misery that sometimes accompanies it. Because men are uncertain of their condition and destiny beyond the grave. How does this fear of death lead men into slavery? Does this passage suggest that men, because of their fear of death, are lured into false religions – only to find themselves even more enslaved in bondage to sin and the devil? Fear of death leads men to be religious, and the devil provides a substitute for God's revealed religion, thereby keeping people in bondage to himself. Unless Jesus delivers men from their subjection to slavery, they will be slaves all their lives.

2:16 -- For assuredly -- It is not all men who experience the freedom that results from Jesus' death. "Assuredly" or "of course" translates *depou*, a word used only here in the New Testament. It makes a strong affirmation and appeals to information already shared by the readers.

He does not give help to angels -- Why did Jesus[73] become a man and experience death like a man can? Because it was men, not angels, whom He planned to help.[74]

Calvary, men who were dead in trespasses and sins can rise to walk in newness of life.

(2) The careful student will have noticed the English translations do not agree on how to render the verbs in this last clause of verse 14. Some read the devil *has* the power of death," others read that the devil" *had* the power of death." This causes us to ponder the question of whether or not some men die physically because the devil decides it is time for that man to die. Does the Devil operate as a sort of independent sovereign who inflicts death upon men at his whim? Does this verse say that at Calvary Jesus took this power away from the devil? He had it once, but since Calvary, he has it no more? Would it also follow that God is now (since Calvary) the One who decides when it is time for a man to die physically? (In Luke 13:7 it is the vineyard-keeper who gives orders that the fruitless tree be cut down. In Revelation 2:22,23 it is Jesus who threatens Jezebel and her followers with sickness and death. In Revelation 1:18 it is the glorified Jesus who claims to have the keys to death and Hades.)

(3) The word translated "devil" suggests the evil one is an "accuser, slanderer, traducer." He continues day and night to accuse the brethren before the throne of God (Revelation 12:10). He once was a good angel (Revelation 12:1-9), but was condemned and cast out, apparently because pride led to his condemnation (1 Timothy 3:6,7). After he was cast out of heaven, the devil plotted and effected the Fall of man (Genesis 3). Today, after the good seed of the kingdom is sown, the devil sows his tares (Matthew 13:38,39). Calvary proved to be a great victory over the devil, and now he is a defeated power who is still exceedingly dangerous, but who eventually will be cast into the lake of fire (Revelation 20:10).

[71] Romans 6:1-14 speaks of a bondage to sin that is the result of a man's committing his first sin. Romans also shows that this bondage is broken when that man is then immersed into Christ.

[72] Jesus' resurrection is not expressly mentioned in this passage. In fact, only in the doxology of Hebrews 13:20,21 is the resurrection specifically mentioned. But it is nonetheless implied. That's how men are delivered from death. Without the resurrection, Jesus' death would never have provided for deliverance (Romans 4:25).

[73] There is no pronoun for "He" in the Greek. While the third person singular verb could be translated "it" (making verse 16 a reference to death -- death didn't take hold of angels; it took hold of men), such a translation ignores the meaning of the verb (see the next footnote), and ignores the context which has been telling us about Jesus. "He," in our opinion, is the proper way to translate in this place.

[74] The word *epilambano* means to lay hold of for the purpose of helping, or to rescue from peril. Compare Matthew 14:31; Mark 8:23; Luke 14:4; Hebrews 8:9. Good angels don't need any help like redemption; the evil angels are beyond rescue.

But He gives help to the descendant of Abraham – In this verse, we would understand that "descendant of Abraham" is not limited to its physical sense (i.e., Jesus died for more than simply the Jewish people).[75] "Descendant of Abraham" elsewhere in the New Testament includes all who exhibit Abraham's faith.[76] It is such believers in particular who experience the deliverance Jesus' death has made available.[77]

2:17 -- Therefore -- "Therefore" shows verses 17 and 18 flow from verse 16 as a consequence. Still in the paragraph where it is being shown that Jesus' suffering does not disprove His superiority to angels, we now enter upon one of the most important facets of Jesus' solidarity with His brethren; namely, how His suffering exactly qualifies Him for His high priestly ministry on their behalf. Further, it is precisely in this role of high priest that it can be seen Jesus is superior to any angel.

He had to be made like His brethren in all things -- No mere pretense of humanity would ever help Jesus understand the people for whom He proposed to function as high priest. His perfect humanity "had to be" – it was an obligation[78] arising out of the work He was undertaking. "All things" means all things[79] essential to perfect humanity. The context says Jesus was not exempt from the suffering and death common to all humanity, nor was He exempt from being tempted.

That He might become a merciful and faithful high priest -- "That" expresses purpose. The incarnation ("made like His brethren") was not aimless; it was for the purpose of Jesus' becoming a high priest. This is the first mention in Hebrews[80] of Jesus being a "high priest."

---

[75] The KJV which reads "took on him the seed of Abraham" might be understood to say that when Jesus became a man, He came of the Jewish race, a descendant of Abraham. However, as observed in previous footnotes, such a translation does not convey the whole sense of *epilambano*. Westcott stresses the absence of the article before "seed" ("descendant") as emphasizing the character of these men rather than their racial identity. (In reply, Kent points out that at John 8:33 the expression "Abraham's descendants" occurs, without the article, and there it certainly has racial overtones.)

[76] Matthew 3:9; John 8:39; Romans 4:11,16; Galatians 3:7,9,29.

[77] The very thing in which men were made "lower than the angels," namely, their mortality, was that which made salvation possible.

[78] The Greek has several words expressing "necessity." *Dei* denotes moral necessity growing out of God's decrees and purposes. *Prepo* (used in Hebrews 2:10) denotes intrinsic fitness and propriety in conformity with divine attributes. *Opheilo*, the word used here in verse 17, expresses obligation arising out of any work or enterprise already undertaken. Since Jesus had voluntarily undertaken the work of redeeming the seed of Abraham from the bondage of sin and Satan, He thereby incurred the further obligation of being made like them. He must be liable to, and must experience, temptation, sorrow, pain, and death. (Milligan, *op. cit.*, p.102)

[79] Scripture stoutly affirms Jesus' sinlessness. He was tempted in all points as we are, yet without sin (Hebrews 4:15). This language about Jesus sharing our humanity also seems to have some bearing on the doctrine of an inherent sinful nature. Jesus didn't have one. Why not? It was not to protect Him from inborn sin that He had a virgin birth. After all, He got His physical body from Mary, and if there is such a thing as inherent sin, how did she avoid it, so as to have none to pass on to her Son? (The Roman Catholic dogma of the immaculate conception will hardly stand scrutiny in the light of Scripture.) That Jesus had a body just like ours, to this commentator, is a strong indication there is no doctrine of total depravity or of an inherited sinful nature taught in Scripture.

[80] The idea of Jesus' priesthood has been implied in Hebrews 2:9,11,14, so we have been prepared for this

We are thus introduced to a theme that will be expanded greatly in the following chapters of Hebrews. Whenever a man needs a priest, he needs one who will be merciful and faithful. "Merciful" speaks of that feeling of sympathy with the misery of another which leads one to act in his behalf to relieve that misery. It is a lack of such a feeling of sympathy that makes officials perfunctory in their duties. The sinner who seeks restoration to the favor of God finds little comfort when the priest simply performs perfunctorily. Jesus can have sympathy because He too has suffered as we do (cp. Hebrews 4:14-16). "Faithful" tells us the priest doesn't quit in the middle of the job of helping the sinner receive forgiveness. In respect to God, Jesus proved Himself faithful. He didn't quit in the middle of the job of redeeming men. In respect to men, Jesus is "faithful;" He is reliable and dependable. What a contrast with the Sadducean high priests (who exhibited very little tender care) to whom the Hebrews were giving serious thought of returning.[81]

In the things pertaining to God -- Perhaps the reference is to the place where Jesus serves as high priest, namely the "true tabernacle" (Hebrews 8:2). Perhaps "things pertaining to God" has reference to such things as are necessary to sustain God's holiness and His government, while at the same time redeeming men and pardoning sin. Once there has been a Calvary, God can be just while at the same time being justifier of those who have faith in Jesus (Romans 3:26).

To make propitiation for the sins of the people -- "Propitiation" speaks of a covering, an atoning sacrifice.[82] It is Jesus, not men, who provided the needed sacrifice. Jesus' death so "covers"[83] the sins of the people that God's wrath does not fall on the sinner. The Old Testament

topic before it is specifically introduced. The suddenness with which the term is introduced here in Hebrews 2:17 suggests the idea is not the invention of the writer of Hebrews, but was a belief already familiar to Christians. See A.J.B. Higgins, "The Priestly Messiah," *New Testament Studies* 13 [1966-67], p.211-39. Though there are no other places in the New Testament, outside of Hebrews, where the term is specifically applied to Jesus' present heavenly ministry on behalf of the redeemed, the idea is implied in numerous verses. See Romans 5:2, 8:34; Ephesians 2:18, 5:2; 1 Timothy 2:5, 1 John 2:1. And there are Jesus' own words where He speaks of Himself as being an intercessor (John 17:9ff; Luke 12:8, 22:32). We therefore affirm the early church learned the idea of Jesus' high priesthood from Jesus and the apostles (and Scripture), not from the Qumran sectarians or some other non-biblical source.

[81] The Sadducean high priests (Annas and Caiaphas were examples of such in an earlier time) were political and ecclesiastical tools and puppets; out of touch with the people, and chosen by Rome. How much better a choice for high priest is Jesus! Such a merciful and faithful high priest as He is ought to be welcomed and embraced by these Hebrew Christians.

[82] See the extended discussion of the word *hilaskomai* (and its cognate *hilasterion*) in the author's commentary on Romans, at Romans 3:25. The same Greek word occurs at Psalm 65:3 where it stands for the Hebrew word which is commonly rendered "make atonement for." See also F.F. Bruce, *Hebrews*, p.41ff, and John R.W. Stott, *The Epistles of John* (Grand Rapids: Eerdmans, 1964), p.84-88. (One of the less-than-biblical ideas currently making the rounds in liberal circles is that Jesus' death was not a "propitiation," was not a covering for sin, but merely an "expiation." That is, it was a good-will offering, but not an objective basis for justification. "Expiation" thus defined is less than the Scriptures teach concerning the death of Jesus.)

[83] The infinitive "to make propitiation" is present tense in the Greek. A present tense verb usually indicates continuing action. Either of the following possibilities may explain this present tense (and it does need some comment, since Hebrews elsewhere emphasizes the complete and final nature of Jesus' sacrifice on Calvary). It may mean that every time a man initially obeys the gospel, down through the ages since Calvary, Jesus' blood covers his sins. Or it may mean that every time a Christian confesses his sins and asks forgiveness, the blood of Jesus Christ covers his sins.

animal sacrifices never could take away sins (Hebrews 10:4), but the sacrifice of Jesus could and did!

2:18 -- For -- Verse 18 is probably to be connected with "might become a merciful ... high priest" (verse 17), by showing how Jesus can sympathize with the erring and tempted. Not only did Jesus deal with the sins of sinners (verse 17), He also deals with the saints (verse 18).

Since He Himself was tempted in that which He has suffered -- "He Himself" is emphatic in the Greek. Contrary to what might have been expected, *He* suffered! And the suffering He experienced (throughout His earthly life, as well as at Calvary) was (every time He suffered) a temptation He had to master. Satan tempted Jesus to avoid the cross (Matthew 4:8,9); Peter, in the spirit of Satan, suggested Jesus avoid the cross (Matthew 16:22,23); Gethsemane was a time of temptation for Jesus (Luke 22:40 implies Jesus was going to be tempted just as were the disciples); the cries of the impenitent thief also were a temptation to come down off the cross (Luke 23:39). Time and again the sufferings He experienced were temptations to quit the mission on which He came to earth. But He resisted these temptations to the end, and set His face steadfastly to accomplish the purpose for which He had come into the world. Now He can sympathize with us. He knows what it is to suffer rather than turning aside from the Father's will. He knows how persuasive temptations can be.

He is able to come to the aid of those who are tempted -- "Come to the aid of" translates a word that means "to run to answer a cry for help." The Hebrews were being tempted to give up Christ, to quit the church, and return to Judaism. How precious to know Jesus was standing ready to run to their aid if they would but cry to Him for help. Further, He knew just what they needed! In His having been tempted lies His special ability to help the tempted; by His sympathy, by His knowledge of the help that is needed, by the position of high priest which He has gained through suffering and death, He is eminently qualified to be our helper.[84] Far from His sufferings proving that Christian doctrine about the deity of Jesus and His superiority to angels was in error, His sufferings and death did just the opposite. They qualified Him to be the only perfect[85] high priest the world has ever known. That's a position and function loftily superior to any angel.

---

[84] The "aid" which Jesus provides when His "brethren" cry to Him may take any one of several forms. It may consist of Jesus doing something to stop the persecutors who are causing the saints to cry for help. It may be a strengthening of the saints to endure the suffering without losing faith. It may be putting a limitation on the duration of the suffering the persecutors are allowed to inflict. It may be a deliverance out of the suffering. Being merciful and faithful, Jesus knows what is best in each case!

[85] To be a "perfect" high priest has several prerequisites. One is sympathy, and Jesus could not sympathize with men unless He entered into their experiences and experienced them for Himself. Jesus did this. Another is mastery of temptation (and perhaps the hardest temptations to master are those that are the result of physical and mental suffering). If Jesus had failed in this area, He would have needed a priest for Himself, rather than being able to enter into God's presence on our behalf. A third prerequisite is a sacrifice that actually avails to take away sins. Jesus' death did that, too. Now He ever lives to make intercession for the saints.

C. Jesus is Superior to Moses. 3:1 - 4:13

1. Both Jesus and Moses were faithful to God. 3:1,2

3:1 -- Therefore -- "Therefore" links chapter 3 to chapter 2. Because Jesus is superior to the angels and because He has partaken of the same flesh and blood that men share, the readers of Hebrews are invited to consider Him in His capacities as apostle and high priest. Near the close of chapter 2, Jesus' priesthood was introduced. We might have expected the writer to continue this topic next in his discussion. But before he does, he takes up the topic that is naturally and historically antecedent to it – the apostleship of Jesus. Just as Moses preceded Aaron in the management of the resources and affairs of Israel in the Old Testament, Jesus appeared as the leader of God's New Testament people before He entered upon the duties of His priesthood.

Holy brethren -- The "holy brethren"[1] whom the author addresses were the Hebrew Christians. They were "brethren" because they were children of the same Father (Hebrews 2:11ff), and they were "holy" because they had been separated from the world as the peculiar people of God (2:11 also spoke of the people who have been "sanctified"[2] by the action of the Sanctifier).

Partakers of a heavenly calling -- Once Jesus has taken part in flesh and blood (Hebrews 2:14), it is now possible for men to take part in a heavenly[3] calling (an invitation from heaven, or an invitation to heaven), that is, an invitation to salvation. By reminding the readers who they are and how they came to be such holy brethren, the writer is recalling the dignity with which God has invested them. To treat such dignity lightly would be insulting to God.

Consider Jesus -- The call to "consider"[4] Jesus is a call to meditate carefully and profoundly on the His nature and character, the apostle and high priest of our confession, who was faithful to God. The readers of this letter, who were giving thought to quitting Jesus and the church, needed just this exhortation. Jesus was faithful! Are you to be unfaithful? Jesus is God! Are you going back to Moses? When you could have Jesus as your high priest, are you going back to one of the Levitical priests?

---

[1] Although the combination of the two terms is not found precisely like this elsewhere in the New Testament (unless the variant text at 1 Thessalonians 5:27 is accepted), each term ("holy" and "brethren") is used to designate members of the Christian community. Believers are often called "brethren" (as in Galatians 1:2,11) and "holy ones" (i.e., saints, as in 1 Corinthians 1:2), and both terms occur together in Colossians 1:2.

[2] "Holy" and "sanctified" are two words that come from the same root, *hagios* or *hagiazo*, which means set apart, dedicated to God. It is the same root word from which our word "saint" comes.

[3] The word "heavenly" suggests the contrast that appears again and again in this Epistle to the Hebrews -- a contrast between the present, visible, material world and that of the truly real world, immaterial, eternal, and heavenly. Christians have been invited to the celestial country, to the land of real and abiding things. They have been invited to share with Christ in His inheritance in heaven just as Jesus shared with them in their human nature (flesh and blood) on earth.

[4] The verb *katanoeo* indicates serious attention, careful study. To get the point of verses 1 and 2, the reader must pay attention to subject, verb, and object of the sentence. "Holy brethren" is the subject. "Consider" is the verb. "Jesus" is the object. "Holy brethren, consider Jesus!"

The Apostle and High Priest of our confession -- "Our confession" reminds the readers that there was a time when they did confess that "Jesus is the Christ, the Son of the living God," or that "Jesus is Lord."[5] Now, before they abandon the church in favor of Judaism, they should meditate on what (and why) they once confessed about Jesus.[6] The Jesus they confessed is both an "apostle" and a "high priest." The word "apostle" means one sent on a mission.[7] The idea the Father sent Jesus into the world on a mission of redemption is an idea found often in the New Testament, especially in the Gospel of John. One who is an "apostle" is God's representative among men. Jesus is also "high priest," an idea that will be developed in detail later in this letter to the Hebrews. A priest is man's representative in the presence of God. Jesus' mission had something to do with helping men with their sin problems, and helping them get to God. The two functions of Jesus, apostle and high priest, are chosen for a special purpose. They introduce the readers to the two great contrasts that are to follow, between Moses and Christ, and between Aaron and Christ.

3:2 -- He was faithful to Him who appointed Him -- As the marginal note in the NASB indicates, the original begins verse 2 with a participle that agrees with Jesus. "Consider Jesus as being faithful to God!" is the idea. It is a present tense participle (continuing action). He *is* faithful – He is now, He was while He was on earth, He always will be. The tasks in which He is faithful are those of "apostle" and "high priest." The Greek word *poieo*, here rendered "appointed," is not the usual word translated "appoint," but the one regularly translated "do or make." It is likely our translators have chosen "appointed" since this reflects what is read about Moses and Aaron at 1 Samuel 12:6, "It is the Lord who *appointed*[8] Moses and Aaron" to their tasks as "apostle" and "high priest" in the Old Testament. Further, the writer has repeatedly affirmed that Jesus is not a created being, but is eternal and co-equal with the Father. So "made"

---

[5] One of the steps in the process of conversion is to make a confession of faith before witnesses. See 1 Timothy 6:12,13; Acts 8:37 (KJV); Matthew 16:16-18 (Christ's church will be built on the rock of similar confessions to the Good Confession which Peter made). To confess means to say the same thing. When we men make a confession of our faith in Jesus, we are saying the same thing about Jesus that God says about Him. Exactly what words made up the content of the earliest Christian confessions (whether "You are the Messiah, the Son of the Living God" as Peter said it, or "Jesus is Lord" as Romans 10:9,10 words it) is probably a matter of little moment, since both are rather synonymous in their meaning.

[6] How often do followers of Jesus make a confession of their faith? There is a sense in which it is a continual thing, for Jesus said (Matthew 10:32), "He who continues to confess me before men, him will I confess once and for all before My Father in Heaven." (*Author's translation*, in which we have emphasized the meaning of the different verb tenses Jesus used, one of which was present tense, continuing action, and the other of which was aorist tense, one act.) Hebrews 4:14 will exhort the readers to "hold fast our confession." Hebrews 10:23 will repeat that exhortation. Whereas some verses speak of continual confession, 2 Corinthians 9:13, in a context dealing with the benevolent offering for the poor at Jerusalem, seems to speak of that act of giving as an evidence of their obedience to the confession of the gospel of Christ, a confession the Corinthians had made (evidently) at an earlier time. Each time we come to a passage in the New Testament that deals with confession of faith, it is a valuable study to attempt to ascertain whether it is the initial confession, or continuing confession, that is in view.

[7] The twelve whom Jesus appointed and who became His special messengers are often called "apostles," because they too were sent on a mission (by Jesus Himself). When one considers that the twelve served as divine spokesmen, some have supposed that included in the designation of Jesus as "apostle" is something similar to what we had in Hebrews 1, where God has spoken through His Son. Jesus, too, was a revealer, a divine spokesman, bringing to men God's final message. "Apostle" is more than merely one sent on a mission. It includes the idea that the person is sent with authority, full authority, to represent the sender.

[8] The Hebrew is *asah,* and the LXX used the same verb *poieo* that is used here in Hebrews 3:2.

would not be the proper sense here; it could be misinterpreted to be saying that Jesus was a created being, when in fact He is not. Jesus was appointed to His official position as apostle and high priest before the incarnation since Scriptures tell us He was a lamb slain from the foundation of the world. His appointment took place in the counsels of God before God ever created our universe.[9]

As Moses also was in all His house -- It should be carefully noted that the writer, as he speaks of Moses, in no way reflects negatively on him. Now Moses was not sinless perfect, and some of his defects could have been recalled to the Hebrew readers' memory.[10] But instead of putting Moses down, the writer lifts up and exalts Jesus. He acknowledges the value of the Mosaic dispensation, and then proves the New is better. Both Moses and Jesus were faithful to the tasks assigned them, but Jesus is still superior to Moses! Rather than risk offending the Jews whose regard for Moses was genuine and deep, the writer sets forth Jesus' superiorities in unanswerable fashion. If you can find no deficiencies in Jesus, why would anyone ever entertain the thought of forsaking Him, as some of the Hebrew readers were doing? How did the writer of Hebrews know Moses had been faithful? Because God Himself bore witness to this fact, in Numbers 12:6-8, "My servant Moses ... is faithful in all My household."[11] God's "household"[12] in Numbers 12:7 is likely a reference to the people of Israel. We suppose the same meaning is to be attached to "His (God's[13]) house" in Hebrews 3:2.[14] The adjective "all"

---

[9] Some of the Latin church fathers believed *poieo* ("do" or "make") here in verse 2 had reference to Jesus' incarnation, and that what was "made" for Jesus was His physical body. While it may be a true doctrine that God did prepare a body for Jesus (see Hebrews 10:5), this is not the proper verse to show it.

[10] An example would the events at Meribah, Numbers 20:7-13, where Moses' behavior was not proper.

[11] A study of the book of Hebrews provides the Bible student with a wonderful opportunity to "brush up" on his Old Testament. Each time a reference is made to an Old Testament passage, it would be a fruitful study to momentarily interrupt our study of Hebrews and take up a study of that Old Testament passage and its context. When we then return to Hebrews, the Hebrew text will jump alive with new meaning for us. For example:
    The occasion of the statement made in Numbers 12:6-8 was Aaron's and Miriam's opposition to Moses and their claim that God had also spoken through them (Numbers 12:2). In response, God says, "Hear now my words: If there is a prophet among you, I the Lord shall make Myself known to him in a vision; I shall speak with him in a dream. Not so with My servant Moses; he is faithful in all My household. With him I speak mouth to mouth ...." In this Old Testament passage, Moses is spoken of as superior to any prophet. They had only subordinate parts of God's will made known to them, and that obscurely by vision and dream. But with Moses, God spoke face to face. Moses had a pattern of the true temple and house of God shown to him on Mt. Sinai. That pattern he reproduced faithfully in the tabernacle (Exodus 40:16-29). What Moses made pointed to the coming Messiah and His work in the true tabernacle in heaven. To leave Jesus and return to Moses would be a serious failure to hear what Moses himself actually had to say about following Messiah when He came.

[12] The word "house" is used with a number of connotations in the Old Testament. The tabernacle, the tent of meeting, might be called the "house of God." The material building in which people lived is called a "house." That neither of these possible meanings is the correct one here in Hebrews is evident from what is said in Hebrews 3:5,6. It is the people, the "household," that is intended by the writer.

[13] It is not easy to decide the antecedent of "his" in the expression "his house." Some have affirmed the reference is to Jesus, so that the writer would be saying that Moses served in Jesus' house. (Were the people of Israel somehow also "Jesus' household"?) A second suggestion is that "Moses" is the antecedent of "his", so that the writer would be saying Moses was faithful in the house to which he belonged and in which he served. Others (as the footnote in the ASV shows) think the antecedent of "His" is God ("Him who appointed ..."). The writer is then saying that both Jesus and Moses were faithful to God who appointed each of them to their offices.

[14] While the identification of "His house" may seem a matter of little moment, lurking in the background is the

may point to a concern both Moses and Jesus had for the whole house. Others, such as prophets, kings, or priests, were concerned only with restricted areas.

2. The Son's superiority to Moses is asserted by appeal to their positions in God's house. 3:3-6

a. Jesus is the builder of the house, Moses was but a part of the house. 3:3,4

3:3 -- For -- Having said both Moses and Jesus were "faithful," the writer goes on to show that the difference between them is really infinite. We suppose that "for" is connected with the exhortation to "consider Jesus" found in verse 1. Consider Jesus, "for" He well deserves your attention! He deserves more honor than you give to Moses.

He has been counted worthy of more glory than Moses -- In this first comparison, Jesus' superiority to Moses (i.e., Jesus is "worthy of more glory, or honor, than Moses") is based on the obvious superiority of the builder to the house. The reason for giving Jesus superior honor is explained on the basis of rank, not faithfulness. Jesus was the builder of the house, whereas Moses was but a member in the house.

By just so much as the builder of the house has more honor than the house -- Men may marvel when they see a beautiful and well-constructed building, but it is self-evident the real credit belongs to the person who planned, constructed, and furnished the building. Applying this illustration to the topic at hand, it is evident the writer does not think of Moses as being the house, but as being a part of the house (verses 2 and 5 tell us Moses was "in" the house). Jesus, the builder, deserves more honor than Moses (one of the members in the house).

3:4 -- For every house is built by someone -- Jesus may be thought of as the builder, the writer goes on to say, since every house is built by someone. No house or household just springs into existence of and by itself. No nation or people just suddenly and spontaneously appear on the stage of history. Every house or thing has its cause, and the writer of Hebrews even teaches there is a First Cause.

But the builder of all things is God – Here is another assertion in Hebrews that Jesus[15] is God!

---

whole question of "covenant" or "covenants" -- i.e., the truth or error of one-covenant theology. Some have tried to say the house Moses was faithful in was "Jesus' house" and therefore they attempt to show there was no difference between the "house" in the time before Calvary and the time after Calvary. Both peoples ("houses"), one-covenant theologians are wont to affirm, are simply called "His (Jesus') house." See further on this matter below in Appendix A, "Covenants and Covenant Theology." We reject one-covenant theology.

[15] Some have supposed the Hebrews writer for a moment has ceased speaking of Jesus as superior to Moses and has for a moment called attention to the sovereignty of God the Father. While it is true Jesus has a unique relationship to the Father ("Son," as chapter 1 has demonstrated), in this commentator's opinion it robs the argument of Hebrews 3 (that Jesus is superior to Moses) of some of its force if we must stop and explain that the import of this illustration is that Jesus, unique as He is, was of course under the Father who was actually the builder of all things. How much easier it is to follow the argument if it is recognized verse 4 is an assertion of the deity of Jesus!

Jesus, who had something to do with building the Old Testament people of God,[16] is Himself God! That's why He is worthy of more honor than Moses. Jesus is not (like Moses) just part of the house; Jesus (Himself God) is the builder of all things.[17]

b. Jesus is the Son over the house; Moses was but a servant in the house. 3:5,6

3:5 -- Now Moses was faithful in all His house as a servant -- The second comparison to show Jesus' superiority to Moses is based on the obvious superiority of a son to a servant. As in verse 2, Moses' faithfulness "in His (God's) house"[18] is again alluded to. Whatever sins Moses committed were more personal than official. He may have been excluded from entering the promised land, but when it came to functioning as God's appointed messenger, Moses always delivered the whole message of God. Further, just as Numbers 12:7 was in the background of verse 2, so also it is in that very passage in Numbers where we find the designation "servant" given to Moses. Now Moses may have been an honored servant; he may have had a special relationship with the Master; but he is still a servant.[19]

For a testimony of those things which were to be spoken later -- Here is where we are told that Moses was faithful when it came to delivering God's message. We suppose the "things which were to be spoken later" refers to the things Moses spoke about the coming Messiah,[20]

---

[16] Jesus' pre-existence has already been alluded to in Hebrews. That Jesus was active at the time of the Exodus and wilderness wanderings is made clear in 1 Corinthians 10:1-4. That it was Jesus whom Isaiah saw high and lifted up (Isaiah 6) is made plain at John 12:36b-41. It should not be thought as something surprising if the writer of Hebrews affirms the pre-existent Jesus had much to do with the building of the Old Testament household of God. "All things," here said to be built by Him, would include creation in general (see Hebrews 1:2 and notes there, and Hebrews 1:10), but in this context where the topic is the household of God, it would certainly include that. ("All things" would not include creating the devil as he is today. The devil was created a good being, who had the power to choose to do evil if he desired. Neither Jesus nor God created evil and sin.)

[17] No Socinian (Socinus, 16th century, denied the full deity of Jesus) or Arian (Arius taught Jesus was a created being, always subordinate to the Father) can ever give us a fair and consistent explanation of Hebrews 3:1-4. Surely the writer never intended to call on his Hebrew readers, or anyone else, to consider Jesus (the Apostle and High Priest of our confession) as merely a *man*! Not in the light of the strong defense of Jesus' deity in chapter 1.

[18] As in verse 2, so here in verses 5 and 6, "His house" is to be understood as meaning "God's house."

[19] This last comment is an attempt to reproduce the difference in meaning of the various synonyms for "slave" or "servant." *Therapon,* the word used here in Hebrews and in the LXX of Numbers 12, implies such ideas as willingness to serve, personal service freely rendered, an affectionate relationship between master and servant, an honorable position. *Doulos,* the word often rendered "slave" (bond slave) does not carry any of these personal ideas. In contrast *to therapon,* a *doulos* often served not because he wanted to, but because he had to. There is a third synonym, *oiketes.* A *therapon* was a more honorable position than *oiketes,* the household servant, the domestic.

[20] For example, see Moses' words, "The Lord ... will raise up ... a prophet like me," recorded at Deuteronomy 18:15. See also the Old Testament types that were fulfilled in Messiah, such as the Passover lamb without spot or blemish, fulfilled in the Lamb of God that takes away the sin of the world. To bear "testimony" of such things was the object of Moses' service.

"Later" in the phrase "to be spoken later" is regarded by some as having more reference to later Messianic predictions made by succeeding Old Testament prophets, rather than to any prophecies made "later" than Numbers 12 and made by Moses himself.

things which had come to pass by the time Hebrews was written. Moses only bore witness to the greater things that were to follow his own day. Therefore, Jesus is superior to Moses by Moses' own admission and prediction.

3:6 -- But Christ *was faithful* as a Son over His house -- The term "Christ"[21] is used here for the first time in Hebrews, and its introduction here is one of the reasons we have opted for the interpretation that verse 5 has reference to Messianic predictions faithfully made by Moses as he served in God's house. Jesus, being "Messiah"[22] as well as "Son,"[23] occupies a position in God's house[24] vastly superior to that which "servant" did. Note that Moses was *in* (Greek, *en*) the house; Jesus was *over* (Greek, *epi*) the house. The NASB translators rightly supplied the verb "was faithful" from the context to complete the sense of this broken sentence.

Whose house we are -- This phrase makes it clear that Christian believers[25] are now members of God's household. But continuing membership in God's house is conditional, as the following phrase indicates.

If we hold fast our confidence and the boast of our hope firm until the end -- The author here adds a most important explanation as to the present composition of the house of God. He is not thinking of Old Testament Israel, nor is he thinking of the Jews as a race. In order to be a part of God's house since Calvary, one must be *faithful* to Jesus. To abandon the Christian religion, to quit Jesus to go back to the Hebrew religion, would necessarily mean one is no longer part of the family (house) of God.[26] "Hold[ing] fast," perseverance, faithfulness, is one of the marks of being a Christian. "If we hold fast" is hardly compatible with the doctrine of

---

We have also tended to disregard the suggestion of those interpreters who think that Numbers 12:8 ("with him I speak mouth to mouth") is alluded to in the last half of Hebrews 3:5. Such a suggestion would make "later" refer to revelations which God gave to Moses in contrast to Miriam and Aaron. We disregard this suggestion because the wording of Hebrews 3:5 is not at all close to the LXX of Numbers 12:8.

[21] "Messiah" is Hebrew, and "Christ" is the Greek word, both of which mean "anointed." Prophets, priests, and kings were anointed. Jesus the Christ (Messiah) is all three -- Prophet, Priest, and King.

[22] "Christ" occurs here (as it does in Hebrews 9:11,24) without any article. Thus it is the quality of Messiah that is emphasized. ("Christ" is used with the article several times in Hebrews, e.g., 3:14, 5:5, 6:1, 9:14,28, 11:26. The expression "Jesus Christ" occurs three times, viz., 10:10, 13:8,21). Here in Hebrews 3, where a name or title of dignity is called for in contrast to "servant," *Messiah* is just such a term.

[23] To get the import of "Son," recall all that was said about Jesus being "Son" in Hebrews 1:4ff.

[24] See comments on verse 2 and verse 5 for the identification of "His house" as meaning "God's house." The KJV added a word in verse 6, so that it reads "But Christ as a son over his *own* house." While the Greek is no different from what is found in verse 2 (there is no word for "own" in the Greek), this added word has led many of the scholars who are commenting on the KJV to suppose there are two "houses" referred to in this brief paragraph. It has been proposed "His own house" is meant to designate a different house than the house Moses served in. While we will reject one-covenant theology as we comment on chapters 8 to 10, we do not need to make a distinction between "houses" (i.e., that Jesus' "house" is different from Moses' "house") here to have reason to reject one-covenant theology.

[25] "We" includes both the writer and his Hebrew Christian readers.

[26] We are not denying faithful men in the Old Testament era were and are counted as part of the house of God. But now that Jesus the Messiah and Son has come, one cannot reject Jesus and at the same time still be counted as one of the "faithful."

"once saved, always saved."[27] "Confidence" (*parresia*) means "freeness and boldness of speech"; metaphorically, it means the confidence which prompts such speech. At one time the "holy brethren" openly made a confession of faith in Jesus (Hebrews 3:1). Such confession must be continued if they are to continue to be counted as members of God's house. "Boast of our hope" likely speaks about being proud of Jesus Who is our "hope."[28] Instead of being ashamed of Jesus and quitting church, the Hebrew readers must "hold fast" to their pride in the Messiah, the Son of God.[29]

SECOND WARNING PASSAGE. 3:7 - 4:13

- ### Warnings and exhortations with respect to our pilgrimage. 3:7-19

3:7 -- Therefore -- Having shown that Jesus is superior to Moses, the writer now pauses to warn against a similar lapse of faithfulness to Jesus as was demonstrated in the days of Moses during the pilgrimage from Egypt to the promised land. The whole point of this second warning passage is this: since Jesus is greater than Moses, the rejection of Jesus involves more serious consequences than any rejection of Moses involved.[30]

---

[27] F.F. Bruce (p.58) has reminded us "the conditional sentences of this epistle are worthy of special attention." We remain God's house (His family) *if* we hold fast, *if* we continue in the Christian life. It is distinctly implied that the Hebrew readers have a possession which they may lose if they do not "hold fast."

[28] This is the first use of the word "hope" in Hebrews. We suppose "hope" and Jesus (whose superiority is the topic of this paragraph) are interchangeable terms here. A number of other suggestions are offered to explain "hope," each of them drawn in some way from the context. Some writers think "hope" refers to heaven, i.e., something hoped for, the future inheritance in glory. Some writers think the thing being boasted about is the Christian's position in God's house; that's something to be proud of, not something to be ashamed of or something therefore one tries to hide. Others try to emphasize the idea that "hope" is an attitude of mind; others try to emphasize the object of our hope.

[29] Though the words are genuine at verse 14, there is considerable doubt that the words "firm until the end" should be included as part of verse 6. The words are not part of verse 6 in P[13], P[46], and Vaticanus. They are found in Sinaiticus, A,D,K,L,M. Perhaps some scribe accidentally interpolated the words into verse 6 from verse 14, from which they then became part of our Bibles in both places.

[30] The careful student will have observed we have a broken sentence here in the Greek. Several ways have been proposed to complete the broken sentence. The KJV, after an introductory "wherefore," puts verses 7 to 11 in parentheses. There were no punctuation marks in the old manuscripts, so the translators have to add them. Sometimes the translators' ideas are correct, and sometimes they appear not to be. In this instance, if verses 7 to 11 are parenthetical, the "wherefore" of verse 7 introduces the subject and verb found in verse 12, and the sense is, "Wherefore ... take care, brethren ...!" The use of parentheses, to us, implies the words included in the brackets are not absolutely necessary to the argument. Such an idea, of course, is hardly true of inspired Scripture. Who would say the words of the Holy Spirit are not important? Those who do not see verses 7 to 11 as a long parenthetical statement think "therefore" introduces the verb found in verse 8, and the sense is, "Therefore ... do not harden your hearts ...!" If we opt for the latter, we must supply some words to complete the broken sentence, something like "Therefore (the state of things stands with us) even as the Holy Spirit says ...." Since, following the quotation, several words and phrases from the quotation in verses 7-11 are repeated and their meanings carefully emphasized, we doubt the Old Testament passage should be treated as a sort of parenthetical thought. The words from the Old Testament are the whole point of the argument in this warning passage. "Therefore, just as the Holy Spirit says in Psalm 95, take care brethren ...!"

Just as the Holy Spirit says -- The quotation from the Old Testament which follows comes from Psalm 95:7-11.[31] The Septuagint ascribes this Psalm to David, and so does the writer of Hebrews (Hebrews 4:7). The writer of Hebrews seems to be saying that the Holy Spirit still speaks[32] to us through the words of Psalm 95. Once he has quoted the passage from Psalms 95, the Hebrew writer (in 3:12ff) will pick out several words in the Psalm and highlight them, lest his readers miss the import of this Old Testament passage.

"TODAY IF YOU HEAR HIS VOICE -- "Today," when David wrote this Psalm, was a reference to his own generation. But, when the writer of Hebrews applies this Psalm to his readers, "Today" means now, right at the present. The very time when the command is heard by the readers is the time it is to be obeyed. God's voice[33] must not be neglected or ignored, or put off till tomorrow. Immediate action is imperative. "Today" is one of the words from Psalm 95 to which the reader's special attention will be directed.

3:8 -- "DO NOT HARDEN YOUR HEARTS -- Here begins the "voice" from God which David wanted his generation to hear, and the "voice" from God the writer of Hebrews wanted his readers to hear. The readers would have to "harden their hearts"[34] before they could abandon Christianity to go back to the religion of the Old Testament. It is also implied that it

---

[31] Milligan nicely summarizes the main ideas of Psalm 95. "The quotation is made from the 95th Psalm, in which David earnestly invites his brethren to worship Jehovah (v.1,2): (1) on the ground that He is above all gods, the Creator of all things, and the good Shepherd of Israel (v.3-7); and (2) on the ground that the neglect of God's word and His ordinances had cost a whole generation of their fathers the loss of Canaan (v.8-11)." It is the last portion of the Psalm that the writer of Hebrews quotes and makes application of. Bruce then writes, "The two parts of the Psalm should not be dissociated from each other; it is a good thing to worship God, but acts and words of worship are acceptable only if they proceed from sincere and obedient hearts" (p.63).

[32] The verb is present tense, "says," not past tense, "said." If it were past tense, one might suppose the writer of Hebrews is affirming the inspiration of David as he wrote Psalm 95. Now the Hebrews writer (in harmony with the New Testament everywhere) does affirm the view that the Old Testament was inspired by the Holy Spirit (see the notes at Hebrews 1:1ff, Hebrews 9:8, 10:15; cp. Acts 28:25). Not only does the New Testament witness to the inspiration of the Old Testament, the New Testament also presents the Holy Spirit as working through the Word, even helping Christians understand the doctrine and their responsibilities. (Compare the statement found at the close of each of the letters to the seven churches in Revelation 2 and 3. "Hear what the Spirit says to the churches!" Though written to an individual congregation, the Spirit would speak to *all* the churches, not just the individual congregation, in each of the letters.) With this latter view the writer of Hebrews agrees. The Holy Spirit, he says, "speaks" to the Hebrew readers through the words of Psalm 95.

[33] In the Hebrew, "If you hear His voice" is a wish: Oh, that you would hear His voice today! If you are going to listen to God, listen now!" All of God's commands relate to *the present*, to this day, to the passing moment. He gives us no commands about the future. He does not command us to repent and turn from sin tomorrow, or ten years hence. His commands are meant to be obeyed when we hear them. It is our duty to turn from sin and love Him now. In fact, it is very likely we shall have to answer for each command we neglect to hear. He very likely will require of us an answer as to why we didn't obey "today."

[34] The Biblical "heart" is the mind. To "harden" the "heart" is to decide (after weighing the evidence) to reject the voice of God, or to decide to refuse to listen. The use of the word "harden" (a word with judicial overtones) should remind the readers that such a refusal tends to make the heart harder, and that God will also harden the heart of the man who refuses to listen. These punishments all are triggered by the man's voluntary refusal to listen in the first place. When we refuse to hear, our heart becomes harder. It is easier to come to Christ today than it will be tomorrow. Someday, we'll not be able to come. Today, it is easier to listen to and heed warnings about the danger of unfaithfulness than it will be tomorrow. (The reader may find a brief presentation of the doctrine of judicial hardening in the author's *Acts Commentary* at Acts 19:9. In comments there, attention is called to three Old Testament passages, Exodus 8:15, 9:12, and 9:35. -- Pharaoh hardened his heart, God hardened his heart, his heart was hard.)

is within the power of a man not to harden his heart.

"AS WHEN THEY PROVOKED ME, AS IN THE DAY OF TRIAL IN THE WILDERNESS -- "Provoked" and "trial"[35] recall several incidents from the period of the wilderness wanderings. (1) Both words were used (Exodus 17:7) with reference to the incident at Rephidim near Mount Horeb during the first or second year of the sojourn, when the Israelites murmured for water. (2) Again, the words were used (Numbers 14:11-23) when the spies returned from spying out the land and ten of the spies persuaded the people to refuse any attempt to enter the promised land. It was on this occasion, about two years after the exodus, when the people were revolting against the leadership of Moses and Aaron and were on the point of choosing a new leader who would take them back to Egypt, that God swore in His wrath the people then living would not enter the promised land (Numbers 14:23). (3) The word "provocation" (*meribah*) also appears at the time Moses disobeyed God and struck the rock at Kadesh-Barnea in the Wilderness of Zin during the 39th year of the Wilderness wanderings (Numbers 20:1-13). Which of these three incidents David had in mind as he wrote Psalm 95 is a question on which expositors are not wholly agreed.[36] Whichever incident we pick, the point is this: What happened in the wilderness wandering was on the verge of happening again. At the time of the exodus and wilderness wanderings, God was tested and provoked by the Israelites. Four hundred years later, when the Psalmist (David) wrote, his own contemporary generation of Israelites was again on the verge of testing and provoking God, and David warned them against such a course lest disaster should overtake them in turn. A millennium later, the writer of Hebrews tries to impress the same warning on his own generation of people.

3:9 -- "WHERE YOUR FATHERS TRIED *ME* BY TESTING *ME* -- "Where" refers to the "wilderness" (verse 8). The wilderness wanderings were the scene of numerous miracles by God, yet the people frequently "tried"[37] God anew, "testing" Him[38] to see if He would do anything about their unbelief. They may not have realized it, but they were putting God's patience on trial, as if they were experimenting to see how much it was possible for God to bear.

---

[35] "Provoked" (or "embittered") translates the Hebrew *meribah*, and "trial" (or temptation) translates the Hebrew word *massah*. The Greek word *peirasmos* also has a double meaning, "trial" (test) or "temptation." Israel's behavior provoked God (they weren't being faithful to Him), and their actions also tested or tempted Him to see if He would do anything.

[36] The whole question is of moment, only in that the decision made determines what comments are offered when explanations are given for certain of the phrases found in Psalm 95 -- such as "provocation" and "trial" and "forty years." In the comments we offer, we reflect the decision that the passage found in Numbers 14 was in David's mind as he wrote. Those who opt for the Exodus 17 passage, do so because the Greek of Psalms 95 (and Hebrews 3) is identical to that of the LXX at Exodus 17. Those who opt for the incident at Kadesh, do so because they believe the phrase "forty years" means the provocation David had in mind was one that occurred after 40 years of wandering.

[37] "Tried" in verse 9 is the same root word as "trial" in verse 8. In spite of all His care and guidance, it seems the people were constantly demanding of God a new demonstration (*dokimazo*, proof, test) that He would honor His promises to provide for them. Such crass behavior borders on insult to God.

[38] As the italics indicate, there is no word for "Me" in the Greek. This opens up the alternative possibility that "My works" in the latter part of the verse is the object of both verbs "tried" and "saw." The verse would then read "Your fathers tried (tempted) ... and saw My works ...."

"AND SAW MY WORKS FOR FORTY YEARS -- What "works" did David have in mind when he wrote this? It seems probable, in this context that provides the readers a warning, that "works" refers to God's judgments upon the disobedient people. They soon learned God does not let disobedience go unpunished.[39] In this verse, the writer of Hebrews puts "forty years" with the word "saw", quantifying how long they saw God's works and yet continued to try Him. Yet in verse 17, the writer does what is found in the Psalm – he puts the "forty years" with the following verb, making it tell how long God was angry with them.[40] Israel's faithlessness was no passing thing, and God's anger was no passing thing. It went on for forty years!

3:10 -- "THEREFORE I WAS ANGRY WITH THIS GENERATION -- The word translated "angry" means to be displeased with, to loath, to be disgusted, to reject, abhor, repudiate.[41] God was offended by the actions of unbelieving Israel.[42] Hebrew readers, are you listening? God is offended by people who harden their hearts and "provoke" and "try" Him. Do you still think it wise to turn away from Jesus when such actions are patently offensive to God and make Him angry?

"AND SAID, `THEY ALWAYS GO ASTRAY IN THEIR HEART -- God's assessment of what He saw in Israel's behavior was a constant wandering or going astray in their thinking.[43] The verb is passive voice in the Greek. Someone else (the devil?) was always leading them astray, leading them aside from the right way. Someone else was always planting erring thoughts in their minds.

AND THEY DID NOT KNOW MY WAYS' -- "Know" can sometimes have the connotation approve. If that is the idea here, then what is indicated is that after they were led astray, they no longer approved or loved what God wanted (i.e., God's ways). "Know" can also have the connotation of acknowledge. Once they were led astray in their thoughts, Israel no longer acknowledged God's ways.

---

[39] That "works" refers to God's judgments seems better than the suggestion that it refers to the continuing evidences God gave the Jews in the wilderness that He was guiding, caring for, and regularly present with them.

[40] Kent offers an intriguing explanation of why the writer of Hebrews, at verse 9, changes the word order found in both the Hebrew and LXX of Psalm 95. "The reason for this change of position is not known. One good possibility is that the writer was conscious of a parallel in years between the forty years of Israel's rebellion in the wilderness and approximately the same period that had now elapsed since the rejection of Christ in AD 30." For forty years the generation in the wilderness tempted God and ultimately missed the Promised Land. Will the Hebrew readers, forty years after Calvary, turn back in their hearts "to Egypt," and thus miss the heavenly promised land? The parallel would provide the readers an opportunity for sober reflection.

[41] We should not miss the reference to the anger of God. The Bible is very clear that God is not impassive or indifferent in the face of human sin. Our God is a "consuming fire" (Hebrews 12:29). His inevitable reaction to unrepented sin is wrath.

[42] "Generation" (*dor*, Hebrew) means clan or race, and sometimes those living at a particular place at a particular time, or those who have the characteristics of a particular age. Here it refers to the wilderness "generation" – the people who lived at that time and had those characteristics that angered God. The writer's own explanation of "generation" is found in verse 17, where we are told it was "those who sinned, whose bodies fell in the wilderness."

[43] "Heart" as used in the Bible does not signify the emotions (as the word tends to signify with us), but stands for the whole inner being -- thoughts, will, feelings. Often the emphasis is on the mind or thoughts. When we remember that this paragraph began with an exhortation to "think right about Jesus" ("Holy brethren ... consider Jesus!"), we are reminded that thinking is important. As a man thinks in his heart, so is he.

3:11 -- "AS I SWORE IN MY WRATH -- To "swear" means to take a solemn oath. It is as though God said, "As long as I live ... they shall not[44] enter!" The seriousness with which God viewed Israel's sin is shown by the fact that God took an oath as He made this threat. And we should not miss the fact that God made this oath when He was wrathful. "Wrath"[45] is a holy God's settled indignation and vigorous opposition to all that is evil. God is not passive when He sees sin; He does care and is bothered when men sin. Sin stirs His Holy indignation and He springs into energetic action to see that the sin is properly recompensed.

"THEY SHALL NOT ENTER MY REST" -- The historical occasion when God swore to exclude the Israelites from entering the promised land was at Kadesh-Barnea, just after the spies returned (see comments at Hebrews 3:8). As David writes Psalm 95, his words are based on Numbers 14:28-30. The word "rest" is not part of Numbers 14,[46] but it is part of Psalm 95:11. As the following verses in Hebrews 3 and 4 will show, "rest" included more than just entrance into the promised land.

3:12 -- Take care, brethren -- Now that the Scripture from Psalm 95 has been called to the readers' minds, the writer of Hebrews will make application of certain key expressions found in the Psalm. The readers are being warned about a possible fate similar (or worse) to that which befell the Israelites during their pilgrimage to the promised land. "Take care" is a present imperative; taking care or taking heed is something the brethren must do constantly. Each believer must constantly monitor his own spiritual condition.

Lest there should be in any one of you an evil, unbelieving heart -- "Heart", as in verse 10, has to do with what a person is thinking. One's thoughts become "evil"[47] if he permits unbelief to be the guiding and controlling idea in his mind.[48] Wrong deeds result from a wrong heart, for "out of [the heart] are the issues of life" (Proverbs 4:23, KJV).

---

[44] In the Greek, the actual words of the oath are "If they shall enter into My rest." This is an elliptical form of the Hebrew negative oath. Such "if clauses" were regularly prefaced or concluded with some statement calling on God. Something like, 'If they shall enter into my rest, then my name is not God!' The obvious meaning is, 'They shall *not* enter.' The same construction is found in Hebrews 4:3 & 5 as the words of the oath are repeated.

[45] Here the Greek word is *orge*, a different word than was used in verse 10 for "angry" (*prosochthisa)*. "Wrath" may not be the perfect word to express one of God's attitudes or actions, for with men, "wrath" implies a lack of self-control and sinful actions, neither of which is true of God. But the word "wrath" also does bring out the idea of God's passionate opposition to evil and His active concern for the right.

[46] While the exact word "rest" does not appear in Numbers 14, it is clear that entrance into the promised land of Canaan was one thing God was denying to that generation of Israel. See what Numbers 14:23,30, and 35 say. "Rest" (*katapausis*) is part of the text of Psalm 95, and it is obvious that "rest" and "promised land" were somehow synonymous. This is corroborated by Deuteronomy 12:9,10, where just before Israel crosses the Jordan River into the promised land, it is said "you are not yet come into the *rest* and inheritance ... but when you go over Jordan, and dwell in the *land* ...." Three passages in Joshua (21:44, 22:4, and 23:1) also show "rest" and "entrance into the promised land" were vitally related.

[47] "Evil" translates *poneros*. The unbeliever, not content with just being bad (*kakos*), does something worse (*poneros*). He tries to drag others into perdition also; he tends to lead others into the same evil.

[48] The KJV reads "an evil heart of unbelief," which is how the Greek also reads ("unbelief" is in the genitive case). This genitive construction can be interpreted in two different ways: it could say the unbelief causes the heart to become evil, or it could say the unbelief is caused by the evil heart. (Cp. the NIV's "sinful, unbelieving heart".) Those who believe Scripture teaches an inherited sinful nature prefer the latter explanation. It is often said by those who believe this way that a man sins because he is a sinner (i.e., a born sinner). The NASB's

In falling away from the living God -- This is one behavior that can issue from an evil heart of unbelief. When the thoughts become evil, men then fall away or rebel against[49] deity. We suppose that "living God" in this passage is a reference to Jesus, rather than to the Father.[50] Perhaps they are reminded that the God with whom they have to do is not a dead idol but a living, eternal, all-powerful being. To call Him the "living God" is intended to impress upon them that God is not dead. What He did in the past, He can and will still do. When He sees unbelief, He punishes it; when He sees faithfulness, He rewards it.[51] Hebrew readers, are you listening? To abandon Jesus and Christianity in favor of returning to the religion of the Old Testament is tantamount to apostasy[52] from God!

3:13 -- But encourage one another day after day – Each reader of this Hebrews letter is to be a daily, habitual encourager of his brethren. When a church member sees another church member, he should give a word of help, a word of exhortation, or a word of encouragement to the other to be true to Jesus! Christians are to be mutually helpful to each other.[53]

---

choice of the former interpretation is the better choice for it is more agreeable with what was said about Israel in verse 10. Israel's going astray in heart was their own action, not the result of an inborn sinful nature. In a passage where Christians are being dissuaded from similar action, the "heart" must work the same way. Unbelief is the thing that makes the heart evil.

[49] "Falling away" may be too weak a translation, for *aphistemi* denotes something more positively deliberate than the English words "falling away" convey. A fall can be an accident, but turning away or apostasy is not. ("Apostasy" is a regular translation of *aphistemi*. Apostasy is defined as the act of someone who has previously subscribed to a certain belief, and who now renounces his former professed belief in favor of some other which is diametrically opposed to what he believed before.) Rebellion comes closer to catching the idea in *aphistemi*. What the Israelites did at Kadesh-Barnea was a deliberate repudiation of the leadership of Moses and Aaron, and in effect a revolt against God. When the Hebrews repudiate the Apostle and High Priest of their confession, similarly appointed by God, that is an even more outrageous revolt against the living God than what Israel did.

[50] Jesus has been called "God" already in Hebrews, so it would not be out of place if verse 12 refers to Jesus when it says "living God." If, however, the reference is to the Father, then we have an idea in Hebrews similar to what we find in John's Gospel, where it is recorded Jesus personally said that people who hate Him, hate the Father also (John 15:23). Jesus also said that men who do not honor the Son, do not honor the Father either (John 5:23). See also John 8:42, 12:26 and 44-45.

[51] When the case of Israel in the wilderness is compared to the case of the unbelieving Hebrews, this is the message: Beware, brethren, of an evil unbelieving heart, such as the Israelites had in the wilderness, lest like them you too apostatize from the living God, and perish on your way to the promised land. Milligan calls attention to three things that are clearly implied in the words of our text: (1) The Hebrew Christians were in danger of apostatizing from the living God, as their fathers had done. (If so, it follows a Christian may fall from grace. Cp. Heb. 6:4-6.) (2) This danger arises wholly from an evil heart of unbelief. (So long as we have unwavering trust in Jesus, all is well!) (3) Every Christian may, through the grace of God, avoid the dangers of apostasy, by keeping his heart with all diligence (Proverbs 4:23).

[52] One can imagine the readers protesting. They were thinking of leaving Jesus, yes; but they were not about to become atheists, they would affirm. "We will still be worshipping God!" they would stoutly maintain. This whole pretense is shattered by the reminder of what Jesus Himself said while here on earth (John 8:47; 10:27, 12:44,45). To reject Jesus was to demonstrate an unbelieving heart that did not know God at all. In the letter writer's presentation thus far, this much has been shown: It is impossible for a man to turn his back upon the highest revelation God has given (i.e., the Son, 1:2ff) and yet possess a true faith in God. When a man repudiates Jesus, he also repudiates God.

[53] Christianity is not merely a private matter between a man and God. Christianity also has corporate implications. Christians may not live in splendid isolation from fellow believers and still fulfill the command found in Hebrews 3:13. When men are alone, they are liable to succumb to subtle temptations that press on them from so many sides. But if they come together regularly for mutual encouragement, if they encourage each

As long as it is *still* called "Today" -- The word "today" is picked up from Psalm 95:7, in order to add a touch of urgency to the imperatives "take care" and "encourage one another." Swift action is needed because "today" does not last forever. The present opportunity the readers have to strengthen each other's faith would soon be gone.[54]

Lest any one of you be hardened by the deceitfulness of sin – The reason for the encouragement was that one of their group (or more than one – the pronoun "any one" is indefinite) might be hardened by the deceitfulness of sin. When a man's heart is "hardened," his spiritual sensitivities are dulled.[55] Before such hardening occurs, much exhortation is needed to gain the upper hand on sin. Sin is deceptive;[56] it promises more than it performs and its dire effects are not usually seen at once. Sin is attractive on the outside, and corrupt within. Appearing to be wise, it blinds men to the truth. Offering promises of gain, it leads inexorably to ruin. George Mark Elliott used to say, "All of Satan's worms have hooks in them!" and "Sin cuts the optic nerve of the soul." It seems likely, in this context, that the arguments[57] presented to the minds of the Christians why it would be wise to abandon Christianity and go back to Judaism are what are called "the deceitfulness of sin." The deceit is so plausible, the mind becomes insensitive to the heinous nature of the act (i.e., by such an act you are falling away from the living God).

3:14 -- For we have become partakers of Christ -- Verse 14 gives a reason why daily encouragement of our brothers to be faithful (verse 13) is so vitally important.[58] Reflecting on our position[59] in Christ[60] will show it is a position to be maintained at whatever effort.

---

other whenever they happen to meet, the devotion of all will be kept warm and their common hope will be in less danger of flickering and dying. What verse 13 calls for is a helpful concern for fellow Christians, and an active involvement in each other's lives. Such help is to be day after day, for the problem that encouragement is intended to overcome exists daily.

[54] See notes at 3:8 for the meaning of the word "Today." The opportunities the Hebrew Christians would have to help one another stay true to Jesus would last but a few more years, and then the congregation at Jerusalem would be scattered as they fled the city to escape the destruction the Romans would wreak on the city (Matthew 24:15ff).

[55] See "hardening" of the heart explained in notes on Hebrews 3:8.

[56] "Deceitfulness" translates *apate*, a word that means trick, stratagem. If sin were always seen in its true aspect when a man is tempted, that sin would be so hateful that he would flee from it with the utmost abhorrence.

[57] The temporary advantages (e.g., easing of social pressures from their Jewish neighbors, and so on) would be made to seem of much more practical importance than the theological implications and the eternal consequences of such a move. One trick the devil uses is to get men to think that temporal and physical safety are more important than spiritual welfare.

[58] Or, perhaps, "for" connects verse 14 to verse 12. If so, it gives a reason for constant watchfulness on each believer's part. "Take care ... for we have become partakers of Christ, if we hold fast ...."

[59] The perfect tense verb translated "we have become" implies a past act with present continuing results. At their conversion they first became partakers with Christ. They continue to share those same privileges if only they do not sever the relationship between Him and themselves. The word translated "partakers" is the same word used in the quotation from Psalm 45:6 (quoted at Hebrews 1:9, where it is rendered "companions") and is the same word used at Hebrews 2:14 and 3:1.

[60] There is some question concerning the proper translation of the genitive construction "of Christ." It could be "in Christ" or "with Christ" or "of Christ." "Of Christ" would emphasize the believers' communion with Him. "With Christ" (NEB, TEV, JB) would emphasize the glory He has won for believers. "In Christ" (NIV, RSV, Mof-

If we hold fast the beginning of our assurance firm until the end -- Continuing in the wonderful partnership with Christ that began in the past is qualified or conditional.[61] "The beginning of our assurance" is likely the assurance or confidence[62] the readers had in Jesus at the time of their conversion. The readers must hold fast to this assurance "until the end"[63] if they would continue to be partakers of Christ.

3:15 -- While it is said -- The NASB translators connect verse 15 with the preceding verses, making verse 15 an explanation of how long "hold[ing] fast ... until the end" (verse 14) lasts. It lasts as long as it can be said, "Today, if you hear his voice ...." On this view, the Hebrew writer takes the words of Psalm 95:7 and makes them part of his own entreaty to his readers. He begs them to take care lest they harden their hearts just like Israel hardened theirs in the wilderness. Other translators would start a new sentence with verse 15, supposing verse 15 begins a second[64] pointed application[65] of Psalm 95 to the readers, showing that what happened to the wilderness generation was not a one-time fluke. If his Hebrew readers likewise demonstrate unbelief, they, too, will perish during their pilgrimage and be excluded from "rest."

---

fatt) would emphasize the idea of spiritual unity with Jesus. Whichever one we opt for, the context is stressing the wonderful privilege it is to be a Christian, something not to be lightly discarded.

[61] At Hebrews 3:6, we had a similar condition stated. Scripture everywhere emphasizes the need for man's voluntary cooperation with God in the matter of salvation and continuing security. Faithfulness, or continuing to believe, is ever the condition of salvation, whether initial salvation or continuing salvation.

[62] The word translated "confidence" at verse 6 was *paressia*. The word here translated "assurance" is *hupostasis*. *Hupostasis* means literally that which stands under, and so, here, emphasizes the ground or basis of hope, that which undergirds the Christian's profession. Have the readers forgotten the evidences that convinced them that Jesus was the Christ, the Son of the living God? They must be forgetting the basis or reason for their earlier confession, else why would they now be giving consideration to quitting Jesus?

(See the comments at Hebrews 11:1, where the word *hupostasis* occurs again, where we are told that "faithfulness" is the "assurance" [or "title deed"] of things not seen.)

(See also the special study on the "Faith that Saves" in the author's *Commentary on Acts*. There it is affirmed that the faith that saves is made up of four parts -- knowledge, assent, *confidence*, and obedience. Hebrews 3:6 and 14 are two places where the "confidence" or "assurance" part is set forth.)

[63] "Faithful unto death" (i.e., faithfulness even if it costs you your physical life) is the condition Jesus Himself required of men who wished to receive a "crown of life" (Revelation 2:10). To begin the Christian life well is good, but it is not enough. It is only those who stay the course and finish the race that have any hope of gaining the prize. The Israelites made a good beginning when they crossed the Red Sea, and praised God for their deliverance. But the good beginning was not matched by their later behavior, and they failed to enter the promised land. That very lesson the Hebrews need to hear! The Bible does teach the security of believers, but only if they continue to be believers. Whether or not these Hebrews reached the "promised land" was conditioned upon their holding fast the beginning of their assurance to the end.

[64] The first application focused on the word "today" (see verse 13).

[65] Three matters of a technical nature make it difficult to decide what comments to make on verse 15. (1) One has to do with the connection of verse 15 to its context. Other ideas, besides those given in the textual comments above, have been proposed to explain the connection of verse 15 to its context. Some connect verse 15 with verse 13 (making verse 14 a parenthesis). Others would connect verse 15 with the beginning of chapter 4 (making verses 16-19 a parenthesis). In our comments we shall opt for the view that the writer quotes a portion of the Psalm again, before drawing attention to certain additional features found in that passage – features also applicable to the Hebrew readers. (2) The second is, how shall we translate the Greek word *tines* that occurs in the first part of verse 16? Shall we treat it as an indefinite relative ("some") or as an interrogative pronoun ("who?")? (3) If we translate *tines* as "who?" how shall we explain the "for" (*gar*) that begins verse 16?

"TODAY IF YOU HEAR HIS VOICE, DO NOT HARDEN YOUR HEARTS, AS WHEN THEY PROVOKED ME" -- Psalm 95:7-11 has already been quoted in Hebrews 3:7-11. The writer now repeats a portion, asking his readers some questions about the meaning of the whole passage, and then (verse 19) making the point he wants to be sure his readers do not miss.

3:16 -- For who provoked *Him* when they had heard? -- We believe the wording and punctuation of the NASB is superior to what is found in the KJV at this place.[66] The NASB makes verses 16-18 a series of questions and answers, with the second question in verses 16 and 17 being the answer to the first.[67] This first question of verse 16 asks the readers to recall who it was the Psalmist says provoked[68] God.

Indeed, did not all those who came out of Egypt *led* by Moses? -- The writer answers his first question with a question, this one so phrased as to expect a "Yes" answer.[69] Yes, it was the very ones who came out of Egypt!   The people[70] (as they came out of Egypt through the

---

[66] The KJV translators treated *tines* as an indefinite relative pronoun ("some"), making it read "For *some*, when they had heard, did provoke." The second half of the verse in the KJV ("howbeit not all that came out of Egypt by Moses" was thought to be a reference to Caleb and Joshua (the two good spies) who did not provoke God, and who did get to enter the promised land. Kent (p.76) objects to the interpretation given to the passage by the KJV: "It is a bit strange to call six hundred thousand men merely 'some,' when the defection was complete with only two exceptions." He also calls attention to the thrust of the present context which is not to show that some were not guilty, but rather that the provocation was wholesale. For reasons such as these, we suppose the NASB translators are correct when they take *tines* as an interrogative pronoun ("who?").

[67] R. Milligan (*op. cit.*, p.127) has included a brief history of the use of punctuation marks and accent marks in the Greek language. (The difference between "some" and "who?" for *tines* rests wholly on where the word was accented. Since we cannot be sure how the autograph would have been accented, the use of question marks by the NASB is, therefore, a matter of interpretation.) About 240 BC Aristophanes introduced at Alexandria an imperfect system of accents and punctuation marks, for use by teachers and scholars of rhetoric. The accent marks were intended to reproduce on paper what previously had been done for years by tone of voice as the teacher helped pupils memorize. The teacher spoke the text and the pupil tried to reproduce the exact words and the exact tone or pitch he heard in the voice of the teacher. Accent marks in written texts were not generally used by Christian writers until after the middle of the 5th century AD, and not until the beginning of the 10th century did the custom of using them become universal. In the mid-5th century, Euthalius, a deacon of Alexandria, divided the New Testament into lines (*stichoi*), each line containing as many words as were to be read without any pause or interruption of the voice. In the 8th century, the use of the comma (,) was introduced, and in the 9th century, the use of the Greek question mark (;) was introduced into the written Greek texts. The present system of Greek punctuation was universally adopted by Greek scholars after the invention of printing in the mid-15th century. So, the accents and punctuation marks we find in current use are additions to the text made by men. Thus, when men make translations, they have a certain right to change what they find in modern printed Greek texts without any accusation being leveled against them that they are changing the Word of God. The Word of God, when first written, did not have any punctuation or accent marks.

[68] "Provoke" translates the verb *parapikraino*, the same verb found in verses 8 and 15. It means to incite to bitter feelings, or to exacerbate, or to exasperate. When a man tempts God, that action promotes strong feelings in God!

[69] In order for the NASB translators to treat both parts of verse 16 as a question, two things must be assumed. One is that *gar* which begins the first phrase must be treated as an exclamatory use of the word, rather than giving it its usual explanatory idea. The other is that *alla* which begins the second phrase must be treated as confirmatory rather than giving it its usual strong adversative meaning. (The KJV translators do give both terms their usual meaning. See footnote #66, above.)

[70] "All" in "all those who came out of Egypt" takes no notice of Joshua and Caleb, but the number of exceptions to "all" is so negligible that the argument is not invalidated. Even though men are at first the recipients of God's great blessings, if He finds unfaithfulness later in their lives, His treatment of those who fall

intermediate agency[71] of Moses) made a good start, only to end up provoking God. In a like manner, the Hebrew readers had made a good start when they first confessed Jesus. Will they, too, now end up provoking God?

3:17 -- And with whom was He angry for forty years? -- The second of this series of three questions is intended to highlight just what the sin was, which those very people committed, which made God angry. The "forty years" covers the duration of the wilderness wanderings after the children of Israel came out of Egypt. The passage seems to say God's anger was aroused over and over again during that whole 40-year period.[72]

Was it not with those who sinned -- The Greek employs *ouchi*, the emphatic negative adverb, in this place. It is not just a "yes" answer that is expected, but an emphatic "yes". There is no doubt the expected answer is yes! There is no doubt it was sin that made God angry. The sin the people committed in the wilderness – the sin that is the topic of discussion here in Hebrews (as in Psalm 95) – is the matter of unbelief so as to fall away from the living God.[73]

Whose bodies fell in the wilderness? -- Instead of entering the promised land, those sinners died and their bodies were scattered here and there all over the wilderness. The temporal punishment for the unbelief of Israel is given in words reminiscent of Numbers 14:29,32. Just as God prophesied would happen (the Numbers passage uses future tense verbs), the Hebrew writer affirms did indeed happen.

3:18 -- And to whom did He swear that they should not enter His rest -- This third question in the series, reminding the readers of the concluding portion of Psalm 95:11, is intended to drive into their consciousness exactly what led to the sin that resulted in those same peoples' being excluded from entrance into rest.

---

away is uniformly consistent. "All" who become unfaithful are excluded from "rest" (verse 19 will affirm). There are no exceptions where unfaithfulness is concerned.

[71] The Greek translated "*led* by Moses" is *dia* and a genitive case, a construction that indicates an intermediate agent who acts on someone else's behalf. (*Hupo* and the genitive [sometimes *en* and the dative] express actual agent.) Moses was but an intermediate agent, a servant (Hebrews 3:5), working on behalf of the Son and the Father.

[72] God's "anger" and God's "wrath" were explained in comments on verses 10 and 11. We've earlier noticed that God was "provoked" on at least three different occasions, from the opening stages to the close of the wilderness wanderings. See notes at Hebrews 3:8. The wrath of God is not something that happens just once, and then one need not worry about it being aroused again. It happened throughout the whole wilderness period. Hebrew readers, are you listening? It can and does get aroused still. Don't be deceived into thinking that what happened years earlier during the wilderness wanderings cannot happen again.

[73] To say those who perished were "those who sinned" does not imply that Joshua and Caleb were sinless perfect (for all men have sinned, Romans 3:23). It only says Joshua and Caleb were not guilty of the particular sin which excluded the others of their generation from the promised land.

But to those who were disobedient? -- There is no other explanation for those peoples' failure except disobedience.[74]   When the generation in Moses' day went "astray in their heart" and "did not know [God's] ways," it was not due to ignorance or lack of information. They had the miracles at the time of the exodus and in the wilderness. They had God's faithful servant Moses telling them God's will. They had the witness of Joshua and Caleb. Their refusal to go where God was leading was a clear case of disobedience. Disobedience, and not anything else, was the reason they were excluded from the promised land. Hebrew readers, are you listening? Did you hear the word "disobedient"? Is the disobedience you are contemplating now as attractive as it formerly was?

3:19 -- And *so* we see that they were not able to enter because of unbelief -- With this conclusion the readers are certain to agree, once they have thought through what the Psalmist said about the behavior of the wilderness generation. Their exclusion from the promised land was not the fault of circumstances over which they had no control, nor was it due to God's intransigence.   They simply failed to meet the conditions God had revealed were His expectations. What was called disobedience in verse 18 is called "unbelief"[75] in verse 19. It is the direct testimony of the Old Testament that disobedience (i.e., unbelief) was the reason they were excluded from the promised land. Chapter four will go on to make the point that what happened to Israel in the days before the cross can also happen to Christians on this side of the cross. There is eternal rest, and people who through unbelief[76] abandon Christianity will find themselves excluded from that rest just as surely as Israel was excluded from the promised land!

---

[74] The verb *apeitho*, translated "disobedience," literally means a stubborn refusal to be persuaded. They would not listen to reason; they were stiff necked and obstinate. The word also includes rebellious action that results from the wrong-headedness. Psalm 95 testified they hardened their hearts, they went astray in their hearts, they did not approve (know) of God's ways. They tested God. All these actions are summed up in the word "disobedience."

[75] Special attention should be given to the juxtaposition of "unbelief" and "disobedient" within this passage. This passage, like John 3:36, shows the close relation in the New Testament between "faith" and "obedience" on the one hand, and "unbelief" and "disobedience" on the other hand. The only way the words "unbelief" and "disobedient" can be treated as synonyms, is if "faith" and "obedience" are also synonymous.

[76] In the Greek, the last word in this paragraph is "unbelief." This word order throws emphasis on "unbelief." *Unbelief.* Think on it; pause, and let that word "*unbelief*" sink into your consciousness. How some can teach unconditional eternal security when we have such passages as this teaching the need for faithfulness, this commentator cannot understand. Just rehearse what the writer of Hebrews has called to our attention in this series of questions (verses 16-19).

- *Warnings and exhortations with respect to the promised "rest."*
  4:1-13.

4:1 -- Therefore -- The following portion of the warning is based on the clear example of what happened to Israel of old. The Israelites experienced God's deliverance from Egypt and heard Him speak the Law at Sinai. But those initial experiences did not keep them from dying in the wilderness or guarantee their safe arrival in Canaan. The point of the historical record is now made plain to the readers of Hebrews. They too had been delivered from bondage (the bondage of sin), and they too were on the way to the heavenly promised land. Like Joshua and Caleb, the readers will be welcomed into the promised land, if they remain obedient believers.

Let us fear -- The "fear" the writer asks of himself and his readers is fear of the consequences of apostasy.[1] Sober and thoughtful men are diligent to avoid a danger when they solemnly recognize that danger for what it is.

While a promise remains of entering His rest -- With these words, the writer takes up the word "rest" found in Psalm 95:11, and thereby introduces the topic that will be the point of discussion through much of chapter 4 – namely, that there was more to God's promise of "rest" than simply entering into and living in the land of Canaan. The Hebrew readers, themselves living in the very land promised to Moses and the children of Israel, still have another promised "rest"[2] to look forward to – a "rest" from which they too are in danger of being excluded if they exhibit the same kind of unbelief Israel did. This "rest" is called God's rest ("His rest") because He presently enjoys it (an idea developed in verse 4), and it is something He bestows or confers on given conditions.

Lest any one of you should seem to have come short of it -- This is the danger about which verse 1 inculcates a healthy fear. Where the NASB has "seem," other translations have "be found" or "be judged."[3] If these other translations are accepted, the passage is talking about

---

[1] Men who have a proper fear of God (Hebrews 12:28ff) need fear none else (Hebrews 13:6).

[2] There are a variety of grammatical constructions found with "promise" in the Greek. Sometimes a genitive case following the word "promise" denotes the one who makes the promise, as in Romans 4:20. Sometimes when a genitive case follows "promise," it denotes the one to whom the promise is made, as in Romans 15:8. Sometimes the genitive following denotes the thing promised, as in Hebrews 9:15. Hebrews 4:1 seems to be the only place an infinitive following the word "promise" is intended to give the content of the promise. The word "promise" is used more times in Hebrews than in any other New Testament book (14 times in Hebrews; Galatians is next with 10 occurrences of the word "promise"). God's promises mean much to the writer, and he wants God's promises to mean much to the readers. It should also be noted that no article occurs with "promise" in this place; this is significant, showing that the reference is not to some specific promise to Israel during the exodus (i.e., it does not read "*the* promise"), but to something which has the same character but is not absolutely identical. The promised "rest" for Christians is not absolutely identical with the "rest" promised to Israel after the exodus.

[3] The verb *dokeo* is capable of many translations, such as "think, suppose, or to have an opinion." It can be used intransitively (which is the construction found here in Hebrews 4:1) to express another's opinion, in which case it may be rendered "to seem, to be accounted, to be reputed." When used impersonally, it can have the meaning of "think, or judge" or "be pleased with or to determine." (Thayer's *Lexicon*, p.154. Arndt-Gingrich *Lexicon*, p.200-201.) Moffatt points out that a meaning like "judge" or "adjudge" is also attested in some passages in Josephus, the LXX, and in Attic Greek.

God's judgment[4] upon unbelief. Just as the wilderness generation was judged and excluded from the promised rest, so, too, possible exclusion from rest is a real danger[5] to the readers of this Hebrew letter. For once God's decision to exclude is made, it is a permanent decision.[6]

4:2 -- For indeed -- The parallel between the Israelites in the Old Testament and the people of God in this Christian age is close enough for the disaster[7] that befell the former to serve as a warning to the latter.

We have had good news preached to us, just as they also -- "We" includes the writer and his Christian readers; "they" refers to the generation that came out of Egypt and perished in the wilderness. The "good news"[8] both have heard is the welcome and gladdening news that a "rest" awaits the people of God.

---

[4] Just as God's decision to exclude Israel from the promised land was something that happened in time, and did not refer to the time of final judgment, so we suppose God's decision on unbelief (disobedience, apostasy) in the Christian age is something that happens in time, and that He does not wait till the final judgment before He makes such a judgment. The New Testament does seem to suggest that God "judges" men's actions every day -- not just at the final judgment. (See 1 Peter 1:17, Romans 3:24 and 4:24, where "justified" and "reckoned" are present tense verbs, indicating continuing action).

[5] The student should be careful at this place, for some versions and most commentators will choose the "translation" for *dokeo* that best harmonizes with what they think the Scripture says elsewhere on the matter of the security of the believer. If they have chosen to defend the doctrine of unconditional eternal security, then this verse will be explained in some way so as to not contradict that cherished doctrine (e.g., the believers mistakenly "think" they may have come short, but of course, we know they have not). Kent's attempt (p.79) to avoid contradicting the doctrine of eternal security is almost convincing. "No one should be misled into thinking that he has come short of God's rest by following Christ alone apart from the Old Testament ritual. The problem was that some of the readers were contemplating a return to Judaism on the false assumption that Christianity was not itself sufficient. They thought they had fallen short unless they resumed all the rites and ceremonies of the Old Testament system. The writer wants to make it clear that this is not so." Kent's explanation has these objections against it: (1) it ignores "therefore" with which verse 1 begins, and by which chapter 4 is shown to be a continuation of the previous warning statement. (Before the translation "think" can be accepted, it must be decided that Hebrews 4:1 does not continue the warning of chapter 3, but instead serves as the thesis of the new section to follow.) (2) "Let us fear" is hardly the same as "Don't be misled." (3) The approach of again emphasizing Law-keeping does not fit what is said in verse 2 about "united by faith." (4) It is not likely that the Hebrew readers are that enamored with the old Judaizing doctrine. (We have seen no evidence that "Judaizer" and "Hebrew" are interchangeable terms.)

Those who believe the Scriptures teach a conditional security may opt for "seem" as the translation for *dokeo* and then explain that the writer of Hebrews recognizes he was not the final judge. While it might "seem" to him they had come short, such a decision was ultimately the prerogative of almighty God.

[6] The verb "come short of" (*husterekenai*) is perfect tense in the Greek, which points to a permanent condition. It is a past action with present continuing results.

[7] "For" with which verse 2 begins shows that verse 2 is connected with something just said in verse 1. Either verse 2 is connected with "let us fear" and gives a reason for "fearing," or it is connected with "judged to come short" and gives the reason why some were so judged. The notes offered on the text assume the second option is the correct one.

[8] Where the NASB has "good news," the KJV reads "gospel." Now the word "gospel" literally means "good news." However, the problem with the KJV is that it leaves the impression the same message of salvation was preached to Israel as what Christians now call "the gospel." (See footnote #14 in chapter 2 for further information concerning the preaching of the gospel in the Old Testament dispensation.) Instead, what was preached to both groups (and what is the topic of this context) is the good news that there is a "rest" (a promised land, a heaven) available.

But the word they heard did not profit them -- Both groups heard "good news."[9] Both groups were expected to act upon it. But the generation that came out of Egypt failed to act upon the good news, and thus did not profit from the message heard. If they had been faithful and entered the promised land, then it could be said they profited from the word they heard.

Because it was not united by faith in those who heard -- Here we learn they were expected to act[10] on what they heard. That very failure to act is what resulted in their exclusion from the "rest" God had promised them. Here is another place in the Bible where it is rather plain that "faith comes from hearing ... the word of Christ."[11] This is the first time the writer of Hebrews has used the word "faith," a term he will employ more than 30 times[12] before the epistle is finished.[13] Here the word points to the right response to the "good news" they heard.

4:3 -- For -- Now the writer sets out to show there is a heaven still awaiting Christians – that is (as verse 1 says), a "promise ... of entering His rest" still remains in effect.[14]

---

[9] The Greek reads "word of hearing," as the marginal note shows. The expression likely corresponds to "good news preached" in the first part of the verse.

[10] This is one passage where it is difficult to harmonize a teaching that "faith" is something God gives to a man and that man is wholly passive under the sovereign action of God, with what the Bible actually teaches. If "faith" is solely a gift of God, rather than a response man makes to what he hears, then the reason the Israelites failed to act properly so as to enter the promised land is God's fault, not theirs. Such a conclusion is monstrous and completely out of harmony with all that has been said by way of comment on Psalms 95.

[11] As the marginal note ("they were not united by faith with those who heard") shows, there is an interesting manuscript variation at this place. Some manuscripts (including P[13], P[46], A, B, C, D, and some minuscules) have the participle *sunkekerasmenous* in the accusative plural. The meaning is that the majority of the wilderness generation were not united in faith with Joshua and Caleb (the familiar, but as-yet unnamed, men who were faithful). While the great preponderance of manuscript evidence favors this reading, the whole context does not well agree with the interpretation that must be given to the words. Other manuscripts and versions (including Aleph, the old Latin, Syriac, Coptic, etc.) have the nominative singular *sunkekerasmenos*. This form would agree with "word" -- the "word of hearing" was not matched by faith on their parts. There are manuscript readings other than the accusative plural or nominative singular forms. In all probability, these numerous readings represent ancient attempts to heal a primitive corruption in the text. (G. Zuntz, The Text of the Epistles. London: Oxford Univ. Press, 1953, p.16.)

[12] By one count, the word "faith" occurs 243 times in the whole New Testament. Only Romans (where "faith" occurs 40 times) has more uses of the word than Hebrews.

[13] *Pistis*, the Greek word translated "faith," can also be translated "faithfulness" (see NASB at Matthew 23:13). It is more than mental assent. It includes obedience to what God has said. "Faith" is doing what God says. Further, it is not a one-time obedience; it is habitual, customary, and repeated obedience.

[14] The problem the writer of Hebrews faced was this – how to show his readers there is a "heaven" without appealing to any New Testament Scriptures. If you didn't have Revelation 21-22 and John 14 – verses we are very familiar with – how would you show there is such a "rest" in the future for the faithful Christian? Worded another way, with only verses from the Old Testament Scriptures to work with (which was perhaps all the Hebrews would listen to), where would you turn to prove "there is yet a rest for the people of God"? We'd have to go to some passages like the ones we are about to look at – passages you have to think about before you see their import and bearing on the subject.

We are about to be given an excellent lesson on one "How-To" of Bible study: do a word study, looking carefully at each of the passages where a certain word is used, in order to ascertain what the Scriptures say on that subject. Furthermore, at times the student must think about the passage for a while before its true import is understood. Remember, for example, what Jesus did one day. He appealed to a passage where it is said "I *am* the God of Abraham, Isaac, and Jacob" to prove life after death and the fact of a coming resurrection. It is a verse you have to think about before you see it. The same method Jesus used, we will find the writer of Hebrews using.

We who have believed enter that rest -- This is a categorical claim that believers in Christ will actually enter into God's rest. It does not say the entrance into rest is already accomplished; rather, that entrance into rest is something in the process of being attained.[15] It is something they might come short of (verse 1); it is something they should make every effort to enter (verse 11). It is believers[16] (faithful Christians) who now may enter God's rest, and these believers may be from any nationality. The promise of rest that still remains in effect is not limited just to members of physical Israel.

Just as He has said -- Once more the writer supports his position by an appeal to Scripture,[17] to the very passage from Psalm 95 that has been in the background since the middle of chapter 3. By analogy of Scripture, the meaning of the word "rest" that occurs in Psalm 95 is going to be unfolded (verses 4 to 8).

"AS I SWORE IN MY WRATH, THEY SHALL NOT ENTER MY REST" -- Here are the words from Psalm 95[18] that imply there is a "rest" which Christians may enter if they are faithful. If the readers will but think about the passage for a moment, they can see there remains a rest for the people of God. When David wrote Psalm 95, the new generation of the people of Israel was already in the promised land. Therefore, "rest" that Psalm 95 threatens exclusion from cannot be a reference to earthly Canaan. If the word "rest" in Psalm 95 is not a reference to Canaan, then it must speak of heaven.[19] If it speaks of heaven, then we see there is a "rest" still in the future for believers.

Although His works were finished from the foundation of the world -- The failure of a past generation to enter God's rest was not because no such rest was yet available; to the contrary, the Bible tells us God has been resting since the creation ("foundation")[20] of the world.[21]

---

[15] "We ... enter" ("we are entering") is a present tense verb. It is something those who believe are in the process of doing.

[16] The aorist participle "believed" looks back over the whole course of a man's life and says the predominant characteristic seen by God is belief. An aorist tense participle simply says the action of the participle precedes the action of the main verb. In other words, in this place, the believing took place before the entering.

[17] The writer of Hebrews here attributes the words of Psalm 95 to God; in verse 7, he attributes the authorship of Psalm 95 to David. Together, these two ideas affirm the inspiration of Psalm 95. Further, the perfect tense "said" puts emphasis on the permanence of what God has said. What God spoke in the past still stands.

[18] For an explanation of the actual wording found in Psalm 95:11, see footnote #44 on chapter 3.

[19] "My rest" in verse 3 is the same thing as "His rest" in verse 1.

[20] The writer did not use *ktisis*, the usual word for creation, but used *katabole*, which means "throw down." Some have thus attempted to render this "from the downfall of the world," thereby attempting to sustain the creation-ruination-recreation interpretation of Genesis 1:1,2. To put such an interpretation on Genesis 1 is unwarranted, and certainly is not needed simply in order to make the Bible record match the age that modern science claims for the universe (i.e., to allow millions of years between Genesis 1:1 and 1:2). (Milligan's acceptance of the idea of an "Adamic Renovation" following Genesis 1:2 is an interpretation not supported either by the Hebrew of Genesis 1 nor by Isaiah 45:18.) Rather, the same expression (*apo katabole kosmou*) is used regularly in the New Testament for the original creation (laying the foundations) of the world. See Hebrews 9:26; Matthew 13:35, 25:34; Luke 11:50; John 17:24; Ephesians 1:4; 1 Peter 1:20; Revelation 13:8, 17:8. The expression "foundation of the world" does not suggest that earth (*kosmos*) has some sort of foundation. "Casting down" or "throwing down" is a figurative expression meaning creation or the beginning of history.

[21] If the writer could have appealed to New Testament verses to make his point about "rest" being available

4:4 -- For He has thus said somewhere concerning the seventh *day* -- When a verse begins with "for," it often gives a reason for something just said. Verses 4 and 5 tie together two Old Testament texts[22] wherein a reason can be seen for what was just said; namely, that there is such a thing as "My (i.e., God's) rest," and that it is still available for people to enter.

"AND GOD RESTED ON THE SEVENTH DAY FROM ALL HIS WORKS" -- The first use of "rest"[23] in Scripture is Genesis 2:2. Since He finished the work of creating, God has been resting[24] from the work of creating.[25] His rest is one of satisfaction and enjoyment because of the sense of accomplishment and completion once the creating work was done.

4:5 -- And again in this *passage* -- Again the writer of Hebrews calls attention to the passage in Psalm 95:11, where the word "rest" occurs.

---

since the time of creation, he could have used Matthew 25:34, where Jesus says "Come, you who are blessed of My Father, inherit the kingdom prepared for you from the foundation of the world."

[22] The indefinite way these passages are cited should not cause concern. Westcott *(Epistle to the Hebrews,* p.96) cites examples from Philo and Clement of Rome to illustrate that such an indefinite way of introducing quotations was not at all uncommon. Kent (p.81) offers the opinion that the indefinite way the first quotation is introduced may be caused partly by the fact the words occur several times in the Old Testament, e.g. Genesis 2:2; Exodus 20:11, 31:17. There is another possibility. Before the Scriptures were divided into chapters and verses, locating a specific verse was not easy. Sometimes a title was given to the whole paragraph, such as "in the bush" (Luke 20:37). Unless it was important, there would be no reason to specify the location of the passage more precisely than is done here ("He has thus said somewhere"). The important thing about the two Old Testament passages here adduced as proof of "rest" is that God spoke the words in both.

[23] The LXX used *katapauo* ("rest") to translate the Hebrew verb *shabath* found in Genesis 2:2. The word *katapausis* (from the same root) is the word found at Psalm 95:11. So to tie together "rest" in Genesis 2:2 and "rest" in Psalm 95:11 is not as farfetched as it might seem.

[24] Some have supposed the Hebrew writer's use of "seventh day" supports the age-day theory for the length of the days in Genesis. The argument (in brief) is this: if God is still resting when Hebrews is written, then it still must be the "seventh day." Now since several thousand years have intervened between Genesis 2 and Hebrews 4, the "seventh day" must extend over a longer period than simply 24 hours. The age-day theory is another attempt to harmonize the Bible and the theories of modern science as to the age of the universe. The student who wishes to study such matters in detail is referred to Bernard Ramm, *The Christian View of Science and Scripture* (Grand Rapids: Eerdmans, 1955). While Ramm's progressive creationism may not be the whole answer, his presentation of the pros and cons of theistic evolution, flood geology, the ideal time view, the gap theory, serves as a good introduction to the whole study.

Kent's footnote (p.82) shows one way to explain the verse about the "seventh day" without having to revert to an age-day theory. Kent's argument is based on the fact that, while each of the first six days of creation were marked by the words "It was evening and morning, day one" (GLR's translation) or "..., day two," this formula "evening and morning" does not occur with the seventh day. "This does not imply that the seventh day was not a literal day with an evening and a morning, just as the previous days of creation. However, the author has used the silence of Scripture on this point to illustrate his argument that God's sabbath rest has never ended. The same method of argument is used in Hebrews 7:3 regarding Melchizedek's absence of recorded birth, parentage, or death."

[25] God's rest is not a rest of inactivity. The Biblical teaching about miracles and providence, as well as Jesus' statement that "My Father is working until now" (John 5:17), indicates that God, even though resting, had not ceased all activity. Nor is the statement that God rested till man sinned, and then went back to work to provide redemption, a wholly correct statement. It ignores His providential activities and the moving of history to a goal. (The Jews who constructed the "traditions of the elders" missed the fact that God's rest was not one of total inactivity. That is why they came up with the Sabbath laws they did, and why Jesus was able to show from Scripture that their interpretation was wrong.) Even in His rest, God is busy sustaining, revealing His will, reigning, forgiving, saving, punishing, matching the wiles of the devil, et al.

"THEY SHALL NOT ENTER MY REST" -- Genesis 2 speaks of God resting. Psalm 95:11, written years later, speaks of God's rest ("My rest"). Comparing these Old Testament passages where the same word appears indicates God is still enjoying His "rest" even in David's time. The next point the Hebrews writer makes will prove "rest" is still available this side of Calvary.

4:6 -- Since therefore it remains for some to enter it -- "It remains" means a promise of rest remains (as Hebrews 4:1 states).[26] With this phrase, the writer summarizes the argument made thus far (based on Psalm 95) before moving on to the next point.

And those who formerly had good news preached to them failed to enter because of disobedience -- God entered into rest thousands of years ago. All that time, He has not allowed *unbelievers* to join Him in enjoying that rest. (Think, for example, of the generation that perished in the wilderness because of unbelief, Hebrews 3:16-19.[27]) But *believers* have entered, and continue to enter, that rest.

4:7 -- He again fixes a certain day, "Today," -- At the time of the wilderness wandering, God offered an invitation to Israel to enter into the promised land; He also excluded unbelievers from entering "His rest." "Again" reminds the readers that Psalm 95 is a fresh invitation from God. Through the words of David, God repeats His invitation to rest, and offers it "today."[28]

Saying through David after so long a time just as has been said before -- Psalm 95 was spoken by God some 400 years ("so long a time") after the wilderness generation was ex-cluded. On that later occasion, speaking through[29] David, God offered the same invitation ("just as has been said before"[30]) to David's contemporaries that He offered to those who made

---

[26] There are some unstated assumptions behind all the statements based on Psalm 95. One is that God's Word (whether promise or curse) is abiding and sure. Another is that God wants to share His rest with men. If God prepared a rest for humanity to enter into, then some are going to enter it and join Him. Count on it! Someone is going to share God's rest. His exclusion of unbelieving Israel was not the end of the matter.

[27] "The idea that the wilderness generation was finally rejected [missed "rest" -- heaven] was one the rabbis found hard to accept. In their writings we find statements such as the following: 'Into this resting place they will not enter, but they will enter into another resting place' (Mid. *Qoheleth* 10:20.1). The rabbis also had a parable of a king who swore in anger that his son would not enter his palace. But when he calmed down, he pulled down his palace and built another, so fulfilling his oath and at the same time retaining his son (*ibid.*). Thus the rabbis expressed their conviction that somehow those Israelites would be saved. The writer of Hebrews, however, has no such reservations about the wilderness generation. They disobeyed God and forfeited their place." Morris, *op. cit.*, p.42.

[28] Compare comments on "today" at Hebrews 3:7.

[29] The Greek reads "in David." This might mean simply in the Psalter (compare Romans 11:2 where "in Elijah" does not imply authorship). On the other hand, "in David" may be an example of instrumental *en*. God used David as His means or instrument. It affirms the inspiration of David as David wrote Psalm 95 (cp. comments on the authorship of Psalm 95 at Hebrews 3:7). One reason Bible students believe the Bible is inspired is because the Bible claims to be inspired. (That claim is either true or false. What is the evidence? When the evidence is examined, there is no reason to reject the claim to inspiration. See Paul Little, "Is the Bible God's Word?" in *Know Why You Believe* [Downers Grove, Ill.: Inter-Varsity, 1970], p.31ff.)

[30] Some explain "just as has been said before" as being the Hebrew writer's recognition that he himself had already mentioned these words in 3:7, 3:13, and 3:15. This commentator thinks a better explanation is the one offered in the notes, that a reminder of the opening words of the passage in Psalm 95 would recall the whole passage (including "My rest") to the minds of the readers. It is on this basis that we have made the comments

the exodus from Egypt, 'Today, do not harden your hearts or you, too, shall not enter My rest.'

"TODAY IF YOU HEAR HIS VOICE, DO NOT HARDEN YOUR HEARTS" -- David appeals to the people of his own time and warns them against the sin of unbelief, lest they, too, like their fathers under Moses, should fail to enter into the enjoyment of the promised rest.

4:8 -- For if Joshua had given them rest -- More was involved in the "rest" promised to the wilderness generation than simply entrance into the promised land. After the disobedient ones perished in the wilderness, the promised land was finally entered by a new generation under the leadership of Joshua.[31] But what they received under Joshua's leadership did not exhaust all that God contemplated when He promised them "rest."[32]

He would not have spoken of another day after that -- If entrance into the land of Canaan exhausted all that was promised in "rest," God would not have used the word "rest" again when speaking to David's generation. That He could promise "rest" to people already living in the promised land indicates that "rest" must include heaven, too.

4:9 -- There remains therefore a Sabbath rest for the people of God. – This is the conclusion[33] to which the writer has been building since verse 3b. "Sabbath rest" (*sabbatismos*) is a new word. Perhaps the writer coined this new word[34] because he did not have a word for

---

about the "same invitation offered" to David's generation as was offered earlier. Refer again to the footnote 46 on chapter 3 where the words "rest" and "promised land" are shown to be somewhat synonymous.

[31] We've earlier noted (footnote #16 on chapter 3) the pre-existent Jesus was active in the Old Testament period. The KJV, at this place, reads "Jesus" ("if Jesus had given them rest"), and this has led some to suppose the pre-existent Jesus had something to do with the entrance of the chosen people into the promised land (perhaps He caused the walls of Jericho to fall). While Jesus may very well have been involved in the taking of the land, we believe that the introduction of such an idea here in Hebrews 4 is beside the point. The "confusion" the KJV "Jesus" causes is removed when it is remembered that "Jesus" is always used in Hellenistic Greek for the Hebrew name "Joshua" (whether the Hebrew spelling is *yehoshua* or *yeshua*). The KJV regularly used the Greek spellings for people's names, even for Old Testament names that occur in the New Testament (cp. Romans 9:25 where the KJV has "Osee" for "Hosea"). The ASV and NASB made an improvement on the KJV, as far as understanding is concerned, when those newer versions consistently use the Hebrew spelling for people's names which occur in both the Old and New Testaments. Whenever two or more people have the same name, the translators had to choose a word that would give the readers the right idea. The use of "Joshua" in the translation of Hebrews 4:8, in our opinion, is the one that gives the correct idea.

The parallel between the Old Testament "Jesus" (Joshua) who led his followers into the earthly Canaan, and the New Testament Jesus (the Son of God) who leads new covenant people into their heavenly inheritance, is a prominent theme in early Christian typology (cf. *Epistle of Barnabas* 6:8ff; or Justin Martyr, *Dialogue with Trypho*, 113, 132).

[32] It is a contrary-to-fact condition in the Greek. What is implied in a contrary-to-fact condition is that whatever is given in the if-clause is admitted to be untrue, or contrary-to-fact. If Joshua had given them rest (but of course he did not), God would not be speaking about another day as He did in Psalm 95.

[33] "Therefore" translates the Greek word *ara*, a word that is inferential. What follows is the logical consequence of the presentation up to now.

[34] No use of the word *sabbatismos* is attested before its use here in Hebrews. The usual Greek word for sabbath is *sabbaton* -- as at Exodus 16:30, Leviticus 23:3, etc. Most commentators suppose, however, that there is some connection between the Hebrew *shabath* ("rest") at Genesis 2:2 and the "rest" (*katapausis*) that is promised to faithful Christians. This new word would immediately call to mind all that has been said about how the Christian's "rest" is like "God's rest."

the kind of "rest" he had in mind. New words catch people's attention. The use of this new word may have been intended to cause the readers to pause and contemplate on the special kind of "rest" still in store for the Christian believer.[35] The expression "people of God" is found elsewhere in the New Testament only at Hebrews 11:25 (though 1 Peter 2:10 is similar, and an expression like "My people" occurs several times). In the Old Testament, the "people of God" were members of the nation of Israel. In the New Testament, the term signifies faithful believers[36] from any nation.

4:10 -- For -- Verse 10, which begins with "for," seems intended as a reason why it is now possible for the people of God (verse 9) to enjoy a future "Sabbath rest." The reason is this: "Jesus, the Apostle and High Priest of our confession" was faithful to the task appointed to Him.

The one who has entered His rest has himself also rested from his works, as God did from His -- The last part of verse 10 is clear enough; it recalls what is learned at Genesis 2:2 where we are told God rested. What is not so clear is who is meant by "the one,"[37] or how to explain the aorist tense verb "rested,"[38] or what is meant by the threefold repetition of "his."[39] The most

---

[35] Mention must be made of several proposed explanations of *sabbatismos* that are to be rejected. (1) The idea that "Sunday" is the sabbath day in the Christian dispensation. Sunday is not the sabbath (the word is not *sabbaton*). Sunday is the Lord's Day! Nor is Sunday necessarily a day of rest for Christians. The "rest" that Hebrews 4 holds out for the Christian is not something the readers are *already* keeping, but something that can be entered in the future (4:1,3,6,10,11). (2) Seventh-Day Adventists (and other seventh-day groups) have used this verse to support their doctrine that Christians are to observe the Sabbath as the day of worship. Seventh-day keepers affirm that the "seventh day" has been the day of "rest" ever since God began resting on the seventh day of creation. Non-seventh-day keepers reply that though God rested on the seventh day, this does not mean that men were required to keep the seventh day each week. They affirm that such an ordinance was not given until the time of the Exodus (Exodus 31:16,17; Deuteronomy 5:15). In the light of the following context in Hebrews 4, which speaks of *heaven*, we doubt that it is proper to interpret *sabbatismos* as something to be done in this present world, as the seventh-day people are wont to do. The writer of Hebrews, who has so much to say about the better hope and the better way of life in the New Covenant, cannot be understood as enforcing the observance of the Mosaic sabbath. On the whole question of "Sabbath or Lord's Day, Which?", see: Richard DeHaan, "Why the Christians Worship on Sunday," *Radio Bible Class*, Grand Rapids, Mich., June 1974; and "Sunday: The Lord's Day" (dealing with why Christians worship on Sunday rather than Saturday), *Radio Bible Class*, 1981. (3) The idea of the Epistle of Barnabas (Chap. XV), that the history of the earth will last 6000 years followed by a 1000-year millennium (on the basis that "with the Lord a day is as a thousand years," and there were six days of creation in Genesis followed by a seventh day of "rest.") This idea that *sabbatismos* teaches a future millennial period has been defended by G.H. Lang, *The Epistle to the Hebrews* [London: Paternoster, 1951], but F.F. Bruce urges that Barnabas is giving Jewish eschatology rather than Christian. What is presented in the book of Hebrews is that the present creation is followed by the new creation, not by a millennium (e.g., Hebrews 9:26-28 and 12:22-28).

[36] Hebrews 3:6,12,14 and 4:3 have demonstrated that the people for whom God's "rest" is awaiting are faithful believers, people who respond in faith to the good news they hear (Hebrews 4:2).

[37] "The one who" or "he who" is the regular way (i.e., as a relative clause) to translate the article and participle. Is there any significance to be assigned to the observation that when believers are referred to in Hebrews 4, the words used are plural ("us" or "we")? Does this make the use of the singular "he" ("the one") in verse 10 noteworthy?

[38] Is this a prophecy of the future made by using a past tense verb (as is often the case with Old Testament prophecies), or is this an historical aorist, the entrance into rest having actually occurred in the past?

[39] The first two instances translate the possessive pronoun *autou*. The third represents the adjective *idios* which means "one's own."

likely explanation, in this commentator's opinion,[40] is the one which suggests *Jesus* is the "one" about whom the verse speaks.[41] "Entered His rest" then refers to Jesus' return to the Father's presence at His ascension and coronation (cp. John 17:5). "Rested from His works" refers to His once-for-all sacrifice for sins being finished. And "as God did from His" says that Jesus now enjoys the same kind of "rest" God has enjoyed since the work of creation was finished.[42] Jesus is introduced at this point because what was true for Jesus is also true for believers.[43] The next verse cites Jesus' example as an incentive for believers to follow, and implies that when they die they will join Jesus and share with Him in God's "rest."

4:11 -- Let us therefore be diligent to enter that rest -- This second warning passage closes with a renewed exhortation to give careful attention[44] to the goal of entering God's rest. Since it is an established fact there is a rest for the people of God still to be enjoyed (4:1-10), let that

---

[40] The other popular explanations both make "one" a reference to believers, either believers in this life or believers at the time of their death.

The first suggestion makes verse 10 say the believer experiences rest in this life, similar to the rest Jesus spoke about in the Great Invitation, "Come to Me all who are weary [who work to exhaustion] and heavy laden, and I will give you rest" (Matthew 11:28). In this view, "rested from his works" is explained as meaning the believer has ceased from his own worthless works. This view has against it not only the fact that it is hard to see how such an explanation in any way explains "Sabbath rest" in verse 9 (remember, verse 10 begins with "for"), but also the fact that the "rest" in this whole Hebrews' passage is something future, not something in this present life.

The second suggestion is the meaning (as shown by their choice of words and capitalization) the NASB, NEB, and NIV translators have thought to be correct. It makes verse 10 say anyone who enters God's rest rests from his own work just as God did from His. That is, happy is the man who reaches heaven. He will enjoy a rest similar to that which God enjoys since He finished His work of creating. The most difficult thing about this interpretation is to try to explain what "works" are meant when it says the man "has himself also rested from his works." It is not unusual to find commentators who adopt this explanation for verse 10 appealing to Revelation 14:13 ("Blessed are the dead who die in the Lord ... they may rest from their labors, for their deeds follow with them") as being a parallel passage. The "works" (i.e., Christian labors on earth before the Christian enters "rest") the believer does are regarded as good, just as God's works at creation were good. Milligan spends a whole page (p.136) urging this interpretation to be the correct one.

[41] Some have objected to this interpretation by saying, "How can 'the one' be a reference to Jesus, when Jesus' name has not been mentioned in the immediate context?" In reply, it can be affirmed that since 3:1 Jesus has been in mind. It can also be said that to interpret verse 10 as a reference to Jesus is in harmony with what will be plainly said in verse 14, a verse that may well serve as a summary of the previous argument.

[42] Of course, "rest" is not inactivity for Jesus any more than it was for God. Jesus' high priestly functions are yet being done, as Hebrews will develop in chapter 5 and following.

[43] We've been told believers share with Jesus (Hebrews 3:14), and we are told Jesus is a "forerunner" Whom Christians may follow into heaven (Hebrews 2:10, 4:14 and 6:20). Hebrews 1 has Jesus sitting at the right hand of God. Chapter 2:9 has Him crowned with glory and honor. If Hebrews 4:10 is a reference to Jesus, we have an interesting parallel between chapters 2 and 4.

In chapter 2, the train of thought was:	In chapter 4 there is a parallel train of thought:
Dominion over creation was assigned to man;	God's rest has been offered to man;
Man has not attained it;	Man failed to attain it;
Jesus has;	Jesus has;
In Jesus, man fulfills his destiny.	In Jesus man may enter God's rest.

[44] "Be diligent" translates *speudasomen,* a word that means strive earnestly, concentrate your attention, to hasten, to exert one's self, to make every effort, to be zealous. In this context "diligent" is contrasted with "unbelief/disobedience."

fact spur the readers to renewed determination to be faithful to Jesus.[45]

Lest anyone fall through *following* the same example of disobedience -- What happened to Israel in the wilderness is treated as an example, a type, of what can happen to the Christian.[46] Disobedience was the reason that earlier generation failed to enter the promised land. Let the readers beware! Unbelief can result in their failure to enter the rest of God. Being faithful to Jesus – deliberately and with planned attention – is the way to be "diligent" and avoid the "same example of disobedience" (compare Hebrews 3:12-14).

4:12 -- For -- Verse 12 gives a reason for being diligent lest any unbelief is permitted to take root in the heart. That reason is the abiding validity of God's Word. The threats and promises one reads in Scripture still come true.

The word of God is living and active and sharper than any two-edged sword -- In this context, "word of God" certainly has reference to the threats, warnings, and promises found in Psalm 95:7-11, the passage that has been in the heart of writer's presentation since the middle of chapter three.[47] "Written Scripture" is designated as the "word of God."[48] "Living and active" means that the promises of Scripture and the warnings of Scripture are ever new. Scripture does not speak only in the past, but also in the present,[49] and it will produce faith if its message is carefully listened to.[50] To say the Scriptures are "sharper than any two-edged sword"[51] is a figure of speech indicating the word of God can cut both ways – it can encourage and it can condemn.

---

[45] Heaven is never obtained but by diligence. No one enters there who does not earnestly desire it, or who does not make a sincere effort to be faithful to Jesus. Hence, we see the duty of constant self-examination while we are endeavoring to work out our salvation with fear and trembling (Philippians 2:12; 2 Corinthians 13:5); for it is God that works in us (Philippians 2:13). His Word tries us, proves us, searches us even to the very center of our being, and will quickly reveal and rebuke any thought of deviation away from Jesus.

[46] In 1 Corinthians 10:1-12, Paul uses the same wilderness generation to present a similar lesson, and he regards the wilderness happenings as types *(typikos,* "example," I Cor. 10:11).

[47] Many of the early church fathers thought "word of God" in this place was a reference to Jesus Himself (remember John 1:1 calls Him the "Word," *logos).* However, the description of the word as "sharper than any two-edged sword" is not suitable to refer to Jesus. The ancients solved this problem by adding the words "his judgment" so that the verse reads "his judgment is sharper ...." In other passages, the "sword" is not Jesus himself, but proceeds out of His mouth (Ephesians 6:17; Revelation 1:16, 19:15; Isaiah 11:4).

[48] Hebrews 3:7 represents the Spirit as speaking still through the words of Psalm 95. The whole point of the use of Psalm 95 is that its words are still valid even for the Hebrews. The line of argument, then, is that the *written Word* (in our day) is living and active. Let us give diligence, for if we slight the word of God, we can have no escape from its irresistible operation; we shall be thoroughly exposed and inevitably judged by it.

[49] That the word "living" can be applied to the word of God reminds us of Stephen's reference to the "living oracles" received by Moses at Sinai (Acts 7:38), and Peter's description of "the living and abiding word of God" (1 Peter 1:23).

[50] That the word of God is "active" reminds us of Isaiah 55:11, where we are told that God's word will not return to Him empty, but will accomplish what it was sent forth to do. Compare also Jeremiah 23:29.

[51] Several writers have suggested that "surgeon's scalpel" or knife is a better translation than "sword," but the Greek is the regular word for the short sword carried by Roman soldiers. "Two edged" is probably better than two-mouthed, though the difference is one of derivation: Was the original *di-stomos* ("two-mouthed," with the word "mouth" given to a sword that devours all before it) or *dis-tomos* ("twice-cutting")?

And piercing as far as the division of soul and spirit, of both joints and marrow -- This is the fourth participle in this verse that agrees with "word of God" and explains its operation. With its clear and convincing insights, the word of God can distinguish between the person who lives in the realm of the spiritual (soul and spirit[52]) and the person who lives only in the realm of the physical (joints and marrow[53]).

And able to judge the thoughts and intentions of the heart -- This last in the series of participles ascribes a fifth activity to the word of God. The word of God (i.e., God speaking through the written word) passes judgment on men's thoughts and motives. Perhaps "heart" is intended to call to mind what was said in 3:12 about an evil heart of unbelief.[54] It seems likely that "intentions" is deliberately chosen to reflect the idea that God knows exactly the real motives that prompted people to consider abandoning the Christian religion.

4:13 -- And there is no creature hidden from His sight -- With the words of verse 13, the second warning passage is completed. At first it may seem as if there has been a change of subject, from "word of God" in verse 12 to God Himself in verse 13. But further reflection will show no real shift. The whole argument based on Psalm 95 has been built on the fact that God still speaks to men through the words of Scripture. And men[55] are such an open book to God that He knows exactly the message men need to hear when they read a verse of Scripture.

But all things are open and laid bare to the eyes of Him with whom we have to do -- "All things" certainly includes any thought of unbelief or disobedience. Such things do not escape God's eyes. There is no way to hide[56] such things from Him. The first beginnings of apostasy

---

[52] This passage is famous for long being the battleground on which the argument of dichotomy versus trichotomy has been fought. Dichotomy says man is made of two parts: physical (body) and spiritual (the spiritual, including "soul" and "spirit" as synonymous terms). Trichotomy says man is made of three parts: body, soul, and spirit (while soul and spirit are both non-physical, they are not exactly the same either). Because this verse clearly distinguishes between "soul" and "spirit," as does 1 Thessalonians 5:23, this commentator has regularly taught trichotomy. The body is the house for the soul which animates the body, and the spirit is intended by God to be the thing that gives directions to the soul as it animates the body. Exceedingly complex are the questions this whole passage raises. What is the proper translation? Is it "dividing soul from spirit, and joints from marrow," or is it "dividing soul and spirit from joints and marrow"? What is the relationship between man's "mind" and his "spirit"? Is the "spirit" a part of the "soul," or a completely separate entity from the soul? The interested student will find a thorough discussion of this matter in Franz Delitzsch, *A System of Biblical Psychology* (Grand Rapids: Baker, 1966 reprint). See also the writer's commentary on Romans, footnote #42 of chapter 1, and notes following.

[53] "Joints" are the places where two bones meet and touch each other, and "marrow" is the soft center of the bones. Since joints and marrow are not contiguous, there is probably no thought that these two are somehow divided or separated by the sharp two-edged sword.

[54] This verse says the "heart" (see comments on "heart" at 3:10) is the seat of "thoughts" and motives ("intentions"). It is one of the verses that tells us the Biblical "heart" is the same as "mind" in our language. A more difficult problem is trying to decide whether "heart" in this verse is coterminous with "soul" or "spirit" in the previous verse.

[55] We suppose that "creature" (literally, created being) is limited to men in this place. Every human being is wholly known to God. All of man's thoughts, feelings, and plans are distinctly understood by God. Nothing remains invisible to Him. God's omniscience is the thing that makes such knowledge on His part possible.

[56] The word "open" translates *gumna*, "naked, without any covering." "Laid bare" translates *trachelizo*, a word that can suggest the throat (trachea) is left unprotected. (Picture the danger to a boxer who leaves his throat unprotected). To have the head back and the throat completely uncovered is a figure suggesting total

are manifest to Him, so be diligent lest there be any tendency to disobedience that would deprive you of the promised rest. The precise meaning of "Him with whom we have to do" is in doubt.[57] It seems to say at least this much: men today have to consider what God says, and they are affected by what God does. God is not off somewhere, leaving men to do as they please. God doesn't wait until the final judgment to get involved in people's lives. He didn't in Old Testament times; He doesn't in New Testament times. God dealt with unbelieving Israel in Moses' time in harmony with a personally delivered message. God dealt with Israel in David's time in harmony with His word spoken in a psalm written by David. Not only has God spoken to us in His Son (Hebrews 1:2), God also speaks with the Hebrews (and us) through His written Word, and then proceeds to act in harmony with His threats and promises, just as He acted in days of yore. He is Someone with whom we have to do.

II. EXHORTATIONS BASED ON THE SUPERIORITY OF THE SON OF GOD'S PRIESTLY OFFICE (which is after the order of Melchizedek). Hebrews 4:14 - 7:28

A. Encouragement to "Hold Fast our Confession," and "Draw Near with Confidence to the Throne of Grace." 4:14-16

4:14 -- Since then -- Commentators have struggled with the outline of the book of Hebrews from this point on.[58] We have chosen to treat 4:14-16 as the transition to a new topic, the high priestly office of Jesus, a topic that is the writer's concern through Hebrews 10:18. This transitional paragraph makes two points: (1) Because of Jesus' greatness, "Let us hold fast our confession" and (2) Because of His human experience, "Let us draw near."

We have a great high priest -- That Jesus functions as a high priest for believers has been stated at 2:17 and 3:1, and perhaps implied as recently as 4:10.[59]   Why are we told again that

---

vulnerability. That's exactly how men are in God's sight. There is no way a man can hide anything from God.

[57] The problem is there is no verb in the Greek expression *pros hon hemin ho logos*, while both *pros* and *logos* can have more than one meaning. Perhaps *pros hon* means "to whom," *hemin* means "to us" and *ho logos* means "the account." *Logos* is attested in the papyri as a word meaning "account" or "reckoning." If we accept this meaning, then the verse says we must give an account to God -- that is, Christians will stand before God at the Judgment. Against this view is the fact the whole warning passage has not been speaking of the final judgment, but rather some decision God makes while men are still living to exclude some from rest. Perhaps *logos* is used to tie verse 13 to verse 12 where *logos* has just been used for the "*word* of God." If we accept this meaning, then the verse says that God deals with us through His Word.

[58] To see the difficulty, the student needs but compare the suggested outlines for the book he finds in the standard commentaries. While most all commentators agree on the outline of the first four chapters, the student will find great diversity of outline suggested for chapters 5 to 10:18. Because the wording of 5:1 would be a rather abrupt way to begin a new thought, we have opted for the view that a transition to the new topic is made in 4:14-16. In the versions of Tyndale, Coverdale, and Luther, what is 4:14 in our Bibles appears as 5:1.

[59] If the interpretation suggested for 4:10 (that it refers to Jesus, who finished His work of redemption and entered into heaven) is correct, it is easier to see how verse 14 can say that the idea of priesthood has been in view in the previous context.

Christians *do* have a high priest? Does this affirmation that Christians *do* have a "great high priest" imply that part of the readers' problem was that they missed the visible and personal ministrations of the Jewish priesthood? Demonstrating that in Jesus we have something better[60] than Aaron or the Levitical priesthood is the thrust of the whole central portion of Hebrews (up to 10:18). No priest in the Old Testament was ever called a "great high priest."

Who has passed through the heavens – It has been observed by many that a knowledge of the ceremonies on the Day of Atonement in the Jewish religion helps readers of Hebrews understand what is being said about Jesus' activities as our great high priest.[61] On the Day of Atonement, the Jewish high priest passed from the altar of burnt offering, through the room called the Holy Place, beyond the veil, into the Holy of Holies.[62] On one of the trips into the Holy of Holies on that day, he carried blood from a sacrificial animal and sprinkled it on the mercy seat on the Ark of the Covenant. In Israel, the sacrifice was not complete when the animal had been killed at the altar of burnt offering. Not until the blood had been sprinkled on the mercy seat was the sacrifice considered efficacious. Likewise, Jesus' atonement was not complete at the cross. Not until He had entered heaven as the High Priest, having made atonement for sin, was His atonement complete (cp. Hebrews 9:12). Not until He passed through the heavens[63] into the very presence of God and there offered, as it were, His blood on the antitypical mercy seat, were men's sins actually forgiven. This is the doctrine that will be developed in chapters 8 through 10.

Jesus the Son of God -- This not only identifies who is the Christian's high priest, but also may well give a reminder of why He can be called "great." "Jesus" reminds us of His humanity, and "Son of God" reminds us of His deity. The great high priest of the Christians is not just a human being, a physical descendant of Aaron, but one much greater, the "Son of God."[64]

Let us hold fast our confession -- Again (compare Hebrews 3:1,6 and 14) the writer voices his exhortation not to slip back into the Jewish religion. The only difference is the reason given

---

[60] The word translated "high priest" is used both for the high priest himself and also for the heads of the twenty four courses of priests. (When the latter is the reference, it is regularly rendered "chief priests"). To say Jesus is a "great" high priest is to distinguish Jesus as greater than all the Old Testament priests put together.

[61] See Leviticus 16:1-34 and Hebrews 10:1-10.

[62] The student who is not familiar with the floor plan of the tabernacle and the location of its rooms and furnishings will find helpful diagrams and explanations in the comments on Hebrews 9.

[63] The canonical Scriptures make reference to three heavens: the atmosphere we breathe, the starry heavens, and the third heaven (the home of the Blessed). See 2 Corinthians 12:2. See also the Old Testament expression "heaven and the heaven of heavens" at Deuteronomy 10:14, 2 Chronicles 6:18, and Nehemiah 9:6. The Targum on 2 Chronicles speaks of *rakiah* (the atmosphere), *shamayim* (the starry heavens), and *shamayim hashamayim* (the place where God dwells). It is after the Greek and Gnostic ideas began to intrude into church circles that we first hear of "seven" heavens -- cf. *Testament Levi* 2:7ff, and *Ascension of Isaiah* 6:13, 7:18ff. Ephesians 4:10, which describes Jesus as "He who ascended far above all the heavens," would preclude any idea there could be four heavens higher than the "third heaven" which 2 Corinthians 12:2 alludes to.

[64] Hebrews 1:2,3,8 have already shown the exalted nature of the "Son." It says that Jesus is God! We should once more take note of the fact that the writer of Hebrews affirms the very thing about Jesus that unbelievers have always had difficulty accepting: that Jesus of Nazareth was actually the Son of God (God in the flesh).

for continuing to make the same confession they made when they first became Christians. A man cannot renounce his confession of faith in Jesus the Christ without renouncing the greatest high priest a man ever had.

4:15 -- For we do not have a high priest who cannot sympathize with our weaknesses -- The negative wording of this statement suggests it is intended to be a reply to a possible objection to the affirmation about Jesus' great high priesthood. Did someone suppose that because He is God He doesn't know how to sympathize[65] with needy worshippers? Did someone suppose that a priest in heaven was no substitute for a priest on earth to whom one could go with his sin problems? The same point about Jesus' ability to understand us and sympathize with us has already been made in Hebrews 2:17,18. "Weaknesses" are not sins, but rather the various physical and moral limitations[66] which often are the occasions for temptations to sin.

But One who has been tempted in all things as *we are* -- God cannot be tempted to sin, but while Jesus was in human form on earth He was tempted the same way all human beings are. The devil has the ability to plant thoughts in men's minds[67] and to stir up the desires of their bodies.[68] Jesus' temptations were real. The devil used every temptation he can use on a man.[69] Jesus' deity did not give Him advantages to overcome temptations which other mortals do not have. He was not a great warrior, with such superhuman powers, that all the temptations bounced off Him like toy arrows. The actual stirring of His emotions, His complete fellow-feeling with our weaknesses, the reality of His actual temptations, all help Him to be sympathetic toward those who share the same humanity He shared.

Yet **without sin** -- Some suppose this phrase explains that there was one respect in which Jesus' temptations differed in power from ours – He didn't have the temptations that come as a result of past failures.[70] There is no hint Jesus' temptations were less powerful than the temptations

---

[65] Exactly why "sympathy" is a desirable quality in priests will be explained in Hebrews 5:1,2.

[66] *Astheneia* sometimes means bodily infirmity, such as disease (see Matthew 8:17; Luke 5:15; John 5:5, 11:4; Acts 28:9; and 1 Timothy 5:23). It is also used of the general weakness of human nature (as Romans 8:26; 1 Corinthians 15:23; 2 Corinthians 12:5,6; 13:4).

[67] On the devil's ability to plant thoughts in a man's mind, see Acts 5:3 ("Satan filled [Ananias'] heart") and John 13:2 ("the devil ... put into the heart of Judas ... to betray Him").

[68] On the devil's ability to stir up the desires of the body, see notes on Romans 6:1-12. It would appear that all temptations a man experiences come from without. First the devil must do his seductive work, then the man will become aware of the temptation and then begin to struggle with it, whether or not he will do what he has been tempted to do. (Even James 1:14, which is sometimes used to prove some of men's temptations come from inside the man and are not therefore the result of a specific temptation, does not seem to support that doctrine. What the verse does seem to say is that temptation results when the man is [first] "carried away" [by the devil] and then is "enticed by his own lust [desires]." In other words, the devil stirs up the desire, and then the man experiences temptations as the desires entice and lure him.)

[69] When we consider the temptations in the wilderness, for example, we can see an appeal to one who is desperately hungry to use improper means to assuage his hunger. (Someone has said, Jesus thus knows the temptation a poor man has to steal so that his family may be fed.) There were temptations to pride, to selfishness, to go some way other than God's way, to avoid the hurt and pain that service to God sometimes carries with it, etc.

[70] Nothing should be affirmed about the *kind* of temptations Jesus experienced that would impinge on the whole point of the sentence; namely, that Jesus can "sympathize with our weaknesses." If the point of "without

offered to us mortals. The moment we begin to think His temptations were somehow different, we have contradicted the whole point of this argument; namely, whether or not Jesus was truly tempted as we are and thus is capable of sympathizing with His human brothers. Therefore, we suppose that "without sin" is the first affirmation in Hebrews of Jesus' sinlessness.[71] While he can sympathize with our weaknesses, Jesus could not be a "great high priest" if He were a sinner Himself.

4:16 -- Let us therefore draw near with confidence -- "Therefore" means since we have in Jesus a high priest who is not only exalted, and is therefore in a most advantageous place, but Who is also perfectly able to be sympathetic because He was once human and tempted. "Let us ... draw near" urges the continuation of an action already going on. In the readers' earlier Christian experience, they had made use of Jesus' good offices as high priest. This exhortation urges a continuation of that previous confidence.[72] Obviously, if they repudiate Jesus and quit the Christian religion, they also forfeit the help of the great High Priest. This is the first use of

---

sin" were that Jesus' temptations were somehow different, it could easily be alleged such a difference renders Him incapable of "sympathizing." If He never experienced the temptations I am experiencing, how could He understand? To represent Jesus' temptations as different from those which we experience is the opposite of the argument the Hebrews writer is making.

In passing, those who think "without sin" is a limitation on the kinds of temptations Jesus experienced often unwittingly make a comment that completely contradicts the idea of a sinful nature inherited from Adam. (E.g., "'Without sin' means that none of His temptations arose out of a sinful disposition, such as all fallen men have since Adam" [Kent, p.92]). If Jesus' body (because He somehow inherited one different from ours) was incapable of offering the same kind of temptations our bodies do, it certainly could not be said He "was tempted in all things as we are." (See the writer's *Commentary on Romans*, p.231ff, for documentation of the historical fact that the idea of an inherited sinful nature, inherited in the accident of our birth, is not a Biblical doctrine.)

[71] Hebrews will elsewhere affirm Jesus' absolute sinlessness in no uncertain terms; we are not dependent on this passage to prove that doctrine. What Hebrews says about the sinlessness of Jesus is in harmony with what is stated elsewhere in the New Testament Scriptures – e.g., John 8:29,46, 10:32; 2 Corinthians 5:21; 1 Peter 2:22; 1 John 3:6. If "without sin" is an affirmation of Jesus' sinlessness, then this is one place in Scripture where we learn that it is not a sin to be tempted. It is only sin if we yield to the devil's temptation. Luther worded it this way, "You can't keep the birds from flying over your head, but you can keep them from building a nest in your hair." We can't keep the devil from planting thoughts in our minds, but we do not have to nurse the idea till it becomes an action.

Some writers suggest that "without sin" implies the temptations Jesus mastered were *stronger* than we mortals experience. When Jesus continued to resist, the devil threw everything he had at Jesus. That Jesus never yielded to temptation might indicate His resistance to temptation involved more, not less, than the ordinary human experiences in temptation. In this commentator's opinion, to say Jesus' temptations were more powerful than our temptations impinges on the whole matter of whether or not He can sympathize, just as much as if His were less powerful. Instead of sympathy, what would keep Him from wondering something like this: 'I put up with more than you. What's the matter with you that you can't handle those little things?'

[72] The "drawing near" is probably not a reference to something the high priest did (e.g., his entrance into the Holy of Holies on the Day of Atonement) since this exhortation is not addressed to Jesus our High Priest. Rather, it is addressed to the readers and urges them to continue to "draw near." In the Old Testament, worshippers had to come to the priest after they had sinned, and the priest decided whether the sin was forgivable or not, and what sacrifice should be offered. In the New Testament, worshippers can depend on Jesus to do this needed task for them. Chapter 5:1, beginning with "for" seems intended to explain what is involved in "draw near."

Some have suggested that "draw near" is something Christians do when they pray for help with their weaknesses, or for forgiveness of their sins. Note that the rest of verse 16 speaks of receiving mercy and finding grace. The exhortation "let us (continue to) draw near" would then be an encouragement to pray for forgiveness of sin and to ask for help with our "weaknesses." For when we pray, our great high priest goes to work on our behalf.

the word "draw near" in Hebrews.[73] In light of what is said in Hebrews 5:1ff, we suppose "Let us draw near" is another way of saying, 'Let Jesus continue to function as our high priest!' Our "confidence" rests upon the assurance of reconciliation with God because of the sacrifice of Jesus, and upon the sympathy of Jesus. It is precisely because it is a throne of grace (and not a judgment seat) that it can be approached with confidence,[74] and without fear of rejection.

To the throne of grace -- "Throne of grace" is a new expression in Hebrews. We've had the word "grace" at Hebrews 2:9, where we learned that grace is sometimes an attitude, and sometimes an action. Perhaps "grace" here is an attitude somewhat synonymous with "sympathize" in verse 15. We've had "throne" used before in Hebrews 1:8 of the place where Jesus is commanded to sit enthroned since His ascension.[75] Putting the two ideas together, we suppose the phrase "throne of grace" says it is Jesus' attitude of grace that one finds when he comes to (i.e., draws near to) the throne where Jesus sits.[76]

That we may receive mercy -- This is one object for which the reader is encouraged to draw near to the throne of grace. But what is mercy? In a context which has spoken about being tempted and "without sin," it seems likely that mercy[77] includes not only sympathy for the one coming for help, but also forgiveness of sins.[78] "Mercy" is what we need first.[79]

---

[73] See 7:19, 10:22 where the verb "draw near" occurs again. "Drawing near" involves a relationship to God resulting from the new covenant, and from Jesus' high priestly functions on behalf of believers. "The exhortation to 'draw near' strikes one of the doctrinal keynotes of the Epistle, for the religion of Christ is the religion of access to God. Under the Old Covenant, only the priests could draw near -- and they only on stipulated conditions. The people could not draw near at all. But Christ's sympathy and suffering for mankind makes access possible. The way to God, so long closed, is now open." Lightfoot, *op. cit.*, p.100.

[74] The word translated "confidence" *is parresia* (on which see comments at Hebrews 3:6), which comes from *pan + resia* = full story. In ancient Greece, the word denoted the right of a full citizen to speak his mind on any subject in the town assembly -- a right that the slave did not have. (Lightfoot, *op. cit.*, p.101)

[75] Our notes assume it is Jesus, rather than the Father, who is being approached as Christians "draw near to the throne of grace." Because Hebrews 8:1 will also affirm Jesus "has taken His seat at the right hand of the throne of the Majesty in the heavens," some commentaries speak of the Father as the one being approached. For example, "When one approaches the 'throne of grace' he is coming to the throne of God where our priest Jesus is seated at His right hand" (Alford), or again, "The throne of grace is a throne on which God sits -- with Jesus at His right hand -- and deals benevolently with all who approach Him" (Lightfoot, *ibid.*).

[76] Throne "of grace" (a genitive construction) more likely means grace is enthroned there than that the throne rests on [or stands on] grace.

[77] After noting the Greek has two synonyms for "mercy," Thayer has this explanation: "*Eleeo* (the word used here in Hebrews 4:16) means to feel sympathy with the misery of another, especially such sympathy as manifests itself in act, less frequently in word; whereas *oikteiro* denotes the inward feeling of compassion which abides in the heart. A criminal begs *eleos* of his judge; but hopeless suffering is often the object of *oiktirmos*."

[78] The reception of mercy that Hebrews 4:16 promises is not the initial reception of mercy from God at conversion (e.g., 1 Timothy 1:16), for the Hebrews were already Christians. Instead, it is what believers need when their weaknesses have led them to succumb to temptation.

[79] In our weaknesses and temptations, we need compassion. When we come to the throne of grace, our first cry should be for mercy. So often in our prayers, we have it all backward. We pray for 5 or 10 minutes about everything in the world, and then end up with "and forgive us our sins, in Jesus name" or "We ask all these things -- along with the forgiveness of our sins -- in Jesus name." The parable Jesus told about the Pharisee and the Publican should instruct us about the importance of asking for mercy first.

And may find grace to help in time of need -- This is a second object for which the readers are encouraged to draw near to the throne of grace. What is the "grace" found at the throne of grace? If "grace" in "throne of grace" is a reference to Jesus' attitude, then we might suppose the "grace" that is found is an action done by Jesus on behalf of His faithful brethren right at the moment they cry for help.[80] "Grace" would be the help (i.e., help with temptations, help with our weaknesses[81]) that is available because our great High Priest is continuing His priestly and intercessory work on behalf of his brethren. Grace is what we need next, after mercy. And having received it, we may serve God acceptably in spite of our weaknesses. If verse 15 gave evidence that our High Priest has perfect knowledge of the help required, verse 16 gives the assurance that the help shall be given as needed, and in the time of need.

---

[80] The Greek translated "in time of need" is *eukairon boetheian*. *Boetheo* is a cry for help in a moment of deep peril. We need help; we want it; we want it badly; we need it now! "Timely" (*eukairon*) may refer back to what 2:18 spoke of, those weaknesses and need of help in time of temptation. If so, this phrase suggests that the approach to the throne of grace is made anytime the believer has a special need. But "timely" could also say that the help each time is specially tailored to their particular need.

If "grace" is an action (as our comments suggest), then we have made a distinction in this passage between "mercy" and "grace." Mercy was an attitude, and grace is an action that grows out of Jesus' sympathetic attitude.

[81] "Grace is the favor, strength, help, counsel, direction, support, for the various duties and trials of life." (Barnes, *op. cit.*, p.109)

B. Jesus is Better Qualified than Aaron to be Our High Priest. 5:1-10

1. The qualifications of Aaron. 5:1-4

5:1 -- For -- The "for" with which this verse begins shows that Hebrews 5:1 and verses following give an explanation or reason for something just said. Thus, the purpose of the first part of chapter 5 is to corroborate the position arrived at in the closing verses of chapter 4; namely, that we *do* have in Jesus a true High Priest sufficient for our needs, and so we should continue to "draw near with confidence to the throne of grace" whenever we need help.

Every high priest -- While this language sounds very general, the fact that the Hebrew readers are addressed, and that the description in verses 3 and 4 specifically name "Aaron," makes it rather obvious that "every high priest" means "every high priest" in the Aaronic or Levitical priesthood.[1] The writer will point out that there were three necessary qualifications to be a high priest: (1) oneness with the people he represents, (2) compassion, and (3) appointment by God. Later in the chapter, the writer will develop his argument about Jesus' priesthood by showing that Jesus had these three qualifications, too.

Taken from among men -- The high priest had to be one of the people whom he represented. This was one of the qualifications. The command to Moses was, "Bring near to yourself Aaron your brother ... from among the sons of Israel, to minister as a priest to Me ..." (Exodus 28:1). Aaron and his successors, who were to represent the nation of Israel in the presence of God, were to be Israelites themselves, so as to be familiar with the conditions under which their people lived, exposed to the same pressures and trials.

Is appointed on behalf of men -- It was not for the benefit of God, but for the benefit of men, that the priesthood was instituted. God doesn't need a priest, but sinning men do! Those who could serve as high priests were appointed[2] by God and set apart to office with great solemnity (see Exodus 29).

In things pertaining to God -- We had this expression at Hebrews 2:17, where it was suggested that it likely has reference to such things as are necessary to sustain God's holiness and His government, while at the same time redeeming men and pardoning sin.

---

[1] By God's original regulation, the Jewish high priesthood was to be a hereditary office, restricted to the family of Aaron and his descendants (Exodus 29:9). After the Romans occupied the promised land, the office became venal (i.e., purchased with money), and the Mosaic regulation was often disregarded. See 2 Maccabees 4:7 and Josephus, *Antiq.* XV.3.1. It was no longer held for life; in fact, several persons might have the title "high priest" at the same time (and this in addition to those who had the title "chief priests" -- see footnote #60 on chapter 4). The word "high priest" (or "chief priest") means simply that the man was a priest of higher rank and office than others.

[2] *Kathistemi* means "appointed to administer an office" (Thayer). As far as the Greek word *kathistatai* is concerned, it could be either middle or passive voice. Though Calvin took it as a middle form, the passive is more likely the correct idea here, as is confirmed by what is said in verses 4 and 5. The idea that there should be a priesthood was something that originated in the mind of God.

In order to offer both gifts and sacrifices for sins -- Part of the divine appointment included instructions concerning the proper offerings to make when men had sinned. The usual distinction[3] between "gifts" and "sacrifices" is that the former denotes meal (or cereal)[4] offerings and the latter denotes bloody sacrifices.[5] Though bloody sacrifices were commonly the offerings when sins or trespasses had been committed, both words ("gifts" and "sacrifices") can be said to be for sins or sin offerings. Meal offerings could serve as sin offerings for the very poor, and on the Day of Atonement the unbloody sacrifice formed part of the ceremony of expiation (Numbers 29:7-11).[6] It was the priest who offered to God the various gifts and sacrifices which the worshippers brought.

5:2 -- He can deal gently with the ignorant and misguided -- Now the second qualification for a high priest, that of compassion, is emphasized. It is not easy to translate *metriopathein* ("deal gently with"[7]). It refers to taking the middle course between apathy and anger. The priest dared not be indifferent to the worshipper's sins, nor could he be too harsh, so that the sinner went away crushed, rather than encouraged. Such a quality of head and heart was peculiarly necessary to every high priest, for to him it belonged to decide, in any given case, whether or not a sacrifice could be legally offered for the sin committed.[8] If the man sinned through ignorance[9] or through error,[10] a sacrifice might be offered and the sin might be forgiven.

---

[3] This distinction is not invariably observed. "Gifts" (*doron*) is used in this epistle (11:4) for Abel's sacrifice which certainly was a "bloody sacrifice," and in Hebrews 8:4 for all kinds of offerings; while *thusia* (here translated "sacrifices") in the LXX denotes Cain's unbloody offering (Genesis 4:3), and in Leviticus 2:1 it is used for a meal (cereal) offering. Still it can be said, in general, that "gifts" when contrasted with "sacrifices" denotes the "unbloody offerings" the Law commanded.

[4] What was the "meal" offering? The vegetable offering, called "meat offering" ("meat" is used in the sense of food, not flesh) in the KJV, and "meal offering" in the ASV, consisted of white flour, or of unleavened bread, cakes, wafers, or ears of roasted grain, always with salt and, except in the sin offering, with olive oil (Leviticus 2:1, 4:13,14, 5:11). In case the worshiper was very poor, this "gift" was accepted as a sin offering in lieu of an animal sacrifice (Leviticus 5:11-13). Sometimes it formed an independent offering; sometimes it was subordinate and accompanied an animal sacrifice. Sometimes it was all burned on the altar; sometimes part was placed on the altar and part was given to the priests (to eat).

[5] Bloody sacrifices involved the slaying of an animal for the sacrifice.

[6] The Day of Atonement is almost always in the writer's thoughts as he refers to the functions of the high priest.

[7] The word is a compound, made up of *metron*, measure, and *pascho*, to suffer. It means to suffer to a measured limit. It denotes a feeling midway between grief and indifference. Thousands of people would come to the priest daily to confess their sins and to have sacrifices offered for those which were forgivable. The high priest must be careful lest he become irritated at sin and ignorance. He must also take care that he does not become weakly indulgent and indifferent. Either unfeeling severity or indifference to sin would disqualify a man from doing the work of high priest as God envisioned its being done.

[8] Leviticus 10:8-11; Deuteronomy 17:8-13, 24:8, 33:10; Malachi 2:7.

[9] Of what were the sinners ignorant? In Numbers 15:22-31, we learn that even sins committed through ignorance of God's commandments had to be atoned for. See also Hebrews 9:7. This was required by the Law as a means of educating the moral perception, also in order to show that sin and defilement might exist unsuspected, that God saw evil where men did not, and that His test of purity was stricter than ours.

[10] In the Greek, there is but one article used with the two words "ignorant" and "misguided." Thus, according to Sharp's rule of grammar, the two words describe one class of people, i.e., those who have gone astray through ignorance. The word translated "misguided" is *planomenois*, and means to go astray or wander from God's ways, yet not deliberately. One suggests the word would cover those who fell into sin through passion.

Not so if the sin was committed with a high hand, that is, in a spirit of haughty insolence or open rebellion against God and His government.[11]   In that case, there was no room for repentance, and none for sacrifice. The presumptuous sinner was to be put to death "at the mouth of two or three witnesses" (Numbers 15:30).

Since he himself also is beset with weakness -- When the sinner comes to the priest, the priest can be gentle since he himself shares in the same weaknesses[12] as the sinners on whom he has compassion. Aware of his own physical and moral frailties, he is better qualified to minister on behalf of guilty and dying men. The human priest, underneath all those gorgeous robes of office, was bound by the same liability to err (and the same need for forgiveness) as were those who appeared before him.[13]

5:3 -- And because of it -- That is, because the human priest[14] is himself a sinner.

He is obligated to offer *sacrifices* **for sins, as for the people, so also for himself** -- Because he, too, sinned, as did the worshippers who came to him, the priest needed some provision, some sacrificial offering, to be made for his own sins. The ritual on the Day of Atonement was so arranged by God that the high priest made atonement for himself before he did so for the people (Leviticus 9:7).[15]

Another suggests the participle might be construed as being in the middle voice, thus the word would mean deceiving themselves.

[11] The writer of Hebrews will treat apostasy from Christ as a sin for which there is no forgiveness, just as was the case with the high-handed sin in the Old Testament. See Hebrews 3:12, 10:26, and especially 6:4-6.

[12] See comments on the word "weaknesses" at Hebrews 4:15. In this context, where the priest is said to have to offer sin offerings for himself, the word certainly includes moral frailty. He was liable to sin, he was subject to temptation, he must die physically and appear before God to be judged. In all these "weaknesses," the priest was just like the men he represented.

[13] Milligan suggests that Aaron's folly in making the golden calf (Exodus 32:1-6) was to himself, no doubt, a source of much grief and painful experience; but it served, nevertheless, to make him deal more tenderly with others who were afterward overcome by similar temptations. A priest did not have to personally experience every type of sin to be qualified to sympathize. All that is needed is a sufficient experience of human weaknesses as would help him strike the proper balance between leniency and severity.

[14] Verse three should not be interpreted to suggest that Jesus sinned and therefore had to offer a sacrifice for Himself. Such an interpretation would be a contradiction of the other plain statements, even in Hebrews, of Jesus' perfect sinlessness (e.g., Hebrews 7:26). All that verse 3 deals with is the human high priest.

[15] It was prescribed by the Law that on the Day of Atonement the high priest was to offer for himself a bull as a sin offering and a burnt offering of a ram (Leviticus 16:6-14). For the congregation, the sin offering consisted of two he-goats and a burnt offering of a ram. Over his own sin offering, the priest made confession of sins, first for himself and his household, and then for the other priests. In the Midrash is found this prayer offered by the priest as he laid his hands on the head of the animal, "O God, I have committed iniquity and transgressed and sinned before thee, I and my house and the children of Aaron, thy holy people. O God, forgive, I pray, the iniquities and transgressions and sins which I have committed and transgressed and sinned before thee, I and my house" (Mid. *Yoma* 4:2). The bull was then killed and the priest passed through the veil with the blood, and sprinkled it on the mercy seat on the Ark of the Covenant. After caring for his own sins, the high priest then killed the goat of the sin offering on behalf of the people, and sprinkled its blood on the mercy seat. (See the whole ceremony described in detail in notes on Hebrews 9:7.)

5:4 -- And no one takes the honor to himself -- The third qualification, divine appointment to the office, is now recalled. The "honor" is likely a reference to the office of high priest. Why could no man take the honor to himself? Because God is holy, and since all men have sinned, where can one be found who can approach God? It would be presumptuous for any sinner to assume the office on his own initiative. If a suitable priest from among men is to be found, it must depend wholly on God's instructions as to what man would be acceptable to serve in that capacity. In point of fact, the Bible records the disasters that befell those who presumed to take it upon themselves to perform priestly duties.[16]

But *receives it* when he is called by God, even as Aaron was -- When the Levitical priesthood was inaugurated, God's call[17] and appointment of Aaron is clearly recorded in Scripture (Exodus 28:1-3; Leviticus 8,9). In fact, no other call to anyone to be a high priest is recorded in Scripture, though the manner in which the high priest was succeeded in office was designated in the Law of Moses (Numbers 16:40, 18:1-7).[18]

2. *The superior qualifications of Jesus Christ. 5:5-10*

5:5 -- So also -- If the writer of Hebrews is to sustain his thesis that Jesus is the Christian's great High Priest, he must produce evidence that Jesus meets the qualifications for the office, the three qualifications just listed. This is now done in the following verses, in reverse order.

Christ did not glorify Himself so as to become a high priest -- *Messiah* (Greek, "*the* Christ") did not thrust Himself, unasked and unwanted, into the great office of high priest. If Jesus were to be a high priest under the Law of Moses, He would have to be a descendant of Aaron and of the tribe of Levi. Jesus was not of the tribe of Levi, but of the tribe of Judah. Nevertheless, He is not an intruder, because (1) the Old Testament taught that Messiah, too, would be a high priest, and (2) of a different order than the Aaronic, namely, the order of Melchizedek. These two points are documented by citing two passages from the Psalms.

But He who said to Him -- The second half of broken sentences (such as we have here) may properly be completed by repeating the verb from the first half. Supplying the verb "glorify" from the previous clause yields the sense, 'He (who spoke the following Old Testament passages) *glorified* Him to be a high priest.' God is the one who appointed Messiah to the office of priest.[19] Messiah thus meets the "divine appointment" qualification for priesthood.

---

[16] See the case of Korah, who was a Levite but not of Aaronic descent (Numbers 16); or Saul, who was of the tribe of Benjamin (1 Samuel 13:8ff); and even Uzzah, who would do what a priest was supposed to do (2 Samuel 6:3-8). One could also cite the case of Uzziah, king of Judah, who intruded into the temple in spite of efforts by the priests to stop him and who was smitten with leprosy as a punishment (2 Chronicles 26:14-23). Any exceptions to the rule of who could serve as priests required an explicit command from God, such as in the case of Samuel who was directed by God to offer a sacrifice at the home of Jesse (1 Samuel 16:1-13).

[17] There is no reference to an internal call by the Holy Spirit to the office. Nor is this verse a proof-text to show a miraculous call to the ministry is essential in this New Testament age.

[18] Aaron's successors derived their divine appointment or commission from his original one. All the sons of Aaron were priests, unless debarred by physical defect (Leviticus 21:16-24).

[19] Cp. John 8:54, where Jesus says, "It is My Father who glorifies Me." See also John 17:1,5; Acts 3:13.

"YOU ARE MY SON, TODAY I HAVE BEGOTTEN YOU" -- If we read this first quotation from the Old Testament with emphasis on the "I," we see that this passage from Psalm 2 does show that God appointed Jesus.[20] Jesus (the Son) did not unilaterally assume the office of Messiah.

5:6 -- Just as He says also in another *passage* -- The other passage about to be quoted is Psalm 110:4. "Just as" shows we must read the two Old Testament passages together to get their full impact. One tells about authority ("*I* have begotten you!"), the other about His office ("a priest ... according to the order of *Melchizedek*"). Since God spoke both, and since both passages were Messianic,[21] both must be true of Jesus, the Messiah.

"YOU ARE A PRIEST FOREVER ACCORDING TO THE ORDER OF MELCHIZEDEK" -- In this quotation of God's words to Messiah, the key words are "priest"[22] and "order of Melchizedek."[23] Psalm 110 clearly taught the Messiah would be a priest and also made it clear that it was not the Aaronic priesthood, but the Melchizedek "kind"[24] of priesthood that He would exercise. God said so! Let no one entertain any idea that Jesus is some kind of

---

[20] Psalm 2:7 has already been explained in notes at Hebrews 1:5, where the author's point was to demonstrate Jesus' "Sonship." The same passage is cited here in connection with Jesus' Messiahship. At first it might seem as though Psalm 2:7 has no bearing on the topic of Jesus' priesthood, but it is the question of divine appointment that is the immediate topic. For that topic, the verse from Psalm 2 is appropriate. In harmony with the conclusions there offered, it seems to follow that the appointment of Jesus to be Messiah and therefore high priest was inseparably connected to His incarnation and resurrection.

[21] As noted in the comments at Hebrews 1:13, where Psalm 110 was used to prove Jesus' superiority to angels, Psalm 110 was Messianic. Verses 1-3 refer to Messiah as king. Verse 4 refers to Messiah as priest. Verses 5-9 refer to Messiah as conqueror. It is cited at Matthew 22:43ff and 1 Corinthians 15:25 to demonstrate the Lordship and victory of Jesus over death. It is cited as averring to Jesus' exaltation to the right hand of God at Acts 2:34; Hebrews 1:13, 10:12. It is cited at Hebrews 5:6,10, 6:7 as evidence of Messiah's priesthood.

[22] In previous verses in Hebrews, the word has been "high priest" (*archiereus*). This is the first use of the word "priest" (*hiereus*) in Hebrews, and it will occur often hereafter. The writer of Hebrews applies it to priests generally (7:14, 8:4), to the Levitical priests (7:20), to Melchizedek (7:1,3), and to Christ (5:6, 7:11,15,17,21, and 10:21). To call Jesus a "priest" is a powerful way to call attention to certain aspects of His saving work for sinning men. All that an Old Testament priest did in offering a sacrifice for men, Christ has done and does. The Old Testament priest only did it symbolically; Jesus our priest truly effects atonement for the sins of men.

[23] We shall save most of the discussion about Christ's priesthood being similar to Melchizedek's until we come to chapter 7. But we might pause to bring out one particular in which there was a striking resemblance between Christ and Melchizedek, a resemblance that did not exist between Christ and any other priest in Scripture. Melchizedek was both *king* and *priest*. None of the kings of the Jews were priests, nor were any of the priests ever elevated to the office of king (at least not till intertestamental times). But in Melchizedek these offices were united. This is a striking resemblance between him and the Lord Jesus.

"The functions of priesthood and throne were carefully distinguished in Israel, with the offices being allocated to different tribes. The practical advantages lay in the avoidance of concentrated power in the Jewish state. Yet there were certainly benefits to be had with a royal priest, provided that the person possessing the office had the integrity to avoid abuses. There were times when a godly priest in the Old Testament was faced with a wicked monarch (e.g., Jehoiada the priest and the evil Athaliah, 2 Kings 11; also Azariah the priest and King Uzziah, 2 Chronicles 26). On other occasions the king was more godly than the priest and had to take the spiritual leadership (e.g., Josiah and his religious reforms, 2 Kings 22, 23). God has planned that Messiah should concentrate in Himself the authority of kingly rule, and this will involve also His spiritual ministration as the great high priest. Because He is the Son of God, believers need not fear that abuse of His power will occur, or that either aspect will be ignored." (Kent, *op. cit.*, p.97)

[24] "Order" (in "order of Melchizedek") may not be an exactly correct translation, since there was no succes-

usurper or vain pretender to the office of great High Priest. All one has to do is read the Old Testament to see that God appointed Messiah to that function! Hebrews 7:23ff will develop the idea that having a priest "forever"[25] makes Jesus a better priest than the Levitical kind of priests whose ministrations were constantly interrupted by death.

5:7 -- In the days of His flesh -- The writer now turns to other qualifications to be a priest – oneness with the people he represents so he can sympathize with them. "In the days of His flesh" recalls what was said about His partaking of flesh and blood" (Hebrews 2:14), and emphasizes again that during the days of Jesus' earthly life[26] He was one with mankind. The long sentence in Greek that begins with verse 7 has as its subject and verb the words (verse 8) "He learned obedience."

He offered up both prayers and supplications -- Most likely the occasion in view is Gethsemane, when Jesus prayed to God, "My Father, if it is possible, let this cup pass from Me; yet not as I will, but as Thou wilt" (Matthew 26:39).[27] "Prayers" are petitions which arise from a sense of need. "Supplications" denote urgent requests for help, protection, or shelter.

With loud crying and tears -- If the occasion in view is Gethsemane, we here learn some things about that ordeal not contained in the Gospels. The Gospel writers do not tell us about tears being shed, or strong outcries being voiced. "Loud crying" describes the screams and yells of someone in extremity crying for help. "Tears" running down the cheeks are visible manifestations of grief or hurt.[28]

---

sion of priests from Melchizedek, and thus no "order." *Taxis* could also be translated as "rank" or "station." Jesus had a rank or station similar to that of Melchizedek.

[25] The word "forever" (*leʿolam*), as in many other Scripture verses, here means "while time endures." Jesus' priesthood is co-extensive with the Christian age, just as the duration of the Aaronic priesthood was co-extensive with the Mosaic Age (Exodus 40:15; Numbers 25:13). At the close of the Christian dispensation, when He shall deliver up the kingdom to God the Father (1 Corinthians 15:24ff), it would appear that He will cease to act as a High Priest, for then the object of His priesthood, as well as of His mediatorial reign, will have been accomplished. In the New Jerusalem there will be no sin, and of course no more need of a priest's ministrations. In the meantime, Jesus' priesthood is superior to the Aaronic order of priests. He has no successor (a fact that will be brought out later in Hebrews).

[26] There is an implied contrast in the expression "in the days of His flesh." Either His pre-existence is contrasted to "the days of His flesh," or the contrast to "days of His flesh" would be found in Jesus' present exalted state. If we opt for the latter, we must be careful, lest we seriously weaken the writer's argument that Jesus *can now* sympathize with sinners who draw near to Him for His priestly help. His present exaltation does not impinge on His ability to sympathize. He is still a priest who understands us!

[27] Because there is information included in Hebrews that is not found in the Gospel accounts of what happened in Gethsemane, some think the time when Jesus offered these prayers and supplications was when He was on the cross.

[28] The commentators do spend time discussing the source of the letter writer's information. Of course, if the occasion is Calvary, the Gospels tell us about Jesus cry with a "loud voice" (Matthew 27:46,50, and Mark 15:34). But if the occasion is Gethsemane, then the source of information about the outcries could be the disciples who, about a stone's cast distant, heard them before sleep overcame them. Did they also see His red eyes when Jesus returned from His hours of agony in prayer, and thus know He had been shedding tears? Was the source of this information a revelation from God to the writer of Hebrews?

To the One able to save Him from death -- Jesus' prayers were directed to the Father in heaven. But, in the light of the words "Let this cup pass from Me," for what was Jesus praying? The Greek *ek thanatou* can be translated "out of death" (i.e., He was praying that He would be raised from the dead), or "from death" (i.e., Jesus prayed that He might avoid dying). If we accept the latter, was it a prayer to avoid Calvary, or a prayer to avoid a premature death in the Garden before He got to Calvary? Every one of the suggested answers to the question for what was Jesus praying has been rejected by some commentators on what (at first sight) seem to be good reasons.[29] No answer is wholly free from difficulty. But on the whole, the traditional interpretation seems the most likely. That is, Mark 14:35,36 plainly shows that the content of Jesus' first prayer in Gethsemane was to avoid the cross altogether. Remember, Jesus was both human and divine. He had a human will and He also knew the Father's will. His prayer shows He is struggling to bring the human will into harmony with the divine. His words "Let this cup pass from Me" and "not as I will" reflect the inevitable shrinking of the human being from such an ordeal as was before Him. The traditional interpretation of the prayer in Gethsemane is no different from what Jesus himself said on the Great Day of Questions, two days before Gethsemane. On that memorable occasion, Jesus struggled with Himself over whether or not to ask God to save Him from this hour (John 12:27ff).

And He was heard because of His piety -- Because Jesus was reverent toward God, because He held God in honor,[30] because He prayed, "Not as I will, but as You will" (Matthew 26:39) is why Jesus' prayer was heard and answered.[31] The Gospels tell us an angel came and minister-

---

[29] The suggestion (made by W.F. Moulton [*Ellicott's Commentary*], Westcott, and others) that Jesus was praying to be raised from the dead has against it the fact that Jesus knew He would rise, and had even predicted it. He would hardly be praying for something He knew to be a certainty, it is alleged. The suggestion (made by A.F. Schauffler [*Expository Times*, 1894-95, p. 433] and W.H. Book [Sermons for the People, p.80]) that Jesus was praying Satan would not be allowed to take His life prematurely (the idea being that the Devil was trying to stop a sacrificial death like the one at Calvary would be, and thus thwart Jesus' whole earthly mission) has against it the fact He Himself said "No one takes it (my life) from me, but I lay it down of my own accord" (John 10:18 NIV). The traditional suggestion (recently reaffirmed by Lightfoot [*Restoration Quarterly* 16 (1973), p.166-73]) that Jesus was praying that if it were possible He might avoid the cross has against it the fact He had on numerous occasions predicted He would die just that way, and also (it is sometimes asserted) it has against it the fact that He did die on the cross, whereas Hebrews says His prayer "was heard." (To suggest His prayer was heard, and the answer was "No!" hardly satisfies the language, it is alleged.) The suggestion (found in the Old Latin Version, and defended by Calvin, Milligan, and others) that Jesus prayed to be delivered from the *fear* of dying has against it the fact that the prepositional phrase that has *eulabeia* (on this view rendered "fear" or "apprehension") in it goes with the verb "heard" not the noun "death.

It is remarkable that this verse (Hebrews 5:7), so filled with imponderables, marvelously explores and exposes much of the theme of the epistle. In it we have a reverential Son, human like all other humans, whose human weakness led Him to pray that He might avoid the pain and hurt that would be Calvary, who was submissive to God even to the point of severe suffering, Who would not have been like brothers in all respects had His prayer to avoid physical death been granted, and Who is therefore qualified to be High Priest and Leader of His people.

[30] In the New Testament, and in Hebrews in particular, *eulabeia* consistently denotes reverence for God, reverent submission, piety. Even though, as the traditional interpretation explains Jesus' Gethsemane prayer, He was apprehensive enough about the suffering and agony of scourging, mockery, and crucifixion to shrink back from it, *eulabeia* is not the word to express that feeling.

[31] Cruden's *Complete Concordance* (p.219) has this to say about God "hearing" prayer. "It is often used in this sense (meaning a "yes" answer, an affirmative answer) in the Psalms and elsewhere. And God is said not to hear when He does not grant one's desires. John 9:31." When Jesus prayed that the Father's will might be done rather than His own, that prayer was given an affirmative answer.

ed to Him.[32]

5:8 -- Although He was a Son -- Just because Jesus was God's unique "Son" (remember what was said in chapter 1), that did not exempt Him from suffering or learning to obey.

He learned obedience from the things which He suffered -- Jesus had to learn to practice obedience just like other humans must learn that virtue.[33] He learned what it sometimes costs a man to obey. And He endured many sufferings because He was being obedient to God. Hebrew readers, are you listening? He understands the temptations to avoid any more suffering for the cause of Christ that you have already experienced. He can sympathize. He is perfectly qualified to be your High Priest.

5:9 -- And having been made perfect -- "Made perfect" does not mean Jesus somehow was less than morally perfect before Gethsemane. The expression here is similar to what was said in Hebrews 2:10, namely, that Jesus' sufferings completely qualified Him to be our Savior and High Priest.[34]

He became ... the source of eternal salvation -- Some of the older translations have "author" at this place, just as at Hebrews 2:10. However, the word used here is not *archegos* as at 2:10, but *aitios*, a word which literally means "the cause." Salvation, "eternal"[35] salvation, can be traced wholly to His suffering and death. The particular way in which this salvation was effected (corresponding to the Old Testament offering for sins) is explained in chapters 8-10.

---

[32] For those who follow the traditional interpretation of Jesus' Gethsemane prayer, exactly what the angel did for Jesus (Luke 22:43) is not easy to explain. (Those who suppose the prayer was to avoid a premature death can suggest the angel performed heart surgery on Jesus to correct an already ruptured heart muscle -- proof of which rupture is alleged to be seen in the bloody sweat.) Did the angel in some way assure Jesus so that He was able to bring His human will into harmony with the Divine, and thus go on to endure the cross? Since the devil was tempting Jesus during the Gethsemane experience ("pray that *you* [emphatic] may not enter into temptation," Luke 22:40-44, implies that Jesus was about to be tempted), perhaps what the angel did was to hinder what the devil was trying to do. By means of an angelic messenger, limits were put on the terrors the devil was able to insinuate into Jesus' thoughts.

[33] We must be careful that we do not read into this verse all of our own experiences. Most of us learn to be obedient because of the unpleasant consequences which follow disobedience. But it was not so with Jesus. He never was disobedient, and so it wasn't just to avoid unpleasant consequences that He decided it was best to be obedient. Jesus did learn what obedience to God can involve, and He learned to practice obedience in the conditions of human life here on earth. Something may be learned as to what was involved in Jesus' obedience from a consideration of Matthew 26:53 (He could have called 12 legions of angels to help avoid being arrested, but that would not have been obedience to the will of God!). See also Isaiah 50:5ff.

[34] See footnote #54 on chapter 2, where it was documented that this word *teleiosis* is used in the LXX with special reference to the consecration of the high priest into office.

[35] The word "eternal" is not very often found connected with the word "salvation" as it is here. Its import is debated in the commentaries. One suggests that the word "eternal" is carefully chosen to reflect the idea that His atoning death was not something that had to be repeated every year, as did the Levitical ritual on the Day of Atonement (cp. Hebrews 6:2, 9:12,14,15, 13:20). Another suggests that it perhaps takes up the idea found in verse 6 where we were reminded that Jesus is a priest "forever," and thus "eternal" is somehow related to Jesus' priestly activities. Still another suggests "eternal salvation" not only includes forgiveness of sins now, but also has something to do with heaven, which shall be a never-ending bliss (see 4:9).

To all those who obey Him – In fact, men do have to do something to be saved.[36] The present tense verb "obey" indicates continuous, habitual action. Continual obedience[37] to Jesus (it could also be called faithfulness) is the condition on which men may participate in the eternal salvation of which Jesus is the cause.

5:10 -- Being designated by God as a high priest -- The word translated "designated" means to address, to give a name publicly. It was in Psalm 110:4 (quoted in verse 6) where God thus publicly called Messiah "priest." This paragraph began (verse 5) with the affirmation that Jesus did not exalt Himself to the office of High Priest.[38] It was a task to which God appointed Him.[39] Therefore, it is on the authority of God the Father that we look to Jesus Christ as our great High Priest.

According to the order of Melchizedek -- This language, taken from Psalm 110:4, as explained in comments on verse 6, implies certain differences between Jesus' priesthood and the Aaronic order. After showing Jesus met all the qualifications expected in a priest, and after reaffirming God "designated" Him as a priest, the writer might be expected to continue unfolding his subject of Jesus' priesthood. Instead, he pauses for another warning passage.

THIRD WARNING PASSAGE. 5:11 - 6:20

- ### Rebuke for having become dull of hearing. 5:11-14.

5:11 -- Concerning Him we have much to say -- The verse from Psalm 110:4 is such an important Old Testament verse that the writer of Hebrews intends to expound its meaning at length. But first, he must make sure his readers are encouraged to put forth the mental effort to appreciate the full significance of His "high priest(hood) according to the order of Melchizedek."[40]

And _it is_ hard to explain -- As the verse will go on to explain, the difficulty was not in the subject itself as though it were abstruse or inexplicable. Nor did the difficulty lie with the writer

---

[36] The Bible never presents the idea of universal salvation for all men regardless of how those men live. God does not save men _in_ their sins; He saves them _from_ their sins. He saves men whose lives demonstrate a tenor of obedience. Jesus Himself worded it this way, "Not every one who says to me `Lord, Lord,' will enter the kingdom of heaven; but he who does [present tense, continuous action] the will of My Father" (Matthew 7:21).

[37] This expression was doubtless intended to dissuade the readers from a wrong course of action. Instead of quitting Jesus, what was needed now was continuing obedience to Him!

[38] The words of God found in Psalm 110 are "Thou art a _priest_ forever ...." In the writer's explanation, the word "priest" is altered into "high priest." It is by this change of word that the meaning of the Psalm is fully expressed.

[39] "High Priest" is to become Jesus' characteristic designation throughout this epistle. This title was not given to Him by men, nor improperly assumed by Jesus Himself, but one conferred on Jesus by God the Father.

[40] The word following the preposition "concerning" can be either masculine (whom) or neuter (which). If it is thought to be masculine, the antecedent would be either Melchizedek or Christ. Melchizedek will be the subject of 7:1ff. If it is thought to be neuter, the term "which" likely refers to the topic of the priesthood of Jesus, which will be expounded at length in chapters 8 to 10.

as though he was not knowledgeable on the material. The difficulty was found in the readers themselves.

Since you have become dull of hearing -- The readers were not always dull of hearing, but recently have gone backward.[41] If they were still the ready listeners they once were, he would not have needed to stop for this third warning passage, but could have plunged into the discussion of Jesus' High Priesthood immediately. However, readers such as these, whose growing interest was in returning to the Levitical priesthood, would be hard to convince concerning the different priesthood, the one according to the order of Melchizedek.

5:12 -- For though by this time you ought to be teachers -- Some considerable time apparently has elapsed[42] since the readers were first converted. After a person has become a Christian, he is expected to teach others what he knows.[43] But how can someone who is considering abandoning Christianity for the old religion of the Jews have anything to say? He certainly will not say anything right about Jesus, and he cannot even explain the real meaning of the Old Testament Scriptures which everywhere pointed to the very Messiah he has just repudiated.

You have need again for someone to teach you the elementary principles of the oracles of God -- The word "oracles" is used regularly to denote the revelations given in the Old Testament Scriptures.[44] "Elementary principles"[45] would refer to the ABC's of divine revela-

---

[41] "You have become dull" says the readers have gone backward. When they first became Christians, the readers possessed a deep interest in everything they could learn about Jesus. Their faculty of hearing had been acute, and at that time a few words and a little explanation, even on a subject such as this, would have sufficed. But since, on subjects about Jesus, their minds have become *nothroi* ("lazy", "sluggish", "apathetic")."

[42] At least the readers had been Christians long enough that they could be expected to understand the explanations of Old Testament Messianic passages that were commonly presented in messages of all Christian preachers. After Jesus opened men's minds to understand all the Scriptures said about Him (cp. Luke 24:25-27, 44-48), it was those witnesses' regular practice to repeat those very explanations of Old Testament prophecies as they presented the good news about Jesus (see Acts 2:24ff, 3:18ff).

[43] There apparently was an office of "teacher" in the early church (Acts 13:1, James 3:1), but we do not believe the writer of Hebrews thinks every reader should become such a "teacher." Nor does this verse prove Hebrews was addressed to just a small group within some congregation, namely those who by now should be functioning in the office of "teacher." Instead, "you ought to be teachers" reflects the truth that every Christian is expected to explain to others what he has learned about Jesus and His kingdom. Parents are to explain such things to their children; neighbors to their neighbors; friends to those who were inquiring about the way of life. To be a "teacher" (as the word is used in this context) meant to the ancient mind one who was able to *think* (the very activity these readers had become sluggish in). See this use of "teach" in Seneca, *Epistle* 33:9.

[44] See Acts 7:38 and Romans 3:2. (One exception to this usage of "oracles" is perhaps 1 Peter 4:11, where the word (NASB95 reads "utterances") is likely not limited to the Old Testament. On the basis of the Peter passage, a goodly number of commentators believe "oracles" here in Hebrews has reference to the gospel, rather than to the Old Testament Scriptures. The problem with making "oracles of God" in Hebrews a reference to the gospel is that Hebrews 6:1 says such "elementary teachings" are to be abandoned. While Jewish things could be safely abandoned, could gospel doctrines ever to be abandoned?) The word "oracle" denotes a message from a deity. The Old Testament Scriptures were a message from God.

[45] The Greek reads "rudiments of the beginning of the oracles of God." "Rudiments" or elements speak of the constituent elements that together make up a thing. The same word (*stoicheion*) is perhaps used at Colossians 2:8,14 of the elements of the Old Testament religion. "Elementary" (beginning) is used again in Hebrews 6:1, where some Jewish "elementary teaching" (first principles) are listed.

tion, the very elementary truths taught in the Old Testament. We suppose (in light of 6:1, "elementary teaching about the Christ") the reference is especially to the Messianic portions of the Old Testament Scriptures. The only way a man could abandon Jesus the Messiah and His religion in favor of returning to the Old Testament religion would be if he were to ignore all the Old Testament itself says about Messiah.[46] Anyone who would contemplate such a move certainly needs to hear again the ABC's of the Old Testament!

And you have come to need milk and not solid food -- "Milk" in this passage is not quite the same as what has been called "elementary principles." Whenever adults who used to be on solid food are reduced to having to eat baby food, it usually signifies they are sick or something is seriously wrong. There was something seriously wrong with the readers if they had to be taught the ABC's all over again, like new pupils[47] (or new converts) had to be taught.[48]

5:13 -- For everyone who partakes *only* of milk -- "For" shows that the writer intends to explain his metaphorical use of "milk" and "solid food." The change of expression from "come to need milk" to "partakes only of milk" (that is, making it their sole food) is significant. Only babies (or sick people) live solely on milk! This is spiritual shock treatment. Gone backward! Babies! An exclusive milk diet! Will the readers admit that this is their real spiritual condition?

Is not accustomed to the word of righteousness -- The spiritual tastes of a babe differ from someone who is more mature (verse 14). The mature person wants the solid food of "the word of righteousness." Because of the use of the word "righteousness," many commentators think Romans 1:16, 17 (where we are told that in the gospel is revealed "the righteousness of God ... from faith to faith") helps us understand what the letter writer had in mind here. If so, "word of righteousness" would be the doctrine or message respecting God's way of saving man, or the way by which men are justified.[49]

------

[46] The thrust of this delicate irony is this -- if you insist on going back to Judaism, you don't even understand the real meaning of the Old Testament, that its sacrifices and institutions all picture Christ. Can't you see this?

[47] Paul is fond of using this metaphor about "milk" and "strong food" (see 1 Corinthians 3:1,2, 14:20; Galatians 4:9; Ephesians 4:14,15). Some have used this similarity as one argument for the Pauline authorship of Hebrews (see Introductory Studies).

[48] Verses 11-12 have indicated the readers have gone backward. When they should have been able to teach others Christian doctrine (using Old Testament Scriptures to explain who Jesus was and why men should follow Him), instead, they need instruction again in the basic ABC's of Jewish doctrine (its Messianic import was elementary). When the Old Testament pointed to Messiah, and when Jesus has been demonstrated to be that Messiah, what will they have left if they go back to an Old Testament stripped of its Messianic elements?

[49] Some have objected that "righteousness" in Hebrews cannot refer to the same "justification" Paul writes about in Romans, for the readers of Hebrews are already Christians and have therefore already had righteousness imputed to them. This objection's flaw is that it is based on the premise that "justification" is a one-time thing, whereas, in Romans, justification is not just an initial act, but a continuing action (cp. footnote #4 on Hebrews 4).

Those writers who think "oracles of God" (verse 12) refers to the gospel (see footnote #44 above, where this idea is rejected) insist that "word of righteousness" has reference to right behavior, right living, the right conduct God expects of believers. The readers, according to this theory, would also have already been justified by faith -- so "word of righteousness" must mean something other than that.

Contrary to both these objections, if in "not accustomed to the word of righteousness" the writer of Hebrews is saying the man who favorably thinks about returning to Judaism is not accustomed to the way God

For he is a babe -- This phrase gives a reason for saying the milk drinker was "unaccustomed" to the word of righteousness. Like little babies, they couldn't handle anything stronger than milk. "Babe" was a term applied to pupils just beginning a course of instruction.[50]

5:14 -- But solid food is for the mature -- "Solid food" in this context is another way of designating the teachings called "word of righteousness." "Mature" indicates there has been some growth in understanding of what was being taught.[51]

Who because of practice have their senses trained to discern good and evil -- One characteristic of maturity is the ability to discern what is good and what is evil. It is through "practice"[52] that a believer's spiritual senses[53] are trained;[54] he then is able to distinguish between good and evil. In this context, remaining true to Jesus would be "good," and returning to the old Hebrew religion would be "evil." "By this time" if the readers really were mature and "accustomed to the word of righteousness," they should have been able to judge what behavior was proper in order to not make any foolish choices.

We have here a rather strong rebuke. The Hebrew Christians who would go back to the Jewish religion had become dull in hearing. Even though they professed devotion to the Old Testament ("the oracles of God"), they did not really hear what it taught, for it everywhere pointed to Christ ("elementary principles"). The Hebrew Christian who would go back to the Jewish religion was really like someone who was sick, who was reduced to living on milk like a baby rather than on solid food like a mature person.

Something must be done to rescue them from their going backward. That something will be explained in chapter 6 as the third warning passage continues.

---

saves man, that would be exactly the point demonstrated in the rest of this warning passage.

[50] The metaphor of "milk" and "solid food" (as the use of "babe" in verse 13, and "mature" in verse 14 show) reflects the rather common usage of the designation infants (*nepios*, babes, sucklings) for new pupils and "mature" for those who had passed beyond the stage of being beginning pupils (see TDNT, I, 645ff).

[51] "Mature" translates the same word rendered "perfect" in Hebrews 2:10 and 5:9. We have learned that each time we come to the word *teleios*, the context must be allowed to determine its meaning. Here in 5:14, the context suggests "adult" ("mature") as compared with "babe." Furthermore, since the context deals with teaching, "mature" would stand for those pupils who have advanced beyond the beginner stage. It is "mature thinking" to abandon the Old Testament religion (6:1ff).

[52] The Greek is *hexin,* meaning "a condition of body or mind, strictly as resulting from practice." The NASB margin has "by habit" or "by perfection" -- skill acquired by experience.

[53] The word rendered "senses" (*aistheteria*) means properly the physical organs of sensation, such as the eyes, the ears, and the fingers, through which we perceive the qualities and properties of things that are material. We have to learn through experience which of the sensations are good and which are bad.

[54] The word *gegumnasmena* means "trained like an athlete is trained." In the infant, the digestive organs, exercised in the beginning on milk, acquire through that exercise the power of assimilating more solid and more complex food. So also in the spiritual sphere. The mental faculties, exercised at first on simple truths ("the elementary principles") found in the Old Testament, should acquire by practice the power of apprehending and distinguishing the higher truths and those harder to be understood. The Christian, after years in the church, should be able to discern the good and evil in doctrine. He should appreciate what is true and reject that which is false or inferior.

- *Exhortation to go forward to spiritual maturity. 6:1-3*

6:1 -- Therefore -- This sentence, as is shown by the inferential conjunction (*dio*) with which it begins, is intended to be an emphatic assertion of the whole gist of the previous illustration drawn from "milk" and "solid food," "babes" and "mature." It says the "maturity" should forget about going back to Judaism.

Leaving the elementary teaching about the Christ -- "Leaving" is the word used by a lover about to be forsaken, 'O, do not leave me!' The readers are thus expected[1] to abandon, to disregard, to let be, the "elementary teaching about the Christ." What is included in this "teaching" that is to be left is disputed in the commentaries. One reason for this dispute is that there is some difficulty, as the marginal reading ("leaving the word of the beginning of the Christ") shows, knowing how to translate the original. Since the first word of chapter 6 shows this is an assertion of a point already made, we presume that whatever "the elementary principles of the oracles of God" in 5:12 meant, this phrase means also. The NASB has tried to show this connection by the repetition of the word "elementary." Another reason behind the dispute is the lack of agreement on the exact nature of the six foundational teachings that are about to be listed as among the things to be abandoned. That is, are they elementary *Christian* doctrines and practices,[2] or are they elementary *Jewish* doctrines and practices,[3] which are to be left behind? It is the understanding of this commentator that the thrust of Hebrews is the readers are to abandon the old covenant's Jewish practices (which were only types and shadows) and in their place embrace the better ideas and the real practices of the new covenant.

Let us press on to maturity -- "Maturity" also shows how closely 6:1 coheres with the preceding, for it is the same word used in 5:14. The verb translated "press on" can be either middle (let us press along for our own benefit) or passive (let us be carried along[4]) in voice. If we take it as middle, the obvious implication is that there is not much personal benefit to be had going back to the old Jewish religion. If we take it as passive, then we might understand the priesthood of Jesus, or the "word of righteousness" (5:13), or "the elementary principles of the oracles of God" (5:12), or even the Holy Spirit, is the agent[5] who would bear the readers[6]

---

[1] The Greek word *aphentes* is an aorist participle, which indicates the action of the participle ("leaving") must precede the action of the main verb, "Let us press on (be borne along) ...."

[2] The KJV writers evidently so interpreted the passage, when they offered "leaving the principles of the doctrine of Christ" for a translation. If it is beginning *Christian* doctrine that is to be left behind, then the foundational items about to be listed should all be given a "Christian" (new covenant) explanation.

[3] The ASV writers evidently so interpreted the passage, when they offered "leaving the doctrine of the first principles of Christ" for a translation. If it is beginning *Jewish* doctrine that is to be left behind, then the foundational items about to be listed should all be given a "Jewish" (old covenant) explanation.

[4] The same word was used in Hebrews 1:3, where we were told Jesus "upholds" (carries) all things forward to their goal.

[5] In a passive voice verb, the subjected is acted upon. The "agent" who does the acting is sometimes specifically identified; at other times, as would be the case here in 6:1, the agent is merely implied.

[6] A question has been raised whether this plural ("Let us") contains an exhortation to the readers, or a declaration of the writer's own purpose. We suppose it should be seen as an exhortation to the Hebrew readers to allow themselves to be carried along to the "maturity" that a knowledge of New Testament truths (as presented by the writer) would provide.

on to maturity.[7]

Not laying again a foundation -- Six foundational items are about to be identified. If the readers were to go back to the Old Testament system,[8] they would be doing the very thing here spoken against. It is not that foundations are worthless,[9] but the readers must not occupy themselves with laying a foundation over and over again.[10]

Of repentance from dead works -- The Old Testament prophets are full of calls to repentance from such dead works, works done without a corresponding attitude of heart.[11] In the Old Testament days, the people often went through the religious rites commanded by the Law, but their hearts were not in their worship. This necessitated the calls to repentance[12] we find in the "burdens" of the prophets. Even in the case of John the Baptist, the forerunner of Jesus, the keynote of his preaching was "repentance" since the Kingdom of Heaven was at hand. Repentance was an important element in the Jewish creed.[13]

---

[7] If it is thought to be a passive form, then "the thought is not primarily of personal effort ... but of personal surrender to an active influence" (Westcott, p.143). What the reader must do is stop putting hindrances in the way (like the hindrance of thinking more highly of old covenant practices than new, or like the hindrance of forgetting that the old covenant Scriptures pointed to the Messiah), and then they will be borne along to the maturity that is expected of each believer within a reasonable length of time.

[8] We are aware that many explain these foundational items as being, not Jewish practices, but the very topics that in the early days of the church formed the catechetical instructions given to prospective converts. As we proceed through the six items, we shall try to show that several do not make sense if we take them as Christian ABC's, while every item in this list can have a place in any fairly orthodox Jewish community.

[9] The Old Testament Scriptures and institutions, rightly understood as preparatory for the coming of Christ, formed an unsurpassed foundation for life and belief. On these beginnings a man could build for time and eternity. "Foundation" and "elementary teaching about the Christ" are two different figures of speech for the same thing.

[10] "Laying again" is a circumstantial participle, present tense indicating continuing action, and either middle or passive in form. In fact, since circumstantial participles can express means, this participle could even be thought of as expressing the agent or means by which being borne along was to be done. 'Let us be borne along *by* not laying again ...' is the idea.

[11] "Dead works" is a unique expression that occurs in the New Testament only here and 9:14. "Dead works" are works that leave the conscience in need of cleansing (9:14). "Dead works" are works that must be repented of (6:1). It is not clear why these works are called "dead." Perhaps they are called "dead" works because they issue in death because they are evil (cp. Romans 6:23, "the wages of sin is death"), or perhaps they are called "dead" because they are works done by men who are "dead in your trespasses and sins" (Ephesians 2:1). That the Jewish people halfheartedly offered their sacrifices, and perfunctorily observed the Sabbath, can be seen, for example, in Amos 5:21-26, and 8:5. The same idea is repeated by Stephen as he rehearsed Old Testament history (Acts 7:43). They had offered sacrifices to God, yes, but they also participated in idolatrous worship. Something was wrong with their hearts, and repentance was surely needed. Compare Malachi 1:8; 1 Samuel 15:22; Micah 6:6-8; and Ezekiel 18, where the people were told their sacrifices (though commanded by God) were unacceptable because their hearts weren't right.

[12] We have defined repentance as a change of mind and a change of action resulting from Godly sorrow for sin, and including restitution where possible.

[13] The teaching of the prophets is faithfully reflected in the sayings preserved in the Talmud: "The perfection of wisdom is repentance." "Repentance obtains a respite until the Day of Atonement completes the atonement." "Without repentance the world could not stand." (Moulton, *op. cit.*, p.302)

And of faith toward God -- Faithfulness toward God was another important element in any summary of Old Testament foundational ideas. That faithfulness was an essential element to Old Testament religion,[14] see the statement that Abraham "believed God, and it was credited to him as righteousness" (Genesis 15:6 as explained in Romans 4:1-5 and James 2:21-24); see also the testimony of Habakkuk 2:4 as quoted at Romans 1:17 that "the righteous man shall live by faith." The readers of Hebrews have already been reminded that it was a lack of faith that disqualified the wilderness generation from entering the promised land.

6:2 -- Of instruction about washings -- "Washings" is the regular word in Hebrews for Jewish "washings."[15] Evidently what is to be left behind are the old Jewish ceremonial washings,[16] for which we find detailed instructions[17] in the Old Testament, even instructions on how to prepare

---

[14] Faithfulness to God and faithfulness to Jesus Christ are also cardinal New Testament doctrines, e.g., Romans 1:17 and Hebrews 11. There was a time when this commentator held the idea that it was *Gospel* ABC's (the teachings given first to new converts) that were to be left as we press on to maturity. But when he made efforts in his preparation for preaching to put into practice what this verse then seemed to say ("not laying again a foundation ... of faith toward God"), did that mean that none-of his sermons to Christians should ever emphasize the need for faithfulness? This hardly rang true to what he found in the epistles and Revelation. Also he noted Milligan, an old Christian church author who understood these foundational items as the *Christian* ABC's (faith, repentance, baptism), had to spend pages explaining that in the steps of salvation, repentance did not really precede faith (a doctrine certain denominations had made popular). While Milligan's explanation of the step of salvation called repentance is excellent, it seems now to be a good example of "right sermon, wrong verse." Once we understand the foundational items are the requirements of the Old Testament *Jewish* system, then we see that "repentance" and "faith" have nothing to do with the steps of salvation for today.

[15] See Hebrews 9:10, "various washings." Compare Mark 7:4, "the washing of cups and pitchers and pots." Observe that the Greek word is not *baptisma* (neuter), the word regularly used for the ordinance of baptism, but *baptismos* (masculine), a word regularly used for the washings, ablutions, lustrations prescribed by the Mosaic Law (Thayer, p.95). (There is a manuscript variation at Colossians 2:12. Some manuscripts [P[46], Aleph[c]] have *baptismos*, while most of the others [including Aleph*] read *baptisma*, even though the context shows the reference is to the ordinance of baptism. Josephus also uses *baptismos* of John's baptism. So we must be careful about saying that *baptismos* is *always* used of Jewish washings.) The word is plural, and thus it is likely the word refers to something other than the baptism commanded in the Great Commission.

Commentators who believe that "baptism" rather than Jewish washings is the thing in view are hard pressed to explain the plural form "baptisms." One supposes the plural must point to the practice of trine immersion. Another supposes "instruction" had to be given to new converts concerning the difference between John's baptism and the baptism of the Great Commission. Another supposes the plural covers baptism in water, baptism of the Holy Spirit, and baptism with fire. Another urges the plural is used for the singular, and that nothing more is really intended than the one ordinance of Christian baptism. Another posits the idea the new converts had to have explained to them the difference between Jewish proselyte baptism and Christian baptism (hardly a live option, since it is certainly doubtful there was a practice of proselyte baptism as early as the writing of Hebrews. See G.R. Beasley-Murray, *Baptism in the New Testament* [Grand Rapids: Eerdmans, 1962], p.18ff.).

[16] First century Pharisaic Judaism practiced ritual immersions in specially built pools called *miqva'ot* (singular, *miqveh*). The pool was constructed with running water in and out (else the water would not be ceremonially clean after the preceding immersion), and it also had a double stairway in and out (one on which the unclean descended, and one on which, after dipping himself, the ceremonially clean person ascended). Such baths were needed, it was thought for example, after returning home from the market, lest contact with gentiles or other unclean persons would leave the Pharisee "unclean." See Wm. S. LaSor, "Discovering What Jewish Miqva'ot Can Tell us About Christian Baptism," *Biblical Archaeology Review* 13/1 (Jan-Feb. 1987), p.52-59. While there is no reason to believe Christian baptism finds its source in the ceremonial baths of the Jews, the article would help us get a picture of the kinds of "washings" the writer of Hebrews urges be left behind.

[17] While the Greek might be translated "baptisms of teaching," such a statement conveys little sense. We opt, therefore, for the view that *teaching* governs *washings* and means "teaching concerning washings."

the water ("ashes of a heifer," Hebrews 9:13). John 3:25ff shows there certainly was a running debate over "purification (ritual washings)" versus John's baptism, and this was all part of the Old Testament (John functioned before Calvary, so he was an Old Testament prophet). As the Hebrews writer summarizes the Mosaic ritual, he identifies "instruction about washings" as a third foundational idea.[18]

And laying on of hands -- This refers to the laying of the offerer's hands upon the sacrificial offerings of the Levitical system.[19] The writer of Hebrews is urging that this obsolete method of dealing with our sins be abandoned.

And the resurrection of the dead -- The Old Testament did teach that in the future there would be a resurrection of dead bodies, but it was very vague.[20] It is in the resurrection of Jesus and in the New Testament Scriptures that a flood of light[21] is thrown on the possibility of resurrection, and what kind of bodies the raised will have. The writer of Hebrews thus is urging his readers to abandon the vagueness of Jewish eschatology for the clear eschatology of the gospel.[22]

And eternal judgment -- While the Jews did learn about a judgment to come from the Old Testament, they also developed numerous erroneous ideas, such as Jews being exempt from judgment while Gentiles are automatically condemned, and confused ideas about the standards

---

[18] For the word translated "teaching, instruction" most manuscripts read *didaches* (genitive case). A few important ones (P[46], B, D, Syr.[P]) read *didachen* (accusative case). With the genitive case, we have six qualities under the heading "foundation," whereas, if the accusative is the correct reading, then repentance and faith are the two foundational qualities and the four terms following are categorized as "instruction" which, while important, are not quite foundational. Moffatt (p.73,74), who suggests the accusative is correct, offers this comment, "The *themelion* [foundation] of instruction consists of *metanoias* [repentance] ... *kai pisteos* [and faith] (genitives of quality), while *didachen*, which is in apposition to it ("I mean, instruction about") controls the other four genitives."

[19] Leviticus 1:4, 3:2, 4:4, 8:14, 16:21. Besides the sacrificial ritual, the laying on of hands was done to appoint someone to public office (Numbers 27:18,23; Deuteronomy 34:9); to bestow a blessing on someone (Genesis 48:14); and in instances of healing (2 Kings 5:11).

 Of course, the laying on of hands was also a practice found in the early church. It had to do with ordination to office (1 Timothy 4:14), with passing on the supernatural gifts of the Holy Spirit (Acts 8:17), with healing (Acts 9:12,17, 28:8), and to set people apart for a special work (Acts 13:3). It would certainly help strengthen the case for the temporary nature of miraculous spiritual gifts if this passage in Hebrews says that "laying on of hands" to impart such gifts is one foundational item that is to be left behind.

 Because of the closeness of this phrase to "baptisms," some see a reference in "laying on of hands" to confirmation. That any such service as confirmation even existed in the apostolic church is not demonstrable.

[20] The Pharisees held such a doctrine because they accepted the authority of the prophets as well as of Moses (Matthew 22:23; Acts 23:8). The Sadducees denied any resurrection, thinking such a doctrine could not be found in the Pentateuch. Jesus accused them of error, and found the doctrine of the resurrection even in Moses (Matthew 22:23-32). Daniel 12:2, and the translation of Enoch also, would give a brief glimpse of such a doctrine, but one must admit the doctrine of resurrection is not enunciated as often in the Old Testament as it is in the New.

[21] 2 Timothy 1:10 says Jesus has abolished death, "and brought life and immortality to light through the gospel."

[22] Acts 17:31 is an example of the clear presentation of resurrection and judgment in the New Testament. Messiah Jesus has been appointed to be the judge of the world, and God Himself has given a pledge that there will indeed be a judgment in that he raised Jesus from the dead. See also John 5:28,29; 1 Corinthians 15:22.

by which God will judge. Jewish ideas of judgment included restoration to Palestine, victories over Israel's national enemies, and national glory for the nation of Israel. The writer of Hebrews urges leaving such ill-founded doctrines, and hearing instead what God Himself says in the clear New Testament presentations.[23]

6:3 -- And this we shall do -- Either pressing on to maturity (6:1) or going on to take up the profound discussion of the high priesthood of Jesus (5:10,11) is the "this" which the writer proposes he and the readers should do.[24]

If God permits -- Will God permit *the writer* to write more? The writer recognizes the necessity of God's involvement in his further writing. It is not as though perhaps God was unwilling to help him write more on the topic. It rather indicates dependence on God. Will God permit *the readers* to be moved along to maturity? That all depends. There are some among the readers that the writer will not be able to help. God Himself (as verse 4ff shows) has excepted some from any such being borne along to maturity.

- *Warning against the consequences of continued spiritual defection. 6:4-8*

6:4 -- For -- "For" shows that what follows is in some way a reason for or an explanation of what was just said. Whether or not the readers can be borne along to maturity depends to a great extent on their own response, i.e., whether or not they leave the elementary teaching about the Christ, or whether they attempt to lay again the old foundation (6:1).[25] Verse 6 will show that in some people's case, there can be no way to "renew them again to repentance."[26]

---

[23] If it is foundational *Christian* doctrines that are to be left, does this phrase exclude all sermons or lessons on the resurrection and the final judgment? It would seem to be so, if it is Christian ABC's rather than Jewish practices that are to be left. This is hard to accept.

Is it possible that one-covenant theology is behind the idea that Hebrews 5:12ff is an exhortation for baby Christians to become "mature" Christians? One-covenant theologians, who say there has only been one covenant since Adam sinned, cannot have you "leaving" what the Old Testament teaches to go to the New, for that would be a denial of their whole system. They must insist that 6:1ff is simply teaching growth in the Christian faith by leaving the ABC's of a new convert's catechism and going on to more mature matters. Not only do we doubt that these six foundational items constituted the core of primitive instruction given to potential converts, but we have not seen much in print explaining what the "mature" items are that Christian preachers and teachers should emphasize, once the foundational items are left.

[24] There is a variation of reading at this place. Some manuscripts read "We shall do" and some read "Let us do." As in verse 1, where it was questioned whether the plural "let us" referred to readers or to the writer, so here, the "we" should probably be explained in harmony with the conclusion given to that earlier question. If they will let the writer bear them along, then the readers will have maturity and an appreciation of Jesus' high priestly activities.

[25] In these verses the Hebrews writer proceeds on the assumption that there are divine means given for going on to maturity, and if these divine means are ignored or abandoned, there is no other way to go on. If the readers persist in going back to Judaism, if they continue to refuse the gospel, if they don't leave the Old Testament elementary principles, there is nothing he or God can do to help them.

[26] The main clause of this long sentence is found in verse 6 in the words "It is impossible to renew them again to repentance." All the rest of the clauses are participial phrases that in some way modify the idea expressed in the main clause.

In the case of those who have once been enlightened -- In verses 4-6 there are seven participles used to describe the people about whom it is said "it is impossible to renew them to repentance." The first five are past tense, the last two are present tense.[27] "Enlightened," if we let the use of the same word at Hebrews 10:32 guide us, means the people in view are thought of as actually having been converted[28] at some time in the past.[29] We also suppose the change from "we" (verse 3) to "those" (verse 4) was done deliberately, not to indicate two separate groups, but to indicate the writer's view that some of the very people addressed (verse 3) could become, if they are not careful, those (verse 4) for whom "it is impossible to renew them again to repentance."

---

[27] Several key problems face the exegete at this place. i) Does "once" go with the first participle only or with all five past-tense participles? ii) Should we insist that the same helping word (such as "if" or "although" or "then" or "in the case of") be used to translate all five past-tense participles? iii) Does the change of tense from past to present require a change of helping word to introduce the present participles? iv) Do the first four participles express four separate ideas, or are participles two, three, and four, explanatory of the first ("enlightened")? v) Does the change from "we" and "us" to "those" and "them" indicate a change in the people addressed?

Kent (p.107) has written a thoughtful introductory paragraph to this long sentence. "The following paragraph is one of the most disputed in the New Testament. Nearly all schools of interpretation face problems in trying to explain the passage consistently. The interpreter is hard pressed to treat it forthrightly without letting his explanations be shaded by his particular theological system. The expositor who approaches each text with a completely neutral mind probably does not exist. The present writer certainly could not claim perfect freedom from such influences. Nevertheless, the attempt will be made to deal fairly with the data confronted here, and then interpret in harmony with other Biblical teaching."

The difficulty in the passage is that it seems to say (1) that for some there is no further hope of repentance; and (2) that some people once saved can later become lost. To avoid one or both of these doctrines, some have gone to one extreme and suggested this is only a hypothetical case; no one ever actually commits such a sin. Others have gone to the other extreme and suggested that even for *one* sin committed after baptism, the man is lost; there is no further possibility of repentance for that. (This latter doctrine is as old as Tertullian *(On Modesty*, 20), who quoted Hebrews 6 to prove there can be no pardon or restoration to communion for post-baptismal sin.) Kenneth S. Wuest, among others, offered the suggestion that the letter writer's concern is with the "unsaved Jew" and that the sin in question is "the act of an unsaved Jew in the first century renouncing his professed faith in Messiah as high priest, and returning to the abrogated sacrifices of the First Testament" [*Bib. Sac.* 119 (1962), p.46]. We reply to Wuest, would an unsaved Jew be thought of as "returning" to the Old Testament sacrifices? Would he ever have left these? And how would you renew "*again*" those who were never renewed in the first place? Wuest's real problem is his adherence at all costs to the doctrine of unconditional eternal security. We shall observe, in the course of the comments on these participles, certain other attempts to prove that the person in question was never saved in the first place.

[28] In the early church, "enlightened" was a term used synonymously with "baptism." (Justin Martyr, *Apol.* I.61,65. *Dial.* c.122). In fact, instead of "enlightened," the Peschito Syriac version (c.425 AD) reads "those who have descended to baptism." It is true that baptism is the point at which one becomes a new creature in Christ. In that act, it might be said the light of Christ has shined upon them (cp. Ephesians 5:8, "you were formerly darkness, but you now are light in the Lord"). Some, following the lead of Zwingli and Calvin, have downplayed the importance of baptism in the process of conversion, attempting to make it but an outward sign of an already-received inward grace. Those writers explain "enlightened" as something akin to regeneration; some even suppose it is something just short of regeneration. Kent (*op. cit.*, p.108) replies to all this in a fine statement: "Although some of the ancients (e.g., Justin) explained this enlightenment as water baptism, and many today explain it of spiritual exposure or illumination short of regeneration, the use of 'once for all' points to something complete, rather than partial or inadequate. The very same participle is used in 10:32, with no hint that there was anything inadequate or tentative about their spiritual enlightenment. Normal understanding of the passage in 10:32 as well as 6:4 would lead us to assume real enlightenment ...." It will just not do to say the people who are thought of as "having fallen away" in verse 6 were never really "enlightened" (verse 4).

[29] Certainly the first participle ("enlightened") is modified by *hapax*, "once" ("once for all"). So, whether or not "once" qualifies all five aorist participles, it without doubt governs the first one. The "enlightenment" was a completed fact.

And have tasted of the heavenly gift -- The gift is "heavenly" perhaps in the sense that it comes from heaven, or has the character of heaven, or is ultimately realized in heaven. It seems probable the "gift" is forgiveness of sins and the new life we enjoy in Christ.[30] As at Hebrews 2:9, "taste" is used in its metaphorical sense of experienced.[31] The people in view in this case are thought of as having been actually forgiven of their past sins. They are saved people.

And have been made partakers of the Holy Spirit -- The writer has used the word "partakers" before at 3:1 and 3:14. This term cannot be diluted so as to make it mean anything less than genuine participation or sharing in the Holy Spirit. The measure of the Spirit that all believers share is the indwelling gift,[32] the help the Spirit gives new converts to live the Christian life. As we read these first three participles, we are reminded that the same things are said at Acts 2:38 – repentance and baptism (enlightened) involves forgiveness of sins (heavenly gift) and the gift of the Holy Spirit (partakers of the Holy Spirit). The three participles in verse 4 cannot properly be applied to any but one who has become a true Christian.

6:5 -- And have tasted the good word of God -- A fourth experience the people have had in this case (verse 4) is that the word of God[33] in the gospel was found to be good and pleasant to the soul. They have found that the gospel does good; it is the power of God to salvation.

And the powers of the age to come -- "Age to come" is normal Biblical language for the Messianic Age, an age that began with the incarnation of Jesus, an age in which the readers were already living. In this case (verse 4) the certain "powers"[34] (predicted in the Old Testament as accompanying the coming Messianic Age) have already been experienced ("tasted") by these readers.

---

[30] Compare Hebrews 2:3-5; Romans 5:15-17, 8:32; John 3:36, 5:24, 6:33,37. Other attempts to specify what the "gift" might be include it being a reference to Christ Himself (cp. 2 Corinthians 9:15, "indescribable gift," and John 4:10), or the gift of the Holy Spirit (cp. Acts 2:38), or some even see a reference to the Lord's Supper. For our own part, we eliminate the possibility the reference is to the indwelling Holy Spirit, for that seems to be the very thing spoken of in the next phrase of this very verse.

[31] "The clause describes vividly the reality of personal experiences of salvation enjoyed by Christians at conversion (baptism)." Behm, TDNT, I. 676. No mere tasting with the tip of the tongue is intended. We cannot use "tasted" as a means of avoiding what seems to be a harsh statement that genuine apostasy (and it was *apostasy* because they had *experienced* -- not just *tasted*) is irremedial -- no repentance is available for it.

[32] We have rejected the idea that "partakers of the Holy Spirit" is a reference to the miraculous spiritual gifts (such as 1 Corinthians 12-14 tells about) since that seems to be what one of the phrases in verse 5 refers to. We have also rejected the idea that "partakers of the Holy Spirit" has exclusive reference to some pre-salvation work of the Spirit (prevenient grace, first work of grace). It is interesting to observe the problem believers in unconditional eternal security have at this place. They usually teach that prevenient grace is irresistible, yet in order to hold onto the doctrine of once-saved, always-saved, they must say these people merely were *exposed* to the Spirit's attempt to convict, but that in this hypothetical case, the Spirit's work was not efficacious. It didn't result in a conversion. Indeed!

[33] "Word" here translates *hrema*, not *logos* (the word used at John 1:1ff, where the reference is to Jesus), so the reference here in Hebrews is to God's Spoken Word, rather than the personal Word (Jesus). Emphasis is on the "Word of God" as uttered; cp. 1 Peter 1:25 and 2:2.

[34] "Powers" is a word regularly used for miracles. (See Matthew 11:20. See also Hebrews 2:4.) We suppose there is specific reference both to the miracles wrought by the apostles, and the supernatural spiritual gifts passed on to certain believers by the laying on of an apostle's hands, and intended to confirm the supernatural character of the message offered in the gospel.

6:6 -- And *then* have fallen away -- "Fallen away" is the last of the five aorist participles found in this series which began in verse 4. There is, therefore, little justification for changing the helping words used to introduce each of these participles.[35] After they used "in the case of" in verse 4 to help translate the earlier participles in this series, the addition (as the italics show it to be) of "then" by the NASB translators can be justified only if it is intended to clarify the idea that on logical grounds the "fallen away" cannot be thought of as simultaneous with the "enlightenment" and "tasted." The verb translated "fallen away" (*parapipto*) is not used elsewhere in the New Testament, though it does occur in the Septuagint in passages dealing with apostasy.[36] It seems obvious that here the word is intended to cover the action some of the readers were seriously considering, namely, abandoning Christianity in favor of returning to Judaism. The person who deliberately repudiates Jesus once he has become a Christian is doing something that renders renewal to repentance an impossibility.[37] It would seem the readers haven't done this woeful deed yet, but it is something distinctly in the realm of the possible, and if they do it, the results are catastrophic.

It is impossible to renew them again to repentance -- Repentance is the result of the action called "renew." "Renew ... again"[38] is an active voice verb, and implies someone or something is trying to bring the person to repentance. But in this instance, there is nothing – no preaching, no communion service, no sacrifice, nothing – that will lead on to needed repentance. And Jesus Himself explained the need for continual repentance when He said, "Unless you repent, you will all likewise perish."[39] The person who does not repent, therefore, forfeits all hope of salvation.[40] "Impossible" stands impressively and emphatically at the beginning of the Greek sentence. It is impossible for God or man to bring about life-changing repentance in the case

---

[35] An "if" is used in the KJV to introduce this fifth participle. "If" is a possible helper to use when translating circumstantial participles, just as "in the case of" (verse 4, NASB) is a possible helper. The only thing objected to is any change of helper that would treat the fifth participle as somehow different from the first four. Milligan (*op. cit.*, p.178) objects to the "if" in the KJV in these words: "Our translators, following Beza, who without any authority from ancient MSS inserted in his version the word *si* (if), ... inserted the word `if' ... that this text might not appear to contradict the doctrine of the perseverance of the saints.

[36] See Ezekiel 18:24, 20:27. Even the writer of Hebrews used a different word (*aphistemi*) for "falls away" (i.e., apostasy) in Hebrews 3:12.

[37] The same contemplated action, and the same sad outcome, is repeated in Hebrews 10:26,27.

[38] When *ana* is prefixed to a word, like it is in *anakainizo*, it does not invariably mean "again," i.e., a return to a previous state or condition. But that likely is the idea here. Repentance would result in a lifestyle as it was before the sin was committed that necessitates repentance.

[39] Luke 13:3,5. The verb in 13:3 is a present tense verb, indicating habitual or continuing or repeated action. Like repeated repentance was needed in Old Testament times (see Hebrews 6:1, "repentance from dead works"), so there are times when repentance is needed and expected of Christians (Acts 8:22; 2 Corinthians 7:9, 10; Revelation 2:5,16). If a man has a low view of Jesus, he is not likely to be careful about being sorrowful for sins against Jesus.

[40] One wonders if "a sin unto death" (1 John 5:16) is the same as the sin the Hebrews were contemplating. It would also seem that 2 Peter 2:21 ("known the way of righteousness" and then "turn away" from it) deals with the same topic. The Bible does seem to present the idea that a person can so sin as to reach a point of no return in his downward slide from God. Possible examples include Judas, when "Satan entered into Judas" (Luke 22:3), and Romans 6:23, in a context where we learn that habitual sin will kill the Christian's spirit, and the result is eternal punishment.

of the man who deliberately repudiates Jesus after having once been one of His followers.[41]

Since they again crucify to themselves the Son of God -- This is why[42] "fallen away" (deliberate repudiation of Jesus) has such dire consequences (i.e., repentance is not possible). They are acting in such a way as to be saying, in effect, 'As far as I am concerned, He deserved to be crucified, for He wasn't doing anything for me when He died!' What else can a man be thinking who rejects Jesus and His religion?   To go back to the Jewish religion implied an

---

[41] Many have been disturbed by this passage, as though it teaches the absolute impossibility of being saved if a man backslides. (Note well: backsliding and falling away are *not* likely synonymous ideas.) Christian instinct, as well as Scripture (such as the calls to repentance in the letters to the seven churches of Revelation), protests against such an interpretation. So extreme care must be exercised at this place lest our explanation discourage sinners who might repent from even trying, because they have been led somehow to suppose they have already committed an unpardonable sin.

The explanations offered for these difficult verses, so that they will not contradict either what is clearly taught elsewhere in Scripture or certain privately-held dogmas, have been numerous. (1) One is that the word "impossible" means no more than great difficulty. Erasmus (16th century) suggested this, and many since that time have urged that "impossible" *not* be taken literally in 6:6. However, the same word is used in Hebrews 6:18, 10:4, and 11:6, where it can only mean "impossible." (2) Another qualifies the meaning by suggesting all things are possible with God, therefore the impossibility must be only on man's part. This suggestion, while it might be corroborated by Matthew 19:26, ignores "If *God* permits" in Hebrews 6:3. (3) Others have supposed Hebrews 6:6 is a hypothetical case that can never really occur. Wuest (*ibid.*), for example, wrote, "The participle is a conditional participle here presenting a hypothetical case, a straw man." Bruce (p.123) rightly notes that the "biblical writers (the writer to Hebrews being no exception) are not given to setting up men of straw." Bruce then continues, "The warning of this passage was a real warning against a real danger, a danger which is still present so long as 'an evil heart of unbelief' can result in 'falling away from the living God' (Ch. 3:12)." (4) Some interpreters, noting that the infinitive "to renew" is without a subject, suggest we should supply a subject from the context of the epistle, such as "the Law of Moses." "It is impossible *for the Law of Moses* to renew again to repentance ...." (5) Lightfoot calls attention to another effort to explain the passage, one that calls attention to the change from past tenses to present tense at this place. The infinitive "to renew" is a present tense, and as such has the force of "to keep on doing a thing." Thus, the passage is interpreted to mean that "it is impossible to keep on restoring them over and over to repentance." They might be restored once, but they cannot be restored again and again without their going outside the bounds of hope. (6) Milligan suggests we can ease some of the disturbance this passage tends to cause by noting that there is a difference between "backsliding" and "apostasy" -- and the thing in view here (for which there is no repentance) is apostasy.

History records some surprising uses to which these verses have been put. (1) "The Montanists and Novatians, on the basis of this passage together with Hebrews 10:26-29, Matthew 12:32, and 1 John 5:16, refused absolution (forgiveness) to anyone who, after baptism (`illumination'), committed one heinous sin" (Moulton, *op. cit.*, p.304). One sin after baptism resulted in the person being eternally lost. "Tertullian ... who believed that Barnabas wrote Hebrews, quotes 6:4-6 and then says: `He who learned this *from* apostles and taught it *with* apostles, never knew of any "second repentance" promised by apostles to the adulterer and fornicator' (On Modesty 20). This was his response to the *Shepherd of Hermas*, which he refers to as `that apocryphal Shepherd of adulteries,' since it allowed *one* opportunity for repentance after baptism (Shepherd, Vision 2.2.4-5). What Hermas actually taught on Hebrews 6 is that there was no repentance for apostates (*Shepherd*, Similitude, 8.6.4)" (Lightfoot, *op. cit.*, p.125). (2) Isabel and Ferdinand started the inquisition against Jews in their realm who had converted to Catholicism, and then reverted to Judaism. They didn't bother Jews who had never converted; those Jews continued to live and do business in their realm. But those who converted and then recanted (and perhaps practiced Judaism secretly from then on) were the ones subject to the inquisition. Later, the inquisition was broadened to involve others besides apostate Jews. This passage was the one they read that triggered the inquisition.

[42] Instead of "since" or "because," as the margin shows, another way of translating present tense circumstantial participles is with the helper "while." "*While* they crucify ... it is impossible to renew them to repentance" might be understood to imply that if they were to quit "crucifying Jesus afresh," then they could be renewed to repentance again. "*Since*" treats this participle as giving the circumstance that makes falling away so bad it precludes any repentance. It is bad because they are crucifying Jesus again, and are continually putting Him to an open shame. A man cannot have a low view of Jesus and at the same time be induced to live for Him.

acceptance of all that the wicked Jews had said and done against the Son of God. "To themselves" says that a man makes an act his own if he approves of it after it is done. To repudiate Jesus now is tantamount to driving the nails into His hands and feet, and doing it gladly.[43]

And put Him to open shame -- This word[44] rouses to mind all the shame and degradation that accompanied being crucified naked. Crucifixion was intended to heap public shame on the victim, and a Christian's apostasy and rejection of the Savior says, in effect, 'He deserves all the public shame and ignominy that can be heaped upon Him.'[45]

6:7 -- For ground that drinks the rain which often falls upon it -- The design of the writer in verses 7 and 8 is to illustrate the consequences of not making a proper use of the privileges which Christians have, and the effect which would follow should such privileges be abused. The Christian is pictured as a field on which frequent rains have fallen, and which continues to produce useful crops.

And brings forth vegetation useful to those for whose sake it is also tilled -- "Vegetation" means anything that is cultivated as an article of food, including grains and vegetables, fodder for animals, plus such crops as flax and cotton. In the Biblical world, many farms were tilled by tenant farmers, and the produce benefited both the owners and the men who did the farming.

Receives a blessing from God -- This phrase shows there is a spiritual application involved in this agricultural illustration.[46] The man who makes proper use of the blessings bestowed by God, and who does not apostatize, meets with the divine favor and approval.

6:8 -- But if it yields thorns and thistles -- It is a continual yielding[47] of thorns and thistles that is in view. After the rains and the work of cultivation, a crop (year after year) of thorns and thistles, neither of which will benefit the farmer or the owner, leads the owner to conclude the land is not worth more work.

---

[43] To turn away from Jesus after once embracing Him is, in effect, joining the ranks of those who actually affixed Him to the cross. It implies an espousal of the bitter hate cherished by the falling nation against Jesus; it is a repetition in spirit of all that the Pharisees had done, and without the mitigating ignorance they could claim since these Hebrew people had the strong evidence of the truth of Christianity -- namely, the true and deep Christian experience indicated in "enlightened, tasted, made partakers, and tasted."

[44] *Paradeigmatizo* is used in Numbers 25:4 (LXX) to describe a public hanging. It is the word used of how the Passover lamb was affixed to a spit in order to be roasted (a "cross" shaped set of sticks -- one lengthwise through the lamb's carcass, the other crosswise at the shoulders, to make it easier to rotate the roasting lamb).

[45] "Now we can see the reason for the impossibility of repentance in the people of this illustration. They have already tried everything God has to offer, and have then turned away from it. Hence there is nothing further that can be done for them. Such will never repent, for God has nothing further to present to them. There will be no additional gospel, no new Messiah. To turn away from God's plan of salvation is to reject the only valid plan there is." (Kent, *op. cit.*, p.111)

[46] The comments offered in the notes (with which Matthew 13:12 might be compared) seem more likely than the explanation which says that God renders the ground more fertile and abundant, though, perhaps, even this explanation can be demonstrated from verses like John 15:2, Genesis 27:27, 49:25, and Deuteronomy 33:13.

[47] Both "brings forth" in verse 7 and "yields" in verse 8 are present tense, indicating continuous action.

It is worthless and close to being cursed -- In the previous verse it was God who did the blessing; we suppose therefore that it is God who is thought of as doing the cursing. The words are reminiscent of Genesis 3:17-18, where the land ever after was cursed to bringing forth thorns and thistles. Isaiah 5 is another Old Testament passage that is called to mind. In that passage, Israel was pictured as God's vineyard, on which He lavished much care and attention, and yet which instead of producing good grapes brought forth only wild grapes, and was therefore abandoned by God. Making the spiritual application, we now see the mortal danger connected with the readers' consideration of the seeming advantages of quitting Jesus. They are getting dangerously close[48] to being "cursed." Such a response by God should not be thought surprising. In perfect harmony with the way He has always acted, and just as recorded in His revealed Word, God's curse rests on the apostate.

And it ends up being burned -- Or as the NASB margin reads, "its end is for burning." The burning hardly suggests a purifying simply to kill any windblown weed seed, in order that the ground may yet bring forth a useful crop. The whole tenor of the passage ("impossible to renew them again to repentance") demands judgment, retribution, and destruction. We assume "burning" is metaphorical language for hell.[49]

- *Encouragement to perseverance based on the certainty of God's promises. 6:9-20*

6:9 -- But, beloved -- The closing sentences of this third warning passage emphasize both God's faithfulness (verses 9-12) and the example of faithful Abraham (verses 13-15) to encourage the readers themselves to continue steadfastly in the Christian religion (verses 1--20). Here in chapter 6, just as in 4:14, the warning is followed by words of encouragement and hope. "Beloved" usually is used to remind readers that God loves them.[50]

We are convinced of better things concerning you -- The "better things" are the alternative spoken of in verse 7. The writer says he[51] believes the Hebrews will yet be blessed by God because they will continue to do the right thing and because, of course, God is faithful. The wording here ("we are convinced," or we trust) is a very personal way to word an exhortation, for implied in the words is the keen disappointment the failure to do as exhorted would cause.

And things that accompany salvation -- The margin reads "things that belong to salvation." The idea might be that these things lead to salvation, or it might be that these things issue from

---

[48] There is no comfort in the words "close to being cursed," for they do not imply a narrow escape, but merely that it has not yet occurred. It indeed will occur if they deliberately repudiate Jesus.

[49] Compare John 15:6; Hebrews 12:29; and Matthew 13:30. The author's meaning is clear -- irrevocable destruction is the destiny of those who turn away from Christ.

[50] Some suppose "beloved" refers to the writer's love for the readers, but verse 10 seems to explain it as meaning God's love for them, since it reminds them of God's dealings with men.

[51] "We" in this case includes the author, and perhaps any associates with him, all of whom were known full well to the readers.

or follow salvation. The New Testament seems to emphasize two facets of good works – sometimes they are the condition of one's salvation,[52] and sometimes they are viewed as the desired response of one who appreciates his own salvation.[53] In the words of this warning passage, "things that accompany salvation" would be "leaving the elementary teachings about Christ," a checking of their tendency to "become dull of hearing," a "pressing on to maturity." These are the things the writer expects of his readers.

Though we are speaking in this way -- "This way" covers the severe warning just uttered, a warning that describes the fearsome consequences of quitting the church to return to Judaism. The readers should not fool themselves: the danger is real! But they do not have to experience it. They can yet decide to be faithful, bring forth useful produce and continue to receive God's blessing. Before they pass the point of no return, they need to check their spiritual defection.

6:10 -- For -- This verse introduces a reason for the confidence just expressed in the previous verse – it rests on God's constancy and their faithfulness.

God is not unjust -- It is a masterly use of understatement to say "God is not unjust." It emphasizes that just the opposite is true. One of God's attributes is that He is perfectly and consistently just. He always does the right thing.

So as to forget your work and the love which you have shown toward His name -- If after revealing that He blesses "ground" which brings forth useful crops (verse 7, i.e., that He looks for evidences of faithfulness in His people[54]) He were to forget what was being done by the readers, that would be unjust on His part. Those who continue to show their faith by their works surely would not end up being burned (verse 8). "Toward His name" reminds us of Matthew 25:40 (KJV), "Inasmuch as ye have done it unto one of the least of these my brethren, ye have done it unto me." Whatever deed of kindness is done to the people of God, God reckons as being done to Him.

In having ministered and in still ministering to the saints -- This is an example of the "work and love" that gave visible expression to the readers' love for God. Hebrews 10:32-34 will detail some of their acts of service or ministering. In days past, before they were scattered by the persecution that arose after Stephen's death (Acts 8:1ff), the Jerusalem church was very generous when it came to meeting the needs of others (Acts 4:32-35). They had demonstrated what James designates as "pure and undefiled religion" (James 1:27). Now this new generation of believers, as is attested in this very letter to the Hebrews, has demonstrated a similar loving

---

[52] Matthew 25:34-40; Galatians 5:22,23; Romans 2:6ff.

[53] James 2:14ff; Galatians 5:6.

[54] There is a behavior characterized by continuing good works that God expects of Christians (Galatians 5:6; Ephesians 2:10; Matthew 25:31ff). It is not possible for a man to meet the condition of faithfulness without also continuing to exhibit good deeds (Romans 2:9,10).

concern for the saints.[55] They demonstrated it in the past, and still are so ministering.[56]

6:11 -- And we desire that each one of you show the same diligence -- The word employed for "desire" suggests an intense longing, as when Jesus spoke to His disciples on that fateful night and said, "How I have longed (desired) to eat this Passover with you before my death" (Luke 22:15, author's translation). In verses 9 and 10, the writer has been speaking to them as a community. Now he wishes that *each individual* would manifest the same diligence in works of love for which he has just commended them as a congregation. Those Christians who were wavering, and tending to quit "ministering to the saints" because they were going back to Judaism, are exhorted to show the same diligence as the people who were showing their faith by their works of love. "Diligence," defined as a strenuous endeavor, ardor, or zeal in work and love and ministry, is the antidote for "sluggish" (next verse) and is an individual matter.

So as to realize the full assurance of hope until the end -- Show diligence in order to make your hope sure is the idea,[57] and continue to show that diligence "until the end," that is, to the end of your lives. Diligence in "ministering to the saints" will result in a growing assurance[58] of hope. "Hope," which is an important word in Hebrews, likely here refers to the thing hoped for,[59] namely, ultimate salvation in heaven. If so, then the verse says that as a Christian contin-

---

[55] We've not had the word "saints" used before (in our English translations of Hebrews), but we have had the word "holy" at 3:1. In the New Testament, a "saint" was a Christian believer, still living on earth, but separated to God's service. It was ministry and service to Christian brethren – ministry in the past, and a ministry continuing in the present – that God would not forget!

This verse has been used by some to argue against a Jerusalem destination for the letter to the Hebrews. Kent, for example has written (p.116), "... the passage does seem to rule out Jerusalem or Judea as the destination of the epistle, inasmuch as the early ministry (Acts 6) was soon curtailed by persecution and their subsequent poverty made them recipients of aid (Acts 11:27ff [sic]; 1 Corinthians 16:1-3) rather than benefactors." Care must be taken here lest we think the Jerusalem church, which began on Pentecost and continued for a few years until its membership was scattered by persecution (Acts 8:1-4), is somehow the same congregation as the Jerusalem church of later years (after Acts 8). The later one was, we understand, made up of new converts won after the original congregation was scattered, and any of the original members (for example, James the brother of the Lord) who may have returned to Jerusalem after the persecution was over. In response to another point made by Kent, while it is true that because of temporary emergencies in the mid 40's (Acts 11) and late 50's (1 Corinthians 16) the Jerusalem saints needed someone else to minister to them, this does not preclude their own ministry to others in times in between and after those emergencies, just as Hebrews here documents. We do not agree that this passage in any way will "rule out Jerusalem or Judea as the destination of the epistle."

[56] The two participles translated "minister" are different tense. One is action previous, the other is action presently being done. The Hebrews have shown fruit and continue to do so (cp. the illustration in verse 7,8), and the writer expects a faithful God to bless those who faithfully continue to produce.

[57] The security of the believer is conditional. Assurance of salvation is conditional. Continuing to show diligence is the condition for avoiding apostasy and the consequent condemnation. Continue to show diligence, and then assurance of God's blessing will grow. We suppose 2 Peter 1:10, "Brethren, be all the more diligent to make certain about His calling and choosing you" is a parallel idea to what is said here in Hebrews 6:11.

[58] "Full assurance" is perhaps the best translation of *plerophoria* in each of its four occurrences in the New Testament (Colossians 2:2; 1 Thessalonians 1:5; Hebrews 6:11 and 10:22). Other suggested renderings include fullness and full development, each of which would result in a slightly different explanation for this verse.

[59] Hope is a complex emotion of the human mind consisting of a desire for some known object and an expectation of receiving and enjoying it. If either the desire or the expectation is missing, it is not "hope", it is just "wishing". When the word "hope" occurs in any passage, it may refer either to the action of hoping or it may

ues to exhibit his faith through his works, thereby comes full assurance of his final salvation. Assurance of the thing hoped for can be expected to follow diligence.

6:12 -- that you may not be sluggish -- Verse 12 is a continuation of the writer's "desire" (verse 11) for the readers. He desires them to show diligence for two reasons: negatively, in order that they "may not be sluggish," and positively, so that they will become "imitators." The word here rendered "sluggish" is the same word translated "dull" in 5:11. "Become dull" there referred to losing interest in Christ and Christianity in favor of going back to Judaism. 'We desire you don't do that,' this verse says.

But imitators of those who through faith and patience inherit the promises -- If the readers show diligence (verse 11), then they would become imitators of those who, because of their faith[60] and patience, are inheriting the promises. "Imitators" (*mimetai*) involves not only following carefully (the English word "mimic" comes from the Greek word) their example of faith and patience, but also (it is implied) inheriting the same reward. Just who are these people who are inheriting the promises and who are to be the role models for the readers? Perhaps the reference is to Old Testament saints like Abraham, who is about to be mentioned in the following verses.[61] Perhaps the reference is to New Testament Christians like Stephen and James,[62] who have already died. Perhaps the reference is to living Christians in the Jerusalem church who instead of becoming dull are examples of faithfulness. "Patience" usually has to do with putting up with provocation caused by people.[63] Persecution because of their faith, such as Hebrews 12:3ff suggests the readers were enduring, would be an example of such provocation. What "promises" are already being inherited[64] depends somewhat on who the role models are. If it is the Old Testament heroes, or even Christians who have died, then the

---

emphasize the object hoped for. The object of the Christian's hope is eternal life, or the "Sabbath rest" that awaits the people of God (Hebrews 4:9). For any Christian, there are still many aspects of salvation yet to be realized. For these blessings he continues to "hope."

[60] Some have supposed that "faith" means believing what God says when He makes promises, and they appeal to the example of Abraham (Hebrews 6:13-15) for evidence this is the correct view. We think "faith" here is to be taken in the sense of *faithfulness*. And while "patience" (perseverance) is sometimes used as a synonym for faithfulness (as for example Romans 2:7), we also think "patience" here in Hebrews is something other than simply perseverance or faithfulness (since a different Greek word is used here than is used at Romans 2:7). "'Faith' is the essential principle through which the blessing is gained, and 'long-suffering' marks the circumstance under which faith has to be maintained" (Westcott, *op. cit.*, p.157).

Paul often uses the trilogy of "faith, hope, love" (e.g., 1 Corinthians 13:13). Those who think Paul is the writer of Hebrews have noticed that familiar trilogy in this paragraph here in Hebrews: love is found in verse 10, hope is named in verse 11, and faith is found in verse 12.

[61] Hebrews 11 will name many of the Old Testament saints and it shows how faithfulness is the reason they have come to be listed in the Scriptures.

[62] Stephen's death is recorded in Acts 7; James' death is recorded in Acts 12.

[63] The difference in the synonyms for "patience" is this: *makrothumia* is putting up with provocations from *people*; *hupomone* is putting up with *things* that are trials; *anoche* is forbearance that is *temporary* in nature. The word here is *makrothumia*.

[64] The participle is present tense, and indicates that the promises are in the process of being inherited, or experienced. They are already the possession of those being blessed.

promises would be those relating to the heavenly rest.[65] If the role models are living Christians, then the promises have to do with present blessings (cp. verse 7) from God who is faithful.

6:13 -- For when God made the promise to Abraham -- "For" seems intended to introduce Abraham[66] as an example of one of those who are inheriting the promises (verse 12). The particular promise to Abraham that the author has in mind is quoted in verse 14. The point of calling attention to Abraham is to show that what happened in the case of Abraham still happens. The same God who made a promise to Abraham and then kept His promise (verses 13-15) has also made a promise to us, and His word is absolutely true. (He cannot lie, verse 16ff.) God's promises are sure and unbreakable and therefore provide a solid foundation for our hope and a strong encouragement to faithfulness. In addition, Jesus, as a forerunner whom others may follow, has already gone within the veil (verses 19,20). By calling attention to Abraham, the writer turns the reader's thoughts beyond the Law of Moses, which was, after all, only a stage in the fulfillment of the promise made to Abraham (Galatians 4:21ff).

Since He could swear by no one greater, He swore by Himself -- There were not many occasions when God took an oath, as far as the Scripture record is concerned. There must, therefore, be a special significance in the fact that as He repeated an oft-made promise to Abraham,[67] God did take an oath. That whole matter deserves special attention. The following verses will unfold the significance of God's swearing.[68]

6:14 -- Saying, "I will surely bless you, and I will surely multiply you" -- The words come from what God said to Abraham on the occasion of the offering of Isaac (Genesis 22:1ff). Genesis 22:16,17 read, "By Myself I have sworn, declares the Lord, ... I will greatly bless you, and I will greatly multiply your seed ...."[69]

---

[65] The Scriptures do indicate that when a good man dies, his soul goes to be with Jesus (Philippians 1:23, 2 Corinthians 5:8). For detailed information on this matter, see the special study on "Hades and the Intermediate State of the Dead" in the author's *Commentary on Acts*. If the role models here called to the readers' attention are the Old Testament saints, then this is one verse which tells us that such men as Abraham, Isaac, Jacob, Moses, Joshua, Samuel, David, Isaiah, Jeremiah, Daniel, are right now enjoying the fulfillment (at least in the intermediate state) of what God promised to the faithful.

[66] This is the second time Abraham is named in Hebrews (see 2:16). He will be mentioned more and more as the book continues. He was one Old Testament character that Christian preachers would appeal to, and the audience would heed what was said.

[67] The promise is recorded in Genesis 12:1-7, 15:5, 17:5-8, and 22:15-18. Included in this promise are the covenant words "In your seed (Jesus) all the nations (Gentiles and Jews both) shall be blessed (have your sins forgiven)" Gen. 22:18. See all this explained in Galatians 3:15ff, Acts 3:25,26, and Romans 4:9ff.

[68] Westcott (*in loc.*) points out the oath itself implied a delay in fulfilling the promise. If God had been about to fulfill His promise immediately, there would have been no reason for God to take an oath. So, from the first, Abraham was faced with the prospect of waiting in hope and faith. Thus, the example of Abraham was fitted to encourage the Hebrews to continue to trust in the unseen.

A recurring topic to which we are paying attention is the whole matter of how the Old Testament is used in the New Testament. How New Testament writers use the Old Testament is surely to be taken as instructive for the church. If (as in the case of God's "oath") there is special significance in such unusual acts, it seems likely our chosen method of interpreting Scripture should also take into account such single acts and words.

[69] The writer of Hebrews substitutes "you" for "your seed" in the last clause because at this point of his argument he is concentrating his attention on Abraham. The Greek "blessing I will bless" is in imitation of the Hebrew construction that lends an emphasis to the statement.

6:15 -- And thus, having patiently waited, he obtained the promise -- At the time the promise was first made by God, and for years thereafter, Abraham was childless. But God was faithful, and Abraham was faithful, and eventually the blessing came.[70] The example of Abraham establishes two things: the certainty of the hope which rests on a promise made by God; and the need for patience before the thing hoped for is received. The idea implied in the verse is this: if Abraham persevered when appearances were so much against the fulfillment of what had been promised, then the Hebrew readers should persevere under the clearer light and with the more distinct promises of the gospel.

6:16 -- For -- With verse 16 the writer begins to impress on his readers the significance of the fact that God took an oath (verse 13). It means the readers, identified as "heirs of the promise" in verse 17, have a double assurance that God's promises will be fulfilled (see verse 18). The promise made to Abraham included more beneficiaries than Abraham alone, and the part of the promise that included other beneficiaries still awaits its ultimate fulfillment.

Men swear by one greater *than themselves* -- Among men, when one takes an oath, it is always implied the appeal is to one of superior power who is able to punish if the oath is violated. The "one greater" by whom men swear is usually God, and was so understood and practiced in both Old and New Testament times.[71] For example, the first recorded instance of an oath appealing to God was taken by Abraham himself (Genesis 14:22, 23).

And with them an oath *given* as confirmation is an end of every dispute -- In the ordinary course of human affairs, an oath has two results – one positive and one negative. Negatively,

---

[70] According to the accepted chronology, 25 years elapsed between the call of Abraham (Genesis 12:4) and the birth of Isaac (Genesis 21:5). The Jews also have Isaac in his early twenties when God commanded Abraham to sacrifice him. So Abraham has already been "patient" for nearly half a century before God reaffirms His promise, this time with an oath. Abraham's grandchildren were not born until another 60 years passed (Genesis 25:26), only 15 years before he died (Genesis 25:7). So it was a wait of many years duration before Abraham began to see the "seed" which God had promised. Of course, the ultimate fulfillment of the promise made to Abraham was never seen during Abraham's earthly lifetime (the Seed [Christ] didn't come till centuries later). As the following verses will show, Abraham (long since having passed from this life) is still seeing some of the things God promised come true. The argument is that Abraham is still in existence, and sees all that is taking place on earth, and that is how he is able to see the promise being fulfilled in the church.

Some have thought they have found a discrepancy between 6:15 ("he obtained the promise") and 11:13,39 ("did not receive what was promised"). The problem may be resolved by explaining chapter 11 as saying the Old Testament heroes died before *all* that was promised (including Messiah's coming) had been fulfilled; but that God never intended *all* the things promised would be realized during this earthly life. Abraham waited a long time, but the promise (by the time the letter to the Hebrews is being written) is finally being realized. In fact, if the underlying idea is that one must wait until heaven to see some of the promised blessings actually come true, it reinforces the argument of chapter 4 that there *is* a heaven (a "Sabbath rest") still awaiting for Christians.

[71] See Genesis 21:23-24, 24:3; Exodus 6:8; Deuteronomy 32:40; Daniel 12:7; Revelation 10:5. In His sermon on the mount, Jesus instructed His followers to "swear not at all" (Matthew 5:34 ASV). James 5:12 has similar language. Yet Paul took an oath in his writings (2 Corinthians 1:23, 11:31). Jesus did not refuse to answer when put under oath while on trial (Matthew 26:63,64). So, we conclude what Jesus was prohibiting were those oaths that come out of insincerity (the oath taker never intended to keep his promise, and was trying to hide that fact in the way he worded his oath) and exaggeration and a life that is generally untruthful and untrustworthy. Judicial oaths, and oaths taken in the name of God on occasions of solemn religious importance, are not excluded by Jesus' prohibition.

it stops all contradiction or disputing.[72] Positively, it establishes or confirms that which it attests.[73] In a courtroom setting, statements given under oath are the ones legally valid, and all lesser statements are disregarded. The sworn statement is the word on which a man stakes his integrity and on which he is willing to be judged and punished by God if it proves false.

6:17 -- In the same way God -- Just like men use an oath to remove all doubt about their truthfulness, so God took an oath in order to remove man's apprehension that His words might not come true. God, of course, did not really need to take an oath; He never speaks anything but pure, holy truth. But He did so to make it absolutely clear to Abraham and the other heirs of the promise that His promise would be fulfilled. It was for others' benefit that God took an oath when He repeated His promise.

Desiring even more to show to the heirs of the promise the unchangeableness of His purpose -- Who are the "heirs of the promise"? Not so much Abraham and the other patriarchs, but those Christians like the writer and his readers, who are Abraham's spiritual offspring (Galatians 3:7, 26-29). What is an "heir"? One who inherits what someone else had. The promise made to Abraham was substantially and really that which embraced all his Messianic hope. Of this the Christians are heirs, i.e., they have become the inheritors of what was promised to Abraham about Messiah. God's plan or "purpose" to have a family who would love and serve Him, a plan that included the death of Jesus to redeem men from their sins, was made back in eternity before He ever began to create.[74] God took an oath when He repeated this information to Abraham so that men (the "heirs" of the promise) would have even more evidence than Abraham had that God wasn't going to change His plan. His purpose was "unchangeable." If God constantly changed His plans, if He were controlled by caprice, if He willed one thing today and another tomorrow, who would confide in Him, and who would have any hope of salvation?

Interposed with an oath – The verb translated "interposed" might also be translated "guaranteed." The two parties to the covenant of blessing[75] were God and man. How was this covenant, then, to be guaranteed? Where was one to be found who could represent the interests of both parties, and guarantee to each party the stability of the covenant? Clearly, no created being could do this.   None but God Himself should so act. So, by His oath, God[76] undertook

---

[72] When two parties are at variance, and doubt the truthfulness of each other's words, an oath binds them to tell the truth, or to adhere to the terms of agreement concluded upon, and thus it puts an end to all strife.

[73] *Bebaiosin* is the word translated "confirmation." That word was used in the papyri for more than 700 years to mean "a legal guarantee" (Deissmann, *Bible Studies*, p.104-109). A man's oath is here called a "guarantee" of the truthfulness of the claim being made.

[74] In Ephesians 1:4ff we are told God wanted a family who would love Him; at Romans 8:28,29 His "purpose" is explained; and at Revelation 13:8 we are told of the Lamb slain from the foundation of the world.

[75] The promise made to Abraham that "in your seed all the nations shall be blessed" is specifically called a "covenant" at Galatians 3:17.

[76] Instead of this being a statement of *God's* imposition, some of the Greek writers (Chrysostom, Oecumenius, Theophylact) thought that "interposed" had reference to *Christ's* mediation. This is the only occurrence of the verb *mesiteuo* ("mediate") in the New Testament, but the corresponding noun form *mesites* does occur at Hebrews 8:6, 9:15, 12:24, where it does speak of *Christ's* mediation. Perhaps that is why the Greek writers tried to make Hebrews 6:17 a reference to Christ also.

to confirm the promise. When He appealed to Himself by an oath, God pledged Himself to do all that was necessary to give the covenant eternal validity.

6:18 -- In order that by two unchangeable things -- The reason the heirs have more evidence than Abraham had is that the heirs have *two* unchangeable things on which to base their confidence in God's faithfulness. The two things are God's oath and God's promise. Both of these are unchangeable. Once God has spoken, it is going to happen that way. God does not lie; God does not swear falsely; God does not break His promises.

In which it is impossible for God to lie -- When God made the Messianic promise to bless the world in Abraham's seed, and when God took an oath to confirm that promise, God was not lying. He cannot lie.[77] "God is not a man, that He should lie" (Numbers 23:19; 1 Samuel 15:29; Titus 1:2).

We may have strong encouragement -- It is "we," says the writer, for whom this "strong encouragement" is intended. In God's promise and oath, the readers may find encouragement to maintain with boldness the position they have taken for Jesus, even though they are temporarily beset with difficulties. If either God's promise or His oath should ever prove to be false, the very laws of His being would be violated, and He would cease to be God. The faithfulness of God is the foundation on which the Christian may rest his hope.

We who have fled for refuge in laying hold of the hope set before us -- "Fled for refuge" reminds us of the Old Testament provision of six cities of refuge to which people who had accidentally killed someone might flee for legal protection.[78] As long as the refugee stayed in the appointed city, he was safe.[79] Applying the figure to the Christians, the idea is that the readers had once been guilty and deserving of death because of their sins, but they had fled to the Redeemer and the hope found in the gospel. Now, if they just remain in Jesus, if they cling to their hope[80] like the man in the city of refuge would cling for dear life to the horns of the altar, then they continue to be safe, and the heavenly rest (centered in Jesus) continues to be held out as an inviting prospect.[81]

---

[77] Some manuscripts have an article before "God," but it should be omitted. The anarthrous form (which emphasizes nature or character) gives the thought, 'It is impossible for one who is *God* (one who has the nature of God) to lie.'

[78] The provision for cities of refuge, three on each side of the Jordan River, may be found in Numbers 35:6,9-32. The verb here translated "fled for refuge" is the very word found in the LXX in Deuteronomy 4:42 and Joshua 20:9 to describe this very flight to avoid revenge by the hands of the dead man's avenger.

[79] There was an additional provision in the Old Testament, that when the high priest died, the one who had fled to the city of refuge could return to his family and home (Numbers 35:28), for it was now against the law for the avenger to seek any further revenge. We have not found any New Testament application of this feature of the cities of refuge.

[80] So far from clinging to some aspect of the *former* life in Judaism, the writer pictures himself and his readers as "laying hold of the hope set *before* (offered)" to them.

[81] The word "hope" was explained in notes at 3:6 and 6:11. It is centered in Jesus, as the following verses in Hebrews 6 indicate. The word translated "set before us" (*prokeimenes*) pictures hope lying before us, spread out like some inviting prospect, and we are encouraged to go to it.

6:19 -- This hope we have as an anchor of the soul -- The figure now shifts from the city of refuge to that of an anchor which storm-distressed sailors cast out of the ship, lest it and they perish on the rocks during the storm. As long as the anchor holds, the ship is safe from drifting to destruction. Hope for heaven is compared to such an anchor. Hope is fundamentally important to a man's soul[82] – it is the antithesis of the despair that can grip a man and cause him to give up. Hope accomplishes for the soul the same thing which an anchor does for the ship – it ensures safety from the dangers of the storm. In the tempests and trials of life, the Christian's mind is calm as long as his hope of heaven is firm.

A *hope* both sure and steadfast -- Two things about anchors are important if the storm is to be safely weathered. One is the anchor's construction: the arms must be strong enough not to bend or twist out of shape or break. Hope, the Christian's anchor, is absolutely reliable. "We have an anchor that keeps the soul, steadfast and sure while the billows roll!" (P. J. Owens)

And one which enters within the veil -- The other important thing about anchors is their placement. On a sandy bottom, the anchor will drag along and still permit the ship to founder on the rocks. The Christian's anchor is placed in the safest place possible –inside the veil,[83] in heaven itself. Abraham rested his hope in the promise and oath of God; but Christians have more than that to rest their hope upon. Christians have the fulfillment of God's promise in the exaltation of Jesus (see verse 20). No wonder the Christian's hope is both steadfast and sure!

6:20 -- Where Jesus has entered as a forerunner for us -- A third figure is introduced, in which Jesus is depicted as a forerunner. As a "forerunner" Jesus differs from all Old Testament priests, who were representatives of men but nothing more. The Levitical priest's entrance into the holy of holies did not make it possible for other men to enter that awesome room. But to call Jesus a "forerunner" indicates that the Christian has the prospect of being where Jesus now is. He is already in heaven, in the presence of the Father, and He entered there "for us." He not only showed the way, He not only atoned for us, but He serves there as our priest in heaven.

Having become a high priest forever according to the order of Melchizedek -- Jesus differs from the Levitical priests. They could enter a little room here on earth. But Jesus, because He belongs to a different order of priesthood, has entered the heavenly reality of which the holy of holies on earth was but a type or a shadow.

At 6:20, with the reiteration of the language of Psalm 110:4, where the Old Testament indicated Messiah would be a priest but of a different order than the Levitical priesthood, we are now back to the point where the writer interrupted his presentation to begin the third warning passage (i.e., 5:10-6:20). The readers will be able to follow the thread of the argument and be positively blessed by the discussion of Jesus' priesthood according to the order of Melchizedek if they have been dissuaded by this warning from "becoming dull of hearing" (5:11).

---

[82] In comments at Hebrews 4:12, the "soul" element of man was discussed. Here in 6:19, it seems that "soul" is synonymous with "life" – and the writer is affirming that hope forms an anchor for a man's whole life. If "soul" refers to a man's whole "life," then the phrase in this verse includes much more than the idea that hope secures the spiritual aspect of man (i.e., that part that animates his body).

[83] The "veil" (or curtain) of the tabernacle and temple separated the holy place from the holy of holies. The place "within the veil," the holy of holies, was a type of heaven (see notes at 9:8,12,24).

C. Further Teaching About Messiah's Priestly Office (after the order of Melchizedek). 7:1-28

1. Jesus' priesthood is a higher order of priesthood than Aaron's. 7:1-11

7:1 -- For this Melchizedek -- With a sentence that begins with "for," the author means to amplify the closing remark of the previous verse, "a high priest forever according to the order of Melchizedek." "This Melchizedek" is the subject of the new sentence, and this sentence is completed in the last words of verse 3, "remains a priest perpetually." That the Melchizedekan priesthood is superior to the Aaronic is shown by three different emphases: (1) Melchizedek was a type of Christ, verses 1-3; (2) Melchizedek was greater than Abraham, verses 4-10; (3) and the Melchizedekan priesthood of Jesus brings in a "perfection" the Aaronic priesthood was unable to provide, verses 11-19. To do a character study of a person in the Bible, it is necessary to look up all the passages about that person. The author of Hebrews does just that. He has already quoted Psalm 110:4. He now goes to the only other place in the Old Testament where Melchizedek is mentioned, Genesis 14.[1]

---

[1] A brief summary of Genesis 14 is this: Four kings (Amraphel, king of Shinar [Babylon], Arioch, king of Ellasar [Lasar was a place in Babylon], Chedorlaomer, king of Elam [a country east of Babylon], and Tidal, king of the nations) invaded the valley where Sodom and Gomorrah were, departing with a great amount of booty and a large number of captives, including Lot, Abraham's nephew. Abraham, with an army of about 300 of his servants, pursued these four kings beyond Dan to the neighborhood of Damascus. God granted Abraham a remarkable victory, and he recovered the spoil and the captives. On his way back to Hebron, he passed Jerusalem, the King's Valley. As he passed, Melchizedek (identified as king of Salem and a priest of the Most High God) came out, bringing bread and wine to refresh Abraham and his soldiers. Abraham gave a tithe of the spoils to Melchizedek, and Melchizedek blessed Abraham. This is all Genesis records of Melchizedek.

Attempts by men to identify this Melchizedek have resulted in numerous conjectures. Josephus regarded Melchizedek as an historical person, and matter-of-factly repeats the Genesis record (*Ant.* I.10.2), and in his *Wars* 6:438, adds additional information as he describes Melchizedek as a "Canaanite chief" whose name means "righteous king," who founded the city of Jerusalem, built a temple there, and officiated as "priest of God." Philo also treats Melchizedek as a historical person, but also gives his usual allegorical interpretation to the details given in Genesis (see *Preliminary Studies* 99, and *Allegorical Interpretation* 3.78ff). Luther and Melanchthon held a view similar to the opinion found in the Jewish Targums (but not the Targum of Onkelos), that Melchizedek was the patriarch Shem who survived the Flood and outlived Abraham forty years. (The Old Testament record proved to be a problem for Jewish interpreters since it obviously makes Melchizedek so much greater than Abraham. By making Melchizedek = "Shem," they relieved some of the pressure they felt, since Abraham would then be ascribing honor to a venerable ancestor.) Others similarly have conjectured that Melchizedek was one of the other patriarchs: Ham, or some descendant of Japheth, or Job, or even Enoch reappearing on earth. Origen and Didymus thought that Melchizedek was an angel. Some Jewish writings (see the Dead Sea Scroll 11Q Melchizedek) suggest Melchizedek was the archangel Michael. Many in the Orthodox Church maintained Melchizedek was none other than the pre-incarnate Jesus on earth in human form in Abraham's day. The Egyptian scholar Hieracas held that Melchizedek was in some way a manifestation of the Holy Spirit. The Melchizedekans (a 3rd century AD sect) held that Melchizedek was not a man but a heavenly being, and this fact made his priesthood superior even to that of Jesus. Jesus' priesthood, they affirmed, was only a copy of Melchizedek's, which was the original order. Therefore, they made their offerings "in the name of Melchizedek." For a summary of views on the identity of Melchizedek, see O. Cullmann, *The Christology of the New Testament*, trans. Shirley C. Guthrie and Charles A. M. Hall (Philadelphia: Westminster,1959), p.83ff.

The writer of Hebrews does not engage in nonsensical conjectures about Melchizedek. He looks at the Old Testament with serious eyes and sees in both Genesis and Psalms a reference to a real, human person. He also tells us the record of Melchizedek was deliberately worded as it was so that Melchizedek could serve as a type of Christ.

King of Salem -- "Salem" is a name given to the city of Jerusalem in Psalm 76:2. The Dead Sea Scrolls[2] and Josephus[3] also identify "Salem" with Jerusalem.[4]

Priest of the Most High God -- "Most High God" is the Septuagint rendering of the Hebrew *'el 'elyon*, a name for Jehovah, in Genesis 14:18.[5] How is it possible for Melchizedek to be a "priest" of Jehovah when there have been no provisions for such a priesthood in the earlier chapters of Genesis? Where did the idea of having a priesthood come from? How did Melchizedek become acquainted with Jehovah? The only satisfactory answer to these questions is that God had made revelations to men which are not recorded in the first fourteen chapters of Genesis,[6] and because of these revelations Melchizedek was functioning as a priest of Jehovah.

Who met Abraham as he was returning from the slaughter of the kings -- We suppose the reason Melchizedek came to meet Abraham was to express gratitude to Abraham for having freed the country from oppressive and troublesome invaders and in order to furnish refreshments[7] to the party which Abraham headed.

And blessed him -- The actual words of the blessing, recorded in Genesis 14:19, 20, are "Blessed be Abram of God Most High, Possessor of heaven and earth; And blessed be God Most High, Who has delivered your enemies into your hand."

---

[2] The Genesis Apocryphon 22,13, found in Cave I, an interpretative translation of Genesis 14, includes the statement that Abram "came to Salem, that is Jerusalem."

[3] Antiquities I.10.2.

[4] Jerusalem would have been on the general route Abraham would have taken on his return from the slaughter of the kings near Damascus. Therefore certain other traditions – for example, that Salem was located on Mt. Gerizim (a Samaritan idea?), or is identical with Shechem (see LXX at Genesis 33:18), or was near Scythopolis (Jerome) – all seem on their face to be improbable.

On the accepted chronology, Abraham is dated about 2000 BC. Before the discovery of the Tell-el-Amarna tablets, negative critics refused to believe what Genesis says about Melchizedek and Salem. They denied that the name of Jerusalem or Salem was known before the time of David (1050 BC). The tablets, found in 1887 about 190 miles south of Cairo, Egypt, are letters written in the 15th and 14th centuries BC and sent to the Pharaoh by the rulers of adjacent territories imploring help against an armed invasion by a people called the Habiru, and pointedly stating that unless Egypt sent aid, the dependent territories would be lost. Among them are seven letters sent by the "King of *Jerusalem*" urging Pharaoh to assist him. So, the assertions of the critics were proven wrong by archaeological discoveries.

[5] There is, of course, no idea that there is any other God who is not most high.

[6] In an earlier chapter of Genesis, we find Cain and Abel offering sacrifices. One sacrifice is acceptable, the other isn't. No statement about sacrifices is found antecedent to their offerings, yet one must certainly have been made since Hebrews 11:4 tells us that it was "by faith" that Abel offered a better sacrifice. Remember, faith comes by hearing the Word of God. A revelation is implied in such language even though no such revelation is recorded in Genesis. Melchizedek knew Jehovah in the same way that Abraham and Job (likely a contemporary of Abraham) knew Him. Those Old Testament heroes were men of faith -- that is, they heard and obeyed God's revelation to them. In the Patriarchal Age, God did make revelations to men face-to-face and through the words of prophets (see Hebrews 1:1).

[7] There is not the slightest evidence that the bread and wine which Melchizedek brought forth were designed to typify the Lord's Supper, as some have supposed. In the bread and the wine, we have nothing more than the ancient rite of hospitality.

7:2 -- To whom also Abraham apportioned a tenth part of all *the spoils* **--** Why did Abraham give a tenth? There is no reason to doubt that the giving of a tithe, as well as the offering of sacrifices, was a regulation of Divine origin.[8] While the offerings given by Abraham to Melchizedek were likely voluntary on Abraham's part, it is reasonable to think he made them in harmony with what he knew to be an existing God-given ordinance.

Was first of all, by the translation *of his name,* **king of righteousness --** Hebrew names had etymological meanings. The meaning of the king's own name and then the name of the place where he ruled are each singled out for special treatment. The king's name, Melchizedek, is made up of two words, *Melchi* meaning "king" and *Zedek* meaning "righteousness." We suppose there is typology involved. One of the interests of any priest is that the worshippers he represents may have a right relationship ("righteousness") with God. Like Melchizedek was king, Jesus, our great High Priest, is also a *king* who is intimately involved in the matter of *righteousness* through His atoning death[9] and His intercessory work. "First of all" tells us that there is even significance in the fact that "righteousness" comes before "peace." Everywhere in Scripture men must be right with God before there can be any peace.[10]

And then also king of Salem, which is king of peace -- "Salem" comes from the same root as *Shalom*, the Hebrew word for "peace." "Peace" is more than the absence of war; it also regularly involves the presence of positive, spiritual blessing from God. Again, we suppose typology is involved. Another interest of any priest is that the worshippers he represents may experience "peace." Jesus, our great High Priest, has bequeathed His special peace to His followers (cp. John 14:27, "My peace I leave with you").

7:3 -- Without father, without mother, without genealogy – Remember, the Levitical and Melchizedekan priesthoods are being contrasted and compared. In the Levitical system, the priest's family tree was of utmost importance. The pedigree of both father and mother clear back to Aaron was carefully recorded.[11] But how different with Melchizedek.

---

[8] The dedication of a tenth of the spoils of war to a deity (on whose behalf the priest acted) was practiced among the Greeks and other nations, though there is no record of it (other than Abraham and Melchizedek) among the Jews (see Herodotus, *History* i.89; Xenophon, *Anabasis* v.3; Livy, *History* v.21). We would assume the Gentile practice reflects an old commandment given by God to men and passed on from generation to generation by word of mouth. This act of devotion on the part of Abraham, as well as the vow of Jacob (Genesis 28:22), clearly indicates the custom of giving tithes to God (for the maintenance of His worship and the support of true religion) was of very remote antiquity, and that it originated in a revelation from God. (Care should be taken here. We have not said, nor does the Scripture suggest, that one of the reasons Cain's sacrifice was unacceptable was because he was not bringing a tenth.)

[9] Jesus was the Righteous One (Acts 3:14), and by His righteous act satisfied the righteousness of God as our substitute, and thus provides peace with God for all believers (Romans 3:21-26; Colossians 1:20; Ephesians 2:14).

[10] See Romans 5:1, 14:17; James 3:18; Hebrews 12:11; Isaiah 33:17; Psalm 72:3, 85:10. R.C. Foster used to observe that one of the fatal flaws in the Ecumenical Movement was that it was trying to produce peace among the denominations without first making sure all groups were right with God (righteousness). Until the Scriptural order – righteousness first, then peace – is observed, the Ecumenical Movement is doomed to failure.

[11] See Leviticus 21:13,14; Ezra 2:62,63; Nehemiah 7:64.

In the sacred writings there is no record made of the name of his father or his mother, nor any of his descendants.[12] It is not that Melchizedek didn't have a father or mother; all it says is that their names are not found in the Scriptures.[13] Furthermore, when the letter writer goes on to say Melchizedek was "made like the Son of God," he is indicating that the omission of the names of ancestors or descendants was done deliberately when God inspired the Scriptures to be written.

Having neither beginning of days nor end of life -- It does not mean Melchizedek was never born or never died, merely that there is no record of his birth or death in the Scripture record.[14] Again, the contrast with the Levitical priesthood is striking. The death of Aaron is carefully recorded, as is the transfer of the priestly office to his son.[15]

But made like the Son of God – The writer of Hebrews here indicates that when the Old Testament record was written, God deliberately led the writers to include and to omit certain facts so that Melchizedek would serve as a *type*[16] of Jesus, the Son of God. The points in which Melchizedek and Jesus correspond as type and antitype are these: he is

---

[12] It would appear that it was common among the Jews to use such terms (without father, without mother) to indicate the father's or mother's names *do not appear in Scripture.* Philo, for example, says that Sarah, the wife of Abraham, did not have a mother (*De Ebrietate*, sect.14), meaning that her mother's name was not found in the sacred records. The Syriac version at Hebrews 7:3 reads "of whom neither the father nor mother are recorded in the genealogies." If "not recorded in Scripture" is the regular meaning of this idiom, then certain views which ignore such a use of terms must be rejected. Among these rejected views are: (1) The writer of Hebrews is intending to say that Melchizedek was some kind of super-human being, based on the fact that among the Greeks the terms "without father, without mother" were sometimes used for deities whom the Greeks supposed had taken their origin from one sex only. (2) The writer of Hebrews is intending to say Melchizedek was an angelic being since angels (being created beings) do not have fathers or mothers.

[13] Melchizedek did have parents and descendants, as Hebrews 7:6 implies. Melchizedek did have a genealogy, a family tree; it just isn't recorded in Scripture. When one comments on the significance of the presence or absence of a family tree in the case of Melchizedek, care must be taken, for the genealogical table for Jesus (the antitype of Melchizedek) is clearly given (Matthew 1, Luke 3). Melchizedek's likeness to Jesus is in his priestly function, not in his human family tree. Further, the human Jesus was born of Mary, died on Calvary, and then arose from the dead. Again, therefore, when we compare Melchizedek and Jesus ("having neither beginning of days nor end of life"), we must limit the discussion to Jesus' priestly functions.

[14] Some have used this phrase ("having neither beginning of days nor end of life") plus the last three words of verse 8 ("he lives on") in an attempt to prove that Melchizedek was an eternal being, and therefore the Melchizedek of the Old Testament must have been Jesus Himself. It is rather common to find the commentaries suggesting Melchizedek was a theophany. We object to such an identification on several grounds: (1) it is strange language to say Melchizedek was *made like* the Son of God if Melchizedek was *actually* Jesus Himself in human form. (2) Further, Psalm 110:4 identifies Messiah as a priest "after the order of Melchizedek." This clearly makes a distinction between Messiah and Melchizedek. The two are not the same person. (3) If Melchizedek was actually a pre-incarnate appearance of *God* in the world, there is no need to spend a whole chapter (Hebrews 7) proving *He* was superior to any mere human patriarch or priest!

[15] Numbers 20:23-29, 33:37-39; Deuteronomy 10:6.

[16] There is a great difference between a *type* and an *allegory.* While Hebrews treats portions of the Old Testament as types, the writer of Hebrews does not allegorize the Old Testament, as did some of his contemporaries. Much has been made of the alleged Alexandrian influence on the writer of Hebrews. In the use of Melchizedek as a type of Christ, there is evidence the writer is *not* treating the Old Testament allegorically, as did Philo, for example. When the Alexandrian school allegorized, they omitted no details; every fact, every item was allegorized. Several important items in the Genesis account are not used in Hebrews. The bread and wine and the fact that the king of Sodom accompanied Melchizedek are completely omitted from Hebrews.

king of righteousness and king of peace; he abides a priest perpetually; he had no ancestors in the priestly office; he has no successors in the priestly office; he is a priest of a different order than Aaron's order; he united in himself the office of king and priest.

He abides a priest perpetually -- As noted earlier, this is the main verb of the Greek sentence that began in verse 1: "This Melchizedek ... abides a priest perpetually." At least as far as the Scriptural record is concerned, there is no account of his death or of his ceasing to exercise his priestly office. Levitical priests did not serve uninterruptedly or continually.[17] Some died and were replaced. Others were hindered by age from continuing to serve (since under the Mosaic Law priests were required to serve from age 30 to 50[18]).

7:4 -- Now observe how great this man was -- Four lines of thought develop the theme that Melchizedek was greater than Abraham (verses 4-10): Abraham gave a tithe to Melchizedek; Melchizedek blessed Abraham; no succession of men followed Melchizedek; Levi (in a sense) paid tithes to Melchizedek. What is the point of showing that Melchizedek was greater than Abraham? The Jews had a profound appreciation for Abraham. If it could be shown that Melchizedek was superior to Abraham, then it would be easy to demonstrate to all Abraham's descendants the superiority of Christ as a priest.

To whom Abraham, the patriarch, gave a tenth of the choicest spoils -- In the Greek, "patriarch"[19] stands at the close of the sentence for emphasis. Think of it – no less than the *patriarch* gave a tithe to Melchizedek! Abraham was a great man indeed. To his neighbors he was a "prince of God" (Genesis 23:6, literally) and God Himself called Abraham "my friend" (Isaiah 41:8). But in the account of Abraham's meeting with Melchizedek, it is Melchizedek who appears as the greater of the two. That greatness is implicit in the fact that Abraham gave the tithe to Melchizedek. "Choicest spoils" reflects the ancient custom, after a battle, of collecting the spoils together, heaping them up into a pile, and then before they were distributed, taking a portion off the top and devoting them to the gods.[20] What Abraham gave to Melchizedek was intended as an offering to God.

---

[17] Different Greek words (*dienekes* and *aion*) are used for "perpetually" and "forever." The word used here, *dienekes*, occurs only in Hebrews (4 times) in the New Testament. It does not so much indicate duration without end as it does duration which lasts through the circumstances indicated in the particular case, i.e., uninterruptedly. Of course, when Melchizedek died, his priesthood was ended. Jesus, also, will cease His priestly functions when the church shall have been redeemed and when Jesus shall have given up the mediatorial kingdom to the Father (1 Corinthians 15:25-28).

[18] Numbers 4:3, 23, 25,43, 47, and 7:24,25. In later periods of Jewish history, men commenced their priestly duties at the age of 20 (1 Chronicles 23:24,25). The high priest also entered office at the age of 30, though it was not supposed that they retired from office at any specific age. High priests served until they died.

[19] "Patriarch" comes from a Greek word meaning "father" and "rule." The "father" (at first, the progenitor, then his first-born or eldest lineal male descendant) was the "head" of the family, tribe, clan, or race. The name "patriarch" is regularly given to those godly men whose lives are recorded in the Old Testament before the time of Moses. The patriarchal dispensation was the period from Creation to Mt. Sinai, and was a time when each patriarchal family head was the priest of his own household, and God communicated with him as such.

[20] See Xenophon, *Cyropaedia* vii.5,35; Herodotus, *History* i.86,90; viii.121,122; Xenophon, *Anabasis* v.3; Dionysius Hal. ii; for the Greek and Roman practices. In like manner it was customary to place the harvest in a heap, and as the first thing, to take off a portion from the top to consecrate as a thank-offering to God. The word *akrothinion* denotes literally the "top of the heap."

7:5 -- And those indeed of the sons of Levi who receive the priest's office -- Lest the point of the argument be missed – that one who receives the tithe is considered greater than the giver – the writer calls attention to this truth as far as the Levitical priesthood[21] was concerned. The right to collect tithes from someone implies a certain authority and thus a superiority. Thus, that Levitical priests received the tithes from the people implies they were superior, in their official capacity, to the people.

Have commandment in the Law to collect a tenth from the people -- The Law of Moses, which vested them with the authority to collect the tithes, thus elevated the priests above the people. Numbers 18:21-32, Deuteronomy 14:22-29, and Nehemiah 10:38 contain the instructions to the Levites to tithe Israel.

That is, from their brethren -- There was a sense in which the Levitical priests had no inherent superiority since they were brothers (kin) of those who gave the tithes. The Levitical priesthood received tithes by positive commandment, not because of any personal superiority. Before this paragraph is finished (verse 10), the writer will show that though the Levitical priests had the right to receive tithes from their brethren, even so they were still inferior to Melchizedek.

Although these are descended from Abraham -- Both the Levitical priests and the Jewish people were descended[22] from Abraham, so the priests had no inherent superiority over the people. Yet by virtue of their position as priests, the Levites did have a certain superiority over the people, even though they were descended from Abraham. The Israelites may have been a special people, God's chosen people, the seed of Abraham, but they still paid tithes; they paid them to priests who by "commandment" were given the position and authority to collect them.

7:6 -- But the one whose genealogy is not traced from them -- Melchizedek is the one intended; he obviously did not trace his descent from Levi since he was a contemporary of Abraham. Since he was not a Levite, Melchizedek's authority (superiority) to collect tithes from Abraham[23] did not derive from any commandment given to Levi and his priestly descendants. If Melchizedek was superior to Abraham, and if by giving a tithe to Melchizedek

---

[21] "The sons of Levi who receive the priest's office" implies not all of Levi's descendants became priests. Only those descending from Aaron were eligible to be priests, and many of these were disqualified by improper marriages, inability to prove their pedigree, or other reasons (Leviticus 21:16-24). Those who did become priests, by that fact, had the responsibility of collecting the tithes from the rest of Israel.

[22] The marginal reading "came out of the loins of Abraham" is an idiomatic expression for descendants.

[23] We are not denying what was said earlier about how Melchizedek came to be a priest of the Most High God. Nor are we suggesting that we believe Abraham had no knowledge of the validity of Melchizedek's priesthood or of the appropriateness of tithing the spoils (i.e., as if such ideas were of human invention rather than Divine revelation). It was Melchizedek's official position as priest of the Most High God that gave him superiority over Abraham. We suppose that position was known to both Melchizedek and Abraham by an unrecorded (in the Old Testament Scriptures) revelation from God. Likewise, Levitical priests had authority and superiority over the Jewish people because of their position. They held their priestly position, not because of any human heredity or other merely human reason, but because God had so commanded in the Law of Moses.

Abraham tacitly admitted this superiority, Melchizedek's superiority rested on some reason other than that on which Levitical superiority rested. Melchizedek's priesthood, and the superiority inherent in that position,[24] rested on a different law than that on which the Levitical priesthood rested.

Collected a tenth from Abraham -- Abraham, though considered (and rightly so) by the Jews to be superior to Aaron and the Levitical priests, was nevertheless inferior to Melchizedek. Unless we admit this surpassing dignity of Melchizedek, how do we account for the fact that Melchizedek received a tithe from Abraham (see Hebrews 7:2), and in return blessed Abraham?

And blessed the one who had the promises -- The idea seems implicit that Melchizedek's act of blessing Abraham was in response to Abraham's giving of the tithe. As he in return conferred the blessing on Abraham, Melchizedek was acknowledging the rightness of Abraham's recognition of Melchizedek's superior position. This is the second point in this presentation about the greatness of Melchizedek as compared to Abraham (see comments on verse 4). What promises did Abraham have? Messianic promises, such as "in your seed all the nations of the earth shall be blessed" and "a father of many nations have I made you." Abraham was an important Old Testament character!

7:7 -- But without any dispute the lesser is blessed by the greater -- In cultures where one seldom sees such a blessing conferred, readers may have difficulty appreciating this argument, that the act of blessing implies superiority.[25] Great as Abraham's privileges were by virtue of the promises he had received from God (see Hebrews 6:13ff), he recognized the superiority of Melchizedek by accepting the blessing at his hands. No one reading the account in Genesis 14 would dispute that Melchizedek, who conferred the blessing (see Hebrews 7:1), was thereby acknowledged to be greater than Abraham who received it.

7:8 -- And in this case mortal men receive tithes -- "In this case" refers to the Levitical priesthood. Under that system, men who will die men receive tithes[26] from the worshipers. Under the Law, the death of the priest was always made a matter of record (cf. 1 Chronicles

---

[24] Not a few commentators suppose Melchizedek's greatness was not so much a function of his priesthood, but rather was a function of who he was in his person. "He was a solitary figure of grandeur" (Morris, *op. cit.*, p.64). "Abraham's act of tithing was voluntary and spontaneous, a tribute to Melchizedek's personal greatness" (Lightfoot, *op. cit.*, p.139). While the fact that he was a king as well as a priest might have led Abraham to recognize his superiority, we have chosen in our comments to attribute Melchizedek's superiority to his official capacity as priest rather than on some personal greatness.

[25] "Melchizedek must have been superior to Abraham so as to be able to bestow a blessing upon him. When he blessed Abraham, his words were not just congratulatory but were an expression of God's approval. Thus at that moment Melchizedek stood between God and Abraham and was the better, while Abraham was the lesser" (Kent, *op. cit.*, p.129). In the Genesis account, Melchizedek makes no claims, and Abraham does not concede anything in words. But their actions spell out exactly what the situation was. The writer of Hebrews is simply drawing attention to what the narrative clearly implies. Melchizedek was superior to Abraham.

[26] The present tense verb "receive" has been used by some to show that when Hebrews was written, the Levitical priesthood was still operational. That priesthood did continue to function until AD 70 when the destruction of Jerusalem by the Romans brought an end to the old system of religious observances.

$6:50\text{-}52$).[27]   We enter here upon the third argument adduced to show Melchizedek's superiority – an argument based on the fact that, according to the record, Melchizedek never had to hand on his authority to someone else. In the Levitical system, priests were continually dying[28] and had to be replaced by others.

But in that case one *receives them* -- "In that case" refers to Melchizedek, who received a tithe[29] from Abraham.

Of whom it is witnessed that he lives on -- As far as the Scriptural record is concerned, Melchizedek could still be living and serving as a priest. There is no specific statement of his death.[30] He does not mean Melchizedek never died, but that the silence of Scripture on this point furnishes the basis for making Melchizedek's priesthood a type of Christ's.

7:9 -- And, so to speak -- This fourth argument for the superiority of Melchizedek (cp. verse 4) seems rather odd, on first thought, to the modern reader, but first-century readers would have been impressed by the compelling force of such a presentation. And on further thought, so will modern readers. "So to speak" says it is not strictly and literally true, but at the same time is not an unfounded exaggeration either.

Through Abraham even Levi, who received tithes, paid tithes -- One might be inclined to suppose the Levitical priesthood was better since it came later than Melchizedek's. Not so, for even Levi paid tithes to Melchizedek (so to speak). How Levi could pay tithes to Melchizedek is explained in the next verse.

7:10 -- For he was still in the loins of his father when Melchizedek met him -- Abraham was actually the great-grandfather of Levi, but "father" is often used in Scripture to mean

---

[27] In the Levitical system, men entered by birth into a state with which the right to receive tithes is associated, and by death passed out of it. No special significance, therefore, attached to the men themselves. It was the *office* that gave them the right to receive tithes from their brethren.

[28] When men are called "mortal," it is a reference to the body which dies. The soul or spirit of man lives on (in the intermediate state) after the body dies.

[29] We have a broken sentence in the Greek, and must supply the verb from the context. Our translators have rightly supplied "receive" from the first part of the sentence.

The reader should be aware that this passage in Hebrews has been used (dubiously, in this commentator's opinion) to prove Christians should be tithers. First it must be interpreted in such a way that Jesus (rather than Melchizedek) is the subject of the sentence. Then the argument is made that Jesus is said to receive tithes, and if the Christian doesn't pay them, who will? Hence, Christians are to be tithers. (Cp. A.B. McReynolds, "God's Solution for Bankrupt Churches" [Talahina, Ok., 1952], p.18.) In this commentator's view, Hebrews 7:8 refers to Melchizedek, and what the New Testament teaches is stewardship, not just tithing.

[30] The writer does not say Melchizedek is actually still living on earth and functioning as a priest (he would have been about 2000 years old when Hebrews was written). He does write that "the witness (testimony)" about Melchizedek is that "he lives on."

This phrase has given commentators exceeding difficulty. It is one of the major reasons some have supposed Melchizedek must be none other than Jesus, for who else but deity would have it said of them that "he lives on" in contrast to men who die?

"ancestor."[31] Levi, the descendant, was not yet born when Abraham met Melchizedek, but what Abraham did affected Levi. This argument is based on the principle that one is affected by the acts of his ancestors.[32] If Jews and Christians use the same argument concerning the blessings promised to Abraham,[33] its use is not objectionable concerning Levi.

7:11 -- Now -- The writer is developing the idea that Jesus' priesthood is superior to the Levitical priesthood. He is in the midst of the first of seven proofs of that superiority, one based on Jesus' priesthood being after the order of Melchizedek. Having shown (1) that Melchizedek was a type and (2) was greater than Abraham (and Levi), he (3) now begins to point out a certain imperfection in the Levitical priesthood (verses 11-19) that made it necessary to replace the Aaronic order with Jesus' priesthood after the order of Melchizedek. To word it another way, the writer is explaining in detail how the demonstrated superiority of Melchizedek to Levi relates to the topic of Jesus' high priesthood.

If perfection was through the Levitical priesthood -- "Perfection" is literally "the making perfect," that is, the full accomplishment of the essential aim of the priesthood, that of bringing men "near to God." "Perfection" means the condition in which men are acceptable to God.[34] The way men become acceptable to God is to have their sins completely atoned for, completely forgiven. This was something the Jewish priesthood could not do, since the sacrifices they had to offer, the blood of bulls and goats, never could take away sin (Hebrews 10:1-4).

(for on the basis of it the people received the Law) -- It is commonly thought that the order was first came the Law, and second, on the basis of the Law, the priesthood rested.

---

[31] The family tree actually was Abraham, Isaac, Jacob, then Levi. The meeting of Abraham and Melchizedek took place about 14 years before the birth of Isaac. Yet the writer of Hebrews calls Abraham the "father" of Levi. This extended use of "father" may be one point against the chronology invented by Ussher. He added together the number of years that Old Testament men lived, in order to arrive at the dates he gave in his chronology. But, if any of the "fathers" were actually "ancestors" two or three generations earlier, then his computation of the total number of years could be off, and creation would be pushed back considerably earlier than Ussher's suggested date of 4004 BC. While not accepting Ussher's date, this commentator does hold to a young earth theory for the date of creation.

[32] The principle is recognized by Jews and Christians alike. Who doubts that what Adam did when he sinned affected the race by bringing physical death on the race? We all died in Adam (1 Corinthians 15:22; Romans 5:12). Who doubts that what Jesus did affects the race? "In Christ all shall be made alive." The number of souls who went down into Egypt in Jacob's time is computed by counting some children not yet born (Genesis 46:21-26). In fact, in the case of Levi and the Levitical priesthood, the principle looks both ways. It was not until after Levi gave birth to Aaron that the Aaronic high priesthood could be established. Yet the point made here in Hebrews is that the Melchizedekan priesthood was greater than the Aaronic because Levi, the great grandfather of Aaron, paid tithes (so to speak) to Melchizedek. This same principle, that what an ancestor does affects his descendants, is true today in the matter of citizenship. When a man becomes a citizen of a country, all his descendants are conferred certain privileges and obligations though they did not personally chose citizenship themselves. This fourth argument, after due consideration is given, is not so unfamiliar after all.

[33] The same Greek phrase "come out of the loins of Abraham" was used in verse 5.

[34] The word here translated "perfection" is *teleiosis*, the same root word translated "mature" in Hebrews 5:14 and 6:1. The "maturity" or "perfection" toward which Christians are to be borne along is the "perfection" available in the sacrifice of Jesus.

But a restudy of the Old Testament record will show that both Moses and Aaron were chosen by God before the Law was given. It was on the basis of the priestly function that God wanted performed that He issued the Law at Sinai, giving the regulations and directions for how the priesthood should function.

What further need was there for another priest to arise according to the order of Melchizedek – This whole question is based on the fact that long after the Levitical priesthood began, and while it was yet still functioning, God made a prediction (Psalm 110:4) that there would one day be another priest[35] after the order of Melchizedek. The writer of Hebrews asks his readers to consider the implications of that later prediction. Lest they miss the point, he spells it out. The very fact that there was a prediction of a coming change of priesthood implied the Levitical priesthood did not accomplish all God required for making men acceptable.[36] If everything needed to make a man perfect had been provided by the Levitical priesthood, there would have been no need to predict a replacement of the Levitical priesthood by the Messiah, whose priesthood *would* make believers perfect.[37]

And not be designated according to the order of Aaron? -- Lest the reader somehow fail to observe the fact, the Hebrew writer is driving home the idea that there is a significant difference between "the order of Melchizedek" (predicted in the Psalm), and the "order of Aaron" (i.e., the Levitical priesthood).[38]

2. Jesus' priesthood means the Law of Moses has been abrogated! 7:12-19

7:12 -- For when the priesthood is changed -- The Greek word *metathesis* is better translated "abrogated" than "changed"; that is, it is replaced by something better.[39] The old

---

[35] "Another (*heteros*, not *allos*) priest" means a priest of a different kind, a different order.

[36] The question is equivalent to a strong denial: there would be no such need if the Levitical priesthood brought "perfection."

[37] We are being introduced to the theme that will be emphasized several times in the following chapters, namely, that the Law of Moses was never intended to be anything but temporary. Even the prediction found in Psalm 110:4 could be fulfilled only if the Old Testament and its priesthood were replaced by something better. If God predicted through David that there would be a priesthood of another kind, then certainly that indicates the Levitical priesthood would be set aside.

[38] F.F. Bruce (*in loc.*) notes that this verse has some bearing on the identification of the readers to whom this letter was addressed. If the readers were of Gentile background, in danger of abandoning the Christian faith, their only response to this argument would have been, 'We never did think there was "perfection" through the Levitical priesthood. We had our own priestly system!' But if the readers were Jewish by birth or religion, now in danger of giving up Christianity in order to go back to the Old Testament religion, then the argument makes sense. 'Are you going to go back to a priesthood that never did (as the Old Testament itself plainly shows) accomplish "perfection" for the worshipers?'

[39] This is the first of three very clear affirmations that the Law of Moses and the Aaronic priesthood have been abrogated. They have been replaced. They are no longer valid. See also Hebrews 7:18 and 10:9.

Aaronic order is replaced by Messiah's priesthood after the order of Melchizedek.[40]

Of necessity there takes place a change of law also -- The abrogation of the Levitical priesthood was a matter of no small moment. If it was on the basis of the priesthood that the Law was given, then when the priesthood is abrogated, so is the Law of Moses.[41] What is written here is in harmony with what the New Testament everywhere else affirms; namely, that the Law of Moses was never intended to be anything but temporary and its validity ceased when Jesus died and rose again.[42] Through verse 25, the writer of Hebrews sets out to show beyond any possibility of contradiction that there has indeed been an abrogation of priesthood and of the Law.[43]

7:13 -- For the one concerning whom these things are spoken – The "one" is Jesus.[44] "These things" refer to the predicted change of priesthood from one order to another. To prove his point (verse 12) that there had been in fact a change of priesthood, the author focuses attention on Jesus' earthly circumstances. If He is going to serve as a priest, it rather quickly becomes obvious that it could never be as a Levitical priest.

Belongs to another tribe -- Jesus descended from or belonged[45] to the tribe of Judah (verse 14), a different[46] tribe than the one designated as the priestly tribe.

---

[40] This verse Mormons find hard to explain. Mormons have both an Aaronic priesthood and a Melchizedekan priesthood in their system. If Hebrews says one replaces the other, how can we have both at the same time? This passage teaches the Aaronic priesthood is a thing of the past when one gets to Calvary, so how can it still be functioning? Furthermore, Jesus is the priest in the order of Melchizedek, not men. How can we have a Melchizedekan priesthood comprised of men, and at the same time not be contradictory to Hebrews' teaching?

[41] We note the NASB capitalizes "Law" in verse 11 (as it regularly does when the reference is to the Law of Moses), and then uses small "l" (law) in verse 12. Is this a place where the theology of the translators has affected their translation? Certainly both verses refer to the same "Law."

[42] See Galatians 3:24,25, "the Law has become our tutor to lead us to Christ ... but now that faith is come, we are no longer under a tutor." See 1 Cor. 9:20, where Paul the Christian affirms he is "not ... under the Law." See Moses' own statement, "God will raise up a prophet like me ... you shall listen to him" (Deut. 18:15). This was a clear prediction by Moses himself that when Jesus came, His words would supersede anything Moses had said. See John 1:17, "The law was given through Moses, grace and truth were realized through Jesus."

It will not do to suggest the Law should be divided into three parts, moral, ceremonial, and judicial, and try to affirm that it is the latter two only that are abrogated. Even F.F. Bruce rejects this means of explanation. "If we like, we may say that Paul (Galatian 3:24) has the moral law mainly in mind, whereas the author of Hebrews is concerned more with the ceremonial law -- although the distinction between the moral and ceremonial law is one drawn by Christian theologians, not by those who accepted the whole law as the will of God, nor yet by the New Testament writers." (p.145). Note this well. Bruce affirms that neither the Jews nor the writers of the New Testament made the distinction that certain Protestant theologians have been wont to make. Such a distinction contributes nothing to a correct understanding of the New Testament claims that the Law of Moses has been abrogated. The point the writer of Hebrews is making is that the Law of Moses was a temporary arrangement, valid only until Christ came to inaugurate the new and better way of "perfection."

[43] A portion of the suggested summary sentence for Hebrews is derived from this section of Hebrews. That sentence, it will be remembered is, "The New Testament is better than, and takes the place of, the Old Testament because the Messenger who gave the New is better than the messengers who gave the Old."

[44] Psalm 110:4 was clearly Messianic, and thus the "one" about whom it spoke is Jesus the Messiah.

[45] See notes at Hebrews 2:14, where the same Greek word is translated "partook of the same."

[46] The word is *heteras*, one of a different kind, not *allos*, another of the same kind.

From which no one has officiated at the altar -- The provisions of the Law of Moses designated the tribe of Levi as the one responsible for officiating at the sacrificial altar.[47]

7:14 -- For it is evident that our Lord was descended from Judah -- The writer calls Jesus "our Lord" again only in Hebrews 13:20. Mostly, the term "Lord" is reserved for the Father. That the word can be used interchangeably for either the Father or the Son points to the deity of Jesus. The "evidences" that the Lord descended from Judah are of two kinds. (1) The genealogies in Matthew 1 and Luke 3 make it clear Jesus was not a Levite, but of the tribe of Judah.[48] Furthermore, (2) the Messianic prophecies of the Old Testament clearly showed Messiah would spring (be "descended") from the tribe of Judah.[49]

A tribe with reference to which Moses spoke nothing concerning priests -- If Jesus sprang from the tribe of Judah, and yet was called a priest by God, that was a clear demonstration that a change had occurred – a change of priesthood and a change of Law. The Mosaic Law cannot be applicable if Jesus the Messiah (from the tribe of Judah) is functioning as a priest.[50]

7:15 -- And this is clearer still -- Just what is it that is "clearer still"? Many answers, each taken from some point made in the preceding verses, have been proposed.[51] We suppose

---

[47] Numbers 16:1 to 18:7. 2 Chronicles 26 tells how God's wrath was kindled on one occasion when Uzziah, of the tribe of Judah, tried to perform a priestly function. Some writers have tried to show that both David and Solomon are contradictions of what is here said about none of the tribe of Judah ever officiating at the altar. Those kings, who were of the tribe of Judah, are said to have offered sacrifice (2 Samuel 6:12-18, 24:25; 1 Kings 3:4, 8:62ff). Leon Morris (*op. cit.*, p.67) has offered several possible explanations for this alleged contradiction. (1) David and Solomon could have "offered" these sacrifices in the sense that they provided the sacrificial victims, while leaving the priests to perform the actual sacrifices. Morris doubts Solomon personally killed 22,000 oxen and 120,000 sheep. (2) Even if the kings did on occasion offer the actual sacrifice, this would not contradict Hebrews which is dealing with the *regular* ministrations of a priest at the altar. This latter, none but the sons of Aaron did in the Old Testament period.

[48] We date the writing of Matthew in AD 45 or 50, and the writing of Luke's Gospel c. AD 60. Thus both were in circulation at the time Hebrews was written. Furthermore, during the years before the Gospels appeared in written form, the Christians seem to have been sharing the same things (to demonstrate Jesus was the Messiah) by word of mouth. Hebrews 7:14 and Revelation 5:5 are the only places in the New Testament, outside the Nativity records in the Gospels, where anything is said explicitly about Jesus being of the tribe of Judah.

[49] See Genesis 49:10, Micah 5:2, Matthew 2:6. The use of the verb "spring" (*anatellein*, "descended") may well be intended to recall the memorable prophecy of Messiah being a "branch" that would spring from the stem of the tree of Jesse (Isaiah 11:1ff; Jeremiah 23:5; Zechariah 3:8). The Jews still admit that the Messiah is to be of the tribe of Judah. Since the destruction of Jerusalem in AD 70, when the genealogical records were destroyed, they have no way of knowing who belongs to the tribe of Judah and who doesn't. But it is held by them that when Messiah does come, the fact that He is of the tribe of Judah will be made known by miracle.

[50] When one acknowledges Jesus as the Messiah of Old Testament prophecy, he has admitted (whether consciously or not) that certain fundamental features that applied under the Mosaic code have been radically altered. All the Mosaic Law allowed were priests after the order of Aaron. If Jesus is now serving as priest, and He is, then either the Law is being disobeyed (an unthinkable option), or the Law is no longer a binding statute.

[51] One supposes it is the impossibility of "perfection" under the Levitical priesthood (verse 11). Another supposes it is the fact that the Law has been abrogated (verse 12). Still another suggests it is the fact that Jesus was of the tribe of Judah, not Levi (verses 13,14). Again, perhaps it is the distinction between orders of priesthood, Melchizedekan v. Aaronic (verse 11). Or, it may be the implication of the prediction found in Psalm 110:4. Or, perhaps, verse 15 is intended to gather up all the previous made since verse 11.

that the point being made "clear" has to do with "What do we read in the Law of Moses?" The last line of verse 14 says we can read precisely nothing in Moses (i.e., the Law of Moses) about the tribe of Judah having anything to do with priesthood.

If another priest arises according to the likeness of Melchizedek -- Not only is it not possible to find anything in the Law of Moses concerning priests from the tribe of Judah (verse 14), it is also impossible to find anything in the Law of Moses[52] about a different priest[53] of the order of Melchizedek. One of the key differences between Jesus' priesthood and the Aaronic priesthood will be emphasized in the next verse.

7:16 -- Who has become *such* -- What Jesus has become is a "different priest."

Not on the basis of a law of physical requirement -- The regulations[54] which set up the Levitical priesthood emphasized fleshly or physical qualifications. In that system, the essentials were physical ancestry, marriages, health, diet, and ceremonial performances.

But according to the power of an indestructible life -- In Jesus' case, His priesthood is different (yea, superior) because it rests on the power[55] inherent in His very life,[56] a life that is indestructible or indissoluble. Nothing can destroy it from within or without.[57]

7:17 -- For it is witnessed *of Him* -- Appeal is again made to Psalm 110:4, the very passage the writer has been building his presentation upon since Hebrews 5:6, to call attention to another thing Psalms clearly teaches.[58] This time, it is the word "forever" that is called out

---

[52] A special study about "Covenants" following comments on chapter 10 will explain that the "Law of Moses" is limited to what one can find in Exodus 20 through Deuteronomy. The Holy Writings (including Psalms) and the Prophets are not technically part of the "Law of Moses," even though the whole Old Testament canon is sometimes called "The Law."

[53] Jesus, of course, is a different (*heteros*) priest, not just another (*allos*) like Aaron.

[54] The Greek reads "a law" rather than "the law." So the reference is not to the whole Law of Moses, but merely to those regulations which dealt with the priesthood.

[55] "Power" is more than authority or regulations (such as those which regulated the Levitical priesthood).

[56] Levitical priests were made priests only because they met the regulations of the Mosaic Law. Inherently, they were no different from their fellow Israelites. But Jesus is priest by virtue of Who He is. His "life" is inherently different from the life of other men. Jesus' "life" is "indestructible;" that is, He inherently "possesses immortality and dwells in unapproachable light" (1 Timothy 6:16). His immortality is underived; it is part of His very essence (Jehovah = self-existent). With men, it is different. Men are not self-existent, but were created beings. Immortality is something the souls of men enjoy only by derivation from the One Who created them.

[57] While not all commentators do so, we have deliberately chosen to wait until verses 23 and 24 (where a different word, "permanently," is used) to discuss the whole matter of how the Levitical priests were subject to death; hence, regulations had to be given for the orderly succession lest the priestly system break down. With Jesus, no such need exists. We have chosen to wait because we think a completely different point is being made when the writer here uses the word "indestructible" and when he later uses the word "permanently."

[58] See the comments at Hebrews 5:6, where this same verse was quoted verbatim. There is a passage in the Old Testament which states the Levitical priesthood would continue "a perpetual priesthood throughout their generations" (Exodus 40:15); that is, to the end of the Mosaic dispensation. But no *individual* priest served the whole dispensation long, while Jesus alone serves as priest for the whole Christian dispensation. "Only a priest

for special attention. That single word is the very word through which God Himself testifies about the indestructible character of the life of Jesus, the new High Priest.

"YOU ARE A PRIEST FOREVER ACCORDING TO THE ORDER OF MELCHIZEDEK -- There *is* a special quality about Jesus' life. Neither does it end, nor can it end. Proof? The single word "forever" in Psalms 110:4.

7:18 -- For -- It is not easy to ascertain with certainty how verse 18 is related to the preceding. Is it a reason why there was a need for a change of priesthood? Is it a further explanation of the conclusion drawn in verses 12 and 16 that there has been an abrogation of the Law of Moses?

On the one hand, there is a setting aside of a former commandment -- "Setting aside" is a stronger word than "abrogate" used in verse 12. This word (*athetesis*) means cancelled or expunged or declared void.[59] The only way Jesus could serve as priest is if the Mosaic Law was no longer valid, since the Mosaic Law called for a priesthood that was exclusively Levitical. People who abide by the Law of Moses[60] have no alternative to the sons of Levi. But with Jesus, the One freely acknowledged by the Hebrew readers to be the promised Messiah, people no longer are limited to that one former[61] alternative.

Because of its weakness and uselessness -- Once more, reason is given why the Levitical system needed to be set aside. There were problems inherent in the Levitical system, which the next verses enumerate. That system was given by God and it served the purpose for which it was designed, namely, to introduce and prepare the way for a more perfect plan to come. Once the better plan (i.e., Jesus and His priesthood) became reality, the Levitical system and the Mosaic Law which rested on it ceased to be valid (see verses 11,12).

7:19 -- (for the Law made nothing perfect) – This parenthetical clause is added for the purpose of explaining the reason why the "former commandment" was set aside (verse 18). "Perfect" means the same thing it did in verse 11, the full accomplishment of the essential aim of the priesthood, that of making men acceptable to God so they may draw near to

---

of an entirely different sort than Judaism was accustomed to could fit the description of this prophetic Psalm [110:4]. It is just this kind of priest – one with a superior kind of life – that believers find in Jesus Christ" (Kent, *op. cit.*, p.135).

[59] Deissmann (*Bible Studies*, p.228ff) has shown that the word *athetesis* was a technical term used in legal documents. The verb means to declare void, to invalidate, to annul.

[60] There is some debate in the commentaries about whether "former commandment" has reference to the whole Mosaic Code, or whether it is limited in its reference to the "physical requirement" (verse 16) concerning the Levitical priesthood. Because of what was said in verses 11 and 12, and because of what is said in the parenthetical statement of explanation in verse 19, this commentator has opted to explain "former commandment" as though it were synonymous with the whole Law of Moses.

[61] The Law of Moses was "former," before something else, namely, before the gospel came. The Law of Moses was part of the revelation God made, but it was not the final revelation. The final revelation ("God ... has spoken to us in His Son," Hebrews 1:1,2) supersedes the former one. The Law of Moses and the Levitical system prepared the way for the coming of Messiah, but it was never intended to be a permanent arrangement.

Him.[62] The Law did curb many excesses, and it did help men to know what things God approved and what things He called sin. But the Law was not sufficient to meet and accomplish God's designs in reference to justification, sanctification, and the redemption of mankind.

And on the other hand -- The use of the particles *men* and *de* ("on the one hand," "on the other hand") in verses 18 and 19 establish a close connection between the thoughts of the two verses.[63] 'While there has been a setting aside of the former commandment ... there has been a bringing in of a better hope.'

There is a bringing in of a better hope -- This "hope" has been detailed in Hebrews 6:11 and 13-20 – namely, the promise and the oath and Christ's priestly function in the presence of God. This priesthood is "better" than the Levitical priesthood, since it can actually do what the Levitical priesthood could only do in type.

Through which we draw near to God -- In comments on "perfection" at verse 11, we tended to make "perfection" and "draw near to God" somewhat interchangeable terms. "Draw near to God" will be further explained at Hebrews 10:19-22. Until a man's sins are actually atoned for, he cannot "draw near to God." It is the blood of Jesus shed at Calvary which actually covered the sins of the people who lived before the cross (Hebrews 9:15); said differently, it is Jesus' blood that gives validity to the Old Testament sacrifices. Now that Jesus' sacrifice has actually atoned for sins, and now that they have Jesus serving as High Priest, it is possible for Old Testament believers,[64] as well as New Testament believers, to get much closer to God than they ever could before.

With this verse we have finished the first of several arguments (see notes at 8:1) designed to show the superiority of Jesus' priesthood to the Levitical priesthood.

---

[62] The Law did not restore things to their condition before God's laws were broken and men became sinners. Romans 8:1-3 is a parallel passage to what we are reading here in Hebrews. What the *Law* could not do (help man out of his sin problem), *God* did. He sent His own Son to become incarnate in the same kind of fleshly bodies other men had, in order that the Son might become a sin-offering that would really and actually atone for men's sins. Besides Romans 8, there are other passages wherein the weakness and inadequacy of the Mosaic Law is explicitly set forth. See 1 Timothy 1:8-10 (it could not create a pure heart), and Galatians 4:9.

[63] The NASB put the first part of verse 19 in parentheses, and treats the rest of verses 18 and 19 as a comparison, one part offsetting the other. (Note the balanced structure: On the one hand, (1) a setting aside, (2) foregoing [temporary], (3) commandment, (4) weakness and uselessness. On the other hand, (1) bringing in, (2) better [final], (3) hope, (4) effectiveness -- draw nigh to God through it.) The KJV treats the passage differently. They treated the Greek *men* in verse 18 as though it were emphatic, and translated it "verily." They then treated the Greek *de* in verse 19 as though it were adversative, making the thought to be in contrast to the first part of verse 19, thus, "For the Law made nothing perfect, but (*de*) the bringing in of a better hope *did*." The KJV translators added the verb "did" to complete what was otherwise, for them, a broken sentence.

[64] The souls of the Old Testament redeemed could not initially enter heaven when they died, but then "Paradise" (where those souls resided) changed locations after the resurrection and ascension of Jesus. Now that an atonement for their sins has been made, the souls of the Old Testament saints have "drawn nearer to God" than they were before, and in fact are now among those on the sea of glass underneath the altar in heaven (Revelation 15:1-4, 6:9ff; 2 Corinthians 12:1-3; Hebrews 12:23 ["spirits of righteous men made perfect"]).

3. Jesus' priesthood is so important it was announced with an oath. 7:20-22

7:20 -- And inasmuch as *it was* not without an oath -- Verses 20-22 form one sentence in the Greek; verse 22 answers verse 20, and verse 21 is parenthetical. The Hebrew writer continues his study of Psalm 110:4 so as to extract from it the last degree of significance for the character of Messiah's priesthood. In this sentence he calls the readers' attention to the *oath* God took as He announced the coming of a priest after the order of Melchizedek. That oath, he says, makes Messiah's Melchizedekan priesthood something special when compared to the Levitical priesthood.

7:21 -- (For they indeed became priests without an oath -- No oath was ever taken by God when He announced the inauguration of the Levitical priesthood.

But He with an oath -- When God announced that Messiah was going to be a priest after the order of Melchizedek, He did take an oath. This adds a solemnity to the announcement, since God is not in the habit of taking oaths when He speaks.

Through the One who said to Him -- God's purpose to have Messiah Jesus function as a priest was so fixed that He took an oath on the matter when He first announced (Psalm 110:4) the future establishment of such a priesthood.

"THE LORD HAS SWORN -- On the matter of God swearing or taking an oath, see comments at Hebrews 6:13-18.[65] All that is said about God's oath there is applicable here.

"AND WILL NOT CHANGE HIS MIND -- When we are told the oath means God "will not change his mind," it is an argument similar to that in 6:17 where we learned that when God took an oath on an earlier occasion, that oath was intended to indicate that His plan to bless Abraham was unchangeable. He intended never to change that part of His plan. In this passage, where God announces Messiah's priesthood, His oath likewise indicates His plans concerning this matter are also fixed and unchanging. This is the way He is going to do it!

"YOU ARE A PRIEST FOREVER") -- The thing being emphasized[66] is that God has no plans to set aside the priesthood of Jesus, as He did the priesthood of Levi, in order to make way for a different order.[67]

---

[65] The oath in chapter 6 was made to Abraham. Here in chapter 7, God is making an oath to Messiah.

[66] The KJV reads "Thou art a priest for ever after the order of Melchizedek." The last five words, though part of Psalm 110:4, are not found in the better manuscripts of Hebrews here at verse 21 (they do occur at verse 11 and verse 17). It is on the basis of their absence, so that the quotation ends with the words "priest forever," that the comments offered in the text are given.

[67] If there is to be no replacement of Jesus' priesthood, does that suggest the Church Age is the last of the series of ages in God's economy of things? Is it possible to harmonize what is here said with certain millennial schemes that have a return to animal sacrifices during an alleged coming millennial age? We think not.

7:22 -- So much the more also -- Every word in verse 22 is important. "So much the more" says Jesus' priesthood is to this greater degree superior to the Levitical priesthood. The oath taken when it was announced, and the permanence of Messiah's priesthood, are gathered up in "so much the more."

Jesus has become the guarantee of a better covenant -- "Jesus" stands last in the Greek text for emphasis. "Has become" is a perfect tense verb, indicating past completed action with present continuing results.[68] "Better" is one of the key words in this epistle.[69] "Covenant" – the idea is introduced, but is not yet developed.[70] "Better covenant" is identical with what is also called the "new covenant" in Hebrews 8:8. "Better" tells us the new covenant is superior to the Mosaic covenant. "Guarantee" or "guarantor"[71] is the one who stands good for a debt: He guarantees *to men* that God will fulfill His covenant of forgiveness, and He guarantees *to God* that those who are believers in Him are "perfected" so as

---

[68] Hebrews 9:15ff will explain when and how Jesus made the inauguration of the "better covenant" possible.

[69] See comments at Hebrews 1:4.

[70] This is the first occurrence of the word *diatheke* in this epistle, and the NASB offers "covenant" as a translation for it. It is a very important word, and the explanation of it will occupy an important part of the next three chapters of Hebrews. Translators have always had a hard time finding a word in the receptor language to express the exact meaning of the Greek (and Hebrew) words. The LXX translators faced a problem trying to find a Greek word to represent the Hebrew word *berith* ("covenant, cut a covenant"). The Hebrew word was used only of the more important class of agreements, at the forming of which a religious ceremony was performed, by which the deity was involved as a party to the covenant, or as the guardian of it. The LXX translators chose *diatheke* as the Greek word that came closest to the meaning of the Hebrew word, but the fact is, they had to pour new meaning into the Greek word to get it to serve for *berith*. The translators of the Bible into English face a similar problem as they try to find a suitable word in English to represent all that *berith/ diatheke* meant in the original. To begin with, there are two synonyms in Greek that can be translated agreement or "covenant." *Suntheke* is an agreement (or treaty) between equals, an agreement negotiated by two parties on equal terms. *Diatheke* is an agreement between unequals, an agreement or arrangement made by one party with plenary power, which the other party may accept or reject, but cannot alter or change. The best the English translators could do is pick an English word that comes close to conveying the idea in *berith/diatheke*. One possibility, "covenant," suggests the idea of an agreement, but also suggests negotiation between equals. That's not quite right for *diatheke*. "Testament" (as in "last will and testament") denotes a one-sided arrangement, but also suggests the death of the one making the arrangement. That connotation is not found in *berith*; God made several "covenants" with people in Old Testament times, but never was there the death of the One who drew up the will before the people received the blessing. "Disposition," "ordinance," "treaty," "agreement," and "arrangement" have also been suggested, but none with any degree of acceptance. Further complicating the matter is the dispute between covenant theologians and dispensational theologians. The former believe there has been but one "covenant of grace" ever since Adam sinned, and therefore want a word reflecting this idea. The latter believe there have been two (or more) covenants (e.g., one confirmed with Moses, another guaranteed by Jesus), and they want a word reflecting this idea. A yet further complication is the dispute between Calvinistic and Arminian theologians. The former want a word that will reflect God's disposition of the case (they often prefer "testament"). The latter want a word that reflects both man's part as well as God's part in salvation (they often prefer "covenant"). We have finally opted to use the word "covenant" and do with it as the Greeks did with *diatheke* – we give a new definition to the word when we find it in the Sacred Scriptures. When we use "covenant," we define it so as to exclude any idea of negotiation by parties of equal authority. (See *diatheke* in Kittel's *Theological Dictionary of the New Testament*, Vol. II, p. 104-134.)

[71] The Greek *enguos* means "surety, guarantor," and is not the same word (*mesites*) translated "mediator" at Galatians 3:19 and Hebrews 8:6. It is not the same word (*bebaiosis*) translated "confirmation" at 6:16. *Enguos* is not found elsewhere in the New Testament, but it is found in the papyri and the LXX. In our legal system, there is a "bondsman," one who pledges his name, his property, or his influence, that a certain thing shall be done. This is what Jesus does to ensure all the requirements of the new covenant shall be satisfied.

to be acceptable and eligible to draw near to God. The idea behind what is said in verse 22 is the same idea written in verse 11: just as the Law of Moses rested on the Levitical priesthood, so the new covenant rests on the Messianic priesthood. Jesus has guaranteed it! As long as Jesus is priest, the new covenant will be in effect – i.e., until the consummation.

4. Jesus' priesthood is a permanent priesthood. 7:23-25

7:23 -- And the *former* priests, on the one hand, existed in greater numbers -- We now begin what some outlines call the third proof of the superiority of Jesus' priesthood (see 7:1). Jesus' priesthood is superior because of the fact that it was not interrupted by death. As the following context shows, the "former priests" are the high priests in the Levitical system. They were more (i.e., they existed in greater numbers) than one.[72]

Because they were prevented by death from continuing -- There were many high priests in the Levitical system because one generation after another of priests had been carried away by death;[73] unable to save themselves, and compelled by death to abandon those who had leaned on them for counsel and sympathy. Successors were needed to keep the priesthood functioning.

7:24 -- But He, on the other hand -- Jesus is the "one" High Priest with whom the "greater numbers" is contrasted.

Because He abides forever -- This fact has been demonstrated during the previous study of the implications of Psalm 110:4 (see verses 15 and 17). Jesus' indissoluble life makes it possible for Him to fulfill to the letter the words "Thou art a priest *forever*."

Holds His priesthood permanently -- Jesus does not have a successor in His priesthood. His priesthood is nontransferable.[74] During this Church Age, whenever men need the services of a priest (and is there ever a time we do not?), we can be assured Jesus is available.

---

[72] There were many high priests. Aaron, the first in the line of high priests, served the people throughout the wilderness wanderings. But the day came when Aaron and his son Eleazar were taken by Moses to the summit of Mount Hor. There "After Moses had stripped Aaron of his garments, and put them on his son Eleazar, Aaron died there on the mountaintop. Then Moses and Eleazar came down from the mountain" (Numbers 20:28). Aaron had been replaced in the office of high priest by his son. Later, after the settlement in the promised land, Eleazar died in his turn (Joshua 24:33), and was succeeded by his son Phinehas. And so the tale went on. Caiaphas (who served from AD 26-36) was the 67th high priest. Phinehas (his name was spelled several different ways), the last who wore the mitre (AD 70), was the 83rd man to serve (Josephus, *Ant.* XX.10.1). The Talmud gives a different figure: it says there were 18 high priests who served during the time the first temple stood, and more than 300 during the second temple period (*Yoma* 9a).

[73] See Hebrews 7:8, "mortal men," for a similar thought.

[74] The Greek word *aparabatos* is not found elsewhere in the New Testament. Etymologically, it means "not passing along (to another)". It is a slightly different word than *akatalotou* ("indestructible") in verse 16. The risen Lord is no longer subject to death; therefore, His priesthood will never be interrupted.

7:25 -- Therefore He is able also to save forever those who draw near to God through Him -- "Therefore" means "in virtue of His holding the priesthood permanently" (verse 24). Instead of using "forever" (a temporal significance) to translate *eis to panteles*, the margin suggests "completely" (to the highest degree possible). While either translation would fit the context,[75] "save completely" would mean Jesus saves in the most comprehensive sense. His sacrifice at Calvary does not depend upon validation by someone else, as did the Old Testament animal sacrifices. Not only that, but in some sense, people who are already Christians still need saving. Jesus can do this, too! That Jesus is "able" to do this "saving" means He has the capacity, which the Levitical priests did not, to bring salvation to all who approach God through His good agency. His priesthood is not automatically universal in its operation. It actually benefits only those who come to God through Him.[76]

Since He always lives to make intercession for them -- This phrase explains the way Jesus' saving ministry is carried on. Exactly what He does as He continually intercedes[77] is not here explained. Perhaps when Christians pray, He constantly presents the merits of His death as a reason why we should be heard and our requests for forgiveness of sins honored.[78] Perhaps when the old accuser accuses the brethren before the throne of God, Jesus does for the believer what He did for Peter ("Satan has demanded permission to sift you like wheat; but I have prayed for you, that your faith may not fail," Luke 22:31,32). Perhaps He does for us what He did for the apostles (John 17:6-26).

---

[75] Those who opt for "forever" note the preceding context has spoken of Jesus holding His priesthood in perpetuity, while the following verses emphasize the fact that once Jesus has died there is no need for repeated or subsequent redemptive acts. (The Greek construction is found in extra-biblical references with the temporal sense that "forever" conveys.) Those who opt for "completely" note the context has spoken about how Jesus can do what the old scheme of things could not do. (The same construction is found at Luke 13:11, where the woman could not straighten herself "completely.") The KJV translators opted for the latter when they rendered it "he is able to save to the uttermost."

[76] The exclusive claims of Jesus, such as found here, remind us of passages like John 14:6, "no one comes to the Father, but through Me."

[77] It is a present tense infinitive, indicating continuing or repeated action. The intercession is something Jesus does in heaven on behalf of believers. The verb *entunchano* can have a variety of meanings: it can mean to light upon, to fall in with, meet with, converse with, talk to, appeal to, petition, pray, or plead for. It is used of lightning that strikes someone. It is used of meeting with books (i.e., reading them). It is used of visiting with someone for a special purpose. It is used in the papyri of prayers (petitions) offered to God. (F.F. Bruce, *op. cit.*, p.154-155 has a brief presentation of the mediatorship work of Jesus. Hebrews 2:17ff speaks of Jesus making propitiation for His people's sins and strengthening them when they are tempted. In 4:15ff, Jesus sympathizes with our weaknesses and supplies mercy and grace to help in time of need. See also Romans 8:27 where the Holy Spirit intercedes for believers, and 8:33ff where Jesus' intercessory work is alluded to.)

Of course, as we make these comments and suggestions, we are careful lest the idea be implied that we believe there is some truth to the Roman Catholic view of what happens in heaven during any observance of the Lord's Supper here on earth. Roman Church teaching has Jesus pleading His sacrifice in heaven while worshipers on earth do the same thing in Holy Communion. Nor do we picture Jesus as maintaining some kind of continuous liturgical action in heaven for our benefit. Such a view is hardly compatible with Jesus being *seated* at God's right hand (Hebrews 1:3,13, 10:12; Ephesians 1:20).

[78] If this is what "intercession" is, then Jesus, our great High Priest, would be doing something similar to what the high priest did on the Day of Atonement, when he joined his fervent intercession with the confessions of the worshipers who had come to have their sins atoned.

5. *It is a priesthood for which Jesus (being sinless) is perfectly qualified. 7:26-28*

7:26 -- For it was fitting that we should have such a high priest -- A further proof that Jesus is superior to Aaron, or to any other Levitical priest, is that He is sinless! After the imperfection (7:11,19) and impermanence (7:23ff) of the Levitical priesthood, men needed just such a high priest Who is complete in His person and work, as the writer here describes. The Messianic high priest is exactly suited[79] to our needs since He is qualified by superior personal fitness to serve as our great High Priest.

Holy -- The Greek word used here, *hosios*,[80] denotes one who is in harmony with the constitution of the universe, one who is loyal to covenant obligations, one who acts always out of regard for God's requirements. In order to be "holy," one must not be outwardly religious and righteous only, but must be pure in heart.

Innocent -- This describes one in whom is no malice or badness of any sort, one who does no evil. He injures no one; he does no wrong to any one – neither to their name, their property, nor their person.

Undefiled -- A third word describing the personal fitness of our great High Priest Jesus says He is morally unstained by any improper desire or passion. His purity goes far beyond mere ceremonial cleanness, such as resulted when the Levitical high priests purified themselves, put on clean garments and observed certain physical taboos, in order to be suitably prepared to officiate on the Day of Atonement.[81]

Separated from sinners -- This expression may be understood in either of two ways, depending on whether it is taken with the preceding context or the following. If it is construed with what goes before, then it extends what was said about Jesus' perfect sinlessness by affirming that while Jesus lived on earth He was separated from their sin. He did associate with them, but He did not partake of their feelings, plans, or pleasures. He mingled with them in order to do them good, not to sin with them. Jesus was so free of sin that He could even ask His enemies, "Which one of you convicts Me of sin?" (John 8:46). If the expression is taken with what follows, it points to the complete separation

---

[79] "It was fitting" is the same word used at Hebrews 2:10.

[80] This is not the word *hagios* that was used at Hebrews 3:1. When we find the negative term *anhosios*, it describes "impious" acts which transgress laws or reject sacred obligations. (See "*Hosios, Anhosios*," in Kittel, *Theological Dictionary of the New Testament*, Vol.5, p.489-493.)

[81] Some have supposed there is an allusion in these descriptive terms in verse 26 to a later Jewish custom concerning the high priest's personal preparation for the ceremonies he would perform on the Day of Atonement. Seven days before the Day of Atonement, the high priest left his house and took up residence in the temple, in order that, having thus separated from men and things unclean, he might, when the day arrived, be free from all defilement. Five washings and ten purifications were required of him on the day itself. And in spite of all these efforts at ceremonial purification, the Levitical priest was still a sinner who needed to be forgiven himself. (See W. Moller, "Atonement, Day of," in *International Standard Bible Encyclopedia*, ed. James Orr, Vol.1, p.327,328. This material is based on the Mishna tractate *Yoma*.)

from sinners that now exists. Our exalted Lord is forevermore removed from a life in the midst of sinners. Because He now resides in heaven, He can carry out His ministry, far removed from any possibility of disqualification because of defilement.

And exalted above the heavens -- Jesus' present exalted position has been alluded to earlier in this epistle. He has passed through the heavens (4:14); He is seated at the right hand of the majesty on high (1:3,13); He is crowned with glory and honor (2:9). Because of where He now is, He is eminently suited to serve as our great High Priest.[82]

7:27 -- Who does not need daily, like those high priests, to offer up sacrifices -- This verse carries on the description of verse 26, presenting what results from the purity and sinlessness we find in Jesus. He has no necessity of making sacrifices for any sins of His own,[83] like the Levitical priests were obliged to do. Once the general thrust of the verse has been recognized, commentators have had some difficulty with the word "daily,"[84] since there is little evidence of such sin offering sacrifices being made by the high priest himself, save once a year on the Day of Atonement. Likely it says Jesus does not have a daily need to offer a sin offering, because He, unlike the Jewish high priests, did not commit sin daily. He did not sin at all! Jesus can intercede daily[85] for His people without first having to make any sacrifices for His own sins.

First for His own sins, and then for the *sins* of the people -- This distinction between "His own sins" and "the sins of the people" is what suggests that the ritual of the Day of Atonement was in the writer's mind as he pens this paragraph.

Because this He did once for all when He offered up Himself -- Since it has been expressly affirmed that Jesus was sinless (4:15, 7:26), this verse cannot be interpreted to mean that somehow what Jesus did at Calvary was a sin offering for His own sins. Rather,

---

[82] There is another possible explanation of the words "exalted above the heavens." It might say He is higher than all other beings in heaven, with the exception of God the Father. Compare Ephesians 1:20-22.

[83] See notes at Hebrews 5:3 concerning the sacrifices offered by the high priest on the Day of Atonement. Aaron and his successors, before they presented a sin offering on behalf of the people, had to present one for themselves.

[84] Attempts to explain "daily" include the following: (1) The writer of Hebrews was unfamiliar with Jewish practices and erroneously supposed the high priest offered the atonement sacrifices every day rather than yearly. This will hardly do, for the writer shows precise knowledge of the ritual in Hebrews 9:7 and 10:1. (2) The other priests, who did make daily sacrifices on behalf of worshippers, acted under the responsibility and as a representative for the high priest. This will hardly do, since the ordinary priests did not have to offer for their own sins daily, before they could officiate on behalf of others. The Old Testament did make provision for the sin offerings of ordinary priests on days other than the annual Day of Atonement (Leviticus 4:3), but there is no Biblical evidence it was to be done daily. (3) Some have tried to explain "daily" as though it meant "on each occurrence of the sacred day," i.e., year after year, on the Day of Atonement, such sacrifices had to be offered. This will hardly do, for if the writer meant to say once a year, he hardly would have used "daily," since he knew how to write "once a year" (9:7, 10:1).

[85] The Levitical high priest interceded for his people once a year on the Day of Atonement. Before he did, he first had to make a sin offering for himself. In the case of Jesus, every time He intercedes for believers (which is not once a year, but every day, i.e., continually, always [Hebrews 7:25]), He has no such need, because He has no sin.

He offered Himself[86] for the sins of the people, and it was such a satisfactory and suitable offering that it had to be done only once![87] He made such an atonement that it was not needful that it should ever be repeated. There was no need for any more blood to be shed to propitiate human guilt.

7:28 -- For the Law appoints men as high priests who are weak -- "Weak(ness)" has been explained before at Hebrews 4:15, 5:2. The Law of Moses gave the qualifications for those who were to serve as priests. Those Levitical priests were not made from some super race, but from ordinary men, with all the moral frailties which characterize ordinary men. Those weaknesses were recognized from the start; God even made arrangements, as He gave the Law, so that the fact of such weaknesses could be taken care of ceremonially (see Hebrews 5:2,3, 7:27; Leviticus 16).

But the word of the oath, which came after the Law -- "But" introduces a contrast: the oath makes the difference. The "oath" is the oath God swore when He announced through David about a coming priest after the order of Melchizedek (see verse 21). That promise (found in Psalm 110:4) was announced more than 400 years after the Law was given on Mt. Sinai. Since the oath came *after* the Law, it cannot be argued that the Law superseded the oath. The oath was the last word, not the Law.

Appoints **a Son** -- Appoints a Son[88] as high priest, is the idea. Actually, the oath did not speak about a "Son," it spoke about the coming Messiah. It was in Psalm 2:7 that we find the designation "Son" (see notes on Hebrews 1:5). But since both Psalms were Messianic, the writer of Hebrews is not to be faulted for applying terminology for Messiah found in one Psalm to the same Messiah spoken about in the other.

Made perfect forever -- Jesus' superior personal qualifications and fitness to serve as High Priest are summarized in this concluding statement. Hebrews 2:10 and 5:9 have already explained in what sense Jesus is "perfect," i.e., perfectly qualified or fully equipped to exercise His priesthood in heaven on behalf of believers. Furthermore, He can do it "forever" (see 7:25), as long as such priestly functions are needed, since His priesthood is nontransferable (7:24) and is never to be superseded (7:16-22).

---

[86] This is the first mention in Hebrews that the sin offering our great High Priest, Jesus, offered was an offering of Himself. To say "what Jesus did at Calvary" is a convenient, if not precisely exact, way to explain just when "He offered up Himself." We are aware the Bible sometimes speaks of Jesus' expiration on the cross as being the propitiation for our sins. We are also aware that Hebrews also tells us that after Jesus died, He "entered through the greater and more perfect tabernacle" to make an atonement for the sins of the world (8:3, 9:11ff, 10:10-14). Perhaps both events are in mind here in Hebrews 7:27, that together they constitute the one great, once-for-all sacrifice for sin.

[87] The Greek word translated "once" is *ephapax*, the more emphatic form than *hapax*. The emphatic form is used repeatedly in Hebrews to convey the absolute finality of Jesus' sin offering. One characteristic we have noted in the writer of Hebrews is that he introduces a subject, but does not elaborate. He then later returns to the thought and develops it. So it will be with the finality of Jesus' sacrificial death.

[88] See Hebrews 1:2 and 5:8 for "Son" as it is applied to Jesus. Absence of the definite article before "Son" emphasizes the *quality* of "son-ness" possessed by Jesus, a quality in which He far surpasses prophets or angels.

III. EXHORTATION BASED ON THE SUPERIORITY OF THE SON OF GOD'S PRIESTLY MINISTRY. Hebrews 8:1 - 10:31

A. His Ministry is Superior Because it Involves a Better Covenant. 8:1-13

8:1 -- Now -- We have chosen to treat chapter 8 as the beginning of a major new point in the presentation of the superiority of the Son through whom God has spoken in these last days.[1] The first five verses are the theme statement of this new section of Hebrews. The emphasis has shifted slightly from the Son's priestly office (4:14-7:28) to His more excellent priestly ministry. Three reasons are then adduced to prove that Jesus' priestly ministry is superior: His ministry involves a better covenant (8:6ff); He serves in a superior sanctuary (9:1ff); and He offers a better sacrifice, for He brings an offering whose efficacy is beyond question (10:1ff).

The main point in what has been said *is this* -- The KJV and NASB treat this statement as though the writer is now going to give a *summary* of what he has already written, and that summary is intended to emphasize the most important point of all that has been thus far written.[2] The RSV and NEB (which reads, "Now this is my main point:") treat this statement as though it introduces a *new point*, and that new point is intended to be the crowning point of the argument, the most important of all the topics the writer discusses.[3] Either way, the consideration of this "main point" is pursued through chapters 8, 9, and 10.

We have such a high priest -- The "main point" is Jesus' exaltation above the heavens (7:26), i.e., Jesus' priesthood is the substance, the real thing, of which the Old Testament priesthood was but a type or preview (see 8:2ff). "We have such a priest" emphasizes both Jesus' present priestly activity on behalf of Christian believers and the fact that Jesus *is* a priest – a fact settled, proven, and indisputable (after what has been written in chapter 7).[4]

---

[1] Not all students of Hebrews begin a major new point at 8:1. Some insist that because the topic since 5:1 is the same (i.e., the high priesthood of Jesus), we do not have a new point, but simply different evidence presented to prove that Jesus' priesthood is superior. In fact, one popular outline of 7:1-10:18 is "Seven Proofs of the Superiority of Christ's Priesthood": (1) He is a priest after the order of Melchizedek; (2) His priesthood was announced with an oath; (3) He is a permanent priest; (4) He is a sinless priest; (5) He is a priest of a better covenant; (6) He serves in a better tabernacle; (7) He offers a better sacrifice.

[2] Some scholars object to treating chapter 8:1ff as a *summary* because the Greek has a present participle (literally, "which we are saying") which does not suit a summary, and there is an introduction of much new material (e.g., "true tabernacle") in the following verses.

[3] Some scholars object to the idea of beginning a whole *new point* in 8:1ff. After all, the writer of Hebrews has been developing some of the implications of Jesus' high priesthood since late in chapter 6. It is precisely because 8:1ff is a continuation of a point already introduced that the writer uses the present tense participle, i.e., the things which we are saying, the discussion presently being conducted. The ideas of a new covenant, of a better sacrifice, and even Jesus' exaltation to heaven where He now serves, are all ideas that already were a part of the argument in chapter 7. The writer now simply unfolds their meaning as he continues his point about Jesus' priesthood. It soon becomes obvious that this is one place in the New Testament where the translator's opinion influences his translation.

[4] "Such" in "such a high priest" may be taken with the preceding, 'such as we have just described in chapter

Who has taken His seat at the right hand of the throne of the Majesty in the heavens -- Jesus doesn't serve on earth, as did Aaron and his successors. He, unlike the Levitical priests, is not continually standing at an altar, offering sacrifices over and over. Instead, He has "taken His seat," an act indicative that His sacrificial work was finished (see Hebrews 10:11-14). "Majesty in the heavens"[5] is a periphrasis for "God."[6] Jesus' session at God's "right hand" is indicative that He is an exalted and kingly High Priest.[7]

8:2 -- A minister in the sanctuary -- "Minister" translates *leitourgos*, a public officer of high rank, an officiating priest, a servant who administers religious functions. Where the NASB reads "sanctuary," the Greek has an article and the adjective meaning "holy," both in the plural. The plural could be translated "of the holy things," and indeed, holy things (think of sacrifices for sin, forgiveness of sinners, mediatorial work between God and man) would make good sense. The plural could be translated "the holies," as in Holy *of Holies*. The NASB translators have shown by their use of "sanctuary" that they think this is the meaning, since "sanctuary"[8] is another name given to the Holy of Holies. Perhaps one reason the translators choose "sanctuary" is because the context seems to be speaking about the place where the high priest serves, and only the high priest could enter the Holy of Holies in the earthly tabernacle. Like the Old Testament priest entered a very holy place

---

7.' Or, "such" may be taken with what follows, 'such that He sat down ... Our priest is so great He may sit in God's presence!'

Behind the current presentation, is there an implication that one reason some readers were tempted to return to the old Jewish system was that they could actually *see* they had a priest who functioned on their behalf at the altar and in the sanctuary? Were some potential defectors thinking, 'Has anyone ever actually *seen* Jesus doing His high priestly work?' The writer of Hebrews then responds, 'Well, men may not be able to see with their physical eyes, but there are proofs that Jesus *is* so serving.' The Bible calls Jesus a *priest,* and that's not merely an honorific title. Priests serve! If Jesus *is* a priest, and the Bible tells us so, then He must be serving (verse 3). Since He is not of the tribe of Levi, but of the tribe of Judah, we would not expect to see Him serving in the tabernacle/temple on earth (verse 4). Instead, we'd expect to see Him serving in heaven. And there is a real "temple" in heaven; the one built on earth was but a scale model (verse 5) of the real thing. Once all these truths are considered, it will no longer be so tempting or so inviting to go back to the old Mosaic system.

[5] "Heavens" is plural here, as it is in seven of ten instances the word occurs in Hebrews. (In Revelation, the singular is used in every case but one. In Ephesians, the word is always plural.) It is our studied opinion there is no substantial difference in meaning when the singular is used rather than the plural, or vice versa. We have the plural in 9:23 and the singular in 9:24, with no apparent change of meaning. As explained in comments on Hebrews 4:14, the Bible speaks of three heavens -- the atmosphere, the starry heavens, and the third heaven which is the home of the Blessed. "Heavens" (plural) is thus a suitable way to refer to the third heaven, the place where God dwells.

[6] Compare what was said about "Majesty on high" at Hebrews 1:3.

[7] Certain millennial theories have Jesus not reigning, not sitting on David's throne, until out in the future, after the close of the Church Age. What are we to think of such a suggestion? Hebrews has Jesus sitting at the right hand of the Father now, during the Church Age. Peter, in Acts 2:30-33, says that at the time he was speaking on Pentecost, Jesus was already on David's throne, i.e., He had received (verse 33) what the Father had promised (verse 30). It is this commentator's understanding that Jesus' being seated on the right hand of the Majesty on high and His sitting on David's throne are references to the same thing, and are occurring *during* the Church Age.

[8] The usual Greek word translated "sanctuary" is *naos*, a word that signifies a place where a deity dwells. When the tabernacle was completed and dedicated, the Shekinah (the visible symbol of the presence of God) came down and filled the Holy of Holies, resting right above the mercy seat on the Ark of the Covenant.

in order to minister, in a similar fashion Jesus has entered into and ministers (officiates as a priest) in the very presence of God. There is no holier place than that!

And in the true tabernacle -- Another reason translators might choose "sanctuary" in the previous phrase is because this second phrase could be rendered "*even* in the true tabernacle." That is, this second phrase of verse 2 is epexegetic, explaining that "tabernacle" is what "the sanctuary (the holies)" in the first phrase actually meant. On the other hand, if we translate it "*and* in the true tabernacle," we seem to imply that "sanctuary" and "tabernacle"[9] are not exactly the same thing. If the first term "sanctuary" had reference to the Holy of Holies, then "tabernacle" could be synonymous with the Holy Place,[10] or it could refer to the whole tent which included both the Holy Place and the Holy of Holies. Whichever way one may prefer to translate, Hebrews 8:2 is saying is that Jesus ministers in the true or genuine[11] place, a far better place[12] than the Jewish tabernacle, which was but a small imitation of the real and genuine thing (see Hebrews 8:5).

Which the Lord pitched, not man -- There is a great difference between the place (i.e., heaven) where Jesus ministers (a place built by the Lord[13] Himself), and the tabernacle in

---

[9] "Tabernacle" translates *skene*, the word meaning "tent."

[10] At this place, the readers of Hebrews are abruptly introduced to the rather nice problem of just exactly what are the names to be applied to the different rooms of the tabernacle and, for that matter, to the whole portable place of worship. Much more will be said on this whole matter at Hebrews 9:1ff. For the moment, it is sufficient to state the Bible is not uniform in its nomenclature. Sometimes the whole structure was called "sanctuary," and sometimes just the Holy of Holies is called "sanctuary." Sometimes the terms used are plural, sometimes they are singular. We have not been able to find any consistent pattern in the uses of the singular or plural, nor have we been able to assign any consistent and distinctive meaning to the singulars and plurals, though some have tried to do so. We suppose the commentator must decide in each instance, by the demands of the context, which specific meaning is suitable.

[11] *Alethinos*, translated "true," means genuine as opposite of counterfeit, real as opposite of unreal or merely apparent. It does not mean "true" as opposed to false; that was the meaning of *alethes* in classical Greek.

[12] The "better place" has reference to heaven itself, see 9:11ff, and 9:22ff. Ignoring what Hebrews itself will say in later chapters, commentaries are filled with human speculations when it comes to attempting to identify what exactly is meant by "sanctuary" and "tabernacle." For example, this commentator is not sure that R. Milligan's attempt (*op. cit.*, p.219-221) to identify the "sanctuary" with heaven and the "tabernacle" with the church here on earth is at all helpful for understanding the argument of Hebrews at this place. When the writer of Hebrews appears to be telling where Christ (the superior priest) serves, it doesn't help to make "tabernacle" mean the church. (In fact, Milligan has to spend considerable time showing that his interpretation does not contradict what the Scriptures say elsewhere. Milligan does not have the church beginning till Pentecost [Acts 2], yet he has Christ our Priest ministering at Calvary before the church ever began. Does this not seem incongruous? He spends time saying that indeed it is not. To avoid all this effort, it is preferable simply to reject Milligan's proposed identification of "tabernacle" with the church.) Another commentary tries to identify the "sanctuary" where Jesus serves as being a reference to His human body. Jesus did call His body a "temple (sanctuary)" at John 2:19-21, so one might argue that "sanctuary" (even though it is not the same Greek words so translated) here in Hebrews is a reference to Christ's "body." It just may be true that Jesus now has something He didn't have before His incarnation, namely, a glorified body (Philippians 2:9 ["highly exalted" is literally "super highly exalted"]; 1 Corinthians 15:48,49), but to make reference to that fact here (in "sanctuary") seems to add little to our understanding of Hebrews.

[13] Leon Morris (*op. cit.*, p.76) has done a word study on "Lord" and "the Lord" in this epistle, and concludes, "In this epistle, the form with the article seems usually to mean Christ, whereas that without the article means the Father." He also expresses his belief that this usual pattern is not followed here (he thinks "the Lord" is a

which the Jewish priests ministered (a place built by men).

8:3 -- For every high priest is appointed to offer both gifts and sacrifices -- This verse assigns a reason for the use of the term "minister" in verse 2. If Jesus ministers as high priest in this authentic sanctuary, what is the nature of His ministry? Verse 3 begins to answer that question. As was taught before (5:1), a high priest is appointed to offer "gifts and sacrifices." The present tense verb "to offer" reflects the idea that "gifts" (unbloody offerings) and "sacrifices" (offerings involving a shedding of blood) had to be repeated over and over by the Levitical priests.

Hence it is necessary that this *high priest* also have something to offer -- If the offering of gifts and sacrifices is part of the very essence of being a priest, we can certainly expect Jesus also had something to offer. The nature of Jesus' one-time offering,[14] already stated in 7:27, will not be elaborated upon until Hebrews 9:12ff. In the meantime, some further points of contrast between the old and new priestly work are explained.

8:4 -- Now if He were on earth, He would not be a priest at all -- If Jesus is our High Priest, and He is, He must exercise a heavenly ministry. As has already been demonstrated in Hebrews 7:13,14, Jesus certainly does not meet the qualifications to be a Levitical priest. Even if He were still on earth, and even if such a priesthood as the Levitical were still valid after Calvary, Jesus could not even be an ordinary priest, let alone a high priest.

Since there are those who offer the gifts according to the Law -- Most writers suppose the present tense verb here is reflective of the fact that when Hebrews was written, the Temple was still standing and the Jewish sacrifices were still being offered. Once the Romans destroyed Jerusalem in AD 70, the Levitical system ceased to be operative.

8:5 -- Who serve a copy and shadow of the heavenly things -- The point of verse 5 is that a priesthood exercised in the earthly tabernacle or temple is far inferior to a priesthood exercised in heaven. Why? Because heaven as it is now is the real thing; the tabernacle on earth was but a copy (a little model[15]) or shadow (a dim outline[16]) of the real thing.

---

reference to God the Father), and he can see no reason for the variation here and at Hebrews 8:11. This commentator would have no problem accepting the idea that verse 2 says *Jesus* ("the Lord") had something to do with fitting up heaven as it now is.

[14] The second time the verb "to offer" occurs in verse 3, it is an aorist tense, indicating one act. The NEB tries to catch the difference by rendering this closing phrase "this One too must have had something to offer." In heaven, Jesus *does* continue to intercede for men; He *does* continue to mediate on their behalf; He does *not* continue to offer "gifts and sacrifices."

[15] *Hupodeigma* (and a nearly synonymous word *paradeigma*) are used in both the LXX and New Testament with the sense of model or copy or example. See John 13:15; Hebrews 4:11, 9:23; James 5:10; 2 Peter 2:6. English words that can carry a similar connotation are likeness, copy, imitation. The copy may be fairly well detailed, but it is not the original; a *hupodeigma* is just an imitation of the real thing.

[16] *Skia* is the regular word for "shadow," whether it be of a man, a house, a tree. The shadow will indicate the form, the outline, the size of the object, but the shadow has no substance or reality. Colossians 2:16,17 speak of other Old Testament institutions (besides the tabernacle) as being shadows of things to come in the Church Age. Many of the Old Testament institutions were types or previews of coming attractions.

Just as Moses is warned *by God* when he was about to erect the tabernacle -- The verse about to be quoted is Exodus 25:40, and it is quoted to prove that the tabernacle was only a copy or shadow of the real thing. Those words, when originally spoken, were a warning or an instruction from God Himself.[17] If *God* says the tabernacle is only a copy, who are we to argue differently?

For, "SEE," He says, "THAT YOU MAKE all things ACCORDING TO THE PATTERN WHICH WAS SHOWN YOU ON THE MOUNTAIN" -- "All things" indicates that not only the tabernacle itself, but the altars, the ark, the candlestick, were all to be exact replicas of what Moses had seen. Moses saw the original (the pattern[18]) while he was up on Mount Sinai, and what was subsequently built, after he came down, was but a copy, a little model of the original. It is instructive to read in Revelation 4-8 the description of heaven as it now is,[19] and compare to that description a floor plan of the tabernacle. Then it becomes very obvious that Moses did build a little model of heaven as it now is.

THE EARTHLY TABERNACLE

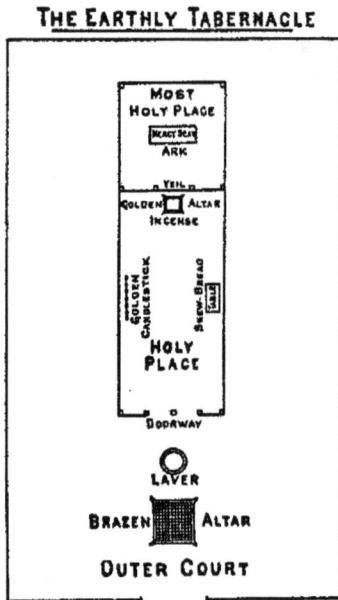

Pictured at left is a floor plan of the tabernacle (with directions changed slightly, so that what actually was located on the east side is located at the bottom of the diagram).

---

[17] The Greek verb is *chrematizo*, a word often found in the New Testament, and regularly with the meaning "divine instructions" or "divinely called" (cp. Acts 11:26), a supernatural revelation from God. That is why our translators have added "by God" in italics. Such an addition is implied by the very word used for warning.

[18] The Greek word translated "pattern" is *tupon* -- type, figure, form, mark, stamp, impression made by a die. The use of the word elsewhere in the New Testament may be helpful to forming an understanding of its meaning here. It is used of the mark made by the nails in Jesus' hands (John 20:25). It is used of the form or shape of a statue (Acts 7:43). It is used of baptism (immersion), which is a form of Christian doctrine (Romans 6:17), picturing the death, burial, and resurrection of Jesus. It is used of an example to be imitated or followed (1 Corinthians 10:6). The word "pattern" implies something more than verbal directions was given to Moses.

[19] Heaven as it now is (Revelation 4-8), of which Moses made a little model, is not the same shape, appearance, or floor plan as will be found in heaven as it shall be after the second advent of Christ (Revelation 21,22).

Below are two different attempts to picture what is read in Revelation 4-8. The similarities in the two are rather quickly obvious. Where the Ark of the Covenant stood in the tabernacle, in heaven one finds the throne of God. Where there were cherubim over the Ark, in heaven are the four living creatures. The seven-branched candlestick stands in the tabernacle, where the seven lamps which are the seven spirits of God are found in heaven. The laver in the tabernacle corresponds to the sea of glass in heaven. And just as there were two altars (burnt offering and incense) in the tabernacle, so there are two altars described in Revelation 8:3. Additional features found in the scene in heaven (which may or may not have corresponding representations in the earthly tabernacle) are the 24 elders around the throne, and the outer circles of beings made up of myriads and myriads of angels and of every creature (animals, birds, etc.?) in heaven and on earth.

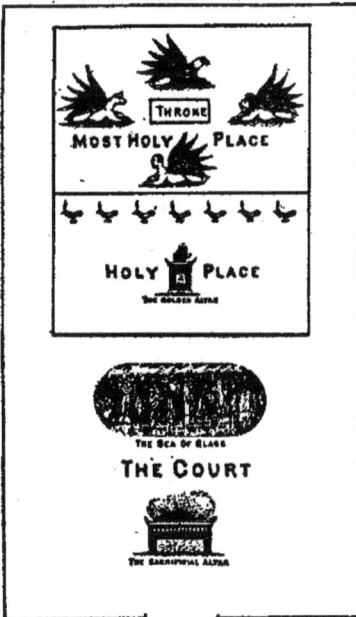

One diagram of heaven as it now is, could be drawn in a rectangular shape, just as was the tabernacle.

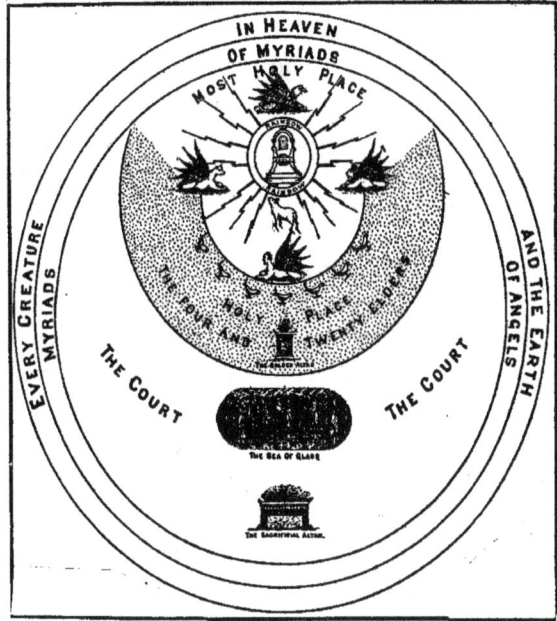

Another diagram by the same artist (E.R. Craven) which attempts to visualize what heaven looks like as it now is – it follows the same general floor plan, save it is no longer rectangular.

Some commentators have objected to the presentation just made, saying it is gross to think of an actual building or furniture (altars, for example) existing in heaven. However, the attempts to spiritualize or allegorize each of the items described in Revelation 4-8 are even less satisfactory, at least to this commentator,[20] for once they are spiritualized, such

---

[20] One example of such spiritualizing reads "All that is implied is that the heavenly truths were represented

words as "copy," "shadow," and "pattern" here in Hebrews 8:5 make little sense.

8:6 -- But now He has obtained a more excellent ministry -- Christians do have a High Priest whose ministry (see verse 2) is superior to that of any Levitical priest (verses 1-5). A further proof of this superiority is found in the fact that the new covenant based on Jesus' priestly ministry is a better covenant than the Mosaic covenant which was based on the Levitical priesthood (cp. 7:11).

By as much as He is also the mediator of a better covenant -- The "better covenant" is the New Covenant (see 7:22, 8:8ff, and 9:15-20). By just as much as the new covenant is "better" than the Mosaic covenant, that's how much Jesus' ministry is more excellent than the Levitical priesthood's ministry. A "mediator" is a middleman, a go-between[21] who gets both parties together and makes possible the agreement. In practically every age, man has felt the need of a mediator to act as a go-between between men and their gods. Under the old Mosaic covenant, the office of mediator was filled primarily by Moses (Exodus 20:19,20; Galatians 3:19,20). After him, it seems the high priest discharged the duties of mediator, standing, as he ever did, between God and the people, especially on the Day of Atonement. In this new covenant age, Jesus is the One who stands between God and men, Who is alike interested in both, Who gets both parties together, and Who makes possible the agreement whereby men are saved and thus qualified to draw near to God.

Which has been enacted on better promises -- The "better promises" will be spelled out one by one in the following verses by means of the quotation from Jeremiah 31:31ff. The "better promises" are the reason the new covenant is "better" than the Old.[22] "Enacted" is a legal word meaning to impose a law, to promulgate a law, to furnish with a law. The same word was used in Hebrews 7:11 where we were told the people "received" the Law of Moses. Here in 8:7, the Greek verb is in the perfect tense, indicating past completed action with present continuing results. In other words, at the time Hebrews was written, the new covenant had already been "enacted" at some time in the past (Calvary), and since then it continues to be the covenant that is valid.

8:7 -- For if the first *covenant* had been faultless -- Should someone wonder why a "better covenant" than the Mosaic covenant was needed, the writer proceeds to explain. That first covenant, the Mosaic, was faulty,[23] he tells us. This is the same argument found

---

in the visual pattern (a blueprint, or an architect's scale model) shown to Moses, and that the resultant tabernacle was a copy of this pattern" (Kent, *op.cit.*, p.150).

[21] "Mediator" translates *mesites,* a different word ("guarantee, guarantor") than was used at 7:22. The verb form *mesiteuo* was used at Hebrews 6:17 ("interposed").

[22] Readers can hardly miss the emphasis of verse 6 that Jesus' priestly ministry was "more excellent ... better ... better." This relentless insistence on the superiority of Jesus' priesthood (and the Christian religion) to the preparatory, shadowy, and typical nature of the Levitical system is intended to fully dissuade the readers from any thoughts that they could defect to Judaism and thereby get something better than what is found in Jesus!

[23] Care must be taken as comments about the first covenant's faultiness are made. This is certainly not tacit support for those who hold to an evolutionary theory for the development of religion in the world, that the new

in 7:11, that there were some things the Levitical priesthood (and the Law enacted on that priesthood) could not do.

There would have been no occasion sought for a second -- As the following context shows, it is God who is pictured as seeking "occasion" for the enactment of the second,[24] the better covenant. After the first covenant had been in force for eight centuries, God used the prophet Jeremiah (who flourished 626-580 BC) to make the classic new covenant prophecy.[25] The very prediction made by God that a new one was coming argues for the failure of the old. The very prediction also implies the new one must be better, for there would have been no point in replacing the old covenant by another no better than itself. A third thing is also implied. The prediction found in Jeremiah argues strongly that at its best the Mosaic covenant was never intended by God to be anything but temporary.

8:8 -- For finding fault with them -- There is a significant manuscript variation at this place, the alternate reading being "finding fault with *it*."[26] Perhaps God found fault with the Mosaic Covenant (cp. verse 7); perhaps He found fault with the people who did not keep His covenant (cp. verse 9). Perhaps both!

He says -- Now (verses 8-12) follows the quotation of Jeremiah 31:31-34, the classic new covenant prophecy.[27]

---

must necessarily have improved on the old just as (because of survival of the fittest) all later forms are superior to earlier forms. The Mosaic covenant was given by God Himself, and was perfect for the time for which it was given. It was holy, and righteous, and good (Romans 7:12). But it could not help a man to keep its provisions (Romans 7:18ff). It could not provide a perfect sacrifice for sin, nor could it actually save a man. It was faulty.

If the Old Testament was faulty and could not save a man, why did God enact it in the first place? Part of the answer to this question is the whole matter of progressive revelation. The Law was added to the promise made to Abraham "because of transgressions" (Galatians 3:19). The Law also was a tutor to lead men to Christ (Galatians 3:24).

[24] Since there have been more than two covenants between God and man, the writer's use of "first covenant" and "second covenant" has resulted in some doubt as to the exact identity of the "first" and "second" ones. It is from verses 8 and 9 that it can be determined that what the writer means by "first covenant" is none other than the Mosaic Covenant, the one made at Mt. Sinai just after the Exodus from Egypt. There is a sense in which the Mosaic Covenant was not the very first covenant God ever made with man (see Genesis 9:9ff for a covenant God made with Noah just after the flood). But there is no real problem here in Hebrews since the writer carefully defines his terms in the verses following. In this context, the "Mosaic covenant" is the "first covenant," and the "new covenant" (the one predicted by Jeremiah) is the "second (covenant)."

[25] During the time the Old Testament prophets functioned, there were other prophecies about a coming new covenant. See this documented in the special study concerning "Covenants" at the close of chapter 10. Jeremiah 31:31-34 was the *classic* one among these predictions.

[26] P[46], Sinaiticus (in the third hand), Vaticanus, Origen, and the Byzantine text all read "it" *(autois)*. Sinaiticus (in the first hand), Alexandrinus, the Old Latin, the Vulgate, the Coptic and Armenian versions, all read "them" *(autous)*.

[27] A brief account of the historic situation in Jeremiah's day may help us to appreciate the prediction that God made through Jeremiah. Jeremiah lived from c. 650 BC to 580 BC. There was turmoil on the international scene as three kingdoms vied for world supremacy. Assyria had ruled the world for about 300 years (during which time the northern kingdom of Israel was taken into captivity) but was growing weak. Babylon was becoming a world power. Egypt, which a thousand years before had been a world power and declined, was again becoming ambitious. Babylon became the world power after defeating Assyria about 610 BC and Egypt at

"BEHOLD, DAYS ARE COMING, SAYS THE LORD -- History has shown that after Jeremiah made this prediction, 600 years passed before Jesus' death on Calvary finally effected, ratified, and validated the promised new covenant. The "days (which) are coming" are the Messianic Age.[28]

"WHEN I WILL EFFECT A NEW COVENANT -- "I will effect" seems to mean something like 'I will bring a new covenant to accomplishment.'[29] "New" translates *kainos*, "renewed." This leads to the conclusion that the new covenant which was finally accomplished is in fact the Abrahamic covenant that had been *renewed* on numerous occasions until it was finally effected or accomplished at Calvary.[30] God had promised Abraham[31] that "in your *Seed* all the *nations* on the earth shall be *blessed*." The Seed was Christ, the nations include Jews and Gentiles, and the blessing is that their sins would be atoned for and forgiven.[32]

"WITH THE HOUSE OF ISRAEL AND WITH THE HOUSE OF JUDAH – The sons of Jacob grew into the twelve tribes by the time of the exodus. Years later, in the time of

---

Carchemish in 605 BC. From the start of his ministry, twenty years before the political situation became clear, Jeremiah unceasingly insisted that Babylon would be the victor. It was during the reign of Josiah that Jeremiah began his ministry, and he witnessed the revival that occurred when the Law was rediscovered in Josiah's eighteenth year (2 Kings 22:3-8). But he saw the spiritual awakening that occurred was not going to be permanent. It was just a matter of time before the southern kingdom would be punished by being taken captive for 70 years by Babylon. It was during the early days of the Babylonian captivity that Jeremiah received the prophecy of the new covenant recorded in Jeremiah 31:31ff. God, speaking through the prophet, said that both Israel and Judah would return from their captivities, and then God would give the suffering nation a New Covenant in which there would be an accomplishment of those things which the Mosaic Covenant was never able to do. (In chapters 50 and 51, Jeremiah also predicted that Babylon, because of her treatment of Israel, would be destroyed, never to rise again as a world power. This the Medo-Persians did, Daniel 5:26-28; Darius I Hystaspes destroyed the city of Babylon itself.)

[28] Hebrews 9:11, for example, will tell us readers that the "good things to come" (the better promises of the better covenant) have already been introduced before Hebrews was written. 9:15ff will show that Jesus' death was the sacrifice that ratified the new covenant and put it into force.

[29] The Hebrew in Jeremiah 31:31,33 and 34:8,15 is *karath berith* (literally, to cut a covenant). For this Hebrew phrase, the LXX uses two different Greek phrases. It reads *diathesomai diatheke* ("I will covenant a new covenant") at both verses 31 and 33. But in 34:8,15, the LXX reads *suntelein diatheken* ("I will effect a covenant"). The writer of Hebrews substitutes *sunteleo* for *diathesomai* in verse 31, but retains the LXX reading at verse 33. *Sunteleo* is the word that suggests a goal being reached, something finally being accomplished.

[30] One writer has suggested that God's words through Jeremiah contained the germ of the future of the spiritual history of mankind, so the words about a "new covenant" are of immense significance. It was to this prophecy that Jesus directed the thoughts of His disciples in the Upper Room as He instituted the Lord's Supper, as being the prophecy which, above all other prophecies, He had come to fulfill by His sacrifice of Himself. In that "new covenant" in His blood, which He solemnly proclaimed at the Last Supper (Matthew 26:28), and which is commemorated whenever men meet to partake of the Supper of the Lord (1 Corinthians 11:25), there was latent the main point of the whole argument of the Epistle to the Hebrews (chapters 8-10), yea, the whole gospel of justification by faith as proclaimed by Paul (Galatians 3:15-17). Some have further suggested that the passage in Jeremiah was one source of the name "new covenant" or New Testament that the church gave to the collected writings of the Apostolic Age.

[31] See Genesis 12:1-3, 22:18.

[32] See all this explained in Galatians 3:16ff; Acts 3:25; Romans 4:1-9, and in the special study on "Covenants" in Appendix A at the back of this book.

Rehoboam and Jeroboam, the tribes split into two groups. "House of Israel" was the name given in prophecy to the northern ten tribes. "House of Judah" was the name for the two southern tribes. In the new covenant prophecy, God was promising all twelve tribes (Israel and Judah[33]) that He would in the coming days effect a new covenant with them, a better one than He made with them at Sinai. While it was promised to the twelve tribes, it was not limited in its benefits to the twelve tribes. Romans and Galatians, in particular, show its benefits were intended for "all the nations."

8:9 -- "NOT LIKE THE COVENANT WHICH I MADE WITH THEIR FATHERS -- The covenant made with the "fathers" of the tribes of Judah and Israel is the Mosaic covenant made at Sinai.[34] God said the new covenant would be *not like* that old one. Verses 10-12 explain some of the ways the new covenant differs from the Mosaic covenant. How anyone can speak of the new covenant being simply a *renewal* of the Mosaic covenant is more than this commentator can understand. The new covenant is not Moses patched up and refurbished; it is a different covenant.

"ON THE DAY WHEN I TOOK THEM BY THE HAND TO LEAD THEM OUT OF THE LAND OF EGYPT -- This is the language that makes it clear the covenant being replaced is the one given at Sinai after Israel had made their exodus from Egypt. "Day" is used metaphorically for the whole period during which God led the people on their way from Egypt to Sinai. "Took them by the hand" is a picturesque metaphor[35] expressing the kindness and love of God, as He delivered the people and led them along.

"FOR THEY DID NOT CONTINUE IN MY COVENANT -- Though the generation of people at Sinai made solemn promises about keeping the provisions of the covenant,[36]

---

[33] Since both house of Judah and house of Israel are mentioned as parties in the new covenant, certain millennial theories think the new covenant won't be effected (the prophecy won't be fulfilled) till the beginning of the Millennium at the close of the Church Age. We reject this presentation for two reasons. (1) It contradicts what was said in 8:6. (2) It eviscerates the argument of Hebrews 8-10. To interpret Hebrews 8-10 as meaning the new covenant will be introduced 2000+ years from now would hardly be any incentive to the readers to abandon their ideas of going back to the Jewish religion. Furthermore, the thrust of Hebrews 8-10 is that the new covenant prophecy has already been fulfilled, and we are now living under the new covenant. That's what makes Jesus' priesthood so superior! That's what makes going back to Judaism so tragic! Only if the new covenant were already in force when Hebrews was written was there any legitimate need to abandon the old.

The modern Identity Movement has advanced a wholly unscriptural and abhorrent idea regarding the new covenant. The Identity Movement says all references in Bible prophecy to Israel are actually references to the white (Aryan) race (who are supposedly the remnants of the ten lost tribes of Israel) and that the new covenant therefore excludes all other races. Especially excluded are the Jews. Is it not rather obvious that there is something wrong with a theory that emphasizes the language about the house of Israel and ignores the language about the house of Judah when both expressions appear in the same prophecy and in the same breath?

[34] Exodus 24:7,8 show that what was done at Sinai was called a covenant. The "book of the covenant" was read to the people, and the "blood of the covenant" was sprinkled on the people who had promised obedience to all the words the Lord had spoken.

[35] Behind the figure of speech is the practice of fathers and mothers taking their little child by the hand and helping the child learn to walk, and helping them to get safely to the place where they are headed.

[36] Exodus 19:7,8, 24:3-8. Exodus 19:5ff shows that the Mosaic Covenant was conditional. If Israel did not faithfully meet the conditions, then God is not to be faulted if He likewise withdrew from it.

neither they nor their children were faithful to their promises. Why was God going to bring in a new covenant? Because the people broke the first one. For 800 years they were constantly guilty of shameful violations of the covenant; they did not comply with its conditions. So in Jeremiah's time, God clearly announced His plans to effect a new covenant.

"AND I DID NOT CARE FOR THEM, SAYS THE LORD -- Since the people did not regard and obey the Laws He had given, God would reject[37] them as His people, set aside the old covenant, and give a new covenant better adapted to save men.

8:10 -- "FOR -- "For" indicates that verse 10ff will explain how the new covenant is "different" (verse 9) and "better" (verse 6).

"THIS IS THE COVENANT THAT I WILL MAKE WITH THE HOUSE OF ISRAEL AFTER THOSE DAYS, SAYS THE LORD -- "After those days" seems to mean after the days when the first covenant was valid, i.e., from Sinai to Calvary. In verse 8, both "Judah" and "Israel" were named as parties in the new covenant. Now, it is simply "the house of Israel." With the reunion of the twelve tribes after the captivity, "Israel" could stand alone as the name of the one united people.

"I WILL PUT MY LAWS INTO THEIR MINDS, AND I WILL WRITE THEM UPON THEIR HEARTS -- Hebrews 8:6 prepared us to find some "better promises" in the new covenant than one could find in the Mosaic covenant. Here begins an enumeration of those better promises. We suppose the promises are four in number.[38] We suppose, also, that "not like the [Mosaic] covenant" (verse 9) gives the key to understanding just what God was promising in these better promises. It leads us to compare the way things were under the Law of Moses with how they are under the new covenant.[39] The *first* difference, the first area where the New Covenant is better, concerns an inward knowledge[40] of God's will versus some commandments written on tables of stone. This first promise seems to refer to the wonderful truth that under the new covenant, men will

---

[37] The writer of Hebrews quotes from the LXX version of Jeremiah 31:31ff, with a few verbal differences of the kind one would find if the passage were being quoted from memory. Of interest, too, is the fact the LXX differs from the Hebrew in places. For example, the Hebrew reads "although I was a husband to them" where the LXX reads "and I did not care for them." Scholars have conjectured why the LXX differs from the Hebrew, and most opt for the explanation that the meaning of the phrase hinges on the meaning given to the Hebrew word *ba'al*. It could mean, (1) to be lord and master over anything; (2) to be husband of anyone; (3) to disdain, reject (when a letter is added). Current evidence is just not extensive enough to make a positive decision on why the LXX differs from the present Hebrew text. The quotation in Hebrews simply follows the LXX at this place.

[38] Some commentators feel there are only three promises. The difference in number depends on how verse 12 is interpreted. Is the second half of the verse a fourth point, or is it a second member of a pair of phrases introduced by "for"? The decision as to whether there are three or four promises does affect (slightly) the explanation given to the phrases in question.

[39] Two of the four areas where the new covenant is "better" are developed in detail in Hebrews, as we shall show in the course of the comments on the verses. We shall appeal to other passages besides Hebrews for the New Testament explanation of the two better promises which are not explained in detail in Hebrews.

[40] "Minds" and "hearts" are likely synonymous terms, since this seems to be Hebrew parallelism.

want to do God's will (His "laws") because of a change in the heart. Under the Mosaic covenant, men had God's commands plainly enough given, but they had no help when it came to trying to obey what God had said. In this matter of help given by God, the new covenant promises something far better.[41]

"AND I WILL BE THEIR GOD, AND THEY SHALL BE MY PEOPLE -- The *second* difference where the new covenant is better concerns the people who can have the experience of having Jehovah as their God,[42] and in turn be His special people. Under the Mosaic Covenant, such an experience was rather limited to the Jewish people. Under the new covenant, the experience is open to both Gentiles and Jews. The use made of similar language in the book of Hosea may be the key to understanding what God was saying in this second promise. The change made in the names of Hosea's children (that's where we find the language similar to this second new covenant promise) enshrined a prophecy of the inclusion of the Gentiles as the people of God.[43]

8:11 -- "AND THEY SHALL NOT TEACH EVERY ONE HIS FELLOW CITIZEN, AND EVERYONE HIS BROTHER, SAYING, `KNOW THE LORD' -- Here begins the *third* difference wherein the new covenant is better than Moses. The new covenant people will "know the Lord" in a far better way than the Old Testament people knew Him, because there would be a better way of learning about Him.[44] In the Mosaic Age, people

---

[41] 2 Corinthians 3:3 is perhaps one passage that helps us to understand this first promise in Jeremiah's new covenant prophecy. In 2 Corinthians 3:3 we have a manifest reference not only to the idea but also to the very words of Jeremiah's prophecy. That passage contrasts what "the Spirit of the living God (has written) on tables of human hearts" with what in the Old Testament was "on tablets of stone." If we let 2 Corinthians guide us, then the work of the Holy Spirit is involved in this inward knowledge. Perhaps there is reference to the regenerating work of the Holy Spirit (as predicted in Ezekiel 36:26,27), an activity similar to the convicting work of the Holy Spirit through the Word (John 16:8-11, 1 Corinthians 12:13), leading men to become Christians, with the result that their "spirits" are alive again (Romans 8:10). Once the "spirit" is alive, the person has a much better opportunity to live as God wishes, because the old slavery to sin has been broken. Perhaps there is reference to the help the indwelling Holy Spirit gives the Christian to live the Christian life. Perhaps we should also think of 1 John 2:20,27, where the Holy Spirit helps men to know what God expects.

[42] When Jehovah promises to "be their God" in the new covenant age, He is promising that He would be their lawgiver, their counselor, their protector, their redeemer, their guide. He would provide for their wants, defend them in danger, pardon their sins, comfort them in trials, and save their souls. Whereas the Gentiles had been estranged from God, and outside the covenants of promise, now they have opportunity to have Jehovah as their God. When Jeremiah made his classic new covenant prophecy, Israel was being punished for disobedience to God's former covenant. But Jeremiah promises there will be an opportunity for Jewish people, too, to be what was really intended when God spoke about chosen people.

[43] See Hosea 1:6-9 and 2:23, and compare 1 Peter 2:10 and Romans 9:25,26. The people who were not God's people (the Gentiles) become God's people; the people who had not received mercy (the Gentiles) now receive mercy. 1 Peter 2:9 uses terms that used to be applied to God's Old Testament chosen people and applies them to God's New Testament people. (Jew or Gentile, once they have become Christians they are God's peculiar possession, a royal priesthood, a chosen people.)

[44] We have taken the words they "all shall know me" as being the heart and soul of this third difference between the new covenant and the Mosaic covenant. By emphasizing other words in this long sentence, some commentators have explained this third area where the new covenant is better as involving: (1) The fact that the new covenant is a *completed revelation* as opposed to all the piecemeal and progressive revelations that were given by Moses and the Prophets. Every time a new revelation was vouchsafed, the prophet had to tell the people to "know the Lord," i.e., here is a new truth you are expected to live by from henceforth. (2) The fact

were born into covenant relationship by physical birth into the descendants of the children of Israel. As the children grew, they had to be taught about the covenant they were already physically a part of. Not only that, but adults had to be called back to God by prophet after prophet.[45] What is so much better about the New Covenant is that now Jesus has revealed the Father (John 12:44ff, 14:7ff, 17:6) in a way that only One as intimate with the Father as Jesus could do (John 1:18).

"FOR ALL SHALL KNOW ME, FROM THE LEAST TO THE GREATEST OF THEM -- One reason men have a better knowledge of God under the new covenant is because Jesus has become flesh and walked among men. "He who has seen Me has seen the Father," said Jesus. Through Jesus we get a better knowledge of God and His will for mankind.[46] Another reason for the better knowledge of God under the new covenant is that the teaching requisite to knowing the Lord is given *before* a person enters into covenant relationship with God. In the process of conversion, first comes teaching, then comes the new birth into the family of God and covenant relationship.[47] However, neither of these possible ways of better knowing the Lord is the one the writer of Hebrews develops. The letter writer develops (in 9:1ff) the fact that new covenant people can "know the Lord" because they have an access to God, yea, the eligibility (that was not available before Jesus died) to "draw near to God"[48] because their sins have been really and actually forgiven.

---

that there is a universality to the gospel ("all shall know me") makes it better than Moses (which was limited primarily to the Jewish people). (3) The fact that all new covenant believers will have a personal (experiential) knowledge of God because of the indwelling presence of the Holy Spirit. (4) Premillennial interpreters, who find the fulfillment of the new covenant prophecy in the coming millennium, say that during the millennium there will be universal righteousness, and the knowledge of Jehovah will cover the earth like the waters cover the sea; so, of course, there will be no reason for anyone to teach another to "know the Lord." (See footnote #34 above for a refutation of this futuristic millennial explanation.)

[45] We trace in these words about every man teaching his neighbor the profound sense of failure to get Old Testament listeners to make any meaningful change in their lives. What good had come of all the machinery of ritual and of teaching which the Law of Israel had provided so abundantly? What good had come of those repeated exhortations on the part of preachers and prophets, down through the centuries, that men should "know the Lord"?

Of course, when God says men won't have to teach their neighbors to know the Lord once the new covenant has been inaugurated, it does not mean that no teachers are needed in the Messianic Age, or that believers have nothing to learn. After all, the writer of Hebrews was teaching his readers by means of this very letter. If we forget to call attention to the differences between the old and new covenants (Hebrews 8:9) as we interpret, we shall very likely offer erroneous comments on some of the individual phrases.

[46] That men come to know God through Jesus is exactly how Jesus Himself used these words from Jeremiah (John 6:45): "It is written in the prophets, `And they shall all be taught of God' [Isaiah 54:13, Jeremiah 31:34]. Everyone who has heard and learned from the Father, comes to Me." John put it this way, "No man has seen God at any time; the only begotten God [i.e., Jesus], who is in the bosom of the Father, He has explained Him" (John 1:18).

[47] The point of difference between the Mosaic and new covenants should not be missed. In the new covenant situation, it is consenting adults who become covenant people, not babies! The new covenant Scriptures everywhere indicate that people must be old enough to "know the Lord" before they become part of God's family by faith, repentance, and immersion.

[48] What it means to "draw near to God" has been explained in notes at Hebrews 4:16, 7:18, and 7:25. See also 10:1,22.

8:12 -- "FOR I WILL BE MERCIFUL TO THEIR INIQUITIES -- This verse begins with "For;" it is intended to give the reason why people under the new covenant will know God better (i.e., be able to "draw near" to Him). It is because sins have been forgiven; He has been "merciful[49] to their iniquities". Wasn't God merciful during the time when the Mosaic Covenant was valid? Yes, very much so. Time and again He "passed over" their sins. But note, He passed over; He did not actually forgive (see Romans 3:25). Furthermore, it must be remembered Jeremiah originally made this new covenant prediction at a time when God was punishing the sins of disobedient Israel. The new covenant prophecy was meant to kindle hope in the sons of Israel. The new covenant, God promised, would ensure believing Israel's restoration to the privilege of drawing near to Him.

"AND I WILL REMEMBER THEIR SINS NO MORE" -- This is the *fourth* of the better promises that make the new covenant better than the Mosaic covenant. Hebrews 10:1ff (especially verses 10-18) will develop this promise, showing the profound difference between Jesus' once-for-all sacrifice and the repeated sacrifices of the Mosaic system. His sacrifice really did atone for sins, whereas the animal sacrifices never did.

8:13 -- When He said, "A new *covenant*" -- Now the writer of Hebrews begins emphasizing several of the truths implied in the new covenant prophecy. First, he highlights the word "new" found in verse 8 (Jeremiah 31:31).

He has made the first obsolete -- At the time God gave this prophecy to Jeremiah, He used the word "new." By the use of that single word, God made the first covenant (the Mosaic Covenant) "obsolete." When God speaks about something "new" coming, the other one must be old, obsolete, about finished, about to be abrogated, superseded.[50] Now, 600+ years after that prediction was first made, the old one is not something the Hebrew readers should go back to with nostalgia.

But whatever is becoming obsolete and growing old is ready to disappear -- This is the writer's comment on the meaning of "obsolete." If Christian doctrine teaches the Mosaic Covenant was but temporary, and has been superseded, that should not be thought to be a strange doctrine. Jeremiah taught it! If the priesthood on which that old covenant had been effected (cp. Hebrews 7:11) should cease to function shortly (it was less than ten years before Jerusalem would be destroyed in AD 70), because that too had been superseded, that too should not be thought to be a strange doctrine. It was implied in God's new covenant prophecy and in Psalm 110:4.[51]

---

[49] The word translated "merciful" *(hileos)* means propitious, favorable, clement. Compare what was said about a similar word *(hilaskomai) in the notes at Hebrews 2:17.*

[50] The writer of Hebrews is pointing out the same connotation we modern readers put on the word "new." After all, what is implied about the old one when we say we are going to get a new car? "Made obsolete" translates *palaioō*, "to treat as antiquated, to abrogate, supersede" (Harper, *Analytical Lexicon*, p.299).

[51] Of course, the old covenant was nailed to the cross (Colossians 2:14). But some years would pass before that truth had been widely disseminated, and men could act upon it by embracing the better promises of the new covenant.

B. His Ministry is Superior Because It Occurs in a Better Sanctuary. 9:1-28

1. The old tabernacle and its imperfect services. 9:1-10

9:1 -- Now -- The general intent of this chapter is the same as in the two preceding, to show that the priesthood exercised by Jesus Messiah is superior to the Levitical priesthood. It is part of the overall presentation which is intended to discourage defection from Christianity back to Judaism; after all, you would be returning to something second best if you were to re-embrace Old Testament religion. In 8:13, the Hebrews writer had shown the first covenant was obsolete and ready to disappear. When one considers what it was replaced with, that disappearance was no calamity.

Even the first *covenant* -- "*Covenant*" is in italics. Some English versions read "first *tabernacle*" because some of the first printed Greek texts had "tabernacle" in the text. All the ancient manuscripts, however, omit any noun after the adjective "first," so from the context we must supply some noun in agreement with "first." Like "covenant" was supplied at 8:7, so "covenant" is supplied at 9:1, since both the preceding and following context show the writer is still developing points suggested by the classic New Covenant prophecy.

Had regulations of divine worship -- Note the past tense "had". The past tense is used since the new covenant has already been inaugurated. The method of worship, the priestly activities,[1] under the Mosaic Covenant was not left haphazard, but was divinely prescribed. God gave the regulations[2] about how this service was to be conducted; it didn't just evolve by human invention. Many of these regulations can be found in Exodus 25 and 26.

And the earthly sanctuary -- God also gave the regulations or instructions how the entire tabernacle structure,[3] in which the priestly services were carried out, should be built. It is called a tabernacle of this world[4] to call attention to the fact that it was material, temporal, perishable, mundane. It was made by human hands, not pitched by the Lord (cp. 8:2); the "earthly tabernacle" was not at all the quality of the heavenly place where Jesus functions.

---

[1] The word translated "worship" is *latreia*, the same root word used at 8:5 to refer to priestly activities.

[2] There is no Greek word corresponding to the English word "divine" at this place. However, *dikaiomata*, translated "regulations," regularly speaks of commands, ordinances, laws, precepts, ceremonies, given by God. See the same word used at Romans 1:32.

[3] In comments at 8:2, we noted the Scriptures are not uniform in the names applied to the rooms or to the whole portable place of worship. It probably can be said that in this immediate context, the singular form (*to hagion*, the Greek construction here translated "sanctuary") is regularly used for the whole structure including the open courtyard. Compare footnote #8 below for more information on the names given to the different rooms.

[4] The Greek word translated "earthly" is *kosmikos*, an adjective formed by adding *-ikos* to a noun. Such a construction emphasizes relation, fitness, or ability. The "tabernacle" was suited for this world; it was not suitable for heaven. (The only other time the word *kosmikos* is found in the New Testament is Titus 2:12 ["worldly desires"], where it has a bad sense. We should not think that the Old Testament tabernacle was bad; rather, it simply belonged to this earth in contrast to the heavenly sanctuary where Jesus ministers [verse 11]. In fact, the translators' use of "earthly" rather than "worldly" helps avoid giving 9:1 a wrong connotation.)

The courtyard (the outer court in the diagram at 8:5) measured 150' long by 75' wide. It was surrounded by a movable cloth fence hung on posts about 7.5' high. The entrance to the courtyard, made of a curtain hung on four posts, was on the east side. Inside this courtyard, in the open eastern half, stood the altar of burnt offering and the laver. Inside the courtyard, in the western half, was where the smaller structure (45' long, 15' wide, 15' high) composed of two rooms (the Holy Place, and the Holy of Holies), was pitched. The two points introduced, "worship" and "sanctuary," are discussed in inverse order in the following verses. Verses 2-5 will cover the sanctuary; verses 6-10 will cover the worship.

9:2 -- For there was a tabernacle prepared -- Whereas verse 1 spoke of the entire structure, verses 2 and 3 describe the two rooms (elsewhere called "the Holy Place" and "the Holy of Holies") of the tent[5] that comprised the inner portion of the whole. God's original instructions for preparing or constructing[6] this whole structure can be found in Exodus 25-40. It is noteworthy that Hebrews throughout refers to the "tabernacle," and not once to the temples (Solomon's, Zerubbabel's, or Herod's) that succeeded it.[7] Though the temples were built on the same general model or floor plan, not everyone was happy with the changes their very design and construction necessitated. No one, however, faulted the original tabernacle, about which we read in detail in the Old Scriptures. The writer's argument could be drawn from it without the force of the argument being evaded by someone saying, 'I never approved of that temple (Herod's, or Zerubbabel's, for example) anyway!'

The outer one ... this is called the holy place -- "Outer one" is literally the first, that is, the first room the priest entered as he went into the two-roomed tent. The dimensions of this first room, the Holy Place,[8] were about 30' long, 15' wide, and 15' high.[9] The outer walls of both rooms were made of boards, 20 for each side (north and south) and 6 for the west end.[10] Each board was 15' long x about 2'3" wide. Each board had 2 tenons at one end, to be stood upright in 2 sockets of silver. Once the boards were stood upright, butting against each other side by side, they were held together with 5 bars or poles run through golden rings in the boards. The boards were overlaid with gold. Ten sheets of cloth, each

---

[5] Each of the two chambers or rooms is called a tent or tabernacle (*skene*, Greek).

[6] The term "prepared" is not the usual word for "pitching" a tent, nor of "erecting" a building, but is the word for the manufacture or original crafting of the tent and its furnishings and equipment.

[7] Some have supposed that the reason the writer makes the tabernacle (rather than the temple) the basis of his argument is because neither the writer nor the readers belonged to the Jerusalem community. They were familiar, so the argument is attempted, with the tabernacle; they were not familiar with the temple. Still others, with not much more success, in this commentator's opinion, urge the use of the tabernacle in the argument as proof that Hebrews was written long after the temple had been destroyed in AD 70. Both these alleged implications ignore the real point the writer is making -- namely, the sanctuary of the old covenant, by its very furniture and services, proclaimed its temporary character. They pointed to Jesus' priestly ministry, a very far better ministry, because of the permanent place, the heavenly place, wherein He serves.

[8] At Hebrews 8:2 we learned the names given to the rooms are not done with consistency. The same word (*hagia*) here translated "Holy Place" is elsewhere applied to the Holy of Holies (8:2, 9:8,12,24,25, 10:19). So the interpreter must determine which room is meant by the demands of the specific context.

[9] The actual dimensions in feet depend on size of the cubit, which varied from 18 to 24 inches.

[10] Exodus 26:23ff describes an additional two boards that were to form the corners at the tent's west end.

42' long x 6' wide, made of blue and white and purple and scarlet linen, with cherubs worked thereon of needlework, were spread over the erected boards, making a sort of ceiling for the rooms.[11] The outside of this structure was then covered by several layers of waterproof materials[12] to protect the furniture inside from the elements.

In which *were* **the lampstand** -- Here begins a list of the furniture found in the Holy Place. The lampstand[13] stood near the south wall of the Holy Place. It was made of pure gold and consisted of an upright shaft, about 6' high, and six branches, three on either side of the upright. Each branch consisted of bowls, knops, and flowers (we are not sure what each looked like). At the end of each branch was a golden lamp, fed with pure olive oil. The lampstand gave the only light there was inside the whole tent.

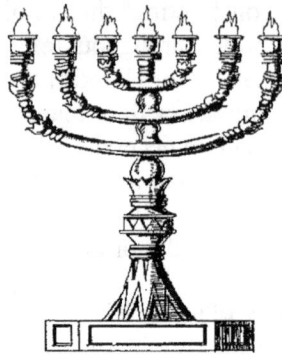

Golden Lampstand

And the table and the sacred bread -- The table, on which the sacred bread (the show-bread) was placed near the northern wall in the Holy Place, across the room opposite the lampstand. The original table, made of wood and overlaid with gold, was about 3' long x 18" wide x about 2' high (remember, it was portable). It was furnished with rings, through which poles were passed and by which the table could be carried, much like a stretcher (four men carried it, one on each end of each pole).[14] Josephus tells us these poles were removed when the table was resting in its place in the Holy Place so they were not in the way of the priests. The dishes and vessels on the table were made of gold. The NASB translators

---

[11] Laid side by side, the 10 sheets formed a cover measuring 60' long x 42' wide. The extra width was to overhang the boards on the north and south sides. The 15' extra length was to hang down on the west end.

[12] One layer was made of goats' hair cloth. It consisted of 11 sheets, each 45' long x 6' wide, with the sheets fastened together with clasps of brass. This whole layer would be 66' long x 45' wide. A second layer was made of red leather from rams' skins. A third layer of covering was made of *tahash* (sealskins or porpoise skins?). Whether or not there was a ridge pole higher than the walls, intended to support these outer coverings in such a way as to make a sloping roof, or whether they laid flat across the top of the boards, is not known for certain. A detailed discussion can be found in the article on the "Tabernacle" in *International Standard Bible Encyclopedia*, edited by J. Orr (Grand Rapids: Eerdmans, 1939), Vol.5, p.2887-2898. For excellent color pictures of the tabernacle and its furniture, see Paul F. Kiene, *The Tabernacle of God in the Wilderness of Sinai* (Grand Rapids: Zondervan, 1977).

[13] The Greek is *luchnia* and the Hebrew is *menorah*. "Candlestick" gives a wrong mental image to most Western minds. Illustrations of the Menorah have been found on Hasmonean coins and in the well-known relief on the Arch of Titus in Rome. (The seven-branched lampstand from the Arch of Titus, which shows the lampstand as it was in Herod's Temple, has been adopted as the coat of arms of the modern state of Israel.) Exodus 25:31-37 describes the seven-branched lampstand found in the tabernacle. (1 Kings 7:49 describes the 10 lampstands used in the temple of Solomon. These were undoubtedly among the treasures carried to Babylon at the fall of Jerusalem and afterward returned, Ezra 1:7.) The lampstand taken to Rome in AD 70, was later taken to Carthage by Genseric, AD 455, then to Constantinople by Belisarius, AD 534. After that, nothing further is known of it.

[14] Exodus 25:23-30, 37:10-16, record the instructions concerning the construction of the table.

have chosen "sacred bread" to translate the Greek, which reads "the setting forth of the loaves."[15] There were twelve of these loaves, one for each of the twelve tribes, stacked in two piles of six loaves each. Hebrew writers describe the loaves, each made from about 7 quarts of fine flour, as being square. The loaves were changed each Sabbath, and on top of each stack was placed a cup of frankincense (Leviticus 24:5-9). The old loaves became the perquisite of the priests, who ate them for food.[16]

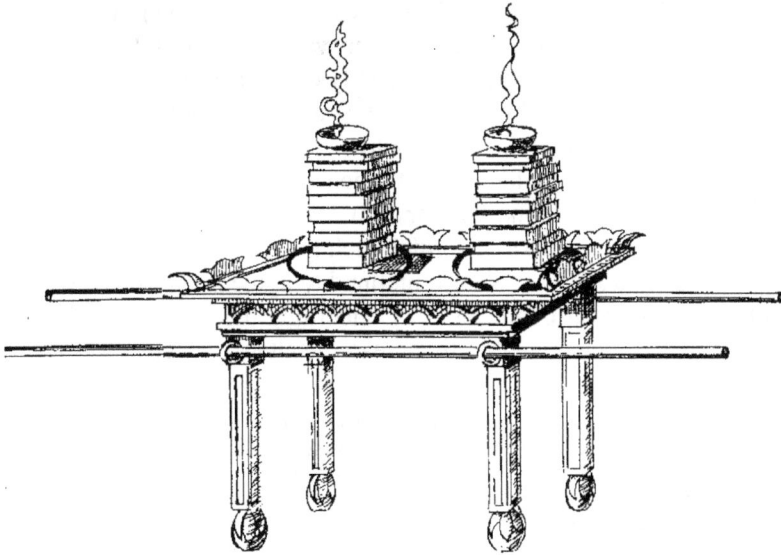

Table of Showbread

There was a third piece of furniture, the altar of incense, located in the first room. Some versions (e.g., the Coptic Sahidic) and manuscripts (e.g., Vaticanus) transpose to this place the word phrase "and the golden altar of incense" found in verse 4 in our version.[17]

9:3 -- And behind the second veil -- The "second veil" separated the two rooms of the tabernacle. It was called the "second veil" to distinguish it from the veil that formed the eastern entrance to the whole tent.[18]

---

[15] Just why the loaves were called "showbread" or "loaves of presentation" (NASB margin) is not certain. The Hebrew expression *lehem happanim* means "bread of the face," and the LXX renders Exodus 25:30 as "loaves placed before my face," while the Douay rendered the expression "loaves of proposition" (i.e., placed before). Various explanations have been offered. Some felt it was so called because the loaves were placed before (in the presence of) God in the tabernacle. Some felt it was so called because it was set out to be seen by men. Another says the loaves were intended to symbolize the nation's gratitude to God for sustenance.

[16] The loaves of showbread were not ordinarily to be eaten by non-priests, though see 1 Samuel 21:1-6 and Mark 2:25ff.

[17] The unusual wording of verse 4, as well as the meaning of the expression, will be explained in due course.

[18] Two distinct words were used in the Hebrew for the two veils. The first one at the outer entrance was *masakh*; the second one between the Holy Place and Holy of Holies was *parokheth*. The Greek version usually uses *kalumma* for the outer veil and *katapetasma* for the second veil (though the LXX is not always consistent

There was a tabernacle which is called the Holy of Holies -- This inner room was cube shaped, measuring 15' in each dimension.[19] This was the room into which no one entered except the high priest, and he only on one day each year, the Day of Atonement.

9:4 -- Having a golden altar of incense -- As verse 2 described the furniture in the Holy Place, verse 4 seems intended to describe the furniture connected with the Holy of Holies. However, this first phrase presents at least two problems: (1) the identity of the *thumiaterion*, and (2) its location or relationship with the Holy of Holies.[20] The first problem, the identity of the *thumiaterion*, is quickly evident from a simple comparison of English versions. The KJV and ERV both translate it "golden censer" (i.e., a metal pot or pan for carrying hot coals on which incense could be sprinkled), whereas the ASV, NASB, NEB, and RSV translate it as "golden altar of incense" (i.e., the little altar[21] that stood in the Holy Place just before the second veil, and on which incense was offered each day at prayer time). While arguments pro and con for each translation have been offered, neither one is entirely without difficulty.[22] We are inclined to agree with the NASB and see it as a reference to the "golden altar of incense." Concerning the second problem, what does "*having* a golden altar ..." mean? Does this mean the altar of incense was located in the

---

in this wording, for *katapetasma* is used for the first veil at Exodus 26:37 and 37:5). Each veil was wrought of blue, purple, scarlet, and fine twisted linen. On the inner veil (suspended by golden hooks on four wooden pillars) which separated the Holy of Holies from the Holy Place were figures of cherubim, in token of the presence and unapproachableness of Jehovah. The outer veil (suspended on five wooden pillars), which was passed by the priests when they entered the Holy Place to minister, lacked any such warning symbols to discourage man's ingress (Exodus 26:31-37). The Rabbis say that the second veil was made of thread six strands double, and that after the erection of Solomon's temple, it was renewed regularly each year.

[19] The name given to this inner room varies. The Hebrew, literally translated, is the "Most Holy." The Greek can be translated Most Holy Place, or Holy of Holies, or Holiest of all. It was considered to be so holy because the Shekinah, the symbol of the divine presence, dwelt therein above the cherubim on the ark of the covenant.

[20] These problems are considered so weighty that many writers have come to the conclusion the writer of Hebrews erred here by saying the altar was in the Holy of Holies, and this problem has also been used as evidence that Paul did not write Hebrews (nor any other apostle, or inspired writer, for that matter).

[21] The altar of incense was made of wood, and overlaid with gold. It was about 3' high x 1.5' square. It was fitted with rings and poles for carrying.

[22] Some insist the reference is to the censer. The LXX regularly uses *thumiaterion* for censer but never for the altar of incense (e.g., 2 Chronicles 26:19; Ezekiel 8:11). From Exodus 30:1-10, it is obvious the altar of incense stood in the Holy Place, not the Holy of Holies; therefore, Hebrews 9:4 (it is argued) which describes furniture in the Holy of Holies, cannot be a reference to the altar of incense. (Others have urged that no difficulties are solved by translating *thumiaterion* as censer here in Hebrews, since it is doubtful if that pan, when not in use, was stored in the Holy of Holies. In addition, it has been observed that since the Old Testament nowhere describes the censer as being *golden* [though such a description has been found in non-canonical Jewish literature], we would hardly expect it to be so described in the New Testament.)

Others insist the reference is to the "altar of incense." If this is not a reference to that altar, no mention is made in Hebrews to that major piece of furniture, and that would be odd, it is argued. (Defenders of the "censer" view note that Josephus does not name the altar of incense when he lists the articles of furniture carried away by the Romans, so its omission in Hebrews is not odd.) There is a different word (*pureion*, "fire pan") used for "censer" in the Pentateuch (Leviticus 16:12, LXX). Furthermore, to use *thumiaterion* to designate the altar of incense was common first-century usage as is evident from the writings of Josephus (*Wars* V.218), Philo (*Who is Heir of Divine Things* 226j and *Life of Moses,* ii.94. 101), Christian writers Clement of Alexandria and Origen, and the versions of Theodotian and Symmachus at Exodus 30:1. Exodus 30:1-10 (the passage that describes its construction) does apply the adjective "gold" to the incense altar.

Holy of Holies?[23] Does the writer of Hebrews simply repeat wording found in the Old Testament concerning the relationship between the ark of the covenant and the altar of incense?[24] Or does it mean that on the Day of Atonement there was a special relationship between the altar of incense and the services conducted in the Holy of Holies? Part of the ritual on the Day of Atonement did call for the high priest to take burning coals from the altar of incense into the Holy of Holies and sprinkle incense on the coals so the smoke would cover the mercy seat, protecting the priest from death (Leviticus 16:12,13).

Altar of Incense

And the ark of the covenant covered on all sides with gold -- The ark of the covenant was a wooden chest, overlaid with gold. It was about 4.5' long x 2.25' wide x 2.25' high. It also had the rings and poles used to carry it. The history of the ark of the covenant is checkered.[25] The last notices in Scripture are from the time of Solomon's temple (1 Kings

---

[23] The use of "having" may be no less explicit than "in which" used in verse 2, since the same word "having" is used to describe the relation of the manna to the golden jar.

[24] Several Old Testament references read much as does Hebrews here, and those verses do connect the *thumiaterion* with the Holy of Holies and the ark of the covenant. In the LXX and the Samaritan Pentateuch at Exodus 30:6, the words "before the mercy seat that is over the testimony" are omitted, so the verse reads "You shall put the altar of gold in front of the veil that is near the ark of the testimony." (The evidence from the Samaritan Bible is weakened somewhat by the fact the whole section dealing with the altar of incense [Exodus 30:1-10] is inserted between Exodus 26:35 and 36, thus locating the *thumiaterion* in the Holy Place.) In addition, both Exodus 40:5 ("you shall set the gold altar of incense before the ark of the testimony") and 1 Kings 6:22 ("the whole altar which was by the inner sanctuary he [Solomon] overlaid with gold"), connect the incense altar with the veil and the ark rather than speaking in terms of the room in which it was located. On this view, that the writer of Hebrews is reflecting Old Testament usage, he cannot be accused of making a mistake regarding the location of the altar of incense. His intimate knowledge of the tabernacle and its services argues strongly that any confusion lies with us readers, not with the original writer.

[25] It, of course, traveled with the Israelites during the wilderness wanderings. After they passed over the Jordan into the promised land, the ark remained some time at Gilgal (Joshua 4:18). Then it was taken to Shiloh (1 Samuel 1:3). From there, it was taken by the Israelites into battle against the Philistines, and was captured by the Philistines (1 Samuel 4). The Philistines eventually returned it on a cow-drawn cart (1 Samuel 7). During the reign of Saul, it was located at Nob (1 Samuel 21:1-6). David brought it to the house of Obed-Edom (2 Samuel 6), and during this trip occurred the famous incident resulting in the death of Uzzah. When Solomon's Temple was dedicated, it was placed in the Holy of Holies, where it remained for many years. Later, the wicked

8:9, 2 Chronicles 5:10) and the reign of Josiah (2 Chronicles 35:3). Its subsequent history is obscured in contradictory traditions.[26] There was no Ark in either Zerubbabel's or Herod's temples; both these buildings contained only a beautifully decorated raised stone platform in the Holy of Holies.[27]

Ark of the Covenant

In which was a golden jar holding the manna -- During the wilderness wanderings, God provided manna when the people were hungry. A small portion was to be kept, put in a container, and stored inside the ark of the covenant.[28] The golden[29] jar held about 4 pints.

And Aaron's rod which budded -- In Numbers 17, it is recorded some rebellious princes questioned the choice of Aaron to be high priest.   To settle the matter, each tribe was to

kings of Judah, having gone into idolatry, set up idols in the Holy of Holies. The priests removed the Ark, and bore it from place to place, to secure it from profanation. When Josiah became king, he commanded the priests to restore the ark to its place in the temple (2 Chronicles 35:3).

[26] Perhaps the ark of the covenant was destroyed when Jerusalem was destroyed by Nebuchadnezzar in 587 BC, or perhaps it was taken with the spoils to Babylon. Jewish tradition has it that Jeremiah hid the ark and other furniture in a cave on Mt. Nebo (2 Maccabees 2:1-8). In Samaritan tradition, the ark and the holy vessels of the tabernacle were hidden on Mt. Gerizim (cp. Josephus, *Ant.* XVIII.4.1).

[27] Concerning Zerubbabel's Temple, see the article on "Temple" in *International Standard Bible Encyclopedia*, edited by James Orr (Grand Rapids: Eerdmans, 1939), Vol. 5, p.2936, which cites the Mishna tract *Yoma* 5.2. Concerning Herod's Temple, see Asher Kaufman, "Where the Ancient Temple of Jerusalem Stood" (Extant 'Foundation Stone' for the Ark of the Covenant is Identified), *Biblical Archaeology Review* 9:2 (March-April 1983), p.40-61. Even before Herod's Temple was built, the ark of the covenant was gone. The Roman general Pompey, who forced his way into the temple in 63 BC, found only the furniture belonging to the Holy Place; there was nothing in the Holy of Holies (Josephus, *Ant.* XIV.4.4; Tacitus, *History*, 5.9; Josephus, *Wars* V.5.5).

[28] Manna would not ordinarily keep very long (Exodus 16:20). Some have supposed that the fact that some could be laid up in a jar in the ark and preserved from age to age appears to have been a perpetual miracle in proof of the presence and faithfulness of God.

[29] The Hebrew text does not describe the urn as golden, but the LXX does.

bring a rod or staff to Moses, with the name of the tribe to which it belonged written on it. These old dead sticks were laid up in the tabernacle overnight, and in the morning Levi's (which had Aaron's name written on it) had budded, blossomed, and put forth ripe almonds. This showed which tribe was to perform the priestly functions. Moses was then instructed to "put back the rod of Aaron before the testimony,[30] to be kept as a sign against the rebels" (Numbers 17:10).

And the tables of the covenant -- These are the two tables of stone on which the Ten Commandments had been written (Exodus 31:18, 32:15, 34:28).[31] They were put inside the ark of the covenant (Exodus 26:16,21, 40:20) and were still in the ark at the time of the dedication of Solomon's Temple (1 Kings 8:9; 2 Chronicles 5:10). The subsequent history of the tablets of stone is unknown. Perhaps they suffered the same fate as did the ark of the covenant itself.

9:5 -- And above it _were_ the cherubim of glory -- The exact form or shape of the cherubim atop the ark of the covenant is not known, but most interpreters think they had bodies somewhat similar to the cherubim described in the Old Testament.[32] There were two cherubs on the ark, made of beaten gold, placed on the lid in such a manner that their faces looked toward each other, and downward at the mercy seat. They stretched their wings on high and covered the mercy seat (cp. Exodus 25:18-22, 37:7-9).[33] "Glory" is evidently a reference to the Shekinah, a luminous cloud, symbolizing the divine presence,[34] which rested above the mercy seat.

---

[30] It is uncertain whether the rod was put *inside* the Ark, or simply laid *beside* it. If it were put inside, it would not have been a very long stick (less than 3.75' long). On the other hand, the other two items in this verse, the pot of manna and the tables of stone, were kept *inside* the ark, and the language for the rod implies the same.

In passing, both the pot of manna and the rod seem to have disappeared before Solomon's time (1 Kings 8:9; 2 Chronicles 5:10), possibly at the time the Philistines captured the Ark (1 Samuel 4:10,11).

[31] Of course, Moses broke the first set of tablets (Deuteronomy 9:9,11,15,17), so the actual tablets put into the ark of the covenant were the second set that God furnished (Exodus 34:1-4).

[32] The word "cherubim" is the Hebrew plural form of cherub (a word that means guardian, keeper). The Old Testament pictures cherubim as being an order of angels who are in the very presence of God (1 Samuel 4:4; Psalm 18:10; and Ezekiel 1:5-14 [the "living creatures" of 1:5ff are identical with the "cherubim" described in Ezekiel 10:10-20, for 10:20 so identifies them]). These angelic creatures are described as having a body somewhat like human bodies, yet they had hands, hooves, and four wings; each one had four faces, the form of their faces being that of a man, a lion, a bull, and an eagle.

Some writers have expressed surprise that the golden cherubim on the ark did not come under the ban imposed by the Second Commandment, a ban on making images (a ban that was ignored when the Jews made the golden bull-calves worshiped at Dan and Bethel). Perhaps the reason the "cherubim of gold" were not prohibited is that their shape was enough different from the actual forms of the living cherubim who inhabit heaven that it can honestly be said their "likeness" was *not* the "likeness of anything that is in heaven above, or that is in the earth beneath, or that is in the water under the earth" (Exodus 20:4 KJV; Deuteronomy 5:8).

[33] In Solomon's temple, the cherubim above the mercy seat were made of wood, overlaid with gold. 15' high, they were so placed that the wing of one touched the wall on one side of the Holy of Holies, and that of the other the other side of the Holy of Holies. Their other two wings met together over the ark. I Kings 6:23-28.

[34] See Exodus 25:22, 40:34; Numbers 7:89; Ezekiel 10:19,20.

Overshadowing the mercy seat -- The "mercy seat" (Hebrew, *kapporeth*; Greek, *hilasterion*) was a cover or lid of pure gold that covered the entire top of the ark of the covenant.[35] The Septuagint choice of *hilasterion* ("propitiatory covering") to translate the Hebrew word *kapporeth* ("covering") probably reflects an attempt to convey to the readers a reminder of one of the major religious ceremonies connected with the lid or cover of the ark. That ceremony, on the Day of Atonement, involved the sprinkling of blood onto the lid (Exodus 25:17, 37:6; Leviticus 16:14) so that the lid served as a covering for sin as well as a covering for the box or chest.

But of these things we cannot now speak in detail -- Enough has been said about the general structure and furniture of the tabernacle, not only to refresh in the readers' minds the whole Old Testament account, but also to enable to the writer to show how Jesus' priestly ministry is superior to anything carried on in such an earthly tabernacle. If the writer had gone into "detail," it likely would have been an exposition of the typological significance of the tabernacle and the priestly services carried on therein.[36]

9:6 -- Now when these things have been thus prepared -- Having described the tabernacle in sufficient detail, the writer proceeds to recall some of the services or rituals carried on therein.

The priests are continually entering the outer tabernacle -- The writer begins with the rituals and ministry performed by the lower priests, the ones who did their work in the room called the Holy Place (cp. verse 2). Such services were performed on a daily basis; they were done continually.[37]

---

[35] The familiar English term "mercy seat" comes from Tyndale's translation, who followed Luther's lead in an attempt to render the Hebrew word into terms easily understood by a modern audience. "Mercy" is a word used regularly of God's attitude that results in forgiveness of sins. Since the blood sprinkled on the *kapporeth* had something to do with sins being passed over, the choice of the word "mercy" was a useful means to call all this to mind. Since the Shekinah supposedly rested right over the ark of the covenant, it was not difficult to picture the cover of the ark as being the "seat," the place where the merciful God was supposed to be seated. Thus the combination of terms "mercy" and "seat" were intended to call several Old Testament ideas to mind.

[36] Hebrews 8:5, 9:9, and 10:1 suggest the tabernacle and its furniture were typical. Acts 7:37 tells us Moses was a type of Christ. Romans 5:12ff shows Adam was a type of Christ. Indeed, very much of the Old Testament was typical. There was a time in Christian Churches that we regularly heard sermons on "types and shadows," and our knowledge of the Scriptures is most likely impoverished now that preachers tend to shy away from such presentations. (Perhaps we no longer study in enough depth to be able to prepare such helpful teaching messages, or perhaps we have been disillusioned by some of the speculations contained in some of those older messages, in which were alleged some rather far-fetched types and shadows [e.g., the table of showbread was supposed to be typical of the Lord's Table; the laver typical of baptism; and the Holy Place typical of the church, through which one must go before entering heaven, the Holy of Holies].) Care certainly should be taken to call only those things "types" which the Scriptures themselves so identify. M.S. Terry, *Biblical Hermeneutics* (Grand Rapids: Zondervan, 1950 reprint), p.334ff has a good chapter on "Interpretation of Types." Some useful tools to begin a study of types and shadows are: V.E. Hoven, *Shadow and Substance* (St. Louis: Bethany Press, 1934). R.E. Milligan, *Scheme of Redemption* (St. Louis: Christian Board of Publication, nd.), chapter 6, "Legal Types." Patrick Fairbairn, *The Typology of Scripture* (Grand Rapids: Zondervan, 1963).

[37] Some have urged that the present tense verb (*"are continually* entering") indicates such services were still being performed when Hebrews was written (i.e., Hebrews was written before the priestly services in the temple were terminated by the fall of Jerusalem, AD 70). This may well be true, but those priests were no longer enter-

Performing the divine worship -- Incense had to be burned morning and evening at prayer time, and the lamps on the lampstand replenished with oil morning and evening (Exodus 30:7,8, Leviticus 24:3,4).[38] The showbread had to be changed weekly (Leviticus 24:5-8).

9:7 -- But into the second -- The second room is the one called the Holy of Holies (cp. verse 3). The "but" marks a contrast where we move from the activities of the ordinary priests to those of the high priest.

Only the high priest *enters* -- By excluding all priests, save the high priest, from entering the Holy of Holies, it appears God was trying to give men an object lesson (cp. verse 8). He was picturing vividly that there was a barrier (unforgiven sin) that kept sinning men from drawing near to His holy presence. In fact, not even the high priest could enter, save on God's terms, and then only if his sins had been (symbolically) taken care of. "Only" or alone says that the high priest was without attendants. Not even a priest was allowed to enter the Holy Place while the high priest was going through the Day of Atonement rituals.

Once a year -- Leviticus 16 details the ceremonies on the Day of Atonement, the one day each year when the high priest dared enter the Holy of Holies. In brief, the ceremonies conducted on that annual day of celebration were these: The high priest brought to the door of the tabernacle a young bull as a sin offering for himself, two goats as sin offerings for the people, and two rams – one a burnt offering for himself, and one a burnt offering for the people. After washing himself at the laver and arraying himself in white linen garments,[39] he cast lots upon the two goats, thus selecting one to be "for the Lord," and the other to be for "Azazel" (the scapegoat). The priest then killed the young bull (his own sin offering), and entered the Holy Place with the blood thereof. Pausing at the altar of incense, he filled the censer with burning coals, and then went within the veil, sprinkling incense on the coals "that the cloud of incense may cover the mercy seat ... lest he die." He then took the blood within the veil; using his finger, he sprinkled the blood on the mercy seat seven times. He then returned outside the tent to the altar of burnt offering and killed the people's sin offering (the goat "for the Lord"). He re-entered the Holy of Holies with its blood, and proceeded as before, save this time he sprinkled the altar of incense as well as the mercy seat. Again he exited from the tent, and this time laid his hands on the head of the scapegoat. As he did this, he confessed over the goat all "the iniquities of the sons of Israel ... lay(ing) them on the head of the goat." The goat was then led away into the wilderness, where it was left to die (all this, it seems, symbolic of taking away of the sins

---

ing the "tabernacle"; they were serving in Herod's Temple. If the verb tense implies the services were still being carried out, the context would also imply they were being done in the "tabernacle," which obviously is not true. Later in the book, the Hebrews writer will point out the fact that having to repeat the old priestly services over and over implies something about their imperfect character or value.

[38] In Luke 1:10, when Zecharias is told he was to be the father of John the Baptist, he was offering prayers on behalf of the people at the golden altar of incense before the veil. We have already commented on the expression "divine worship" in our notes at Hebrews 9:1.

[39] The white linen garments (Exodus 28:39-43) were not the ordinary official dress worn by the high priest, which was blue colored (Exodus 28:31-35).

of the people). Re-entering the courtyard, the priest put off the white linen garments, washed at the laver, and put on his official dress. He then sacrificed the rams as burnt offerings, first his own, and then the people's. The dead bodies of the two sin offerings (the young bull and the goat "for the Lord") were taken outside the camp, and there entirely consumed by fire. After this (according to the Mishna), the priest put on the white linen garments again, went into the Holy of Holies, brought out the censer, and then changed back into his ordinary costume.[40] A whole year would then pass before anyone again entered the Holy of Holies. The annual Day of Atonement fell on the 10th day of Tishri, roughly equivalent to our month of September.

Not without *taking* blood -- Going into the Holy of Holies, into (as it were) the very presence of God, was a most dangerous thing. Only if the high priest were carrying blood was he safeguarded from danger.[41]

Which he offers for himself -- As explained above, the blood from the young bull served as the sin offering for the high priest. That he had to offer for himself kept impressively before his own mind and the mind of the people the fact that even priests of the highest order were sinners, needing forgiveness just like other men.

And for the sins of the people committed in ignorance -- According to Numbers 15:27-31, only sins done "in ignorance" would be forgiven by God. On the Day of Atonement, when the priest made his second trip into the Holy of Holies, carrying in the blood of the people's sin offering, that offering "covered" only sins "done in ignorance."[42]

9:8 -- The Holy Spirit is signifying this -- "Signify" means to indicate clearly. In the Old Testament record of the ritual of the tabernacle and its services, the Holy Spirit had a lesson to teach,[43] namely, that throughout the whole Mosaic Age, there was no such thing as open and direct access to God. The way to the throne room of God was barred for all men; for Israelites and even for the high priest himself.

---

[40] In the light of the above discussion, "once a year" in verse 7 does not mean the priest went into the Holy of Holies only one *time* each year. What it does mean is that he went in on only one *day* each year, the contrast being with the daily activities of the ordinary priests in the outer room. Except for that single day, the approach to the Holy of Holies was closed to all, even the high priest.

[41] In the light of the above discussion, which has the high priest making several trips into the Holy of Holies on the Day of Atonement, this passage does not seem to affirm that the priest had to carry blood on every trip he made into the Holy of Holies. But it does say that on that one day each year on which he did enter, one of his responsibilities was to carry blood from the sin offerings, or he would not have come out alive.

[42] There was no sacrifice that could be made for sins committed "defiantly (with a high hand)," i.e., sins done in open defiance and contempt for God's law, deliberate sins like willful apostasy (cf. Numbers 15:31,32, and Hebrews 10:26).

[43] Perhaps the Holy Spirit's message was broadcast as He inspired the original written records about the tabernacle and its services. Perhaps the Holy Spirit is viewed as speaking through the written record to the people of the old covenant era. Perhaps the Spirit is viewed as using the rituals themselves as the medium of broadcasting His message. Either way, we have here an affirmation of Holy Spirit's activity in the Mosaic Age.

That the way into the holy place has not yet been disclosed – Which "holy place" is intended by the writer? The west room of the tabernacle on earth or the real "Holy of Holies" in heaven? We think it is a reference to heaven itself. If so, this verse says the way into heaven, the way into the presence of God, the way for men to draw near to God was not disclosed or clearly revealed as long as the Levitical priesthood's sacrifices provided the only blood that was available. The way did not become obvious until after Jesus came, died, was buried, arose from the dead, and ascended to heaven. When Jesus died, the veil of the temple was rent in twain from top to bottom (Matthew 27:51) and henceforth the way into heaven is perfectly evident. Hebrews 9:15ff will speak of how Christ's blood made the promise of eternal inheritance and access to the Father come true.

While the outer tabernacle is still standing -- "Still standing" means literally having a standing, i.e., retained its status. As long as the only priestly services available were those done in the earthly tabernacle,[44] the way into the presence of God was not open. But when Jesus passed through the heavens (Hebrews 4:14, 9:24) and offered His blood in the real "Holy of Holies," the earthly structure lost its status or standing or any real significance; more than that, the way into the Father's presence is now open!

9:9 -- Which *is* a symbol for the present time -- *Parabole*, here translated "symbol," is the word elsewhere translated "parable," something thrown alongside to illustrate, represent or compare, "an earthly story with a heavenly meaning."[45] This word says the "outer tabernacle" (verse 8) was intended (like an object lesson) to represent important realities, things which would be revealed more fully at a future period (a time subsequent to when the tabernacle was first erected and used, a time subsequent to "the time *then* present"[46]).

Accordingly both gifts and sacrifices are offered -- Not only was the tabernacle a symbol, so were the gifts and sacrifices.[47]

---

[44] The careful student will have observed that we have treated "outer tabernacle" (literally, the first tent) differently here in verse 8 than we did in verses 2 and 6. Those who try to explain the terms the same way throughout the whole chapter will offer this comment on verse 8 -- "As long as the tabernacle existed with two chambers, the position of chamber one barred the way to chamber two." We admit we have assigned a different meaning to "first tent" here than we did earlier, but we also plead that the Greek translated "holy place" in this verse is plural, and we have regularly used the plural to refer to the Holy of Holies (rather than simply to the holy place). See also the use of the plural in 9:12,24,25 to mean Holy of Holies.

[45] As noted at verse 5, much of the Old Testament has typical or symbolical significance. Though "symbol" is not exactly the same as type, verses 9 and 10 will show both the tabernacle and its services had typical (symbolic) significance.

[46] While the NASB95 reads "the present time," the earlier editions read "for the time *then* present." The italics indicated there is no word for "then" in the Greek. Its use or omission depends on how we translate the Greek verb tenses at this place. The less likely choice for a translation would be "the time *now* present," i.e., the time when the letter is written, or now that we have seen the work of Jesus as our Priest and when, therefore, the real meaning of the tabernacle can be understood. The more likely choice, "the time *then* present," has reference to the Mosaic Age. The whole verse then reflects how things were before Jesus came.

[47] For the meaning of the words "gifts and sacrifices," see notes at 5:1 and 8:3. There is a manuscript difference at this place. According to the Greek text followed by the KJV, the antecedent of "which" is "time." The text behind the original NASB (which reads "according to which both gifts ...") makes "which" agree with "symbol," and this is the text behind the notes offered above. The present tense "are offered" may be an historical present, or (even though they were no longer valid) it may say that the same sort of offerings were

Which cannot make the worshiper perfect in conscience -- During the Mosaic Age, the people offering the sacrifices[48] were aware[49] something more was needed to make them "perfect." The immediate context will go on to explain the Old Testament sacrifices resulted merely in ceremonial purification, not in actual forgiveness of sins. Only if sins are actually forgiven does the worshipper have a sense of being "perfect."[50] The Old Testament worshipper went away from the services conscious of the fact that even though he had been obedient to the Law, the sacrifice he had offered was not sufficient to meet the needs.[51] The blood of bulls and goats did not take away sin, and they knew it.

9:10 -- Since they *relate* only to food and drink and various washings -- The original simply reads "in addition (to something)" the "food and drink and various washings" are "regulations for the body."[52] Perhaps the best way to understand this is to say the "gifts and sacrifices" (verse 9) as well as the "food and drink and various washings" are all regulations for the body. "Food and drink" remind us of the ordinances pertaining to what was clean and unclean.[53] "Various washings" (the same word as 6:2) are ceremonial washings.[54]

Regulations for the body -- These sacrifices and ceremonial rules[55] did nothing to make

---

still being presented in the temple at Jerusalem.

[48] "The worshiper" translates an article and a participle in the Greek, *ton latrueonta*, "the one serving," which likely is a reference to the priest's function in helping the people offer their gifts and sacrifices.

[49] Both here and in verse 14, we suppose "conscience" is used in its secondary sense of awareness (rather than in its primary sense of prompter or accuser). The word "conscience" should be given the same meaning each time it occurs in this context. What the blood of bulls and goats could not do (verse 9) for a man's awareness, the blood of Christ did (verse 14).

[50] Hebrews 8:11-14 and 10:1 will affirm the sacrifices, especially those on the Day of Atonement, did not give assurance of perfect reconciliation with God. But (being a symbol or an object lesson) they did supply the worshiper with a good hope of coming forgiveness.

[51] Because we have explained "conscience" as awareness, we have been led to reject the view sometimes taught that the Old Testament worshipper went home without having a clear conscience. In the primary sense of the word (prompter or accuser), a clear "conscience" would be one not accusing the worshiper of having done something wrong. The Old Testament worshiper's conscience would not accuse the man who had offered the gifts or sacrifices which the Lord commanded, even if he was aware his sins had not actually been forgiven.

[52] "Foods" and "drinks" are plural in the Greek. The clause is introduced by a preposition *epi* ("in addition to"), and the construction of the sentence is somewhat obscure since it is not easy to decide what the antecedent to *epi* is. Possible antecedents include "perfect," "the worshipper," and "gifts and sacrifices."

[53] Since the context talks about "cleansing of the flesh" (verse 13), it seems more likely that the thrust here deals with ceremonial cleanness rather than (as some have suggested) "food and drink" offerings or the diet connected with the Nazirite vow. The laws concerning clean and unclean foods are found in Leviticus 11. Regulations concerning "drink" are not so prominent in the Old Testament. Priests were to abstain from alcoholic drinks while engaged in their ministry (Leviticus 10:8,9); no one was allowed to drink from an unclean vessel (Leviticus 11:33ff); and there were libations accompanying some sacrifices (Numbers 6:15,17, 28:7ff).

[54] Ceremonial washings were performed by the priests in their ministry (Exodus 19:7-13); that's what the laver was for. The officiating priest had to wash his hands, the victim being offered was washed, the helpers around the temple and even the vessels used in the temple had to be washed. The high priest had to bathe himself before officiating in the Day of Atonement celebration (Leviticus 16:4). In addition, there were a variety of washings for ceremonially defiled people (Leviticus 15:4-27, 17:15,16; Numbers 19:7-13).

[55] "Regulations" translates the word *dikaioma*, the word also translated "ordinances" (see notes at Hebrews

the "conscience" perfect (verse 9); they simply took care of the flesh (body), and that only in a ceremonial or ritualistic way.

Imposed until a time of reformation -- The tabernacle, its services, and the ceremonial rules were only ever intended to be temporary. They were imposed only until the "time of reformation" dawned. The word rendered "reformation" means improvement, emendation, new order. It speaks of putting things right, making it better. What used to be faulty (8:6,7) is now put right.[56] The Gospel Age, the new covenant Age, is the "time of reformation," as the following verses will make abundantly clear. Since Jesus has come and offered Himself as the final and perfect sacrifice, there is no reason for anyone to be satisfied with the mere ceremonial cleansing offered by the Levitical services.

2. The heavenly tabernacle and the superior services of Jesus. 9:11-28

9:11 -- But when Christ appeared -- The first coming of Jesus as a sin offering inaugurated the "time of reformation." We are now beginning that part of the argument wherein Christ's superior service in heaven is contrasted with the old tabernacle and its imperfect services (9:1-10). The writer starts out with a reminder that the long-awaited Messiah has come! Messiah has appeared, he affirms.

As **a high priest of the good things to come** -- "Good things to come" is another way of saying "time of reformation," another way of designating the "better promises" of the new covenant (8:6-12). From the Old Testament people's standpoint, Messiah's better services were a thing looked forward to; since Messiah has come, what was once anticipated (Christ's priesthood, Psalm 110:4, and the new covenant) is now a present reality.[57] Before He came, it was fit and right that the Levitical services be carefully observed. But now that He has come, the things that were types and shadows are no longer necessary.

He entered **through the greater and more perfect tabernacle** – The rest of verse 11 and the first part of verse 12 must to be read together.[58]   Just as the Jewish high priest passed

---

9:1). These "regulations" were God-given rules and requirements.

[56] The expression "time of reformation" is a description of the Messianic Age from an Old Testament standpoint. The people living under the old covenant, aware of its inadequacy, looked forward to the day when things out of order would be put right.

[57] There is a manuscript variation here. Some (Sinaiticus, Alexandrinus, a majority of the Byzantine text manuscripts) have a present tense participle (*mellonton*, about to come), and some (Vaticanus, Beza, P[46]) an aorist tense participle (*genomenon*). If the present tense is correct, then the "good things" are not yet being experienced; they will not occur until sometime out in the future after the Hebrews read this letter. If the aorist tense is correct, then the "good things" are already available to the readers, and have been for a while. Our comments assume the aorist is the correct reading. The "good things" have already come. (Even if the present tense is correct, it should be noted that not a few commentators still explain it as being a reference to the Gospel Age, for the Gospel Age was future to the time when the Levitical priesthood and its services were valid.)

[58] The NASB translators have attempted to show this by picking up the verb from verse 12 and inserting it in italics here in verse 11.

through the holy place on his way into the Holy of Holies, so Jesus is pictured as passing through a greater and more perfect tabernacle than the Jewish priest passed through. Not only that, Jesus has entered a better place, the heavenly Holy of Holies.

Not made with hands, that is to say, not of this creation – Why is the "tabernacle" Jesus passed through called "greater and more perfect"? Because the holy place through which Jesus passed was not made with human hands as was the building erected by Bezaleel and Oholiab and their helpers.[59] It is not part of this earthly creation. Hebrews 9:24 explains what Jesus did in even clearer language. When we remember what was said in 8:2 about where Jesus serves and the picture of heaven as it now is (see notes at Hebrews 8:5),[60] we can see Jesus passing by the sea of glass and the altar of incense, right up to the throne into the presence of God. The place where Jesus our great High Priest serves is a far better sanctuary than the one in which the Levitical priests served!

9:12 -- And not through the blood of goats and calves, but through His own blood -- Not only is the place where Jesus serves a great improvement, but so is the blood He offers, by virtue of which He enters.[61] "Goats and calves" (bulls, verse 13) were the animals whose blood was used on the Day of Atonement (see 9:7). Jesus own blood is inestimably more valuable.

He entered the holy place once and for all – The "holy place"[62] here is a reference to heaven. "Once and for all" speaks of the finality of Jesus' sacrifice. With such an offering

---

[59] Exodus 35:30-35, 36:1-4, 38:22,23.

[60] Since Hebrews regularly explains that Jesus serves in the real place of which the earthly tabernacle was but a copy and shadow, we have opted for this means of explaining the identity of the "greater and more perfect tabernacle." Certain other suggested explanations are less than satisfactory. Among these which we have rejected are R. Milligan's, who sees the "tabernacle" through which Jesus passed as being the *church* (*op. cit.*, p.253). Against this explanation is the fact that when Jesus ascended to heaven, the church had not yet been established, and would not be till the day of Pentecost some days after His resurrection and ascension. Also rejected is the idea of Grotius and others that the word "tabernacle" has reference to Jesus human *body*. We reject it even though Jesus did speak of His body as being a "temple" (John 2:21), and even though a possible interpretation of Hebrews 10:20 might support such an idea. Several arguments against "tabernacle" being a reference to Jesus' body, have been offered. (1) The tabernacle is "not of this creation", yet Jesus' body was certainly just like ours (Hebrews 2:11,14). (2) Jesus entered His body before He made His sacrifice, not after.

[61] The writer of Hebrews uses the same preposition (*dia*) for blood that he did for "*through* the greater tabernacle." This has caused commentators to ponder the possibility of whether the preposition is used with two different meanings in expressions so close together. Some (cp. the RSV, TEV, JB, "He entered, taking not the blood of goats and calves, but his own blood") have understood that when Jesus entered the heavenly Holy of Holies, He actually carried His own blood into the very presence of God, there to offer it on behalf of us believers. These commentators press the analogy, suggesting that indeed it was not until Jesus ascended from the earth and made atonement for us in the antitypical Holy of Holies that the salvation of men was accomplished. Others have preferred to attach some meaning such as "by virtue of" to *dia*, and then explain that the Levitical priests went into the Holy of Holies by virtue of the blood of bulls and goats, but Jesus went into heaven by virtue of His own blood. These commentators urge that even though the Jewish high priest's offering was in two parts -- the blood first shed in the court, and then brought into the Holy of Holies -- it is improper to think of Jesus' offering as being two parts, one on Calvary, and the other later in heaven. They believe His sacrifice was completed at Calvary. This commentator tends to agree with the first group. It seems Jesus did (in some way) offer His blood to the Father in heaven as a reason why He should be permitted to return to the Father's presence, and as a reason why access for believers to the Father's presence should now be open.

[62] The form is plural in the Greek, the regular language for the Holy of Holies (9:25, 13:11).

as "His own blood," now that the time of reformation has come, there is no need for a continual repetition of His sacrifice as there was need for an annual repetition of the services on the Day of Atonement.

Having obtained eternal redemption – The following verses will explain "redemption" by showing that Jesus' blood (1) produces internal purification, not just external, ceremonial purification such as was effected by the Levitical services, (2) serves as the propitiation for sins committed in Old Testament times as well as New, and also (3) ratified or inaugurated the new covenant. "Eternal" seems to say that this method of redemption[63] covers past, present, and future. It is valid until the end of the new covenant Age, i.e., for the rest of the period of human history. God has no intention of replacing it, as He replaced the Levitical priesthood and its sacrifices.

9:13 -- For -- Three ideas were introduced in verses 11 and 12 that are explained in detail in the paragraphs following. 9:13-22 will explain the necessity of Jesus' death; 9:23-28 will explain the necessity of His presence in heaven; 10:1-18 will explain His "once and for all" offering for sin.

If the blood of goats and bulls -- Here is repeated what was said in 9:7,12 concerning ceremonial cleansing resulting from the services on the Day of Atonement.

And the ashes of a heifer sprinkling those who have been defiled – Besides the blood of bulls and goats, another arrangement for producing ceremonial cleansing was prescribed in Numbers 19:2-10. This one was for the benefit of the people, whereas the other one was for the priests. Both call attention to the kind of purity or cleanness the Old Testament priesthood provided. It was external and ceremonial, ritual not actual. The ashes were prepared by killing the animal, burning its carcass completely (together with cedar, hyssop, and scarlet), and storing the ashes for future use. When a person became ceremonially unclean (i.e., "defiled" by touching a dead body, or being in a tent in which someone died), there was no need to wait until an animal could be killed, and the ashes prepared. All that was needed was to mix a portion of the already stored ashes with water and then sprinkle the water on the unclean person. A branch of hyssop would be dipped into the container holding the water of purification; then the water would be tossed over the person defiled. When unclean persons were cleansed, they could rejoin the congregation of Israel (Numbers 19:13,20).

Sanctify for the cleansing of the flesh – The blood and the ashes of purification had nothing to do with internal spiritual defilement. Remember the statement about "regulations for the body" (9:10). The real purpose of such a ceremony was to cause men to think of the need they had to be cleansed (inside) from the defilement of sin, and to awaken in their minds the idea that God could and would provide the needed purification.

---

[63] "Redemption" translates *lutrosis*, a word from the world of slavery, which suggests that one who was a slave has now been freed or released. The doctrine of this verse is that the blood of Jesus is the means of redemption for as long as time shall last. (See the author's *Commentary on Romans* at 3:24 for an explanation of some of the more difficult theological questions involved in the word *lutrosis*.)

9:14 -- How much more will the blood of Christ -- The blood of Jesus the Messiah is infinitely more efficacious than the blood of an animal could possibly be. It is no mere ceremonial cleansing that is effected by the blood of Jesus.[64]

Who through the eternal Spirit offered Himself without blemish to God -- Animals intended for sacrificial purposes in the Old Testament ritual had to be physically perfect (without blemish[65]), a fact that seems to have had symbolic significance. It helped men to look forward to what would be needed and expected when the sacrifice for sins that would actually be efficacious finally came onto the scene of history. Jesus, that sacrifice, had a spotlessness far beyond any animal's, for His perfection was not only physical but moral. He was sinless! Further, no animal could do what Jesus did – He "offered Himself". What Jesus did was deliberately voluntary, a self-sacrifice, not the bloodshed of a passive victim. The verse seems to say the Holy Spirit[66] had something to do with Jesus' offering; either He helped Jesus offer Himself[67] to God, or the Spirit had something to do with the fact Jesus was without blemish.[68]

Cleanse your conscience from dead works -- "Dead works," as explained both at 6:1 and in this very context, are those Levitical sacrifices that never could leave the worshiper with

---

[64] The "blood of Christ" is likely another way to say Jesus' death was a sacrifice (offered to God) for sin. This is the argument of the whole context in Hebrews 9 and 10. The word "blood" points to death (Leon Morris, *The Apostolic Preaching of the Cross* [Grand Rapids: Eerdmans, 1965], chapter 3).

[65] Leviticus 1:10, 22:19-22.

[66] "Eternal Spirit" is an unusual name or title for the Holy Spirit. A few manuscripts do read "Holy Spirit," and though these show the opinion of some scribe or scribes that the reference indeed is to the third person in the Godhead, the reading is of not sufficient authority to establish "holy" as the true reading. Some (Lenski, Alford, Milligan, Rotherham, Moffatt) have called attention to the fact there is no "the" before "eternal Spirit" in the Greek, and have used this to support the view that "eternal spirit" is a reference to Jesus' own divine nature. Appeal is made to 1 Peter 3:18 for a similar reference to all that was divine in Jesus, and the explanation offered is something on this order: Since Jesus was eternal, the Son of the Living God, He could offer Himself as a sacrifice that would satisfy the holy justice of God. (This interpretation, which does not find this to be a reference to the Holy Spirit, is not as objectionable as some other present-day denials of any reference to the Holy Spirit. Many present-day writers are disinclined to see a trinitarian reference here in verse 14 out of a growing antipathy to the whole idea of a plurality in the Godhead, even though it is a plain teaching of Scripture. Of course, if there are not three distinct persons to whom the Scriptures ascribe deity, this verse could not be a reference to such a belief.) Others have urged that the absence of the article in a prepositional phrase is not definitive, since prepositions tend to make a noun definite. Thus the KJV, ASV, NASB, Bruce, Kent, Denney, and many others capitalize "Spirit" and (appealing to Acts 10:38 or Isaiah 42:1 for corroboration) urge that this verse says it was by the help of the Holy Spirit that Christ's death was a satisfactory sin offering. (Isaiah 42:1, one of the Suffering Servant Poems, specifically says "Behold My servant ... I have put My Spirit upon Him." The Scriptures consistently present the idea that the Holy Spirit was helping Jesus during His earthly ministry.) As to why attention should be called to the fact that the Spirit is "eternal" at this place, the answer may be this: what the Spirit helped Jesus do was in complete harmony with the plan made back in eternity by Jehovah God, a plan with which the Spirit (Who was there when the plan was made) was in perfect harmony and agreement.

[67] The Greek word order would incline one to believe that what the Holy Spirit did was to help Jesus through Calvary. Exactly of what this help consisted, the New Testament does not make clear.

[68] Our Lord's complete holiness, His active obedience to God, is essential to the efficacy of His sacrifice. Had He sinned, Jesus could never have been an acceptable atoning sacrifice. See this developed in James Denney, *The Death of Christ* (London: Hodder and Stoughton, 1911), p. 129ff.

an awareness[69] his sins had actually been atoned for. They could cleanse the flesh (verse 13), but they never took care of the heart. Legal ceremonies do not give life to the inner man. But what those old sacrifices could never do, the death of Jesus does. From among all the Jewish rites, in verses 12-13 the Hebrews writer selected those which most fully represented the purification from sin available under the Levitical system. He used these to show that in Christ there is an *actual* forgiveness of sins, which is far better than the Old Testament arrangement for covering sins.

To serve the living God? -- Believers who avail themselves of Jesus' sacrifice are not only cleansed in conscience, they are also put into a position for offering an acceptable service to God.[70] Jewish worship left the believer with the awareness that something more than animal sacrifice was needed (i.e., complete forgiveness) to provide access to God. The Christian, who knows the blood of Jesus, has no such awareness. Nothing more is needed to provide complete access to God.

9:15 -- And for this reason -- The reason is because Jesus' sacrifice is so much better than the Levitical sacrifices (verses 11-14).

He is the mediator of a new covenant – The writer here reasserts the same thing he wrote in 8:6.[71] We do learn some additional facts about this "new covenant"[72] at this place, including the fact that Jesus' sacrificial death is the basis of His mediatorship functions, that the death of Jesus atoned for sins committed before Calvary, as well as after, and that His death served as the covenant sacrifice which ratified the new covenant.[73]

---

[69] We are defining "conscience" here the same way we did in verse 9, since what we have in verse 14 is a direct contrast to what was said in verse 9. The manuscript evidence is rather evenly divided between "*your* conscience" (Aleph, D^c, 33, Byzantine Text) and "*our* conscience" (A, D, K, P). Codex Vaticanus is not extant beyond the word "cleanse" (the final pages of Hebrews and all of Revelation having been lost), so it cannot help us determine the correct reading. By explaining "conscience" as meaning awareness, we are also required to take the word "cleanse" here in verse 14 in the same sense it was given in verse 13. If this is true, the fact that the awareness needed to be cleansed probably is not exactly synonymous with the idea that the "conscience" (which is "defiled", 1 Corinthians 8:7) also needs to be cleansed.

[70] "Serve" is the same root word translated "worshiper" in verse 9.

[71] At 8:6, we learned a "mediator" (*mesites*) is one who gets two parties together and pledges that both parties will carry out the conditions of the covenant. What was there called a "better covenant," and was immediately explained as being the "new covenant" foretold by Jeremiah, is here simply described as the "new covenant." The use of the term "mediator" shows that this is the Hebrew idea of "covenant" and not the Roman idea of testament. A mediator is involved where there is a covenant, but a mediator has no place where the idea is a last will and testament. Neither does the death of a person making a will (testament) possess any of the sacrificial character which is referred to in verses 15-22.

[72] It is evident from 10:15-17, as well as 9:15ff, that Jeremiah's classic new covenant prophecy, which has been quoted at Hebrews 8:6-13, dominates the whole discussion in chapters 8 to 10 of Hebrews.

[73] Hebrews 9:14 is a climax to the Hebrews writer's argument concerning the significance of Jesus' sacrificial death. At this point, some commentators on Hebrews have noted the close correspondence between the ideas just written in 9:14 and the ideas in 10:18. Those who look for similarities between Hebrews and the Pauline letters observe that it was not unlike Paul to go off at a word, make a long digression, and then later return to the idea from which he departed. It has been be argued the present passage from 9:14 to 10:18 is a typical Pauline digression. It has alternatively been argued this is not a digression; instead, it must be assumed the verses in between 9:14 and 10:18 make a very important point, namely, to make it perfectly clear that the new

In order that since a death has taken place – The death that has taken place is the death of Jesus,[74] the God-appointed sacrifice to atone for the sins of the world. The phrase that begins with "in order that" will be completed by the closing words of this verse. It says that one result of the death of the mediator is that "those who have been called may receive the ... inheritance" from which they otherwise would have been excluded.

For the redemption of the transgressions that were *committed* under the first covenant -- The Mosaic Covenant, "the first covenant," supplied no real propitiation for sin. The animal sacrifices merely made ceremonial purification (verses 10-13), while God "passed over the sins previously committed" (Romans 3:25).[75] What formerly had been "passed over," what formerly had been done only in a ceremonial sense, is now actually a "redemption."[76] A "redemption of the transgressions that were committed under the first covenant" would have direct reference only to those who lived under the Mosaic covenant. But what about those who, during all those centuries, were still living under patriarchal rules? We suppose, in the light of the more general language of Romans 3:25, the retroactive validity of Jesus' death extended to faithful men from the patriarchal age as well.

Those who have been called may receive the promise of the eternal inheritance -- This is one conclusion to which we have been building. It states one of the blessed results of the death of the Mediator. The "called" include those who have listened to God under both old and new covenants.[77] To "receive the promise" means to actually receive what had

---

covenant has indeed superseded the Mosaic. If there is to be a new covenant, there must be the death of the covenant sacrifice since no covenant was ever in force until the covenant sacrifice was offered. The readers must be helped to understand that is exactly what has happened when Jesus died. It is only because the covenant sacrifice has been killed that the new covenant relationship with God can exist at all.

[74] 'Why did Jesus have to die?' was a hard question for Jewish readers to understand. The writer's answer is at least two fold: (1) Jesus' death was a sacrifice, a sacrifice that really did atone for sins. Thus, it was a sacrifice more efficacious than the death of animals under the old covenant, which only took care of ceremonial purification of the flesh. (2) If there is a sacrifice that really takes care of sins, that implies a new covenant is in effect, too. He became the covenant sacrifice that validated or inaugurated the new covenant.

[75] The verb "passed over" in Romans 3:25 has a meaning halfway between punishment and forgiveness. "Passed over" differs in two ways from forgiveness: (1) The passing over was but temporary -- it was provisional. (2) It was something done in the forbearance of God -- it was a temporary delay of deserved punishment, God temporarily suspending the punishment the sinners deserved.

[76] "Redemption" is a word we've already had at Hebrews 9:12. Remember, Jeremiah 31:34 predicted "I will forgive their iniquity" -- something not done under the old covenant by the blood of bulls and goats (Hebrews 10:4). The writer of Hebrews seems to be saying the promise of forgiveness encompasses not only the people who live in the new covenant Age, but also involves a blessed effect upon the guilt of those who lived in the Mosaic Age, too. Leon Morris (*op. cit.*, p.88) has observed that while the idea of redemption was widespread in the ancient world, the actual word used regularly for "redemption" in the New Testament is a rare word, a fact Morris thinks may reflect the conviction that the redemption Christians know is not simply another redemption among many. It is unique!

[77] "Called" brings to mind the writer's earlier designation of Christians as those who are "partakers of a heavenly calling" (3:1). Not every physical descendant of Abraham was included in the salvation, only those who were the "remnant" (Romans 11:5), those who were the spiritual sons of Abraham. "Called" is language similar to what occurs in some of Jesus' parables, in which men are invited ("called") to the kingdom (cp. Luke 14:16-24; Matthew 22:1-14).

been promised.[78] Before anyone could rightfully inherit what was promised (an eternal[79] inheritance, he calls it) and claim it as his own, the covenant through which it was to be provided had to be sealed and ratified with the blood of Jesus (verse 14). The "inheritance" (i.e., Canaan per 1 Kings 8:36) assigned to Israel under the provisions of the first covenant was held by them but "for a little while" (Isaiah 63:17,18). The "inheritance" promised in the new covenant, which includes access to God, is eternal.

9:16 -- For where a covenant is – There is a marginal note here offering "testament" as an alternative translation for *diatheke*.[80] Shall we translate it "testament"[81] or "covenant"[82]? While the answer to this question makes little difference to the general thrust of the argument, it does affect the comments offered at certain key places in the following phrases. The NASB translators believed the reference is to the new covenant since there is a definite contrast with the first covenant (see verse 18); we tend to agree with them.

There must of necessity be the death of the one who made it – It was the known and regular practice among the Hebrews that a sacrifice be offered in order to ratify a covenant.[83] There were many covenants made in Old Testament times, but only animals (never

---

[78] The idea of "promise" (and some of the things involved in this idea) was already introduced in 6:15-17.

[79] "Eternal" is an adjective the writer of Hebrews often uses. In 13:20, he says the new covenant itself is "eternal." In 9:12,15, he says the redemption Jesus' death provides is "eternal." In 9:14, the Spirit who helped Jesus provide the atoning sacrifice is identified as being "eternal." In 5:9 Jesus is spoken of as the author of "eternal" salvation to all who obey Him. History is said to conclude with an "eternal" judgment, Hebrews 6:2.

[80] Readers are reminded the word *diatheke* first occurred in Hebrews at 7:22, where certain notes were offered by way of introduction to this whole problem. There is no consistency in our English translations when translating the 33 occurrences of *diatheke* in the New Testament. Some versions (NASB) use "covenant" all the way through; some (Latin Vulgate) use "testament" all the way through; some (KJV, ERV, ASV, RSV) use "covenant" part of the time and "testament" part of the time. Where there is such a lack of consistency (and key passages to check are Hebrews 9:15-20 and Galatians 3:15-17), it is very difficult to do a word study from the English. J. Barton Payne, *The Theology of the Older Testament* (Grand Rapids: Zondervan, 1962), p.71ff, urges that "testament" is the preferred translation of *berith* as well as *diatheke*. B.F. Westcott, *The Epistle to the Hebrews* (Grand Rapids: Eerdmans, 1952), p.298ff, has one of the outstanding presentations of the view *diatheke* should be translated "covenant" throughout the Bible, even at Hebrews 9:16ff.

[81] Some of the standard proofs given to support this translation include: (1) the use of the word "inheritance" in verse 15; (2) this is the standard meaning of *diatheke* in *classical* Greek; (3) and the use of the words "the death of the one who made it."

[82] Some of the proofs for this way of translating *diatheke* include: (1) The whole context is dominated by the classic new *covenant* prophecy of Jeremiah 31:31ff. (2) "Mediator" (verse 15) does not fit the idea of "testament". (3) Though the idea of "testament" is familiar to us, we must not forget that the idea of "testament" (i.e., a *will*) was unknown to the Jews until the Romans introduced it. (4) It will hardly do to have Jesus simultaneously designated both as the "executor" (mediator) of the *will* and the "testator" (the one who died). Such a dual role for the same person would not be out of place, however, in a *covenant*. (5) The fact that verses 18ff are intended to illustrate the sentiments of verses 15-17 surely point to "covenant" as the proper translation. How could the fact that a *will* (verse 16) is not binding until he who makes it is dead be a reason why a *covenant* (verse 18) should be confirmed with blood? But if we suppose the writer is stating a general principle that in all covenant transactions with God, the death of a sacrificial victim is necessary, then everything is plain.

[83] For example, in the covenants made with Abraham (Genesis 15:1-18) and with Israel at the foot of Mt. Sinai (Exodus 24:3-8), covenant-victims were slaughtered before the covenant was officially recognized as being in force. Hebrews 9:17 will go on to explain a covenant is never valid until the covenant-sacrifice is dead. A covenant's conditions and promises could be revealed by God, and the people hearing those conditions could

man, never God) died to ratify them. For "the death of the one who made it," we would suggest "the death of the covenanter" or "the death of the covenant sacrifice."[84] Jesus is the covenant sacrifice and until He died, there was no way the new covenant could be in force.[85] Verse 17 will go on to explain in greater detail this whole idea of the need for the death of the covenant sacrifice.

9:17 – For a covenant is valid *only* when men are dead -- The margin indicates the Greek reads "only over the dead." "Dead" is an adjective; we must supply the noun. A better word to supply (since it better suits "covenant") than "men" would be "victims" (i.e., the sacrificial victims).

For it is never in force while the one who made it lives -- "The one who made it" is the same word used in verse 16. A covenant was never in force as long as the sacrificial victim was still living.[86] It is well to observe, in passing, that the verses just studied (9:16,17) have been used by Christian Church teachers almost as much as Acts 2:38 as we have attempted to help people understand the difference between the Mosaic and Christian dispensations – i.e., the difference between the Law and the Gospel (old covenant and new covenant). The import of these verses, yea, of this whole section (chapters 8-10), in Hebrews cannot be ignored. It is one of the key passages for showing that the Law of Moses ended and the new covenant came into force when Jesus died. A new priesthood, a covenant sacrifice like Jesus' blood, means we live under a *new* covenant. The temporary and preparatory one (Mosaic) is now a thing of the past!

9:18 -- Therefore -- Much of the Old Testament, we have learned, was typical, intended to prepare men for the coming of Messiah. Perhaps verse 18, which introduces a rehearsal of how the Mosaic covenant was inaugurated, is intended to say even that event should help the readers to understand the need for the death of Jesus.

Even the first covenant was not inaugurated without blood – As in 8:7 and 9:1, where the same terminology occurred, "first covenant" is a reference to the Mosaic Covenant. As in those previous verses, so here it is the following context which makes clear exactly what covenant is in the writer's mind.[87] The following verses recall what was written in Exodus

---

agree to live by the conditions so that they might receive the things promised. But the covenant was not in force until the sacrificial victim died and its blood was sprinkled.

[84] The difficulty within verse 16 concerns two disputed words – *diatheke* ("covenant" or "testament") and *diathemenou* ("the one who made it" or the "sacrificial victim"). Basically, a translator must decide to give one word its primary sense, and the other its secondary sense. If *diatheke* is given its secondary sense ("testament"), then *diathemenou* is given its primary sense. If *diatheke* is given its primary sense ("covenant"), then *diathemenou* is given its secondary sense ("sacrificial victim"). Since a choice must be made, this commentator prefers the latter approach.

[85] Compare 1 Corinthians 11:25, "this cup is the new covenant in My blood." I.e., 'My blood,' says Jesus, 'is the thing that establishes the new covenant.'

[86] The ERV treats the last part of verse 17 as a question: "Doth it ever avail while he that made it liveth?" F.F. Bruce (*op. cit.*, p.207) urges that this translation does more justice to the negative *me* (in *mepote*, "never"), which is the usual way of asking a question that expects a negative answer.

[87] Which "covenant" did the writer of Hebrews have in mind? After all, there was a covenant made with Noah

24:1-8. Moses has come down from the mountain and reported to the people all the Lord had declared, and the people promised to do all the words which the Lord commanded. Moses then wrote down all the words (found in Exodus 20-23[88]) in a book (called "the book of the covenant" in Exodus 24:7). The next morning Moses erected an altar at the foot of the mountain and twelve pillars, one for each of the tribes of Israel. Burnt offerings and peace offerings were offered to the Lord. Half the blood of the sacrificial victims was sprinkled on the altar, half was collected in basins. Moses then read to the people the words he had written in the book of the covenant, and again the people said "All that the Lord has spoken we will do, and we will be obedient" (Exodus 24:7). At this point Moses took the blood collected in the basins and sprinkled it upon the people, saying as he did so, "Behold, the blood of the covenant, which the Lord has made with you in accordance with all these words" (Exodus 24:8). By these acts – by the killing of the sacrificial victims and the sprinkling of the blood – the covenant had been officially inaugurated.

9:19 -- For when every commandment had been spoken by Moses to all the people according to the Law -- "For" shows verses 19ff are an explanation of verse 18's assertion – that the first covenant was dedicated, inaugurated, and ratified with blood. "According to the Law" says Moses set out the terms and conditions of the covenant (the terms and conditions given by God), making plain to the people the requirements of the covenant. They would have no doubt what a covenant relationship with God demanded of them.

He took the blood of the calves and the goats -- Careful students of the Scriptures have noticed certain differences in the accounts in Hebrews and Exodus 24. Exodus 24 makes no mention of the blood of goats,[89] the water, the scarlet wool, the hyssop, or the sprinkling of the book.[90] Hebrews makes no mention of the building of the altar, the twelve pillars, or the kinds of offerings which were offered.

With water and scarlet wool and hyssop – Though not mentioned in Exodus 24, some means would be needed for sprinkling the blood. Water would be used to increase the quantity of fluid available and to keep it from coagulating.　The scarlet wool[91] would be

---

and another made with Abraham and the patriarchs; both of these were earlier in time than the Mosaic covenant. So even though the writer speaks of the "*first* covenant," there is no doubt which covenant he is talking about since he carefully defines his terms. It is the one made at Sinai, the one that had the Levitical priesthood, the one referred to in Exodus 24 (not Genesis 9 or 12-17). Although the Mosaic covenant is not chronologically the "first," we have no doubt which one the writer is calling "first."

[88] The Ten Commandments were written on the tables of stone. Whether or not they were repeated in the book of the covenant is a matter not entirely clear.

[89] The words "and goats" are omitted from P[46], Aleph[c], K, L, etc. They are found in Aleph, A, C, D, Coptic, Old Latin, and the Byzantine Text. If we omit the words, then the text of Hebrews agrees with the text of Exodus 24:5, which mentions "young bulls" but not goats. Those who find no problem including the words do so on the basis that, according to Leviticus 1:10, 4:23, 9:2, goats could be used for burnt offerings.

[90] Suggestions for the source of the letter writer's information include: (1) oral tradition; (2) a revelation from God; (3) we do not know where this information came from, yet there is nothing improbable about any of it.

[91] The original word denotes crimson or deep scarlet (note the margin, "purple"). The color was obtained from a small insect (about pea size) which was found adhering to the shoots of a species of oak in Spain and in Western Asia. It was regarded as the most valuable of the colors for dyeing, and was very expensive.

attached to the forked end of a branch of hyssop,[92] making an instrument that would absorb a quantity of the blood and water that were to be sprinkled, and then would serve as a sort of shaker by which the blood could be flung on the people and the book.

And sprinkled both the book itself and all the people – The "book" is the book of the covenant. The sprinkling of the book was not mentioned in Exodus 24, but since it was written by men, it would need to be cleansed of any ceremonial defilement they might have been conveyed to it. We suppose Moses, standing in front of groups of the people, would dip the hyssop in the mixture of blood and water then fling the mixture over the people.[93]

9:20 -- saying, "THIS IS THE BLOOD OF THE COVENANT WHICH GOD COMMANDED YOU" – Each time Moses flung some of the mixture over the people, he explained the significance of the blood. The point of the quotation from Exodus 24:8 is to show that shedding of blood was necessary for the confirmation and establishment of the first covenant.[94] Further, the use of both the words "covenant" and "commanded" shows the Mosaic Covenant was not a mere compact or agreement made between equals. It was an arrangement proposed by God Himself and presented to the people for their acceptance. They could acquiesce to the terms of the covenant but could not change any of them.

9:21 -- And in the same way – That is, using a mixture of blood and water, and an instrument made of scarlet wool and hyssop.

He sprinkled both the tabernacle and all the vessels of the ministry with the blood – This ceremony, of course, had to be at a later time than the occasion on which the Mosaic Covenant was first ratified. At the time Moses sprinkled the book of the covenant and the people, the tabernacle and its furniture had not yet been constructed. The Old Testament records an anointing of the newly built tabernacle and furniture with oil (Exodus 40:9), but does not specifically mention the use of blood.[95] However, in Numbers 7:1, we are told Moses "anointed it and consecrated it," and the latter term (we presume) involved a sprinkling with blood, just as Hebrews says it was.

---

[92] Hyssop was a low shrub, regarded as one of the smallest of the plants. In some cases a bunch of hyssop was fastened to a stick of cedar wood by means of a scarlet band, then the bunch would be wrapped around with the scarlet wool. Such a tool was used for sprinkling the blood of the paschal lamb on the doorway (Exodus 12:22), and to sprinkle the "blood" on persons who had become ceremonially unclean (Numbers 19:18), and its use is reflected in the language of Psalm 51:7, "Purify me with hyssop, and I shall be clean."

[93] We do not know whether every individual in Israel was actually spotted by some of the blood and water, or whether as Moses flung the mixture toward the groups it fell, in fact, on only a few in each group.

[94] Again, the reader is reminded of comments made at Hebrews 9:16, especially footnote #85. The similarity between what Moses said as he inaugurated the first covenant and the words spoken by Jesus as He was about to die to inaugurate the better covenant is striking.

[95] The silence of Moses is not conclusive proof that no blood was used in the dedication of the tabernacle and its vessels. There are several facts (not recorded in the Old Testament) about Old Testament events that we learn from the New Testament -- Abraham's call from Ur of the Chaldees, the names of Jannes and Jambres, and the prophecy made by Enoch. So, if here in Hebrews we learn about things not recorded in Exodus, that is not a thing unheard of. Again, the instructions about the sprinkling of Aaron are given in Exodus 40:12ff. Nothing is said about blood, yet as we know from Leviticus 8:30 that blood as well as oil was used. Josephus, *Ant.* III.8.6, mentions the same facts as does the writer of Hebrews.

9:22 -- And according to the Law, *one may* almost *say* – I.e., 'As far as the whole record found in the Old Testament is concerned, it is almost universally true.' There were some things purified by water (Leviticus 15:10) and some by fire (Leviticus 5:11-13; Numbers 31:22-24), but those were exceptions to the general rule. "Almost" allows for exceptions, but they were clearly exceptions. The normal method of purification was blood.

All things are cleansed with blood – It was clearly established by Old Testament precedent that if there was to be forgiveness of sins, there must be the shedding of blood. We should not, therefore, wonder why Jesus had to die. Instead, we should think of His blood as the best sin offering ever offered.

And without shedding of blood there is no forgiveness – Though some things were purified with water or fire, when the matter pertained to the forgiveness of sins it was universally true that no sins were pardoned except by the shedding of blood.[96] Every sin required an atonement, and no atonement could be made without blood.

9:23 -- Therefore -- In 9:11,12 three ideas were introduced that are worked out in detail in the verses following. We begin here a consideration of the second of these ideas, the need for Jesus' presence and superior services in heaven. Perhaps the readers have been thinking the idea of an unseen priest functioning on our behalf in heaven was not nearly so attractive or impressive as the ceremonies presided over by the visible Levitical priest. Lest such negative ideas become influential, three points are emphasized in the following verses in an attempt to show the importance and necessity of Jesus' ministry in heaven.

It was necessary for the copies of the things in the heavens to be cleansed with these -- "Copies of the things in the heavens" refers to the tabernacle and its vessels (verse 21). "Copies" is the word used at Hebrews 8:5 where we learned Moses built a scale model of what heaven looks like now. If the copies had cleansing prescribed for them, and that cleansing required the shedding of blood, the reality in heaven must also have a cleansing.

But the heavenly things themselves with better sacrifices than these – Why should heaven (as it now is) need[97] a cleansing? That should not be thought to be a problem; it is consistent with other New Testament teaching. There was war in heaven when Satan and his angels rebelled (Revelation 12:7-9). His act defiled heaven, such that heaven itself needed cleansing.[98] It would take better blood than that of bulls and goats – it would take

---

[96] The worshiper who was too poor to offer even little birds as a bloody sacrifice could substitute a mixture of flour and oil (Leviticus 5:11-13). Furthermore, this substitute offering was burned "on the altar, with the offerings of the Lord by fire" (Leviticus 5:12), which evidently pictures this offering being placed on top of bloody offerings already on the altar.

[97] That there was a "need" for the heavenly things to be cleansed is implied in the grammar of the original, though not specifically so worded in the NASB. Grammar would teach us to repeat the verb from the first part of the sentence as we translate the second part, so that it reads "just as it was necessary for the copies ... to be cleansed ... so it is necessary for the heavenly things themselves to be cleansed."

[98] Some deny that heaven as it now is needed cleansing. To avoid such an interpretation, the expression "heavenly things" is explained to refer to God's people rather than to the place called heaven. F.F. Bruce (*op.*

the blood of Jesus – to cleanse the heavenly things.[99]

9:24 -- For Christ did not enter into a holy place made with hands -- "For" shows this verse is intended as further explanation of what has just been said. We are reminded of Hebrews 9:11's affirmations when we are told again about the better tabernacle, not made by human hands, in which Jesus offers His superior services. Jesus did not enter an earthly tabernacle to perform His priestly services. Only Levitical priests could enter that structure, and it has already been demonstrated Jesus could never qualify to be a Levitical priest.

A *mere* copy of the true one -- Readers of Hebrews, are you listening? The tabernacle is just a *copy*. It is not the real thing (see notes at 8:5); the real thing[100] is in heaven.

But into heaven itself -- In order to perform His superior services, Jesus (after His death) has entered into heaven itself.[101]

Now to appear in the presence of God for us -- Jesus has not entered a smoke-clouded chamber as the high priest did on the Day of Atonement, where there was only an ark of the covenant and a visible symbol of God's presence. Jesus' ministry on our behalf[102] is

---

cit., p.219), for example, warns his readers against thinking of the heavenly dwelling place of God in something like material terms. He appeals first to verses where God's people are called His habitation, and then to verses in Hebrews which have talked about the need for peoples' consciences to be cleansed, and he thinks these explain what "cleansed" means in verse 23. Another interpretation of "cleansed" in verse 23 is that it is not so much the removal of impurity that is talked about but rather this word is expressive of a consecratory or inaugural process. We see no compelling reason to think of the "heavenly things" as being anything other than the heavenly tabernacle, wherein Christ performs the superior functions of His ministry. We see confirmatory evidence in verses like Ephesians 6:12, which speaks of "spiritual forces of wickedness in the heavenly places," Colossians 2:15 which tells that Christ "disarmed the rulers and authorities ..." triumphing over them by the cross, and Colossians 1:20, where we learn that it was God's will, through Jesus, "to reconcile all things to Himself ... whether things on earth or things in heaven, having made peace through the blood of His cross."

[99] While this verse has a plural ("better sacrifices"), the following context makes it clear there was only *one* superior sacrifice. What is stressed is that where atonement really matters, namely, in heaven itself, something better than the sacrifices used in the Jewish system was needed.

[100] The word translated "copy" here is *antitupos* (antitype); the word translated "pattern" in 8:5 was *tupon* (type). This shows how the terms type and antitype have changed meanings through the years. In the Greek, *tupos* is the original, and *antitupos* is the copy of the original. While the English words are derivatives of the Greek, the distinction between the Greek words has become lost in English, so that the word "type" has come to be ambiguous and may mean either the original or the copy. To add further to the confusion, the other word is sometimes spelled with an "e" instead of an "i" (antetype vs. antitype). Although these words have different etymological connotations, English speakers have tended to use them as if they were interchangeable. Thus, whenever one uses the words *type* or *antitype*, he must carefully define the words for the readers or hearers.

[101] The Greek word translated "heaven" in this epistle is usually plural. Here, however, it is singular. Morris (*op. cit.*, p.91) thinks there is no difference in meaning. We tend to agree. This is the writer's own explanation of what he means by "heavenly things" in verse 23.

[102] "For us" translates the preposition *huper*, which in this context signifies "in behalf of" or "in the place of." Jesus is not just sitting at the right hand of God, doing nothing. He is appearing on our behalf. One old-time illustration goes like this: The devil is the prosecuting attorney; Jesus is the attorney for the defense; God is the Judge. Jesus appears for us like a defense attorney does for his client. Whether or not this illustration helps us understand exactly what Jesus is doing on our behalf, we do suppose what is here written in Hebrews is another way of saying what is written in Romans 8:34 and Hebrews 7:25.

performed in the very presence of God Himself. The word "now" expresses the duration of time from Jesus' entrance into heaven after His death and resurrection, until the consummation of all things results in the judgment and final entrance into heaven of the redeemed.

9:25 -- Nor was it that He should offer Himself often -- Here begins the second point intended to demonstrate the importance and necessity for Jesus' ministry in heaven (see notes at 9:23). His superior ministry in heaven involves nothing less than the fact that sin has been dealt with once and for all. "Nor" continues the negative found at the beginning of verse 24. 'Jesus did not enter a man-made tabernacle ... nor does He have to keep entering again and again.' "Offer Himself" refers not to the death on the cross, but to Jesus' presentation of Himself before the heavenly mercy seat after accomplishing the atonement. It answers to the high priest's yearly entrance with blood of a sacrifice previously made.

As the high priest enters the holy place year by year -- The high priest's entrance into the Holy of Holies[103] on the annual Day of Atonement is the thing being compared to Jesus' entrance into heaven.

With blood not his own -- When the Levitical high priest entered the Holy of Holies to appear on behalf of himself and the people, he carried the blood of others – that of bulls and goats. When Jesus presented Himself in the Father's presence in heaven, He offered His own blood. Jesus' offering is superior in that He does not press into service some offering like the blood of some non-cooperating, non-comprehending animal. He uses His own blood, all the while doing it voluntarily and knowing exactly what He was doing.

9:26 -- Otherwise -- If Jesus had to present the blood of His sacrifice every year (like the Jewish priest did on the Day of Atonement), that would mean Jesus would have to go to Calvary every year. The Hebrews writer now shows such a continuing repetition of His sacrifice is not needed,[104] nor is it possible if Jesus is to be like humans who die but once.

He would have needed to suffer often since the foundation of the world -- We have seen earlier (verse 15) that Jesus' atoning death covered sins committed by men in the ages before His incarnation and death on Calvary. Sin was committed by the devil before Adam fell; very shortly after the creation of the universe,[105] Adam began sinning. So did Adam's offspring. If an atoning sacrifice was needed for all those sins (and one was!), and if Jesus' once-for-all sacrifice had not been superior to the sacrifices that had to be repeated on the annual Day of Atonement, then Jesus would have had to die often. And such a death would have been needed long before He finally did come into the world to go to Calvary.

---

[103] At Hebrews 8:1 and 9:2,8 we have noted the inconsistency in Hebrews of the name given to the inner room of the tabernacle, the room we regularly call the Holy of Holies. The Greek is plural here, and in harmony with the demands of the context, we understand the reference is to the Holy of Holies.

[104] As far as grammar is concerned, the use of *epei* and an imperfect tense verb introduces a contrary-to-fact condition (though it is an unusual way to write such a conditional sentence). Any idea that Jesus needed to suffer more than once is contrary-to-fact.

[105] "Foundation of the world" is synonymous with creation. See Hebrews 4:3.

But now -- "Now" is logical, not temporal. The adversative "but" tells us that to suppose Jesus' priestly service requires repetition presses the Levitical type too far. There was a vast difference in efficacy between the two offerings, those of animals and His own blood.

Once at the consummation of the ages -- "Once" says Jesus had to become incarnate only one time to effectively deal with sin. "Consummation of the ages"[106] seems to say the Christian Age is the last in the succession of ages in God's management of history.[107] It was at the beginning of this last of the series of ages that Jesus came to deal with sin.

He has been manifested -- When He became incarnate, Jesus became visible to human eyes. The verb translated "manifested" is perfect tense, indicating past completed action with present continuing results. His incarnation (manifestation) is past when Hebrews was written.

To put away sin by the sacrifice of Himself – This phrase explains the purpose of His incarnation: Jesus came to put away sin. He came to die. Compare 1 John 3:5, "You know that He appeared (was manifested) to take away sin." "Put away" is the same word translated "setting aside" at Hebrews 7:18. It means to annul, cancel. Since there are still acts of sin in the world, it does not mean to abolish it from the earth. It does say that Jesus atoned for it, made it powerless,[108] He provided a way of pardon. No longer do men need to fear the punishment due their sins if they have surrendered to Jesus and remain faithful. The words "the sacrifice of Himself," like "His own blood" (9:12), are emphatic, and mark once more the contrast between Jesus' priestly action and that of Aaron and his successors. Some of what is involved in "the sacrifice of Himself" will be unfolded in 10:5ff.

9:27 -- And -- This is the third point (see notes at 9:23) relating to Jesus' superior ministry in heaven. It has to do with His Second Advent and the salvation that event will introduce.

---

[106] The first editions of the NASB read simply "at the consummation." Later editions read "the consummation of the ages." Since there is no manuscript evidence whatever for the omission of "of the ages," we must presume the printers of the first edition simply made a mistake now corrected in later editions. The expression here translated "consummation of the ages" is not found in this precise form elsewhere in the New Testament, though similar expressions are found. "End of the age" at Matthew 13:39,40,49, 24:3, 28: 20, likely refers to the end of the present Christian Age. "The ends of the ages" occurs at 1 Corinthians 10:11, and "fullness of time" at Galatians 4:4. "In these last times" is found at 1 Peter 1:20, where the expression may mean either the end of the Old Testament Age, or the beginning of the final age of history.

[107] The NEB calls it "the climax of history." What happened at Calvary was the focal point of all redemptive history. Here is where all the various facets of God's plan for saving man came together. What He had been doing in the Patriarchal and Mosaic Ages previous to this all led to Calvary.

[108] "Sin" is sometimes singular in the Bible, sometimes plural ("sins"). Much has been written in an attempt to explain what might be the difference, if any, when Bible writers use one or the other of these words. (Those writers who suppose the Bible to teach that there is such a thing as an inherited sinful nature are often likely to say that "sin" [singular] refers to this sinful nature, while "sins" [plural] refers to acts of sin that spring from the old nature. In the author's *Commentary on Romans*, it has been documented that the idea of an inherited sinful nature comes from Greek philosophy, not from Scripture. So, this suggestion for "sin" and "sins" is likely not valid.) In Romans, the Greek expression "the sin" (cp. 5:12ff) occurs regularly; the expression seems to be personification. We have suggested it almost equals "the devil" in many passages. Such an explanation of "sin" (i.e., the devil) would, in fact, yield an intelligible sense even here in Hebrews 9:26.

Inasmuch as it is appointed for men to die once -- "Inasmuch" introduces an analogy drawn from the fact that Jesus' humanity is just like all other men's. ("He had to be made like His brethren in all things," 2:17.) By divine appointment, each man's physical life ends in death.[109] By divine appointment[110] each man lives and dies but once.[111] If Jesus' sacrifice were not superior to those repeatedly offered by the Levitical priests, if Jesus had to become incarnate often and die often, He would no longer be like "His brethren."

And after this comes judgment – For men, once physical death has ended life here on earth, the next thing to be faced is the final judgment.[112] If He is in all points "like His brethren," we would expect a similar schedule for Jesus, too. Instead of having to become incarnate again, we would expect the Second Advent and final judgment to be the next thing on His calendar. That is exactly what will be affirmed in the next verse.

9:28 -- So Christ also -- As men die but once, so it was proper for Jesus to die but once.[113]

Having been offered once to bear the sins of many -- Note the writer's repetition of "once" (once for all) throughout these last three verses of chapter 9. Jesus' sacrifice was so effective that everything He came to do in regard to being a sin offering has been settled

---

[109] There are exceptions to this rule that is normative for human beings. Enoch and Elijah did not die physically, and the generation of men living on earth when Jesus returns will not die physically at all. We also suppose that those folk raised from the dead from time to time (i.e., Dorcas, Lazarus) probably died twice. These supernatural interventions, however, do not mean the rule will be broken for the rest of us.

[110] Physical death is the result of Adam's sin (Genesis 3:19); what Adam did affected all his descendants (Romans 5:12ff, 1 Corinthians 15:22). All this was because that is the way God so arranged it.

[111] Reincarnation (an idea held by many ancients as well as moderns) is flatly contradicted by what is here written in Hebrews. Men live and die but *once*! The "once for all" (*hapax*) often used of Christ's sacrifice is here used of man's physical death. There is an indisputable finality about it. (Cases of resurrection, such as Lazarus and Dorcas, differ from reincarnation. They came back in the same bodies. In reincarnation, it's a different body and a different life.) (Because of recent writing on out-of-body experiences, some have asked, 'What about OBE's? Do they not die twice [or more]? Are not these experiences a contradiction of what is here written in Hebrews?' Perhaps the problem is in our definition of death. When a person experiences what is called an out-of-the-body experience, perhaps it is imprecise to say he has died. Perhaps he was only in the process of dying, but that process was not completed.) We understand Scriptures to teach that physical death ends man's opportunities to alter his circumstances and destiny. He does not get a second chance, nor a second life.

[112] Not everyone in the ancient world anticipated existence beyond physical death, but Scripture has always indicated death does not end a man's existence. The body may be buried, but the spirit continues to experience conscious existence in the intermediate state. The intermediate state will end when, according to God's timetable, it is time for the final judgment. (Some have supposed the judgment which Hebrews 9:27 references is not the final judgment, but rather a judgment alleged to occur at the time a man dies and which results in his soul's removal to either Paradise or Hades [torment]. We do not doubt such a removal occurs at death [see Luke 16:22,23; 2 Corinthians 5:1,8], but we see little evidence it requires some formal "judgment" – a kind of preview of coming attractions as a precursor to the final judgment. Scripture teaches a man is either saved or lost right now, while he lives on earth [John 3:16,36]; it does not require God to make some decision *after* this life is over before it is known which portion of the intermediate state will be the soul's lot while it awaits the final judgment.) Hebrews elsewhere uses the term "judgment" to reference the final judgment (see 10:27, 12:23).

[113] There is a perfect parallelism between verses 27 and 28. Each deals first with the present world, then secondly with last things. The work of redemption was so ordered as to correspond to the course of man's history. As man must die once and then face the judgment, so Jesus died but once; what remains is for His return in judgment, which He Himself will administer and at which He will grant heavenly salvation to His people.

and finished for all time. Sin-bearing, a concept found only here and in 1 Peter 2:24 in the New Testament, is found frequently in the Old Testament where it plainly means "to bear the penalty for sin." In fact, we think both New Testament occurrences of this language are intended to echo what we read in the fourth Suffering Servant poem ("He will bear their iniquities," and "He Himself bore the sin of many," Isaiah 53:11,12). The writer of Hebrews says Jesus took upon Himself the consequences of the sins of many.[114] He suffered what was an appropriate sacrifice for the sins of others.

Shall appear a second time – We live in an open universe. Jesus is going to appear on the scene of history again, just as He did when He came to be a sin offering. There is going to be a Second Coming of Jesus!

Without *reference to* sin – The original reads simply, "without sin." That is, He is not coming the second time to be a sin offering. When He comes the second time, He is not coming to die a second time. Far from it!

To those who eagerly await Him – Every eye shall see Him – for the wicked will see Him, too, as He returns. But the righteous, the ones said to be eagerly awaiting Him, are the ones especially in view here in Hebrews. How does a man wait or look for Jesus to come? By being faithful unto death (Revelation 2:10, and the thrust of the whole epistle to the Hebrews). By loving His appearing (His first advent) as the most desirable thing (2 Timothy 4:8). By longing for it and praying, "Come, Lord Jesus!" (Revelation 22:20). By building one's self up in the faith and keeping one's self in the love of God (Jude 20,21). By making wise preparation for the future (Luke 16:1-13).

For salvation -- When Jesus appears the second time, it will result in eternal rewards for those who eagerly are awaiting His return. Concerning the adverse judgment which He shall pass upon "the adversaries" (Hebrews 10:27), this verse does not speak. Christ's superior ministry in heaven and His reappearance signify His work has been accepted by God.[115] It ensures a favorable verdict at the judgment for those who are in Christ.[116] Then the redeemed will see the final fulfillment of all the blessed results of Jesus' once- for-all sacrifice for sin. Then, His superior services will be more than obvious!

---

[114] It should not be thought strange that it says "many" rather than all men. Jesus did die for all men (potentially), but not all men will be saved. Or, as the close of verse 28 words it, not all are eagerly awaiting His return. But for the many who are eagerly awaiting Him, His death did serve to bear their sins. (In light of the contrast between the "One" and the "many" [i.e., mankind] in Isaiah 53, it is certainly not a proper use of this language to make it a proof-text for the doctrine of limited atonement.)

[115] Perhaps a reminder of Levitical practices will help our understanding here. On the Day of Atonement, the Israelites, who watched their high priest enter the sanctuary for them, waited expectantly for his emergence from the tabernacle. His reappearance was a welcome sign that he and the sacrifice which he presented had been accepted by God. So the writer of Hebrews thinks of Jesus as going into heaven itself, right into the very presence of God, with a sin-offering consisting of His own blood. Would it and He be accepted? They expectantly wait to see if He returns from the heavenly sanctuary. When He does appear the second time, all doubts will be removed and the blessings He won for His people at His first appearing will be theirs to enjoy in perpetual fullness forever thereafter.

[116] A few manuscripts (69, A, P, etc.) read "unto salvation *through faith*." Compare 1 Peter 1:5. While the added words are not likely original, the idea is implied in "those who eagerly await Him." It is the faithful who will be benefitted and blessed when Jesus returns.

C. His Ministry is Superior Because It Offers a Better Sacrifice. 10:1-18.

10:1 -- For -- A reminder of the thread of argument may be useful. At 8:1, the writer began an exhortation based on the superiority of the Son of God's priestly ministry – a superiority based on a better covenant, a better sanctuary, and, we're now told, a better sacrifice. "For" indicates we are being given a reason or an explanation of something just said.[1]

The Law -- The main idea of this verse is, "For the Law ... can never ... make perfect" (according to our English versions). However, in the better manuscripts, the verb "can" has a plural subject (cp. NASB marginal reading, "*They* can never"). The plural pronoun "they" is most probably to be understood as a reference to the "regulations for the body" spoken of in 9:10, or the "priests" who labor under the law (9:6). "Law," here, has reference to the whole Old Testament with particular reference to the sacrificial system.

Since it has *only* a shadow of the good things to come *and* not the very form of things -- See 8:5 for the words "shadow" and "copy," and how these words express the comparative worth of the Old Testament sacrificial system versus the once-for-all sacrifice of Christ. Christianity is far superior to the Jewish system. "The good things to come" refer to the blessings conferred on men by the gospel, which were yet future when viewed from an Old Testament standpoint.

Can never by the same sacrifices year by year – Each year, on the Day of Atonement, the same rites that were unavailing last year are repeated. Though unavailing, this is all the Law had to offer. The animal sacrifices were unable to effect the putting away of sin.

Which they offer continually – Shall we take this phrase[2] with what precedes (the same sacrifices are repeated endlessly) or with what follows (can never bring the worshipers to perfection "for all time," 10:14)?

Make perfect those who draw near -- "Make perfect" has reference to remission of sins, as explained in notes at 7:11 and 9:6. "Draw near"[3] is a term synonymous with "worshipers" (as 10:2 will explain).

---

[1] At Hebrews 8:1 we entered into the presentation of the fact that the new covenant has replaced the Mosaic covenant. In 9:11,12 three statements vital to the new covenant were made, which are then explained in detail. 9:13-22 deals with Christ's death. 9:23-28 deals with His presence in heaven. Now 10:1ff deals with His once-for-all offering. The contrast between the old and the new may be outlined in this manner:

The Inadequacy of Mosaic (animal) sacrifices. v. 1-10
Shown by repetition. 1-4
Shown by direct Scriptural statement. 5-9a
Shown by replacement of the former system. 9b-10

The Efficacy of Christ's offering. v.11-18
Shown by Christ's present exaltation (the finality of His sacrifice). 11-14
Shown by the testimony of the Holy Spirit (direct Scriptural statement). 15-18

[2] *Eis to dienekes* was used at 7:3 and translated "perpetually." It indicates something permanent.

[3] See notes on the term "draw near" at 4:16 and 7:25.

10:2 -- Otherwise, would they not have ceased to be offered -- "They" refers to the Levitical sacrifices. The question expects an affirmative answer. Yes, if they had made the worshiper perfect, they would not need to be repeated! The very repetition of the ceremony was a testimony to its imperfection. The desired cleansing had not been affected. No amount of repetition could transform the shadow into reality.[4]

Because the worshipers -- "Worshipers" comes from *latreuo*. It is the same word used at 9:6 of the priestly service and at 9:9 for the priests who officiated at the worship services. On the other hand, at 9:14 the verb "serve" is used of all Christians (all Christians are priests, 1 Peter 2:9). So whether the "worshipers" here are the priests or the people whom the priest led in worship (i.e., "those who draw near" in 10:1), is not easy to decide.

Having once been cleansed – The verb is a perfect tense in the Greek, denoting a past completed action with present continuing results. The point is that in the life of the Jewish worshiper, there never was this "once" when they were cleansed. The Old Testament sacrificial system did not provide actual forgiveness of sins.[5]

(The worshipers) would no longer have had consciousness of sins? -- "Conscience" (as the KJV translates *suneidesis*) is used here as it was at 9:9 in the sense of "consciousness", or awareness. Even though the Old Testament worshiper had performed the divinely prescribed animal sacrifice, he went home with the awareness that something more than animal sacrifice was needed if sins were actually to be forgiven.

10:3 -- But in those *sacrifices* – These are the animal sacrifices referred to in verse 1. The strong adversative "but" (*alla*) puts this verse in contrast to what might have been if the sacrifices had cleansed and removed consciousness of sins.

There is a reminder of sins year by year -- The Day of Atonement ceremonies each year reminded people[6] of the fact something needed to be done about sin since sin offerings (verse 4 will tell us) did not remove the guilt. Sin offerings were made whenever needed throughout the year; that is, whenever men sinned and needed "forgiveness" for those transgressions. On the Day of Atonement a special sin offering for the nation was offered, an offering concerned with the *same* sins for which sin offerings had *already* been offered earlier in the year. It would not take a man long to realize the earlier sin offerings had not taken away sin. If they had, why the need for another offering on the Day of Atonement?

---

[4] Some interpreters have sensed an implication in this language that the sacrificial ritual was still being practiced in the temple at Jerusalem when this letter was written to the Hebrews. Others urge that the verse has little bearing on the date of Hebrews, the argument simply being that if perfection were attainable under the Levitical system its sacrificial system would have come to an end long ago.

[5] Someone has said the faithful man in Old Testament times had a *covering* for sin (Christ's death at Calvary would eventually provide the sacrifice they really needed to be forgiven), but no *cleansing* from sin. That there was a "cleansing," a "forgiveness" (conditioned on Jesus' death at Calvary) of sins committed during Old Testament times is clearly stated at Leviticus 4:20,26,31,35, at Romans 3:25, and at Hebrews 9:13-15.

[6] Some suppose the Day of Atonement activities were a reminder *to God* that something needed to be done about sin.

10:4 -- For it is impossible for the blood of bulls and goats to take away sins -- This verse gives a reason for what was just said in verse 3 about the yearly ceremonies being ineffective as far as actual forgiveness was concerned. On the one hand, since God had commanded such sacrifices, there would have been no forgiveness granted had the people refused to meet the conditions God had revealed. At the same time, those animal sacrifices were temporary and typical – the real forgiveness depended on Christ's sacrifice at Calvary to which they pointed. The constant repetition of the sin offerings showed their inadequacy to effect the actual removal of sin, so that sin would no longer factor into the situation.

10:5 -- Therefore – Now we enter the section of this chapter where the writer argues from Old Testament Scripture concerning the inadequacy of animal sacrifices.

When He comes into the world, He says – The writer will quote a portion of Psalm 40. The words are spoken by Christ to God,[7] giving the reason for the incarnation.

"SACRIFICE AND OFFERING YOU HAVE NOT DESIRED -- "Sacrifice" often speaks of an animal victim, while "offering" denotes the grain, meal and drink offerings.[8] In the words of the Psalmist, Jesus is saying He recognizes that the sacrifices commanded by the Old Testament did not satisfy the mind of God as far as forgiveness is concerned.[9]

"BUT A BODY YOU HAVE PREPARED FOR ME -- The "body"[10] God had prepared for Jesus was the human body He inhabited after His birth at Bethlehem. In that body, Jesus could make the kind of sacrifice God "desired" if sins were to be satisfactorily atoned. The body God had prepared for Messiah is given back to God as a living sacrifice. The leading point of the argument is, not that a body was prepared, but that Messiah came to do the will of God with reference to how sin should be forgiven in the mind of God.

---

[7] In its original setting, the Psalmist (not Messiah) is talking to God. But the Psalmist, who often typified Messiah, was often inspired to say words that later exactly suited what Messiah would say. Instead of accusing the Hebrews writer of quoting the Psalm in a sneaky way (a suggestion which undermines the force of the whole argument), it is better to say the writer used the verses in a generally recognized way. These quoted texts would not have carried force if the readers were being asked to accept a peculiar interpretation of certain Bible verses.

[8] "Sacrifice" in Hebrew is *zebah*, and may refer to "peace offerings" -- offerings intended to knit a broken fellowship. "Offering" translates the Hebrew *minhah*, a word used in Genesis 4:3 of both Cain's vegetable sacrifice and Abel's animal sacrifice. The Hebrew word denotes the "offering" as a sanctifying consecration.

[9] Did not the Old Testament require sacrifice? Yes! Then why does it say God "has not desired" them or "has no pleasure" in them? Certain liberal theologians have used language like this to support their theory of the evolutionary development of Old Testament doctrine: Moses instituted sacrifice, then years later the prophets and psalmists (as they evolved to a higher knowledge) came to realize there was something better than sacrifice, so in their preaching improved on Moses by showing that these really were of no avail. Liberalism then thought of Jesus improving on the prophets' work; Paul improved on Jesus; and we with our advanced knowledge can improve on Paul as we forge a religion for modern man. But the verse does *not* say God did not require them; rather, it says He has no desire for, no pleasure in, them. Given the argument of Hebrews 10:4, this means the sacrifices, though required, never did atone for sins. When the Old Testament prophets made statements similar to the Psalmist's (see 1 Samuel 15:22; Isaiah 1:11-17; Jeremiah 7:21-23; Hosea 6:6; Micah 6:6-8), they were saying God had no pleasure in the sacrifice when the worshiper's heart was not right.

[10] The Hebrew text of Psalm 40 reads "ears thou hast digged out for me." The LXX substituted the whole ("body") for the part: God made the ear, He also made the whole body. The Hebrews writer used the LXX text.

10:6 – "IN WHOLE BURNT OFFERINGS AND *sacrifices* **FOR SIN YOU HAVE TAKEN NO PLEASURE** – The two terms in verse 5 were quite general, whereas the two in verse 6 are specific. The first term speaks of voluntary sacrifices brought to the altar of burnt offering by grateful worshippers. The second term speaks of the sin and trespass offerings.[11] "Pleasure" has to do with the forgiveness of sins, so God can again look with pleasure on the sinner. In Old Testament times, sins were covered not cleansed; they were "passed over" (Acts 17:30; Romans 3:25). Until Calvary, God's actions were halfway between punishment and forgiveness.

10:7 – "THEN I SAID, `BEHOLD, I HAVE COME ... TO DO YOUR WILL, O GOD' – Messiah now tells God that He is willing to do whatever God wills in order that sins may be atoned. That is the whole reason for the incarnation, for Jesus coming to earth the first time. What the blood of bulls and goats could not do, Jesus would do by giving His life on the cross. What God desired and had pleasure in, as far as forgiveness being made available, Jesus knew and would do voluntarily.

"(IN THE SCROLL OF THE BOOK IT IS WRITTEN OF ME) – What book[12] was it in which the author of the Psalm had read about obedience? And in what book was it said that Jesus, during His stay on earth, would do God's will? In the Psalmist's case, perhaps the reference was to the Mosaic Law (e.g., Deuteronomy 6:5), or perhaps this phrase is a reference to an already existing collection of the Psalms of David. If the author of Psalm 40 was David,[13] then the book or volume which was quoted must be some book of Scripture written before David's writing of Psalm 40. Concerning Messiah, in the books written before the Psalms were collected, this language ("I have come to do thy will") is not literally found. The meaning must be that there were verses where it was implied or typified respecting the Messiah. Many of the sacrifices and institutions of the Old Testament economy were types, each presenting the idea that a Savior would hereafter come to do the will of God in making atonement for the sin of the world.

10:8 – After saying above – Read verses 8 and 9 together, to see how the writer of Hebrews repeats two phrases from Psalm 40, isolating them and emphasizing what they say, in order to call attention to the point the Psalmist made.

"SACRIFICES, OFFERINGS, WHOLE BURNT OFFERINGS AND sacrifices FOR

---

[11] The Hebrew here is *hatta'ah*, which the LXX regularly renders as *peri hamartias*, i.e., "sin offering."

[12] The expression translated "scroll" literally means "little head" and apparently had reference to the little knob on the end of the stick around which the scroll of Scripture was wound. By metonymy the term stands for the scroll itself. "Scroll of the book" is a reference to some scroll of Scripture. F.F. Bruce (*op. cit.*, p.234) urges that the words in the next verse (Hebrews 10:8), "according to the Law," clarify what is meant by "the roll of the book." The whole phrase is in parentheses in our English version, perhaps because the Hebrew original admits two renderings. (1) "Then said I, Lo, I am come! In the roll of the book it is written of me ...." or, (2) "Then said I, Lo, I am come with the roll of the book that is written concerning me ...."

[13] The author of the Psalm is not named in the heading of the Psalm 40, but it is included in "book one" of Psalms (Psalms 1-41), most of which are attributed to David. See the *Wycliffe Bible Commentary*, p.495, on the division of the Psalms into "five books" and on the authorship of the Psalms in "book one."

SIN YOU HAVE NOT DESIRED, NOR HAVE YOU TAKEN PLEASURE in them -- The first part of the quotation from Psalm 40 says God did not desire animal sacrifices; they were not the divinely appointed way to forgiveness of men's sins.

(Which are offered according to the Law) – Those animal sacrifices were indeed prescribed by the Law of Moses,[14] and without faithfulness to the commands of the Law a man would be lost. Nevertheless, even when offered just as the Law directed, the sacrifices still did not provide a perfect atonement for sin.

10:9 -- Then He said – The writer now emphasizes the second key phrase in Psalm 40.

"BEHOLD I HAVE COME TO DO YOUR WILL" -- In Jesus case, the doing of God's will included His death to atone for sin. As explained in verse 7, in His pre-incarnate state, Jesus knew that the sacrifices commanded by the Mosaic covenant were not adequate to atone for sin, and He knew something would have to take their place. So He volunteered to intervene personally and give Himself as the sin offering.

He takes away the first in order to establish the second -- "The first" was the Old Testament sacrificial system. "The second" is Christ's way of dealing with sin, which was in tune with the will of God. The old is "taken away," a strong word denoting total abolition. The second is established, or made firm. The Hebrews writer is saying, 'Study Psalm 40:6-8, and you will see this truth exactly. The Mosaic system was only ever intended to be temporary. The Christian system is set over against the Mosaic and is superior to it.' The old system of Mosaic sacrifices has been replaced by something better.

10:10 -- By this will -- Goodspeed renders the phrase, "And it is through His doing of God's will that we have been once-for-all purified from sin ...." It refers to the "will" of God concerning how sins were to be atoned, the very will of God which Jesus came to do when He became incarnate.

We have been sanctified -- Sanctification (in Jewish thinking) cleansed an unclean person so he could approach God in worship. The death of Christ actually accomplishes for us what the Old Testament did only ritually for the Jew.[15]

Through the offering of the body of Jesus Christ once for all -- "Once for all"[16] speaks

---

[14] "Law" is anarthrous here. Some insist the change from "the Law" to "law" is intentional, as if the writer had in mind the contrast between external ritual and the principle of inward obedience. This same matter of anarthrous *nomos* must be dealt with when studying Romans, and one's beliefs about whether or not saving faith includes works of obedience flavors the comments given not a little (both in Romans and here in Hebrews). (The student who wishes to pursue this matter should consult the author's *Commentary on Romans* at 2:13ff.)

[15] Sometimes, especially in Paul's epistles, sanctification is rather synonymous with growth and development in Christian character. Since the verb translated "we have been sanctified" implies a one-time act in the past, the reference here in Hebrews is not to spiritual growth after one becomes a Christian. It rather speaks of the initial setting apart to sacred service that is possible because of the death of Christ.

[16] Be careful lest the emphasis on the once-for-all nature of Christ's atonement, a point oft repeated in Hebrews (see 9:12,26,28), is missed!

of the finality of the atonement.[17] What a contrast to what the Levitical priests could do –
with their repeated offerings year after year! The "body of Jesus" is that body which was
prepared for Him at His incarnation (verse 5).

10:11 -- And -- According to the outline suggested at the beginning of this chapter, we are
now entering into a discussion of evidences that the sacrifice of Jesus was a one-time
sacrifice, eternally effective. Verses 11-14 point to the present exaltation (He is *sitting* in
the presence of God!) of Jesus as one of these evidences.

Every priest – We suppose the writer has the Levitical priests in mind.[18] "Every" suggests many priests were needed over the years, itself a mark of inadequacy (Hebrews 7:23).

Stands daily – This does not literally mean *every* priest did this every day; the priests took
turns according to their courses. The point is that the offerings were done *daily*. There
was no end to the routine. As Hebrews emphasized earlier, the constant repetition of the
sacrifices was evidence of their imperfection. In 10:1, the repetition of the ritual of the
Day of Atonement "year by year" was alluded to. Here, as in Hebrews 7:27, the reference
is to the daily offering of the sacrifices. Standing was a posture appropriate to the Levitical
priestly service, for it implies yet more work (more "sacrifices") to be done.

Ministering and offering time after time the same sacrifices -- "Ministering" speaks of
performing religious duties as the priests helped the worshippers who came bringing sin
and trespass offerings. "Same sacrifices" reminds us that under the old economy the same
sacrifices were offered morning and evening every day, and that in addition to the sin and
trespass offerings offered for individuals repeatedly. The sacrifices were ever the same –
offered at the same place, in the same way, for the same sins. To what effect?

Which can never take away sins -- The Greek verb means "to take from around." Man
is wrapped in his sins; he weaves day by day a terrible robe for himself (Psalm 35:26,
Psalm 109:18). This enveloping robe was never really stripped off by the sacrifices offered
by the ministering priests. If they had dealt with the basic problem (the removal of sin),
they would not have needed endless repetition (Hebrews 10:2).

10:12 -- But He -- Jesus' work is now contrasted to the Levitical priests'. He offered one
sacrifice – just *one*! – and then He sat down!

Having offered one sacrifice for sins for all time -- Christ's death on the cross is that "one

---

[17] "It matters immensely that this one offering, once made, avails for all people at all times. This contrasts sharply with the sacrifices under the old covenant as the author has been emphasizing. But it contrasts also with other religions. Hering *(in loc.)* for example, points out that this distinguishes Christianity from the mystery religions, where the sacrifice of the god was repeated annually. In fact, there is no other religion in the world in which one great happening brings salvation through the centuries and through the world. This is the distinctive doctrine of Christianity." Morris, *op. cit.*, p.100.

[18] A few manuscripts (e.g., A P 69) read "high priest" *(archiereus)* instead of "priest" *(hiereus)*, but the text as we have it is probably correct.

sacrifice" (Hebrews 7:27, 8:1, 9:26). Some English versions put the word "forever" ("for all time") with the following phrase, but those that put it with this preceding expression (as does the NASB) are probably right. The way the NASB reads, the emphasis is on the idea that Christ's priestly offering is finished; it will never have to be repeated. Such a magnificent offering, so well done, and so acceptable; it is good for all time!

SAT DOWN AT THE RIGHT HAND OF GOD – What does Christ's sitting at the right hand of God indicate? Levitical priests stood (verse 11 told us), for their work was not done but instead went on. Christ sits because His work is done. Sitting is the posture of rest, not of work. That Christ has sat down indicates there is no more work (no more sacrifice, no more atoning work) to do. Where He sits is important, too. "At the right hand of God" is the place of highest dignity and honor.[19]

10:13 – Waiting from that time onward – As evidence that no more sacrificial work remains for Jesus to do, the writer appeals to Psalm 110:1.[20] The next thing on the heavenly agenda is not another Calvary, but the subjugation of all the enemies of Christ. As Psalm 110:1 records, "The Lord (God the Father) says to my Lord (Jesus), 'Sit at My right hand until I make Your enemies a footstool for Your feet'."

UNTIL HIS ENEMIES BE MADE A FOOTSTOOL FOR HIS FEET – Christ is represented as calmly and patiently waiting for the fulfillment of the promise made to Him. The last enemy to be destroyed is death (1 Corinthians 15:26), and that will be done at the final resurrection accompanying Christ's second coming. The "footstool" image had its origin in the custom of conquerors putting their feet on the necks of their enemies to symbolize the enemies' thorough defeat. Jesus remains in heaven, at the Father's side, until that time in the future when all His enemies will have been thoroughly and completely subdued.

10:14 -- For -- He is able to sit down and wait "For" no repetition of His offering is needed.

By one offering He has perfected for all time those who are sanctified -- The idea in the word "perfected" has been explained at Hebrews 2:10, 7:11,19,28, and 10:1. Only what Jesus has done makes it possible for the beneficiaries of His sacrifice to come near to God. Those beneficiaries are here called "those who are sanctified." Evidently, the sanctified here are the same as in Hebrews 2:11. As a present tense[21] verb, it speaks of those who are

---

[19] "We should remember that to be seated at God's right hand is to be in the place of highest honor. Even angels are not said to have attained to this: angels stand in God's presence (Luke 1:19). When Jesus claimed this place for Himself (during His trials on the night before the crucifixion), the high priest tore his robe at what he regarded as blasphemy (Mark 14:62-63). The author is combining with the thought of a finished work the idea that our Lord is a being of the highest dignity and honor." Morris, *op. cit.*, p.101.

[20] This is the third time Psalm 110:1 has been used in Hebrews (see 1:3,13). Psalm 110:4 has also been used extensively to prove Christ's priesthood after the order of Melchizedek (see 5:6,10, 6:20, 7:11,15,17).

[21] In Hebrews 10:10, "sanctified" was a perfect tense verb form (implying a past completed act with present continuing results). Sanctification in the New Testament has three aspects for believers. (1) The *past* aspect (indicated by a past tense verb) was accomplished by the blood of Christ shed on man's behalf. Thus, every believer can be called a saint (Hebrews 13:12; 1 Corinthians 1:2). Past sanctification is positional, admitting no

in the process of being sanctified.[22] "For all time" translates the same Greek phrase as did the words "for all time" in verse 12. The argument the author of Hebrews sets forth would have been understood through all the New Testament churches. Many of the converts to Christianity had come from a religion where worship involved continual animal sacrifices; this was true whether they were Jewish or Gentile converts. Now, in their new religion, Christianity, there was no continuation of such sacrifices. They knew what Jesus had done was of abiding validity; the need for any further sacrifice was obviated.

10:15 – And the Holy Spirit also bears witness to us – Verses 15-18 call attention to the Holy Spirit's testimony in Scripture regarding the efficacy of Christ's sacrifice, about how much better it is than any the Levitical priesthood could offer. The writer of Hebrews insists the Holy Spirit is the author of the Scripture about to be quoted. "Also" likely means the Spirit adds His testimony to that of Christ previously referred to in Psalm 40:6-8.

For after saying – The passage cited in verses 16 and 17 is taken from Jeremiah 31:31ff. As he did in verses 8 and 9, the writer divides the quotation into two parts in order to call special attention to the second part. When Jeremiah's classic new covenant prophecy was quoted earlier in Hebrews (8:8-12), it was used to highlight God's intention to replace the Mosaic covenant with the new covenant. From the same passage, attention now centers on the verse predicting that when the new covenant was in force, the sins of the people would be actually forgiven. Since sins were to be completely remitted, the implication of the verse in Jeremiah was that no further need for continual, repeated sacrifices remains.

10:16 – "THIS IS THE COVENANT THAT I WILL MAKE WITH THEM AFTER THOSE DAYS, SAYS THE LORD: I WILL PUT MY LAWS UPON THEIR HEART, AND UPON THEIR MIND I WILL WRITE THEM" – See notes at Hebrews 8:6-12 for an explanation of this verse. It is repeated here simply to set up the next verse, which is the one the writer wanted to emphasize.

He then says – English translations[23] have added words here to help direct our thinking to the language of the prophecy found in verse 17. Jeremiah's original passage contains a number of phrases between the two quoted by the Hebrews writer, but enough was quoted to show the new covenant passage was the one he wanted his readers to think about again.

---

degrees. At the time of new birth, every believer receives the benefits of past sanctification and has as much right to God's presence as any other Christian. (2) The *present* aspect (indicated by a present tense verb) is progressive throughout the Christian's life (John 17:17; Ephesians 5:25,26), something akin to spiritual growth. It is practical rather than positional, and is accomplished as believers submit to the indwelling Spirit's help and walk in the light of God's Word (1 Peter 1:15). (3) The *future* aspect (indicated by a future tense verb) occurs at the second coming, when the sanctification of believers will be completed (1 Thessalonians 3:12,13, 5:23).

[22] Not all writers are convinced verse 14 here speaks of the process of sanctification that takes place in each individual believer's life. They explain the present tense verb as referring to the progressive occurrence in this age as one after another responds to the gospel and is thus set apart to sacred service.

[23] Earlier translators and commentators, since the Reformation, made the break in the middle of verse 16. They put a period after "days," and started the second statement with the words "*Then* the Lord says ...." The thought was that even though the words "says the Lord" were actually part of the quotation from Jeremiah, the author of Hebrews was using the words to separate the two parts of the passage.

10:17 – "THEIR SINS AND THEIR LAWLESS DEEDS I WILL REMEMBER NO MORE" – Now we see how those who are sanctified are "perfected for all time." God remembers their sins no more. Those sins are wholly forgiven. The men are completely pardoned. No further sacrifice is needed, once the death of Christ is taken into account.[24]

10:18 – Now where there is forgiveness of these things – This verse shows that "forgiveness" and "I will remember (their sins) no more" are synonymous expressions. The meaning of the word "forgiveness" was discussed at 9:22.

There is no longer *any* offering for sin – The distinctive feature of the new covenant is the fact God remembers sins and iniquities no more. The constant repetition of sacrifices within the old covenant system demonstrated that the sin question was not settled. The once-for-all offering of Messiah shows that sin is paid for and put away.[25] Having demonstrated the superiority of the Son of God's priestly ministry (Hebrews 8:1ff), now follows an exhortation to live their lives in light of this great truth about Jesus' superior ministry.

FOURTH WARNING PASSAGE. 10:19-31

- *Encouragement to use the new access to God which Christ's priesthood affords. 10:19-25.*

   Three exhortations are offered in this paragraph. (1) Draw near in faith, v.19-22. (2) Hold fast the hope, v.23. (3) Encourage one another to love, v.24,25.

10:19 -- Since therefore – The practical encouragement that follows is based squarely upon the superiority of the Christian system. If the Mosaic religion is all shadow and no substance, if there are no true advantages in the old covenant, if forgiveness of sins comes only in the once-for-all sacrifice that inaugurated the new covenant, if only Christ's priesthood makes perfect fellowship with God possible, then clearly there are some duties which follow and are incumbent upon the Christian. Verses 19-21 summarize some of the truths learned thus far in our study of Hebrews, and on these truths the exhortations of v.22ff rest.

Brethren – The writer identifies himself with his readers, with all being recipients of the

---

[24] Not infrequently the language of Jeremiah, "I will remember their sins no more," is thought to mean that in the final judgment those sins that have been forgiven will be completely forgotten and not brought up at all as men's lives are compared to the Word of God. We doubt the language from Jeremiah should be applied to the final judgment. All through Hebrews (let the writer of Hebrews explain the real import) this language "I will remember their sins no more" has reference to the new covenant provision concerning an efficacious sacrifice for sins, so that sins may be completely forgiven in the first place.

[25] "The logic should have been compelling to every reader. First century recipients of this letter, particularly those Jewish Christians who were toying with the notion of returning to Judaism, should recognize the foolishness of such a step. Since Christ's offering secured complete remission of sin, no further need exists for Levitical sacrifices or any other kind. The argument is no less relevant to modern readers. When a large segment of Christendom regularly re-offers the sacrifice of Christ in the Mass, it is obvious that the forthright implications of this verse need to be more clearly understood and proclaimed." Kent, *op. cit.*, p.195.

special benefits available in the Christian religion.

We have confidence to enter the holy place by the blood of Jesus -- The word "confidence" (boldness) was explained at 3:6 and 4:16. Christians can approach God confidently, feeling completely at home in the situation created for them by Christ's saving work.[26] The "holy place" is the place where God dwells.[27] The "blood of Jesus" recalls all that Hebrews has said about the once-for-all atoning sacrifice Jesus offered on Calvary. Believers all need forgiveness of sins. "By the blood of Jesus" we may boldly enter God's presence, make our confession, and find the forgiveness we need.

10:20 -- By a new and living way -- The two terms modifying "way" are meaningful. "New" is a translation of *prosphaton*, a word that means "recently slaughtered." When Hebrews was written, less than a generation after Calvary and within the lifetime of many of the original readers, the sacrifice of Jesus was still just newly killed, it had just recently happened. "Living" reminds us that Jesus rose from the dead. It is no slain and hence lifeless animal on whom we depend for our way of access into God's presence (a "way" "to enter the holy place"). It is on the risen, exalted, seated, and royal High Priest, who ever lives to make intercession for the saints. "Living" also reminds us that the way is forever available – it is perpetual and constant, like a fountain that always flows.

Which He inaugurated for us through the veil -- "Inaugurated" translates the verb *enkainizo*, which means to initiate, to consecrate, to sanction.[28] Christ has opened the way "for us" into the presence of God. Once more, the writer of Hebrews uses Old Testament symbolism to explain new covenant truths. Entrance into the Holy of Holies could only be gained by passing through the second veil (Hebrews 9:3). So for us, entrance into God's presence could only be gained by Christ. The way Christ opened is forever opened.

That is, His flesh – The difficult problem here is to decide with which word ("way" or "veil") this explanation is in apposition.[29] We prefer to say it is the *way* into the presence

---

[26] No longer do forgiven people need be afraid when in God's presence. Nadab and Abihu died while offering incense (Leviticus 10:2), and it had become the custom for the high priest not to linger in the Holy of Holies on the Day of Atonement, lest he do something wrong, or the people become terrified. Because of the saving work of Jesus, Christians have a new attitude towards being in the presence of God.

[27] Cf. Isaiah 57:15, "For thus says the high and exalted One Who lives forever, whose name is Holy, `I dwell on a high and holy place, and also with the contrite and lowly of spirit'." "Holy place" here refers to the Holy of Holies" (see notes at 9:8) which was the antitype of the earthly tabernacle's Holy of Holies. The words in the next verse "through the veil" (Hebrews 10:20) tell us that the inner room is in the writer's mind.

[28] It is the word translated "dedication" in the expression "Feast of Dedication" (John 10:22). The same word was used in Hebrews 9:18 of the inauguration of the Mosaic covenant. Behind the word is the hint of sacrifice. The KJV chose "consecrated" to translate *enkainizo*. KJV-based commentaries sometimes give an incorrect idea, as though the way had previously existed but was now being dedicated. *Kainos* in the middle of *enkainizo* does not mean brand new -- that's the word *neos* -- as we learned when we talked about the "*new* covenant" in 8:8,13. In the argument being made by Hebrews, the implied contrast "is not between a new, unfrequented path, and an old one, familiar and well-trodden; but rather between a new way and no way at all" (Bruce, *op. cit.*, p.245).

[29] The student who wishes to examine the arguments in favor of either rendering will find them listed in Bruce, *op. cit.*, p.247ff.

of God that the "flesh" (incarnation) of Jesus opened up.[30] So explained, Hebrews 10:20 harmonizes nicely with what was earlier presented about Christ's entering "through the greater and more perfect tabernacle" at Hebrews 9:11.

10:21 -- And since *we have* a great priest over the house of God -- Believers are not only reminded of the benefits of the "new and living way," they are also reminded that they have the services of an incomparable priest. "Great" applied to Jesus may reflect Hebrews' presentation that Christ's priesthood is *greater* than the Aaronic priesthood. "House of God" is likely a reference to the church, the community of God's people (cp. Hebrews 3:6). "Even though He has opened the way for our direct approach to God, Christ does not cease His ministration on our behalf. He continues as our great priest, guiding, strengthening, encouraging, and interceding."[31]

10:22 -- Let us draw near – Having begun with a brief summary of the epistle (verses 19-21), now come three exhortations each introduced by the words "Let us," each of them a present tense verb, indicating continual encouragement. Draw near to what? Evidently to God and the throne of grace (cp. 4:16, 7:25). 10:19 has spoken of "confidence to enter the holy place." The believers are encouraged to continually draw near.

With a sincere heart in full assurance of faith – What is a true or "sincere" heart? Does it speak of all false ways and false ideas (e.g., let's go back to the Jewish religion) being rejected? If so, this phrase says there should be no wavering, no longing looks back at the old system. Is there a contrast to the Old Testament system which only cleansed the flesh (Hebrews 9:10), but didn't help with the heart? Does it suggest all self-righteousness should be renounced? "Full assurance of faith" has reference to a firm and immovable persuasion concerning the priesthood of Christ, and the superiority of the new covenant to the old. Proper understanding of the doctrinal portion of this epistle should give objective grounds for this assurance, for faith comes by hearing and is based on evidence.

Having our hearts sprinkled *clean* from an evil conscience – The right to "draw near" and the "full assurance" result from certain conditions being met. Two are specified in this phrase and the next. "Conscience" here likely has the same meaning it did in 9:9,14.[32] According to 1 Peter 1:2, the sprinkling of the blood is something God does or is something that happens in God's mind. In Old Testament symbolic language (where the ceremonial cleansing with blood was required of the Jewish priests, Hebrews 10:22), it would remind

---

[30] Some have felt the identification of "veil" and "flesh" poses a problem, for it would imply Christ's incarnation was a barrier to entrance into God's presence, an idea that seems to be the exact opposite to what Hebrews has been arguing. Even though the Greek word order might favor taking "flesh" as an explanation of the "veil," it raises a further problem of having to explain that passing through does not mean leave behind. Jesus did not leave His flesh behind when He passed through the veil, since the Bible elsewhere (see note #12, p.126 above) suggests Jesus *now* has His risen and glorified body.

[31] Kent, *op. cit.*, p.199.

[32] The word rendered "conscience" (*suneidesis*) may mean here, as in Hebrews 9:9,14, either conscience or consciousness; either the moral faculty of the soul or the state of mind resulting from the exercise of this faculty. R. Milligan, *op. cit.*, p.281.

us that where the blood of Christ is sprinkled, the consciousness is cleansed.[33]

And our bodies washed with pure water -- The Old Testament ceremony had the priest washing at the laver before entering the Holy of Holies. Just as the Levitical priest had to wash before drawing near to God, most commentators refer to the truth that baptism (immersion in water) is here identified as a second condition that must be met before men have free access to God's presence. Notice that salvation here has two parts – God's part (sprinkling the heart) and man's part (bodies washed).[34] The two perfect participles ("sprinkled" and "washed") might suggest the two acts take place at the same time. It is when a penitent believer is immersed that his heart is "sprinkled;" that is, at immersion the benefits of Christ's atoning sacrifice are applied to his personal sin problem. This would be in harmony with what the New Testament elsewhere presents, that baptism is the beginning of the Christian life, the point at which men's sins are forgiven in the mind of God.[35]

10:23 -- Let us hold fast the confession of our hope -- This is the second of the three exhortations based on verses 19-21. In our comments on Hebrews 6:19,20, we learned Jesus is the basis of the Christian's hope.[36] He is the new way of access; He is the intercessor. If we quit confessing Him, we have no hope! If the first exhortation (verse 22) dealt with what happens at conversion, then "hold fast the confession[37] of our hope"[38] would be tantamount to "be faithful until death."[39]

---

[33] Some commentators suppose "hearts sprinkled clean from an evil conscience" is a reference to repentance. This would imply the blood is applied at repentance, so that forgiveness also takes place at repentance (before baptism), a view that seems to contradict what Scripture says elsewhere about when "sins are washed away" (e.g., Acts 22:16) and the "spirit is alive" (e.g., Romans 8:10). B.F. Westcott (*op. cit.*, p.323) saw what he calls a faint allusion to the Lord's Supper. In this commentator's opinion, Westcott's view is fanciful.

[34] A word about the punctuation marks in our English Bibles is needed at this place. Notice that between the last two participial phrases in verse 22, the KJV and NASB insert a comma. The ASV used a semicolon. The punctuation of the ASV, which has a heavy stop between the last two phrases, causes us to attach the first ("having our hearts sprinkled ...") to the preceding exhortation, "Let us draw near," and to attach the second ("having our bodies washed...") to the following exhortation, "Let us hold fast." This change of punctuation may have been due to a feeling that there is something incongruous in correlating the figurative sprinkling of the heart and a literal washing of the body. The same feeling of incongruity has led some expositors to maintain that "our bodies washed" is as figurative as "hearts sprinkled," and to deny it has any reference to baptism. (Cf. G.H. Lang, *Epistle to the Hebrews*, London, 1951, p.167). While the majority of commentators see a reference to baptism, Calvin was one of the exceptions. He explained that "bodies washed with pure water" was a reference to the "Spirit of God" (*Calvin's Commentaries* [Grand Rapids: Baker, 2005 reprint], Vol.22, p.237).

[35] See Acts 2:38, 22:16; Romans 6:3,4; 1 Corinthians 12:13; Galatians 3:27; Colossians 2:12; 1 Peter 3:21.

[36] "Hope" has been one of the main themes of Hebrews. Included in this hope which each believer cherishes is the knowledge that God is "bringing many sons to glory" (2:10); that believers are "partakers of a heavenly calling" (3:1); they can boast in their hope (3:6); they are looking for Christ to return (9:28); they are seeking a city that is yet to come (13:14); and that hope is an anchor for the soul (6:11,18-20).

[37] See notes on "confession" at 3:1 and 4:14. In fact, 4:14 has the same exhortation, "Let us hold fast our confession!"

[38] Although the KJV reads "profession of *our* faith," it is without manuscript support. Nestle-Aland list no alternatives for the reading "confession of hope" (save the possible addition of "our" before "hope"). Even the Textus Receptus reads "hope" at this place.

[39] "Hold fast" is a continuous action verb. "Let us keep on making the confession of our hope without wavering!"

Without wavering -- The Greek adjective unwavering may agree with either "confession" or "hope."[40] Either it says we are to be constant in their hope, or it says we are to be unswerving in our confession, bending to neither side. If we opt for the second idea, then it is implied the readers have some irresolution of mind concerning continuing to make the good confession. The exhortation is to give up this irresolution and replace it with resolute purpose of mind to be unswerving in their loyalty to Jesus. They were to cease being influenced to stop confessing by whatever difficulties or opposition they faced.

For He who promised is faithful -- Is it God the Father,[41] or Jesus the royal priest,[42] who made the promise? And what was promised? A hope of "rest"? A hope of "forgiveness"? A promise of being "confessed" before the Father in heaven? Whatever is intended, this much is sure – Christians will not be disappointed if they hold fast their confession without wavering, because the One who promised can be thoroughly relied upon.

10:24 – And let us consider how to stimulate one another to love and good deeds -- This is the third in the series of exhortations based on verses 19-21. The readers will be more apt to confess their hope courageously and unhesitatingly if they are encouraged constantly by their brothers and sisters in Christ. The emphasis is not on "consider how" but on "consider ... one another" so as to be able to stimulate each other.[43] It involves carefully taking into account the circumstances and weaknesses of "one another"[44] (each brother and sister in Christ) to ascertain just what support is needed. Once the needed support is determined, what is needed next is "stimulation" or provocation[45] to "love and good deeds." "Love"[46] is likely love for Christ, so that brethren do not avoid the meeting (verse 25) where Jesus is worshiped. The "good deeds" would be the cups of cold water given in Jesus name (Matthew 10:42), the "ministering to the saints" 6:10 spoke of.

---

[40] The ASV made it plain that "wavering not" modified one of the nouns. The NASB, RSV, NEB, render the word in such a way that it seems to the English reader as though "without wavering" modifies "us" or "our." The translators must have supposed that if a confession wavers it is because the confessor wavers.

[41] The faithfulness of God is an oft-repeated theme in the Bible. See 1 Corinthians 1:9, 10:13; 1 Thessalonians 5:24; Hebrews 11:11. The majority of commentaries this commentator has checked interpret this last phrase of verse 23 as though it were another reference to this same topic of God's faithfulness.

[42] The topic of this verse is "confession" and Jesus spoke on this topic, promising to confess before the Father those who, during their earthly sojourn, continually confess Him (Matthew 10:32).

[43] The English infinitive is intended to represent a preposition and infinitive in the Greek, a construction that expresses purpose. Christians thus are to "consider ... one another" with this purpose in mind, namely, the incitement of love and good works in their lives.

[44] This is the only place in Hebrews where we find the expression "one another," though it is frequent elsewhere in the New Testament. Christians cannot be selfish, caring merely for their own interests! There is a mutual activity expected of those who are part of the family of God, wherein we encourage one another. It is not just the leaders, it is every brother and sister who are to encourage and stimulate one another.

[45] The Greek word *paruxmos* (cp. the English paroxysm) is a strong word used elsewhere in the New Testament, e.g., at Acts 15:39 to describe the "sharp contention" between Paul and Barnabas over who should be the helper on the second missionary journey. The KJV translates it "provoke," a word that has changed meaning since 1611. To us, "provoke" means to offend, to irritate, to incense. In 1611 it meant to arouse, to excite, to call into action, to stimulate to action. The word is also used at Acts 17:16 and 1 Corinthians 13:5.

[46] The only other place in Hebrews where "love" is mentioned is at 6:10.

10:25 -- Not forsaking our own assembling together -- Apparently, some of the wavering believers had begun absenting themselves from the regular weekly assembly.[47] A continual forsaking[48] is the thing prohibited, and the Greek prohibits the continuance of an act already going on, 'Stop forsaking the assembling ....'" It is interesting to note the emphasis here is not on what a believer *gets* from the assembly, but rather on what he can *contribute* to the assembly (as he considers the others, in order to stimulate them to love and good works). A man who attends the public worship[49] only for what he can get, and whose attendance becomes more and more sporadic because he thinks he is getting nothing from attending, has not yet grasped the significance of this oft-memorized passage from Hebrews. Indeed, he may need encouragement (we all do!), but he also needs to be an encourager, and that encouragement is best given when the believers have all assembled.[50]

As is the habit of some – Several reasons have been offered in the commentaries why some were getting into the habit of missing church. Some may have been deterred by the fear of persecution. Some may have become sleepy spiritually. Some may have neglected the services from self-confidence (they were good enough without going to church regularly). Some may have overlooked the fact that the assembly is an opportunity for stimulating others. Some may have had disdain for the church assembly compared with the earthly glory of the temple and its services. Behind these reasons was a forgetfulness of who Jesus is and that He expected His followers to confess Him consistently and continually.

But encouraging one another – Encouraging one another to do what? Perhaps the answer is to meet together. As the "day" (next phrase) drew nearer and nearer, they were to encourage one another to meet together. Perhaps the answer is "to love and good deeds (verse 24). There is a vital connection between "assembling together" and "encouraging one another." One function of public worship, according to 1 Corinthians 14:26ff, is the edification of all who come together. Opportunities for such edification, such encouragement, such stimulation, are missed when the potential encourager misses the public worship.

---

[47] The "assembly" would be what we know as the regular Sunday service. Because the term translated "assembly" is *episunagoge* (the word for "synagogue" plus the preposition *epi*), some have supposed Christians were attending a Christian worship service in addition to (*epi*) to the regular synagogue services. (It has even been suggested the Christian assembly was appended to the Sabbath services in the synagogue rather than being held on the Lord's Day. This last idea is certainly too much to find in the simple preposition *epi*.)

[48] A matter of considerable importance here is the exact connotation of the verb translated "forsaking" (*enkataleipo*). Its primary meaning is "to abandon, to leave behind, to forsake, to desert" (BAG, p.214). Yet the context following seems to indicate the readers have not completely forsaken the church, but there was a danger they soon would if they continued in their absenteeism. Thus the idea seems to be they were breaking ranks from the group, they were neglecting the assembly with some regularity.

[49] While some interpret "assembling together" as referring to the society of Christians, or the church, and then think that the writer here prohibits quitting church, it is more likely, in this commentator's opinion, that the term (as is commonly interpreted) refers to the weekly public worship assembly. He also freely admits that if one misses public worship too often and for very long, he is dangerously apt to quit church altogether.

[50] In the Restoration Movement, verse 25 has often been used to promote the idea of regular or perfect attendance at the worship services. But it has often been missed that verse 24 tells us one of the most important activities that should be a central part of the service once the brethren are present. Worded another way, verse 25 tells us to assemble; verse 24 tells us what to do when we assemble. How much better is a positive attitude of helpfulness toward others than the abandonment of the assembly.

And all the more, as you see the day drawing near – The encouragement was to be more spirited, more intense ("all the more") as the "day" drew nearer. But what day is it, whose approach can be seen? (1) Some say the day of the destruction of Jerusalem.[51] The signs of the near approach of the destruction of Jerusalem had been given by Jesus (Matthew 24:3-28), and people could see these coming to pass. How disappointing and spiritually devastating it would be to go back to the Jewish religion, only to have the temple and the sacrifices abruptly ended, and that within about seven years after Hebrews was written. (2) Some say the day of the second coming of Christ.[52] When that "day" does dawn, there is a judgment to be faced, and who then would want to explain to Jesus why they had quit church? The "day" would be drawing near in the sense that Paul speaks of it in Romans 13:12, "The night is far gone, the day is at hand."[53] If it be asked how they could "see" the day of the second coming approaching, the answer is that "see" is used in a similar way at Hebrews 2:9. If they could "see" Jesus crowned with glory and honor, it would be no problem to "see" the day of the Lord was also getting nearer and nearer. (3) Some say the Lord's Day (Sunday, the "first day of the week,"[54] the regular day when the Christians assembled for worship) is the "day" that was approaching. Each week, as the day of worship comes nearer, Christians are to encourage one another to be present at the assembly.

- *A reminder of the fearful consequences of apostasy. 10:26-31*

10:26 – For – This verse begins to delineate the fearful consequences to which such "forsaking" (thus missing the encouragement and stimulation, verses 24-25) may lead.

If we go on sinning willfully -- "Willfully" is the first word in the Greek sentence, placing a vivid emphasis on it. The verse says it is "sinning," deliberately sinning, to absent one's self from the assembly as some of the readers were doing. The sin is found in the reason for the absence; namely, a deliberate choice to cease confessing Christ, a deliberate rejec-

---

[51] R. Milligan, *op. cit.*, p.284.

[52] Lightfoot, *op. cit.*, p.193. This is the view generally held by most recent commentaries and translations (RSV, NEB, TEV).

[53] This commentator is not in agreement with the scholarly reconstruction of first-century beliefs that says in the first decades after the resurrection and ascension, the believers (mistakenly) thought the Second Advent would be very soon, and only after they became disillusioned about the return did such passages as Hebrews 10:25 have to be written. Some scholars have assigned this disappointment over the apparent postponement of the Parousia as a reason why the Hebrews were weakening in their confession and becoming sporadic in their attendance. Nor does this commentator agree that some New Testament epistles (say those written earliest) present the Second Advent as being soon; and then, when it became apparent Jesus would not return soon, later New Testament epistles present a different eschatology (it will be a long time, don't grow weary in waiting!). Such a reconstruction impinges on inspiration and the truthfulness of the records. Not even Jesus knew the time of His return (Matthew 24:36), so His pronouncements alternate between soon and a long time. The New Testament writings (whether written early or later) present the same uncertainty as to the time. They are not uncertain about the *fact* of the return; only about the *time* when it would occur.

[54] The "first day of the week" was the day of assembly for early Christians (Acts 20:7; 1 Corinthians 16:2; Revelation 1:10). (This commentator has no real reason to doubt "Lord's Day" in Revelation 1:10 refers to Sunday.) See the evidence presented in the author's *Commentary on Acts*, p.764 that the early church worshiped on Sunday long before Constantine (c. AD 321) officially changed the day of worship for his whole empire.

tion of the gospel truth after it had been received. The present tense participle "sinning" indicates a repeated or continuing action,[55] not a single sin. If they continue in this sin of rejecting Jesus, if they deliberately persist in this sin,[56] the consequences are grave!

After receiving the knowledge of the truth – This language reminds us of the warning in 6:4-8. To receive the knowledge of the truth is synonymous with becoming a Christian, and the past tense verb indicates the conversion to Christianity here in view was a thing of the past. These are Christians (people who know[57] the truth[58]) who are warned about the grave danger of "sinning willfully." If "enlightened" men (Hebrews 6:4) persist in "falling away from the living God" (3:12), if they continue to abandon Christ and repudiate the new covenant which His blood inaugurated (10: 20), there is for them no way of forgiveness.

There no longer remains a sacrifice for sins – Idolatry's sacrifices never were valid. The Mosaic sacrifices, the author has shown, although divinely commanded, never took away sins. If the once-for-all sacrifice[59] of Christ is thought so worthless as to be safely ignored or abandoned, to what would a man go to get help with his sin problem? Nothing is left! If salvation is only in Christ (Acts 4:12), to abandon Christianity[60] brings final damnation.

10:27 -- But a certain terrifying expectation of judgment – This is what remains for the man who (once a Christian, now) turns his back on Jesus. The Greek word *tis* ("certain")

---

[55] This passage was destined to have repercussions in Christian history beyond what our author could have foreseen. Probably something similar to what he had written before was intended. In 2:2, despising the message spoken by the Son brings more severe penalties than despising the Law of Moses did. In 3:12 he spoke of "falling away from the living God." In 6:4-6 he wrote about the consequences of renouncing Christianity to return to Judaism. And Hebrews 10:29 likely shows that this warning deals with outright apostasy from Christ. But, as was noted in comments at 6:4-6, one of the problems the early church faced was the matter of forgiveness of sin after baptism. Using chapters 6 and 10, some in the early church taught there was no forgiveness for any post-baptismal sin. (They read the verb tense as though it were one act, rather than continuing action.)

[56] Oftentimes in our New Testament studies, we come to the expression "sins of ignorance" (cp. Numbers 15:30,31), and we have puzzled over how one decides what is a sin done in ignorance (and therefore forgivable) and what is a sin done deliberately (and therefore unforgivable). May it now be said that Hebrews 10:26ff explains what is a willful sin that is unforgivable? What the Hebrews were about to do was to deliberately repudiate Christ, to abandon the Christian religion. For that, there is no remedy. There is no other way to be saved. The fearful consequences of repudiating Christ can be nothing but damnation.

[57] The word translated "knowledge" is *epignosis*, a word which means more than mere objective knowledge (*gnosis*) of the truth. It rather denotes a full experiential knowledge of the truth.

[58] "Truth" stands for "the content of Christianity as the absolute truth" (BAG, p.35). The people in question know what God has done in Christ; their acquaintance with Christian teaching is more than superficial. Morris, *op. cit.*, p.106.

[59] "The once-for-all nature of Christ's *sacrifice* is a two-edged sword. On the one hand, it is so effective that it does not need to be repeated (Hebrews 7:27), but, on the other hand, it cannot be repeated, even if needed." G.W. Buchanan, *To the Hebrews* (Garden City, NY: Doubleday, 1972), p.171.

[60] Observe once more that "sinning willfully" is not a one-time act; it is a habit pattern. This verse does not mean the man who backslides (sins occasionally) is lost. The context is saying that a Jewish Christian (or any other Christian) who decides to *give up* Christianity and *go back* to Judaism (or any other religion), would be lost. Such a decision and resulting lifestyle is the kind of willful, deliberate, habit of sin being warned against. The only atonement that will ever be made for sin has been made -- and if a man turns his back on Jesus Christ, there is nothing left for him but hell! There is no other way to be saved. Jesus *is* the only way (John 14:6)!

is an indefinite pronoun that leaves it somewhat open to the reader's imagination[61] to fill in the terrifying[62] details of what that judgment[63] will be like.

And THE FURY OF A FIRE WHICH WILL CONSUME THE ADVERSARIES -- God's judgment on the wicked is often described as coming with fire.[64] The ASV has "fierceness of fire;" the KJV has "fiery indignation;" a literal translation might be "jealousy (zeal) of fire." That is, the fire is represented as being anxious to receive this one about to be cast into it. The fire reaches out to engulf.[65] The one who sins willfully (verse 26) is the one here designated as an adversary by God. One who abandons the Christian religion does not thereby become neutral in his relationship to God -- he becomes an *adversary*!

10:28 -- Anyone who has set aside the Law of Moses -- Verses 28 and 29 form an argument from the lesser to the greater. If it was a serious matter to break the Mosaic Law, how much more serious is it to ignore the provisions of the new covenant? The passage alluded to is Deuteronomy 17:2-7 (as shown by the words "two or three witnesses"). The sin particularly in view was the sin of idolatry after one had forsaken Jehovah.[66]

Dies without mercy – The one found guilty of forsaking Jehovah was put to death. There was no delay in executing the sentence, no opportunity for repentance and forgiveness, once guilt had been established beyond a shadow of a doubt.

On *the testimony of* two or three witnesses – When the required number of witnesses (one was not sufficient in capital cases) had established the fact of a sin of presumption (Numbers 15:30,31), the death penalty by stoning was carried out without any reprieve or right of appeal or opportunity to offer a sacrifice. No sacrifice was provided because the sin was that of rebellion against God and disregard for the Law which God had given. The guilty sinner was summarily executed.

10:29 -- How much severer punishment do you think he will deserve – The penalty is

---

[61] Although *ekdoche* has not been found elsewhere in Greek literature with the meaning "expectation" as used in our translations; that sense is rather required here and is so listed in the lexicons (e.g., BAG, p.238).

[62] The adjective *phoberos* is unusual; it occurs elsewhere in the New Testament only at Hebrews 10:32 and 12:21, and conveys the idea of "frightening." It is first of all sobering, then scary or frightening, to think what the judgment (and the sentence) of the person who repudiates Jesus will be.

[63] Some futurist interpreters think of numerous judgments in the future (e.g., the judgment of the nations, the judgment seat of Christ, the great white throne judgment). But there are no passages difficult to harmonize with the idea of one general judgment at the second coming of Christ, at which all men will be judged.

[64] See Isaiah 66:15-16; Zephaniah 1:18; Romans 2:8; 2 Thessalonians 1:7-10; Hebrews 12:29.

[65] The English translations found here for *esthio* ("eat"), such as "devour" and "consume," should not be pressed into service to defend the doctrine of conditional immortality (for the righteous) and the annihilation of the wicked, as has been done, e.g., Curtis Dickinson, *Man and His Destiny* (Lubbock, Tex.: published by the author, 1970[?]), p.26.

[66] The passage in Deuteronomy deals with one who "does what is evil in the sight of the Lord ... by transgressing His covenant, and has gone and served other gods and worshiped them, or the sun or the moon or any of the heavenly host."

more severe than physical death[67] because Jesus is greater than Moses (3:1-6) and His new covenant is greater than the old (8:6-10:18). If apostates from Israel's God suffered physical death as retribution for their deeds, how much greater should be the punishment[68] for defectors from the Son of God? The reason the punishment is more severe is because of the three terrible deeds they have done, which are detailed in the phrases that follow.

Who has trampled underfoot the Son of God – This is the first crime of which the Christ-rejecter is guilty. He treats God's *Son* (remember what Hebrews 1 said about "Son") with disdain. To "trample underfoot" is a strong expression for contempt or disdain.[69]

And has regarded as unclean the blood of the covenant – This is the second crime of which the Christ-rejecter is guilty, and which makes a "much severer punishment" suitable recompense. The "blood of the covenant" is shorthand to denote the blood (the sacrifice) which ratified, sealed, or established the new covenant, which was explained in Hebrews 9:15-20. To treat that blood as "unclean" or unholy or common is to take the position that the death of Jesus was no different from the death of any other man. Common means 'As far as I am concerned, there was nothing efficacious or atoning about His death. The covenant for which He was the sacrifice does not interest me.' 'His death did nothing for me!' is the thinking of the man who rejects Jesus.

By which he was sanctified – The meaning of "sanctified" in such a context has been explained at Hebrews at 9:13,14 and 10:10,14. It refers to making a man suitable or qualified to enter the presence of a holy God, and it was accomplished by the blood of the covenant. The man whom the writer of Hebrews has in mind as "sinning willfully" (repudiating Jesus) is one who at a previous time had been "sanctified."[70]

---

[67] Calvinistic interpreters, who must attempt to defend the doctrine of unconditional eternal security, find themselves in a peculiar difficulty here. They must explain the "much severer punishment" as something other than loss of salvation, or punishment in hell, or elsewise must give up their cherished doctrine. Not a few try to explain the "much severer punishment" as being some sort of chastening this side of death, even though the contrast with Deuteronomy 17 seems to say the punishment the writer of Hebrews has in mind for the defecting Christian is something that follows physical death (it is something more severe than death by stoning).

[68] With the words "do you think?" the writer invites the readers to work out for themselves how much more serious is the punishment of the man who once confessed Christ and then repudiates Him.

[69] The verb *katapateo* (to trample under foot, deny, despise) "denotes contempt of the most flagrant kind" (Moffatt, *Hebrews*, p.151). The source of the word picture is debated. Some think it means to treat like dirt -- as one would do when walking down a salt covered path (Matthew 5:13), or when trampling down seed that had been sown (Luke 8:5). Others think the language comes from the custom of ancient conquerors who tread on the necks of their enemies in token of their being subdued. Still others point to Greek writings where the word was used of laws or oaths that were trampled down, i.e., that were disobeyed or unkept or deliberately ignored.

[70] Because this passage, when understood of the apostate, is so difficult to harmonize with the doctrine of unconditional eternal security, it is not uncommon to find the explanation in the commentaries that the "he" who was sanctified is not the sinner but *Christ*! Such an interpretation raises more questions than it answers. Since (as Hebrews has often emphasized) Jesus never sinned, He had no need to be "sanctified" (in the sense of needing a cleansing before He was eligible to be in the Father's presence). Indeed, Jesus once said, "for their sakes I sanctify Myself" (John 17:19), but there is no instance in which He says He was sanctified *with his own blood*. The topic Hebrews is covering is the crime of the man who turns away from Jesus after once being a Christian. "He was sanctified" naturally refers to the one apostatizing, and not the Lord Jesus. Some groups

And has insulted the Spirit of grace? – This is the third crime of which the one "sinning willfully" is guilty. The word "insulted" is *enhubrizo*, and denotes personal hostility, arrogance that tries to inflict wanton injury, insolent self-assertion, to treat with contempt. The name "Spirit of grace" recalls that one of the Holy Spirit's[71] tasks is to lead men to Christ, where they find the grace they need. To have once been led to Christ, only to later repudiate Him, is tantamount to a deliberate and callous attempt to hurt or wound the Spirit.[72]

10:30 – For – With its two Scripture quotations, this verse seems to be the Biblical evidence for the assertion in 10:29 about "severer punishment" for those who sin willfully.

We know Him who said, "VENGEANCE IS MINE, I WILL REPAY" – Deuteronomy 32:35 is cited.[73] The Hebrews writer affirms the inspiration of the Old Testament passage when he tells us "God" said these words. The writer and readers of this letter "know" God through Jesus, through Scripture, and through countless evidences of His actions in history. The God who spoke these words through Moses was no stranger to the writer or the readers. "I will repay" tells us God's judgments are appropriate recompense for men's deeds, so it should not be thought that the "severer punishment" for the Christian who repudiates Jesus is too strong a statement. The Old Testament displays a terrible side, as well as a gracious side, to the revelation of God; and many times, it was His own people who suffered, not just the apostate.[74] In its original setting in the Song of Moses, the words about vengeance and requital are spoken to apostates in Israel who had sacrificed to demons and rejected the true God (Deuteronomy 32:17). How astounding that God views apostasy from Jesus in this same light, and threatens the same punishment, as to the apostates in Israel.[75]

---

try to make a distinction between professing and true Christians. They are wont to say that only professing Christians can fall away; the true ones cannot. That idea, too, is hard to square with verse 29. When God says a man is sanctified, does that mean anything but truly saved? If sanctified cannot mean simply professing, then this passage once and for all puts the lie to the doctrine of unconditional eternal security.

[71] As at 9:14, where some doubt *pneuma* ("spirit") has reference to the Holy Spirit, so some have tried to explain verse 29 as though it too were not a reference to the Holy Spirit. But in a context where the contrast is with the Law of Moses (Hebrews 10:28; cp. John 1:17), the translators are evidently correct capitalizing "Spirit."

[72] While it is true there is not much emphasis on the work of the Holy Spirit found in this epistle to the Hebrews, that is not unexpected in an epistle in which the person and work of Jesus is the particular topic of concern. Yet even the few references to the Spirit (such as here in verse 29) show the Spirit is a person, not an influence or a thing, for it is only a person who can be insulted.

[73] The quotation differs from both the Hebrew ("To me vengeance and recompense") and the LXX ("In a day of vengeance I will recompense"), yet is worded exactly the same as the other time this Deuteronomy passage is quoted in the New Testament, at Romans 12:19. Either the quotations were taken from a form of the text not extant today, or the writer of Hebrews used Romans as his source, or Paul wrote both passages. (See George Howard, "Hebrews and the Old Testament Quotations," *NovTest* 10 [1968], p.208-16.) The additional phrase, "says the Lord," appearing here in the TR is likely an interpolation from Romans 12:19.

[74] The privileges Israel enjoyed as God's covenant people meant their responsibilities were greater than those of their religious neighbors who were still living under Patriarchal rules. Therefore, their retribution would be the more severe if they gave themselves up to unrighteousness. "You alone have Me among all the families of the earth; Therefore, I will punish you for all your iniquities" (Amos 3:2). The same reasoning (greater privileges, greater responsibilities, so greater punishment) is true of the Christian as compared to the Israelite.

[75] "To Jewish readers the citation should have been all the more impressive as it reminded them that many

And again, "THE LORD WILL JUDGE HIS PEOPLE" – This second quotation is found in Deuteronomy 32:36 and Psalm 135:14. The word translated "judge" can also mean "vindicate" (give a favorable judgment). "Vindicate" is the rendering used in the RSV for those Old Testament passages where it is the deliverance of faithful people that is in mind. But even in the Old Testament, God does not vindicate His people when they are unfaithful. His impartial judgment according to righteousness demands that unfaithfulness be punished as much as that faithfulness be rewarded. Thus, the writer of Hebrews has not misused or misapplied the passage from the Old Testament in this context where "severer punishment" for willful sinners is the topic.

10:31 -- It is a terrifying thing to fall into the hands of the living God – This fourth warning passage (10:26ff) about the fearful consequences of apostasy is brought to an end with this somber warning. It is a most awesome prospect[76] to face the punitive judgment of the living God! "To fall into the hands" is to come under a person's authority and be incapable of further resistance. When that person is the "living God,"[77] such a fate is daunting.[78] This summary sentence is one of the most powerful words in Scripture.

IV. EXHORTATIONS BASED ON THE IMPERATIVE OF FAITHFULNESS TO THE SUPERIOR REVELATION MADE THROUGH JESUS, THE SON OF GOD. Hebrews 10:32 - 13:17

A. Encouragement to Endurance in the Faith. 10:32-39.

10:32 – But – The Greek word *de* ("but") sometimes emphasizes a contrast,[79] but it can

---

of their ancestors experienced the vengeance of God because they were not true spiritual seed of [faithful] Abraham. When God finally moves in retribution, His judgment will not be forgetful of the enormity of men's rejection of Christ's perfect sacrifice." Kent, *op. cit.*, p.208. [The word "faithful" was added by this commentator to correct Kent's opinion that such apostasy is only hypothetical, and could not really happen.]

[76] "Terrifying" is the same word used in verse 27.

[77] "Living God" occurs repeatedly in the Bible as a synonym for "Jehovah." The phrase is often used of Jehovah as He stands in opposition to idols. God always lives. His power is capable of being always exerted. He is not like the idols of wood and stone which have no life, and which are not to be dreaded: HE LIVES!

[78] Not a few students of the Bible are reminded by verse 31 of something David once said, recorded in 2 Samuel 24:14 and 1 Chronicles. 21:13. David had sinned when numbering the people, and God must punish sin. God gave David three options: 7 years of famine, 3 months of flight before his enemies, or 3 days of pestilence. Instead of making the decision by himself, David preferred to look to God to do right by saying, "Let us fall into the hand of the Lord, for His mercies are very great." Some have supposed the expression in Hebrews 10:31 contradicts 2 Samuel 24:14. But there is no contradiction, because the cases are not parallel. David had sinned, but he was not apostate. To the believer it is a wonderful thing to be left in the hands of God. But to fall into the hands of the Lord, after having despised His mercy and rejected His salvation, is perfectly dreadful! The punishments, too, are not the same. In David's case, it was something temporal. In the apostate Christian's case, it is something eternal ("these shall go away into eternal punishment," Matthew 25:46).

[79] If we treat it as adversative, the rest of chapter 10 is set over against what was just written about the fearful consequences of apostasy (10:26-31). After detailing the consequences of apostasy, this fourth warning passage would end on a note of encouragement to continued faithfulness. The tone would then be similar

also provide a transitional particle with no contrast intended ("now"). *De* can even be used to resume a discourse that has been interrupted.[80] This paragraph introduces the fourth major theme of Hebrews, and includes at 10:37,38 the passage from Habakkuk that forms the basis of the following appeal to faithfulness. What is needed is for the readers to give up thoughts of quitting Christ, and determine instead to live a life of faithfulness to Jesus.

Remember the former days – This reminder of how things were in the past implies (as did 5:12ff) that the people addressed have been Christians for some time. The Greek verb is a present imperative, meaning continue to remember, or keep remembering. In those early days they had done well. Are they going to do otherwise now?

When, after being enlightened – As at 6:4, "enlightened" refers to their conversion to Christ.[81]

You endured a great conflict of sufferings – Shortly after the readers had been converted, they had experienced a period of persecution. This persecution is described figuratively as a contest; the Greek is *athlesin*, from which we get our word "athletics."[82] Their enemies, or perhaps the persecutions themselves, are pictured as the opponent against whom the new converts were fighting. However, the writer's emphasis is not so much on the contest as it is on the endurance. Persecution back then[83] did not cause them to think about quitting church. Why let persecution now be such a temptation?

10:33 – Partly – This verse partially describes the "conflict of sufferings" alluded to in the previous verse. The word "partly" occurs twice in this verse: "sometimes ... at other times ..." may refer to one group of people having two experiences, or it may mean two groups ("some of you ... others of you") each with their own particular kind of suffering.

By being made a public spectacle through reproaches and tribulations – The first group had been subjected to verbal insults and other forms of pressure or severe troubles. That they were made a "public spectacle" does not have to be understood literally, as though they were actually put on display in some amphitheater, though it could have so

---

to what was found in the warning passage in chapter 6. There, after some solemn words about the impossibility of renewing apostates to repentance, the writer offers an encouraging word on how to avoid such apostasy.

[80] See Bauer-Arndt-Gingrich, *A Greek-English Lexicon of the New Testament*, p. 170.

[81] The comments on this word at 6:4 would be true here, also.

[82] The word came to be widely used of the Christian as a spiritual athlete, and it also implies the strenuous nature of the Christian's daily life in the face of the enemies of the cross.

[83] Commentators have difficulty identifying the persecution endured by the Hebrews. Some point to the persecution of the Jerusalem church that occurred after the martyrdom of Stephen (Acts 8:1-4, 12:1-3). Others, supposing the readers were Hebrew Christians living in *Jerusalem*, object to identifying the readers with that group of Christians because that persecution scattered them away from Jerusalem. However, if we identify the readers as Hebrew Christians living in *Palestine*, we have partially answered the use sometimes made of this paragraph to deny a Holy Land destination for this book. But even granting a Palestinian destination, we still are not able to identify either the exact persecutors or the exact time or place of the trials referenced in verses 32-34 from any extra-Biblical or Biblical source.

happened.[84] Used figuratively, the word means "general exposure to disgrace." This would be a painful reminder that when they accepted Jesus as the Messiah, immediately they were the brunt of attacks of all kinds by their unconverted countrymen as well as by civil and religious authorities. "Tribulations" may refer to subtle, everyday troubles and pressures, or it may refer to physical abuse as they were kicked and tortured and scourged.

And partly by becoming sharers with those who were so treated – The second group suffered, not because they were the primary objects of attack, but because of their willingness to associate with the first group as they tried[85] to carry out Jesus' instructions regarding visiting those in prison (as verse 37 will explain).

10:34 – For you showed sympathy to the prisoners – "For" tells us that verse 34 is a further explanation of what was just said about "becoming sharers" of their brothers' mistreatment. In reverse order it gives specific examples of those sufferings. Jesus taught His followers to "visit" those in prison (Matthew 25:36), and in days past the Hebrews had done just that.[86] Ancient penal systems did not provide food and clothing for prisoners. Thus, prisoners who had no means of their own were liable to starve unless their friends brought food and whatever other form of help they required. Of course, anyone visiting and aiding prisoners ran the risk of being imprisoned themselves because the persecutors could immediately identify the helper as a friend and sympathizer of the prisoner.

And accepted joyfully the seizure of your property – Not only had they been sympathetic with their suffering Christian friends, but in the spirit of Matthew 5:12 they accepted suffering when it affected them personally. "Seizure of your property" could refer to an official action by the authorities or it could speak of looting by mob action.

Knowing that you have for yourselves a better possession and an abiding one – This explains their joyful attitude at the loss of earthly possessions. Evidently the "better possession" they looked forward to was heaven.[87] The heavenly possession was better (it was worth more, and gave more comfort) and more abiding (it is not subject to rust or moth, or

---

[84] Those who argue for a Roman destination for this letter (e.g. Bruce) urged that "public spectacle (exposed in the theater)" be taken literally, referring to the persecution of the Christians in the Circus Maximus there. Such exposure was the lot of Christians during the Neronian persecution, but we have suggested in the Introductory Studies that the letter to the Hebrews antedates the Neronian persecutions.

[85] There is a meaningful change of tense in the participles. "Being made a public spectacle" (present tense) is something they were habitually exposed to. Every day they were exposed to public reproach and ridicule. "Becoming sharers" (aorist tense) suggests on some special occasion they had in heroic fashion identified themselves with some Christian prisoners, willingly and unhesitatingly accepting whatever persecution might cost, when they could have avoided any hurt by simply failing to come to their fellow Christians' aid.

[86] Several different readings appear in the manuscripts at this place. Some read "to the prisoners (on them in bonds)" (cp. ASV, NASB) and some read "on me in my bonds" (cp. KJV). In the Introductory Studies, it was noted the KJV reading tends to support the Pauline authorship of Hebrews, for during Paul's two-year imprisonment at Caesarea (Acts 24:27) the Hebrews would have had ample opportunity to minister to Paul's needs.

[87] The KJV carries the words "in heaven" after the word "you have," and though the manuscripts will hardly support this as the original reading, it nevertheless seems to be the meaning of this passage where the earthly possessions that could be seized are contrasted to future possession that cannot be taken away from them.

to petty robbers, Matthew 6:20) than all the earthly possessions they could ever amass.

10:35 – Therefore – Having recalled the inspiring record of their faith in the past, the writer now appeals to them concerning the present.

Do not throw away your confidence – "Throw away" is the opposite of "hold fast" (3:6,14; 10:23) and conveys the thought of a reckless rejection[88] of something very valuable. "Confidence" is a word used earlier in Hebrews, reminding us of the firm assurance with which the faithful Christian may approach the throne of grace (4:16, 10:19), and also of the open and fearless way believers in Jesus continue to confess Him before men (3:1-6). Neither the wonderful privilege of access to God, nor of confessing Jesus before men, should be carelessly cast aside! The readers are thus warned about losing their convictions about the truth of the Christian faith, which would result in the loss of boldness in their witness and boldness in their response to their persecutors.

Which has a great reward – The word here translated "reward" was translated "penalty" at Hebrews 2:2. There is a relationship or correlation between men's deeds in this life and the reward (or punishment) to be received in the next world. Again, we are reminded of the words of Jesus: "Blessed are you," He said, "when men hate you, and ostracize you, and insult you, and scorn your name as evil, for the sake of the Son of Man. Be glad in that day, and leap for joy: for behold, your reward great in heaven" (Luke 6:22,23). Here, the thought of reward is intended as a motivator, an encouragement to faithfulness.

10:36 – For – Once more the writer explains that "endurance" is the revealed way the readers would go about avoiding the throwing away of their confidence.

You have need of endurance – "Endurance" or perseverance is synonymous with faithfulness.[89] What was done in the past may be commendable, but Christians "need" more than a good past record. It is something absolutely necessary (not just merely desirable) that the Christian persevere in his commitment to and confession of Jesus.

So that when you have done the will of God – "Have done"[90] looks back over the Christian's whole life from the standpoint of the final judgment. When God's record shows a

---

[88] Such reckless throwing away can be illustrated by the conduct of terrified soldiers who in the day of battle threw aside their shields and turned their backs and ran from the enemy. It was the sentiment of the ancients that such behavior by soldiers was so dishonorable that even if they escaped and came home, they were not allowed to be present at the sacrifices nor to attend the public assemblies of the townspeople.

[89] See comments on the word "patience" at Hebrews 6:12. "Patience" is also a good translation of *hupomone*, provided it is understood that what is denoted is not a passive reception of whatever comes upon us, but is rather an active, positive, deliberate action. It is taking adverse circumstances and using them as stepping stones or springboards to greater deeds of service for Christ.

[90] Because of a misunderstanding of the argument in Romans about "works of law" not saving, not a few commentators have written paragraphs here to "safeguard" against the idea that "works" or "deeds" are any kind of a condition of salvation at all. More will be said on this whole matter when in chapter 11 we examine what is involved in the "faithfulness" God expects of His people. Suffice it to say here that "having done the will of God" and "faithfulness" are not two different and antithetical ideas. You cannot have one without the other.

Christian's whole walk was one that could be characterized as doing of His will, then the believer will hear, "Well done, good and faithful slave!" In this context, what God wills may be that Christians "suffer according to the will of God" (cp. 1 Peter 4:19), or it may be the "need of endurance" even if they are persecuted. While the specific thing willed may not be the same in each case, we remember the writer has spoken of Jesus Himself as being anxious to do the will of God (Hebrews 10:7,9). Now he makes the point that Christ's followers must be similarly focused.

You may receive what was promised -- The thing promised is doubtless what was described earlier (Hebrews 4:1,9) as "entering His rest," or "a better possession" (10:34) or "a great reward" (10:35). After a life of faithfulness, there is a rest for the people of God! Let the readers be bold in their confession, let them be faithful in their service, and this rest and its great reward will be theirs. Hebrews 10:36 recapitulates the leading ideas in the epistle – the need for faithfulness (rather than quitting Christ), the doing of God's will (as revealed in the better covenant), and the reception of the promised rest.[91]

10:37 – "FOR – The writer's exhortation to "endurance" is supported by a quotation from the Old Testament which teaches the same truth.

"YET IN A VERY LITTLE WHILE – These words are taken from two Old Testament passages. Verse 37a apparently is taken from Isaiah 26:20; verses 37b and 38 are from Habakkuk 2:2-4. In its original setting in Isaiah, "a very little while" had specific reference to Jesus' second advent, a point the writer of Hebrews also seems to have in view in the context.[92] The language "very little while" points to a short period; the Greek expression *mikron hoson hoson* is unusual, literally "a little, how very, how very"). The argument is that the readers ought not throw away their confidence (hang on just a little longer!), lest their behavior during the "very little while"[93] cost them a heavenly reward.

"HE WHO IS COMING WILL COME -- Milligan argued this "coming" has reference to the destruction of Jerusalem in AD 70, not the second coming of Jesus.[94] We are inclined

---

[91] R.C. Foster, in *Classnotes on Hebrews and James* (Cincinnati: Standard Publishing Co., 1925), p.52.

[92] We have interpreted what the Hebrews writer wrote about "receive what was promised" and "have done [past tense] the will of God," as though we were standing at the final judgment. That interpretation rests in part on the Isaiah passage in its original setting, and also on the interpretation of the Habakkuk passage about to be quoted and studied in verses 37b-38.

[93] In comments on Hebrews 10:25, we have already commented on the (in our view) mistaken notion of some that for a few decades in the early church even the Scripture writers anticipated the second coming in their own lifetimes. The same point is often found in comments on these passages from Isaiah and Habakkuk. In reply, if in Isaiah's time (8th century BC) the second coming was but "a very little while" away, how much shorter was the time when the New Testament was written.

[94] Luke 17:26-30 and Matthew 22:7 may be examples of passages that indeed refer to the then-future destruction of Jerusalem. The city was to be destroyed when it was because Christ in heaven moved and caused events to happen ("armies to be sent") in the physical world. Milligan's presentation (*op. cit.*, p.293) that Hebrews 10:37 cannot be a reference to the second coming further rests on what he finds in earlier epistles of Paul, such as 2 Thessalonians, and on his deliberately- and studiously-held post-millennial eschatology.

not to agree, even though not a few scholars have been troubled by the writer's interpreting Habakkuk as though it were Messianic.[95] The same Habakkuk passage is treated as Messianic in Romans 1:17 and Galatians 3:11; there is no reason to question its Messianic import here in Hebrews. "He who is coming" or the coming One was a common designation of Messiah, even at His first coming. Because of the close association of the Isaiah and Habakkuk passages, we think this passage speaks of His second coming.

"AND WILL NOT DELAY – Perhaps the context's emphasis is on this phrase. Should the readers ask "How long must we endure?" the answer is, "The time is not long. Isaiah says it will be 'a very little while'; Habakkuk says 'He who is coming will not delay.' "

10:38 – "BUT MY RIGHTEOUS ONE SHALL LIVE BY FAITH – "My[96] righteous one" speaks of the kind of person *God* thinks of as "righteous." The man who is "faithful" is "My (kind of) righteous one," says God. This mention of "faith" (= faithfulness) leads onward to the most sustained treatment of the subject in the New Testament. The term "faith" occurs again in the next verse, and then is repeated often throughout chapter 11. If "faith" (endurance) and "shrinking back" are antonyms, "faithfulness" is a translation that catches the idea at this place, and this verse sets the tone for chapter 11. The "righteous one" is the obedient believer who has been justified by faith (see the argument of Romans). The condition God looks for before He counts a man as "righteous" (justified) is "faithful-ness." "Live" covers both the Christian life now and the heavenly reward hereafter.[97]

"AND IF HE SHRINKS BACK – The person being warned about shrinking back is the same person designated as "righteous" in the previous phrase. It is possible for a person to

---

[95] In its original setting, Habakkuk was faced with the coming of the Chaldeans (Habakkuk 1:6), who would be God's instruments of judgment on Judah. What Habakkuk wanted to know of God is what judgment would He visit on the Chaldeans. The prophecy in chapter 2 was given in answer to that question, to assure the prophet judgment would eventually come. With the same kind of freedom that we assume when quoting freely from Scripture, the Hebrews writer freely quotes from the LXX of Habakkuk without altering the sense in any basic way. The chief differences are as follows: (1) There is an additional article *ho* added in Hebrews; making the passage more specifically Messianic than the LXX is at first reading. (2) The writer of Hebrews transposes the last two clauses of Habakkuk 2:4. (3) The writer inserts an emphatic *mou* ("My") before the word "righteous one." The writer's use of the text of Habakkuk is very much in the same spirit as the LXX. While the Hebrew text of Habakkuk refers to a vision of deliverance that will not tarry, the LXX speaks of a personal deliverer: "Though he should tarry, wait for him; for he will surely come, and will not tarry" (*The Septuagint Version, Greek and English Old Testament with the Apocrypha* [London: Samuel Bagster, nd] p.1107).

[96] There is considerable variation in the manuscripts at this place regarding the use and location of the pronoun "My." The Hebrew text does not have the possessive in Habakkuk, while the LXX uses it with "faith" rather than with "righteous one." Among the Greek manuscripts of Hebrews, some (P[46], Sinaiticus, and Alexandrinus) have the pronoun with "righteous one"; one (Ephraemi) has it with "faith"; and some (P[13] and the corrector of Ephraemi) omit it altogether. In some of the Greek manuscript copies of Hebrews, one might assume assimilation of the reading "my faith" as found in the quotation of Habakkuk in Romans 1:17 and Galatians 3:11. The real problem is whether the original writer of Hebrews put the pronoun after "righteous" or whether our present manuscripts that so read are already showing a copyist's mistake. Fortunately, the argument of the passage does not hinge upon any one of the variant readings.

[97] The student is directed to the writer's commentary on Romans, where there are copious notes of explanation about this important prophecy found in Habakkuk and quoted often in the New Testament. The Christian should not miss the meaning of this key passage!

be once justified and later to shrink back and be lost. Through Habakkuk, God warned of this possibility hundreds of years before Christ first came. As has already been noted, the Hebrews writer reverses the order of the two clauses from Habakkuk. He finishes with the words about shrinking back because he wants to make special application of that idea to his readers who were, it seems, seriously contemplating shrinking back from Christ and returning to the Jewish religion. Referencing Habakkuk, the writer warns his readers such behavior is a good way to fall out of God's pleasure.

"MY SOUL HAS NO PLEASURE IN HIM – God says He finds no pleasure in the one who "shrinks back." What pleases God is "endurance" (verse 36), or faithfulness. To incur God's displeasure is the same as to incur His wrath. If in Habakkuk's time the righteous man who pleased God was the one faithful and tenacious in clinging to God, then fidelity and fortitude must be even more required of the follower of Jesus who wants to please God.

10:39 -- But we are not of those who shrink back to destruction -- This encouragement to endurance in the faith ends like the others before it, with a clear note of hope and optimism. The writer of Hebrews expresses hope that neither he nor the readers will "shrink back." To couch an exhortation in words of "hope" is a very strong way of wording an exhortation; it makes the appeal as exceedingly personal (from one heart to another) as can be expressed in human language. "Shrink back" has a rich word picture background.[98] It means to draw in or contract, as someone might furl a sail, or as a dog tucks its tail. Then it means to avoid, or abstain from. It then is used of a person who has never completed anything he started, one who has stuck at nothing. That's the idea here: Christians are not to be quitters, but are to stick at it, to persevere in faithfulness. The use of the word "destruction" (*apoleia*) as the threatened punishment for those who shrink back makes it clear the judgment in view in this context is not just temporal chastening of God's people, but the final destruction in hell. *Apoleia* is the regular word used of perishing in hell.

But of those who have faith to the preserving of the soul – In harmony with what we read everywhere else in Scripture, "faithfulness" is the condition on which salvation is granted. The Greek word *peripoiesin* has several meanings: "obtaining" (1 Thessalonians 5:9), or "possession" (1 Peter 2:9), or "preserving." The word is used here in contrast to "destruction," so to possess or preserve one's soul is the same as salvation and entrance into the eternal rest. Though different Greek words are used, we wonder whether the writer of Hebrews here reflects something Jesus once said, "By your endurance you will gain your lives (souls)" (Luke 21:19).[99] In the verses following in chapter 11, we shall see that "faith" (= faithfulness) has always been the way to please God. A man's security (i.e., the preservation of the soul) is conditioned on faithfulness.

---

[98] The verb "shrink back" is used in Galatians 2:12 to describe the timid conduct of Peter. After certain Jews came from Jerusalem, Peter "withdrew" and no longer ate with Gentiles. See also the use of the verb in the middle voice in Acts 20:20,27.

[99] The context for Jesus' statement was the coming destruction of Jerusalem in AD 70 and the need in the meantime for His followers to be faithful. While the topic of Hebrews 10 appears to be the second coming rather than the destruction of Jerusalem (cp. footnotes #92 and 93, above), the principle is the same. Jesus' followers still need to exhibit faithfulness.

B. A Reminder that Faithfulness Has Always been the True Characteristic of God's People. 11:1 - 12:3

1. Preliminary view of the consequences of faithfulness. 11:1-3

11:1 – Now faith is – Verse 1 is *not* a definition[1] of faith, but a description of what faith does. In the light of 10:39, we affirm that "faithfulness" (as in Matthew 23:23, NASB) is a better translation of *pistis*.[2] In fact, if it were so translated, no one would think verse 1 is a definition of faith. Because a man was determined to be faithful, see what happened! The implication is 'See what will fail to be accomplished if you readers prove to be faithless (if you "shrink back," 10:39)?'

The assurance of things hoped for – Perhaps a better translation for *hupostasis* ("assurance") would be title deed.[3] A man who is faithful to what God has commanded has a title deed to all God has promised for the future. Hebrews has had much to say about "hope"; see 3:6, 6:11, 7:19, 10:23. Most writers are reminded of Revelation 2:10, "Be faithful until death, and I will give you the crown of life." Such an appeal to continued faithfulness with its corresponding reward is what the writer of Hebrews is emphasizing.

The conviction of things not seen – In this place, one's theology is likely to influence both translation and comments. Calvinist theologians prefer the translation "evidence" (as the KJV, taking *elengchos* objectively) since they tend to teach that "faith" is something God gives to the elect, and is therefore "proof" (evidence) of salvation. Non-Calvinistic theologians, who have learned from Scripture that saving faith comes by hearing, and that man is not wholly passive in salvation, tend to prefer the translation "conviction" (as the NASB, taking the Greek word subjectively), and then they tend to write about an inward persuasion that has an effect on the soul. Faithfulness[4] (when a man can look at his life in light of God's revelation in the Word and in Christ and see a consistency in doing right) will result in the inner persuasion that what God has promised continues to be his possession.

---

[1] We might offer as a *definition* of faith the one suggested by E.J. Carnell *(An Introduction to Christian Apologetics* [Grand Rapids: Eerdmans, 1952], p.66). "Faith is whole-souled trust in God's Word as true because of the sufficiency of the evidence." You commit your whole life to what God has said because you can count on His Word.   An easier definition is, "Faith is habitually doing what God says." In the different dispensations (Patriarchal, Mosaic, Christian) what God has said (commanded, prohibited, even promised) has often differed, but the response He expects from mankind has always been the same – persistence in doing what He has said. That's faith!

[2] We affirm that chapter 11 is very closely connected with the last verses of chapter 10, where a determination to be faithful, rather than "shrink back," is the attitude inculcated.

[3] We've had *hupostasis* before in Hebrews, and with different meanings. For its use in the objective sense ("nature") see notes at 1:3. For its use in the subjective sense ("assurance") see notes at 3:14. If we reject the idea of title deed, then we might observe that *hupostasis* means that which stands under, and thus Hebrews 11:1 says that faithfulness is the substructure of all the Christian life involves. If a man misses the supreme importance of this topic (faithfulness) he has missed the heart of the Christian lifestyle. He is building his life on shifting sand, not on some solid substructure!

[4] Preachers and teachers, commenting on this phrase, must be careful lest they present "faith" as merely a subjective thing, something akin to credulity. That's *not* the *pistis* that is a "conviction of things not seen"!

11:2 – For by it – That is, by the "faithfulness" described in 10:39ff. Verse 2 gives a reason for what was just said about "faith" being "assurance" and "conviction."

The men of old – The Old Testament heroes about to be listed in chapter 11.

Gained approval – They were immortalized in Scripture. God testified in the pages of Scripture that these people were pleasing to Him. Their faithfulness is the key to having God's approval. And the point of the verse is that similar faithfulness will result in God's approval for the readers of Hebrews.

11:3 – By faith we understand – If we render *pistis* as faithfulness all the way through this section, then verse 3 says, 'Because we are determined to be faithful, we exercise the mind by way of discernment ... even from the very first page of Scripture!'[5] When God speaks, it is truth; that's the way it really is. Faithfulness involves taking God at His word.[6]

That the worlds were prepared – The word translated "worlds" literally means "ages." God is responsible not only for the physical universe but also for its progression of ages – Patriarchal, Mosaic, Christian. If we render it "worlds," there is something similar to Genesis 1:1, "God created the heavens and the earth." The expression at the close of the verse, "things which are visible," tends to cause us to think that the created world (rather than the ages) is in the writer's mind.

By the word of God – "Word" here translates *rhema*, so it is doubtful this is a reference to Jesus (as John 1:1ff calls Him the "Word" – but "Word" is *logos*.) Rather, this expression in Hebrews refers to God's spoken word. He spoke and it was done! See Psalm 33:6.

---

[5] This commentator admits that verse 3 offers the most difficulty in his attempt to translate *pistis* as faithfulness throughout this entire section. On first reading, something less than persistence in lifestyle (i.e., faithfulness) seems to be the meaning of *pistis*, at least when it comes to understanding and appreciating the Old Testament accounts of the creation of the universe. Is this not a verse where a more suitable translation of *pistis* would simply be "faith" -- i.e., a mental assent? Perhaps, but on further reflection, is it not just possible that such a simple explanation causes us to miss the whole point of the verse?

[6] Once more, the thoughtful student will observe that one's definition of "faith" will greatly color a person's comments on the various verses. Those who think of "faith" as merely mental assent will have one set of comments. Those who think of works of faith as naturally resulting after a man is initially justified by faith will have a completely different set of explanations. This commentator has attempted to include several factors in his conclusion about the meaning of "faith" in this classic passage: (1) He has tried to let the context define what is meant by "faith," and then tried to carry that idea through all the verses that are intended to be an illustration of the thesis about the necessity of "faith." (2) He has also tried to take into account the fact that not only does one find the simple dative case ("by faith"), but we also read occasionally "according to faith" (*kata pistin*) and also "through faith" (*dia pisteos*). It is doubtful that all three constructions mean the very same thing, though some commentators affirm they do. (3) In addition, as one reads through chapter 11, he notes the times when what God commanded or expected might (on first sight) seem unprecedented and even unreasonable, yet the heroes persisted in doing what God said and let Him work out the seeming difficulties. (4) Furthermore, in a number of instances the fact that the reward for their obedience was not experienced in this lifetime must be taken into account. Now, in light of these factors, this commentator has opted for the explanation offered; namely, that "by faith" means "Because they were determined to be faithful to God" the following remarkable things happened, and these men had their names inscribed in Holy Scripture as an example and encouragement for us. "Because they were determined to be faithful to God" is the unifying note that ties all these verses together -- it is the one idea running through all the verses.

So that – As a result of God's speaking, the visible world came into being.

What is seen – Our physical universe.

Was not made out of things which are visible – Creation *ex nihilo* is herein affirmed, and by it the writer of Hebrews repudiates first-century ideas about the origin of the created universe.[7] It was by the creative fiat of God without using previously existing materials.[8] The point of verse 3 seems to be that unless we deliberately and consciously take into account what God has revealed about Himself (i.e., He is a Supreme God Who not only created but who sustains the visible universe and is moving it toward a goal), we may well miss one of the greater incentives to faithfulness. Over and over, the following examples will underscore the truth that God does what He says He will do. The ancients did not miss this fact – it was an important component in their determination to be faithful to Him.

2. Faithfulness in the age before the flood. 11:4-7

11:4 – By faith Abel – Abel's history is recounted at Genesis 4:1-15. "By faith" – because he was determined to be faithful – is why Abel acted as he did on that memorable occasion.

Offered to God a better sacrifice – Not that it was of greater monetary value,[9] but it was accepted by God because it was offered "by faith." Matthew 23:35 and 1 John 3:12 tell us Abel was "righteous" and his deeds were righteous. Abel's heart was right in the sight of God, and his offering was a demonstration of his faith. This verse implies that the idea of sacrifice was of divine origin, for "faith" always comes by hearing a revelation from God. Without such a revelation, there is no way that what Abel did could have been "by faith."

Than Cain – By implication, the problem with Cain's offering is that he was not being faithful to what God had taught. A lack of faithfulness always gets a man in trouble with God.

Through which – This pronoun can refer either to "faith" or to "sacrifice." Since the topic of chapter 11 is faithfulness, we incline to the understanding that "which" refers to "faith."

He obtained the testimony that he was righteous – It was from God that this testimony came. Faithfulness is the condition God looks for when He would pronounce any man "righteous" – i.e., in right standing with God.

---

[7] Milligan, *op. cit.*, p.302, shows some of the ancient evolutionary ideas (Thales, Plato, Aristotle) repudiated by this statement about creation.

[8] If a man is ever to know what really happened at creation, since none of us were there to see it, we are utterly dependent on God to tell us. And if we reject His revelation, we are left without any certain understanding of earth's or human origins.

[9] The use of "better" to characterize Abel's sacrifice has puzzled commentators. Some prefer to translate it literally, saying Abel gave God "more" -- i.e., greater value, greater quantity.

God testifying about his gifts – Abel's faith was demonstrated by his offering and by the fact that God accepted his offering. God looks on the heart, not just at the gifts.

And through faith, though he is dead, he still speaks – Abel speaks to us as we read in the account of his life about of the vital importance of faithfulness in God's sight.

11:5 – By faith Enoch – See Genesis 5:21-24. Again, 'by faith" means 'because he was determined to be faithful.' Faithfulness is the condition on which God confers His blessing.

Was taken up so that he should not see death – Enoch passed into the intermediate state without experiencing physical death. "Walked with God" (Genesis 5:22) suggests something similar to what happened in Elijah's case (2 Kings 2).

AND HE WAS NOT FOUND BECAUSE GOOD TOOK HIM UP – This expression indicates a search was made for him by his friends, but they could not find him. Compare 2 Kings 2:17 in the case of Elijah.

For he obtained the witness that ... he was well pleasing to God – Genesis 5:24 in the LXX (instead of "walked with God") reads "was well pleasing to God." The next verse shows it was Enoch's *faithfulness* that pleased God.

11:6 – And without faith it is impossible to please *Him* – The Old Testament record does not tell us Enoch was faithful, so the writer of Hebrews goes on to explain why he can speak of Enoch's "faith" so confidently. Enoch's faithfulness is implicit (implied, though not actually expressed) in the Genesis account. The Old Testament may not specifically mention Enoch's "faith," but it does say he was "pleasing to God." Since it is not possible to please God without faithfulness, Enoch must have had it. Faithfulness is absolutely necessary. He does not say simply that without faith it is *difficult* to please God; he says without faith it is *impossible* to please God. Hebrew readers, are you listening – no one can please God unless he is faithful!

For he who comes to God – Perhaps "comes to God" speaks of prayer, worship, entrance into His presence, or having right standing with God.[10] "For" gives a reason for the statement just made about the necessity of faith on man's part if he is to be pleasing to God.

Must believe that He is – No meaningful coming to God is possible without first believing that He exists. Such "belief"[11] is based on the kinds of evidences that are the substance of many Theistic arguments within the field of apologetics.

---

[10] One "who comes to God" renders the participle of the verb *proserchomai*, the word used in Hebrews 10:1 of coming near to God in worship.

[11] Here is one passage where "belief" and "faith" are not quite synonymous terms, for in this context "faith" speaks not just of an awareness that God exists, but rather of a life characterized by consistently living in harmony with His revealed will. On this whole matter of the content of the "faith" that saves, as well as a presentation of the different grammatical constructions in the original (i.e., *pisteuo* followed by an accusative case v. *pisteuo* followed by a prepositional phrase) see Special Study #16 in the author's *Commentary on Acts*.

And *that* He is a rewarder of those who seek Him – Our belief must also include the idea that God keeps His promises. He maintains a moral government of the universe. Enoch's faith led to a reward including the blessing that he "walked with God." "Seek" is a present participle, indicating continuous and repeated action.

11:7 – By faith Noah – See Genesis 6-9 and Ezekiel 14:12-14. As before, "by faith" means 'because he was faithful to what God had spoken on other occasions, and was determined to continue to be faithful. '

Being warned *by God* – The Greek verb is *chrematizo* and it speaks of divine revelation.[12]

About things not yet seen – I.e., the flood. Perhaps also rain and a sea-going vessel. Certainly he had never seen anything like a worldwide judgment (Genesis 7:11,12).

In reverence prepared an ark – "Reverence" is Godly fear. He paid careful heed to God's warning to get ready for the flood. Noah found grace in the eyes of the Lord because of his faithfulness, so God warned him. See Genesis 6:14-16 concerning the ark.

For the salvation of his household – Faithful obedience to what God said led Noah to build the ark with this purpose in mind, namely, to ensure that his family (wife, three sons, and their wives) would survive[13] the flood.

By which he condemned the world – As in verse 4, where "which" was ambiguous, so here "which" could refer either to the ark or his faith condemning the world. (Noah was also a preacher of righteousness, 2 Peter 2:5, and he certainly must have told his contemporaries why he was doing such an extraordinary thing as building an ark there on dry land.) His faith (lifestyle) was so different from the disbelief of his contemporaries[14] that their habitual disobedience stood out in stark contrast and their guilt was inexcusable.

And became an heir of the righteousness which is according to faith – "Righteousness ... according to faith" (right standing with God on the condition of faithfulness) is something that happens in this life. Compare Romans 1:17 and 3:21,22. God imputes righteousness to a man when He sees the looked-for condition He has set – namely, faith. Noah is the first man to be called "righteous" in the Bible (Genesis 6:9). See Genesis 7:1 also for the fact that Noah was "righteous" during his life on earth before the warning and the coming of the flood. Then, after a life of faithfulness, Noah became an "heir" – he began to enjoy the inheritance reserved for the righteous. There is an inheritance to be enjoyed after an earthly life characterized by "righteousness" is over, and the Old Testament people knew about it.

---

[12] The same word is translated "called" (divinely called) at Acts 11:26. See further comments there on this Greek word in the author's *Commentary on Acts*.

[13] "Salvation" here seems to refer to deliverance from disaster, more than it does to another meaning the word sometimes has, salvation from the guilt and consequences of sin.

[14] "The world" here likely signifies the totality of mankind in his day who did not obey God.

3. Faithfulness in the Patriarchal Age. 11:8-22

11:8 – By faith Abraham – The account of the faithful life of Abraham is found in Genesis 11:26 - 25:11.   Abraham was not sinless perfect, but he was a man whose life was characterized by a determination to be faithful ("by faith").[15]

When he was called – Abraham's call before he left Ur of the Chaldees is recorded in Nehemiah 9:7,8 and in Acts 7:2,3. His later call to leave Haran is recorded in Genesis 12. Perhaps the reference here in Hebrews is to his call to leave Ur. We perceive that Abraham was a man of faith before God ever called him to leave Ur.[16]   That life of faithfulness simply continued, and the man grew in faith as the years passed.

Obeyed by going out to a place which he was to receive for an inheritance – It was only after Abraham left Ur and Haran and arrived in Canaan, a trip of over 1500 miles, that Abraham was told the land would belong to his descendants (Genesis 12:6,7).

And he went out, not knowing where he was going – At the beginning, Abraham was ignorant of the exact country to which God was leading him. Perhaps the idea of such an unseen destination is related to the "things not seen" and "hoped for" that Hebrews 11:1 holds out for the Christian.

11:9 – By faith he lived as an alien in the land of promise – The years of living in the land came and went, yet Abraham continued to be faithful to God. There was no quick fulfillment of God's promise to Abraham. Abraham never had a permanent residence (he always was an "alien") in the promised land.[17] Milligan shows Abraham sojourned for 100 years in Canaan – all the while being an example of faithfulness. A hundred years! Hear that my Hebrew readers!

As in a foreign *land* – Abraham had to live in the land of promise as though he were living in a "foreign land." He had no rights. He and his household lived in tents, in temporary dwellings. The whole land had been promised to him, but to the end of his life the only piece of the country he owned was a field he purchased as Sarah's burial place (Genesis 23). God "gave him no inheritance in it, not even a foot of ground" (Acts 7:2,5).

---

[15] Abraham is one of the great heroes of God. The Jews prided themselves on their descent from Abraham, and the great patriarch is mentioned a number of times in the New Testament as one who had faith and who acted on that faith (Acts 7:2-8; Romans 4:3; Galatians 3:6; James 2:23). In line with this, the writer of Hebrews gives more space to Abraham than to any other individual in this list. He sees Abraham as an excellent example of what he has in mind. It was a faith that could not always see where it was going -- an obedience when God's promises and God's commands seemed contradictory. Abraham just went on doing what God asked of him. That is faithfulness!

[16] "When he was called" translates a present participle that indicates a very prompt obedience. "He obeyed the call while (so to say) it was still sounding in his ears." B.F. Westcott, op. cit., p.358.

[17] "The promised land" (literally, "the land of promise") is an expression found only here in the Bible. As the context shows, the reference is to the land we call Canaan or Israel. (Verse 10 may also show that the "promised land" includes a reference ultimately to heaven, too.)

Dwelling in tents – "Dwelling" is *katoikeo*, to settle down, dwell permanently. "In tents" denotes a very temporary kind of dwelling place. All during his stay in the land of promise, he moved first here to there, then to another place – Shechem (Genesis 12:6), Bethel (12:8), Hebron (13:18), Beersheba (22:19).

With Isaac and Jacob – "With" means 'as did.' It does not say all three were contemporaries living under the same tent, though they might have. It does say they all lived in tents.

Fellow heirs of the same promise – God renewed the same promise ("In your seed all the nations of the earth shall be blessed") to each of them (Genesis 26:1-5 and 28:10-15) that He earlier had made to Abraham.

11:10 – For he was looking for the city which has foundations – This verse is the secret behind Abraham's determination to be faithful. The Greek says "He *kept* looking for the city which has *the* foundations." It is the same city we Christians have described for us by John in Revelation 21:9-27, especially verse 14. The implication is that the patriarchs had information about the future (things not yet seen, but hoped for) revealed to them beyond what is recorded in detail in Genesis or any other part of the Old Testament. Still, when speaking of heaven to come, the Old Testament prophets often spoke of "Jerusalem" – with which one should compare Hebrews 11:16, 12:22, 13:14, and Galatians 4:26 – for these verses will help us understand what the Old Testament prophets were predicting when they spoke of "Jerusalem" to come.

Whose architect and builder is God – "Architect" (*technites*) is the word for planner or designer. "Builder" (*demiourgos*) is a word meaning craftsman, master builder, maker. The expression is intended to stress the excellent and abiding quality of the heavenly city.[18] This city, the heavenly Jerusalem, is regarded in Scripture as the final home of God's people, and it has been prepared since the foundation of the world (Matthew 25:34). We wonder, was it built at the time when God created the "heavens" (plural) and the earth?

11:11 – By faith even Sarah herself – See Genesis 17,18. Some writers have felt uncomfortable trying to harmonize this statement about her faithfulness ("by faith") with Genesis 18:10-15, where we are told she laughed (in unbelief?) following the announcement that Isaac's long-promised birth would now finally occur just a year later. But it should be remembered she was a woman of 90 years, and considerable faith was involved in her cooperation in the birth of Isaac.[19] Furthermore, faithfulness is never a condition synonymous with being sinless perfect. It would be entirely possible for her to doubt at one time or another in her life and still be one the tenor of whose life could be called faithful.

Received ability to conceive – Note the marginal reading. The Greek points to the male's

---

[18] Other references in Hebrews to this heavenly city are 11:16 where God is said to have prepared it; 12:22 where it is called the "city of the living God, the heavenly Jerusalem"; and 13:14, which refers to the city "which is to come." Galatians 4:26 speaks of "Jerusalem above."

[19] Some manuscripts read, "Sarah, being barren" (*steira*). The manuscript evidence is probably against including this characterization of Sarah at this place in the text.

sexual function, depositing of seed, not the female's. Several ideas are advanced to explain this seeming difficulty. (1) Perhaps we should read "with Sarah" (dative, rather than nominative[20]). (2) Perhaps *eis* should be rendered 'in connection with' or 'in regard to.' Thus, Sarah received power with regard to Abraham's depositing seed. We remember, in either case, that Sarah was barren (sterile, Genesis 11:30, Galatians 4:27) and past age of childbearing (Romans 4:19). Isaac's birth was miraculous.

Even beyond the proper time of life – Sarah was 90 (Genesis 17:17 compared with 18:11) and Abraham was 99 when God stepped in and the promised heir was conceived.

Since she considered Him faithful who had promised – Sarah (or is it "Abraham"?[21]) was convinced God keeps promises. God had promised a son. A son they would have!

11:12 – Therefore, also, there was born of one man – Abraham, who was 100 years old by the time Isaac was born (Genesis 17:1,17 and 21:5), is the "one man." "Therefore, also" introduces the inevitable result. Because God had promised, and because Abraham and Sarah were faithful, the consequence naturally followed.

And him as good as dead at that – For "at that" the marginal reading is "in these things." Abraham was "dead in these things" as far as men were ordinarily concerned. Abraham had about as much probability of fathering a son as a dead man would have.[22]

As many descendants **AS THE STARS OF HEAVEN IN NUMBER, AND INNUMERABLE AS THE SAND WHICH IS BY THE SEASHORE** – As far as Abraham's "descendants" being innumerable, this is in accord with the promise given to Abraham recorded in Genesis 15:5 and 22:17. Both stars and grains of sand were proverbial for multitude, so the general meaning is that Abraham's descendants would be too many to count. The New Testament helps us see that not just physical descendants are involved, but spiritual as well (Galatians 3:29).

11:13 – All these died in faith – The writer pauses for a moment in his treatment of Abraham to emphasize some general conclusions about "all these (people)," i.e., those spoken of just previously – Abraham, Isaac, Jacob, and Sarah. "In faith" is a different Greek construction than the "by faith" that we have been reading at the beginning of many of these verses. The preposition here is *kata*, in accord with. They didn't die "by faith," but in a manner consistent with faith. That is, they were faithful to death. They remained true to God all their lives. Hebrew readers, are you listening?

---

[20] In the Uncial manuscripts, there would have been no iota subscript, so it is not possible to determine with certainty whether the Greek words ΑΥΤΗ ΣΑΡΡΑ should be read as nominative (no iota subscript), or as dative (with an iota subscript under the last letter of each word).

[21] The verb is a third person singular, and could be translated "he" (Abraham) as well as "she" (Sarah).

[22] What of his sons by Keturah (Genesis 25:1ff)? Does it not suggest Abraham was 120 when he married her and produced this whole new family? F.F. Bruce (*in loc.*) argues "It is reading too much into the text to suppose that he married her after Sarah's death; in 1 Chronicles 1:32 she is called `Abraham's concubine'." Compare the author's notes in his *Commentary on Romans* at Romans 4:19.

Without receiving the promises – They had received verbal promises from God, but they had not received the *things* promised; namely, the land, the coming of Messiah. (There is no contradiction to Hebrews 6:15, where it reads "he obtained the promise" – for that refers only to the birth of Isaac.)

But having seen them and having welcomed them from a distance – The patriarchs understood that what God promised was to be fulfilled far out in the future – and that their full participation in these promises would require life after death (and resurrection, too?).

And having confessed that they were strangers and exiles on the earth – Abraham made this confession at the burial of his wife (Genesis 23:4). Jacob spoke these words to Pharaoh (Genesis 47:9). A "stranger" (pilgrim) is a traveler with a destination. The patriarchs kept confessing that they were on a journey to another place, the heavenly city. They were men of steadfast faith.

11:14 – For those who say such things – I.e., that they are "strangers" and "exiles."

Make it clear that they are seeking a country of their own – A fatherland is a fixed and permanent residence. Such a confession as these men made was a clear indication that on earth they had not found a dwelling place that could provide permanent satisfaction. A fatherland is a true homeland, from which one springs, and where one really belongs. Not even the land of Canaan fulfilled all that God had promised; only heaven can do that. The next verse explains that these men were looking for the city that has the foundations. Their hearts were not in Mesopotamia, or even Canaan, for that matter. Single mindedly, they walked the path that led to the New Jerusalem – that's faithfulness!

11:15 – And indeed, if they had been thinking of that *country* from which they went out – One should not think that because Abraham did not settle in Canaan, nor that he did not regard Canaan as his "country," that he still regarded Mesopotamia as his fatherland. That wasn't the country he was longing for.

They would have had opportunity to return – If the patriarchs had desired to return to Ur of Chaldees, or to Haran, there was nothing that prevented doing so. They had plenty of opportunity – for example, when Abraham sought a wife for Isaac, or when Jacob spent 20 years in Mesopotamia – but Mesopotamia was not the fatherland.

11:16 – But as it is, they desire a better *country* – They sought a country better than Mesopotamia or Canaan, not an earthly one, but a heavenly one. This verse is the conclusion of the discussion about the fatherland for which they were looking.

That is a heavenly one – Their true homeland wasn't on earth at all! "The eternal values involved in the promises of God made them willing to regard their earthly experience as a pilgrimage, and kept them from despair even when it was evident that death would overtake them before fulfillment came."[23]

---

[23] Homer Kent, *op. cit.*, p.229.

Therefore God is not ashamed to be called their God – Jehovah frequently designated Himself as "the God of Abraham, Isaac, and Jacob" (Exodus 3:6; Acts 7:32). Because these men acted in faith, it was fit and proper that He should be a Benefactor, Protector, and Friend to them, to show His approval of them by calling Himself their God.

For He has prepared a city for them – This is the same city mentioned in Hebrews 11:10. It is also the same as the "better country" spoken of earlier in this verse. The reminder that God has prepared[24] a city emphasizes that God rewards those whom He approves.

> The example of the patriarchs is intended to guide the readers of the epistle to a true sense of values. Like the elect sojourners of the Dispersion addressed in 1 Peter, they are to live as "aliens and exiles" (1 Peter 2:11). Like the Philippians to whom Paul wrote, their "citizenship" is in heaven (Philippians 3:20) ... There is, of course, no difference between the heavenly country and the city of God. Words could hardly make it clearer that the patriarchs and the other men and women of God who lived before Christ have a share in the same inheritance of glory as is promised to believers in Christ of New Testament times.[25]

11:17 – By faith Abraham, when he was tested – The writer now returns from the patriarchs in general to Abraham in particular. The "binding of Isaac" (Genesis 22) is referred to in two places in the New Testament – here in Hebrews and at James 2:21ff. In both places it is given as an example of faith, obedient faith, faithfulness. The word *peirazo* can be translated either tempted or tested. It is not that Abraham was tempted to sin, but was subjected to a test, to a trial to test the genuineness of his faith. Of what the test consisted has been answered in several ways: (1) The natural revulsion any father would feel toward killing his own son; (2) Abraham is too old to have another child – he was already old when Isaac was born, and that took a miracle! (3) The apparent contradictions in revelations given to Abraham: Isaac is the heir, the line, the promised seed v. kill him![26]

Offered up Isaac – The perfect tense verb – past completed action with present continuing results – perhaps speaks of the deed as being completed in Abraham's mind, though events would so be arranged that it was not done in actuality.

And he who had received the promises – Abraham was the receiver[27] of the promises.

---

[24] "Prepared" – Do not miss the use of the past tense verb here. It is not that God will one day prepare their city, but that He has already done so.

[25] F.F. Bruce, *op. cit.*, p.307.

[26] We are apt to see this as a conflict between Abraham's love for his son and his duty to God. But for the Hebrews writer, the problem was Abraham's difficulty in reconciling the different revelations made to him. God had promised a numerous posterity through Isaac; yet now God was calling on him to kill Isaac as a sacrifice. How then could the promise be fulfilled? Though he might not understand the how, Abraham knew how to obey, and he was determined to be faithful to what God asked of him. (Adapted from Morris, *op. cit.*, p.122.)

[27] The word for "received" is *anadechomai*, an unusual word, found again in the New Testament only at Acts 28:7. Moulton and Milligan *(The Vocabulary of the Greek Testament* [London: Hodder & Stoughton, 1963], p.32) find many examples of its use in the papyri in the legal sense of undertake, assume. They say "the

Was offering up his only begotten son – Josephus tells us (*Ant.*I.13.2) Isaac was 25 years old at the time of the sacrifice. "Only begotten" is not always the proper translation for *monogenes*. Ishmael had been born previously to Isaac, and others were fathered later by Abraham. But there was something special, something unique, about Isaac – of all the sons, he was the one through whom the "descendants" ("seed") was to come.[28]

11:18 – *It was he* **to whom it was said, "IN ISAAC YOUR DESCENDANTS SHALL BE CALLED"** – We have already alluded to the fact of the seemingly contradictory revelations. The son to be sacrificed is none other than one through whom the "descendants" (who for so many years had been promised) were to come. This is the very one he was in the process of offering when God stayed his hand (note the second use of "offering" in verse 17 is an imperfect tense verb in the Greek).

11:19 – He considered that God is able to raise *people* **even from the dead** – Abraham treated it as God's problem. It was for God, and not for Abraham, to reconcile His promise and His command. The solution to the seeming contradiction, as Abraham viewed it, was that God would raise Isaac from the dead, once Abraham had killed him in obedience to God's command. Thus he was able to say to the servants left behind to guard the pack animals, "We will go yonder and worship and *we* will return to you" (Genesis 22:5). Abraham's anticipated solution to the problem is all the more remarkable when it is remembered that he had no precedent to appeal to. As far as the record is concerned, there had never been any such thing as a resurrection from the dead!

From which he also received him back as a type – For "as a type"[29] the Greek reads "in a parable," that is, figuratively speaking. It was obviously not a literal resurrection, but as Abraham had given him up for dead, his receiving Isaac back was a type of resurrection.

11:20 – By faith Isaac blessed Jacob and Esau – Genesis 27:1 - 28:5. Because he was being faithful to God, Isaac blessed Jacob and Esau.

Even regarding things to come – The blessing promised to Jacob (Genesis 27:29) did come true, as did the blessing promised to Esau (Genesis 27:40).[30] God must have put

---

predominance of this meaning suggests its application in Hebrews 11:17. The statement that Abraham had 'undertaken' or 'assumed the responsibility of' the promises would not perhaps be alien to the thought." Abraham was not passive; he undertook the responsibility of being the man through whom God would work out His promise of a coming Messiah.

[28] There are times in the New Testament where *monogenes* does mean the "only begotten son" or only offspring of the parents (Luke 7:12, 8:42, 9:38). The term *monogenes* is also used of Jesus as the only one like Him that the Father has had (John 1:14,18, 3:16,18, 1 John 4:9). Because of what the Bible says elsewhere about who Jesus is, we should beware of versions like the RSV which translate *monogenes* simply by "only."

[29] This unusual expression has led many to suggest that the sacrifice of Isaac is a type of the sacrifice of Christ – including a literal death and resurrection. And it was on the same mount, for Mount Moriah (where Abraham went to sacrifice Isaac) is the same hill we call Calvary.

[30] The trickery by Jacob to get the blessing is seen by some as a difficulty here, even tending to mitigate against the statement that Isaac did it "by faith." But it must be recognized that Isaac did believe the promises God made to Abraham, then renewed to him, and he wanted to transmit that blessing to his sons.

these words into Isaac's mouth! The ultimate difference in the blessings is that the one to Jacob was spiritual, and the other one to Esau was earthly.

11:21 – By faith Jacob – Genesis 47:28 - 49:33.

As he was dying – Even in his dying hours, Jacob did not waver in his faithfulness. He believed God would fulfill His promises, and so acted in harmony with what God had said.

Blessed each of the sons of Joseph – Just why these two sons, Ephraim and Manasseh, are singled out in Hebrews, when Genesis shows Jacob blessed *all* his sons, is not clear. Perhaps it was to show the grandsons, born in Egypt, to an Egyptian mother, were just as important as the sons Reuben and Simeon (cp. Genesis 48:5). Jacob also bestowed the preferential blessing on Ephraim, the younger son, in spite of the protestations of Joseph.

And worshiped, *leaning* on the top of his staff – Genesis 47:31 in the LXX reads "staff" rather than the Hebrew "bed."[31] We should picture an old man, leaning reverently on his staff,[32] as old men do, to help support himself. It should also be observed that this "worshiping" took place at a time *before* the occasion when he blessed Ephraim and Manasseh; namely, when Joseph had sworn to his father that he would not bury him in Egypt.

11:22 – By faith Joseph – Genesis 50:22-26. Joseph is another Old Testament example of how men who are being faithful to God act.

When he was dying, made mention of the exodus of the sons of Israel – Joseph also was a sojourner, looking for the fulfillment of God's promises. Joseph spent the whole of his life, apart from the first 17 years, in Egypt, but Egypt was not his homeland. Even when the rest of his family came down to Egypt at his invitation, he knew their residence in that land would be temporary. God promised, even before the beginning of the Egyptian captivity, that the people would come back to Canaan to serve Him there (Genesis 15:13-16). God had predicted the exodus[33] years before, so exit from Egypt they would!

And gave orders concerning his bones – Joseph made those around his death bed swear they would carry his bones up with them to the promised land whenever the exodus was made (Genesis 50:25). Hundreds of years later at the exodus, Moses faithfully carried out Joseph's wishes (Exodus 13:19).

---

[31] The consonants for "bed" and "staff" in the Hebrew are the same, and the Masoretic text has mistakenly (?) added the vowel pointing for "bed." Beware. The Latin Vulgate reads that Jacob "adored the top of his staff," i.e., he was bowing down to his staff as to an image! This is not the only place in Hebrews that the Vulgate rendering has led the Roman Church down a wrong path.

[32] There is no word for "leaning" in the Greek, but there is a preposition *epi* (on, "upon") and so we must supply something like "leaning" to make sense of the expression "*on* the top of his staff."

[33] "The departing" in the Greek is "exodus" -- the event we call the Exodus of the children of Israel from Egypt. With Isaac, Jacob, and Joseph (note that each made statements about what would happen after their deaths), the significant thing was their firm conviction that their physical deaths would not make any difference in whether or not God carried out His purposes. God would continue to work His will long after they had passed from the scene of history, so they could speak with confidence about what would happen after they had died.

4. *Faithfulness in the Mosaic Age. 11:23-40*

11:23 – By faith Moses – Exodus 1,2. It was the faith of his parents,[34] Amram and Jochebed, which is here referred to. Exodus 2:2 says it was the mother who hid Moses. Harmonizing Hebrews with Exodus, we learn that the father concurred in and helped in this hiding – all because they wanted to be faithful to God.

When he was born, was hidden for three months by his parents – While the Hebrew text at Exodus 2:2 has the mother as the active party in circumventing Pharaoh's decree, the LXX says that both parents hid him (in the LXX the verbs in 2:2 are plural).

Because they saw he was a beautiful child – Compare Acts 7:20, where Stephen speaks of him as "lovely in the sight to God." There was something in the child's appearance, or something in what God had told the parents about the child ('This baby is special to Me'), that caused the parents to believe God had special plans for Moses. Amram and Jochebed had some appreciation of the divine purpose that was to be fulfilled through Moses – and because they were faithful people, they acted to preserve the child alive.

And they were not afraid of the king's edict – Pharaoh had called for the execution of all newborn sons (infanticide), Exodus 1:22. Had their defiance of the law been discovered, Amram and Jochebed would have been severely punished; but "they[35] were not afraid." Faithful men have always obeyed God rather than men, when the two conflict. When the three months were up, they no longer hid the baby at home, but committed him to an ark of bulrushes, floating on the Nile, where he was seen and adopted by the daughter of Pharaoh (Exodus 2:3-10).

11:24 – By faith Moses – It is no longer the parent's faithfulness, but the faithfulness of Moses himself that is the topic of consideration. The writer of Hebrews will recall five different occasions on which Moses' faithfulness to God was significantly evident.

When he had grown up – Moses was about 40 years old when he fled Egypt following his killing of an Egyptian (Acts 7:23). The writer of Hebrews seems to be saying the decision reached by Moses (when he "refused to be called the son of Pharaoh's daughter") was that of a mature man, not the decision of a child or rebellious adolescent. In full knowledge of what he was doing, because he wished to be faithful to God, he threw in his lot with the downtrodden Israelites.

Refused to be called the son of Pharaoh's daughter – There is little agreement among scholars of Scripture and Egyptian history on the identity of this "daughter." Philo iden-

---

[34] We are aware that some believe Exodus 6:20 does not speak of parents but only his ancestors. We are not inclined to agree -- thus we call Amram and Jochebed his parents.

[35] Is there an implied contrast to the Hebrew readers, who were frightened by the severe penalties Christians were facing at the hands of unbelieving Jews?

tifies her as Hatshepsut.[36] Another tradition identifies her as Thermuthis.[37] Whoever the daughter was, it meant Moses could become the next Pharaoh of Egypt whenever the daughter's father had died. Moses might have stayed in Egypt, and his name could have been perpetuated in history as one of the greatest Pharaohs who ever lived – but it would have been a reputation beneath what he in fact attained by making the great refusal! Whether this refusal was an official repudiation of some prominent position offered to him or merely was implied when he identified himself with the slaves (unmistakable proof that he was a Hebrew, not an Egyptian) is nowhere recorded.

11:25 – Choosing rather to endure ill-treatment with the people of God – Perhaps this verse is an explanation of Moses' refusal referred to in the previous verse. He could not identify himself with both the Israelites and the Egyptians; he had to choose one or the other. By worldly standards, the choice he made would seem to be nothing but folly. But Moses knew those slaves of Pharaoh were a people of destiny, appointed by God; and he himself would be a part of that destiny.

Than to enjoy the passing pleasures of sin – It is doubtful that the word "sin" indicates that Moses, while living in the court of Egypt, spent his time in riotous living and vicious self-indulgence. But the privileges and advantages of one in his position provided enjoyment in stark contrast to the life of Pharaoh's Hebrew slaves. Nor does this passage say such privileges and advantages as are attached to high rank or political power are sinful in themselves; they can be used very effectively to promote the well-being of others and help the underprivileged. Rather, sin is transgression of God's revealed will. Once Moses knew God's revealed will, it would have been sin for him to stay in the court of Egypt; to remain would have meant repudiation of his God-appointed work as Israel's deliverer (Acts 7:25). This kind of enjoyment resulting from the sin of abandoning God's will and God's people is what Moses refused. (It is probably true, from this passage, to say there is a temporary pleasure or enjoyment in sinning – but it is only temporary.)

11:26 – Considering the reproach of Christ – Compare Hebrews 13:13. Suggested meanings: (1) Perhaps the reproach Moses suffered was the same kind of reproach Jesus

---

[36] Philo, *Life of Moses*, I.13. According to the data furnished by the Old Testament itself, the exodus occurred 480 years before the 4th year of Solomon's reign (1 Kings 6:1). Solomon's 4th year can be fixed at 966 BC which yields a 1447-6 BC date for the exodus, a date this commentator accepts without question. Moses was 80 years old at the exodus (Exodus 7:7), so he must have been born, hidden, found, and adopted by Pharaoh's daughter c. 1527 BC. According to the generally accepted Egyptian chronology, in 1527 BC, Thutmose I would have been Pharaoh, Pharaoh's daughter was Hatshepsut, and the Pharaoh of the exodus was Amenhotep II. However, according to Artapanus (quoted by Eusebius), the Pharaoh who ruled upper Egypt when Moses was born was Khanefrere (Sobek-hotep IV) and the woman who found Moses was named Merris, the daughter of Pharoah Palmanuthes who ruled in the Delta and Goshen. Manetho's King List and the Royal Canon of Turin name Dudimose as Pharaoh of the exodus. (Since the traditional chronology cannot be squared with ancient records, perhaps the chronology needs revision. Until more work is done in this area, there is no way to be sure of the actual names of the Pharaoh or the daughter involved with Moses.)

[37] See Jubilees 47:5, and Josephus, *Ant.* II.ix.5. Intertwined amongst all this debate is also the question of the date of the exodus. On the basis of the currently accepted chronology of the Egyptian kings, one would hold to a 1225 BC date for the exodus if he were to identify Thermuthis as the daughter of Pharaoh who adopted Moses (cp. what is said in footnotes #36 and #39, and also consult the author's *Commentary on Acts* at 7:18.)

Himself suffered; (2) Perhaps it is a general expression to denote sufferings endured for the cause of revealed religion; (3) Perhaps it speaks of reproach suffered on account of Christ; (4) Perhaps there is reference to sufferings that fell on Moses because he was God's anointed; (5) Perhaps it is a reminder that Christ was present among God's Old Testament people and suffered along with them. This commentator might opt for #3. Moses did understand a great deal about the coming of Messiah (Deuteronomy18:15,18), though the time when all this was first revealed to him is not made clear in the Old Testament. Even Abraham possessed an awareness of coming Messianic events (John 8:56), and this knowledge was passed on to his descendants. The Messiah was known to be coming, and to help prepare for Him Moses and others were willing to suffer (Psalm 89:50,51). The phrases "ill-treatment with the people of God" and "reproach of Christ" are certainly intended to reflect the situation being faced by the readers of Hebrews. Will they be as faithful as Moses in the face of similar treatment?

Greater riches than the treasures of Egypt – To get some idea of the wealth and opulence of the 18th dynasty, see the accounts of the treasures found in Tutankhamen's tomb,[38] remembering that, according to generally accepted Egyptian chronology, Tutankhamen was a later Pharaoh in the same dynasty that Moses would have been in.[39] Moses made a deliberate choice: he saw more worth, greater value, in the reproaches suffered for Christ than in the gold and silver of Egypt. There is a wealth inherent in the reproach of Christ, a wealth explained by the next phrase.[40]

For he was looking to the reward – This tells us why Moses made a choice to put the treasures of Egypt beyond his reach. It was not personal dissatisfaction in Egypt, nor even the escape of his people to Canaan, so much as he was determined to share in the ultimate reward to be experienced in the life to come. Moses had the same "city" in mind that Abraham and the other patriarchs did (Hebrews 11:10,13-16).

11:27 – By faith he left Egypt – Moses left Egypt twice – once when he fled to Midian (after killing the Egyptian), and once when he led the exodus. Since Exodus 2:14,15 shows the first flight was because he feared the wrath of the king, we might opt for the exodus being the time in view in this verse.[41]

---

[38] See National Geographic's *Ancient Egypt*, p.20ff, and *National Geographic Magazine*, Mar.'77, p.305ff.

[39] This identification of the 18th dynasty as the one Moses was involved with is based on the traditional reconstruction of the list of Egyptian kings, and also assumes a 1447 BC date for the exodus. If continuing study and research on the Egyptian king lists causes adoption of a different numbering for the dynasties (and studies by Velikovsky, Courville, and Rohl may result in such a renumbering), then the statement that Tutankhamen and Moses were involved with the same dynasty may need to be modified. Still, Tutankhamen's is a fair representation of the "treasures of Egypt" during most of the dynasties.

[40] While Moses knew what the "treasures of Egypt" were worth, they were not as valuable as the "reward" that follows a life of faithfulness to God. Moses had a right sense of values!

[41] Several commentators give neat summaries of the arguments pro and con for both of the occasions when Moses left Egypt. The reader who wishes to pursue this may find such convenient listings either in Kent, *op. cit.*, p.240,241, or in Leon Morris, *op. cit.*, p.127.

Not fearing the wrath of the king – The wrath of Pharaoh was aroused immediately after Israel's departure, and Moses certainly must have anticipated it (Exodus 14:5). But he did not fear it, for he was confident in his Protector.

For he endured – Hear this, Hebrew readers! Moses endured in faith! Let Moses' example challenge and encourage you to remain faithful.

As seeing Him who is unseen – The participle can be understood as giving a reason for Moses' actions: he saw God. "The Old Testament has a good deal to say about Moses' close relationship with God. 'The Lord would speak to Moses face to face, as a man speaks with his friend' (Exodus 33:11; cf. Numbers 12:7,8). This close walk with God sustained Moses through all the difficult days."[42] Moses followed where God led, trusting Him to protect the chosen people from the human forces arrayed against them. In fact, he trusted God to use means not always present to human eyes when danger or trouble came.

11:28 – By faith he kept the Passover – Better, he *instituted* the Passover, and the perfect tense verb implies that it has been kept (celebrated) ever since.

And the sprinkling of the blood – Using hyssop to dip the blood of the lamb out of the containers it was caught in, the blood was sprinkled on the doorposts and served to protect the homes of the Israelites from the death of the firstborn (the tenth plague, see Exodus 12.) This "sprinkling of the blood" is another illustration of faith. Nothing in the previous experience of either Moses or the Israelites presaged this action. Had there ever been anything like the passing over by a death angel, or the sprinkling of blood as defense against such a plague? Moses had nothing to go on but his knowledge that it was God Who had directed him. Doing what God says, taking Him at His word, is the essence of faith.

So that he who destroyed the firstborn might not touch them – The identity of the destroyer is disputed. Exodus 12:23 attributes the plague to "the destroyer" while Exodus 11:4 attributes the smiting of the firstborn to God Himself.[43] "He who destroyed" was an angel sent as an agent of God.

11:29 – By faith they passed through the Red Sea – Exodus 14:21-29.[44] Who is included in "they" who are here called "faithful"? Since a vast part of the nation perished because of unbelief (Hebrews 3:12,18,19, 4:2,6,11), some have thought only the leaders – Moses, Aaron, Caleb, and Joshua – are here included in "they." Others have urged that there was a portion of the whole nation who remained true to the faith.

As though *they were passing* through dry land – With a wall of water on both sides, the

---

[42] Morris, *op. cit.*, p.127.

[43] Consult commentaries at 1 Corinthians 10:10 concerning the identity of the "destroyer."

[44] See notes at Acts 7:36 in the author's *New Testament History: Acts,* for detailed comments about the crossing of the Red Sea, as well as certain mediating positions offered by liberal theologians. J.W. McGarvey's *Lands of the Bible,* p.438ff, has a delightful description of the probable location of this historic event.

people who followed God's indicated plan walked across the sea bed just as they would walk across land where there was no water.

And the Egyptians, when they attempted it, were drowned – Pharaoh and his chariots, attempting to follow the same channel through the sea (Exodus 14:26,27), were destroyed to the last man (Exodus 14:28), swallowed up as the walls of water crashed back over them.

11:30 – By faith the walls of Jericho fell down – Joshua 6:12-20. Here is another example of God's using means not visible to human eyes. God told them what to do, and they endured for all seven days. Remember, nothing happened on days 1 to 6. Only a firm belief that God would do what He said can explain why the Israelites behaved ("by faith") as they did.[45]

After they had been encircled for seven days – That is, after Israel had marched around the city each day just as God instructed. "Faith" is continuing to do what God has said.

11:31 – By faith Rahab – Joshua 2:1-24, 6:22-25. She became the great-grandmother of Jesse, the father of David, and one of the ancestors of the Messiah (Matthew 1:5).[46]

The harlot – Some have softened the word (*porne*, prostitute) into inn-keeper, or hostess. But there is no reason to take the word other than literally.[47] That she is here called "faithful" implies she repented of her old ways, changed her lifestyle, and was adopted into the commonwealth of Israel. We would affirm she has changed *before* the spies were welcomed into her home, for she already knows a great deal about Jehovah and the marvelous victories He accomplished years earlier in the plagues and at the Red Sea (Joshua 2:9,10). Just as Moses sang (Exodus 15:1ff) and just as God had said ("that my name may be declared throughout all the earth", Exodus 9:15,16 KJV), the news about what God had done preceded Israel to Canaan, and already had borne fruit in the changed life of Rahab.

Did not perish along with those who were disobedient – This speaks of the other inhabitants of Jericho. They resisted God's will – a will that was by now well-known, as evidenced in Rahab's words, "we have heard ...." No specific act of disobedience by the other inhabitants of Jericho is recorded, but if Rahab had enough revelation to become a woman of faith in Jehovah, so did they.[48]

---

[45] Is there, in this allusion to the fall of Jericho's walls, another implication that reason may not always see the wisdom of what God asks or commanded be done? Yet men are to continue to do what God has said – and let God work out the apparent difficulties.

[46] The New Testament says Rahab was the wife of Salmon, and the mother of Boaz. How we are to explain the Jewish tradition that has Rahab marrying Joshua and becoming the ancestress of eight priests (Tal. *Megillah* 14b), this commentator is not able to tell.

[47] The Hebrew word translated "harlot" (*zanah*) signifies a secular prostitute, not a temple prostitute.

[48] "Rahab is certainly a rebuke to unsaved people who give excuses for not trusting Christ. 'I don't know very much about the Bible,' is an excuse I often hear. Rahab knew very little spiritual truth, but she acted on what she did know ... Another excuse is, 'What will my family think?' Rahab's first concern was *saving* her family, not opposing them. She stands as one of the great women of faith." W. Wiersbe, *Be Confident*, p.128.

After she had welcomed the spies in peace – The fact that Rahab lied to the men who were pursuing the spies (Joshua 2:4,5) has caused some people difficulty. They wonder about Biblical ethics that, at times, permit lying, while at the same time depicting the liar's lifestyle as being one of faith. In Old Testament times, strict truthfulness was not likely known as a necessary virtue. We have another similar case of lying in the Old Testament, when Michal lied to Saul's messengers in order to save David's life (1 Samuel 19:11ff). The person who serves God honestly, up to the measure of his knowledge, is blessed and encouraged.[49] Rahab, at great personal risk, wanted to be identified with God's people, so she hid the spies while acting in accordance with her new belief.

11:32 – And what more shall I say? – The writer cannot continue to give every example of faithfulness in such detail[50] After all, scrolls on which books were written were only so long!

For time will fail me – The writer has amply made his point about how God looks for and rewards faithfulness. To save time, he simplifies by grouping the following examples (not chronologically, but, we suppose) by office – judges, kings, and prophets. He uses bold strokes to paint the picture.[51]

If I tell of Gideon – It has been noted that the masculine gender of "If I tell" indicates the writer of Hebrews was male, thus ruling out Priscilla as the author.[52] Gideon's history is described in Judges 6,7.

Barak – Judges 4,5.

Samson – Judges 13-16.

Jephthah – Judges 11,12.[53]

Of David – The kings of Israel are represented by one, the illustrious David. See 1 Samuel 13 to 2 Samuel 7.

---

[49] Such Old Testament passages ought not to be used by men (who have God's New Testament Scriptures) to defend the sophistry that the end justifies the means or that little white lies are sometimes acceptable.

[50] Depending on how *ti* is translated (it can be either what? or why?), the question says, 'What more shall I say?' or 'Is there any need to say more?'

[51] Beginning Bible students can find a good, detailed summary, with the pertinent Old Testament passages where the men's lives are recorded, either in Milligan or in the *Westminster Dictionary of the Bible.*

[52] See the Introductory Studies to Hebrews, for an in-depth study of the problem of human authorship of this book.

[53] "Calvin points out there were defects in the lives of these four (just) named people. Gideon was slow to take up arms; Barak hesitated and went forward only when Deborah encouraged him; Samson was enticed by Delilah; and Jephthah made a foolish vow and stubbornly kept it. Calvin comments (in loc.), 'In every saint there is always to be found something reprehensible. Nevertheless although faith may be imperfect and incomplete it does not cease to be approved by God'." Morris, *op. cit.*, p.130. Calvin's comment may need a bit of rewording – faithfulness and sinless perfection are not equated in the Bible – but the general thrust is correct.

And Samuel and the prophets – Samuel was the last of the judges and the first of the prophets. There was considerable personal risk when Samuel anointed David as king (1 Samuel 16:13), but he did it because he was faithful to what God had revealed.

11:33 – Who by faith conquered kingdoms – "Who" speaks of those specified in the previous verses and others like them. Joshua subdued Canaan; Gideon the Midianites; Jephthah the Ammonites; David the Philistines, Amalekites, Jebusites, Edomites. "By faith" might better be translated "through faith."[54] "The achievements of these heroes of faith stand enshrined in Scripture as evidences of God's power, and also of God's honoring of those who will trust Him and do His will."[55]

Performed *acts of* **righteousness** – Perhaps it speaks of personal lives that were characterized by righteous conduct (just as God had revealed), or perhaps it speaks of official policies of these Israelite leaders (cp. 2 Samuel 8:15, where David administered "justice and righteousness for all his people."

Obtained promises – It may mean they obtained verbal promises from God, or it may mean they obtained the blessings promised by God. There is no contradiction with Hebrews 11:13,39 (which reads they "did not receive what was promised") since the thing being promised in the various verses is not the same.

Shut the mouths of lions – Daniel (Daniel 6:16-23), David (1 Samuel 17:34,35), Samson (Judges 14:5,6), and Beniah who killed a lion in a pit on a snowy day (1 Chronicles 11:22) come to mind. God was blessing these men because they were being faithful to Him.

11:34 – Quenched the power of fire – Shadrach, Meshach, and Abednego (Daniel 3:13-30). Their faithfulness was honored, even to the extent that they got to meet Jesus in the furnace with them (Daniel 3:25).

Escaped the edge of the sword – It might refer to emerging unscathed from battle, or it might refer to personal escapes from execution, as in the case of Elijah who was delivered from Jezebel (1 Kings 19:1-3), or Elisha who was delivered from Jezebel's son Jehoram (2 Kings 6:15-17), or Jeremiah who escaped Jehoiakim (Jeremiah 36:19,26).[56]

From weakness were made strong – They were enabled to perform exploits beyond their natural strength. Samson's feats of strength are well known. Hezekiah (2 Kings 20; Isaiah 36-39) was raised from a dangerous sickness by God. Clement of Rome (I Clement 55:3) speaks of Esther as an example of a woman who was made strong.

---

[54] Until now, the writer has used the dative "by faith" (with one case of *kata pistin*, "according to faith," accusative case). Now there is a change of construction to "through faith" (*dia pisteos*, genitive). The NASB's rendering of both the dative and genitive constructions as "by faith" does not reflect this change in the Greek.

[55] Kent, *op. cit.*, p.248.

[56] One writer's suggestion that "escaped the edge of the sword" means they ran away to avoid being executed, seems out of character with the context.

Became mighty in war – Think of Joshua, Barak, David.

Put foreign armies to flight – The Philistines, Ammonites, Moabites, Assyrians, and several invaders who were routed throughout the time covered by Old Testament history are included in this summary statement. Time and again a small number of Israelites (think of Gideon's 300, or of the tiny armies of Israel "like two little flocks of goats", 1 Kings 20:27) fought at God's direction against vastly superior forces and defeated them.

11:35 – Women received *back* their dead by resurrection – One of the most perplexing problems facing the exegete of Hebrews 11 is whether or not this and the following verses reflect events before Malachi's time (and the close of the Old Testament canon), or whether the writer of Hebrews reflects events in the intertestamental period.[57] Since none of the following examples *requires* a reference to the Apocrypha, this commentator is hesitant to say the writer of Hebrews has inter-testamental examples of faithfulness in mind as he writes the remainder of chapter 11. The widow of Zarephath (1 Kings 17:9-24) and the Shunamite woman (2 Kings 4:8-37) are examples of women who saw a resurrection from the dead in their families.

And others were tortured – Notice the emphasis changes from achievements resulting from faith to a willingness to suffer for their faith. Not everyone was delivered. Sometimes, "through faith," others accepted torture rather than release in order that they might gain a better resurrection. Is this shift of emphasis something the Hebrew readers needed to consider, implying they have not till now been very willing to suffer for their faith, if, indeed, they are seriously considering abandoning the Christian religion in favor of returning to Judaism? "Tortured" (*etumpanisthesan*) means to stretch and torture on the tympanum (a drum or wheel). The victims were stretched, then beaten to death with rods. The rods would cut deeper and the gashes, open to the air, would increase the pain and shock, eventually resulting in the death of the person being tortured.

Not accepting their release – They would be asked to quit their faith in Jehovah; if they did so, they were promised that the torture would stop.[58]

In order that they might obtain a better resurrection – A resurrection better than what? Better than the resurrection just spoken of in the first part of the verse (performed by Elijah and Elisha)? Or is there a contrast between the final resurrection of the just, and the deliverance from death offered to these victims if they would just recant? Or is there a

---

[57] The importance of this question can be understood with but a moment's thought. It has often been given as one of the arguments for the omission of the Old Testament Apocrypha from the canon of the Bible that those works were never quoted by Jesus or the apostles. That argument is true only if the following examples in Hebrews 11 are *not* taken from the Apocrypha. If this is an allusion to the Old Testament Apocrypha, then we may need to restudy, and perhaps revise, our estimate of the canonicity of those intertestamental books often found in Catholic editions of the Bible, but not (usually) in Protestant editions.

[58] "Not accepting their release" literally is "not having accepted redemption" (*apolutrosis*). It is important to give that word its regular meaning if we are to understand this phrase. The people were not offered unconditional freedom. There was a price they were expected to pay -- and that price was renunciation of their faith in Jehovah. It was too high a price to pay for release as far as the faithful were concerned.

contrast between the final resurrection of the just and the unjust? Those who failed in their faithfulness will find themselves raised from the dead, but among the unjust. Not a good prospect! (Also observe that this language implies the Old Testament martyrs had revelation about the final resurrection from the dead and the glories to follow. Indeed, "better resurrection" may imply they knew *all* would be raised, but that the prospects of the unfaithful after the resurrection are grim, much more so than torture or painful death now.)

11:36 – And others experienced mockings and scourgings – Elisha was mocked (2 Kings 2:23), as were others.[59] The word *empaigmos* often implies cruel mockery, derisive torture, brutality. Scourgings were beatings in which whips (not rods) were used. Jeremiah endured such twice (Jeremiah 20:2, 37:15).

Yes, also chains and imprisonment – Hannani (2 Chronicles 16:7-10), Micaiah (1 Kings 22:26,27), and Jeremiah (Jeremiah 20:2, 37:15, 38:6) are examples in the Old Testament.

11:37 – They were stoned – Zechariah, the son of Jehoiada the priest, was so killed in the temple court (2 Chronicles 24:20,21). Tradition had it that Jeremiah too suffered such a fate.[60] Stoning was a characteristic Jewish form of execution, so what is implied here is that the faithful sometimes suffered at the hands of their own countrymen.

They were sawn in two – According to the Talmud, Isaiah was so executed during the reign of Manasseh, king of Judah. The same is recorded in Justin Martyr, *Dialog with Trypho*, c.120, and in pseudepigraphical literature also.

They were tempted – This clause has given commentators much trouble, since it seems rather mild in the midst of the other tortures listed. In fact, a manuscript variation exists at this place, some omitting any word at all (see the marginal note in NASB).[61] Some have conjectured we should read "they were burned" instead of "they were tempted," (a change of one letter in the Greek), but there is no manuscript authority for such a conjectural emendation. If we read "tempted," it likely is the temptation to apostatize presented to the martyrs just before they were killed. Considering the eternal destiny consequent on such a failure in faithfulness, this is not something that should be considered mild.

They were put to death with the sword – We are told in verse 34 that some escaped the sword, but not all did. 85 priests were slain by Doeg (1 Samuel 22:18). A number of God's prophets were slain in the time of Ahab and Jezebel, about which the prophet Elijah complains (1 Kings 19:9,10). The prophet Urijah was brought out of Egypt to king Jehoiakim, "who slew him with a sword" (Jeremiah 26:23).

---

[59] Again, some commentators are confident that verses 36-38 speak of the period of time following the age of the Old Testament prophets – the intertestamental period, the time of the Maccabees – and their references and illustrations of such mistreatment of God's people will reflect references to the Apocrypha. See comments in footnote #57 on this matter.

[60] Tertullian, *Scorpion Antidote* 8.

[61] RSV and NEB omit any word at all here. ASV, NASB, Phillips read "tempted."

They went about in sheepskins, in goatskins – Though such garments were the normal dress of certain prophets (1 Kings 19:13, 2 Kings 1:8), it is obvious the writer of Hebrews is saying the persecuted faithful had nothing else to wear after they had been driven from their homes and been despoiled of their possessions.

Being destitute – They lacked what most would consider as the barest necessities of life.

Afflicted – Troubled, distressed, burdened, oppressed. Think of the additional work piled on the Hebrews in Egypt; or think of the thankless actions toward the faithful by the very ones for whose benefit the faithful ministered.

Ill-treated – Maltreated, tormented. This evil, too, may have been inflicted on the faithful by their fellow countrymen who did not appreciate what the faithful were trying to do for them.

11:38 – (*Men* of whom the world was not worthy) – This is the letter writer's comment. To tell the great, the mighty, the wealthy, the rulers of the world that they were not worthy of the society of such heroes is the very opposite of the attitudes of those who despised the heroes. The despisers thought they were too good to be found in the company of those they afflicted and ill-treated. But when it comes to benefiting their own society, the despised and ill-treated group of servants of God was of greater real worth than all the rest of humanity put together. This parenthetical note also suggests that it was by the grace of God such heroes had been sent to help Israel – who hadn't earned or deserved such help.

Wandering in deserts and mountains and caves and holes in the ground – This description resumes the list of hardships God's people endured while they were being faithful to Him. "Deserts" are uninhabited places (the Greek does not necessarily denote sand and dunes, as the English word does). David fled to the mountains to get away from Saul. Caves were used by Obadiah to hide 100 prophets from the wrath of Jezebel (1 Kings 18:4,13) and by Elijah (1 Kings 19:9). "Holes in the ground" abound in Palestine; they were intended for hiding places for valuables, for granaries, and cisterns. That men had to use such for their homes indicates the meager circumstances to which they had been reduced. "Faith in God carries with it no guarantee in this world; this was no doubt one of the lessons which our author wished his readers to learn. But it does carry with it great 'recompense of reward' in the only world that ultimately matters."[62]

11:39 – And all these – All the faithful persons referred to in this chapter, whether named or unnamed, from Abel onward.

Having gained approval through their faith – They obtained a testimony; they had their names entered on the Old Testament record. In example after example, God specifically said their "faith"[63] was the reason for His special treatment of them. (See 11:4,5,7, etc.)

---

[62] Bruce, *op. cit.*, p.342.

[63] The Greek behind "through faith" is again *dia ten pisteos*. See notes at Hebrews 11:33.

Did not receive what was promised – Again, there is no contradiction to what is affirmed in 6:15 and 11:33. These men did not receive all that was promised. They lived all their lives without seeing the fulfillment of "what was promised" (the word here is singular) relating to the personal coming and reign of the Messiah. This helps us to see the character of their faith. (Hebrew readers, are you listening? You have seen the One promised. Will your faith endure, for you have more evidence than the Old Testament heroes did? Hebrew readers, are you listening? Though some promises made in the Old Testament were not fulfilled until far in the future, still God was true of His word. In a similar way, Christians must look forward in faith to certain fulfillments still future. Will you follow their example of endurance, because you too are convinced that God keeps His promises?)

11:40 – Because God had provided something better for us – "Us" means us Christians. Now, in this Christian Age, the promise (of Messiah's coming to deal with sin) has been fulfilled. The age of the new covenant has begun. The Christ to whose day they looked forward has come, and by His self-offering and His high priestly ministry in the presence of God, has procured perfection for all of us, Old and New Testament faithful alike. With all these "better" things, what an encouragement to faithfulness!

So that apart from us they would not be made perfect – Comparison should be made with Hebrews 12:23, which speaks of the Old Testament saints, long dead, whose "spirits" have been brought to perfection.[64] Those saints are now in heaven. They know Christ's sacrifice opens the way to complete forgiveness and access to the presence of God. Their spirits (disembodied?) rest in perfect fulfillment, awaiting the resurrection of their bodies and the beginning of eternal bliss.

This passage accords entirely with the argument the writer has been pursuing. He is urging the Hebrew Christians to not apostatize from the Christian faith. The argument is this: The saints in Old Testament times, even under fiery trials, sustained their faith in God, even though they had not seen the fulfillment of the promise of a coming Messiah. If they, under the influence of a mere promise of future blessing, were able to thus live lives consistently faithful to God, how much more reason is there for us to persevere in faithfulness, whatever the cost, since we have been permitted to see Messiah's coming.

"Provided" involves the idea of planning, making provision. God's better plan was that only in company with us Christians should those Old Testament faithful saints reach their perfection. "They and we together now enjoy unrestricted access to God through Christ, as fellow-citizens of the heavenly Jerusalem."[65]

---

[64] See notes at Hebrews 10:1, where we learned perfection was not available through animal sacrifices. It took the death of Christ to bring the blessings of perfection and the new covenant, Hebrews 8:6-13. God's plan (we have been told) provided that the "faithful" throughout the ages before the cross should not be "made perfect" apart from us Christians. Real salvation from sin is something Christ made available for the people who lived in the Old Testament ages as well as in the New Testament age.

[65] Bruce, *op. cit.*, p.344.

5. *Jesus, the perfect example of faithfulness.* 12:1-3

12:1 – Therefore – We are coming to the conclusion of the writer's reminder that faithfulness has always been the true characteristic of God's people. "Therefore" is an inferential particle, drawing an inference from what has been written earlier.

Since we have so great a cloud of witnesses surrounding us – The "cloud[1] of witnesses" are the Old Testament saints, just listed in chapter 11. In what sense they are witnesses – are they watching us Christians from the stands in heaven,[2] or in the sense that they had testimony borne to them[3] by God as to what pleases Him? – is not easy to decide.[4]

Let us lay aside every encumbrance – With all those witnesses, it is important for the readers of Hebrews to run well. Therefore they are to get rid of "every encumbrance"[5] – anything that hampers spiritual progress.[6] In the case of the Hebrew readers, it may be a reference to ancestral religious traditions.

And the sin which so easily entangles us – The sin is unbelief in Jesus. The reference in this verse is not necessarily to sensual gratification. Note that this sin "easily entangles"[7]

---

[1] The word "cloud" may speak of a mass of clouds in the sky, for it translates *nephos*, whereas the usual word for a single cloud is *nephele*. "Cloud" is also used metaphorically for a vast throng.

[2] The word translated "witness" is *marturon*, and "spectator" is not a basic meaning of the term, though it might have such a meaning at 1 Timothy 6:12 and Hebrews 10:28. A "witness" is usually defined as one who tells what he knows. Nevertheless, the imagery of the present passage favors the idea of spectator, for the writer goes on to picture athletes in a race, running for the winning post; they are urged to look at Jesus as they race, suggesting they are not looking to the "witnesses," but that the "witnesses" are watching the racers. If we opt for the spectator meaning, then the passage implies the departed dead know and see what goes on back on the earth they have left -- an idea suggested as indeed true by such passages as Luke 16:27ff (the rich man knew his brothers were still in need of warning) and Revelation 6:9 (the souls under the altar in heaven know what is happening to their brothers who are still living on earth).

[3] This too is a rather loose rendering of *marturon*. Notwithstanding, not a few would argue "the point is that these Old Testament heroes were approved for their faith by the testimony of God, and their experience now stands as a testimony to us as to what pleases God." Kent, *op. cit.*, p.257.

[4] Morris, *op. cit.*, p. 133, writes "both ideas may be present," and urges his readers to think of something like a relay race where those who have finished their leg of the race have handed on the baton to the next runner and then are watching and encouraging their successors.

[5] The word translated "encumbrance" is *ogkon* which originally meant crooked or hooked, and then came to mean something attached or suspended by a hook, hence "weight" (KJV). Some have supposed the athletic metaphor is to training when excess weight is worked off. Others urge that it is not training but the race itself, and that the figure behind the language is the taking off of the excess clothing (actually, Greek runners ran naked) that might slow the runner, causing him to be defeated.

[6] It is doubtful that this phrase has reference to *any* specific acts of sin -- for "sin which so easily entangles" is specially mentioned in the next phrase. "Some things that are not wrong in themselves hinder us in putting forth our best effort, so the writer urges us to get rid of them." Morris, *op. cit.*, p.134.

[7] The word translated "easily entangles" is found nowhere else. It is made up of three parts that mean, respectively well, around, and stands. Most language students accept some such meaning as "easily surrounding" or "easily entangling." Instead of "easily besets" (*euperistaton*), some manuscripts (including P[46]) read "easily distracts" (*euperispaton*). If this alternate reading is accepted, the idea is anything that distracts the athlete's concentration will put him out of the running.

a man; that is, it limits a man's freedom and forms a crippling hindrance to good running.

And let us run with endurance the race that is set before us – The sin that easily entangles is an ever-present threat which calls for steadfastness, faithfulness in the race.[8] The same trait was found in the Old Testament heroes whose examples were called to mind in chapter 11, and was also alluded to in 10:36.

12:2 – Fixing our eyes on Jesus – Contemplate[9] His example, so that we might be encouraged by its greatness. Have no eyes for anyone or anything but Jesus!

The author and perfecter of faith – Jesus has blazed the trail[10] and has completed[11] the course. He carries our salvation on to perfection. Is it "*the* faith" (i.e., the kind of faithfulness the writer has been encouraging[12]) or "*our* faith"[13] (as the KJV reads)? In this context, Jesus is a better example of faithfulness than any of the examples in chapter 11.

Who for the joy set before Him endured the cross – The joy of seeing many men return to God through faith and obedience.[14] Jesus' faithfulness to God required "endurance," the same kind of endurance Christians are to exhibit (Hebrews 12:1).

Despising the shame – He did not allow its shame to dissuade Him or cause Him to waver in His faithfulness.[15]

---

[8] "The author is not thinking of a short, sharp sprint, but of a distance race that requires endurance and persistence. Everyone has from time to time a mild inclination to do good. The author is not talking about this but about the kind of sustained effort required of the long-distance runner who keeps on with great determination over the long course." Morris, *op. cit.*, p.134.

[9] It is no casual glance at Him, but a firmly fixed gaze that is meant. *Aphorao* means to look away from all else and give Jesus our undivided attention.

[10] We had the word translated "author" at Hebrews 2:10, where we learned it could mean originator or leader or pioneer. And at Hebrews 6:20, we were told Jesus is a forerunner who has opened the way for us to follow.

[11] "Perfecter" translates *teleiotes*, a word whose etymology indicates bringing something to its goal or completion. Thus some commentators speak of Jesus' activity at the close of the Church Age when He will bring all of God's creation to the goal He had in mind before He ever created. Others are reminded of the ever-living Christ's activities in heaven as the Christian's high priest (see Hebrews 10:14, 9:9, and 7:25).

[12] The article before "faith" in the Greek would be the article of previous reference.

[13] Based on the reading "our faith," some write about how Jesus is the author and finisher of the Christian faith, the Christian religion (i.e., taking faith in its objective sense, as a body of doctrine). Others write about how Jesus originates men's personal faith, and then also brings it to perfection (a doctrine often taught in denominational circles, even though it is difficult to find any verse that teaches that anyone's personal faith is something given to him by God. The Bible speaks of personal faith coming as a result of hearing the Word of God). Both these alternatives are rendered needless by the explanation offered in the notes, namely, that "*the* faith" is a reference to Jesus as the greatest example of "the faithfulness" that has been the topic since the closing verses of chapter 10.

[14] The Greek preposition behind "*for* the joy" is *anti*. It can be translated "instead of" or "for the sake of." If we take the former meaning, the verse says that instead of the joy He had in heaven before His incarnation, Jesus endured the cross. If we take the latter reading, the idea is that He looked beyond Calvary to the joy He would have once He was back in heaven with the Father, joy at seeing many men now able to come to God.

[15] If one is "despising" or scorning something, that normally means he has nothing to do with it. Such a

And has sat down at the right hand of the throne of God – See comments at Hebrews 1:3. The perfect tense verb "has sat down" points to a permanent result. Christ is seated at the right hand of God until the last enemy has been put under His feet (Hebrews 10:12,13).

12:3 – For consider Him – Examine minutely and from all angles the example He has given us.

Who has endured such hostility by sinners against Himself – "Hostility" in word and deed, rebellion. The enemies resisted His plans, perverted His sayings, and ridiculed His claims, but none of these caused Him for a moment to deviate from His course.[16] Jesus "endured". Do the readers find themselves in a position similar to the one Jesus Himself experienced? Will their reaction be the same as His?

So that you may not grow weary – The purpose for considering the example of Jesus is that the readers may draw strength and encouragement for their own race. "Grow weary" translates a verb that describes fatigue after a long effort.

And lose heart – Get discouraged so as to no longer pursue a certain course of behavior – in this case, faithfulness to Jesus.[17]

C. Exhortation Concerning Perils that Threaten a Life of Faithfulness. 12:4-17

1. Misunderstanding of the nature and value of suffering. 12:4-13.

12:4 – You have not yet resisted to the point of shedding blood – Is it strenuousness or martyrdom implied in this figure of speech? Though either idea can be harmonized with this call to faithfulness even in the face of suffering, it is this commentator's judgment that "strenuousness" is the idea being illustrated.[18]

---

meaning will not suit here. What this expression says is that Jesus thought so little of the pain and shame involved with Calvary that He did not bother to avoid it.

[16] There is a manuscript variation here. Most of the oldest manuscripts (including Sinaiticus and P⁴⁶) read plural "against *themselves*" instead of the singular "against Himself" (which has been adopted as likely the correct reading by Kurt Aland in the 25th edition of the Nestle text and in the UBS text). The plural may imply that the sinners, while opposing Jesus, were in fact also hurting themselves. They were just asking for retribution from the Living God!

[17] "Several commentators point out that the two verbs used at the end of the verse ("grow weary" and "lose heart") are both used by Aristotle of runners who relax and collapse after they have passed the finishing post. The readers were still in the race. They must not give way prematurely. They must not allow themselves to faint and collapse through weariness. Once again there is a call to perseverance in the face of hardship." Morris, *op. cit.*, p.135.

[18] R. Milligan, *op. cit.*, p.345, quotes Barnes' suggestion that there has been a change of imagery from the race to combat such as boxing. Boxers' hands were so wrapped that blows often left the opponents bloodied. But you didn't stop the match simply for a bloody nose or a cut above the eye. "'Resistance unto blood' showed

In your striving against sin – "Striving against" (*antagonizomai*) seems to continue the imagery of the athletic games.[19]   Some commentators write as though "You have not resisted ..." is an emphatic expression in the Greek, implying that Jesus so resisted, whereas the readers have not. But the Greek is not emphatic. However, implicit in this language is a warning that the readers still have more persecution and suffering[20] to face before their lives on earth are over; they will have more temptations to quit Christianity than they have heretofore faced and successfully resisted. It is not clear whether the "sin" the writer has in mind is the *readers'* potential sin of abandoning Christianity or the *oppressors'* sin as they tried to terrorize the Christians into abandoning their faith.

12:5 – And you have forgotten the exhortation – The first phrase can either be indicative ("you have forgotten") or interrogative ("have you forgotten?"). The "exhortation" (or word of encouragement) he reminds them of is found in Proverbs 3:11,12.

Which is addressed to you as sons – If they would recall the words of Proverbs, they would be better able to view the persecution and suffering they were experiencing in proper perspective. It is "sons" who are thus exhorted.[21]   The implication is that the present experience of persecution is not proof God no longer loves them, nor is caring for them.[22]

"MY SON, DO NOT REGARD LIGHTLY THE DISCIPLINE OF THE LORD – The correction which the Lord administers. The opposition and persecution the readers were experiencing (because they were determined to be true to Jesus) at the hands of sinners is also viewed as being "the discipline of the Lord." Though God is not responsible for the evil which wicked men were bringing upon the Christians, He surely permitted the wicked men to so act. In His providence, He did not exempt His "sons" from such hostility and suffering. At the same time, the "sons" should not despise or treat it lightly.

"NOR FAINT WHEN YOU ARE REPROVED BY HIM – There are two wrong ways

---

a determination, courage, and purpose not to yield" (Barnes wrote).

[19] Writers who suppose the language is no longer an athletic metaphor but is rather a reference to "martyrdom" in turn use this interpretation to argue against a Palestinian destination for the epistle to the Hebrews, since some of their members (think of Stephen, James the apostle, and those who died as a result of Saul's persecution) had been martyred in days gone by. Milligan replies that even if we think martyrdom is the figure, the writer is speaking to readers still living; he is not referring to generations gone by. It is the *present* generation he is exhorting to faithfulness.

[20] Interpreters of Hebrews must keep sharp in their thinking at this place. It is not *all* suffering in general that is the writer's theme, but suffering because of righteousness sake, suffering experienced because they wish to remain true to Christ.

[21] A father would spend much more care and patience on the proper upbringing of a "son" than he would on someone else's child. It is on the child whom the father wishes to be a worthy heir, and for whom a future of honor and responsibility is envisioned, that the father spends so much effort.

[22] W. Wiersbe, *Be Confident!* (p.138ff), suggests the following verses give three proofs that such chastening as the Hebrews were experiencing are indications of God's continued love for them: (1) the Scriptures, 12:5,6; (2) personal experience (how a father disciplines his child), 12:7-10; and (3) the blessed results (peaceable fruit of righteousness), 12:11-13.

a man can react to God's discipline: "regard lightly" and "faint"[23]. Affliction or persecution can be overruled by God and used for the training of believers[24] if it serves as a rebuke concerning their sins.

12:6 – "FOR THOSE WHOM THE LORD LOVES HE DISCIPLINES – This verse gives a reason why Christians should not regard chastening lightly, nor faint because of it. Instead, they should look at what is happening as "discipline" at the hands of a loving Father.[25] Proper training must include correction of faulty behavior. Earthly parents do not "discipline" their children every hour, nor even every day, but only when some fault needs correcting. Likewise, it is not all suffering a Christian faces,[26] but those occasional corrections administered by the Heavenly Father, that form the topic here discussed.

"AND HE SCOURGES EVERY SON WHOM HE RECEIVES" – To scourge is to flog with a whip or lash. Implied is the idea that some of God's "discipline" will hurt! The correction of faulty behavior must be memorable or it is apt to be repeated. It is the son who is disciplined, and "every son" at that. The Bible elsewhere suggests Christians are God's adopted sons. Perhaps that is what is alluded to when it says He "receives" sons. Then again, perhaps "receives" simply serves as another word to say God *loves* His sons.[27]

12:7 – It is for discipline that you endure – It is for the purpose of training that you are asked by God to undergo suffering.[28] The emphatic position of the words "for discipline" is important. God isn't trying to make His sons miserable; it is not just an accident; it is "discipline." This is how Christians should view persecutions they are called on to face.

God deals with you as with sons – It is part of the Father's program of educating His sons. His aim is to foster spiritual growth and prevent further sinning. Observe that it is Christians who are called God's "sons."[29]

---

[23] The word translated "faint" here is the same word translated "lose heart" in verse 3.

[24] The word for "discipline" combines the ideas of chastening (punishment), education, training, and correction. When a parent "disciplines," he is trying to teach the child something.

[25] "Those whom the Lord loves" comes first in the Greek, and this gives a certain emphasis to it. God disciplines those he loves. Those disciplined are not those toward whom He might be said to be indifferent.

[26] Romans 8:23 indicates some suffering a Christian experiences is simply a part of the creaturely suffering all creation experiences since Adam's fall.

[27] The last part of the verse adopts the reading of the LXX. The Hebrew text reads "even as a father the son in whom he delights." "Delights" may be no more than Hebrew parallelism, matching the word "loves" in the first part of the verse.

[28] The KJV follows a manuscript reading that has "if you endure chastening" (*ei paideian hupomonete*, indicative). The NASB translates a better supported reading, "endure unto discipline" (*eis paideian hupomonete*, imperative).

[29] In an earlier part of the twentieth century, it was popular in certain liberal theological circles to speak of the Fatherhood of God and the brotherhood of man. What was implied is that all men are "sons" of God, and that there was no special relationship to God as a result of accepting Christianity. Such a broad application of the term "son" is not in harmony with the view of the writer of Hebrews, who clearly sees only "believers" as the "sons" of God. (Compare notes at Hebrews 12:5 and at 12:9 under "Father of spirits.")

For what son is there whom *his* father does not discipline? – The writer appeals to a generally accepted practice among human fathers to illustrate his point about God's discipline in the spiritual realm. The first century was not like the permissive society of the twentieth century; it was unthinkable to the writer and his readers that a father would not discipline his sons.

12:8 – But if you are without discipline – Sometimes children receiving parental discipline envy those who escape such discipline. Christians are mistaken if they think it better to be without any opposition or persecution (i.e., "discipline"). The contrast between what is said here in verse 8 and what is said in verse 9 shows that the "discipline" in view here in verse 8 is discipline which comes from the hand of God (cp. verse 5).

Of which all have become partakers – All God's children can expect to be disciplined at some time or other.

Then you are illegitimate children and not sons – Illegitimate offspring often have no one who cares enough to train them. Don't be envious of the person who is not disciplined. Surprisingly, a complete lack of discipline is not indicative of a privileged position. It may indicate the person is not really a child of God.

12:9 – Furthermore, we had earthly fathers to discipline us – "Earthly fathers" literally is fathers of our flesh.

And we respected them – The discipline received from our earthly fathers did not cause us to think they didn't love us, nor did it cause us to lose our respect for them. It is not usual for a spanking to be the thing that causes a child to leave home.

Shall we not much rather be subject to the Father of spirits – "Father of spirits" is an unusual expression, found only here in Scripture. The exact identity of the "spirits" of whom He is the Father is debated,[30] but the best idea seems to be that it has reference to the spirit part of man which is "born again" (John 3:6) as he becomes a Christian. "Spirits" certainly is contrasted to that which is natural or "earthly" (previous phrase),[31] and is therefore to be taken in a non-physical sense. "Be subject to" reminds us a child can rebel when disciplined; if so, the discipline does no lasting good. Christians who rebel will not be profited by God's discipline either.

---

[30] The "spirits" might be those of "righteous men made perfect" (Hebrews 12:23). In some verses (e.g., Hebrews 1:7,14), angels are designated by the term "spirits." Others have urged that since there is no "our" in the Greek (it does not read "our spirits," as some English versions render it), "spirits" is a reference to all men, and then the verse has been used as a foundation for references to God's universal Fatherhood. In a passage where what happens to God's "sons" (not something that happens to all men descended from Adam) is the topic, "spirits" must have some reference to the spiritual nature of the subjects of God's special discipline.

[31] It is doubtful that what is here written should be used as proof of either creationism or traducianism. Creationism holds that God creates each human spirit at the time the physical body is conceived by the parents. Traducianism holds that the entire person (body, soul, spirit) is descended from Adam and is procreated by the parents. If our comments are correct, it is not the entrance of the spirit into the body at physical birth, but the rebirth of the spirit, that is behind the expression "Father of spirits."

And live? – "Live" may be an allusion to abundant life in the present or it may be used of the glory of the life to come. Shortly the writer will speak of "holiness," and that may be a reference to life here and now. On the other hand, when this life is over, "sons" who have been profited by the Father's discipline have a citizenship in heavenly Jerusalem to enjoy.

12:10 – For they disciplined us for a short time – Now the writer contrasts the duration and the quality of the discipline meted out by earthly fathers and by the heavenly Father. Childhood, when the children are subject to parental discipline, is a comparatively short time, perhaps 20 years, more or less.

As seemed best to them – Earthly parents sometimes make mistakes as they attempt to train and discipline. Not God! His wisdom surpasses that of earthly fathers.

But He *disciplines us* for *our* good – God's discipline is not haphazard. His discipline is always for His children's "good" (Greek, *sumpheron*, profit, benefit, advantage).

That we may share His holiness – This is the purpose[32] God has in mind when He disciplines. "Holiness" here is one of God's attributes, one that believers are to reproduce and reflect. At 1 Peter 1:15,16 this attribute of "holiness"[33] is explained to mean that God is *different* from the pagan Roman and Greek gods. Christians are disciplined, this verse says, that they may learn to be different from the pagans around them.

12:11 – All discipline for the moment seems not to be joyful – Whether administered by our earthly or heavenly Father, at the time it is being received, it is not a joyous affair.

But sorrowful – *Lupe* speaks of grief or pain. If there is no pain, there is no chastisement.

Yet to those who have been trained by it – God's purpose in discipline is realized only if there is an appropriate response in the sufferer. The sufferer must be sensitive to God's purposes,[34] instead of reacting in bitterness or complaint or rebellion.

Afterwards – In the future life? Or just after the disciplining is over?

It yields the peaceful fruit of righteousness – "Righteousness" (right living) is the fruit produced by God's disciplining. It is produced in a soul at peace[35] with God, in one who

---

[32] "That we may share" translates *eis* and an infinitive. This Greek construction expresses purpose. It indicates God does not discipline people aimlessly. Rather, He has a definite purpose in view.

[33] The Greek at 1 Peter 1:15,16 (*hagios*) is the same root as the word *hagiotes* (holiness) found here in Hebrews 12. When added to an adjective, the suffix *-tes* emphasizes quality. Thus "holiness" speaks of one of God's attributes or qualities.

[34] "Trained" translates *gegumnasmenois*, another metaphor taken from athletics. God's discipline is likened to training for an athletic contest. Those who refused to submit to the toil and pain and drudgery of training were not the victors. The victors in the games could see that the training was a very great benefit toward their winning. The perfect tense participle reflects a long process, not a minor practice session or two.

[35] "Peaceful" in the Greek is an adjective, a fact not apparent to the reader of the NIV where it reads as

knows all is right between him and God.

12:12 – Therefore, strengthen the hands that are weak – "Therefore" means 'since it is to be expected that God's sons will be disciplined.' But whose "hands" are the readers called on to "strengthen"? Are Christians being called on to help *others* when they are being "disciplined", or is the Christian being called on to prepare *himself* so as to profit from God's discipline when it comes?

And the knees that are feeble – The language of this verse is perhaps drawn from Isaiah 35:3, where the words refer to the Jews' on their return from Babylon to Jerusalem. Applied spiritually, the writer of Hebrews may be thinking of Christians on their way to heavenly Jerusalem. If the idea of training (verse 11) is continued, then the one who will benefit from God's discipline dare not be out of shape. There must be the strengthening of the inner resolve if Christians are going to face victoriously the challenges to quit Christianity.

12:13 – And make straight paths for your feet – The Greek can be translated "with your feet" or "for your feet." The exhortation is for the readers to make a straight path *with* their feet so others can follow, or to plan the straight and honorable path *for* their own feet.

So that *the limb* which is lame may not be put out of joint – If one's limbs are "lame," special care must be taken that the way on which they travel be free of dangerous obstacles lest the hurt will be aggravated.[36] Perhaps the underlying metaphor is still the image of a company of persons marching onward to heavenly Jerusalem. Some are lame, weak, and disheartened because of the many obstacles on the way. Lest such travelers drop out, the writer admonishes his stronger readers to do all they can to help their hurting brethren.

But rather be healed – The aim of our response to discipline, whether in ourselves or as we see it happening to our brothers, is that the lameness may be cured, rather than aggravated. Opposition and persecution the Christian faces because of his faith will not hinder his faithfulness if the Christian makes a proper response to the suffering. That response includes: (1) see it as "training" (discipline); (2) view it as God the Father helping His children; (3) be submissive to the Father, and live; (4) know that God does not make mistakes; (5) cooperate with God's effort to produce only righteousness; and (7) help the Christian brothers when they are being disciplined.

2. Failure to pursue peace and sanctification. 12:14-17

12:14 – Pursue peace with all men – Here begins the second peril that can threaten a life of faithfulness. If a Christian does not actively "pursue peace," his faithfulness will suffer,

---

though peace were another kind of fruit produced by discipline. Perhaps the "peace" is contrasted with the violence experienced while the discipline is being administered. Perhaps (as reflected in the comments above) "peace" speaks of the relationship the "son" has with his "Father" -- he is at peace with God.

[36] The word translated "out of joint" is the regular medical term for "dislocated." The lameness is aggravated and becomes a dislocated limb.

since the New Testament contains a number of exhortations to be at peace with one another (Matthew 5:9, Mark 9:50, Romans 12:18). But who are included in the "all men"? All believers, or all persecutors, or all men in general? And what does it mean to "pursue peace"? Is this an exhortation against being selfish and abrasive in our actions toward others? Or does "peace" include soul-winning, so that we are at peace with each other because we are both at peace with God?

And the sanctification – "Sanctification" here is synonymous with spiritual growth,[37] and is presented as being a continuous process, to be "pursued" throughout the Christian's life on earth. The Greek speaks of "*the* sanctification," and perhaps means "the well-known sanctification every follower of God knows about" (cp. "holiness" in Hebrews 12:10).

Without which no one will see the Lord – Note the imperative of sanctification, of submitting one's life to the Spirit's guidance. Without sanctification, there is no eternal life with the Father. The pursuits of peace and sanctification are not optional for the Christian!

12:15 – See to it – Look at one's own heart and life, and be concerned too about the spiritual welfare of others.[38] The writer goes on to specify four areas where believers are to have a concern for one another.

That no one comes short of the grace of God – This is the first thing to be concerned about. The language has to do with defecting from the Christian religion, the result of which is to be excluded from further blessings that God's grace might bestow.[39]

That no root of bitterness springing up cause trouble – The second thing that should be a concern is the possibility of a bitter root springing up in their midst. The image behind "root of bitterness" is that of a plant that starts with a root, after a while grows to maturity, and then bears bitter fruit. Some have thought this alludes to Deuteronomy 29:16-21, where Moses admonished his brethren to beware of the sin of idolatry. If so, this is another instance where the writer of Hebrews, warning of the seriousness of abandoning the church, uses Old Testament language that warned the Jews not to go into idolatry (cp. Hebrews 3:12). If one believer is enticed away from the faith, that example in doctrine and action could become a source of infection to others. It may not immediately be apparent, but in due time its bitter fruit appears, and the whole community will be troubled.

And by it many be defiled – Defection in doctrine or in conduct is usually contagious. Such "bitterness" defiles people and makes them unfit to stand before God.

---

[37] For an in-depth look at "sanctification," see the special study in the author's *Commentary on Romans*, p.243ff. Barclay, *Romans*, p.92,93, notes that all Greek nouns ending in -*asmos* describe, not the completed state, but a process. "Sanctification" represents the Greek word *hagiasmos* and describes a process.

[38] The verb is *episkopeo*. It conveys the idea of oversight, to care for, and is formed from the same root word from which we get our word bishop.

[39] After the long discussion at Hebrews 6:6, it seems unnecessary to spend further time on the topic of the possibility of falling from grace after once being saved.

12:16 – (See to it) that *there be* **no immoral or godless person like Esau** – "Immoral" is the third thing the brethren are to be concerned about (see verse 15). The ASV reads "fornicator," a word that may be either literal or figurative (speaking of idolatry). The fourth thing[40] the readers are to be concerned about is that none of them becomes "godless." The ASV reads "profane," that is, one who treats spiritual values with contempt, one who is more concerned with temporal and material matters than with spiritual things. "Esau" is an example of a man in whose life there is a lack of pursuing sanctification, and his example should warn us not to disregard our spiritual privileges or slight the favors of the gospel.

Who sold his own birthright for a *single* **meal** – In Esau's time, the firstborn had important rights and spiritual responsibilities toward the rest of the family. Genesis 25:27-34 records an example of Esau's being "profane." He relinquished his opportunity to exercise those spiritual rights and responsibilities in order to satisfy his immediate physical hunger; if carried out, the spiritual would have been more eternally meaningful and satisfying.

12:17 – For you know that even afterwards – The word "know" may be either imperative ("know!") or indicative ("as you know"). If indicative, the writer appeals to knowledge common to himself and his readers. If imperative, it sharpens the warning against being a godless person, for what happened to Esau will also happen today to men who are profane. The penalty is to be "rejected"! You will miss the things that really satisfy.

When he desired to inherit the blessing – Evidently the "birthright" (verse 16) and the "blessing" are not precisely the same thing. Esau himself complained of *two* areas wherein Jacob had supplanted him – both the birthright and the blessing (Genesis 27:36). The birthright had to do with inheritance (a double portion) and with responsibility for authority over and leadership of the family, including priestly functions. The blessing had to do with a close and favored relationship with God, especially with reference to the fulfillment of the covenant promises. At Rebekah's prompting, Jacob had tricked Isaac, and Isaac had pronounced the blessing on Jacob. Shortly after, when Esau came in from the hunt, and learned what had happened, he "cried out with an exceedingly great and bitter cry" (Genesis 27:34) and begged for a blessing, any kind of blessing (Genesis 27:36,38).

He was rejected – The blessing had been pronounced on Jacob. There was none left to give to Esau, though Jacob did make a prediction about Esau's future (Genesis 27:39,40).

For he found no place for repentance – Though Esau pleaded, evidently there was no way *Isaac* could change his mind and give the blessing to Esau. (It is doubtful the verse says *Esau* sought to repent, but was unable.[41]) What had been done could not be undone.

---

[40] The division of this verse into two dangers (immorality and godlessness) is based on an interpretation which does *not* have Esau accused of being immoral, only godless. Philo, the Palestinian Targum, and references in rabbinical literature indeed accuse Esau of fornication (see the references in Bruce, in loc.), but no such loose behavior is attributed to him in the Old Testament, unless the term is considerably stretched to include his marrying many wives, and particularly foreigners, the daughters of Canaan (Genesis 26:34,35, 36:2).

[41] Even if it were interpreted that Esau found no place to repent of his own *sin*, such an idea (namely, that a man can reach the place where he has no further opportunity to repent) is not foreign to Hebrews. Remember

Though he sought for it with tears – "It" is feminine in the Greek, and thus the antecedent could be either "blessing" or "repentance," since both are feminine nouns. We suppose it was the "blessing" that Esau sought with tears (cp. Genesis 27:38).

FIFTH WARNING PASSAGE. 12:18-29

- *The joy and happiness associated with Mount Zion (compared with the terrors associated with Mount Sinai). 12:18-24*

12:18 – For you have not come to *a mountain* that may be touched – "For" shows this warning is connected with what precedes. Perhaps it gives a reason why Christians should pursue peace and sanctification (verse 14) or be solicitous of each other (verse 15ff). Think seriously about heeding what God has spoken through His Son, for Christianity has superior privileges. You would be throwing away considerably more than Esau ever did, were you to turn out to be profane and come short of the grace of God. The allusion in "a mountain[42] that may (not) be touched" is to Mount Sinai, when the children of Israel arrived there following the exodus from Egypt. The sound and the sights produced terror in the Israelites. It was a day unequalled in Jewish history. After a few verses, the writer will compare the terrors associated with the giving of the Law at Sinai with the joys and glory associated with Mount Zion, the heavenly Jerusalem. This comparison leads into a paragraph where the truth is enforced that great privilege also carries great responsibility.

And to a blazing fire – The phenomena listed in this and the next few phrases were all associated with the giving of the Law at Sinai. See Exodus 19:9-25, 20:18-21, and Deuteronomy 4:10-24. "The rugged heights of Sinai rocked with thunder and crackled with lightning which set the mountain aflame."[43]

And to darkness and gloom and whirlwind – Three Greek synonyms for "darkness" are used. "Darkness" is *gnophos*, the darkness which accompanies a storm. "Gloom" is *zophos*, the gloom of twilight. "Whirlwind" translates *thuella*, a cyclone or tornado.

12:19 – And to the blast of a trumpet – The trumpet, possibly blown by an angel, is spoken of again and again at Sinai, and it grew louder and louder. Exodus 19:16,19 and 20:18.

And the sound of words which *sound was such that* those who heard begged that no further word should be spoken to them – The "sound of words" was produced as God spoke (Deuteronomy 4:12, 5:24). The voice was so loud and terrifying the Israelites begged Moses to henceforth serve as the messenger who would deliver God's message to them, rather than having God speak directly to them (Exodus 20:19).

---

what was written at Hebrews 6:4-6, "it is impossible to renew them again to repentance ...."

[42] Though the oldest manuscripts have no word for "mountain," there can be no doubt the events that occurred at Sinai are in mind. In fact, "mountain" is found in the Byzantine and Western texts.

[43] Kent, *op. cit.*, p.269.

12:20 – For they could not bear the command – What was being commanded were the regulations regarding the people's conduct while at Sinai (Exodus 19:9-13).[44]

IF EVEN A BEAST TOUCHES THE MOUNTAIN, IT WILL BE STONED – The decree recorded in Exodus 19:12,13 commanded that nothing, neither man nor straying animal, touch the mountain under penalty of death.[45] We suppose this restriction was intended to impress on the Israelites that the majestic and holy God is to be held in awe.

12:21 – And so terrible was the sight – Is the reference to when Moses went up onto the mountain, or when he came down from the mountain? This quote from Deuteronomy 9:19 is not part of the Sinai narrative, but occurs at the time of the golden calf. This alleged Biblical difficulty has led to several proposed solutions. (1) The terror Moses felt may have been known to the writer by tradition, or by revelation from God. (2) The writer may have telescoped several events together ("shook with fear" at the burning bush [Acts 7:32] and Moses' apprehension when he saw what the people were doing around the golden calf [Exodus 32:30-35]) to show that similar events at Sinai produced fear. (3) Exodus 19:16 states "all the people … in the camp trembled," and that certainly included Moses.

That Moses said, "I AM FULL OF FEAR AND TREMBLING" – If Moses (the one who had an especially close relationship with God, Exodus 33:11) was himself terrified, no wonder the people were terrified. It was awesome to be at Sinai!

12:22 – But – "But" (*alla*) is the strong adversative and introduces a marked contrast between the people who came to Mount Sinai and those who come to Mount Zion. It is not such a terror-inspiring experience that Christians face. Mount Zion is a serene and glorious and happy place! The point of the contrast is that Christians have a greater privilege (and a correspondingly greater responsibility) than did Israel of old.

You have come to Mount Zion – Mount Zion was one of the hills on which the city of Jerusalem had been built, and in time came to be a name for the whole city. But in this place, it is not *earthly* Jerusalem being referenced. Rather, the *heavenly* Jerusalem is signified, as the following phrases explain. "You have come" (a perfect tense verb, indicating past completed action with present continuing results) is a surprising word. The readers of Hebrews were still living on earth. How could it be said they have already come to Mt. Zion? It is in the same way that the writer of Ephesians can affirm that saints on earth are already experiencing the blessings "in heavenly places."[46] A child of God already

---

[44] Some English versions enclose verses 20 and 21 in parentheses in order to help the reader to see that these verses also are intended to assign the reason why the ancient Hebrews felt so much terror and alarm as they stood at the foot of Mt. Sinai. The commands concerning the people's behavior not only dealt with not touching the mountain, they included restrictions against sexual relations immediately prior to God's visiting them (Exodus 19:15), and they also required the people to wash their clothes and sanctify themselves (19:10).

[45] In Exodus 19:13, the death of the offending animal or man was to be accomplished without touching the offender. Stoning was the means if the offender was near enough; otherwise darts or arrows could be used so that those taking part in execution of the penalty need not touch the mountain themselves. The KJV adds the phrase "or thrust through with a dart" in Hebrews 12:20, but the phrase is lacking in all the older manuscripts.

[46] Ephesians 1:3,20, 2:6, 3:10, and 6:12.

has eternal life abiding in him; all that remains is for him to be faithful until he dies, and entrance into the heavenly Jerusalem is guaranteed!

And to the city of the living God – This phrase and the next are further designations of "Mount Zion." Heaven is frequently pictured as a magnificent city where God and the angels live.[47] Perhaps He is called "the living God" to emphasize the thought that the heavenly Jerusalem is no dull, static place. It is the city of a vital, dynamic, living Being, who is doing things.

The heavenly Jerusalem – The new Jerusalem has not yet come down (Revelation 21:10), but in the spiritual realm Christians already have access to it. The privileges of its citizenship are already enjoyed by the faithful. The Hebrews writer has already spoken of "the city which has (the) foundations whose architect and builder is God" (Hebrews 11:10).

And to myriads of angels – Angels, so numerous they are called a "host" (Luke 2:13), form one group of the inhabitants of the heavenly Jerusalem. Daniel saw "thousands upon thousands" who attended God, and "myriads upon myriads"[48] who were standing before Him (Daniel 7:10). The number of angels whom John saw around God's throne was "myriads of myriads, and thousands of thousands" (Revelation 5:11). The Hebrews writer has earlier said much about angels (Hebrews 1:4ff), showing they are "ministering spirits" sent to minister to the heirs of salvation (1:14). When, therefore, Christian believers come to the myriads of angels, it is not to worship them, but to worship God just as they do (1:6).

12:23 – To the general assembly – *Panegurei* means a festive gathering.[49] Scholars differ as to whether this word goes with "angels" in verse 22, or with "church" in verse 23 (as does TEV, "You have come to the joyful gathering of God's oldest sons"). We prefer to take these words with what precedes, so that Christians are said to come to myriads of angels in joyful assembly.[50] There were angels present at Sinai where they helped leave an impression of awesome majesty (cp. Hebrews 2:2). It is different on Mount Zion, for there the angels are involved in a festive celebration. Heaven is a joyful place. Why would anyone want to miss the celebration there?

And church of the firstborn who are enrolled in heaven – Christians enjoy the rights of

---

[47] Hebrews 11:10,14-16, 12:28, 13:14; Galatians 4:26; Revelation 3:12, 21:2,10-27. In the Psalms, generally, the holy hill of Zion is viewed as the Lord's immovable abode, where He is surrounded by thousands of angels, and from whence He succors His people (Psalms 48, 68, 125, 132). When the Old Testament prophets spoke about the future Messianic blessings as being connected with "Jerusalem," we certainly are to think of heavenly Jerusalem as the scene and center of those blessings. In Revelation 14:1, "Mount Zion" is the place where the Lamb (Christ) stands along with the 144,000.

[48] The word "myriad" originally meant "ten thousand," one of largest numbers in the Greek language. "Myriads of (times) myriads" thus comes to mean a very large number.

[49] The lexicons show that this word originally denoted a national festive assembly to honor some god, and then came to mean, generally, any festive assembly.

[50] As one reads the original, he sees that the writer of Hebrews seems to use *kai* (and) to introduce each of the leading ideas of this majestic sentence. If so, then "festive gathering" goes with angels.

first-born sons, and though still living and assembling[51] on earth, they form a select group. Their names are already enrolled (in the book of life?) on heaven's citizenship list.[52]

And to God the Judge of all – It might better be translated "and to the Judge, God of all." The emphasis is on the fact that it is to a *judge* to whom the Christians have come. There is no other God; hence, all men can expect to be judged by Him. This reminds the readers their destiny still depended on God; they should be careful not to provoke His wrath, which they would be sure to do if they abandoned Jesus. This phrase echoes earlier references in Hebrews to the One "with whom we have to do" (4:13), and "it is a terrifying thing to fall into the hands of the living God" (10:31).

And to the spirits of righteous men made perfect – The reference seems to be to the Old Testament saints with whom Christians share salvation. Disembodied "spirits" is likely the idea.[53] While they still lived on earth, they were "righteous;" that is, they were "justified by faith" (Habakkuk 2:4, see also what was written about their faithfulness in Hebrews 11), but it remained for Christ's death on Calvary to guarantee the forgiveness of their sins. Now, they have been "made perfect" because Christ's sacrifice for sins has removed their sin, and their spirits have been admitted to the world of glory. (Revelation 6:9 and 15:2 locate the souls of the redeemed on or beside the sea of glass in front of the throne of God.) Most Christians have friends or family who have already joined this throng of the righteous ones in glory. The appeal to those still living here on earth is to live so as not to be separated from them by the Judge discerning some continuing unfaithfulness in us.

12:24 – And to Jesus, the mediator of a new covenant – The climax of this majestic list is now reached. Men in former ages had God's promise concerning the coming of Jesus; the Christian has the blessing of having seen those Messianic promises fulfilled. On Jesus being the "mediator" of the new covenant, see Hebrews 8:6 and 9:15-17. Recall, too, how chapters 8 to 10 presented in detail how the "new[54] covenant" is better than the Mosaic.

---

[51] "Church" (*ekklesia*, assembly) is a word often used elsewhere for the church on earth. This whole phrase has caused problems for the commentators. They doubt that "church of the firstborn" (the Greek word translated "firstborn" is plural) has reference to believers who have already died and whose souls are in the presence of God, for it seems that group of people is specially mentioned later ("spirits of righteous men made perfect"). Some have supposed "first-born (ones)" is another designation for angels (having been created before men were), but it would be unusual to speak of angels as "enrolled in heaven." On the other hand, to make "church of the firstborn (ones)" a reference to the church militant still on earth would have the readers coming to themselves, for they would be part of that "assembly."

[52] The readers of this epistle would know what is intended by "enrolled in heaven" if they have been made aware of what Jesus used to say, "Rejoice that your names are recorded in heaven" (Luke 10:20), or if they have heard Paul tell about men "whose names are in the book of life" (Philippians 4:3). Also see Revelation 20:12 and 21:27. Though Revelation was written after Hebrews, the ideas included there are not being introduced for the first time; they evidently had been preached by the apostles long before John wrote them.

[53] While some think the use of "spirits" to refer to the departed is unusual, we remember that "spirit" in Acts 23:8 is used of the Sadducees' beliefs that rejected any conscious existence after death.

[54] "New" here is *neos* (brand new, new in point of time), whereas in all other places in Scripture, it is *kainos* (renewed, refreshed, new in quality) that is translated "new." "The choice of *neos* here emphasizes the fresh and recent character of the revelation in Jesus Christ." Kent, *op. cit.*, p.274.

And to the sprinkled blood – See Hebrews 9:18-23. Perhaps the idea behind this phrase is of Christ's blood which inaugurated, or validated, the new covenant. Or perhaps it speaks of hearts now cleansed (cp. 1 Peter 1:2) because they have been sprinkled with better blood (Hebrews 10:22).

Which speaks better than *the blood* of Abel – Christ's blood speaks of redemption (rather than revenge, as in Abel's case, Genesis 4:10).

- ### *The consequent responsibilities of Christians. 12:25-29*

12:25 – See to it – Repeating an expression used at 12:15, the writer begins to make application of what has been written since verse 18. Since Christians have not come to Mount Sinai (something imperfect, terrifying, alarming), but have instead come to Mount Zion (where all is perfect, winsome, and alluring), they now have real motives for perseverance.

That you do not refuse Him who is speaking – Evidently God is the speaker in the writer's mind (remember, Hebrews 1:2, "God ... has spoken!"). Several times in this letter, Judaism and Christianity have been contrasted. Here the contrast is between the way God spoke of old and the way He now speaks through Jesus. If we worded this exhortation positively, it would be, 'Pay heed to the voice of God!'

For if those did not escape – Israelites who were disobedient to what God had spoken at Sinai experienced various temporal judgments.

When they refused him who warned *them* on earth – Time and again throughout the years following Sinai they failed to pay heed[55] to the God's commands.[56] The word translated "warned" (*chrematizo*) denotes divine instruction. When God spoke, it was a warning given "on earth"[57] because it was connected with the revelation He made at Sinai.

Much less *will* we *escape* – We are reminded of the warnings in Hebrews 2:1-3 and 10:29, where the writer used the same kind of how-much-more exhortation. "We" is a reference to Christians in contrast to the "they" (Jews) of the previous phrase. Christians who disobey the gospel will have greater punishment than those who disobeyed to the Law, because the Christians have had greater privileges and opportunities.

---

[55] "Refused" is an aorist participle, but it may be that it looks at a whole series of events as now completed. We are reminded of the Psalmist observing that the wilderness generation provoked God by their disobedience (Hebrews 3:8-10), and that Jeremiah (hundreds of years before Christ's first coming) already accused the Israelites of breaking the commands of the covenant given at Sinai (Hebrews 8:9).

[56] Some would make the personal pronoun "him" in this phrase refer to Moses, and write about how God spoke through Moses. Then when they read the next phrase, they make the "him" who speaks from heaven refer to Jesus, and write about God speaking through Jesus now.

[57] The word order in the various manuscripts is not uniform. In some ancient manuscripts, "on earth" immediately follows "did not escape," suggesting the idea that they did not escape on earth, i.e., there were certain temporal punishments for sin. P[46] and the Textus Receptus have an order that connects "on earth" with "Who warned them," a word order that has in its favor the obvious parallel with "from heaven" in the next clause.

Who turn away from Him who *warns* from heaven – 'How shall we escape if we are turning away?' is the idea. Too often, those who hear a warning think it is intended for someone else. This one is written in a way that makes it personal. "Turn away" indicates that the point of no return has not yet been reached (just as Hebrews 6:4ff indicated). But if the process[58] continues, it will not be long until it is reached, and God's severer punishment will then be inevitable. Is it the ascended, glorified Christ who warns from heaven,[59] or is it God speaking through Christ? If we take the latter option, then God has addressed us in the gospel as truly and as actually as He addressed the Israelites from Sinai.

12:26 – And His voice shook the earth then – There was an earthquake at Sinai when the Law was given (Exodus 19:18; Judges 5:4,5). This earthquake that accompanied God's speaking made such an impression it was celebrated in the Psalms (e.g., Psalms 68:7,8, 77:18, 114:1-4). This brief statement recalls all that has been said about the awe-inspiring nature of what happened when the Law was given. At the same time, the "shaking" allows the writer to connect to another Old Testament passage which also speaks of a "shaking."[60]

But now He has promised, saying – The passage that follows is from Haggai 2:6-9. Haggai's sermons were intended to encourage the rebuilding of the temple after the return from the Babylonian captivity. This second temple may not be the glorious structure that Solomon's temple was, he admitted, but "the desire of all nations" (Haggai 2:7 KJV) was to come and fill this house with glory. Haggai worded it this way, "For thus says the Lord of hosts, 'Once more in a little while, I am going to shake the heavens and the earth, the sea also and the dry land. I will shake all the nations; and they will come with the wealth of all nations [Heb., the desire of all nations shall come], and I will fill this house with glory,' declares the Lord of hosts. 'The latter glory of this house will be greater than the former,' says the Lord of hosts, 'and in this place I will give peace,' declares the Lord of hosts." The "desire of all nations" is evidently a reference to the first coming of Messiah.[61]

"YET ONCE MORE I WILL SHAKE NOT ONLY THE EARTH, BUT ALSO THE HEAVEN" – The key problem faced by exegetes is to decide whether or not this "shaking" has already taken place. Some let the language "earth" and "heaven" cause their minds to look forward to the second advent, when there will be a new heavens and a new earth. But to make Haggai 2:6 a reference to the second advent seems to rob this passage of its real emphasis – namely, the prediction that the Mosaic covenant was to be shaken (removed)

---

[58] "Turn away" is a present participle, indicating continuing action.

[59] Those who object to the idea that God is the speaker in both instances (cp. footnote #56) note that it is difficult to explain the difference between "on earth" in the first instance, and "from heaven" in the second. Bruce, *op. cit.*, p.382, offers a possible explanation: "It was from an earthly hill that God proclaimed the statutes which formed the basis of the old covenant, it was from the heavenly Zion, from His unseen throne, that He speaks in the Gospel."

[60] The writer's method of alluding to Old Testament passages by emphasizing certain key words common to all has already been discussed in comments on chapters 1 and 4.

[61] Even Jewish writers regarded this passage as Messianic. "There are several rabbinic passages that show that Habakkuk 2:6 was frequently considered in discussing messianic questions, notably the date of the coming of the Messiah. Tal. *Sanhedrin* 97b, Exod R. 18:18, Deut R. 1:23." Morris, *op. cit.*, p.145.

by the first coming of Christ. This emphasis is seen in the next two verses, which are the writer's own explanation of what the Haggai prophecy meant.[62]

12:27 – This *expression*, "Yet once more," denotes the removing of those things which can be shaken – The writer picks up the words "yet once more" to stress the fact that the new shaking mentioned by Haggai will be the final one. The Mosaic covenant with its priesthood, tabernacle, animal sacrifices, and annual remembrance of sins was to be removed,[63] for these things were only ever intended by God to be but temporary.

As of created things – "Created things" are temporary (see Hebrews 1:10-12). So were the things which could be shaken, i.e., the Mosaic system.[64]

In order that those things which cannot be shaken may remain – "In order that" introduces a purpose clause. It was God's purpose that when Jesus came the temporary things would be removed so that the permanent things could remain. If our comments are correct, the permanent things are the new covenant with its superior sacrifice and its superior priesthood and its superior "tabernacle not made with hands, not of this creation." These "cannot be shaken"; they never were intended to be temporary. Instead, they are to last to the end of time. Hebrews has taught that Jesus offered one sacrifice for sins for all time and that He is now sitting down at the right hand of the Father; His work is done. God does not find fault with the new covenant like He did the old (Hebrews 8:7,8), so no more shaking is needed as far as the removal and introduction of covenants is concerned.

12:28 – Therefore – Verse 28 is the conclusion the writer of Hebrews draws from Haggai's prophecy and its fulfillment.

Since we receive a kingdom which cannot be shaken – Believers are now receiving (it

---

[62] Writers who think the second advent and the renovation of the universe are in Haggai's words object to the metaphorical interpretation offered above. Kent (*op. cit.*, p.275) voiced his objection this way: "Although some interpret the prophecy metaphorically as referring to the upheavals accomplished by Christ's first coming in its effect upon Jewish worship and politics, the parallelism with the former shaking makes this view unlikely. The first shaking was physical and geographical at Sinai. There is no good reason to take this second shaking of the earth and the heavens above it in any less literal sense. The reference is to the second coming of Christ, which will involve great physical judgments as foretold by the prophets in both the Old and New Testaments."

[63] The word translated "removing" is the same word used in Hebrews 7:12 and translated "changed." But "removing" is also a possible translation, and seems better suited to this context.

[64] It is a little difficult to see how the expression "created things" can be somehow a reference to the Law of Moses, as our comments suggest. In fact, not a few writers note that the verb *poieo* is often used of God's creative activity, and infer from this that it is the physical creation that Haggai predicts will be removed. But observe that it reads "*as* of created things." The writer of Hebrews says there is a similarity between the "things which can be shaken" and "created things." We suppose that similarity is in the temporary nature of both. (The Bible does teach the temporary nature of the physical creation. It speaks of how heaven and earth will pass away, and the elements melt with fervent heat. Even here in Hebrews, we have been told that "they will perish, but You will remain," 1:10-12. But if our interpretation of Hebrews 12 is correct, the passage in Haggai is not one of the passages to use when attempting to show this transitoriness. Further, Romans 8:18ff teaches a renovation of the universe, not its annihilation. This being true, we would not want to translate the verb *metatithemi* by the English word "remove"; we'd have to use the word "change" even though the idea involved in "change" is not exactly synonymous with "renovation" as comments at 7:12 have shown.)

is a present participle) an unshakable kingdom.[65] Here is one verse that indicates that the "kingdom" was already in some sense begun before Hebrews was written, and the writer and readers both were already receiving it. The writer of Hebrews looked at reality in terms of God's sovereignty, God's rule, and also affirms that the present economy, unlike the Jewish economy, is unshakable (that is, it is not a temporary thing needing to be replaced). So certain is he that the new covenant was never intended to be a temporary thing that he writes, not "will not" but, "cannot be shaken."

Let us show gratitude – The KJV reads "Let us have grace."[66] The NASB margin reads "Let us have gratitude," i.e., let us be grateful. Both "grace" and "gratitude" are legitimate ideas found in *charis*. So the writer may be saying, 'Let us hold fast the grace we have received (in Christ),' or, 'Let us be grateful enough for all the blessings associated with Mount Zion to continue serving Him as He has appointed.'

By which we may offer to God an acceptable service with reverence and awe – "By which" seems to mean that it is by means of *charis* that we are able to offer to God an acceptable service. Whether *latreuo* should be rendered worship or "service" in this place is unclear. "Whether the meaning is service in general or worship in particular, it must be done with 'reverence and awe'."[67] It is not a one-time service; the present tense verb indicates continuous action. Such service is a happy and blessed privilege, but it must always be accompanied with reverence (i.e., taking care lest we break His commands) and awe, for we must never forget who He is. If these attitudes are present, our service (worship) will be done in an acceptable manner, a manner well-pleasing to God.

12:29 – For our God is a consuming fire – Verse 29 gives a reason for serving God with reverence and awe. If we scorn the present dispensation of grace, the day of judgment will be a day of terror (Hebrews 10:26,27). The language in this verse may be taken from Deuteronomy 4:24. If so, it says God is not to be trifled with any more in this age than He was of old. He is still a "consuming fire" now, just as He was then. We need not be filled with terror like the people of old at Sinai, if we are believers who continue to serve Him in reverence and awe. Yet even then, we need a healthy respect for His holiness, enough so that we have been reproducing it in our own lives. As then, so now, there is a real danger inherent in forgetting the covenant of the Lord. God is no more a friend of willful sin now than He was then. Any temptation to quit Christ and His church should be weighed soberly in the light of this fifth and final warning passage in Hebrews.

---

[65] It is an amazing that this verse in Hebrews has seldom figured in the now century-long debate about the identity of the "kingdom." The student is reminded of the comments offered about the "kingdom" in the author's *Commentary on Acts* at Acts 1:3. Before Pentecost (Acts 2) the "kingdom" was spoken of as still future, but after Pentecost, it is regularly referred to as already in existence. In addition, it is emphasized that orientals would think more of the rule of God, than of the people or territory ruled, when they used the word "kingdom."

[66] There is a manuscript variation here, some (including P[46], Sinaiticus, and 33) reading indicative ("we have grace") and some (including Alexandrinus and Claromontanus) reading subjunctive ("Let us have grace!"). There is a one letter difference in spelling of the two forms, and they were often confused by scribes writing as someone else dictated. Commentators tend to favor the subjunctive because of its suitability to the context.

[67] Morris, *op. cit.*, p.145.

D. Exhortation Concerning the Performance of Christian Duties. 13:1-17

1. Social Duties. 13:1-6

a. Brotherly Love. 13:1-3

13:1 – Let love of the brethren continue – Display kindness, sympathy, helpfulness.[1] "Brotherly love" is no mere sentiment. It can be a very costly thing (1 John 3:16-18). "Let ... continue" indicates there was a danger these Hebrew Christians' love for their brothers in Christ was about to be interrupted, or was in danger of being interrupted.[2] There is a tendency in times of persecution to allow one's brotherly love to cool, to show indifference to those being persecuted, and thus escape any suffering ourselves. Two specific areas where brotherly love can be shown follow.

13:2 – Do not neglect to show hospitality to strangers – Hospitality for local brethren and for travelling brethren is incumbent on all Christians.[3] Public accommodations were not always safe, often were morally offensive to Christians, and could be expensive. (Why ask travelling preachers and brethren to spend resources for housing when it could be provided for them, rather inexpensively, by their brethren, thus leaving resources free for other worthy projects?) The prohibition (*me* and a present imperative) forbids the continuance of an action already in progress. Stop neglecting hospitality!

For by this – That is, by showing hospitality.

Some have entertained angels without knowing it – Abraham, Lot, Gideon, and Manoah (the father of Samson) are Old Testament examples.[4] God is pleased when this sort of brotherly love is displayed. And the host sometimes receives an unexpected blessing.[5]

13:3 – Remember the prisoners – "Remember" means more than merely to think about

---

[1] Brotherly love is a most important virtue, if we may judge from the number of times it is emphasized in the New Testament (cf. Romans 12:10; 1 Thessalonians 4:9; 1 Peter 1:22; 2 Peter 1:7).

[2] These comments reflect a studied conclusion that chapter 13 is an integral part of the work that makes up the first 12 chapters. There is no justification from either internal or external evidence for regarding it as in some way a separate writing (perhaps by an author other than the one who wrote the first 12 chapters) that somehow became attached to the first 12 chapters at some later date. In fact, 13:9-14 reflect what is written earlier about the cross of Jesus, and the concluding doxology (13:20,21) reflects a number of the key ideas from earlier chapters of the book.

[3] Matthew 25:31-46; Romans 12:13; 1 Peter 4:9, teach hospitality as a vital way to express one's love to "strangers." One of the mandatory qualifications to be an elder is that men were to be "hospitable" (1 Timothy 3:2; Titus 1:8). Hospitality is a grace expected of all, not just those who would be elders.

[4] See Genesis 18:1-3, 19:1,2; Judges 6:11-24; 13:2-20.

[5] "Entertained angels" seems to be figurative language for receive unexpected blessings. It is doubtful the language implies such angelic visits still occur, as they occasionally did in Bible times.

them. It means continue to give whatever assistance you can to your brethren who have been imprisoned. These brethren likely have been imprisoned because of their Christianity. To attempt to meet their needs will take more effort than showing hospitality to strangers, for strangers may come unbidden, but prisoners must be actively sought out.

As though in prison with them – Express human kindness toward them, doing the same for them you might wish others to do for you, were your circumstances reversed.

And those who are ill-treated – In the ancient world, prisoners were not cared for by the state. They depended – often even for necessities like food and clothing – on friends and acquaintances who, by coming to the prison to show human kindness to the prisoner, would call attention to themselves. Such attention might bring the wrath of the authorities onto the sympathizer, even if the sympathy lay not with the cause (crime?) for which the prisoner was accused, but simply for his everyday physical needs. The writer of Hebrews calls for "remembering" not only the prisoners, but also "those who are ill- treated."[6]

Since you yourselves also are in the body – Perhaps "body" speaks of the physical body, and the idea is that you are liable to similar treatment and will need help, then, too. Perhaps the reference is to the body of Christ, in which case the idea is that they are just like members of your own body, and we try to help those who are hurting (1 Corinthians 12:26, "if one member suffers, all members suffer with it").

b. Fidelity to the marriage relationship. 13:4

13:4 – Let marriage *be held* in honor among all – The words in italics show that we must supply the verb. Make it an exhortation, and let the rest of the verse (which begins with "for") be seen as a reason for the exhortation.[7] Having made it an exhortation, the verse then becomes a command to purity and fidelity to the marriage relationship. "Among all" may be either masculine (among all men) or neuter (in all circumstances).[8]

And the *marriage* bed *is to be* undefiled – The "marriage bed" is a euphemism for sexual intercourse. Christians are to have a mindset (honor the married state as the only proper place for intercourse) on this matter that directs and informs all their behavior. "This was a novel view to many in the first century. For them chastity was an unreasonable demand to make. It is one of the unrecognized miracles that Christians were able not only to make

---

[6] This is a New Testament passage that shows Christians are to have a certain respect for the dignity of human life. Not only is it implied that such maltreatment and injury of others is to have no place in the Christian's own behavior, but the Christian is specifically exhorted to sympathetically get involved helping those who have been ill-treated by others.

[7] The KJV which makes it read as a statement is the result of the translators beliefs that this verse is intended to be a refutation of asceticism, or celibacy.

[8] If we read all circumstances, does this exhortation then have some application to everyday literature and opera and movies and TV? Does it not require that the high view of the God-approved place for sexual activity is the only view the Christian should tolerate?

this demand, but to make it stick."[9]

For fornicators and adulterers God will judge – "For" seems to say this phrase is intended as a reason for the exhortation just given. Fornication is sexual sin before marriage. Adultery is infidelity after marriage. Both are offenses against the exhortation to honor the marriage relationship. Both sins "defile the bed." Contemplation of such extra-marital behavior is evidence the proper mind set about the "marriage bed" is absent. "God[10] will judge" says that violations of the marriage relationship may be undetected by men here on earth, but they do not avoid God's notice, nor His eventual condemnation.

c. Contentment. 13:5,6

13:5 -- Let your way of life be free from the love of money – Covetousness ("love of money") is another area[11] where a man's selfish desires can quickly lead him away from the way of life that pleases God. "Free from the love of money" is another characteristic that, while given as a qualification for elders (1 Timothy 3:3), is expected of all Christians.

Being content with what you have – Contentment is the thing being urged in verses 5 and 6. The writer is saying our trust and confidence in God should be such that we will be satisfied with our condition.[12] The Christian finds his satisfaction not in some hoped-for wealth, but in the things at hand and the Lord's companionship. Wealth alone, without God's personal presence, will not solve our problems.

For He Himself has said – Here follows a reason why covetousness is needless and foolish. What is an abundance of things compared to God's personal presence and care?

"I WILL NEVER DESERT YOU, NOR WILL I EVER FORSAKE YOU" – The exact source of this quote is debated.[13] Perhaps it is from Deuteronomy 31:6,8 or Joshua 1:5 or 1 Chronicles 28:20. Perhaps it reflects our Lord's own teaching, "Is not life more than food,

---

[9] Leon Morris, *op. cit.*, p.147.

[10] "God" comes last in the Greek word order, and is therefore emphatic. Sexual sinners may go their way here on earth, careless of all others. But in the end they will be judged by none less than God!

[11] One wonders if a possible reason why sexual impurity and covetousness are often linked together in the same passage of Scripture is because behind both is a selfishness that pursues its selfish aims (whether sexual or financial), without regard to the rights of others.

[12] Milligan, *op. cit.*, p.373, indicates this exhortation does not forbid all lawful endeavors to improve our condition and that of others. Such a prohibition would be inconsistent with what is plainly taught in many other passages (e.g., Romans 12:11; Ephesians 4:28; 2 Thessalonians 3:11). 1 Timothy 6:9,10 should to be read in this context, too.

[13] The words do not correspond exactly to any Old Testament passage. There are several that are rather like it. What adds to the enigma is that the same quotation in the same words is found in Philo (*On the Confusion of Tongues* 166). "Rather than suppose the author [of Hebrews] to have utilized Philo, it is more likely that this saying from the Old Testament had acquired usage as a proverb, and that both Philo and Hebrews employ this prevalent form." Homer Kent, *op. cit.*, p.280. Morris, *ibid.*, suggests both Philo and the writer of Hebrews may have quoted a version of the LXX that has not survived.

and the body more than clothing" (Matthew 6:25-34)? Or "Beware, and be on your guard against every form of greed; for not even when one has an abundance does his life consist of his possessions" (Luke 12:15). Since God has promised to help His own, to be their constant companion, covetousness in all forms is out of character for anyone who knows Him. God's people should find their security in Him, not in the things of this world.

13:6 – So that we confidently say – The Christian who knows God's care and companionship may[14] confidently make the words of the Psalmist his own. The following quotations are from Psalm 118:6. There are three points that may be confidently affirmed.

"THE LORD IS MY HELPER – The first point the Psalmist and the Christian realizes is that the Lord is my helper. This continues (yea, expresses more succinctly) the thought introduced in the previous verse, that the believer counts on the Lord's assistance. Psalm 118 is a Messianic Psalm. Perhaps Jesus Himself is here promised as help for Christians.

I WILL NOT BE AFRAID – The second point is that with the Lord's help, the believer has no reason to fear.

WHAT WILL MAN DO TO ME?" – The third point is that while men may do[15] many things – ill-treat, persecute, ostracize, spoil their goods, martyr – to Christians, none of these causes the Christian's confidence in the final outcome to waver. "Fainthearted Jewish converts who were tempted to forsake Christ and return to Judaism through fear of persecution should take note that such an act would be to turn away from the attitude of the Old Testament psalmist also."[16]

2. Religious Duties. 13:7-17

a. Imitate the faith of their former leaders. 13:7,8

13:7 – Remember those who led you – Former leaders are in view here, including the apostles and such men as Stephen, James, and other faithful preachers[17] who led the Hebrews in the years before this letter was written. It is because of the past tense verbs in this place that we speak of former leaders.[18] These few words (verses 7,17) about "leaders"

---

[14] On the construction introduced by *hoste*, E.A. Abbott says that it "rather suggests what we *may* say than states what we *do* say." *Johannine Grammar*, 2203b.

[15] The modern versions are divided on how to render this question. Some (ASV, NASB) read, "What will man do to me?" Others (NIV) read, "What can man do to me?" Now it seems that it is the actual performance, not just the capacity to perform, that the Psalmist has in mind.

[16] Kent, *op. cit.*, p.280.

[17] The word translated "led" is *hegeomai*, a general word for "lead" occurring three times in chapter 13 – here, at verse 17, and again at verse 24. Because it is a general word, it is not possible to identify a certain function (such as elder, evangelist, apostle) and say that it is this which is in the writer's mind.

[18] KJV readers ("Remember them which have the rule over you") are left with the impression the "leaders"

and the way Christians should treat their leaders are important, for there is not much on this topic elsewhere in the New Testament.

Who spoke the word of God to you – "Word of God" is a comprehensive expression for the whole Christian message, the gospel. That it came from God reminds the readers that the gospel by which they became believers was not of human invention, but was of divine origin. Further, if they will follow the example of those who planted the church and fostered it by this message from God, all will be well with them.

And considering the result of their conduct – "Result" ("issue," ASV) is likely a euphemism for death,[19] and implies that something good happened to them after they died. When they died, they entered into blessedness. "Conduct" in this clause and "faith" in the next complement each other. They were men who had run the race with endurance (12:1); they had held fast the beginning of their assurance firm until the end (3:14). What they did, their converts could do also!

Imitate their faith – Continue imitating their example, and the outcome or "result" of your life will be the same as theirs. These former leaders' example of faithfulness is held up as the good example to be followed (instead of allowing the temptation to unbelief and to falling away from Christ to prevail).

13:8 – Jesus Christ is the same yesterday and today, yes and forever – Verse 8 may be taken with what precedes, or it can be taken with what follows. If taken with verse 7, the idea is that what Jesus did for the faithful people who led you in the past, He will do for you if you too are faithful. Jesus will not act differently, now or in the future, than He did in the past.[20] When those who are faithful to Him exit this life, it is to enter into His pres-

---

of verse 7 are still living. This reading is based partly on the fact that in the first phrase of verse 7, the article and participle translated "those who led you" is a *present* participle in the Greek. Remember that *tense* in an indicative mood indicates two things: both the time and the kind of action. But *tense* in *participles* indicates only the kind of action, and that only in relation to the time of the leading verb. Thus an aorist participle indicates action that happened before the action of the leading verb occurred. A present participle indicates action contemporaneous with the action of the leading verb (cp. J G. Machen, *New Testament Greek for Beginners*, p.105-6). Applied to verse 7, this means the "leading" is conceived as occurring at the same time as the speaking. Since "spoke the word" is a past tense, so too the leading is something done in the past, contemporaneous with the speaking. Those who believe verse 7 refers to *former* leaders make these points: "(1) The readers are urged to *remember* them. (2) Present leaders are referred to in verse 17. (3) "Result" *(ekbasis)* is used elsewhere in the sense of "death" (Wisdom 2:17), and that meaning is readily understandable here. (4) The present participle *(ton hegoumenon)* is often used as a substantive: 'leaders'." Kent, *op. cit.*, p.281.

[19] *Ekbasis* occurs only here in Hebrews, and but one other time in the New Testament, at 1 Corinthians 10:13, where it is rendered "way of escape." Some commentators (e.g., Westcott, Moffatt) think it refers specially to a martyr's death, but that may be adding more to the word than it actually implies. It is not necessary to think all the former leaders were martyred; all that is needed is to say that, like the heroes of chapter 11, these former leaders had "died in faith" (cp. Hebrews 11:13).

[20] While "yesterday" seems to be contrasted with "forever" (unto the ages in the future; cp. comments on Hebrews 13:21) and thus would speak of Christ's pre-existence, care must be taken lest this impressive statement about His unchanging nature be stretched too much. We do not for a moment teach Christ was always subordinate to the Father as He was during His incarnate state, or that He always will be subordinate. Philippians 2:6-11 shows that He temporarily "emptied Himself" of the independent exercise of the prerogatives

ence, a life of bliss and happy activity in God's presence, where Jesus has gone as our forerunner (Hebrews 6:20). If Jesus' behavior is consistent, as is here affirmed, then it is ever true that "He is able to save forever those who draw near to God through Him" (Hebrews 7:25), and He is the source of eternal salvation to all who obey Him (Hebrews 5:9). If we take 13:8 with 13:9, then this statement gives a reason why our doctrine about Him should always be the same.

b. Be steadfast in the teachings of Christianity. 13:9-15

13:9 – Do not be carried away by varied and strange teachings – Christians are to have fixed and settled points of belief.[21] Compare Ephesians 4:14. "Strange" translates *xenais*; "foreign," foreign to the gospel, evidently is meant. The "varied ... teachings" are probably Jewish – see the reference to "foods" in the following phrase, and the topic of the whole letter, namely, do not revert to Judaism at the expense of abandoning faith in Christ.

For it is good for the heart to be strengthened by grace, not by foods – The false teachings that threatened to carry them away were apparently attempting to elevate Judaism at the expense of true Christianity, urging Law rather than grace. "Foods" may be a reference to the Jewish dietary laws with their clean and unclean foods. The "heart" stands for the whole inner spiritual life of a man. This part of a man cannot be sustained by certain diets,[22] but must be sustained by grace.[23]

Through which those who were thus occupied were not benefited – The spiritual value of foods is neither negative nor positive. Diet is not what helps a man grow spiritually strong. "Food will not commend us to God," Paul writes in a related passage on 'foods.' "We are neither the worse if we do not eat, nor better if we do eat" (1 Corinthians 8:8).

13:10 – We have an altar – "We" is we Christians, as distinguished from the Jews. It seems (if we may read underneath the surface of what the writer here says) that some were taunting the Christians, 'You do not have any dietary laws to help you grow; you do not have any altar; you do not have a temple to worship in; you do not have any sacrifices to offer. What kind of religion is that?' One may even infer that these taunts were part of the reason the Christians were thinking of returning to Judaism. Answering the taunts, the

---

of deity when He became incarnate: He became subordinate in function but not in nature or essence for He always "exists (so the Greek, literally) in the form of God." Philippians 2 also shows He has now been "super highly exalted" (again, so the Greek, literally). None of these expressions contradict what is said in Hebrews 13:7, for the topics being discussed are not the same.

[21] When it is the "word of God" that leads a man to change his beliefs, this prohibition against changing ("do not be carried away") is not applicable. It is "strange teachings" that are to be rejected in a person's convictions.

[22] "Rules about food, imposed by external authority, have never helped people maintain a closer walk with God. (Voluntary fasting, in the spirit of our Lord's instruction in Matthew 6:16ff, is quite a different thing, but that is not the subject here.)" Bruce, *op. cit.*, p.398.

[23] Milligan, *op. cit.*, p.376, suggests "grace" here means "the gracious truths and influences of the Gospel."

writer affirms, "We (do) have an altar!" And not only so, our altar[24] (explained in verses 11 and 12 to be a reference to Jesus) is better than anything the Jews have.

From which those who serve the tabernacle have no right to eat – Christians have exclusive rights and privileges. Adherents[25] of the old Levitical system are not eligible to participate in the benefits of Christ's sacrifice; not, that is, until they too become Christians. If the Jewish ritual was only a type and shadow of things to come (Hebrews 10:1), and if a man cannot see that the ceremonies were intended to point to Christ, then Christ will mean nothing at all to him, and he is not eligible to participate in the "altar." By pointing out the Christian's privileges, the writer has offered another warning against defection from Jesus.

13:11 – For the bodies of those animals whose blood is brought into the holy place by the high priest *as an offering* for sin – "For" shows that verses 11 and 12 are intended to be an explanation of something just said. We suppose it explains that "altar" has reference to Jesus' suffering (crucifixion).[26] As has often been said, the reader of Hebrews will be aided in his understanding by keeping in mind the rituals on the Day of Atonement (see Hebrews 7:27, 9:7,25, 10:1-3). In many Jewish sacrifices, portions of the animals offered in sacrifice were later eaten by the priests (Leviticus 4:22-35, 6:25,26). But the flesh of any sin offering whose blood was carried into the Holy of Holies[27] by the high priest on the Day of Atonement was not to be eaten. Instead it was to be carried outside the camp and there entirely consumed by fire (Leviticus 16:27).

Are burned outside the camp – "Outside the camp" reminds us of the situation of Israel in the wilderness, living in tents in a "camp." It was out in the wilderness, away from the

---

[24] The exact identification of the "altar" has been debated through the centuries. (1) Greek Orthodox and Roman Catholic theologians affirm that the "altar" is to be identified with the communion table. This is the verse that has led both those churches to call the table an "altar." (Such an interpretation is a curious way of explaining this passage given the point just made about "foods." Would the Hebrews writer deny that one kind of physical food [clean or unclean meats] is of benefit to the heart, only to affirm another kind [the loaf and the cup] is? Would the writer who has constantly pointed to the heavenly realities in contrast to the Jewish physical types and shadows now substitute another physical table for the Jewish altar?) After interpretting "altar" to mean Lord's Table, it is then observed that this passage teaches non-Christians are to have no part in the Lord's Supper. Actually, in this commentator's opinion, there is no reference to the Lord's Supper in Hebrews at all, not even in the bread and wine brought by Melchizedek to Abraham. (2) Not a few Protestants identify the "altar" with the cross of Calvary. An altar was a place where a sacrifice was offered. Christ's sacrifice was offered on the cross. Thus the cross may properly be spoken of as an "altar." (3) Others identify the "altar" with Christ Himself. These affirm the reference is not to the place of sacrifice, but to the sacrifice itself.

[25] "Those who serve the tabernacle" need not be limited to the priests. Since the word *latreuo* can mean worship or serve, the expression can have reference to Jewish worshippers in general.

[26] To connect verses 11 and 12 with "altar," the main clause of verse 10, rather than to "those who serve in the tabernacle," a subordinate clause, would seem the better choice. Morris, *op. cit.*, p.150, however, opts for the latter when he writes, "'For' ... leads from the general idea of serving the altar to a specific example, one taken from the Day of Atonement ceremonies in all probability."

[27] Some commentators express doubt that the reference here in Hebrews 13 is to the Day of Atonement since the word translated "holy place" is used in Hebrews 9:2 to refer to the first room of the tabernacle, not the Holy of Holies. It will be recalled that in our comments at 9:2,3, it was observed there is no uniformity in the Sacred writings when it comes to the names for the tent itself, or for its different rooms. So by interpretation we conclude "holy place" here has reference particularly to the Holy of Holies, as it does in Hebrews 9:3.

camp, that the bodies of the sacrificial victims were to be burned. The writer is building toward the next verse where he suggests that Jesus fulfilled a type by suffering outside the gate. No one partook of the typical sin offerings on the Day of Atonement; but of the true sin offering, all may partake, if they just go outside the camp to where Jesus is.

13:12 – Therefore Jesus also – "Therefore" now draws the inference from the Old Testament event just referred to, where an "altar" for sacrifice was used. This is the verse that seems to identify Jesus' suffering with the "altar" referred to in verse 10.

That He might sanctify the people through His own blood – Christ's death fulfilled the sin offering ritual of the Jewish Day of Atonement. His purpose[28] was to set the people apart to God's service by removing their guilt. "Sanctify" means to set aside for God, and we remember that in 10:29 we have been told Christ's blood[29] ratified the new covenant, by which the privilege of sonship was restored to men.

Suffered outside the gate – Christ's crucifixion was outside the city walls of Jerusalem.[30] There was disgrace involved in what happened to Jesus (compare "bearing His reproach" in the next verse) in the eyes of those without spiritual discernment.

13:13 – Hence – Here is the application of the type and fulfillment. If Jesus could bear reproach,[31] is it too much to ask His followers to willingly suffer similar disgrace, should being faithful to Jesus bring such reproach from those who lack spiritual discernment?

Let us go out to Him outside the camp – This is a call to separation. Christ is outside the camp of the Judaism that refused to acknowledge Him as the long-awaited Messiah. The readers are encouraged to go to Him outside the camp. This is a stirring challenge to forsake the camp of Israel, to leave Judaism behind. The old way has been superseded in the

---

[28] The conjunction *hina*, translated "that," introduces a purpose clause. Jesus' suffering was not purposeless; He had a specific purpose in mind, namely, to "sanctify the people."

[29] This setting apart of a people was effected through "His own blood." This expression may put some emphasis on the fact that Christ did not need an external victim like the Jewish priests had to use, but rather brought about the setting apart by the sacrifice of Himself.

[30] The Gospels imply the crucifixion took place outside the city; they read "He went out bearing His cross" (John 19:17; see also Matthew 27:32, Mark 15:20). Endeavoring to locate the place of the crucifixion, some have used this passage to cast doubt on claims made by the Church of the Holy Sepulchre that it covers the site of the crucifixion and the tomb, since it is *inside* the *present* walls of Jerusalem. If it lay outside the *ancient* walls of the city, and we do not know for certain the location of the second north wall, its claim might be valid.

[31] Kent, *op. cit.*, p. 284,285, has a succinct note that catches the meaning of the key words in this analogy. "As the animal carcasses were burned outside the camp of Israel (Lev. 16:27), Jesus also experienced something quite similar. He suffered outside the gate of Jerusalem. The analogy was not meant to be pressed, and that may be why the author used the word suffered (*epathen*) rather than 'died.' The Old Testament sin offering was actually slain *within* the tabernacle precincts, and only after its blood was sprinkled on the altar was the carcass carried outside the camp for burning. In the case of Jesus, of course, His death occurred outside the city. The main point in view is the disgrace involved. The burning of the animal carcass outside the camp was not part of a burnt offering ritual, for that would have occurred on the brazen altar. It was rather to picture the removal of sin from Israel, and also the disgraceful character of sin and its repudiation. In the instance of Christ, the author is using the analogy to demonstrate the ignominy of His death."

program of God. Forget it – even if it means taking on yourselves the "reproach" of Christ.

Bearing His reproach – "Reproach" is the same word used at 11:26, where Moses is said to have been willing to suffer "reproach for Christ." To align oneself with Christ could well result in becoming an object of scorn, reproach, contempt, and derision. Nevertheless, belonging to Christ is well worth it – a point made over and over again in this epistle.

13:14 – For here we do not have a lasting city – "For," with which this verse begins, seems to suggest that it is a reason for what was just said about going out to Christ. Even if the reproach of Christ means we are driven from our homes, and become refugees who have had to flee from earthly Jerusalem, remember that our real home is not here on earth, but in heaven. It is vain to seek refuge in Jerusalem and its temple, for when AD 70 comes, those places will have ceased to last. (Does this verse imply that part of the struggle the readers faced was the attractiveness of the Jewish temple, and its ancestral traditions and elaborate rituals, compared with the simple services found in Christianity?)

But we are seeking *the city* which is to come – In Hebrews 11:10,13,16, and 12:22, we became acquainted with heavenly Jerusalem. Like Abraham, our motivating purpose is to live in that city. "Seeking" translates *epizeteo*, a word that suggests earnest endeavor to live in that city. Only if they would once and for all leave earthly Jerusalem's attractions and the errors and corruptions of Judaism, and go to Christ (who Himself was "outside the camp"), could they be considered to have sought "the city which is to come" and thereby meet the conditions that would secure for themselves a place in the heavenly Jerusalem.

13:15 – Through Him then – "Him" is emphatic in the Greek. It is through Jesus, and through Him alone (not through any Jewish priests, or any other priests for that matter), that men may offer sacrifices that God views as acceptable.

Let us continually offer up a sacrifice of praise to God – Christians *do* have sacrifices to offer[32], and they are not limited to a few annual festivals. Other sacrifices a Christian offers are noted in Romans 12:1,2 and Philippians 4:18. It may well be intimated that sacrifices of animals are no longer the kind of sacrifices God accepts.[33] A "sacrifice of praise"[34] is a sacrifice that consists of praise, a special thanks offering, voluntarily offered.

---

[32] Compare notes at verses 10 and 14. Had the opponents of the readers said not only, 'You have no altar,' but also 'You have no sacrifices'? Is such an objection what is now answered by the writer of Hebrews? He says, 'We do have sacrifices to offer, and something better than animal sacrifices.'

[33] The idea of offering animal sacrifices originated in a revelation from God. That patriarchal tradition was passed on so that such sacrifice is almost a universal religious practice (at least in those cultures that have not been influenced by modern Judaism or by Christianity). With such a mindset toward sacrifice, are Christians to have nothing to offer? Indeed, Christians do have sacrifices to offer -- and they are the kind that please God! Christ's suffering "outside the camp" has altered everything. God long ago revealed that sacrifices of bulls and goats was not the way to atone for sins; further, Jesus came to do God's will in this matter by the sacrifice of Himself on Calvary (Hebrews 10:5-10). Instead of offering animals in sacrifice, people who know God through Jesus Christ show their appreciation for what God has done by praise, good deeds, and sharing out of love.

[34] This may reflect the vocabulary of Leviticus 7:11-13, which describes the Old Testament peace offering which was offered when a worshipper wanted to offer special thanks to God.

This kind of "sacrifice" is something Christians can offer up "continually."

That is, the fruit of lips – Out of the mouth proceeds what is in the heart (Matthew 12:34). If our hearts are full of gratitude to God for what He has done in Jesus, we will express it with our lips. "Fruit of (our) lips" may be language taken from Hosea 14:2.[35]

That give thanks to His name – Margin, "confess" to His name. The "name" often stands for the person himself. Confession or thanks given to God Himself is the thing here called "fruit of (the) lips." And it should not be overlooked that this confession is something done continually (it is a present tense verb). There is no way a person who abandons Christ in favor of Judaism can continue to make such an approved confession.

c. Benevolence encouraged. 13:16

13:16 – And do not neglect doing good and sharing – The writer identifies two more examples of the sacrifices Christians may offer which will please God. Christians are to be benevolent, to share liberally with others. It is not enough just to praise God with our lips. We honor Him with our substance by being helpful to our brethren (and fellowmen) as we have opportunity. We also honor Him by "sharing." The word is often translated fellowship, i.e., participating in a common cause. We wonder if there is another reflection on what would be lost if the readers forsake the assembling together: how would they then be involved in any "sharing," any participation with their brethren in the common cause related to Jesus? And if there was no such "sharing," how could there be any pleasing of God, for they would no longer have one of the sacrifices that please Him in this age?

For with such sacrifices God is pleased – This reminds us of James 1:27. Such words of praise and thanksgiving, and such deeds of love (as verses 15 and 16 have called for) are evidence of spiritual vitality; these please God (more than Levitical rituals and sacrifices).

d. Obedience and submission to spiritual leaders. 13:17

13:17 – Obey your leaders – The readers' present leaders are intended.[36] (Verse 7 spoke

---

[35] The writer of Hebrews reflects the LXX reading of Hosea 14:2 rather than the Hebrew. "The Hebrew Masoretic text ... has the expression `calves of our lips.' The difference is caused apparently by two different ways of dividing the consonants in the Hebrew text, which would yield the two words in question. The Masoretic text we now possess has done it one way. The Septuagint may be based upon a Hebrew text which did it differently. It is also possible that the Septuagint was intended to be a paraphrase interpreting the Hebrew 'calves.' Whatever may have caused the Septuagint to translate it as 'fruit,' the point of the passage is clear. God is primarily interested not in calves slain upon material altars, but in 'calves of our lips'; that is, the spiritual sacrifice of lips devoted to the acknowledgement of God and the praise of Him." Kent, *op. cit.*, p.287.

[36] Again (as in verse 7) "leaders" is a general term. Thus it is not possible to limit this exclusively to one particular office, say, to the elders. Still, elders are certainly included, as would be evident when "watching for your souls" is compared to instructions given to elders in Acts 20:28-32 and 1 Peter 5:1-5.

of former leaders.) Continually "obey" (present tense imperative) their directions, when those directions are in harmony with the Word. In light of the theme of this whole letter, may we not suppose the present leaders have been urging faithfulness to Christ?

And submit *to them* – When they teach the oracles of God, when they plead for faithfulness to Jesus, we yield our contrary opinions in favor of their guidance. Habitual submission (present tense imperative) is the thing commanded.

For they keep watch over your souls – "For" gives a reason why the readers should obey and submit. We are reminded of Ezekiel 3:18-21. The guidance the present leaders[37] give is the result of watchfulness,[38] and is intended to be spiritually beneficial.[39]

As those who will give an account – It is no simple matter to have the responsibility (stewardship?) of watching over the flock of God. At the final judgment these leaders will give an account – a solemn reminder to leaders and members alike of the awesome responsibility leaders have.

Let them do this with joy – Is it the watching or the giving account that is in view? The present tense subjunctive verb "do" (something they do continuously) may show that the emphasis is on watching.[40] The response of the people can make a great difference in the joy (or heartbreak) of the leader. By this exhortation, the readers are invited to cooperate with their spiritual overseers, and thus make their task joyful.

And not with grief – If the watching (or the accounting) brings "grief"[41] to the leaders, it is certain the members of the flock will be in trouble when they too give "account" to God.

For this would be unprofitable for you – If either the watching or the giving account is done with "grief," it is evidence the attempted leadership has not produced the spiritual profit the leaders and the Lord desired. In such cases the rebels will do more than groan.[42]

---

[37] "They" translates a pronoun in the nominative case in the Greek. With nominative case pronouns, there is emphasis on that pronoun, an implied contrast. "They, and no one else, watch for your souls" is the idea. Just who is in the writer's mind as he rules out others as being interested in their souls is not easy to determine. Perhaps those who reproached and persecuted the Christians until they were giving serious thought to quitting Christ. 'Well, don't do it,' the writer says. 'They aren't interested in your souls like your present leaders are!'

[38] "Keep watch" (*agrupneo*) means literally "keep oneself awake, be awake" (BAG, p.13). The word may well reflect the fact such leaders have spent sleepless nights because of their concern for their people.

[39] Commentators are divided on whether "souls" is simply a periphrasis for "you," or whether the thought is of the "spiritual life" in particular. In view of the similar use of "soul" in 10:39 ("to the saving of the soul") it may be that here in verse 17 there is deliberate reference to spiritual well-being, the deep needs of the people, and not simply what lies on the surface.

[40] We would understand that the accounting that leaders will give at the final judgment is a one-time thing; thus the present tense "do" seems not to be appropriate for a reference to the judgment.

[41] "Grief" translates *stenazontes*, a burden, a groaning.

[42] "Unprofitable" is perhaps a deliberate understatement, in order to heighten the effect of the point being made. The rebels will stand before God in the final judgment. And it appears that this language threatens more

CONCLUSION: INSTRUCTIONS AND GREETINGS.
Hebrews 13:18-25

A. A Request for Prayer. 13:18,19

13:18 – Pray for us – Is "us" a reference to the author (a literary plural) or to the author and his associates (a true plural)? The identity of the author is no secret to the readers.[43] They are exhorted to keep on praying for "us."[44] The writer has rebuked the readers, warning them five times of the danger of abandoning Christianity. Nevertheless, he now shows he depends on them to support him with their prayers. In the following phrases, he gives a reason why it is proper for them to continue to pray for him, and then he specifies the exact thing he wants them to pray for.

For we are sure that we have a good conscience – One reason why a request for their prayers is proper is the fact that his conscience does not accuse him of false conduct.[45] A man's "conscience" will accuse him if he has failed to carry out a known duty or if he does what his mind thinks is wrong.[46] If he had been guilty of flagrant sin, or if his appeals to them to abandon Judaism proceeded from selfish or sinister motives, then his conscience would have bothered him, and the request about to be specified would have been out of place, since he would have no right to claim their sympathy and their prayers.

Desiring to conduct ourselves honorably in all things – His activities had always been motivated by a firm determination[47] to behave honorably. This is a second reason why he

---

than simply loss of some reward a saved person might have had (as in 1 Corinthians 3:13-15). It appears rather that what is here threatened is not different from the "certain terrifying expectation" that Hebrews 10:27 has affirmed awaits those who "shrink back to destruction" (10:39).

[43] The plural ["us"] in this verse is followed by a singular ["I"] in verse 19, and exactly opposite conclusions about the import of the word "us" has been drawn from all this. Westcott and Kent think the plural is genuine and that the writer is asking for prayer not only for himself but also for all his associates. Bruce, Hewitt, and Morris think the following singular pronoun shows that the plural is nothing more than a literary plural.

[44] Such requests for prayer are found in many of the New Testament epistles (e.g., 1 Thessalonians 5:25; 2 Thessalonians 3:1; Colossians 4:3; Ephesians 6:18,19; and Philemon 22). The verb "pray" is present imperative, thus calling for a continuing activity.

[45] This is the only place in the New Testament that the adjective *kalen* ("good") is applied to conscience. On first thought, the fact that the writer has a "good conscience" is an unusual reason for requesting prayer. If he had specified certain difficulties that made such a prayer request proper, it would be easier to understand. Such language about "good conscience" implies someone has made an accusation against the writer, an accusation he knows about, also one he knows to be patently false. Has someone attributed his continuing absence to unworthy motives? Has he been accused of some crime, concerning which he thus avers his innocence? Whatever accusation has been made, the writer declares it is untrue. His conscience does not accuse him of the crime; therefore there is no reason they should be hesitant to pray for him.

[46] We suppose "conscience" in this verse speaks of that innate faculty that prompts a man to do what his mind thinks is right and accuses him when he does what his mind thinks is wrong. The mind, of course, is correctly informed only when it thinks in harmony with what God has revealed. (Compare what is said about "conscience" at Acts 23:1, 24:16; 1 Timothy 1:5.)

[47] "Desiring" is the NASB rendering of *thelontes*. The verb expresses more than a wish. It is a set of the

is not hesitant to asked to be included in the readers' prayers on his behalf.

13:19 – And I urge *you* all the more to do this – "All the more" indicates the readers have already been petitioning God for this particular favor. Now, the writer asks for more.

That I may be restored to you the sooner – For the writer to make such a request indicates his conviction that the fervent prayer of righteous men avails much. It also reveals his hope that he will soon be able to visit the readers again.[48] Some considerable obstacle was in the way of this hoped-for reunion. Is the writer's absence due to imprisonment, illness, or something else? Whatever the reason for the separation, both writer and readers know the Lord does providentially dispense the affairs of men according to the prayers of the saints.

B. A Prayer for the Readers. 13:20,21

13:20 – Now the God of peace – The verb that completes this request to God does not follow until early in verse 21. May "God ... equip you ..." is the main idea. After asking for their prayers for himself, the writer prays for them. He addresses this prayer to "the God of peace,"[49] thus recognizing that God is the author and source of peace – an idea very comforting to the churches of Judea which were threatened with many dangers. Verses 20 and 21 have often been called a magnificent doxology which gathers up a number of the themes that have been unfolded throughout the course of this epistle.

Who brought up from the dead the great Shepherd of the sheep – This is one of the few references in Hebrews to Jesus' resurrection. While the writer has implied it before, he has not specifically mentioned it. In some New Testament passages, Jesus' resurrection is attributed to His own power; He is said to have arisen.[50] More commonly, though, we read that God raised Him. Jesus, "even Jesus our Lord", is the One designated as "the great Shepherd of the sheep."[51] There may be an allusion to Isaiah 63:11, where Moses is a shepherd of God's Old Testament flock. But we have already learned that Jesus is superior to Moses (Hebrews 3:1ff), so Jesus is the "GREAT Shepherd of the sheep." Did the readers yet have doubt about who their real leader was? When it is remembered that God raised

---

will, a firm determination that is indicated.

[48] "Restored" implies the writer had once lived or worked among the readers. If Paul wrote this letter, as was advocated in the Introductory Studies, we must admit it is uncertain whether this desire for reunion was ever realized. Per the Prison Epistles and early Christian literature, after release from his first Roman imprisonment, Paul traveled throughout the middle Mediterranean world, but we know nothing of a visit to Jerusalem.

[49] This designation for God is used six other times in the New Testament, always by Paul (Romans 15:33, 16:20; 1 Corinthians 14:33; 2 Corinthians 13:11; Philippians 4:9; 1 Thessalonians 5:23). The expression "Lord of peace" occurs at 2 Thessalonians 3:16. Most of these references occur in a context where there is some difficulty faced by the readers, and convey the blessed truth that men find their ultimate peace and harmony in the service of God. See comments on the word "peace" (the Hebrew *shalom*) at Hebrews 7:2.

[50] Compare comments in the author's *Commentary on Romans*, at 4:24 and 6:4.

[51] See John 10:1-18, 1 Peter 2:25, and Matthew 26:31 for further development of the "Shepherd" theme.

Jesus from the dead, that stupendous event, without doubt, should answer with certainty any question about His leadership.

Through the blood of the eternal covenant – Jesus' better blood, His better sacrifice has been one of the major themes of this epistle. "Covenant" has reference to the "new covenant" (discussed at 8:6-13 and 9:15-10:18), another of the major themes of this epistle. This covenant lasts to the end of the Christian Age (the idea in "eternal" is to the end of the age); it will never be replaced by another as the Mosaic covenant was replaced. Commentators must decide whether to take this phrase with what precedes or with what follows. If taken with what precedes, it says Christ's resurrection was made possible because His sacrifice (that inaugurated the new covenant) was accepted. If taken with what follows, it says God would equip His servants through their covenant relationship.

Even **Jesus our Lord** – This phrase is intended to identify who the "great Shepherd of the sheep" is. He is the One in whom both "lordship" and "humanity" are combined.

13:21 – Equip you in every good thing to do His will – "Equip"[52] is the main verb in the sentence that began in verse 20. May "God ... equip you ..." is the idea. The writer is praying that God will mend or restore in the readers whatever[53] was necessary in order that they may do His will.[54]

Working in us that which is pleasing in His sight – Evidently the "us"[55] in this phrase is to be distinguished from the "you" in the previous phrase.[56] God's equipping work in the readers is somehow related to what God does in the writer,[57] perhaps even in this letter. It is likely the writer is aware that what he has written was inspired, was something worked in him by God, so that if the readers hearkened to what God worked in the author, the result would be that their lives would continue to be well pleasing[58] in His sight.

---

[52] The verb "equip" (*katartizo*) is used of mending what is broken, of putting in order what is amiss, of restoring, or preparing. Perhaps the writer's prayer is that God will put right what is amiss in the spiritual lives of the readers.

[53] The NASB reads "good thing." Following a different manuscript reading, the KJV has "good work." "Good" is evidently neuter (rather than masculine), but there is no noun. We must supply the noun. Exactly what "thing" the writer has in mind is not absolutely clear. Perhaps the prayer means, 'May God correct or mend those areas of your doctrine and life that are out of harmony with all the better things that have been presented in this letter.'

[54] Doing the will of God is another theme found in this epistle.

[55] The KJV reads "working in *you*," but that reading is not as well attested as the NASB's "working in *us*." If the KJV were the correct reading, then the prayer includes a request that the readers may be wholly surrendered to God, so that what He might wish to do will not be hindered by their hardness or rebellion.

[56] We suppose that the "us" in this verse is not different than the "us" in verse 18. It is doubtful that the thrust of this prayer is that God will somehow (mystically?) work on the hearts of the readers, so that their resulting behavior will thus be well pleasing to Him.

[57] The circumstantial participle (*poion*) perhaps should be rendered "by working ..." Thus the sentence reads, "May God ... equip you ... by working in us ...."

[58] To illustrate the use of "(well) pleasing," it might be observed that *euarestos* is used in Titus 2:9 of a slave whose work was such that he pleased his master.

Through Jesus Christ – The mediatorship of Jesus (i.e., no longer will the ceremonies of the Mosaic system serve men's needs for a mediator) is also necessary for this equipping which will result in a true relationship with God.

To whom *be* **the glory forever and ever** – Is this doxology addressed to the Father (the subject of the sentence, which was given at the beginning of verse 20), or to Jesus Christ (the nearest antecedent)? Either is appropriate. And both are to be praised through all eternity, "forever and ever"[59] – literally, "unto the ages of the ages". And whether it is glory to God or glory to Jesus, these, too, have been themes elaborated in this letter.

Amen – It is curious that doxologies should end with an "Amen" since the word usually denotes the speaker's assent or agreement with what has just been said. Some suppose this "Amen" was added at a later date, after it had become the custom of congregations, as they heard the letter read aloud in worship services, to respond with an "Amen" at these places.[60] Perhaps a better explanation is that the writer, conscious that what he has just written has been not of his own initiative, but was the result of Holy Spirit inspiration,[61] adds his own note of assent. "I am in hearty agreement with what has just been said about God equipping you through what He has done in me so that your lives will be pleasing to Him."

C. An Exhortation to Heed the Things just Written in this Epistle. 13:22

13:22 – But I urge you, brethren – Instead of rendering *de* by "But" as the NASB has done (which would consider verse 22 to be a contrast to what has just been written), we would follow the example of the KJV, translating it as "and," thus making this verse a continuation of the thought already begun in the prayer of verses 20 and 21. To the prayer about God "working in us" (verse 21), the writer adds his own word of entreaty.

Bear with this word of exhortation – Some strong things have been said in the course of this letter, so it is not likely all the readers would immediately respond favorably to this word of encouragement. So the writer urges them to "bear with" it, to receive it with feelings of kindness.[62] We suppose "word of exhortation" is reference to the whole letter,

---

[59] P[46] and a few other old uncial manuscripts omit the words "and ever," while they are in part of the text in Sinaiticus and Alexandrinus. "It is the kind of addition scribes would naturally insert if it was lacking in the text before them. There seems, however, to be no reason for anyone to omit it if it were original; so the shorter reading should probably be preferred." Morris, *op. cit.*, p.156.

[60] Before such a scenario regarding how "Amen" came to be a part of the doxologies is accepted, it should be observed that any claim that they were not part of the original letter as it proceeded from the pen of the human author impinges on the doctrine of inspiration. Do commentators really mean to say the "Amen" was added by uninspired human copyists simply because they learned (from church practice) that "Amen" is a proper response to a doxology?

[61] Such a prayer, which as we have suggested is Holy Spirit-inspired, would be appropriate to the Holy Spirit's work in this age, which is ultimately to bring glory to Christ and to the Father (John 16:14).

[62] In 2 Timothy 4:3, the same word here translated "bear with" is used (with a negative adverb) to characterize people who will refuse to heed or receive "sound doctrine."

rather than just to the last three (practical) chapters or just to the five warning passages.[63] The "exhortation" that runs all through the letter is the appeal to remain faithful.

For I have written to you briefly – "Briefly" means in few words compared to the greatness of the theme.[64] The whole phrase gives a reason why they should receive it gladly. After all, such a momentous theme deserves a fair hearing.

D. Information about Timothy. 13:23

13:23 – Take notice that our brother Timothy has been released – Translating the initial verb as imperative, "Take notice," rather than indicative, is probably the right idea, for we presume the writer is giving new information about Timothy. If we were to translate it as indicative, it would mean that the writer was simply repeating something they already knew. "Timothy" is doubtless the companion of Paul, since we know of no other first-century person with the name "Timothy." Whether "our brother" means simply brother in Christ or whether it reflects association and ties with both the writer and readers is not known.[65] "Released" from what? From imprisonment? From duties with some other church (cp. Philippians 2:19-24 which tells about Timothy's mission to Macedonia, a mission some believe Hebrews 13:23 says is completed)?

With whom, if he comes soon, I shall see you – Timothy has already been "released" but he was not with the writer at the moment. The writer hopes the two can together make a joint visit upon the readers. How much can we learn from this about the writer's own condition? Is the author himself (on the assumption it is Paul) a prisoner at the time he writes this letter, yet all the time confidently expecting release[66] so that he will be free to

---

[63] In Acts 13:15, the expression "word of exhortation" seems to be an invitation to Paul and Barnabas to give the sermon after the reading of the Law and Prophets in the synagogue service. Thus, some think Hebrews is a written sermon. (For more detailed information on the form of Hebrews, whether it is an epistle, a treatise, or a sermon, see the Introductory Studies.)

[64] "Some commentators think such a description [i.e., 'briefly'] can scarcely apply to an epistle as long as this one, and so suggest that perhaps chapter 13 (or part of it) was added to some previously existing writing, and that this expression refers only to the 'addition.' Against that, it is hard to see why anyone would bother to apologize for writing anything as short as this chapter. It is better to see it as applying to the whole. For the letter *is* short, considering the subject matter." Morris, *op. cit.*, p.157.

[65] If the letter is by Paul, as we tend to think, and if it is addressed to Christians in Judea ("to the Hebrews") as we also tend to think, this reference to Timothy is not out of place. The Jerusalem church knew Timothy, for in AD 58 Timothy had accompanied Paul to Jerusalem at the close of the third missionary journey (Acts 20:4), helping to carry the offering to Jerusalem. After that we have no further information about Timothy's activities until he is associated with Paul in the writing of the Prison Epistles (Philippians 1:1 and 2:19; Colossians 1:1; and Philemon 1), which we believe were written during Paul's first Roman imprisonment, AD 61-63. Timothy will, at a time later than we have dated Hebrews (see the Introductory Studies concerning the date of Hebrews), be involved in doing the work of an evangelist at Ephesus, about AD 65 (1 Timothy 1:1,2, 18, and 6:20). He is still at Ephesus when 2 Timothy is addressed to him, about AD 67. But if our dating of Hebrews is accurate, his ministry at Ephesus cannot be the thing from which he is "released."

[66] Compare what Paul writes in the Prison Epistles. To Philemon he urges prayers that he may visit Colossae soon, and even urges Philemon to get his guest room ready. Similarly, as he wrote Philippians 2:23,

travel with Timothy? Or is the author (whether Paul, or someone else) not a prisoner, so that his visit hinges only on Timothy's coming, not on his own release from custody? It has already been observed, in comments on Hebrews 13:19, that if the writer is Paul, the likelihood is slim that he ever did get to complete this anticipated visit with the Hebrews.

E. Final Greetings and Benediction. 13:24,25

13:24 – Greet all of your leaders and all the saints – Give them my regards. This is the third time the "leaders" have been mentioned in this chapter. That the leaders (i.e., their present leaders, see verse 17) are to be greeted by the recipients of this letter suggests that when it was first read, those leaders[67] were not all expected to be present. "All the saints" might reflect the situation in a large city where instead of one central meeting place, there would be a number of house churches, each with its own membership. If this is what "all the saints" implies, then we may say Hebrews is addressed to a definite community, rather than being a circular letter. Though addressed to a definite community, it was not intended for the hearing and edification of just one congregation. "Saints" was a common New Testament appellation for God's people, still living in the flesh on earth,[68] but set apart to God's purposes.

Those from Italy greet you – Is the writer in Italy, or are there some Italians with the writer wherever he is,[69] or is the writer sending greetings to Italy? In the Introductory Studies, we have opted for the conclusion that the Italian Christians who are in Rome with the author are sending their greetings "to the Hebrews" living in and around Jerusalem. They know about this letter being written, and, we suppose, have asked the writer to include their greetings to their brothers in Christ. We can even surmise that in this greeting is another exhortation to faithfulness. In so many words, it says, the Christians in Rome are watching. Let your example (an example that they likely will follow) be a good one!

Paul believed he would shortly know how things would go with him there at Rome. Concerning his expectations of being freed from the first Roman imprisonment and the regular Roman practice of freeing accused prisoners if their accusers did not appear within two years, see the "epilogue" to the author's *Commentary on Acts.*

[67] If the "leaders" are "elders," we might expect them to be present in the congregational meeting when this letter was read. Yet if they are present, why would the writer's salutation need to be carried to them by the readers? If, on the other hand, the leaders are men whose function was not limited (like the function of elders is) to one congregation, if they were, say, apostles or evangelists, then it is easily conceivable some would not be present in the meeting when the letter was first read.

[68] Where the Roman Catholic Church has found Biblical evidence for their doctrine that the word "saint" is reserved for people now dead, but who (sometime after their exemplary lives were completed) have been canonized, is hard to understand. In Scripture, "saints" are not people long dead, but are people still living on this earth.

[69] Sometimes a Scriptural analogy can help us determine what another Biblical phrase likely means. Such, alas, is not the case here, for the usage elsewhere in Scripture of similar phraseology is not determinative. In Acts 10:23, "from Joppa" names people still in Joppa. In Acts 17:13, "of (from) Thessalonica" names people still living in Thessalonica. A different meaning attaches to similar phraseology in Acts 21:27, where "from Asia" speaks of people from Asia who were visiting in Jerusalem. Hence, the phrase determines the people's origin; it does not determine their present place of residence. Thus, the "Italians" could be anywhere the writer is.

13:25 – Grace be with you all – We are not under Law, but under grace! May you all come to appreciate all this[70] means!

New Testament letters normally end with a prayer by the writer on behalf of the readers. In Paul's letters, it was his custom to take the pen in hand himself (after the amanuensis had finished the main body of the letter) and add this closing prayer in his own handwriting.[71]

Let us hope the epistle succeeded with its first readers. And let us make certain that its purpose continues to be accomplished in us.[72]

---

[70] The word "grace" has occurred several times in the course of this letter to the Hebrews. See 2:9, 4:16, 10:29, 12:15, and 13:9.

[71] In the "Historical Allusions" portion of the Introductory Studies, it was observed some manuscripts carry a subscription, which has then found its way into some editions of the King James Version. In small size type, those editions have this phrase, "Written to the Hebrews from Italy by Timothy." Such subscriptions are all post-apostolic, representing, as they do, some early scribes' attempts to add a brief introductory note to the letters to help the readers understand from whence the letters came and to whom they were addressed. In the subscriptions, the by-line does not indicate *authorship*, but rather indicates (in the scribe's opinion) who was responsible for *carrying* the letter to its destination. In this case, the opinion appears to be contrary to what is written in 13:23. If Timothy was absent from the place of writing, how could he be either the writer or the bearer of the letter? (The exact wording of the subscription to Hebrews varies very much depending on the manuscript being consulted. In D, M, 1, m, there is no subscription at all. In Sinaiticus, Ephraemi, and 17, it reads simply "to the Hebrews." In Alexandrinus, it reads "Written to the Hebrews from Rome." And in the Syriac and Coptic versions, in K, and d, it reads just as does the KJV.)

[72] There is no book of the New Testament that would be more missed if it were absent than this epistle to the Hebrews. Every Bible student needs such a guide as this to help with his understanding of the Old and New Covenants. And what a boon it will prove to be if the exhortations to faithfulness are favorably received and acted upon!

APPENDIX A

COVENANTS AND COVENANT THEOLOGY

Reminder: Materials on "covenants" have been introduced at Hebrews 7:22 & 8:6-10.[1]

A. KEY IDEAS IN KETCHERSIDE'S BOOK *THE DEATH OF THE CUSTODIAN: THE CASE OF THE MISSING TUTOR*[2]

Chapter 1. God is a covenant making and covenant keeping God. He has chosen to relate to man on the basis of covenants (plural).

Chapter 2. The Noahic Covenant
This is the first covenant so called in the Bible. Genesis 6:18, Genesis 9:11.
God sets the conditions (*diatheke*).
God gives the terms of the covenant.
Sign of the covenant (rainbow) -- God remembers His covenant.
(The first use of the word "grace" in the Bible is found at Genesis 6:8, KJV.)

Chapter 3. Covenant with Abraham
Ketcherside says there were two sides to the covenant made with Abraham -- one was fleshly and temporal; the other was spiritual and lasting.

Genesis 15 and 17 record the covenant God made with Abraham (a repeat of what was said earlier, Genesis 12:1-3).

Purpose -- to constitute a nation for the preservation of the great truth of monotheism.

Chapter 4. The Mosaic Covenant (Called "the first covenant" in Hebrews 8:7, 9:15,18.)
All God's covenants are based on some act God has done prior to inaugurating the covenant. In Israel's case, the act was deliverance from Egypt.

The Mosaic covenant, given at Sinai, was a national constitution by which the people will be governed. (Just as one can read the *text* of the Constitution of the United States of America, so one can read the *text* of the constitution of the nation of Israel in the tables of stone and the book of the covenant [Exodus 20-23].)

Chapter 5. Analysis of the Mosaic Covenant
The first 39 books in our Bibles do *not* make up the text of the old (or Mosaic) covenant. (Nor do the 27 books of the New Testament make up the text of the new covenant.

---

[1] Consult the notes at Hebrews 7:22 on the word "covenant" as a translation for the Hebrew *berith* and the Greek *diatheke*. See also the notes at Hebrews 8:6-10 on the classic New Covenant Prophecy found in Jeremiah 31:31, and the (three or) four "better promises" it contained.

[2] The book was reprinted in 1983 under the title *That the World May Believe ... A Study of the Covenants.* The reader is encouraged personally to read this book. It is available on the Internet. The summary is provided for those who do not have access to the original work.

The title page of the KJV may lead us astray when it says "The Holy Bible containing the Old and New Testaments.")

The Ten Commandments (plus perhaps the "book of the covenant" [Exodus 20-23]) are the text of the old, or Mosaic, covenant.

The rest of the Old Testament –history, poetry, and prophecy – are not part of the text of the covenant. They are old covenant Scriptures, but not the covenant itself.

Chapter 6. The Covenant of Law

Nothing written before the tables of stone were written, and nothing written after the giving of the tables (with the possible exception of the "book of the covenant") is part of the Mosaic covenant.

Proof: Deuteronomy 4:11-13. "Covenant" is equated with the "ten commandments."

Five arguments to show the Mosaic covenant does not include all the words one reads in the first 39 books in our Bibles.

1) The two tablets of stone are distinctly said to be "the tablets of the covenant," Deuteronomy 9:11.
2) The chest containing the tablets was called "the ark of the covenant," Numbers 10:33.
   (Consider, too, that the ark had disappeared before many of the books of prophecy were even written. How could they be thought to be part of the Mosaic covenant which long before was kept in the ark?)
3) The Mosaic covenant was distinctly said (Deuteronomy 5:2) to have been made and given at Mt. Horeb (Sinai).
   (Most of the rest of the Old Testament Scriptures were written in Palestine, Babylon, Persia. Therefore they could not be part of the covenant, if the covenant was written at Mt. Horeb.)
4) The covenant was said to have been made when God "took them by the hand to bring them out of the land of Egypt." Jeremiah 31:32.
   (Most of the other old covenant Scriptures were written much later in time.)
5) Jeremiah's prophecy was no part of the "first covenant," for by the time Jeremiah wrote, the people had already broken the covenant of God. Jeremiah 31:31.

Nature of the system of law:
   a) One who seeks to be justified by law must keep it perfectly. Galatians 3:10.
   b) The Law was added to the promise (made to Abraham) "because of transgressions," "until the seed (Christ) should come." Galatians 3:19.

Chapter 7. The Weakness of the Law

The weakness was not in the law, but in the flesh of men. Romans 8:1-3. (Hebrews 8:8 – "finding fault with *them*" [NASB].)

The Law couldn't justify, give life, make the worshiper "perfect," nor provide a perfect sacrifice for sins.

Jeremiah 31:31-34 is the classic new covenant prophecy – Special features were to be:
1) Forgiveness of sins.
2) Direct personal access to God.
3) Reconciliation ("I will be their God, and they shall be My people").
4) Internality ("I will write [My laws] upon their hearts" – Ketcherside identifies the "laws" as being "Love God!" and "Love men!")

Chapter 8. The Time of Reformation. Hebrews 9:10
The Mosaic covenant was temporary – John 1:17; Romans 6:14; 2 Corinthians 3:4-11; Galatians 3:23-26; Hebrews 9:10 – until Christ came.

Chapter 9. The Freedom of Maturity
Christians have liberty in Christ. No longer are God's people under a code of laws.

It is difficult for some of Ketcherside's readers to accept this:
a) It cuts across traditional patterns of thinking (i.e., that 27 books make up the text of the new covenant).
b) Some would rather be under law than under grace.
c) We no longer have a blueprint or pattern for the church (Ketcherside affirms).

Chapters 10,11. Answering Objections.
(Whose objections are these? They are objections made by Ketcherside's non-instrument brethren, who were offended the book's thesis. Why were they offended? It scuttled many of their arguments for the "church of Christ" legalistic doctrines.)

Chapter 10 – Answers to verses that seem to indicate Christians are still under "law."

Chapter 11 – Answers to verses that seem to say Jesus has given us commandments to keep, therefore we must be under law yet.
(Ketcherside suggests Christians are to live by the Law of God, which is "love." It is an internal rule, not imposed externally. Christian churches have been erroneously trying to impose the 27 books of the New Testament as an external code of laws.[3])

Evaluation of Ketcherside's presentation:

1. First 8 chapters are fantastic!
   His handling of the Mosaic covenant, and the fact that the books of our Bible are not the "text" of the covenants, seems precisely right.

2. It is difficult to follow his train of thought in the remaining chapters (though we have

---

[3] See these seed thoughts voiced by Ketcherside fleshed out in Boyce Mouton's books listed in the Bibliography on Covenants and Covenant Theology.

attempted to reproduce it [with some adaptation] in the above summary of key ideas).

REASON: He does not cite Scriptures to show that his identification of the "text" of the "new covenant" is either Christ Himself or the new commandment of love.

3. The book serves to stimulate our thinking about "covenants" and "covenant theology."[4]

B. OLD TESTAMENT PREDICTIONS OF THE NEW COVENANT

1) Hosea 2:18-23.

    In the 8th century BC, the prophet Hosea was granted a specific revelation concerning a newer "covenant" than the Mosaic under which the people were then living. The prophecy he makes shows the new covenant has both an external and internal aspect.

2) Isaiah 42:6; 49:8 (KJV)

    Isaiah elaborates on the internal portion of Hosea's revelation. In his messages of comfort to Judah, subsequent to the devastating attacks by Sennacherib in 701 BC, Isaiah spoke of the deliverance that would be accomplished through God's Suffering Servant (Jesus Christ, Luke 22:37, Acts 8:32-35, especially verse 35).

    One line in Isaiah 42:6 reads, "I will appoint You as a covenant to the people, as a light to the nations."

    > Not that Jesus is Himself the covenant. Rather, Jesus is not only the everlasting Son of God who *establishes* the covenant, He is the priest who at the same time *officiates* at the death (52:15). He is also the testator (sacrificial offering), the offering that *dies* (53:8), and He is the *inheritance* that is bestowed (49:6).

3) Jeremiah 31:31ff

    In the year 597 BC, after Jerusalem's depopulation had commenced (Jeremiah 29:1,2), God revealed through Jeremiah more detailed truth about His "new covenant." Jeremiah identified four primary elements in the "new covenant" (see comments on Hebrews 8).

4) Daniel 9:24-27

    Daniel's prophecies provided God's date for the termination of the animal sacrifices that played so great a part in the old covenant, and for the confirmation of the covenant previously made with many (i.e., with "Israel". This is not the "new covenant" of Jeremiah 31:31-34). It was to be 490 years later. He showed that the termination of the Mosaic sacrifices involved the rejection of the Messiah.

---

[4] W. Adams Brown, "Covenant" in *Hastings Encyclopedia of Religion and Ethics* (p.216), recognizes an important distinction between the covenant idea and Covenant Theology. The covenant idea permeates Biblical thought, while Covenant Theology represents a "special type of Christian thought which gives this idea a central importance not elsewhere assigned to it, and uses it as the organizing principle of the entire theological system."

5) Malachi 3:1ff

Malachi, the last of the Old Testament prophets, spoke of Moses (Malachi 4:4-6) and yet at the same time of the need for that future "covenant" which had been foreseen by Hosea and his successors. He anticipated the "messenger of the covenant" who was the Lord Himself (3:1c), whose coming would be preceded only by another human messenger, namely, "Elijah the prophet" (3:1a, 4:5,6), whom Jesus in New Testament times identified with John the Baptist (Matthew 17:11-13).

C. NEW TESTAMENT STATEMENTS THAT THOSE NEW COVENANT PROPHECIES ARE ALREADY FULFILLED

1) Matthew 26:28; 1 Corinthians 11:25 – Jesus says the cup of the Lord's Supper symbolizes His blood that is the sacrifice that ratifies, or inaugurates, the new covenant that the Old Testament prophets envisioned.

2) Galatians 3:14 – Christians have received the thing promised by the Spirit (i.e., the thing promised in the covenant made with Abraham about all the nations of the earth being blessed in his seed [Christ]).

3) 2 Corinthians 3:6 – Christian preachers are ministers of a new covenant, not ministers of the letter which kills (i.e., Mosaic Covenant).

4) Hebrews 8-10 – Christians are already participating in the benefits of the new covenant.

Hebrews 10:9,10 – The old way of dealing with sin is taken away; the second is established.

Hebrews 8:13 – The former (Mosaic) is obsolete and is ready to disappear.

Hebrews 10:9-23 – Here are thirteen startling, searching, revolutionary truths (see them listed in Ashley Johnson, *Two Covenants*, p.173), none of which was true or could be true under Moses (under the first covenant).

Under the first covenant: many priests, many offerings, no real remission of sins, no good conscience.

Under the second: one Priest, one Offering, sin forever blotted out, good conscience, all by the new way! Where is the man who, in view of these things, would desire to re-establish the old covenant, or would go back and live under its provision (even if that were possible), or who says the new is just a continuation of the old?

5) Hebrews 7:12 – Where the priesthood is changed (and it has been, from the Levitical to Jesus' priesthood), there is also a change of Law. See also 7:18, where the Law is already set aside by the time Hebrews was written.

D. INTRODUCTION TO COVENANT THEOLOGY

God is a covenant-making and covenant-keeping God. To that extent, all Biblical theology deals with the matter of covenant or covenants.

> Covenant (or federal) Theology,[5] however, refers quite specifically to a type of theology prevalent in the Reformed or Calvinistic tradition in which everything (all Bible doctrine and history) is systematically organized around the idea of covenant.

Covenant theology is a development distinct not only from the early reformers, particularly John Calvin, but also from the Reformed Scholasticism that arose a generation after him.

> Calvin knew but one covenant, the covenant of grace, which he believed was of the same substance in both the Old and New Testaments. (*Institutes*, II, 11, 2-4). He did not speak of a pre-lapsarian covenant of works.

> It was apparently Ursinus, Olevianus (16th century), and Cocceius (17th century) who first advocated federalism (covenant theology).

> Federalism found able exponents in William Ames (1575-1633) and Hermann Witsius, whose *Economy of the Covenants Between God and Man* (1685) represents covenant theology in its "later and more developed form."

Covenant theology was the predominant theology among churches of the Reformed tradition from the 17th to the 19th centuries.

> It was the theology of the Westminster Confession of Faith (Questions 30-32) which clearly distinguished between the covenant of works and the covenant of grace.

> It came to fruition in English Puritanism in the last half of the 17th century.

> It was the prevailing theology on the American frontier at the time the Restoration Movement began.[6]

E. THE OUTLINES OF COVENANT THEOLOGY

The definitive idea in covenant theology is the concept of a **covenant of works** as being the original covenant with man.

---

[5] Covenant Theology is also called "federal theology" (from the Latin *foedus*, league, treaty, compact), since the prevailing idea behind the theology is that of a compact or covenant made between God and some other party.

[6] Some have mistakenly believed that Alexander Campbell taught covenant theology, but this is a misunderstanding of Campbell's emphasis on God's covenants. See Wm. J. Richardson, *The Role of Grace in the Thought of Alexander Campbell* (Los Angeles, Calif.: Westwood Christian Foundation, 1991), p.1. Many of the following explanations of what Covenant theology teaches are drawn from Richardson's book.

Webster's (2nd ed.) definition of federal theology: "The theological system which rests on the concept that before the Fall, man was under a covenant of works, wherein God promised him (through Adam the federal head of the race) eternal blessedness if he perfectly kept the law; and that since the Fall, man is under a covenant of grace, wherein God of His free grace promises the same blessings to all who believe in Christ (the federal head of the church)."

Federal theologians frequently developed quite elaborate distinctions within those two general categories – covenant of works and covenant of grace.

Some tended to make distinctions between the Mosaic covenant (the old covenant) and the new covenant – even dividing the old into three periods (from Adam to Abraham, from Abraham to Moses, from Moses to Christ) – and then also dividing the new into three periods (from the advent to the resurrection, from the resurrection to the second coming, and from the second coming to the final consummation). (Harvey, *Handbook of Theological Terms*, p.62)

Others came quickly to see that any theory treating the old and new covenants as two radically different covenants (and indeed some appealed to New Testament passages where Moses was alleged to be called a covenant of *works* – and made little distinction between it, and what Adam was supposed to have before the fall) contained within itself the seeds of its own destruction.

So, for a century or more, the course of federal theology was marked by acrimonious debate over this matter – a debate that after a century of being dormant is beginning to heat up again.[7]

Covenant theologians divided human history into two periods, each known by the type of covenant that defined man's relation to God.

1. THE COVENANT OF WORKS

The first period of human history, the *covenant of works*, was made in the beginning with Adam and through him with the whole human race.[8]

It promised life on the stipulation of perfect obedience to the Ten Commandments, thought to be identical with the law of nature and engraved upon the heart of man. (This accounts for the designation *Foedus Naturale*.)

---

[7] Not only is there a revival of Puritan theology, but a heated debate over the ramifications of covenant theology has led to a revision of the footnotes in the Scofield Reference Bible, so that all notes found in the earlier edition which tended to make the Law of Moses a "covenant of works" have now been replaced.

[8] Heinrich Heppe, *Reformed Dogmatics, Set Out and Illustrated from the Sources*. Revised by E. Bizer, Trans. by G.T. Thompson. (London: Allen & Unwin, 1950), p.241. Hosea 6:7 is said to prove such a covenant relationship between God and Adam, when it reads "but like Adam they have transgressed the covenant."

For the most part, federal theologians preferred to translate the Hebrew *berith* by the Latin *foedus* or *pactum*, both of which are bilateral in import. The covenant was a contractual agreement, a divine/human *quid pro quo*.

Having been given to mankind at the beginning, the stipulations of the Decalogue are perpetually binding upon the whole of mankind, whether of the elect or not.

One factor in the original rise of covenant theology was the concern of 16th and 17th century political philosophers to find a theological basis for the duty of man in the natural realm.

The covenant of grace (see below) as conceived by the early reformers involved only the elect; hence, it laid no basis for a social-political theory for society as a whole.

By invoking the idea of a prior covenant (the covenant of works), one in substance with the law of nature, a basis for structuring society could be found which was incumbent on all men, saved or not.

It was apparently the Rhineland theologians, Ursinus and Olevianus, who developed this mode of thought – i.e., a *foedus naturale* between God and Adam and his descendants – into a rationale for political-social structure.

Edward Fisher, author of the *Marrow of Modern Divinity* (1645), endeavored to show that in eating the forbidden fruit Adam broke all of the Ten Commandments.[9]

But Adam's sin lay not alone in violating the Law; it was a denial of God's authority, hence, a breach of fellowship. The consequences of the fall were guilt, corruption of human nature, and alienation from God, leaving man subject to indignation, wrath, and judgment.[10]

Prominent Puritan theologians refined the concept of corruption of human nature to mean that "depravity touched the whole range of human faculties, not that the total functioning of any or all the faculties was depraved."[11]

Some writers call this position natural depravity in distinction to Calvin's total depravity.

Adam and his descendants were still obliged to keep the Law but in their lapsed state could not hope thereby to receive life.

---

[9] Edward Fisher, *Marrow of Modern Divinity*. (Boston: Green, Bushel and Allen, 1743), p.17,18.

[10] Johannes Cocceius, *De Foedus*, III. 63.

[11] John Von Rohr, *Covenant of Grace in Puritan Thought* (Atlanta, Ga.: Scholars Press, 1986), p.42.

2. THE COVENANT OF GRACE

Once the fall had occurred, even before their expulsion from the garden, God announced to Adam and Eve the *covenant of grace* (Genesis 3:15), to be in effect until the final judgment and which promises eternal life to the elect.

This covenant of grace was based on a previously made covenant between God and Christ as the Second Adam, through whose perfect obedience these benefits are imputed to elect believers.

A fundamental feature of federal theology is the belief that justification (under the covenant of grace) rests upon a pre-temporal pact between Father and Son[12] in which, in McGrath's words, "God exacted from Christ the condition of perfect obedience to the Law in return for the elect as His inheritance."[13]

The Biblical record from Genesis 3:15 onward is the story of the covenant of grace.

Both the Old Testament and the New Testament are economies of the covenant of grace – one in substance although different in administration.

Covenant theologians are wont to make little distinction between the Mosaic covenant and the new covenant.

Thus, we hear expressions to the effect that the Sermon on the Mount really does not set aside the Law of Moses – it *elaborates* and *emphasizes* its real meaning.

Covenant theologians are wont to say that since Adam's fall, there has been but *one* covenant by which men may have a relationship with God, namely, the covenant of grace.

The agreements with Noah, Abraham, and David, as well as the Mosaic covenant, are not viewed as distinct covenants. Rather, they are renewals of the one covenant of grace. Even the new covenant is but a renewal of the covenant of grace.[14]

---

[12] See notes below for elaboration on this pre-temporal pact which is called "the covenant of redemption."

[13] Alister E. McGrath, *Iustitia Dei: A History of the Doctrine of Justification* (Cambridge: Cambridge U. Press, 1986], Vol.2, p.42.

[14] For example, a typical expression of one-covenant theology is as follows: "Throughout the Old Testament period there were successive proclamations of this covenant of grace. We find it in the protevangelium of Genesis 3:15. Certain of its provisions were later revealed to Noah (Genesis 9), and Abraham (Genesis 12) ... Although the New Testament is described as *new*, such passages as Romans 4 and Galatians 3 show that it is essentially one with the covenant under which believers lived in Old Testament times." (Geo.Collins, "Covenant Theology," *Baker Dictionary of Theology* [Grand Rapids: Baker, 1960], p.144)

While Karl Barth is not a one-covenant theologian, he did cut his theological teeth in the Calvinistic tradition, and his writings tend to reflect some one-covenant ideas. While he refuses on critical grounds to fix the origin of the covenant in time, he still insists there is but one covenant of grace in Scripture. In language reminiscent of the reformers he writes, "What is done away ... is only its 'economy,' the form in which [the covenant] is revealed and active in the events of the Old Testament." *Church Dogmatics*, IV, 1, 31.

The covenants are alike in these particulars, according to Herman Witsius:

> (1) The contracting parties, God and man, are the same.
> (2) Both promise eternal life.
> (3) Both have the same conditions, faith and obedience to the law.
> (4) Both have the glory of God as their final end.
> (5) The church is the same institution in both Testaments.[15]

In the federal theology system, the covenant of grace begins at the time of the *fall* of Adam. This helps distinguish federal theology from the common belief in two basic covenants (one before and one after *Calvary*), which the covenant theologians in fact reject.[16]

Although the elect are saved by God's mercy under the terms of the covenant of grace, the Law continues to play a foundational role. From creation onward all mankind are subject to its mandates.

> But there is a difference in the way the Law's role was viewed, a difference of great importance to covenant theologians. Fisher sought to clarify this matter in *Marrow of Modern Divinity*, in a dialogue between Evangelistica, Nomista, Antinomista, and Neophitis.

> He distinguished the Law of Works, the Law of Faith, and the Law of Christ; but the Ten Commandments were the substance of each.

> > The *Law of Works* was the covenant made with Adam, promising life on the basis of perfect obedience. This covenant failed with Adam's disobedience.

> > The *Law of Faith* is the covenant of grace by which Christ entered into the same covenant of works that Adam did and perfectly fulfilled it on our behalf. This is the gospel.

> > The *Law of Christ* is the Ten Commandments, now serving as the rule of life for the elect. Hence, Fisher concluded, the Ten Commandments are the "matter of both covenants, only they differ in forms."

---

[15] Witsius, *Economy of the Covenants*, Book I, Ch.I, XV.

[16] A fairly representative (but not one-covenant theology) presentation of the idea of "covenants" is as follows: "The Bible is divided into two main sections, the Old Testament and the New Testament. Because the Bible is so divided, it is commonly believed [by non-covenant theologians] that it tells how God has made (at least) two covenants with men. The 'first covenant' was concluded on Mt. Sinai through Moses with the people of Israel (Exodus 19,20). In it God offered salvation in return for obedience to His law. The 'second covenant,' the 'new covenant,' was concluded at Calvary with all mankind through Christ. In it, God offers salvation in return for faith in Christ. The first was a covenant of law. The second is a covenant of grace (i.e., undeserved favor) because it delivers man from the obligations of the law." It is this common belief in two basic covenants, with the change occurring at Calvary, rather than in the Garden of Eden, which advocates of one-covenant theology, in fact, reject. For one-covenant theologians, the covenant of grace began in Eden, not at Calvary.

3. THE COVENANT OF REDEMPTION

The covenant of grace, announced to Adam immediately after the Fall, is actually grounded in an earlier pact between Father and Son. Via this *Covenant of Redemption*, even before creation Christ agreed to be the redeemer of the elect and their mediator.

Thus the covenant of grace has both pre-temporal and temporal aspects – pre-temporal in that it was a pact entered into before creation, temporal in that it was implemented after the Fall.[17]

(Some theologians distinguish the Covenant of Redemption from the Covenant of Grace. Witsius, however, preferred to see these two as periods of one covenant, the first being in the eternal counsel of the Trinity, the second in history immediately upon the fall of man.)

What significance are we to see in this conception of the role of Christ in fulfilling perfectly the Law and incurring the penalty of disobedience to it – all on our behalf? Admittedly, as John von Rohr states (p.44), it "gave a Christological foundation to the covenant of grace." But it is difficult to resist the conclusion drawn by David Alexander Wier that the covenant of grace is "really therefore the covenant of works in disguise."[18]

For several pages, we have been following Richardson's explanation, in broad outline, of "Covenant Theology." What was behind the development of such a theology?

F. COVENANT THEOLOGY (Its Defenders Believe) HELPS EXPLAIN BOTH OLD AND NEW TESTAMENTS

Calvinist theology starts with the sovereignty of God, but it has trouble harmonizing the sovereignty of God with man's desire for assurance of salvation, and with the numerous Biblical exhortations that men need to be faithful. Covenant theology has helped some Calvinists reconcile these apparent contradictions in their system.

Assurance. Covenant theologians believe that man as a sinner has no rights before a holy, sovereign, omnipotent God. Man ought to be perfectly obedient to the will of God, but even then there is no reward to be earned. Fellowship with God comes only through a voluntary divine agreement establishing a relationship which is not necessarily according to nature. This was done by the covenant, which causes God to act in a

---

[17] Covenant theologians have spoken of the "covenant of redemption," by which they mean an engagement entered into between God the Father and God the Son, back in eternity, whereby the former secured to the latter a certain number of ransomed sinners, as His church or elect body, and the latter engaged to become their surety and substitute. (It is not easy to find verses of Scripture that show such a covenant relationship between the Father and Son, though some of the other ideas are in a measure Biblical.)

[18] *Foedus Naturale: The Origins of Federal Theology in Sixteeneth Century Reformation Thought.* Unpublished Doctoral dissertation, University of St. Andrews, 1984, p.7.

kindly way, thus removing the uncertainty from dealing with the Almighty.

Exhortations to faithfulness. It is alleged God's dealings with Israel (Old Testament) cannot be understood without the presupposition of covenant theology. Because of His covenant with Abraham *and his descendants*, God continues to deal graciously with a wayward and rebellious people. On the basis of this continuing covenant, God requires His people to obey His law (Deut. 29:29). Because the Israelites are God's covenant people, the prophets can plead so strongly with them to turn from their wickedness.

New Testament. The same principle is found – men are required to obey because they are involved in that continuing covenant.[19]

G. ARGUMENTS ADVANCED TO SUPPORT ONE-COVENANT THEOLOGY

1. Support for the view of some kind of continuity in the history of God's dealings with man is found in the record of the life of Abraham, and in the covenant which God first made with him (Genesis 12:1-3, 15:5) and then renewed from time to time.

2. Romans 4, which references the covenant with Abraham, is appealed to as proof that there has always been just one way of salvation. Abraham, they argue, was not saved by works (circumcision, sacrifice of Isaac), but by faith – just as the covenant of grace theory would expect. The promise made to Abraham was entirely dependent on God's grace (Romans 4:13-22). The same is true of the Christian believer today (Romans 4:23-25). Only one way of salvation is proof of one covenant, it is believed.

3. Galatians 3 takes the argument further. One-covenant theologians tend to identify the covenant made with Abraham with their alleged "one covenant of grace" made after Adam's fall. They then affirm that this covenant (renewed to Abraham) is the primary source of all understanding of God's dealings with men (3:7-9). The covenant at Sinai followed 430 years thereafter (3:15-18). One-covenant theologians affirm that the purpose of the Sinaitic covenant was not to contradict what God had already said, but to drive the Israelites to experience the utter futility of trying to earn their own salvation, thus preparing them to receive what He freely offers (3:19-22).

4. Hebrews, one-covenant theologians affirm, makes the same point – the "old covenant" is by no means the original *covenant*, but a shadowy foretaste of the full *blessings* God wishes to grant (10:1). Even in Old Testament times, faith was always the essential basis of man's relationship with God. (Remember, one-covenant theologians make a distinction between "works" and "faith" as the conditions for the two covenants.)

5. Galatians 3:8 – God preached the gospel before to Abraham. Thus, one-covenant theo-

---

[19] In all this is an attempt to give a reasonable explanation to the need for "exhortations to faithfulness" if people once saved are always saved -- one of the key doctrines of Calvinism. If a saved person can't be lost, why make any such exhortations? The Calvinist answers, because they are covenant people.

logians affirm the same thing is found in the ages both before and after the cross.

6. Jesus' declared (Luke 16:17) heaven and earth will pass away before the Law would. [*Reply*: "... until all is accomplished (fulfilled)," Jesus said (Matthew 5:18). And on the cross, "knowing that all things had been accomplished to fulfill the Scripture ..." (John 19:28). Once fulfilled, the Mosaic covenant was set aside, as the New Testament Scriptures plainly show elsewhere (e.g., Hebrews 7:12).]

7. The identity of the covenants is argued (by one-covenant theologians) from the standpoint that there is one God and one object of each covenant. [*Reply*: We may admit with this without agreeing there has been but one covenant since Adam sinned.]

8. Some assert that baptism replaces circumcision – thus the covenants are identical.

   [*Reply*: Baptism did *not* take the place of circumcision, for the following reasons:

   a. Circumcision was a mark in the flesh (Genesis 17:23-25). Baptism is not a mark in the flesh.

   b. Circumcision was proof (the "seal") of membership in the covenant (Genesis 17:10-12). Baptism is not the evidence that a man is a member of the church – the indwelling Holy Spirit is the seal of the new covenant (Ephesians 1:13).

   c. Circumcision was administered when the child was 8 days old (Genesis 17:12). Baptism is for repentant believers, something 8-day old children cannot do.

   d. Those circumcised were debtors to do the whole Law of Moses (Galatians 5:2,3). Will advocates of the theory that baptism takes the place of circumcision affirm that those who are *baptized* are debtors to keep the *entire* Law of Moses?

   e. Circumcision was not a type of baptism. It was a type of a circumcised heart and life (Romans 2:28,29, Colossians 2:10-13).

   If baptism does not take the place of circumcision, then the two actions should not be used to prove that the covenants (Mosaic and New) are identical.]

9. If God made a "faulty" covenant with Israel and then set it aside, can it not be said (one-covenant theologians want to know) that God is "trifling with men"? [*Reply*: Not by any means! The idea of discarding the old and accepting the new is part of the progressive development of the Kingdom of God. Compare Mark 4:2629.]

10. "Why did Jesus and the apostles endorse the Law if the Gospel is so different from the Law?" is another defense put forward by one-covenant theologians.

    [*Reply*: Jesus simply urged people to keep the Law because it was still binding, and would be till Calvary. Then it was nailed to the cross.

Reply: The apostles did so out of expediency – being all things to all men, in order to win them. If someone tried to make the Law a test of fellowship, the apostles did *not* endorse it! See the Jerusalem Conference (Acts 15, Galatians 2), for example.]

11. The New Testament says Christian ethics may be defined in terms of the "*royal law*" (James 2:8-11, 4:11,12; cp. Romans 13:8-10). Does this not refer to the Law of Moses?

[*Reply*: James also talked about "the perfect law, the law of liberty" – James 1:25, 2:12. The two are not the same, for the Mosaic Law was a ministration of death, whereas the new covenant is a ministration of life and liberty.]

H. ONE-COVENANT THEOLOGY REJECTED

1. Many theologians would reject out of hand the entire argument that Scripture reveals one covenant of grace behind both the Mosaic and new covenants. They would stress the discontinuity and contrast between the covenants.[20]

God, speaking through Jeremiah, promises a "new covenant ... *not like the covenant* which I made with their fathers ..." (Jeremiah 31:31,32). On the night before His death, Jesus said, "This cup is the *new* covenant in My blood" (1 Corinthians 11:25). Paul, writing to the Galatians, makes a great deal of *two* covenants (Galatians 4:24[21]). And the book of Hebrews is filled with the idea that the new covenant is better (Hebrews 8-10, especially 8:6 and 9:15). The Law (Old Testament) was a schoolmaster to bring us to Christ (Galatians 3:24).

2. Others would not object to the premise (one covenant of grace, accepted by faith, underlying both Testaments), but they would argue the covenant made with Abraham included two distinct elements – one physical and the other spiritual.[22]

For example, it promised a literal portion of land (Genesis 12:7); but it also promised a heavenly city (Hebrews 11:10,16).

The word "seed" or "descendants" had a double meaning: Abraham's *physical* descendants (Genesis 12:7), and also his *spiritual* descendants (Romans 4:16).

Similarly, the rite of circumcision had two purposes: to mark out a special nation-

---

[20] This first point is an outright rejection of Calvinistic, reformed, one-covenant theology.

[21] "Galatians 4:24, 'which things are an allegory: for these are *two covenants*; the one from Mount Sinai, which gendereth to bondage, which is Hagar ....' How many covenants? Two! ... Not one as a continuation of the other, not one as an outgrowth of the other, not one grafted on another, but two! One from Mount Sinai ... which gendereth to bondage ... The other was dedicated at Jerusalem, began at Jerusalem, was unfolded at Jerusalem, was administered at Jerusalem the first time in its history." A. Johnson, *Two Covenants*, p.145-146.

[22] This second view, the one expressed substantially in Milligan and Ketcherside, is a mediating position between point #1 (above) and point #3 (following).

ality, but also to symbolize a moral and spiritual characteristic.

3. One-covenant theology is vigorously opposed by Lutherans on the ground that it destroys the Law/Gospel structure of Scripture – a principle fundamental to Lutheran hermeneutics and theology.

    How does Paul view the status of the Law, now that Christ has come? Luther himself denied the *usus normativus* of the Law, but Lutherans now generally affirm it.

    > Especially in Romans, Paul contrasts justification by faith in the Gospel with justification by works of Law (Protestants are wont to affirm). Harvey (*op. cit.*, p.143,144) explains briefly:

    > The Reformers, especially Luther, made this Pauline distinction the basis of their theology. Luther said that the distinction between Law and Gospel "contains the sum of all Christian doctrine." By the Law, Luther meant the total claim of God on human life, the "Thou shalt," whether it appears in the Mosaic law or in the Natural law, or even in the Sermon on the Mount. The demand of this Law is perfect love. Just because it demands such love, Luther believed it impossible for sinful man to fulfill it. Therefore, Law only intensifies man's sin and despair instead of bringing him into fellowship with God. Law exposes sin but cannot cure it. By the Gospel, Luther means the message that God has revealed Himself in Christ not as a tyrant or lawgiver, but as an infinitely compassionate savior. With this in mind, Luther speaks quite critically of the Law as an enemy of faith. On the other hand, since Luther regarded the inner meaning of the Law to be love, and this presupposes a gracious God, it is not easy for him to place Law and Gospel in such a sharp contrast. Therefore, Luther often speaks of Law and Gospel as but two sides of one coin, the Law being a demand and the Gospel a gift, but both having the same content. Only insofar as the Law tempts man to trust in works is it disparaged, which is to say (if we are fairly representing Luther's view), it requires interpretation in the light of the Gospel.

    Lutherans, generally, affirm a more normative function to the Law than did Luther.

    > Lutherans teach three kinds of law in the Old Testament – moral, ceremonial, and judicial.[23]

    > Some Lutherans teach that the Ten Commandments are binding on all men today – as the moral law which sets forth our duties to God and man.[24]

    > Some Lutherans teach that baptism takes the place of circumcision.[25]

    Still, Lutherans make a distinction between the old and new covenants at *Calvary*, sharply rejecting the Reformed/Calvinistic view of one-covenant theology.

---

[23] *Luther's Small Catechism.* Questions and Answers, #18.

[24] *Luther's Small Catechism.* Questions and Answers, #21.

[25] *Luther's Small Catechism.* Note under question 335.

4. One-covenant theology was also condemned by the Council of Trent, AD 1543.

5. Calvin claimed that Christ abrogated the ceremonial law, but not the moral law.

6. Modern pre-millennialism opposes one-covenant theology "on the grounds that there are seven dispensations and several specific covenants (*[Old] Scofield Reference Bible* lists 8, p. 1297), and the harmony of Scripture is achieved by the proper division of Scripture into dispensations and covenants; to mix or confuse covenants and dispensations is a major error of one-covenant theologians."[26]

    Note: There has been in recent years a continuing dialog between one-covenant theologians and dispensational theologians, especially at Dallas Theological Seminary. One of the results can be seen by the man in the pew if he were to compare the footnotes in the old Scofield Reference Bible and the New Scofield Reference Bible. For example, in the old edition, the Mosaic covenant is described as a covenant of works. But covenant theologians insist there has been no covenant of works made with man since Adam sinned. Therefore, the New SRB changes the presentation of the Mosaic covenant. The note now matches one-covenant theology's "covenant of grace." To see this change, compare notes at John 1:17.

    Another place you can see the results of the dialogue is in the 1952 revision of the Dallas Seminary Statement of Faith. The fifth article sought to clarify how dispensationalism affirms that salvation in every age is simply by faith through grace – i.e., no longer is the Mosaic covenant called a covenant of works.

7. It is difficult to speak of renewals of a single covenant – as though the new covenant were similar to the Mosaic – as one-covenant theologians are wont to do (see for example, "Covenant" in *Zondervan Pictorial Encyclopedia of the Bible*).

    a) Jeremiah 31:31 specifically says the "new covenant" will *not be like* the one God made with Israel when He brought them out of Egypt.

    b) It is hard to see how the Mosaic covenant could be called a renewal of the one covenant (covenant of grace) always in force since Adam sinned, when Hebrews 7:18 speaks of it being completely set aside (abrogated).

    c) It is hard to see how the Mosaic covenant could be called a renewal when Galatians 3:15ff speaks of it as being something added to the Abrahamic covenant, and which did not alter or set aside that continuing covenant. The Mosaic was something added to – not just a renewal of – the Abrahamic covenant.

8. Call Bible things by Bible names.

---

[26] Bernard Ramm, *A Handbook of Contemporary Theology* (Grand Rapids: Eerdmans, 1965). p.28.

There is a kernel of truth behind one-covenant theology, namely, that something runs all through history. But the Bible calls this the *purpose* of God, not a covenant.

Should we not then speak of His eternal "purpose" (cp. Romans 8:28) rather than a "covenant of redemption"? (Even covenant theologians admit we cannot find God's eternal deliberations called a "covenant" in the Bible.)

9. Evidences of no continuity, no identity, between the Mosaic and new covenants.

   a. The Law of Moses, using the phrase in its most comprehensive sense, was never absolutely necessary to salvation. (Romans 4:13 – what was true for Abraham was true for others.)

   b. If the new covenant is a continuation, or identical with the Mosaic, how shall we explain that there was no indwelling Holy Spirit in the Old Testament age? (Galatians 3:1-14; John 7:37-39; Acts 19:1-6.)

   c. 2 Corinthians 3:6. (See notes on this passage above on page 257.)

   d. Instead of a covenant of grace extending from Adam's time, it would be better to say that grace was introduced by the incarnation of Jesus.[27]

      John 1:17 – The law came by Moses, but grace and truth came by Jesus Christ. The Law and grace are not identical.

      Romans 6:14 – "You are not under Law, but under grace" (now that Christ has come).

   e. At the Jerusalem Conference, it was taught that the Law of Moses is *not* binding anymore! (Acts 15:19-21) Likewise say the books of Romans, Galatians, Hebrews, and 2 Corinthians. In light of these presentations, how do some say the gospel just continues the Law?

   f. It is not possible to affirm only the ceremonial portions of the Law ended but that the oral and judicial portions continue.

      Acts 15 (the conclusion of the Jerusalem Conference) shows such an attempted distinction is a faulty and unacceptable explanation of Scripture.

      Notice this, that [the apostles at the conference] declare that they gave no such commandment as that the Law of Moses should be kept. The Gentiles were never under it and [the apostles] were determined that [the Christians] never should be under it, and in order that [the Christians] might have further assurance [the apostles] sent chosen men with Paul and Barnabas to carry the news among the Christians everywhere.

---

[27] This statement about a covenant of grace is not contradicted by the fact "Noah found favor (grace) in the eyes of the Lord." The Genesis account says nothing about that "grace" being the result of a covenant of grace.

Oh well, says one, I see where you are mistaken. That was the ceremonial law. You cannot find such a statement inside the lids of the Bible. We might as well pull the thing up root and branch. Oh, you say, the idea is there. Well, if the idea is there, the words ought to be there. But for argument's sake, I will grant it and I will take the thing up by the roots still. Hear me! Hear the Word, rather, "Forasmuch as we have heard, that certain which went out from us have troubled you with words, subverting your souls, saying *ye must* be circumcised, and keep the Law; to whom we gave no *such* commandment"(Acts 15:24).

He did not tell them to be circumcised, and did not tell them to keep the Law -- and let's see what we can make of that. Beside it, I lay Paul's statement about keeping the law and circumcision. Then we will know, because Paul said he did not learn it from Peter or the other apostles, he learned it from God ... "Behold, I Paul say unto you, that if ye be circumcised, Christ shall profit you nothing. For I testify *again* to every man that is circumcised, that he is a debtor to do the whole law" (Galatians 5:2,3).

What does he say "again" for? Because from Jerusalem to the regions round about Illyricum he preached the Gospel of Christ and testified that they were not under the Law of Moses, but under Jesus.

It could not be the ceremonial law simply that they were contending had passed away. It could not mean the statutes of Israel simply, it could not mean the ten commandments merely, because Paul says if a man is circumcised he is debtor to do the WHOLE LAW.

That means every word in the ritualistic or ceremonial law if you ... put it that way, and also the ten commandments and the statutes. There is no way out of it. All or none. Every word, every jot, every tittle, every sentence, every statue, or none. Which will you take? Peter, Paul, all the apostles, Jesus – all agree the First Covenant is no part of the New.[28]

No continuation, no identity!

10. It is very difficult to find any Biblical evidence of a pre-temporal inter-trinitarian pact (the so-called covenant of redemption) between Father and Son.

    (We do teach that back in eternity, when God formed His eternal purpose [plan], Jesus volunteered to be the one to become the redeemer if one were needed.)

    A covenant of works made after there was a covenant of redemption in place, "would tend to make the covenant of redemption a second or third thing, a wretched expedient of God in face of the obvious failure of His plan."[29]

    Did God need to make a pact with the Son in order to guarantee or establish the unity of the Godhead in relation to man? Such an idea impinges on our understanding of the being of God.

---

[28] Johnson, *Two Covenants*, p.117,118.

[29] Karl Barth, *Dogmatics*, IV.64

11. It is certainly unbiblical to speak of one covenant only when the language of the Holy Spirit is plural -- *covenants*.

> "To the Israelites pertain the adoption, and the glory, and the <u>covenants</u>, and the giving of the <u>Law</u>, and the service of God, and the <u>promises</u>." Romans 9:4.[30]

> Besides the law and the promises, there was a *plurality* of covenants given to Israel.

> From a study of God's dealings with Abraham, we find no less than three made with him – two based on the first promise, and one based on the second.

> a) The dealings of God with Abraham (concerning Christ) are called covenant. "Brethren, I speak after the manner of men; though it be but a man's covenant, yet if it be confirmed, no man disannuleth, or addeth thereto. Now to Abraham and his seed were the promises made. He saith not, And to seeds, as of many; but as of one, even thy seed, which is Christ"9 (Galatians 3:15,16 KJV). He continues, "What I am saying is this: the Law, which came 430 years later, does not invalidate a covenant previously ratified by God, so as to nullify the promise." Nothing can be more clearly expressed. A covenant is named, described, dated. (430 years before Sinai brings us to Abraham's 75th year, i.e., his departure from Ur.)[31]

> b) We find another dealing of God with Abraham called a covenant in Genesis 15. This is 10 or 12 years after the first covenant (Genesis 12). This one had respect to the promised land. Before Abraham's descendants would come into possession of the land, the Lord tells Abraham his descendants will be sojourners, strangers and oppressed in a foreign land, till a time 400 years from now. "In the same day," says Moses, "the Lord made a *covenant* with Abram, saying, Unto thy seed have I given this land, from the river of Egypt to the great river, the river Euphrates" (Genesis 15:18 KJV). Alexander Campbell fixed this covenant in the 86th year of Abraham; because immediately after it, we are informed of the birth of Ishmael, who was 13 years old at the date of the covenant of circumcision.

> c) We find another covenant at Genesis 17:10, called the covenant of circumcision by Stephen (Acts 7:8). This covenant was made one year before the birth of Isaac, in the 99th year of Abraham, and 24 or 25 years after the covenant concerning Christ.

> We have three distinct covenants made with Abraham in a period of 25 years, and no man can convert these three into one covenant. In this Romans 9:4 passage, the "covenants" are different from the "giving of the Law," and also different from the "promises." Now the Jews, besides the Law, had no covenants but the Abrahamic.

---

[30] The general thrust and wording of much of this point are taken from Alexander Campbell's presentation in the *Campbell-Rice Debate* (reprint Rosemead, Ca: Old Paths Book Club, 195[?]), p.306-307.

[31] See details of this on page 307 of the *Campbell-Rice Debate*.

Therefore, Campbell could assert that he could properly quote the verse to prove a *plurality of covenants* with Abraham.

I.   THOUGHTS ABOUT THE NEW COVENANT

1. Of the divine covenants mentioned in Scripture, first or chief place is due to that one which is emphatically styled by Holy Spirit as the "*better covenant*" (Hebrews 8:6).

    This better covenant is sometimes called an "everlasting covenant" (Isaiah 55:3, Hebrews 13:20).

    Jehovah sometimes called it "My covenant" (Genesis 17:19, etc.). (Exercise care here, since the Mosaic covenant is also styled "My covenant" at Jeremiah 31:32.)

    It is sometimes called the "second" or "new" covenant, to distinguish it from the Mosaic covenant.

2. Other covenants, such as the Noahic and Adamic, were separate covenants from the Mosaic. And unlike the Mosaic, which was temporary, the Noahic and Adamic are still in force, just like the new covenant is.

3. The NEW covenant is the Abrahamic Covenant RENEWED.

    There were renewals of that covenant with Isaac, Jacob, and perhaps David (2 Samuel 7:8-17).

    It would not be proper to say that the Noahic and Mosaic covenants are simply renewals of (as some allege) the "covenant of grace." The Noahic is not a renewal; it is a separate covenant altogether. And the Mosaic and the Abrahamic (= new covenant) are completely different covenants (Jeremiah 31:31ff).

    The only Old Testament passage where the expression "new covenant" appears is Jeremiah 31:31. The unique appearance of the word "new" in that passage stimulated Origen to name the last 27 books of the Bible "The New Testament."

    Do not misunderstand Jeremiah's and Christ's use of the word "new." Both the Hebrew *hadas* and the Greek *kainos* frequently mean "to renew" or "to restore."[32]

    Kainos is the word used in the expressions "new commandment" (which is actually an old one, John 13:34, 1 John 2:7, 2 John 7); the "new moon," the "new creature" in Christ, the "new heart," and the "new heaven and new earth."

    Actually, the Hebrew word *hadas* has to serve for both the ideas of *neos* (new

---

[32] *Neos* is the Greek synonym meaning "new in time." *Kainos* is the synonym meaning "new in quality."

in point of time) and *kainos* (renewed). It is therefore the New Testament vocabulary that helps us decide which is meant in Jeremiah 31:31ff.

4. The key to understanding the "better covenant" of Hebrews 8:6 is to observe the equation -- **ABRAHAMIC = DAVIDIC = NEW COVENANT**.

It is better than the Mosaic covenant, which was a temporary addition to the covenant made with Abraham, renewed (or repeated) in David (2 Samuel 7, "the sure mercies of David"), and renewed again in this age (when the death of Jesus, the covenant sacrifice, validated it).

Compare Acts 3:25, "You are the sons of the covenant God made with Abraham."

THE TEXT OF THE NEW (RENEWED) COVENANT IS FOUND IN THESE WORDS: "**In your seed all the nations of the earth shall be blessed.**" (Genesis 22:18)

The "seed" is Christ. (Galatians 3:16)
"Nations" includes both Jews and Gentiles. (Galatians 3:8)
"Blessed" has to do with sins being atoned for and forgiven. (Romans 4:6-8)

5. There are some elements in the renewed phase of the covenant made with Abraham that become clearer, now that we can look back on what happened and is happening.

a) Since "nations" includes Gentiles (Galatians 3:8) as well as Jews, we have a guideline for interpreting "house of Israel and house of Judah" in Jeremiah 31:31. The new covenant is not limited to Jews.

b) The phrase "I will write [my laws] in their hearts" (Jeremiah 31:33) evidently involves the indwelling of the Holy Spirit to help covenant people live the Christian life – a help not available in the Mosaic age or earlier.

c) The promise of God "I will be their God and they shall be My people" (Jeremiah 31:33) includes not only present, direct access to God but also a future tabernacling of God with men. Revelation 21:3, Hebrews 9:15.

d) The church age is the last of the ages in God's carrying out of His eternal purpose.

God's grand plan, announced in the Abrahamic = Davidic = New Covenant, continues to be implemented as God causes history to flow to its consummation.

J. A CONSIDERATION OF OBJECTIONS TO THIS PRESENTATION OF COVENANTS AND NEW COVENANT

1. Where are God's dealings with Abraham called a *covenant*, so that it is possible to speak of the new covenant being the Abrahamic covenant renewed?

    What was spoken to Abraham is often called a *promise*. See Galatians 3:16. Is there any place where this same "promise" is called a covenant?

    Several places: see 1 Chronicles 16:15-17; Galatians 3:17, Galatians 4:24 (where the "promise" is called a "covenant," in fact, one of *two* covenants); Acts 3:25 (where after calling the hearers "sons ... of the covenant" he quotes the "promise" – "in your seed all the families of the earth will be blessed.")

2. If the new covenant is not written with ink, if it is of Spirit and not the letter (2 Corinthians 3:3-6), how can it be said the "text" of the New Covenant is "in your seed shall all the families of the earth be blessed"?

    2 Corinthians 3:3 does not say the new covenant is not written with ink. It says the Corinthian *Christians* are a letter dictated by Christ, not written by ink, but by the Spirit on the hearts.

    Nor does 2 Corinthians 3:6 ("new covenant, not of the letter, but of the Spirit") say the "new covenant" will not be written *anywhere*. It rather says the motivation to keep the new covenant will not come from tables of stone (letters), but from the indwelling Spirit.

3. If the above presentation is true (that the first recorded use of the word "covenant" appears in Noah's time and that there is no verse that says God made a covenant in Adam's time[33]), then perhaps the chart sometimes drawn by this commentator (showing the covenants and their duration[34]) is faulty in its presentation of an Adamic "covenant" (Genesis 3:14-21).

    This may be a valid criticism. Nevertheless, what was said to Adam is still binding – it is not part of the Mosaic covenant which is presented in the New Testament Scriptures as being temporary. After all, it was not until later at Sinai, years after the words spoken to Adam, that there even was a Mosaic covenant.

---

[33] Compare what is written in footnote #8 above.

[34] The chief issue with the chart is where to locate the New Covenant. Shall we draw another arrow from the cross to the second coming (indicated by the dotted line at the top of the chart), or shall we add another label to the line designated "Abrahamic Covenant" and call it the New (renewed) Covenant?

BIBLE COVENANTS AND THEIR DURATION

"Covenants" (plural) -- Rom. 9:4, Gal. 4:24, Eph. 2:12

SECOND COMING

New Covenant (?)

Christ Now Reigns
Acts 2:33,
I Cor. 15:25

SINAI — Mosaic Covenant (Exodus 20-23)

Davidic Covenant
(Psm. 89:3,4, 132:11,
2 Sam. 7:11-16)

Covenant of Circumcision
(Gen. 17:8-13)

New Covenant (?)

Abrahamic Covenant
(Gen. 12:3, 22:18, etc.)

FLOOD — Noahic Covenant
(Rainbow, Gen. 9:8-17)

FALL — Adamic Covenant
(Gen. 3:14-21)

CREATION

SELECTED BIBLIOGRAPHY ON THE

COVENANTS AND COVENANT THEOLOGY

Baker, D. L., *Two Testaments: One Bible*. Downers Grove, Ill.: Inter-Varsity Press,
  What is the relationship between the two Testaments which constitute our Bible? Is the Old more important than the New? Is the New more important than the Old? Are the two of equal importance and authority? This book surveys the principal modern solutions to the problem -- most of the modern writers cited are of liberal theological persuasion -- and the proposed methods of answering the question of relationship will challenge the reader's presuppositions. He closes this volume (his PhD thesis) by discussing the idea of tension between continuity and discontinuity between the Testaments.

Baker, J. Wayne, *Heinrich Bullinger and the Covenant: The Other Reformed Tradition*. Athens, Ohio: Ohio University Press, 1980.
  Chapters include "The Zurich Origins of the Covenant Idea," "Predestination and Covenant in Bullinger's Thought," and "'Looke from Adam': The People of God in Old Testament Times."

Behm, J., and Quell, G., "Diatheke, Diathithemi," in *Theological Dictionary of the New Testament*, edited by Kittle and Friedrich. Grand Rapids: Wm. B. Eerdmans Pub. Co., 1964 -. Vol.2, p.104-137.

Brown, W. Adams, "Covenant Theology," in *Hasting's Encyclopedia of Religion and Ethics*. New York: Charles Scribners and Sons, 1912. Vol. 4, p.216-224.
  An excellent introduction to the topic for the beginning student. Covers the nature of covenant theology, the history of covenant theology, and shows how other doctrines found in Calvinism grew out of the covenant theology debates.

Buis, H., "Biblical Covenants," in *Encyclopedia of Christianity*, edited by Philip Edgecombe Hughes. Marshalltown, Del.: National Foundation for Christian Education, 1972. Vol.3, p.219-229.
  This article evidently is an attempt to balance the treatment given in this Encyclopedia between pro-one-covenant theologians and anti-one-covenant theologians.

Cottrell, Jack W., *Covenant and Baptism in the Theology of Huldreich Zwingli*. Th.D. dissertation. Princeton Theological Seminary, 1971.

DeJong, Peter Y., *The Covenant Idea in New England Theology, 1620-1874*. Grand Rapids: Wm. B. Eerdmans Pub. Co., 1945.

Fuller, Daniel P., *Gospel and Law: Contrast or Continuum?* Grand Rapids: Wm. B. Eerdmans Pub. Co., 1980.
  The hermeneutics of dispensationalism and one-covenant theology. The rapprochement of the two previously disparate schools of theology is here documented, as students of the two disciplines interact, especially at Dallas Theological Seminary.

Hendriksen, William, *The Covenant of Grace*. Grand Rapids: Baker Book House, 1978.
A strong defense of Reformed, one-covenant theology, and its consequences.

Johnson, Ashley S., *The Two Covenants*. Delight, Ark.: Gospel Light Publishing Co., nd. (A reprint of a volume originally published in 1899), 1949.
Twenty years before originally publishing this series of sermons, the author had prepared and debated on the subject. The series of sermons analyzes the law and the perfect way of faith -- the new covenant. He shows the necessity of living under the law of liberty. A classic in its field.

Kaiser, Walter C., Jr., "The Old Promise and the New Covenant: Jeremiah 31:31-34," in *Journal of the Evangelical Theological Society*. 15:1 (Winter 1972), p.11ff.

------, "The Davidic Promise and the Inclusion of the Gentiles (Amos 9:9-15 and Acts 15:13-18): A Test Passage for Theological Systems," in *Journal of the Evangelical Theological Society*. 20:2 (June 1977), p.97ff.

Kent, Homer A., "The Church and the New Covenant," in *The Epistle to the Hebrews: A Commentary*. Winona Lake, Ind., BMH Books, 1972, p.155-160.
A brief introduction to the following questions: Has the church replaced Israel as the participant in the new covenant? Is the new covenant with the nation of Israel only? Were there two covenants, one with Israel and one with the church? Did the new covenant include both Israel and the church?

Ketcherside, W. Carl., *The Death of the Custodian: The Case of the Missing Tutor*. Cincinnati: Standard Publishing Co., 1976.
Reprinted in 1983 under the title, *That the World May Believe ... A Study of the Covenants*, by World Literature Crusade, Studio City, Calif. A readable presentation of the identity and purpose of the Mosaic Covenant, and thought provoking in its presentation of the New Covenant, as well as in the answers given to the usual objections (especially from Church of Christ circles) to the presentation contained in the book.

McCaig, Archibald, "Covenant, The New," in *New International Standard Bible Encyclopedia*, edited by Geoffrey Bromiley. Grand Rapids: Baker Book House, 1979-. Vol.1, p.795-797.

Mouton, Boyce, *By This Shall All Men Know*. Joplin, Mo., College Press, 1979.
This book is a sequel to *These Two Commandments*, and in it the author seeks to apply the principle of love for men to the very practical problems that perplex the Christian world. (What is the church? What is the task of the church? How should the church be organized? What can the church own? Whom can the church hire? Who runs the church?) His chapter on "Two Covenants" is a good summary of the arguments found in Ketcherside's book.

------, *These Two Commandments*. Joplin, Mo.: College Press, 1979.
This book attempts to show that all the commands God has recorded in both the Old and New Testament Scriptures can be summarized under two heads -- either "Love God" or "Love Men." One of the chapters towards the close of the book shows that if the thesis is accepted, we are left without a "pattern" to try to reproduce in the 20th century church. (This is one of the very things that makes it hard for Restoration Movement readers to accept the thesis of this book.). The 27 books of the New Testament Scriptures give us ways to learn whether or not we are "loving" as we should.

Murray, John, *Covenant of Grace*. London: Tyndale Press, 1953.

Murray, John, "Covenant Theology," in *Encyclopedia of Christianity*, edited by Philip Edgecombe Hughes. Marshalltown, Del.: National Foundation for Christian Education, 1972. V.3, p.199-219.
> This article attempts to explain the covenant of works, the covenant of grace, and the covenant of redemption in terms the layman can understand. Murray's presentation is sympathetic to the one-covenant theology position.

Payne, J. Barton, *The Theology of the Older Testament*. Grand Rapids: Zondervan Publishing House, 1962. p.66-95, 115-119, 463-478.
> Written from a decidedly Reformed (Calvinistic) point of view.

------, "Covenant (in the Old Testament)," in *Zondervan Pictorial Encyclopedia of the Bible*, edited by M. C. Tenney. Grand Rapids: Zondervan Publishing House, 1975. Vol. 1, p.1001-1010.

------, "Covenant, the New," *op. cit.*, p.1012-1016.
> The last two encyclopedia articles nicely summarize the federal theology presentation of one-covenant-of-grace ideas, which are presented in more detail in the same author's work, *The Theology of the Older Testament*.

Robertson, O. Palmer, *The Christ of the Covenants*. Grand Rapids: Baker Book House, 1980.
> Although covenant theology is well-established in many Protestant circles, the classic works on covenant theology have been those of the older theologians. This volume is a modern statement of one-covenant theology that admits weaknesses in the older expressions of that system, and refines them. The dialogue with dispensationalism is at once firm and courteous.
>
> He attempts to show that there has been a covenant relationship between God and men even in eras when the Bible does not call the divine-human relationship a "covenant" in the specific passages where they were instituted.
>
> He appeals to Jeremiah 31:20,21,25,26 and Hosea 6:7, to prove there was a "covenant" in the pre-Noahic period. He takes "Adam" as a reference to the man rather than to the city named at Joshua 3:16. We reply -- why not take the Hosea 6:7 meaning "as at Adam"?
>
> He changes terms -- instead of speaking of a "covenant of works" and a "covenant of grace," he prefers "covenant of creation" and "covenant of redemption."
>
> He speaks of the unity and diversity in the divine covenants, and sees the promise of redemption as being the unifying theme through all the diverse covenants.

Schaff, Philip, ed., "The Westminster Confession of Faith, A.D.1647," The Creeds of Christendom, 4th edition. 3 Vols. New York: Harper and Brothers, 1877. Vol. III, p.598-673.
> A good source to find the text (both their original language, and a translation) of the historic creeds.

Schell, William G., *The Better Testament: Or the Two Testaments Compared*. Moundsville, W. Va.: Gospel Trumpet Publishing Co., 1899.

> Written by a first-generation Church of God preacher, this volume "demonstrates the superiority of the Gospel over Moses' Law according to the Epistles of Paul, especially that addressed to the Hebrews." While the underlying purpose of the volume is to show there is a second work of grace that results in holiness (and the last half of the book is taken up with this theme), the chapters in the early part of the book do a fine job showing the superiority of the New to the Old Testaments.

Smith, Mont W., *What the Bible Says About Covenant*. Joplin, Mo.: College Press, 1982.

> He traces the meaning of "covenant" through history, comparing Biblical covenants with the ancient concept of treaty and exposing the false presuppositions of the Greeks upon which much faulty theology has been based. He sees covenant as essential to understanding New Testament theology and Christian service. Smith emphasizes that *Christ Himself is the new covenant*. His treatment of the change from Old to New Covenant is devastating to modern dispensationalism's idea that fleshly Israel is still God's chosen people.
>
> (Many will find unsatisfactory Smith's identification of the new covenant with Christ, his views on election, and his ascription to Greek philosophy the understanding that the New Testament distinctly teaches the basic corruption of the natural man.)

Thompson, J. Arthur, "Covenant (OT)," *New International Standard Bible Encyclopedia*, edited by Geoffrey Bromiley. Grand Rapids: Wm. B. Eerdmans Publishing Co., 1979- . Vol. 1, p.790-793.

Van Til, Cornelius, "Covenant Theology," in *Twentieth Century Encyclopedia of Religious Knowledge* (being volume 1 of the two-volume supplement to *The New Schaff-Herzog Encyclopedia of Religious Knowledge*). Grand Rapids: Baker Book House, 1955. p.306

Vos, Geerhardus, "The Epistle's Conception of the *Diatheke*," *The Teaching of the Epistle To the Hebrews*. Grand Rapids: Wm. B. Eerdmans Pub. Co., 1956. p.27-45.

Vos, Geerhardus, "Hebrews, the Epistle of the *Diatheke*," *Princeton Theological Review*. 13 (1915), p.587-632 and 14 (1916), p.1-61.

Wing, C. P., "Federal Theology," *Encyclopedia of Biblical, Theological, and Ecclesiastical Literature*, edited by McClintock and Strong. New York: Harper and Brothers, 1891. Vol. III,, p.515-520.

APPENDIX B

SUGGESTED SERMON OUTLINES

In hopes of encouraging more preaching from the book of Hebrews, we offer several suggested expository outlines. The ideas introduced both as main points and as sub-points can be found explained in detail in the commentary section of this book.

* * * * * * * *

HOLY BRETHREN, CONSIDER JESUS!

Hebrews 3:1, Hebrews 1:1-3

INTRODUCTION
A. The Book of Hebrews has been tragically ignored in recent years in the Restoration Movement.
B. God has spoken. Hebrews 1:1-3. Is anybody listening?
C. Outline of the whole book (to see where this and later messages fit)
  1. A SUPERIOR PERSON -- CHRIST. Hebrews 1-6
      a. Better than the prophets. 1:1-3
      b. Better than the angels. 1:4 - 2:18 (*Warning.* 2:1-4)
      c. Better than Moses. 3:1 - 4:13 (*Warning.* 3:7 - 4:13)
      d. Better than Aaron. 4:14 - 6:20 (*Warning.* 5:11 - 6:20)

  2. A SUPERIOR PRIESTHOOD – ORDER OF MELCHIZEDEK. Hebrews 7-10
      a. A superior order. 7
      b. A superior covenant. 8
      c. A superior sanctuary. 9
      d. A superior sacrifice. 10 (*Warning.* 10:26-39)

  3. A SUPERIOR PRINCIPLE -- FAITHFULNESS. Hebrews 11-13
      a. The great examples of faithfulness. 11:1 - 12:3
      b. The perils that threaten a life of faithfulness. (*Warning.* 12:14-29)
      c. Exhortations to perform certain Christian duties faithfully. 13

Purpose of message: Highlight truths about Jesus emphasized in this book of Hebrews. *(We learn more about Jesus from Hebrews than from any other New Testament book!)*

I.   JESUS IS SUPERIOR TO THE PROPHETS. Hebrews 1:1-3

   A. Some famous men were prophets. None of these men was great enough to be called "Son" of God.

   B. The Person of Jesus Christ
     1. He is the radiance (effulgence) of His (the Father's) glory. 1:3
     2. He is the exact representation of His (the Father's) nature. 1:3

C. The Work of Jesus Christ
    IN HIS PRE-INCARNATE STATE
        1. He is appointed Heir of all things. 1:2
        2. He is the creator. 1:2 (through whom God made the world [ages])

    IN HIS WORK SINCE HE CAME INTO THE WORLD THROUGH THE
    MANGER IN BETHLEHEM
        3. He upholds all things by the word of His power. 1:3
        4. He made purification for sins. 1:3

    IN HIS PRESENT GLORIFIED STATE
        5. He sat down at the right hand of the Majesty on high. 1:3
D. God has spoken – Are we listening?
    1. He is there, and He is not silent!
    2. Finality of the revelation in Jesus Christ. "God has spoken!"
    3. Greater than the prophets. (Hear this, as compared to Islam and modern
        religious liberalism).
    4. Creator, Prophet, Priest, and King – Jesus Christ is superior to all of the
        prophets and servants of God who have ever appeared on the sacred pages of
        the Scriptures, or walked down the corridors of time and history.

II. JESUS IS SUPERIOR TO THE ANGELS. Hebrews 1:4-14

    A. A Word about Angels
        1. Their nature -- they are created beings, 1:6.
        2. Their appearance
        3. Their ministry, 1:7,14.

    B. What is said about Jesus in this section (that can't be said about angels)
        1. He is the Son, 1:4,5.
        2. He is the firstborn who receives worship, 1:6.
        3. He is served by the angels, 1:7.
        4. He is God enthroned and anointed, 1:8-9.
        5. He is creator, eternal and unchanging, 1:10-12.
        6. He sends the angels to serve the redeemed, 1:13,14.

    C. What does it mean -- this unanswerable evidence that Jesus is superior to angels?
        1. Those misguided religious groups who say that Jesus was once but an angel
            himself -- albeit an archangel -- are mistaken.
        2. Jesus Christ is greater than the angels, and this means the message He brings
            is also greater than the Law which angels helped deliver to the people in Old
            Testament times.

III. HEED THE WORD AND DON'T DRIFT! Hebrews 2:1-4

    A. This is the first of five warning (exhortation) passages in the book of Hebrews.

B. What does a Christian have to do to be lost? NOTHING! ("Neglect the great salvation")

C. The penalty for faithlessness in the Church Age is severe.

CONCLUSION
A. Consider Jesus Christ!
B. How shall we escape if we neglect this great salvation?
C. Drifters -- beware!
D. Invitation

* * * * * * * *

JESUS CAN MAKE A MAN OUT OF YOU!
Hebrews 2:5-18

INTRODUCTION
A. We learn more about Jesus in Hebrews than in any other book of the Bible.
B. Jesus' Deity was emphasized in chapter 1.
C. His Humanity (and His humiliation) are emphasized in chapter 2.
D. Our text answers Jewish objections to the lofty Christian doctrine of who Jesus is.
E. Jesus is superior to prophets and angels – a messenger from God to be listened to.

Purpose of message: To help each of us grasp the Biblical view of man, and appreciate Jesus' contribution to our manhood.

I.   MAN, AS GOD MADE HIM. Hebrews 2:6-8. Psalm 8:4-6.

A. It is by no means easy to grasp the meaning of Hebrews 2:5-9.
B. "What is man?"
C. Man is someone special!
D. Man's splendid origin. "Thou hast MADE HIM ..."
E. Man's exalted position in the order of created beings. "A little lower than the angels" and "crowned with glory and honor"
F. Man's lordship over creation.
G. Man's fellowship with God. "Man, thou art mindful of him ... thou visitest him!"
H. Man's destiny to be higher than the angels. "Thou madest him, for a little while, lower than the angels."
I. F.B. Meyer on man as God made him.

II. MAN, AS SIN MAKES HIM. Hebrews 2:8c

A. The Hebrew writer's commentary on Psalm 8.
B. Man sinned – and all was lost.
C. Not only did Adam sin. Our own personal sin degrades and debauches us.
D. F.B. Meyer on Man as sin makes him.

III. JESUS, AS MAN, WAS JUST WHAT GOD INTENDED MAN TO BE.

  A. The Bible tells us that Jesus was perfectly human while on earth.
    1. Hear what the Gospels say about Jesus' humanity!
    2. Hear what the Epistles say about Jesus' humanity!
    3. Hear what Hebrews 2 says about Jesus' humanity!
            Verse 11 – He and humans are all of one *father*.
            Verse 11 – Jesus calls men His "brothers."
            Verse 14 – Jesus partook of flesh and blood
            Verse 17 – Jesus was made like His brethren in all things

  B. Jesus' humanity -- it was just like ours.
    1. "God sent His own Son IN THE BODY OF FLESH OF SIN" – Romans 8:3 (literally)
    2. He was "tempted in all things as we are, yet without sin." Hebrews 4:15
    3. Jesus used no powers to overcome temptations other than those we also can use!
    4. He was (temporarily) made a little lower than angels – if He was just like us.

  C. A Word about the Temporary Subordination of Jesus to the Father.
    1. Standard argument to prove Jesus is not God ….
    2. Reply to this argument
      a. Jesus has always existed in the form of God, John 17:5; Philippians 2:6.
      b. When He was born into a human body at Bethlehem, He emptied himself, Philippians 2:6,7. He temporarily gave up the independent exercise of the prerogatives of deity, John 5:19.
      c. He, one day, will take up again the independent exercise of the prerogatives of deity, 1 Corinthians 15:22-28.
      d. In the meantime, since his resurrection and ascension, He has been crowned with glory and honor, Hebrews 2:7.

  D. A Word about the Necessity of the Incarnation.
    1. It was not degrading to become a man, 2:5-9.
    2. It was fitting (becoming) for God to redeem man this way, 2:10.
    3. It was necessary for the redeeming work of Christ, 2:9, 11-16.
    4. It resulted from His desire to be more than a Savior from sin, 1:17,18.
    5. It was the only way God could reach us!

IV. WHAT MAN CAN BECOME IN JESUS CHRIST.

  A. Some of the Results of Jesus' humanity (Incarnation) can now be seen!
  B. Jesus is the Sanctifier, and believing men are the sanctified, 2:11.
  C. Jesus is no longer (like other humans) lower than the angels.
  D. His Humanity Enabled Him to Regain Man's Lost Dominion, 2:5-9.
            "Not to angels (but to Jesus) did God subject the world to come."
            Jesus is the "Pioneer" -- Who has blazed the trail that others may follow.

E.   His Humanity Enables God to bring Many Sons to Glory, 2:10-13; Rom. 8:28-30.
F.   His Humanity Enabled Him to Disarm Satan and deliver us from death, 2:14-16.
G.   His Humanity Enables Him to be a Sympathetic High Priest to His people, 2:17,18.
      "He is able to come to the aid of those who are tempted"
      He makes "propitiation for the sins of the people."

CONCLUSION
A.   Summary:
B.   Let us:
      1.   Cherish the Scriptural idea of man's dignity.
      2.   Remember that we can realize our destiny only in Christ.
      3.   Seek a saving interest in His atoning death.
      4.   Consecrate soul and life to His service.
      5.   Imitate Him as the pattern Man.
      6.   Live in a manner befitting the great hope we have in Him.
C.   Consider:
      1.   The guilt of those who reject the help Christ offers is greater than that of fallen
            angels.
      2.   The blessedness of those who accept the help of Christ will be greater, in some
            respects, than that of the holy angels.
D.   The devil has made a fool of us -- less than human. Let Jesus make a man out of you.
E.   Invitation

* * * * * * * *

THE REST WE DARE NOT MISS
Hebrews 4:1-13

INTRODUCTION

A.   Sometimes we can get by without resting – but there is a rest we dare not miss.
B.   The possibility of missing God's "rest" should fill the mind with awe.
C.   Hebrews is addressed to people who are genuine Christians, and is full of warnings
      about the eternal consequences of a lack of faithfulness to Christ.
D.   Our text is part of the "second warning passage," Hebrews 3:7 - 4:19.

Purpose of message:
      1.   Make sure the hearers understand and appreciate Hebrews 3 and 4.
      2.   See a method of Bible study the Hebrews writer used, and encourage our use of it.
      3.   Teach the conscious steps we must take, lest we miss the rest a man dare not miss.

I.   FIRST, WE NEED A BRIEF REVIEW.
      A.   A review of the argument of Hebrews, thus far.
      B.   A review of Hebrew history, after their exodus from Egypt.
            1.   The exodus and wilderness wanderings took place about 1400 BC.
            2.   David lived and wrote his Psalms about 1000 BC.

II. THERE IS A HEAVEN (GOD'S "REST") INTO WHICH MEN ARE INVITED TO ENTER!

    A. The problem for the Hebrews writer – How to prove to his readers there is a place called "heaven" without appealing to the New Testament Scriptures, or the words of Jesus.
        Do a word study!

    B. Hebrews 4:1-9 is a written record of that word study on the word "rest. Let us review what is there written.
        1. The first place we find the word "rest" is in the account of the creation. Gen. 2:2
        2. The next place we find the word "rest" is in those verses that tell about the exodus and the wilderness wanderings.
        3. Years later, we find the word "rest" in David's writings.
        4. The Hebrews writer draws a conclusion from his study – Hebrews 4:8-11

    C. What we learn from this word study about heaven.
        1. God's "rest," when He rested from the work of creation, is the kind of rest which He invites men to share.
        2. How shall we harmonize Genesis 2:2 and John 5:17?
        3. Psalm 132:13-14
        4. God has provided a rest. Some will enter it! Some will not!

    D. God's Rest -- God's provision -- God's Eternal purpose -- is implicit in the words of Hebrews 4:1, "a promise remains of entering His rest."
        1. God's eternal purpose, Ephesians 1:4-11; Romans 8:28-30.
        2. The historic fulfillment of this plan.

    E. God never intended to live in heaven all by Himself. He planned to share it with people!

III. REST WAS OFFERED TO, AND FORFEITED BY, ISRAEL. Hebrews 4:2

    A. They had good news preached to them, but "the word they heard did not profit them, because it was not united by faith in those who heard."
    B. It happened in Moses' time. Remember the incident recorded in Numbers 14!
    C. David warned it could happen in his time. Psalm 95:7-11
    D. The point being made to the Hebrews readers is that it could happen to them, just as it happened before.

IV. IN THIS CHRISTIAN AGE, REST IS STILL OFFERED TO THE PEOPLE OF GOD
    A. There is a place of rest, called heaven, Hebrews 4:1,3,9.
    B. The persons for whom the rest is designed are "the people of God."
    C. The reason Christians have a promise of heaven is because Christ made good man's failure, Hebrews 4:9,10
    D. In the gospel, God offers rest to believers in Christ.

V. WE PAUSE IN OUR PRESENTATION, TO ENCOURAGE A BIBLE STUDY.
    A. Make a review of Old Testament history.
    B. Do a word study.
    C. Carefully identify persons and things whose names are the same, or similar.

VI. THE SURE WAY TO FIND REST
    The expected response God looks for in the people He would have join Him in His rest.

    A. By giving diligence, 4:11.
    B. By taking care ("heed" KJV), 3:12.
    C. By letting the Living Word judge the thoughts and intents of the heart, 4:12,13.
    D. By holding fast our confession, 4:14-16.
    E. By offering encouragement to others to be steadfast, 3:13.
    F. By fearing, 4:1,2.
    G. "Do not harden not your hearts," 3:8.
    H. Faithfulness until death, 3:14.

CONCLUSION

A. Beware lest you fail to reach the promised land!
B. Man's need for God's rest is urgent.
C. Today, if you hear His voice, do not harden your heart!
    There are certain great warnings here:
    1. God makes men an offer.
    2. But to obtain the blessings of God, men must make a certain response.
    3. The immutability of God's demands.
    4. To the offer of God there is a limit.
D. Only today is yours!

* * * * * * * *

ARE YOU LOSING YOUR HEARING?
Text: Hebrews 5:11 - 6:12

INTRODUCTION
A. In the physical world, one of the accompaniments of old age is often the loss of hearing. It is something over which we have little control.
B. In the spiritual world, the loss of hearing leads to a Christian's being lost.
C. In the spiritual world, the loss of hearing *IS* something over which men have control.

Purpose of message: Examine what Hebrews has to say about the doctrine of Eternal Security, to see if it harmonizes with what the Bible says elsewhere, and to encourage all of us to make sure we are listening when God speaks.

I. DULLNESS OF HEARING CAN OVERTAKE CHRISTIANS.
    A. Hebrews 5:11
    B. Hebrews 6:12
    C. Symptoms and evidences of "loss of hearing."

II. DULLNESS OF HEARING CAN RESULT IN GREAT MISTAKES AND HURTS.
    A. It can lead to embracing an obsolete religion, Hebrews 6:1,2.
    B. It can lead to falling away and the impossibility of repentance, Hebrews 6:4-6.
    C. It can lead to thoughtless and shameful treatment of man's only Savior, Hebrews 6:6.
    D. It can lead to eternal punishment, Hebrews 6:7,8.
    E. The world loses opportunity to hear about our Savior, Hebrews 5:12.

III. CAN A CHILD OF GOD SO SIN AS TO LOSE HIS SALVATION?

    A. Theologians have taken several positions on this question.
        1. Christians can sin, but God will not allow them to die guilty of sin. Rather He
            will preserve and chastise them until they repent. They may lose some
            opportunities for further service for God, but not their eternal salvation.
        2. Some have insisted that salvation is all the work of God. If someone could
            later be lost, it would take another act by God to get the person lost.
        3. A child of God dying in a sinful and impenitent condition will be saved despite
            that condition. They won't lose salvation, but will lose some of their reward.
        4. Christians are expected to be faithful, and a careless disregard of God's
            commands will lead to an adverse judgment and sentence from God. Once
            saved, yes. Later lost, yes.

    B. Which of these several theological views does Hebrews seem to teach?
            Hebrews 2:1-3 --
            Hebrews 3:12,13, 4:1 --
            Hebrews 5:9 --
            Hebrews 6:4-6 --
            Hebrews 6:7-8 --
            Hebrews 10:26,27 --
            Hebrews 10:28,29 --
            Hebrews 10:36-39 --
            Hebrews 12:15--
            Hebrews 12:25 --
            All these Hebrews passages support view #4.

    C. Which of these theological views do the rest of the Scriptures seem to teach?
            Matthew 13:3-8, 18-23; Luke 8:4-15 ... The Parable of the Sower --
            Matthew 25:14-30 --
            John 15:2-6 --
            Romans 2:6,7 --
            Romans 8:13 --
            Romans 11:17-23 –

1 Corinthians 6:9-11 --
1 Corinthians 8:1-11 --
1 Corinthians 9:27 --
1 Corinthians 10:1-12 --
Galatians 6:7-9 --
1 Timothy 4:1-2 --
1 Timothy 1:19 --
1 Timothy 5:12 --
James 5:19,20
2 Peter 1:10 --
2 Peter 2:20-22 --
Revelation 2:4,5 --
Revelation 3:15,16 --
All of these harmonize with view #4, that eternal security is conditional.

IV. AN EXAMINATION OF TEXTS THAT SEEM TO CONTRADICT "CONDITION-
AL" ETERNAL SECURITY.

We know Scripture does not contradict other Scripture, so what is the explanation of
these passages?
John 5:24, 6:37, 10:27-29 --
Romans 8:35-39 --
1 Corinthians 3:15 --
1 Peter 1:5 --
1 John 2:19, 3:9 --
Jude 24 --
*All these passages are easily harmonized with the doctrine elsewhere taught that
continuing salvation is a conditional thing with God.*

V. WHERE DID THE DOCTRINE OF "ONCE SAVED, ALWAYS SAVED" COME
FROM?
A. Augustine (who baptized Greek philosophy into Christian theology)
B. Calvin (who continued Augustine's non-Biblical emphases)

VI. WHAT CONSTITUTES SALVATION?
A. God's part in salvation.
B. Man's part in salvation.

CONCLUSION:
A. Check your hearing! It is dangerous, eternally so, to become and remain dull of hearing!
B. Julian the Apostate
C. Were the serpent's subtle words to Adam and Eve the first teaching eternal security?
D. The construction of the New Testament implies the danger of falling away from grace.
(Are there not 21 epistles to encourage a man to life a consistent Christian life?)
E. Exhortation and invitation

JESUS CHRIST -- A PRIEST LIKE MELCHIZEDEK
Read Genesis 14:14-24, and Hebrews 7:1-28

INTRODUCTION
A. A brief summary of what is recorded in Genesis 14.
B. The presuppositions behind this presentation of Jesus as a priest like Melchizedek:
   1. The basic idea is that religion is access to God.
   2. God gave revelations of His will for man to make continuing access to God possible.
   3. The priesthood (and sacrificial system) existed to make access to God possible.

Purpose of message:
   The Hebrews readers are commanded to "consider" how great a man Melchizedek was so they will have a better idea of how great Jesus is. We, too, need to make this study!

I. CHARACTER STUDY OF MELCHIZEDEK
    A. He was king of Salem.
    B. He was a priest of the Most High God.
       1. The phrase "Most High God" explained.
       2. First instance of anyone being a "priest" in the Bible.
       3. How did Melchizedek know anything about being a priest?
       4. What does a priest do?
       5. Canaan was not wholly idolatrous. Some people had things right.
    C. He was both king and priest.
    D. He met Abraham, returning from the slaughter of the kings, blessed him, and provided bread and wine.
    E. To Melchizedek, Abraham gave the tenth of the chief spoils.
            Tithing did not originate with Moses.
            By tithing, Abraham expressed his gratitude to God.
    F. His name is significant, Hebrews 7:2.
            In the Bible, names and their meanings are often important.
    G. His family history is different – no "pedigree," Hebrews 7:3.
            Melchizedek's priesthood was not hereditary, as the Jewish priesthood was.
    H. The non-transferable character of Melchizedek's priesthood, Hebrews 7:24.
    I. "Observe how great this man was," Hebrews 7:4-10.
    J. He was a priest for all men.

II. WHAT LESSONS MAY WE LEARN ABOUT JESUS FROM THE PARALLELS BETWEEN MELCHIZEDEK (the type) AND JESUS (the antitype)?
    A. From verse 3, we learn that Melchizedek was a type – "Made like the Son of God."
       Give a brief explanation of how types worked, and how they are to be interpreted.
    B. Jesus is king of righteousness.
    C. "King of Salem." "Salem" (Jerusalem) is Jesus' capital city.
    D. Jesus is Priest of the Most High God.
    E. Jesus is "first king of righteousness, then king of peace."

    F. Jesus is King and Priest at the same time.

    G. Christ's followers contribute gold and treasures to the cause of His kingdom.

    H. Without father, mother – the Son of God is.

    I. Jesus "remains a priest forever."

    J. Christ rewards and refreshes His followers.

    K. Unites Jew and Gentile – He is a world-wide priest, a priest for all men.

III. SOME APPLICATIONS OF THE DOCTRINAL TRUTHS FOUND IN THE BIBLICAL RECORD OF MELCHIZEDEK AND JESUS.

    A. "Observe how great this Melchizedek was!" v.4 (Consider how great Jesus is!)

    B. The accounts of Melchizedek in the Bible are one of the most remarkable proofs of the divine inspiration and unity of the Scripture.

    C. Deal with Calvin's and non-instrumental groups' use of the argument from silence.

    D. If there was perfection by the Levitical priesthood, why was there another priest after the order of Melchizedek? v.11

    E. What is the fate of the unevangelized?

    F. Righteousness must precede peace.
        1. Righteousness – with God and men.
        2. The peace Jesus can give.
        3. Stop looking for peace the wrong way.
            (Won't find it in escape, evasion, compromise – only in Jesus.)

CONCLUSION

A. In several particulars we have seen Melchizedek "made like the Son of God," Hebrews 7:3.

        In office both are king-priests.

        In character and conduct righteousness, the aim of divine government, is magnified.

        In service there is self-giving for the peace and happiness of men.

        The eternity of their personality is a pledge of success and permanence of the divine program for the world.

B. All hail, King Jesus! All hail, Emmanuel!
    King of kings, Lord of Lords, bright morning star.
    Throughout all eternity, we'll sing your praises,
    And forevermore we will reign with Him.

C. Invitation

TYPES AND SHADOWS – PREVIEWS OF COMING ATTRACTIONS
Hebrews 8:5, 9:23, 10:1

INTRODUCTION
A. The study of types and their fulfillment shows that the Bible is a truly remarkable book, unlike any other ever written.
B. We Restoration Movement people used to make a regular study of types and shadows.

Purpose of message:
   1. To encourage you to make a study of the types recorded in the Bible, for your own personal enrichment.

   2. To use types to call our attention to a whole range of impressive evidence of the divine origin of the Bible. If we miss these systems of types and antitypes, we miss a wondrous evidence which distinguishes the Bible from all other books.

I. MAN'S NEED OF DIVINE INSTRUCTION

   A. Sin separates, and men's foolish hearts become darkened.

   B. Without a revelation from God, we would not have the foggiest idea what God's plans are, or what His will is for us.

II. GOD'S METHOD OF INSTRUCTION

   A. NT Age –
      1. God has spoken through His Son, Hebrews 1:1,2
      2. Revelation, Inspiration, Illumination, 1 Corinthians 2:6-16.
      3. By words, Psalm 32:8.

   B. OT Ages – "God spoke ... to the Fathers in the prophets in many portions and in many ways," Hebrews 1:1.
      1. It was a progressive revelation ("many portions").
         a. God's revelation has been progressive.
         b. The necessity for such a gradual (progressive) revelation.
      2. It was presented in many different ways.
         a. Mysteries – Things not very clearly revealed in the OT, but now are.
         b. Prophecies – A message given (spoken) by inspiration in the vernacular of the people.
         c. By object lessons – Types, shadows, copies, allegories, parables.

III. A BRIEF OVERVIEW OF BIBLICAL "TYPES"

   A. Definition
       A type is a mere shadow or faint outline-picture of something pertaining to the future. They are previews of coming attractions.

B. Examples of (classification of) types
    1. Personal types
    2. Historical types
    3. Ritual (or legal) types

C. Several things are implied by these definitions and examples:
    1. There will be some resemblance or analogy existing between type and antitype.
    2. The likeness is but partial.
    3. The points of resemblance were designed and preordained by God.
    4. Every type is a sort of prophecy. They all relate to the future.
    5. All types are found in the OT Scriptures, rather than in NT writings.

D. Biblical types have both a *present* and *future* significance.

E. The design or purpose for using types.

F. How much of the Old Testament is typical?

G. A word on the interpretation of types.

IV. A STUDY OF SEVERAL HELPFUL TYPES

A. Adam was a type of Christ. Romans 5:12-21
    1. In some ways Adam and Christ are alike.
    2. In some ways Adam and Christ are opposite.

B. Moses was a type of Christ. Hebrews 3:1-6; Acts 3:22-26 and Deuteronomy 18:15
    – "a prophet like me"
    1. Providentially preserved. Exodus 1:15-2:15; Matthew 2:13-15.
    2. Sent as a deliverer. Exodus 3:10
    3. Officiated as lawgiver and mediator. Exodus 18:13,14
    4. Worked as (builder)?
    5. Served as ruler and intercessor. Exodus 24:3; Deuteronomy 1:3.
    6. Was a distinguished prophet (represented God to men). Acts 3:22,23,
        Deuteronomy 18:15-18

C. Priesthood of Melchizedek. Hebrews 7:1-3 – "made like Son of God" (*see previous
    sermon*).

D. Tabernacle – type of heaven. "Make all things according to pattern," Hebrews 8:5.
    1. Hebrews 8:5
    2. This helps us to understand many other verses in the Bible (e.g., Rev. 4-8).

E. Ceremony of the Day of Atonement.
    1. Leviticus 16
    2. Jesus' ministry in heaven, Hebrews 9:11-18.

F. The Law was only a shadow of the good things to come. Hebrews 10:1ff.

V. WHAT THE STUDY OF TYPES WILL DO FOR OUR FAITH.

  A. The study of types and their fulfillment affords a very impressive evidence of the divine origin of the Bible.

  B. We shall appreciate the singular truths God has been teaching from age to age.

  C. We shall find it easier to recognize the truth of Messiah and His religion.

CONCLUSION
A. Encouragement to begin your own study of types and antitypes, shadows and substance.
B. Invitation

* * * * * * * *

THE BETTER COVENANT, *or*
THE LAST WILL AND TESTAMENT OF JESUS CHRIST
Hebrews 9:13-17

Purpose of message:
  This passage is important to our understanding of the Bible, our faith, and our practice. It needs to become one of our everyday working passages from which we approach our Bibles, as we would learn ourselves and as we would teach others.

  A. Christian church people used to know Hebrews about as well as they knew Acts.
  B. Background of the text
  C. The problem of translation (cp. NASB v. KJV). "Covenant" or "Testament"?

I. CHRIST'S LAST WILL AND TESTAMENT
    What does this passage teach if we translate it "testament" as does the KJV?

  A. Who is the testator?

  B. Some truths concerning wills or testaments.
    1. Everyone who owns any possessions should make a will.
    2. Who are the heirs?
    3. The latest will made supersedes all previous wills.
    4. Before his death, the testator may dispose of his property as he wishes.
    5. The testator must die before the will has any force, or takes effect.
    6. After the death of the testator, the will may not be altered or revoked.
    7. Proof of the death of the testator.
    8. A testator appoints executors of his will.

  C. Think of the gospel as the last will and testament of Jesus Christ.
    1. In human wills, it is necessary that we have it in written form.
    2. It is not enough that a will and testament be written, it must be attested.
    3. There is also a need that the terms of the will must be published and made known.

    D. What are the legacies conveyed by this testament?

    E. A will may be conditional or unconditional.

II. THE BETTER COVENANT
What does this passage teach, if we translate it "covenant" all the way through?

    A. What is a covenant?
        1. Words translated "covenant" or "testament" (Hebrew, *berith*; Greek, *diatheke*).
        2. In any covenant there are two contracting parties.
        3. Covenants are God's promises.
        4. Some conclusions drawn from the nature of such covenants.

    B. God is a covenant-making and -keeping God. (Covenants are promises, in a sense.)
        1. Covenants with Noah (Genesis 9:8-13) and with David (2 Samuel 7:4-16).
        2. Two major covenants, with which most of the books of the Bible are concerned.
          -- The Mosaic Covenant, made at Sinai, 1447 BC. Exodus 19-24, esp. 24:1-8.
          -- The new covenant (the Abrahamic covenant renewed), made at Jerusalem,
              AD 30. Jeremiah 31:31ff (Hebrews 8:8-13); Acts 3:25; Galatians 3:8ff.

    C. God's covenants were always sealed by the death of a sacrificial victim.
        The first, or Mosaic, covenant was thus sealed, Hebrews 9:18-22.
        The new covenant has been sealed by the death of Christ, Hebrews 9:15.

    D. The three-fold effect of the death of Christ:
        1. An actual atonement for sins. Verse 12 speaks of eternal redemption in His blood.
          Verse 15 speaks of a redemption of transgressions in Old Testament times.
          Verse 14 speaks of the blood of Christ cleansing men's consciences.
        2. A call of believers to an eternal inheritance, verse 15.
        3. Became the mediator of the new covenant, verse 15.

    E. The new covenant is not (like Moses') something temporary.
        It cannot be shaken, Hebrews 12:27-29.

    F. God's covenants are conditional.

    G. If men are to have a relationship with God, it will be on the basis of "covenant."

III. APPLICATION. What does this mean to me? How does all this affect me?

    A. Under either way of explaining this important passage in Hebrews, the Law of Moses is no longer a valid or binding covenant.
        Patriarchal ⇨ Mosaic ⇨ Christian dispensations.
          God dealt with a family, a nation, then all peoples.
        New covenant, the Christian dispensation, starts with the death of Christ.
        What was taken out of the way?

B. Are the covenants of equal importance and authority to us who live in the Christian dispensation? Certainly not. See these verses: Hebrews 1:1,2, 2:1-3; 2 Corinthians 3:6-11; Galatians 3:19-25; Ephesians 2:14,15; Colossians 2:6-17.   See the Transfiguration account (Matthew 17:1-8), too.

C. THE NEW TESTAMENT IS OUR RULE OF FAITH AND PRACTICE!

D. Effect on Bible Study – the new covenant should be studied in contrast with the Old.
> Better promises, better sacrifice, better priest.
> The Old and the New contrasted.

E. Understand how sin is atoned for.

F. Mosaic covenant – if over-emphasized – gets us into trouble.
> Example from Seventh Day Adventism.
> Example from the practice of infant baptism
> Example from ethics. (Leniency. Harsh austerity.)

G. Importance to the Christian of the old covenant Scriptures.
> There is a spiritual benefit to the study of the old covenant writings.

H. Instruction at Lord's Supper – cup reminds us of the blood of the covenant.

CONCLUSION.
A. Mark and memorize our text.
B. The importance of the new covenant to our relationship to God.

Several Restoration Movement preachers have produced charts to help their audiences understand what the Scriptures say about Bible covenants and their duration. Preachers may find it helpful to copy them and hand them out to their audiences as they preach on this topic.

THE TWO COVENANTS

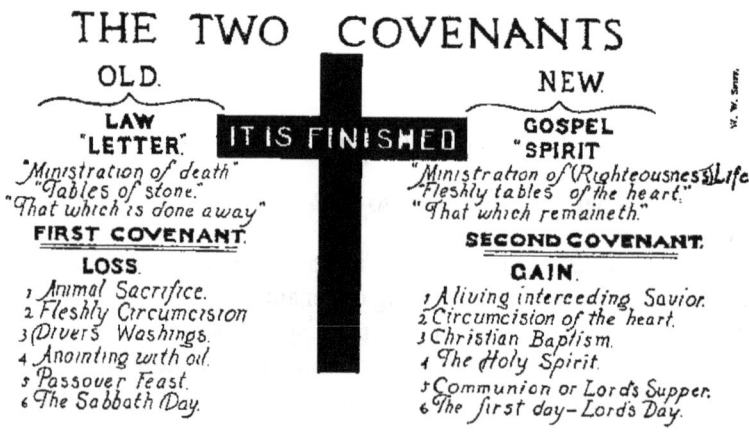

THE DIVINE LIBRARY.

PATRIARCHAL DISPENSATION, Creation to 1447 BC
JEWISH DISPENSATION, 1447 B.C. to Cross.

Mosaic Covenant (Ex. 20-23)

CHRISTIAN DISPENSATION,
From Cross to End of Time.

Better Covenant (Heb. 8-10)

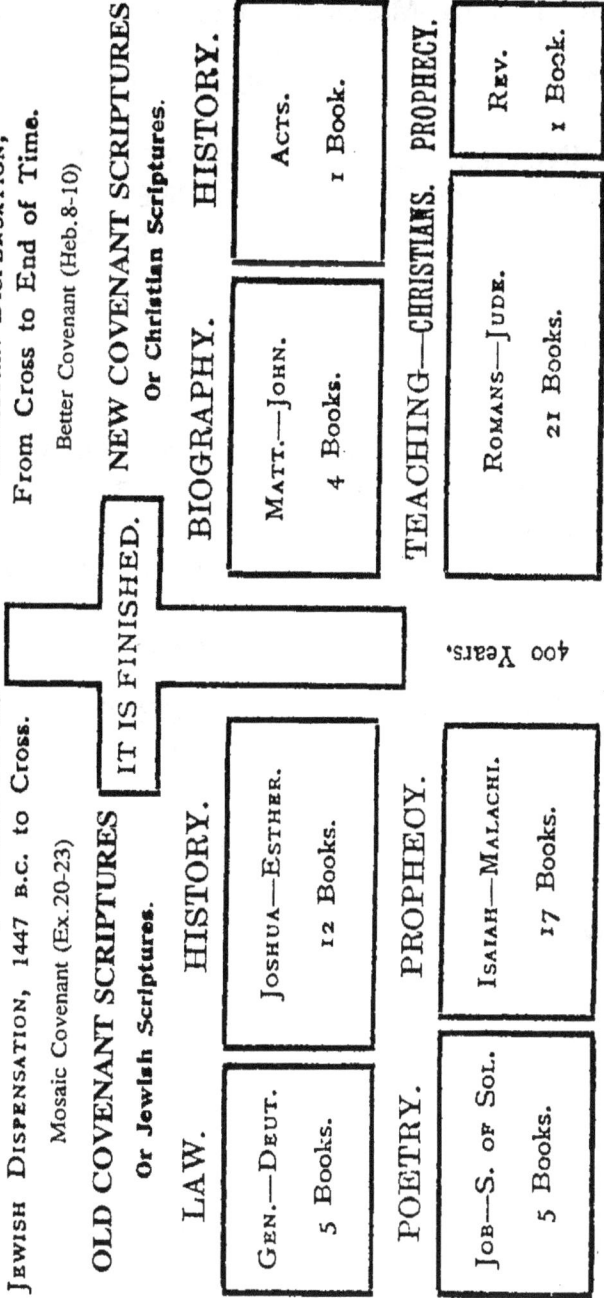

OLD COVENANT SCRIPTURES
Or Jewish Scriptures.

NEW COVENANT SCRIPTURES
Or Christian Scriptures.

IT IS FINISHED.

LAW.
GEN.—DEUT.
5 Books.

HISTORY.
JOSHUA—ESTHER.
12 Books.

POETRY.
JOB—S. of SOL.
5 Books.

PROPHECY.
ISAIAH—MALACHI.
17 Books.

BIOGRAPHY.
MATT.—JOHN.
4 Books.

HISTORY.
ACTS.
1 Book.

TEACHING—CHRISTIANS.
ROMANS—JUDE.
21 Books.

PROPHECY.
REV.
1 Book.

400 Years.

WHO SPEAKS?   TO WHOM SPOKEN?   WHAT PURPOSE?   WHAT DISPENSATION?

THE "BETTER PROMISES" OF THE NEW COVENANT

NEW COVENANT	OLD COVENANT
1. INWARD KNOWLEDGE OF GOD'S WILL. "I will put my laws in their minds ... hearts." Indwelling Holy Spirit. Regeneration makes a difference.	1. WRITTEN ON TABLES OF STONE. 2 Cor. 3:3
2. RECONCILIATION -- "I will be their God, and they shall be my people." Gentiles included. Access to God.	2. LAW MADE NOTHING PERFECT. Limited to Jews Unforgiven sins barred access to God.
3. COMPLETED REVELATION "They will know me" Must believe in order to become covenant people. Nothing temporary about the New Covenant revelation.	3. PROGRESSIVE, INCOMPLETE REVELATION Born into covenant relationship, then had to be taught its obligations. Was temporary.
4. ACTUAL FORGIVENESS OF SINS -- "Their sins I will forgive, and remember no more." One perfect sacrifice for sins.	4. SINS WERE "PASSED OVER" "Animal sacrifices were a reminder of sins" 10:3 Repeated sacrifices never did make the worshippers "perfect."

THE COVENANTS

OLD COVENANT		NEW COVENANT
MOSES		**CHRIST**
THE LAW		THE GOSPEL
MT. SINAI		MT. ZION
ONE NATION		ALL NATIONS
TYPES		ANTITYPES
FLESH		SPIRIT
CIRCUMCISION		HOLY SPIRIT
SABBATH		LORDS DAY
EARTHLY		HEAVENLY
TEMPORAL		ETERNAL

J. H. GORDINIER.

SOMETHING TO CONSIDER

Hebrews 10:19-25

INTRODUCTION
A. Background – hy the Hebrews needed encouraging.
B. Every one of us needs encouraging
        Non-Christians do.
        Even Christians do.
C. Hebrews is full of encouragement. 3:13, 6:18, 10:25, 12:5, 13:22

Purpose of message: If encouragement is so important, we need to know what it is and how to do it.

I.   ENCOURAGEMENT – THE MISSING INGREDIENT TO OUR WORSHIP
     (There's more to worship than what most of us do.)

     A. What is worship?
         Common answers – hymns, prayer, putting money in a plate, sharing communion, hearing special music, listening to a sermon, and perhaps witnessing an immersion.

         That is incomplete. Where was there anything about "encouragement"?

     B. Spend a few moments thinking through what our text for the day says.
         1. What we have
                 Confidence to approach God, verse 19
                 A priest (Christ) who gives us access to God, verse 21
                 What stupendous and magnificent benefits these are!
         2. What we are to do
                 Let us draw near, verse 22.
                 Let us hold fast, verse 23.
                 Let us consider how to stimulate one another ..., verse 24.
                     (This is the missing ingredient in worship.)

II. WHAT IS "ENCOURAGEMENT"?

     A. It is not an easy word to explain.
         Tell what others have said on "encouragement"

     B. A study of antonyms may help.
         Discouragement is the opposite of encouragement.
         What do you have to do to discourage someone? Do the opposite to encourage him.

     C. "Encouragement" is the act of inspiring others to renewed courage, spirit, or hope.
         ("Encouraging" in Hebrews 10:25 is the same root word [*parakaleo*] as used for the Holy Spirit, John 14:26, 16:7).
                 Give examples of calling someone alongside to help.

D. Barnabas – son of encouragement, exhortation, consolation, Acts 4:36,37, 11:22-24.
  Rescued Paul, Acts 9:26,27.
  Rescued John Mark, Acts 15:36-40.
  Now there's an example for us!

III. SOME SUGGESTIONS ON HOW TO GO ABOUT ENCOURAGING EACH OTHER

A. The beautiful thing about encouragement is this: Anyone can do it!

B. "Consider (think)" at Hebrews 10:24 is a present imperative. All must do it, and do it continually. This is the expectation of the writer of Hebrews.

C. Some helpful scriptures
  James 2:14-17
  1 John 3:17
  Romans 15:5
  Philippians 2:1-5

D. By watching others, I can get more ideas.
  1. What we can do as congregations, together:
    Encouragement cards -- written during worship services.
    Call for volunteers to give special attention to absentees
  2. Things we can do on a one-to-one basis:
    "See you in church, Sunday!"
    Compliment admirable character qualities you see in another.
    Correspondence
    Phone calls
    Notice a job well done, and say so.
    Pick up the tab in a restaurant
    Be supportive of someone you know is hurting.
    Recall the important people who had a part in your life years ago, and contact them with a thank-you.
    Encourage young people about full-time Christian service.
    Encourage people who are having trouble with a particular sin, Hebrews 3:13.

IV. THE STRATEGIC SIGNIFICANCE OF ENCOURAGEMENT

A. Encouragement will keep people from drying up spiritually.

B. Encouragement will help hurting people to recover from their wounds.

C. Encouragement will protect us from taking people for granted.

D. Encouragement helps people reach their real potential.

E. Many times a word of praise or thanks or appreciation or cheer has kept a person on his feet. (Job's friend -- "your words have helped the tottering to stand.")

CONCLUSION
A. Summary – something to consider, something to think about -- be an encourager!
B. Hebrews is a letter of encouragement, encouraging the readers to be encouragers. Are you an encourager? Is this something among your priorities you consider important?
C. The habit of being an encourager can be learned in the home.
    Allow me to challenge you to have a family that is different.
    And you will be a happier person.
    And pretty soon this will be an encouraging church.
D. Develop personally the habit of being an encourager.
    We've listed some ideas how to go about it.
    Which one have you decided to do this week?
    Which one are you going to begin doing today?
E. Invitation – We encourage you to confess Jesus and become a Christian.

* * * * * * * *

FAITHFULNESS – IT'S THE ONLY WAY TO LIVE!

Text: Hebrews 10:35-11:2   (Sermon covers 10:36 to 12:3)

INTRODUCTION
A. Certain words stand out – "endurance," "patience," "faith" or "faithfulness."
    "Faith" and "faithfulness" are interchangeable words.
    "Endurance" and "patience" are synonyms for faithfulness.

B. Background of Hebrews

C. Several verses deserve to be memorized!

Purpose of message: Remind us of the absolute imperative of faithfulness.

I.   FAITHFULNESS – WHAT IS IT?
    A. Taking God at His word. "Faith comes by hearing the Word of God," Romans 10:17.

    B. Faithfulness is the continual, habitual doing of what God says.
        "Having done the will of God" (10:36 ASV) and "faith" or "faithfulness" (10:38) are not antithetical ideas.

    C. It is from the Reformation (Luther and Calvin) that we have learned the mistaken notion that no "works" at all are expected of us by God.
        Luther and Calvin were objecting to the works that Rome said a church member must do, not the works that God had commanded.

Works commanded by men are no value when it comes to pleasing God.

But works commanded by God are altogether important and cannot be ignored.

D. There are works that are useless when it comes to being saved (Cain's example).

E. Of course, none of us would be saved without Calvary.

F. Faithfulness is not synonymous with not sinless perfection.

The faith that saves operates quite simply.

"Faithfulness" is the habitual, consistent, practice of what God has revealed to us that He expects of His creatures.

II. GOD HAS ALWAYS REQUIRED FAITHFULNESS.

A. Faithfulness in the Old Testament

A lack of faithfulness kept Israel out of the promised land. It is lack of faithfulness that will keep us out of heaven!

Micah 6:8 – "What does the Lord require of you, but to do justice, to love kindness, and to walk humbly with your God?"

B. Faithfulness in the New Testament

Faithfulness is still expected by God. *This is the gist of chapters 10 and 11.*

The closing words of Jesus' Sermon on the Mount stress faithfulness. "He that **does** the will of My Father," Matthew 7:21.

Romans 2:6-16 tell what God's standards will be at the final judgment. It is faithfulness, not sinless perfection.

1 Peter 3:10,11 – "If you would have a life you can love, then turn away from evil and **do good** ..."

James 4:17 – "To one who knows the right thing to do and does not do it, to him it is sin."
Not a one-time act – both "do's" are present tense, denoting continuous action.

C. God has always required faithfulness.

III. FAITHFULNESS – AS PRESENTED IN HEBREWS 10:35-39

  A. 10:35 – One reason to remain faithful is consideration of the nearness of the reward, herein called a "great reward."

  They were now nearer the fulfillment of God's promise than ever before.
  This was no time to turn back.
  This was no time for reckless rejection of God's Word.

  "Confidence" reminds us of the firm assurance with which the faithful Christian may approach the throne of grace (Hebrews 4:6, 10:19), and also of the open and fearless way believers in Jesus continue to confess Him before men (3:1-6).

  B. 10:36 – What they need is endurance – the determination to remain faithful under persecutions rather than seeking to escape them by denying Christ.

  Continuing to do the will of God is the thing called for – i.e., faithfulness.
  Endurance or perseverance is a synonym for faithfulness.

  Endurance is the way to "receive what is promised."
  "What was promised" likely = entrance into heavenly rest (Heb. 4:1,9).

  The Bible does not say salvation is unconditional, but it does say rewards to the faithful are conditional.

  Ironside's note is an attempt to justify unconditional election and eternal security. "Salvation is ours by grace, and is ours from the moment we believe in the Lord Jesus Christ – but it is at His coming that we shall receive our reward. He said, 'Behold, I come quickly, and My reward is with me, to give unto every man according as his work shall be.' " (*Studies in the Epistle to the Hebrews*, p.128)

  Faithfulness is the way to "receive what is promised." No faithfulness – no receiving. It is as clear as that!

  C. 10:37-38 – Contains a quotation from Habakkuk 2:3,4 (in the LXX), intended to give Biblical evidence for this very point.

  Perhaps the first few words "Yet a very little while" are taken from Isaiah 26:20, which in its original setting in Isaiah has specific reference to the second advent of Christ, a point which the Hebrew writer has in view in the context (rewards, receive what is promised).

  The idea is, "do not throw away your confidence" (Hang on just a little longer!), lest your behavior during the "very little while" costs you your heavenly reward.

  The rest of verses 37 and 38 come from Habakkuk 2:3,4.

D. 10:38 – A final incentive to steadfast endurance is the fear of God's displeasure.

> Continuing the quotation from Habakkuk, the author shows that the life that pleases God is the life of faith. "My righteous one shall live by faith."

>> This same text is also quoted in Romans 1:17, and Galatians 3:11. (In Romans, the emphasis is on "righteous." In Galatians, the emphasis is on "shall live." In Hebrews, the emphasis is on "faith(fulness)."

>> We are not just saved from our sin (in the first place) by faith; we must also *live* by faith.

>> "MY righteous one" = the kind of person God thinks of as "righteous." The man who is *faithful* is my kind of man, says God.

> The righteous will live by his faith, Habakkuk 2:4.
> "Righteous one" (Hebrews 10:38) is the man whom God counts as saved.
> "Live" both now and hereafter – the abundant life.
> "Faith(fulness)" – is the condition.
>> If "faith" (endurance) and "shrinks back" are antonyms (and they are in verse 38), then "faith" is synonymous with faithfulness.

>> So … Faithfulness is the condition!

> This mention of "faith" leads to one of the most sustained treatments of the subject in the whole New Testament.

>> This is the life that pleases God.

>> On the other hand, the life that displeases God is that of the man who renounces the Messiah and returns to the obsolete sacrifices of the temple: "the one who shrinks back, My soul has no pleasure in him."

>> (It is hardly right to say that the man who turns back proves he never had any real faith.)

E. 10:39 – The writer encourages his readers to be men of faith, by expressing his hope that both he and they are men who will not shrink back.

> What is "destruction (perdition, KJV)"? It is the word for perish, for Hell. It is the opposite of the "preserving (saving, KJV) of the soul."

> A Christian who does not walk by faith, but goes back to his own way, perishes!

F. The presentation of faithfulness is the same in Hebrews as we find elsewhere in the Holy Scriptures.

IV. A MAN'S SECURITY (the preservation, salvation of his soul) IS CONDITIONED ON FAITHFULNESS.
> *We can see this by studying what God has approved and rewarded in the different ages of history.*

A. Faithfulness in the AGE BEFORE THE FLOOD.

The Faithfulness of Abel. 11:4
1. His offering commended. "By faith Abel offered to God a better sacrifice than Cain." (They had revelation from God about sacrifice.)
2. His righteousness attested. "Through which he obtained the testimony that he was righteous"
3. His gifts accepted. "God testifying about his gifts"
4. His testimony perpetuated. "And through faith, though he is dead, he still speaks." (His faithfulness speaks to us of the need for faithfulness.)

The Faithfulness of Enoch. 11:5,6
1. Miraculous translation. "By faith Enoch was taken up"
2. Marvelous deliverance. "So that he should not see death"
3. Missing patriarch. "And he was not found"
4. Mighty power. "Because God took him up."
5. Magnificent walk. "For he obtained the witness that before his being taken up he was pleasing to God." (You can read this in the OT, at Genesis 5:24, where the LXX says Enoch "was well pleasing to God." Enoch walked with God for 300+ years, and God testified that He was pleased with Enoch's faithfulness.)
6. "He was pleasing to God" implies Enoch's faithfulness.
   You cannot please God without faithfulness.
   Enoch was a man who continually and diligently sought God.

> *One must believe that God rewards those who are faithful. Many of these Old Testament heroes in Hebrews 11 had some idea of the life to come, and that is why they walked consistently before God.*

The Faithfulness of Noah. 11:7
1. The basis of faith. "Noah (was) warned by God"
2. The realm of faith. "About things not yet seen"
3. The reverence of faith. "In reverence" ("moved with godly fear" ASV)
4. The response of faith. "Prepared (constructed) an ark"
5. The quest of faith. "For the salvation of his household"
6. The effect of faith. "By which he condemned the world"
7. The reward of faith. "Became an heir of the righteousness which is according to faith."

Perhaps many of the Jewish Christians to whom Hebrews was written often wondered why, if they were right, they were such a small minority. Noah steps out from the pages of the Old Testament to remind them that in his day only 8 people were right, and all the rest of the world perished.

B. Faithfulness in the PATRIARCHAL AGE

The Faithfulness of Abraham. 11:8-12 (17-19)
1. Unhesitating obedience to an unusual call. "By faith Abraham, when he was called, obeyed by going out to a place he was to receive for an inheritance"
    He had already been a man of faith before God called him.
2. A century long pilgrimage. "He lived as an alien in the land of promise, as in a foreign land, dwelling in tents ...."
    Do you hear, my Hebrew readers! 100 years he proved faithful!
3. The reason for his faithfulness – "He was looking for the city which has (the) foundations, whose architect and builder is God."
4. Sarah shared Abraham's faithfulness. "By faith even Sarah herself received the ability to conceive." (Old, and barren.)
5. Abraham became the father of the faithful. "Therefore there was born even of one man as many descendants as the stars of heaven."
6. Determined to be faithful, he offered Isaac, Hebrews 11:17-19.
    God's command, at first, surely seemed unbelievable. This was the heir, the one through whom the seed was to come. He was their only child, and if it was rather unexpected they would have a son 20 years ago when Isaac was born, wouldn't it be quite much to start over again now? Abraham was about 120, and Sarah was about 111. Isaac wasn't even married yet, nor did he have any sons. Where would the line of descendants come from? (Yet Abraham figured God would raise Isaac from the dead – so he went about doing what God said.)

Abraham's faithfulness has been summarized: (Wiersbe, *op. cit.*, p.124)
a. Abraham obeyed when he did not know *where* God was leading him.
b. Abraham obeyed when he did not know *how* God's will would be accomplished (too old to have children, sacrifice your son).
c. Abraham obeyed when he did not know *when* God would fulfill His promises.
    (He never did live to see the promised Seed come. Abraham was dead about 2000 years before Jesus finally came to earth.)
d. Abraham obeyed when he did not know *why* God was so working (when Isaac's sacrifice was demanded).

The Faithfulness of Isaac, Jacob, and Joseph. 11:20-22. (13-18)
1. These men were all faithful until they died. "All died in faith," 11:13. In Jacob's case, it was when he was dying that faith shone out most triumphantly. He may have lived a checkered life, but his closing days find him faithfully carrying out God's plan.

Joseph, too, late in life, gave evidence he was being faithful to God. How are we doing – late in life?

2. They didn't live to see the promised Messiah on earth. (So we have more reason to be faithful than they had.)
3. Their pilgrim confession. "They confessed that they were strangers and exiles on the earth."
4. They could have quit. "If they had been thinking of that country from which they had went out, they would have had opportunity to return."
5. They were faithful – and so have God's approval. "God is not ashamed to be called their God; for He has prepared a city for them."

In Abraham, Isaac, Jacob, and Joseph, we see four generations of faithfulness. These men sometimes failed, but basically they were men of faith. They were not sinless perfect, but the tenor of their lives was right. They were devoted to God, and continually sought to do what He said.

C. Faithfulness in the MOSAIC AGE. 11:23ff.

The Faithfulness of Moses' Parents. 11:23
1. His parents perceived "he was a beautiful child", special in God's sight. Such language bespeaks a revelation from God concerning the destiny of this child. They acted on that revelation.

The Faithfulness of Moses. 11:24-28
1. He refused Egypt's fame (the luxury of the palace, gold and silver, and power – and Egypt was the greatest nation in the world at the time.)
2. He repudiated Egypt's pleasures, rather than "to enjoy the passing pleasures of sin." This is what Moses would have done, had he refused to be the faithful man God wanted him to be – the leader out of exile.
3. He chose to share ill-treatment with God's people.
    The result: He does not occupy a line on some obscure cuneiform tablet – he is memorialized in God's eternal Book. Instead of being in a museum as an Egyptian mummy, he is famous as a man of God.
4. Moses left the palace and never went back to the old way of life! He identified with God's people, and that is where he stayed.
5. Because he was faithful, he instituted the Passover and sprinkled the blood, so the destroyer of the firstborn might not touch them.
    By so doing, he repudiated Egypt's religion. He separated himself from the idolatry of the Egyptians forever. He flung down the gauntlet in defiance of their religious establishment.

The Faithfulness of Israel at the Red Sea, and at Jericho. 11:29,30.

The Faithfulness of Rahab. 11:31
1. She became a worshipper of Jehovah, abandoning the false religion of

Canaan. (She heard what God did in Egypt and at Red Sea, which was 40 years earlier.)

2. She did not perish with those who were disobedient.
3. She would stand on the Lord's side, even if it meant doing something no one else in her country did.
4. She became an ancestor of Jesus. Not only was Rahab delivered when Jericho fell to Joshua and the Israelites, but she became a part of the nation of Israel, married Salmon, and gave birth to Boaz, the ancestor of David (Matthew 1:4-6). Imagine, a pagan harlot has become a part of the ancestry of Jesus. But that is what faithfulness to God can do!

Other Examples of Faithfulness in Mosaic Age. 11:32ff.
1. Gallant Heroes – Gideon, Barak, Samson, David, Samuel.
2. Thrilling triumphs – (Daniel – lions' mouths stopped; Hebrew children in the fiery furnace.)
3. Tremendous trials and difficulties were overcome. Faithfulness helps men through hard times, intense suffering, and bitter persecutions.
4. Not all experienced miraculous deliverance. Some were tortured and died! (verses 36-38). It takes more faith to endure than to escape.
5. Faithfulness enables us to be more interested in the approval of God than in the approval of the world.

D. JESUS – THE GREATEST EXAMPLE OF FAITHFULNESS. 12:1-3

1. "Witnesses" – Perhaps it means the Old Testament faithful are watching us to see how we do. Or, maybe it means that others have done it – so can you. They are testifying to you that it can be done.

2. Get rid of encumbrances.
   Lay aside every weight
   Such weights might be material possessions, family ties, the love of comfort, lack of mobility.

   In the Olympic races, there is no rule against carrying a supply of food and beverage, but the runner would never win the race that way.

   Lay aside the sin which so easily besets (entangles, clings so closely).
   In this context, it is the sin of unbelief -- the lack of faithfulness.

3. Persevere
   Run with endurance the race set before us.
   We must guard against the notion the race is an easy sprint, that everything in the Christian life is rosy.

   We must be prepared to press on with perseverance through trials and temptations.

Some runners get weary and faint, and quit the race before they get to the finish line. There is no prize for them.

4. Keep our eyes on Jesus. (Look away from every other object, and keep your eyes on Jesus.)
   a. Pioneer – He blazed a trail for us to follow
      He has provided us with a perfect example of what a life of faithfulness should look like.

   b. Perfecter – The finisher of our faith
      Jesus is the perfect example of faithfulness to God -- even to the end. He not only started the race, but He finished it triumphantly!
      For Him, the course stretched from heaven to Bethlehem, then to Gethsemane and Calvary, then out of the tomb and back to heaven.

   c. His motivation – For the joy that was set before Him.

      While Jesus was on earth, during His earthly ministry, He did not use His divine powers for His own personal needs. Satan tempted Him to do this, but He refused.

      How then did He manage to remain faithful? He kept his eyes fixed on the coming glory, when all the redeemed would be gathered with Him eternally. His thoughts of being with the Father is what enabled Him to keep on being faithful to God.

   d. His endurance – He endured the cross.
      That is something more bitter than any of the readers would face.

   e. His attitude – He despised the shame

   f. His honor – He is now seated at the right hand of the throne of God.

CONCLUSION

A. Have we seen the Biblical emphasis on faithfulness?

B. Have we taken inventory of our lives in order to see how our "race" is going? Have we begun to listen to the Word, so we can know what He wants?

   Are we being faithful, enduring, or are we growing weary and starting to faint?

C. Hear the Word of the Lord! **"Without Faith it is impossible to please Him."**
   This kind of faith grows as we listen to God's Word (Romans 10:17), and fellowship in worship and prayer.

   Faithfulness is possible to all kinds of believers in all kinds of situations.

   It is not a luxury for a few elite saints. It is a necessity for all God's people!

D. *SONG*: LORD, I WANT A DIADEM

Lord, I want a shining diadem, when I reach Your heavenly land.
What must I do, my Lord, to gain a diadem, when I reach that golden strand?

O, you must run, run the race that's set before you,
You must run right straight, and never turn aside to the right, to the left,
    and keep your eyes on Jesus –
That's the way to win a shining crown.

Lord, I want a shining diadem, when I reach Your heavenly land.
What must I do, my Lord, to gain a diadem, when I reach that golden strand?

O, you must fight, fight the world, the flesh, the devil, never falter, nor grow weary in
the strife, for the Lord hath trod the bitter way before thee –
That's the way to win a shining crown.

    O, a shining crown, yes, my Lord, a starry crown.
    I'm gonna win my crown, so help me Lord, and glorify thy name!

When I gain my shining diadem on the blessed heavenly shore,
I'm goin' to cast my diadem at Jesus' feet, and adore Him evermore.

To Him be power, honor, love and adoration, Let my soul ascribe all glory to His name;
When the race is run, and every battle's over,
At His feet I'll lay my shining crown.

    O, a shining crown, yes, my Lord, a starry crown.
    I'm gonna win my crown, so help me Lord, and glorify thy name!

* * * * * * * *

PILGRIMS SHOULD MAKE PROGRESS!

Hebrews 12:14-29   Hebrews 11:13-16

INTRODUCTION
A. What do you think of when you hear the word "pilgrim"?
B. And what does *Pilgrim's Progress* suggest?
C. Abraham – the Biblical example of a pilgrim.
D. A pilgrim is a temporary resident, on a journey to his real homeland.

Purpose of message: Who am I? Why am I here? Where am I going? All answered
when we recognize that we, too, are pilgrims, and are making progress.

I. CHRISTIANS ARE PILGRIMS
    A. Philippians 3:17-20
    B. 1 Peter 1:1,17, 2:11
    C. Hebrews 13:14
    D. *Song* – "I am a stranger here, within a foreign land ...."
    E. Song – "I must needs go home by the way of the cross ... Then I bid farewell to the way of the world ...."

II. PRIORITIES FOR PILGRIMS. 12:14-17 and 12:25-29

    (The matter of establishing priorities is always hard. Let Hebrews help!)

    A. Attitude toward God
            Do not refuse Him who speaks from heaven, 12:25
            Follow holiness, without which no one will see God, 12:14

    B. Attitude toward men – Pursue peace, 12:14

    C. Attitude toward fellow Christians – Watchfulness. "See to it that ..."
            No one comes short of the grace of God – help the laggards.
            No root of bitterness – no going after strange gods
            No immoral person
                No godless (profane, ASV) person, like Esau. (It can become too late to change!)

III. PRIVILEGES OF PILGRIMS. 12:18-24 -- Mt. Sinai vs. Mt. Zion

    A. Mount Sinai – fear, terror, God is unapproachable is the message, 12:18-21.

    B. Mount Zion – joy, confidence, God is approachable through Jesus, 12:22-24.
        1. You are come to Mount Zion, heavenly Jerusalem, the city of the living God.
            "Law will go forth from Zion, and the word of the Lord from Jerusalem," Isaiah 2:3
            "Beautiful for situation, the joy of the whole earth," Psalm 48:2.
                Song – "The hill of Zion yields a thousand sacred sweets, before we reach the heav'nly fields, or walk the golden streets"

        2. You are come to myriads of angels in joyful assembly, 12:22.
            Song – "That's what makes the angels rejoice"

        3. You are come to the church of the firstborn who are enrolled in heaven, 12:23
                It is a privilege to belong to the church. It is something special!

        4. You are come to the Judge, the God of all.
                "Shall not the Judge of all the earth deal justly?"
                It is a privilege to be on intimate relations with the Judge of the whole world.

5. You are come to the spirits of righteous men made perfect, 12:23.
    Spirits – righteous men – made perfect.
    It is a privilege to have fellowship with the saints.

6. You are come to Jesus, the mediator of a new covenant, 12:24.
    Mediator –
    New covenant –

7. You are come to sprinkled blood ..., 12:24.
    Heaven is purified with a better offering, Hebrews 9:23
    Hearts are sprinkled from an evil conscience, Hebrews 10:22
    There is real forgiveness.

8. You are come to a kingdom that cannot be shaken.
    The religion of Jesus is not temporary, as was the religion of Moses.

C. Now we can appreciate the words of the chorus:
    Well, I wouldn't take nothing for my journey now,
    Gotta make heaven somehow!
    Though the devil tempt me and try to turn me away.
    He's offered everything that's got a name,
    All the wealth I want and worldly fame.
    But even if I could, still I wouldn't take nothing for my journey now!

IV. PILGRIMS ARE TO MAKE PROGRESS!

A. "See ..." 12:15. Watchman. Progress in your abilities as a watchman (looking for ways to help others on their journey).

B. "Pursue ..." 12:14. Hunter. Progress in the pursuit of peace and holiness.

C. "Confess ..." 13:14-16. Progress in confession that we are pilgrims.

D. Pilgrims keep right on the road to the fatherland.
    We're marching to Zion, beautiful, beautiful Zion.
    We're marching upward to Zion, the beautiful city of God.

CONCLUSION
A. Summary
B. *Song* – a "There is a habitation built by the living God ... O Zion, Zion, I long thy gates to see!"
C. Have you already started on your pilgrimage? One day the journey will be ended. Keep on making progress!
D. Do you need to begin your pilgrimage today? Invitation.

SOME EVERYDAY CHRISTIAN ACTIVITIES
Hebrews 13:1-21

INTRODUCTION
A. Which would you rather, in the town where you live –

   1. That Bertrand Russell's accusations about hypocritical lives among followers of Jesus be found true? *or* –

   2. That Pliny the Younger's admission of exemplary lives being lived by the Christians be true?

B. The New Testament is filled with exhortations about everyday Christian living.

C. The importance of giving a consistent witness.

D. Why, then, is it that critics can find examples of inconsistent living?

   The reason critics regularly can find some bad examples is that few of us have a well-thought-out system of ethics by which we live every day.

Purpose of message: Understand the only possible foundation on which a consistent system of ethics can be built, and then examine whether our own personal ethics (and our everyday Christian activities) reflect the ethics taught in the Scriptures.

I. THE BASIS OF CHRISTIAN ETHICS

   A. The two-point outline of many New Testament epistles is doctrine + practice.

   B. What do we mean by ethics?

   C. The only solid basis for any behavior is found in the revelation from God made through Jesus Christ.

   D. Included in the Christian's ethics are social duties and religious duties.

II. SOME SOCIAL DUTIES. Hebrews 13:1-6

   A. Let love of the brethren continue, 13:1.
      1. Jesus is the source of this ethical principle.
      2. Love of the brethren – what is it?
      3. Who is my brother?
      4. How is brotherly love to be cultivated?
      5. Love of the brethren – some ways to show it.
         a. Do not neglect to show hospitality to strangers, 13:2
         b. Remember the prisoners, 13:3

B. Let marriage be held in honor, 13:4.
    1. Marriage is an honorable estate.
    2. Scripture gives at least three reasons for marriage.
        a. One is the propagation of children.
        b. Marriage is provided as a means of preventing sexual sin.
        c. Marriage is provided for companionship.
    3. "Let the marriage bed be undefiled!"
        a. God is serious about sexual purity. You and I should be, too!
        b. The world today is obsessed with sex, because God's will is repudiated.
        c. When Christians are immoral, the immediate consequences may even be worse, because the testimony of the gospel is polluted.
    4. "Fornicators and adulterers, God will judge." 13:4
    5. Marriage can be held in honor in many ways.

C. Be free from the love of money, 13:5.
    1. What is covetousness?
    2. Covetousness is a sin to which few of us have ever admitted.
    3. Love of money is one of the most common forms of covetousness.
    4. The love of money can take many forms.
    5. Is it not humiliating that the best of Christians should need to be cautioned against this worst of sins?
    6. Be content with what you have.

III. SOME RELIGIOUS DUTIES. Hebrews 13:7-17

A. Remember your former leaders and imitate their faith, 13:7,8
    1. "Remember those who led you."
    2. Consideration should also be given to the outcome of their way of life (13:7) – their exodus from this life.
    3. The duty to imitating the faith of the primitive teachers of Christianity.
    4. How to honor the saintly dead.

B. Be steadfast in the teachings of Christianity, 13:9-15
    1. Do not be carried away by varied and strange teachings, 13:9
        a. Purity of doctrine
        b. The "varied and strange teachings"
        c. Stay away from false teachers.
        d. One of the marks of small children is lack of discernment.
        e. So demand doctrinal preaching. Participate in Bible studies, Sunday School classes, etc., because the Bible is the source of strength and growth in the church.

    2. Be completely separated and dedicated to Jesus, 13:10-14
        a. Christians faced taunts about the Christian religion.
        b. "We have an altar ...."

      c. "Let us go to Him (Jesus) outside the camp, bearing His reproach," 13:13
      d. What "separation" involves, 13:13,14
      e. True separation is costly.

C. Continually offer up new covenant style sacrifices, 13:15,16
    1. The sacrifice of praise.
    2. The sacrifices of benevolence.

D. Be obedient to and submit to present spiritual leaders, 13:17
    1. "Your leaders" ("those who have the rule over you," KJV)
    2. "Obey" your leaders
    3. Submission is desirable:
      a. Because church leaders represent God.
      b. Because church leaders watch for church member's souls.
      c. Because church leaders are accountable to God.
      d. Because it is profitable.

IV. ENJOY GOD'S BENEDICTION. Hebrews 13:20,21

A. This benediction seems to gather together the major themes of Hebrews
B. The writer calls on God to equip the readers for "every good work" (KJV).
    1. What does the word "equip" ("make you perfect," KJV) mean?
    2. How does He equip us?
      a. Through the blood of the eternal covenant
      b. Through Jesus Christ our Lord
      c. Through "us" – the apostles and their writings.
C. "To whom be the glory forever and ever."
D. The thing we must contribute to the Christian life is willing yieldedness. All we have to do is open the channel of our wills and let God's power work through us.
E. What a difference it would make in our lives if we would turn Hebrews 13:20,21 into a personal prayer each day. "Lord, equip me for every good work to do Your will. Work in me that which is pleasing in Your sight. Do it through Jesus Christ and may He receive the glory."

CONCLUSION
A. Hebrews teaches some thrilling truths about Jesus Christ.
B. Hebrews shows that God expects followers of Jesus to be men of faithfulness.
C. Faithfulness includes ethical standards and actions.
D. Become a Christian, and you can begin to live as God would have you to live.

SELECTED BIBLIOGRAPHY FOR HEBREWS

Alford, Henry, "Hebrews," in *Alford's Greek Testament*, Vol. 4. London: Rivingtons, 1871. Revised and reprinted by Moody Press, Chicago.

> Probably still the best complete commentary on the Greek text by a single author. It has a critically revised text, a digest of various alternate readings, marginal references, introductory studies, and a critical and exegetical commentary.

Anderson, Robert, *Types in Hebrews*. Grand Rapids: Kregel Publications, 1978.

> A rewarding study of Old Testament types which Hebrews explains as being fulfilled in the church.

Attridge, H. W., *The Epistle to the Hebrews. A Commentary On The Epistle To The Hebrews*, ed. by H. Koester, in the Hermeneia Series. Philadelphia: Fortress Press, 1989.

> In a 32-page introduction, Attridge deals with authorship, date, addressees, literary characteristics, aim and message, relation to Judaism and early Christianity, and text. Attridge pays special attention to the structure and outline of Hebrews (his conclusions are disappointing!); yet in the future, this is one source anyone writing on that aspect of the book will have to consult. It includes fourteen special studies (on sonship in Hebrews, the Christological pattern in 2:10-18, the language of perfection, etc.). Attridge believes Hebrews is a masterpiece of early Christian homiletics ("a word of exhortation," 13:22) addressed to believers in Christ who are in danger of becoming lax in their commitment. He maintains that no single strand of Judaism provides a clear and simple matrix within which to understand the thought of the author and his text.

Barclay, William, *The Letter to the Hebrews*, Daily Study Bible Series. Philadelphia: Westminster Press, 1957.

> The author is neo-liberal in theology, so the reader must be careful. The Daily Study Bible Series is of value for the word studies and abundant quotations from sacred and secular writers.

Barmby, J., "Hebrews," in *The Pulpit Commentary*, edited by H. D. M. Spence and Joseph Excell. Grand Rapids: Wm. B. Eerdmans Co., 1962 and many times.

> The verse-by-verse comments in Pulpit Commentary are one of the first sources this teacher regularly checks whenever beginning a study of any Bible book. The set makes a good backbone for any preacher's library since it is well indexed.

Barnes, A., "Hebrews," in *Notes on the New Testament*. Grand Rapids: Baker Book House, 1953.

> A verse-by-verse coverage of the text, with practical applications of the chapters given at the close of each. Barnes (1798-1870) was an American Presbyterian minister. In the division between strict Calvinists and New School Presbyterians, he sided with the latter. He preached total abstinence from alcohol, the abolition of slavery, held the doctrine of unconditional election, and held to the Calvinistic doctrine of the perseverance of the saints.

Boatman, Don Earl, *Helps from Hebrews*. Joplin, MO: College Press, 1960.

> Originally titled *Preaching and Teaching Helps from Hebrews*, it includes verse-by-verse comments, a paraphrase by Macknight, chapter summaries by T.R. Applebury, and numerous questions to guide adult-level Bible study.

Boll, R. H., *Lessons on Hebrews*. Louisville, KY: Word and Work, 1947.

> A series of 25 lessons prepared for home Bible classes. They are presented with a simplicity that appeals to the average reader. Each lesson closes with questions and suggestions for the next lesson, intended to guide the student's study before the next class meeting.

Borchert, Gerald L, et al., "Hebrews" in *Review and Expositor*. 82:3 (Summer 1985), p.317-440.

> This Baptist theological journal's treatment outlines Hebrews as follows: A Superior Book: Hebrews; A Superior Model, Hebrews 1:1-4:13; A Superior Priesthood, Hebrews 4:14-7:28; A Superior Covenant, Hebrews 8:1-10:18; A Superior Faith, Hebrews 10:19-12:2; and A Superior Life, Hebrews 12:3-13:25. The comments are followed by helps for preaching and teaching Hebrews.

Brown, Raymond, *Christ Above All*. Downers Grove, IL: Inter-Varsity Press, 1982.

> Brown divides the epistle as it was done traditionally, into the great doctrine (1:5-10:18) and the great duty (10:19-13:17). The doctrine refers to the superiority of Christianity to Judaism, and the duty is the believer's faithfulness to Christ and to Christian living.

Bruce, Alexander Balmain, *The Epistle to the Hebrews*. Edinburgh: T & T Clark, 1899. Reprinted by Klock and Klock, 1980.

> A thorough interpretation of the epistle based on the premise that it is a formal defense of the Christian faith. Though readers will not always agree with Bruce, they will find this is a valuable contribution to their study of this epistle. Neil Lightfoot says A.B. Bruce is indispensable for his book "reveals the soul of the book of Hebrews."

Bruce, Frederick Fyvie, *The Epistle to the Hebrews*. New International Critical Commentary on the New Testament. Grand Rapids: Wm. B. Eerdmans Publishing Co., 1964.

> A thorough exposition based on the best Greek text. Bruce, an English evangelical, doubts the Pauline authorship, but opts for no one author in particular. Bruce seeks help from recent archaeological discoveries concerning understanding the Greek language. Extensive footnotes. One of the best commentaries on Hebrews in English.

Bullinger, Ethelbert W., *A Great Cloud of Witnesses*. London: Lamp Press, 1956.

> A series of studies on Hebrews 11 by the "father" of modern ultra-dispensationalism. Preachers may find these studies helpful, especially since they quite regularly include Greek word studies.

Calvin, John, *The Epistle of Paul the Apostle to the Hebrews*. Grand Rapids: Wm. B. Eerdmans Publishing Co., 1963.

> Calvin's closely knit theological reasoning shows here as the Law and Gospel are considered in their office and relevance. The reader will need to get acquainted with covenant theology in order to understand and evaluate what he reads.

Cockerill, Gareth L., *Hebrews: A Biblical Commentary in the Wesleyan Tradition*. Indianapolis, IN: Wesleyan, 1999.

> The thrust of the comments is that "we can no longer do our own thing" as is popular in this current age, but rather points out the practicality of Hebrews which has a vital message for today's "pluralistic age who believe in the relativity of truth and morality." As to authorship, after examining the usual possibilities, he feels it is unknowable; as to recipients, he opts for a congregation in Rome that had numerous Jewish believers in it. There are numerous diagrams in the book to help the reader see the flow of thought.

Coffman, James Burton, *Commentary on Hebrews*. Austin, TX: Firm Foundation Publishing House, 1971.

> This is one of a set called *Firm Foundation Series of Commentaries on the New Testament*, produced by the Churches of Christ. Coffman regularly gleans the more succinct comments from the old masters and weaves them together for his comments. Sets are being purchased and sent free to Church of Christ missionaries for their use -- purchased by various large congregations for their living-link missionaries. The use of this volume is a quick way to get a general idea of problem passages and various proposed solutions.

Crouch, Owen L., *Expository Preaching and Teaching -- Hebrews*. Joplin, MO: College Press, 1983.
> Mr. Crouch makes a division of Hebrews into 23 parts for the purpose of exposition; each section begins with Crouch's own translation of the text, along with a theme which he has assigned to it. He diagrams each of the sections of the text to help the expositor see the major ideas in the paragraph -- a necessity for any who would preach through a book, and who would get the ideas of the Biblical text firmly in mind.

Davidson, Andrew Bruce, *The Epistle to the Hebrews*. Grand Rapids: Zondervan Publishing House, 1950. Edinburgh: T & T Clark, 1959.
> Originally published in 1882, small in size, but containing many valuable insights into the truths contained in this epistle. The "additional notes" are helpful.

DeHaan, Martin Ralph, *Hebrews*. Grand Rapids: Zondervan Publishing House, 1959.
> A collection of studies first presented on the radio program known as "The Radio Bible Class." It contains ideas for emphases in sermons.

Delitzsch, Franz, *Commentary on the Epistle to the Hebrews*. 2 Vols. Edinburgh: T & T Clark, 1868-70. Reprinted in Minneapolis: Klock and Klock, 1978.
> An extremely fine exposition of the Greek text. The writer draws upon older literature for many of his ideas, and uses Talmudic source material to highlight the meaning of the text.

DeSilva, David, *Perseverance in Gratitude: A Socio-Rhetorical Commentary on the Epistle `to the Hebrews.'* Grand Rapids, MI: Eerdmans, 2000.
> Viewing Hebrews against the supposed cultural background of a society that takes as its pivotal values honor and shame, DeSilva argues that the author of this sermon attempts to insulate his audience "from the shaming strategies of non-Christians." "Hebrews reads more naturally in a pre-70 setting" and its author is understood to be "a member of the Pauline mission whose task is to nurture and preserve the work of the apostolic leader." DeSilva deploys the strategies of classical Greco-Roman rhetorical practice to exhort the readers to make the right choice "between pursuing friendship with God and friendship with one's unbelieving neighbors." As a key to understanding Hebrews, socio-rhetorical criticism fails to unlock all the riches of the divine-human relationship revealed in the letter to the Hebrews.

Dods, Marcus, *The Epistle to the Hebrews*. Expositor's Greek Testament, Vol. 4. Edited by W. Robertson Nicoll. Grand Rapids: Wm. B. Eerdmans Publishing Co., 1967.
> A commentary based on the Greek text, including information for making decisions where the various manuscripts differ in their readings. A student, who wishes to keep his Greek fresh would find that working through this book would be a great help, while at the same time throwing insight into his study of Hebrews.

Ellingworth, Paul, *The Epistle to the Hebrews: A Commentary on the Greek Text*. New International Greek Testament Commentary series. Grand Rapids: Eerdmans, 1993.
> This volume is a detailed word-for-word treatment of the Greek text of Hebrews. Ellingworth urges that the author certainly was not Paul (the letter should remain "anonymous"), and was probably written to a church in Rome made up predominantly of Jewish believers. He dates the work between AD 64 and 69. Written for Greek readers, there is no running English translation in this commentary, and Greek words are translated only to show specific interpretations. Ellingworth also attempts to unveil the alleged "discourse structure" of this carefully written letter.

Eubanks, David L., and Shannon, Robert, *Hebrews* in the Standard Bible Study Series. Cincinnati: Standard Publishing Co., 1986.
> This is a two-level approach to the study of Hebrews. The first level is a passage-by-passage exegesis of the text, done by Eubanks. The second level is an illustrative exegesis at the end of each chapter, entitled "Lessons From Chapter ____," done by Shannon. Sunday school teachers, preachers, leaders of home Bible studies will find help here. An accompanying workbook was written by Michael D. McCann.

Foster, Rupert C., *Class Notes on the Epistle of Hebrews and the Epistle of James*. Cincinnati, OH: Standard Publishing Co., 1925.

> This is an outline of the epistle, plus a number of questions on each verse, intended to aid and encourage independent study of the Scriptures on the part of the student. Use these questions to guide your study.

Fudge, Edward, *Our Man in Heaven*. Athens, AL: C. E. I. Publishing Co., 1973.

> A summary of the central emphasis of the letter to the Hebrews, that the human family has in the presence of God an acceptable Representative. It shows how the message in Hebrews is astonishingly up-to-date, speaking directly to the condition of Christian existence in this uncertain world.

Gordon, Robert P., *Hebrews* in Readings: A New Biblical Commentary series. Sheffield: Sheffield Academic Press, 2000.

> Gordon documents his "continuing suspicion that the addressees were originally converts from Judaism [to Christianity]," and if the "Hebrews" give up their Christianity, far from returning to Him, they would be turning away from God (3:12). Jesus is presented as the Son of God (6:6, 10:29) precisely to focus attention on the very issue that may prevent the readers from defecting. Gordon argues that 11:32 rules out a female author for Hebrews. Admitting the slenderness of the internal evidence for a pre-70 date of writing, he nevertheless favors a date in the late 60s, arguing that 8:13, 10:2, and 10:25 all point to a date before the destruction of Jerusalem and its temple. In an interesting affirmation, Gordon argues that "there is no point in trying to deny the charge that *Hebrews* is supersessionist," and he goes on to affirm that "*both* Judaism and Christianity are supersessionist in relation to the Old Testament" (p.27,28).

Gouge, William, *A Commentary on the Whole Epistle to the Hebrews*. Grand Rapids: Kregel Publications, 1980.

> This is a reprint of an 1866 edition, which itself was a reprint of a 1650 work. Special emphasis is placed on both the sublime statements of Christ's deity found in the epistle and on the moving exhortations to faith and service. The author lived and wrote in the 17th century, and was a renowned Puritan theologian and preacher.

Guthrie, Donald, *The Letter to the Hebrews. An Introduction And Commentary*, in The Tyndale New Testament Commentaries. Grand Rapids: Eerdmans, 1983.

> This commentary forms part of the updating of this series, superseding (in this instance) T. Hewitt's volume on Hebrews. Guthrie concludes that the unknown author "gives us the clearest discussion of the Christian approach to the Old Testament of any of the New Testament writers"; that the first readers were probably Jewish Christians in Rome; that the letter was written before AD 70; and that its purpose was to prevent "some kind of apostasy to Judaism." Guthrie follows the older pattern of outlining the book, which divides it after 10:18 between a doctrinal section and a section of exhortation. Guthrie treats Hebrews as a source of primitive (and therefore normative) Christian teaching. He is more concerned than Morris, and much more concerned than Hagner, to "solve" historical and theological problems in a harmonistic direction (though sometimes his arguments are somewhat convoluted).

Guthrie, George H., "HEBREWS" in *The NIV Application Commentary*. Grand Rapids: Zondervan, 1998.

> Many of the conclusions set forth in his earlier work *(The Structure of Hebrews: A Text-Linguistic Analysis* [Leiden: Brill, 1994]) appear here. The letter, Guthrie concludes, was written to Rome. The readers were of Jewish background worshiping in a synagogue in Rome. The date is given as the mid-60's AD, before the Neronian persecution. Apollos is suggested as the author. Modern discourse analysis is used to determine the outline of the book. Preachers working their way through Hebrews will find helpful ideas for contemporary application of the letter.

Hagner, Donald A., *Hebrews: A Good News Commentary*. San Francisco: Harper & Row, 1983.

> This commentary in many places complements that of Leon Morris. Like Morris, Hagner adopts the majority view that Hebrews was probably written before AD 70 from Rome to Jewish Christians, but he states more strongly that none of these judgments is more than a hypothesis. Hagner's commentary is based on the Good

News Bible translation and does not often explicitly disagree with it, but frequently goes behind GNB to offer a more literal translation, thus revealing he has some question about the accuracy resulting from the use of a dynamic equivalent theory of translation. Hagner's additional notes have numerous references to materials in secondary literature.

Harvill, J., "Focus on Jesus: Studies in the Epistle to the Hebrews." *Restoration Quarterly* 22:3 (1979), p.129-140.

To achieve a focus on Jesus there is no better place than Hebrews and no better way to begin than by surveying the names and titles attributed to Jesus in this epistle. At least 17 names or titles are ascribed to Jesus, each adding its own distinctive element to the exceeding rich doctrine of Christ. Five major titles, High Priest, Son, Christ, Jesus, and Lord, lay stress on the character of Jesus. The remaining titles, Sanctifier, Source, Apostle, Author, Surety, Heir, Minister, Mediator, Shepherd, Forerunner, and Finisher, relate to Jesus' person or define His work and function.

Hastings, James, ed., *The Epistle to the Hebrews*. The Speaker's Bible. Grand Rapids: Baker Book House, 1961. Reprint

A wealth of excellent seed thoughts for the preacher who would preach a series of expository messages from Hebrews. Recommended!

Heen, Erik M., and Philip D.W. Krey, eds., *Hebrews* in the Ancient Christian Commentary Series. Downers Grove, IL: InterVarsity, 2005.

Every time the prevailing worldview changes, some scholars have attempted to invent a method of Scripture interpretation that harmonizes with the new worldview. Since Post-modernism has become the popular worldview, with its dictum that "all truth is relative," several new methods of Scripture interpretation have been introduced. Deconstructionism (one key theme of postmodernism) is one approach to ancient events and writings, attempting to convince today's readers that past events and writings have no intrinsic meaning, so what the original authors may have intended is irrelevant. What matters, instead, is what we think of what they wrote. Attempts are made to revise the past to conform to current politically correct views. What is lost is any idea of the Scriptures being absolute truth or that they are authoritative. One current method of study (reflected in ACCS), which ignores authorial intent, is to collect and collate what ancient writers thought about the Scriptures. Included in this volume are selected, reworked, and arranged interpretive extracts on the text of Hebrews from the first eight centuries of Church Fathers. The comments from the Fathers reveal a different world of exegesis from the contemporary critical approaches that dominate modern linguistic and social science criticism approaches to the Bible books. The comments of the Fathers often deal specifically with practical and theological issues contemporary to the time in which they lived.

Henrichsen, Walter A., *After the Sacrifice*. Grand Rapids: Zondervan Publishing House, 1979.

Over two dozen charts, useable in preaching or teaching, to help visualize the contents of Hebrews, accompany the chapters that tell of the Person, Position, Priesthood, Promises, Perfection, of Christ.

Hoyt, Herman A., *Christ: God's Final Word to Man*. Winona Lake, IN: Brethren Missionary Herald Books, 1974.

A book which the preacher will welcome, this study guide to Hebrews gives an analytical outline, followed by comments.

Hughes, Philip Edgcumbe, *A Commentary on the Epistle to the Hebrews*. Grand Rapids: Wm. B. Eerdmans Publishing Co., 1977.

This volume is a good source to use to become acquainted with the very latest in critical and scholarly opinion on such matters as authorship, occasion, date, purpose, place of writing, and destination. Based on the RSV. Special studies include, "The Blood of Jesus and His Heavenly Priesthood," "The Doctrine of Creation in Hebrews 11:3," and "Hebrews 6:4-6 and the Peril of Apostasy."

Jewett, Robert, *Letter to Pilgrims: A Commentary on the Epistle to the Hebrews*. New York: Pilgrim Press, 1981.
> Jewett's thesis is that Hebrews, like Colossians, was written against angel-worshipping heretics in the Lycus River valley; that Hebrews is the "Letter to the Laodiceans" mentioned in Colossians 4:16, and that its author was Epaphras. Many of the arguments used to arrive at these conclusions are rather obvious examples of circular reasoning.

Johnson, Luke Timothy, *Hebrews: A Commentary* in the New Testament Library Series. Louisville: Westminster/John Knox, 2006.
> Included is a fresh translation of Hebrews "from the best available ancient manuscripts" along with brief textual notes concerning alternative readings in major Greek manuscripts. Johnson's answers to standard introductory questions include the date of writing ("likely between AD 50 and 70"), and authorship (he favors Apollos over Barnabas as the best two options). Johnson provides no outline for the book of Hebrews (so much for "careful attention to the literary design" of the book – one of the emphases of this whole series). What sets this work apart is Johnson's insistence that the author of Hebrews was unduly influenced by contemporary Platonic thought (Johnson thinks Hebrews reflects a Judaism influenced by a Platonic worldview, similar to Philo in Egypt).

Johnson, Richard W., *Going Outside the Camp: The Sociological Function of the Levitical Critique in the Epistle to the Hebrews*. Sheffield: Sheffield Academic Press, 2001.
> Social-science criticism is just beginning to be adopted as a method of explaining New Testament books. In this early attempt to apply the method to Hebrews, Johnson employs Mary Douglas' group-grid model to analyze the author's critique of the Levitical system. Johnson attempts to flesh out the type of society implied or projected by the critique, and to note the differences between this ideal society and the first-century Hellenistic Judaism from which the author and audience emerged. Douglas' method, used by Johnson, is to appeal to the function of rituals to determine the character and cosmology of a given society.

Kay, William, "Hebrews" in *The Bible Commentary* edited by F.C. Cook. New York: Charles Scribner's Sons, 1886. Reprinted in Grand Rapids: Baker Book House, 1981.
> This whole set is excellent and should be in every preacher's library. These are notes by Anglican scholars on the Greek text, with additional notes where helpful to enlarge on topics introduced in the comments.

Kent, Homer Austin, *The Epistle to the Hebrews: A Commentary*. Winona Lake, IN: Brethren Missionary Herald Co., 1972.
> Gives an analytical outline of the book, and builds exposition upon a very delightful exegesis of the text. Also emphasizes the theological themes found in Hebrews.

Ketcherside, W. Carl., *That the World May Believe*. Studio City, CA: World Literature Crusade, 1983.
> Originally published under the title The Death of The Custodian (Cincinnati: Standard Publishing Co., 1976), this little volume includes such thought-provoking questions as "What is the Nature of the New Covenant?" "How does the New Covenant Compare with the Old Covenant?" "Is the New Testament a Code of laws for the Christian to follow?"

Kistemaker, Simon J., *Exposition of the Epistle to the Hebrews*. The New Testament Commentary. Grand Rapids: Baker Book House, 1984.
> This is the first volume in the continuation of Hendriksen's *New Testament Commentary* series, after the death of the original author. Simon Kistemaker's contribution to the series is not up to the quality of the original. He dates Hebrews in the early 80's, thinks the work was written to a congregation in Rome, and is less than satisfactory on the question of authorship ("authorship is not important [Apollos? Barnabas? Priscilla? Paul?]; it is content that matters.") At Hebrews 6:4-6, he defends unconditional eternal security, and proposes this verse means that "the church is unable to bring a hardened sinner back to the grace of God." He treats

6:1-3 as being standard instruction given to new church members about Christian baptism, the laying on of hands, and other basic Christian doctrine and practice.

Koester, Craig R., *Hebrews. A New Translation with Introduction and Commentary* in the Anchor Bible Series. New York: Doubleday, 2001.

Rhetorical analysis is used to discern the supposed outline of "this compelling speech." Koester supposes it was likely addressed to Rome, somewhere between AD 60 and 90. Because Koester makes 2:5-9 the proposition of the sermon (followed by three points -- 2:10-6:20; 7:1-10:25; 11:1-12:27) he suggests that the main theme of Hebrews is not the priesthood and deity of Christ, but God's purposes for His people. "Hebrews identifies the question of God's intention for humanity as the crux around which the speech is structured" (p.97). God's people are on a journey to the promised land of heavenly rest, even though their present earthly experience might seem to indicate there is nothing glorious about being one of God's people.

Lane, William L., *Call to Commitment. Responding to the Message of Hebrews*. Nashville: Nelson, 1985.

This volume is a by-product of what was then the forthcoming commentary on Hebrews in the *Word Biblical Commentary* series. It was first delivered orally on cable television. Its message is essentially practical; several of the chapters end with summaries which go beyond exposition to application. Lane argues that Hebrews was written to a house church in Rome whose members had suffered hardship under Claudius in AD 49, and were now frightened by the persecution of other congregations by Nero following the great fire of Rome in AD 64. Lane pays particular attention to the structure of Hebrews, with the result that this book enables the reader to follow the thread of the argument. It quotes in full Lane's own translation of the Greek text.

-----, *Hebrews 1-8* and *Hebrews 9-13* in the Word Biblical Commentary series. Dallas, TX: Word Books, 1991.

One of the valuable features of this series is that every paragraph includes a rather thorough bibliography of both monographs and serial articles from the past century (and in some cases more). It is a useful tool for serious research on any of the knotty problems and issues raised in Hebrews.

Lenski, Richard Charles Henry, *The Interpretation of the Epistle to the Hebrews and the Epistle of James*. Columbus, OH: The Wartburg Press, 1937.

A conservative Lutheran exposition based on the Greek text. The author does not burden the reader with a mass of textual criticism and technicalities, but gives him the results of careful and thorough textual study of the Greek original. Interacts with and often times supplies additional comments to the results arrived at by the better commentators before him.

Leonard, William, *Authorship of the Epistle to the Hebrews*. Rome: Vatican Polyglot Press, 1939.

Through the years since the Reformation, in opposition to the position taken by Luther, Calvin, Melanchthon, and the Geneva School, all of which doubted or denied the Pauline authorship, the Roman Catholic Church has championed the Pauline authorship of Hebrews. This volume is perhaps the last full-scale defense of the Pauline authorship of Hebrews which the Roman Catholic Church has published. The book was first the author's doctoral thesis, and Leonard interacts with the scholars who have influenced the whole scholarly world toward more liberal theological conclusions. He shows that the theology, the vocabulary, the literary elegances, the distribution of Scripture in the epistle, the mode of Scriptural citations, the LXX use in Scriptural quotations, and even the modes of exegesis of Old Testament Scriptures found in Hebrews are exactly paralleled in the Pauline epistles. On none of these grounds, Leonard affirms, must we question or deny the Pauline authorship of Hebrews.

Lightfoot, Neil R., *Jesus Christ Today: A Commentary on the Book of Hebrews*. Grand Rapids: Baker Book House, 1976.

A commentary intended for college-university level work and for serious students of the Bible. Reference is regularly made to scholarly works and books that would be helpful and accessible for English students. Summaries and additional notes (many are technical word studies) in addition to exegetical and theological notes based on the RSV. Lightfoot shows acquaintance with Vanhoye's structural analysis of Hebrews, but follows a more conventional outline.

MacArthur, John Jr., *Hebrews*. The MacArthur New Testament Commentary. Winona Lake, IN: Brethren Missionary Herald Books, 1983.

> This contemporary radio-TV preacher is beginning to publish a set of commentaries on Bible books. The introductory studies are unsatisfactory. Authorship is "unknown." Destination is "outside Israel." Date is "65-70 AD." There is an attempt to defend unconditional eternal security (three groups of people are addressed, Hebrew Christians, Hebrew non-Christians who are intellectually convinced, and Hebrew non-Christians who are not convinced) as chapter 6 is written to show the church she can't help unbelievers who are not convinced. The author teaches that the new covenant is made with Israel, not the church (though Gentiles benefit from the new covenant). Chapter 6:1-3 are instructions that Jewish activities and beliefs are to be left behind.

MacLeod, David J., *The Epistle to the Hebrews*. Dubuque, IA: Emmaus Correspondence School, 1998.

> MacLeod believes the initial recipients of Hebrews were Jewish Christians living in Palestine. He suggests AD 67-68 as a likely date. It was written to establish the supremacy of Christianity, to exhort a break with Judaism, to encourage the renewal of effort, and to emphasize the danger of apostasy. The so-called warning passages are addressed, he maintains, to nonbelievers who have heard the gospel but have not embraced it. For instance, Hebrews 6:1ff encourages those who have heard the gospel not to depart ("fall away") from it, that is, not to fall from their as yet non-genuine "faith." The strong emphasis in Hebrews on the person and work of Christ is beautifully highlighted in this book. Multiple-choice questions on each chapter in Hebrews are included at the back of this correspondence-course textbook.

McCullough, J.C., "Some Recent Developments in Research on the Epistle to the Hebrews," *Irish Bible Studies* 2 (1980), p.141-165, and 3 (1981), p.28-45.

> The first installment is a survey of research on Hebrews which summarizes earlier contributions and assesses more recent ones, especially those made during the past twenty years. The areas considered are authorship, religious background (Philo, Qumran, gnosticism, Merkabah mysticism), date and destination, literary genre, and literary structure. The second installment considers the use of the Old Testament: what text the author of Hebrews used, and what exegetical principles he followed. This second installment also focuses on the meaning of *diatheke* in the epistle, and on the interpretation of Hebrews 6:4-6.

Milligan, George, *The Theology of the Epistle to the Hebrews, With a Critical Introduction*. Minneapolis: Klock & Klock, 1978.

> First published in 1899, this is one of the most significant works to be reprinted in years. It treats concisely matters of authorship and date, and then systematizes the theology of the epistle in the light of God's covenants with Israel.

Milligan, Robert E., *The Epistle to the Hebrews*. Des Moines, IA: Eugene S. Smith, 1875. Reprinted many times by many companies.

> Probably the best commentary on the book of Hebrews by a scholar of Christian Church background. Supports the Pauline authorship of the epistle and expounds the text in the light of the clear distinction between the old and new covenants.

Moffatt, James, *The Epistle to the Hebrews*. International Critical Commentary. Edinburgh: T&T Clark, 1957.

> Espouses the non-Jewish character of the recipients of this letter. Based on the Greek text, the work tends to be liberal in theology.

Moll, C.B., "Hebrews" in *Lange's Commentary on the Holy Scriptures*. Grand Rapids: Zondervan Publishing House, nd. (Moll's work was originally published in 1861.)
> Exegetical, doctrinal, and homiletical notes afford the student a comprehensive and practical view of the verses under consideration. It is a thorough commentary, and the student often needs to know Hebrew, Latin, and/or Greek to handle this commentary. Should be consulted by advanced students.

Morris, Leon, *Hebrews*. Expositor's Bible Commentary series, edited by Frank E. Gaebelein. Grand Rapids: Zondervan Publishing House, 1981.
> Morris is rather noncommittal on such matters as author ("a second generation Christian" [2:3]), destination (Jewish Christians in Rome), and date for the letter. Comments are based on the NIV. Critical notes are kept separate in an effort to make this work of value to a wider readership. This volume provides an exposition of the epistle covering such paragraphs as the excellence of Christ, the promised rest, a great high priest, the danger of apostasy, a priest like Melchizedek, a new and better covenant, faith, and Christian living.

Moulton, W.F., *The Epistle of Paul the Apostle to the Hebrews*. Ellicott's Commentary on the Whole Bible, Volume 8. Grand Rapids: Zondervan Publishing House, 1970. Reprinted many times.
> Ellicott's commentaries are among the first this writer checks when wanting to know in depth what one of the New Testament letters likely means. It has a number of notes based on the Greek text, including the meaning of words and the impact of verb tenses.

Owen, John, *An Exposition of the Epistle to the Hebrews*. 4 Volumes. Wilmington, DE: Sovereign Grace Publishers, nd.
> Perhaps the most exhaustive work available on Hebrews, this Puritan work was first published between 1668-84

Pink, Arthur Walkington, *An Exposition of Hebrews*. 3 Volumes. Grand Rapids: Baker Book House, 1954.
> Sometimes tends to verbosity. If the student exhibits patience, he will find helpful expository values.

Rotherham, Joseph B., *Studies in the Epistle to the Hebrews*. Joplin, MO: College Press, [?]. Also reprinted earlier in the Restoration Reprint Library Series, Delight, AR: Gospel Light Publishers.
> Not, strictly speaking, a continuous commentary, these 16 studies do attempt to set forth the main ideas in the epistle. The text given is Rotherham's "Emphasized" version. First published in 1906. Bound together in the same volume are Ashley Johnson's *Thirteen Expository Sermons on the Book of Hebrews*, originally preached at Johnson Bible College in 1895-96.

Salevao, Iutisone, *Legitimation in the Letter to the Hebrews: The Construction and Maintenance of a Symbolic Universe*. Sheffield: Sheffield Academic Press, 2002.
> Another attempt at applying social-science criticism to the interpretation of Hebrews. Salevao tries to reconstruct the socio-historical situation of the readers (an audience located in imperial Rome, in danger of "relapse" back into Judaism) as he attempts to prove his thesis that the Hebrew writer deliberately constructed his theology in such a way as to provide a justification for the readers' community. He sees the readers as being harassed both by an "out-group conflict" and by an "in-group conflict." Salevao chides contemporary scholars for neglecting Hebrews as they try to understanding the parting of the ways between Christianity and Judaism late in the first century.

Saphir, Adolph, *The Epistle to the Hebrews*. 2 Volumes. New York: Gospel Publishing House, nd.
> Warm expository studies by a converted Jew. A reprint of a work originally published 1874-76. Calvinistic in places.

Sauer, Erich Ernst, *In the Arena*. Grand Rapids: Wm. B. Eerdmans Publishing Co., 1955.
> Delightful reading, emphasizing the Christian life as set forth in Hebrews 12.

Schenck, Kenneth, *Understanding the Book of Hebrews: The Story Behind the Sermon*. Louisville: Westminster/John Knox Press, 2003
> Schenck uses the principles of narrative criticism to explain the implicit "story" behind Hebrews. He classifies Hebrews as being a "sermon." He identifies the plot of the story, and the main characters, and the setting. In the process, he argues that Hebrews does NOT affirm the pre-existence, or the eternality, or the deity of the Son of God. Christ's ministry is intercessory. Schenck argues there is no place in Hebrews that clearly affirms that Christ's sacrifice was offered in heaven. Rather its offering on earth gained Christ access to God's presence where he intercedes as our high priest. Schenck's Jesus is neither true to the teaching of Hebrews nor adequate to procure our salvation.

Schneider, Johannes, *The Letter to the Hebrews*. Grand Rapids: Wm. B. Eerdmans Publishing Co., 1957.
> Generally conservative, the author is a European Baptist theologian. The preacher, working expositorily through the epistle, will find help here.

Seiss, Joseph Augustus, *Lectures on Hebrews*. Grand Rapids: Baker Book House, 1954.
> 36 delightful sermons which exalt the deity of Christ, stress the necessity of studying the Word, expound the fundamental doctrines of the Christian faith, and exhort believers to a closer walk with Christ.

Stedman, Ray C., *What More Can God Say?* A Bible Commentary for Laymen. Glendale, CA: Regal Books, 1974.
> The author's emphasis is that the book of Hebrews was written to produce Christians who really lived what they said they believed. He believes it was addressed to a group of Jewish Christians who were starting to drift back to their pre-Christian ways. Hebrews focuses more directly on Jesus Christ than any other book in the Bible.

-----, "Hebrews" in *The IVP New Testament Commentary Series*. Downers Grove, IL: InterVarsity, 1988.
> Stedman's commentary on Hebrews leans toward identifying Apollos as its anonymous author, Jewish Christians as its readers, and the late AD 60s as its date. The famous problem text in 6:4-8 is handled from a Calvinistic perspective, and is documented with a three-page appendix. The author bases most of his documentation on three evangelical commentaries. Many will question his perspective that the tabernacle and its furniture were a type of humans' three-part nature.

Stibbs, Alan Marshall, *So Great Salvation: The Meaning and Message of the Letter to the Hebrews*. Exeter, England: Paternoster Press, 1970.
> Helpful to the preacher or teacher who wants ideas for practical application of the precepts in Hebrews.

Stuart, Moses, *A Commentary on the Epistle to the Hebrews*. Andover, MA: Warren F. Draper, 1860.
> A concise, conservative commentary based on the Greek text. Its introductory studies are extensive and rewarding.

Thomas, William Henry Griffith, *Hebrews: A Devotional Commentary*. Grand Rapids: Wm. B. Eerdmans Publishing Co., 1962.
> 41 devotional messages from various paragraphs of Hebrews, stressing the need for spiritual progress in the Christian life.

Thompson, James, *The Letter to the Hebrews*. Living Word Commentary Series. Austin, TX: R. B. Sweet Co., 1971.
> This commentary is based on the text of the RSV. Introductory studies are a bit unsatisfactory on date and alleged sources and influences on the writer.

Trentham, Charles A., "Hebrews," in *The Broadman Bible Commentary*. Nashville: Broadman Press, 1975.
> Trentham, influenced by the discovery of 11Q Melchizedek among the Dead Sea Scrolls, thinks the original readers were Jewish Christians who were tempted to leave Christianity and return to the old sect. He thinks the work was originally a sermon (or sermons) delivered in Alexandria, then later put in writing and sent to Rome. He denies the Pauline authorship of the letter, but offers no alternative save it was some "pilgrim upon earth ... some displaced person." For the time of writing he opts for a date between AD 68 and 70, just when the Qumran community was destroyed (thus the readers had no continuing city to which they could return).

Trotter, Andrew H., *Interpreting the Epistle to the Hebrews*. Grand Rapids: Baker, 1997.
> One of the Guides to New Testament Exegesis series, a series intended to help "college religion majors, seminarians, and pastors who have had at least one year of Greek." The volume is not a commentary on Hebrews, but does seek to provide tools to help the reader interpret the text either to teach or preach Hebrews. Part one of the book provides background material, historical and cultural context including readership and then date, then authorship (he suggests either Barnabas or Apollos), genre, structure, and interesting particulars of the Greek text. Part two of the book enables the reader to do word studies in Hebrews, and notes the grammar, its various styles of speech, and finally the theology that comes from the text – the doctrines of Scripture, Christology, eschatology, sanctification, and perseverance.

Turner, George Allen, *The New and Living Way*. Minneapolis: Bethany Fellowship, 1974.
> A brief survey of Hebrews, containing helpful word studies and a concise explanation of the text. The author writes from an Arminian position.

Vanhoye, Albert, *La Structire Litteraire De l'Epitre Aux Hebreux*. Paris: Desclee, 1963.
> Noted Jesuit scholar, building on an earlier suggestion of Vaganay, has found a carefully constructed literary structure to the book. Lane nicely summarizes this man's voluminous writings in English *(Word Commentary on Hebrews 1-8)*. See also Black, "Literary Structure of Hebrews," *Grace Theological Journal* 7:2 (1986), p.163-77. There is, however, one outstanding difficulty in the scheme of Vanhoye, namely, his conjecture that 13:19 and 13:22-25 were later added to the original work (i.e., Hebrews does not enjoy integrity). In the light of the studies presented by Tasker, "The Integrity of the Epistle to the Romans," *Expository Times* 47 (1935-6), p. 136-38, the defense of the authenticity and integrity of chapter 13, Vanhoye's conjecture can scarcely be accepted. (Vanhoye omits these verses because he must in order to secure the perfect symmetry – the kind of structure he thinks must have originally lay behind our epistle.)

Vine, W.E., *The Epistle to the Hebrews*. London: Oliphants Ltd., 1952.
> Each chapter begins with a brief summary, then an analytical outline of the outline of the chapter, followed by brief but delightful notes, many being Greek word studies. Through it all he develops the theme that Christ is all excelling.

Vos, Geerhardus, *The Teaching of the Epistle to the Hebrews*. Grand Rapids: Wm. B. Eerdmans Publishing Co., 1956.
> A series of lectures emphasizing the central theme of the letter, including "the distinctive character of the epistle," "the concept of *diatheke* (covenant)," "the philosophy of revelation and redemption."

Westcott, Brooke Foss, *The Epistle to the Hebrews*. Grand Rapids: Wm. B. Eerdmans Publishing Co., reprint.
> One of the best treatments of the Greek text. First published in 1889. A must for the serious student. The notes on Melchizedek, the tabernacle, the Christology of the epistle, the use of Old Testament quotations by the writer of Hebrews, are well worth the price of the book.

Wiersbe, Warren W., *Be Confident* (Hebrews). Wheaton, IL: Victor Books, 1982.

> A series of twelve sermons based on the book of Hebrews. Some delightful titles ("Is Anybody Listening?" "Pilgrims Should Make Progress," "Stay in the Running!" and "Pardon Me, Your Faith is Showing," and others), and some helpful illustrations.

Wilson, R. McL., "Hebrews" in the *New Century Bible Commentary*. Grand Rapids: Wm. B. Eerdmans, 1987.

> In his Introductory Studies, Wilson discusses the inclusion of Hebrews in the New Testament canon, its authorship, destination and place of writing, date, and background of thought and ideas. Headings such as prologue (1:1-4), the superiority of the Son to angels (1:5-15), the danger of neglect (2:1-4), the supremacy of Jesus (2:5-9), serve as an outline to the book. Wilson describes Hebrews as "a book with a message of encouragement, inspiration, hope, and assurance."

Word, Archie L., *61 Soul-Winning Sermon Outlines from Hebrews*. Joplin, MO: College Press, 1962.

> The outlines vary in length from two to four pages, and include illustrations. The book will prove helpful to the student who would preach through the book after having studied it thoroughly. Some few of the outlines will need adaptation, especially in certain well-known difficult and disputed passages where the student may disagree with Word's interpretation.

Zeitlin, Solomon, *The Rise and Fall of the Judean State*. Volume 3. Philadelphia: Jewish Publication Society, 1978.

> A useful volume which documents the change that occurred in Jewish religious life from keeping the Laws of Moses to observing the traditions of the Pharisees.

INDEX OF AUTHORS

INDEX OF SUBJECTS, PERSONS AND PLACES

OTHER BOOKS BY GARETH L. REESE

New Testament History: Acts   (097-176-5235)

New Testament Epistles: Romans (097-176-5200)

New Testament Epistles: 1 Corinthians (097-176-5251)

New Testament Epistles: 2 Corinthians & Galatians (097-176-5278)

New Testament Epistles: Paul's Prison Epistles (978-0-9984518-0-0)

New Testament Epistles: 1 and 2 Timothy & Titus (097-176-5227)

New Testament Epistles: 1 and 2 Peter & Jude (097-176-5243)

New Testament Epistles: James & 1,2,3 John (097-176-526X)

Order from:
Scripture Exposition Books
803 McKinsey Place
Moberly, MO., 65270
www.glreese@cccb.edu

www.ingramcontent.com/pod-product-compliance
Lightning Source LLC
Chambersburg PA
CBHW061958090426
42811CB00006B/972